Emerging Research and Trends in Gamification

Harsha Gangadharbatla
University of Colorado Boulder, USA

Donna Z. Davis
University of Oregon, USA

A volume in the Advances in Multimedia and
Interactive Technologies (AMIT) Book Series

Managing Director:	Lindsay Johnston
Managing Editor:	Keith Greenberg
Director of Intellectual Property & Contracts:	Jan Travers
Acquisitions Editor:	Kayla Wolfe
Production Editor:	Christina Henning
Development Editor:	Brandon Carbaugh
Typesetter:	Kaitlyn Kulp
Cover Design:	Jason Mull

Published in the United States of America by
Information Science Reference (an imprint of IGI Global)
701 E. Chocolate Avenue
Hershey PA, USA 17033
Tel: 717-533-8845
Fax: 717-533-8661
E-mail: cust@igi-global.com
Web site: http://www.igi-global.com

Library of Congress Cataloging-in-Publication Data

Emerging research and trends in gamification / Harsha Gangadharbatla and Donna Z. Davis, editors.
    pages cm
  Includes bibliographical references and index.
  Summary: "This book brings together innovative and scholarly research on the use of game-based design and technology in a variety of settings, including discussions from both industry and academic perspectives"-- Provided by publisher.
  ISBN 978-1-4666-8651-9 (hc) -- ISBN 978-1-4666-8652-6 (eISBN) 1. Games--Social aspects--Research 2. Computer games--Social aspects--Research. I. Gangadharbatla, Harshavardhan. II. Davis, Donna Z., 1959-
  GV1201.38.E64 2016
  794.80072--dc23
                          2015015652

This book is published in the IGI Global book series Advances in Multimedia and Interactive Technologies (AMIT) (ISSN: 2327-929X; eISSN: 2327-9303)

British Cataloguing in Publication Data
A Cataloguing in Publication record for this book is available from the British Library.

For electronic access to this publication, please contact: eresources@igi-global.com.

Advances in Multimedia and Interactive Technologies (AMIT) Book Series

Joel J.P.C. Rodrigues
Instituto de Telecomunicações, University of Beira Interior, Portugal

ISSN: 2327-929X
EISSN: 2327-9303

MISSION

Traditional forms of media communications are continuously being challenged. The emergence of user-friendly web-based applications such as social media and Web 2.0 has expanded into everyday society, providing an interactive structure to media content such as images, audio, video, and text.

The **Advances in Multimedia and Interactive Technologies (AMIT) Book Series** investigates the relationship between multimedia technology and the usability of web applications. This series aims to highlight evolving research on interactive communication systems, tools, applications, and techniques to provide researchers, practitioners, and students of information technology, communication science, media studies, and many more with a comprehensive examination of these multimedia technology trends.

COVERAGE

- Audio Signals
- Internet technologies
- Digital Watermarking
- Gaming Media
- Web Technologies
- Multimedia Services
- Digital Games
- Social Networking
- Digital Images
- Digital Technology

IGI Global is currently accepting manuscripts for publication within this series. To submit a proposal for a volume in this series, please contact our Acquisition Editors at Acquisitions@igi-global.com or visit: http://www.igi-global.com/publish/.

Titles in this Series

For a list of additional titles in this series, please visit: www.igi-global.com

Cases on the Societal Effects of Persuasive Games
Dana Ruggiero (Bath Spa University, UK)
Information Science Reference • copyright 2014 • 345pp • H/C (ISBN: 9781466662063) • US $205.00 (our price)

Video Surveillance Techniques and Technologies
Vesna Zeljkovic (New York Institute of Technology, Nanjing Campus, China)
Information Science Reference • copyright 2014 • 369pp • H/C (ISBN: 9781466648968) • US $215.00 (our price)

Techniques and Principles in Three-Dimensional Imaging An Introductory Approach
Martin Richardson (De Montfort University, UK)
Information Science Reference • copyright 2014 • 324pp • H/C (ISBN: 9781466649323) • US $200.00 (our price)

Computational Solutions for Knowledge, Art, and Entertainment Information Exchange Beyond Text
Anna Ursyn (University of Northern Colorado, USA)
Information Science Reference • copyright 2014 • 511pp • H/C (ISBN: 9781466646278) • US $180.00 (our price)

Perceptions of Knowledge Visualization Explaining Concepts through Meaningful Images
Anna Ursyn (University of Northern Colorado, USA)
Information Science Reference • copyright 2014 • 418pp • H/C (ISBN: 9781466647039) • US $180.00 (our price)

Exploring Multimodal Composition and Digital Writing
Richard E. Ferdig (Research Center for Educational Technology - Kent State University, USA) and Kristine E. Pytash (Kent State University, USA)
Information Science Reference • copyright 2014 • 352pp • H/C (ISBN: 9781466643451) • US $175.00 (our price)

Multimedia Information Hiding Technologies and Methodologies for Controlling Data
Kazuhiro Kondo (Yamagata University, Japan)
Information Science Reference • copyright 2013 • 497pp • H/C (ISBN: 9781466622173) • US $190.00 (our price)

Media in the Ubiquitous Era Ambient, Social and Gaming Media
Artur Lugmayr (Tampere University of Technology, Finland) Helja Franssila (University of Tampere, Finland) Pertti Näränen (TAMK University of Applied Sciences, Finland) Olli Sotamaa (University of Tampere, Finland) Jukka Vanhala (Tampere University of Technology, Finland) and Zhiwen Yu (Northwestern Polytechnical University, China)
Information Science Reference • copyright 2012 • 312pp • H/C (ISBN: 9781609607746) • US $195.00 (our price)

www.igi-global.com

701 E. Chocolate Ave., Hershey, PA 17033
Order online at www.igi-global.com or call 717-533-8845 x100
To place a standing order for titles released in this series, contact: cust@igi-global.com
Mon-Fri 8:00 am - 5:00 pm (est) or fax 24 hours a day 717-533-8661

List of Reviewers

Michael B. Armstrong, *Old Dominion University, USA*
Laura Bright, *Texas Christian University, USA*
Jacqueline Carpenter, *SHAKER, USA*
Raul Ferrer Conill, *Karlstad University, Sweden*
Carmen Costa-Sánchez, *University of Coruna, Spain*
Nicole Dudley, *SHAKER, USA*
Zeynep Tanes Ehle, *Duquesne University, USA*
Mike Fancher, *University of Oregon, USA*
Jared Z. Ferrell, *SHAKER, USA*
Jolene Fisher, *University of Oregon, USA*
Scott Goodman, *SHAKER, USA*
Michael Hanus, *Ohio State University, USA*
Heath Hooper, *Shorter University, USA*
Toby Hopp, *University of Alabama, USA*
Nathan Hulsey, *North Carolina State University, USA*
Yowei Kang, *Kainan University, Taiwan*
Michael Karlsson, *Karlstad University, Sweden*
Richard N. Landers, *Old Dominion University, USA*
Julia Largent, *Bowling Green State University, USA*
Darcy Osheim, *Maine Maritime Academy, USA*
Selcen Ozturkcan, *Istanbul Bilgi University, Turkey*
Gregory Perreault, *Missouri School of Journalism, USA*
Mimi Perreault, *Missouri School of Journalism, USA*
Teresa Piñeiro-Otero, *University of Coruna, Spain*
David Staton, *University of Oregon, USA*
Sercan Şengün, *Istanbul Bilgi University, Turkey*
Daly Vaughn, *SHAKER, USA*
Shefali Virkar, *University of Oxford, UK*
Stephen Ward, *Murdoch University, USA*
Bartosz W. Wojdynski, *University of Georgia, USA*

Table of Contents

Detailed Table of Contents

Section 1
Designing Successful Gamification

This chapter is a critical-conceptual introduction to the topic of gamification from the standpoint of game studies (the study of games) and ludology (the study of play). A secondary task is to move the definition and conceptual history of gamification away from essentialist notions of play and games and towards a more nuanced understanding of gamification as a philosophy of design with situational outcomes. By examining the controversy surrounding gamification as a complex history of concepts, the chapter aims to give the reader an overview of how gamification aligns with or deviates from various definitions of games and play. Gamification can be controversial when using traditional ludological concepts largely because traditional ludology is pre-digital, and does not account for the current technological and cultural shifts driving gaming and gamification. Finally, the chapter ends with the suggestion that the current cultural turn in game studies provides a way to analyze gamification as an example of the "gaming of culture."

Gamification is the concept of infusing elements of gameplay (competition, incentives, story/narrative, collaboration, problem-solving, etc.) into non-game activities in order to make those activities more compelling. Recently, game designers have begun stressing the need for greater "maturity" in the field of gamification with greater focus on the importance of designing applications for optimal user experience. One hurdle to achieving maturity in the field is the fact that even gamification experts question "What exactly are the essential elements of gameplay that optimize user engagement and enjoyment?" Thus, the goal of the current chapter is to provide a comprehensive listing of the elements of gameplay that are essential to user engagement, and to provide examples of how each of those elements has been applied successfully in game design in the past. The chapter reviews 14 essential gameplay elements including: chance, control, creativity, completion, spectacle, status, strategy, unification, rules, narrative, recognition, collaboration, escapism, and enjoyment.

Chapter 3

Selcen Ozturkcan, Istanbul Bilgi University, Turkey
Sercan Şengün, Istanbul Bilgi University, Turkey

This chapter enhances the dyadic gain-loss concept by presenting findings of a research project on uncovering whether the efficiency component of gamification could be better attained by balancing a shift from gain to loss, or completely avoiding it altogether. The gamification of any system requires a good selection and balance of game design elements to make the overall experience fun, as well as gaming emotions to keep it intrinsically rewarding. However, if not designed properly, participators of a gamified system that expect the prospect of gaining rewards, may ultimately realize a shift of engagement from gain to avoiding losses any earned status, badge, experience, or popularity often defined within the periphery of the gamified system. Findings reveal changing levels of motivation within different participatory foci, where loss avoidance (punishment scenarios) generates more motivation than the prospect of gaining rewards.

Chapter 4

Yowei Kang, Kainan University, Taiwan

Digital game is an essential part of digital creative industries around the world. This chapter aims to develop H.I.R.E. scales that can be used to explain and understand users' responses to digital creative contents. Although multiple methodologies have been used to study gameplayers' experiences and interactions with different genres of digital games that lead to their gamifications, this chapter is based on a rhetorical theoretical tradition by arguing that gameplay interactions are a rhetorical process in which players interact with game designers as well as other players in the same guild through a series of persuasive manipulations. H.I.R.E. scales are developed to explain how gameplayers have different experiences when playing a digital game that contributes to their gamifications. Because digital game is an important branch of contemporary digital creative industry, the development of the H.I.R.E. scales will help researchers and practitioners to study and develop better digital games and other digital creative contents.

Section 2
Gamification and Business

Chapter 5

Kartik Pashupati, Research Now, USA
Pushkala Raman, Texas Woman's University, USA

This chapter presents an overview of gamification in the domain of market research, with a specific focus on digital data collection methods, such as online surveys. The problems faced by the market research industry are outlined, followed by a discussion of why gamification has been offered as a possible way to overcome some of these challenges. The literature on gamification is reviewed, with a focus on results from empirical studies investigating the impact of gamification on outcome variables such as data quality and respondent engagement. Finally, the authors present results from an original study conducted in 2013, comparing differences between a conventional (text-dominant) survey and a gamified version of the same survey.

Chapter 6

Gamification promises to deliver more motivating, engaging, and, ultimately, effective human resource (HR) processes. The following chapter presents an overview of key motivational theories supporting the potential effectiveness of gamifying HR processes. Key motivational theories underpinning the success of gamification include Need Satisfaction Theories, Operant Conditioning, Flow, and Goal Setting Theory. After providing a theoretical framework supporting the effectiveness of gamification, emphasis will shift to an examination of key game elements used to improve four large categories of HR processes: recruitment, selection, training, and performance management. Case studies will be leveraged to provide real-world examples of organizations using gamification to improve HR initiatives. Finally, the chapter will cover key considerations and best practices that should be followed when developing and implementing gamified HR initiatives.

Chapter 7

Game-thinking is beginning to appear in a wide variety of non-game contexts, including organizational support settings like human resource management (HRM). The purpose of this chapter is two-fold: 1) to explore the opportunities for game-thinking via gamification and serious games in HRM based on current and previous HRM literature and 2) to identify future research areas at the intersection of game-thinking and HRM. Prevailing HRM theories will be applied to the use of game-thinking in different sub-fields of HRM, including recruitment, selection, training, and performance management.

Section 3
Gamification of Education

Chapter 8

Video games and gamified applications have been used for various purposes including helping businesses (in commercial marketing), or helping the individual, community or society (in social marketing). Video games are systems with rules, play structures, and narratives; while gamified applications utilize game elements, mechanics, and ways of thinking to generate meaningful, playful and fun experiences. Both video games and gamified applications require a learning process including learning to play, and learning through the game. This chapter advocates that learning is an inherent component of video games and gamified applications. The main purpose of this chapter is to examine the concept of 'game learning' from three major theoretical positions, namely Behaviorism, Cognitivism, and Constructivism. In doing so, this chapter first explains, compares, and contrasts these three positions, then elaborates on how learning takes place in specific games designed for commercial and social marketing with the lens of these three positions.

Chapter 9

Gamification continues to grow in popularity, and has significant application to education and student motivation. Because gamification is a large, encompassing concept it may be best to assess its effects by breaking down its composite features and assessing the positive and negative effects of these features. This chapter takes features including immediate feedback, use of narrative, tailored challenges, and displays of progress, and discusses popular current theories in communication and psychology to discuss the potential benefits and drawbacks of each feature, placing a focus on student motivation, comparison, and self-perception. This moves to discuss practical ways to best employ gamification features, and discusses the impact of digital technology on gamification in the classroom and should be useful for researchers interested in the topic and for teachers considering how to best gamify their classrooms.

Chapter 10

Students need the classroom in order to educate in a way in which they can relate, and grow bored when that does not happen. Gamification employs game mechanics, techniques, and theory in areas that traditionally are not set up to function like a game, and many instructors and administrators at the university level are eager to use gamification to encourage students to learn. However, gamification is not a generic fix to the problems found in the classroom. Instructors should gain insight on how successful games work, and gamify specific classroom functions to retain the deep learning required for subject mastery. The author employs the method of heterotopian rhetorical criticism and the methodology of autoethnography to analyze World of Warcraft and re-imagine experiences in the game through critical communication pedagogy to enact change in the traditional college classroom. A general definition emerged: Gamification must consist of high-choice, low-risk engagements in a clearly structured environment.

We live in an age of networks: transportation networks, computer networks, economic networks, research networks, energy networks, social networks, the list goes on. Each consists of nodes connected to each other to manage the production and distribution of output to network users. Two large networks that share some particularly interesting overlap are gaming networks and advocacy networks. This chapter encourages an understanding of the potential overlap of these types of networks – both of which involve many millions of users, countless hours of interaction and billions of dollars of investment – and explores the intersection and impact of games designed to matter and gamified advocacy efforts. The chapter concludes with a proposed common planning framework from the field of advocacy network building and explores how gamification may more deeply help drive advocacy and social change, while advocacy work also opens new, valuable and more meaningful interactions and ideas for game designers.

This chapter constructs a historical overview of digital games used for international development. While the decade long use of digital games in this field has seen mixed results, a trend towards gamification has continued. The various approaches to international development taken in these games are analyzed alongside the gaming goals, platforms, and narrative structures. Broadly, this chapter argues that the field of digital development games breaks down into three categories: Developing Developers, Digital Interventions, and Critical Play. Because these games are tied to larger frameworks of development thought, they are an important part of the development discourse and should be critically analyzed, regardless of their success at the level of individual attitude and behavior change. Such an analysis presents a useful way to think about what's happening in the current development field and how the trend towards gamification may impact its future directions.

Gamified self has many dimensions, one of which is self-tracking. It is an activity in which a person collects and reflects on their personal information over time. Digital tools such as pedometers, GPS-enabled mobile applications, and number-crunching websites increasingly facilitate this practice. The collection of personal information is now a commonplace activity as a result of connected devices and the Internet. Tracking is integrated into so many digital services and devices; it is more or less unavoidable. Self-tracking engages with new technology to put the power of self-improvement and self-knowledge into people's own hands by bringing game dynamics to non-game contexts. The purpose of this chapter's research is to move towards a better understanding of how self-tracking can (and will) grow in the consumer market. An online survey was conducted and results indicate that perceptions of ease of use and enjoyment of tracking tools are less influential to technology acceptance than perceptions of usefulness. Implications and future research directions are presented.

Section 5
Gamification and Journalism

Chapter 14

The competition for online news page views increasingly involves strategies designed to promote the "viral" nature of content, and to capitalize on the content's spread by ensuring that the content does not quickly lose timeliness or relevance. As a result of the pressure for these stories, news experiences which can be revisited by consumers are at a premium. In this ecosystem, interactive games and quizzes which can be played to receive different feedback or reach a different ending offer promise for news organizations to receive ongoing and widespread reward for their efforts. This chapter provides an overview of the state of gamification in journalism, challenges and opportunities for the growth of games in online news, and discusses evidence for the impact of increasingly gamified news content on how users process and perceive news information.

Chapter 15

Traditional news outlets are on the decline and journalism has embraced digital media in its struggle to survive. New models of delivering news to the public are being explored in order to increase the levels of readership and user engagement. The narrative of this chapter focuses on the future of journalism and media, and the potential benefits and dangers of gamifying journalism. Since gamification is a new trend, a thorough look at the intersection between the enhancements of public mobility, the digitalization of news services, and the engagement of gamified systems can bring better understanding of future channels of reading news to the users, to researchers, and to the industry. This chapter aims to bridge the gap between gamification as an emerging practice in news distribution and yet a vastly uncharted area or research.

Preface

People have been drawn to the act of gameplay perhaps since the earliest days of humanity. Historians reported evidence of the first board games dating back to 3100 BC (Piccone, 1980) and the earliest iterations of chess in 200 B.C. (Murray, 1913). Even then, games were used to establish hierarchy, to entertain, to learn or to escape the mundane. To better understand these motivations, theorists and psychologists have debated what makes games appealing for decades (Huizinga, 1950; Caillois, 1961; Spariosu, 1989; and Fink, 1968). Ultimately they agree the core tenets of games are that they are voluntary, games have rules, they challenge players with obstacles and they require imagination, strategy, and the ability to cooperate when the game involves team play (Caillois, 1961).

Today games continue to engage players in similar ways as in the earliest days of chess or backgammon, but now often with additional stimulus of immersive environments, internationally and digitally connected players and an unprecedented ability to create and distribute games via digital platforms. Quite significantly, today online games alone represent an economy of $41.4 billion in U.S. dollars, up from $13.8 billion a decade ago (Statistica.com, 2015).

FROM GAMES TO GAMIFICATION

In recent years, games have found a new application, as the era of "gamification" launched. The first use of the word "gamification" dates back to 2008 (Paharia, 2010) with many alternate terms like "productivity games," "playful design," "alternate reality games," and "exploitationware" used to describe this phenomenon (Deterding, Dixon, Khaled, and Nacke, 2011). One important question about gamification is whether it represents something significantly different from previous phenomena in area of research on games and gaming. Deterding et al. (2011) argue and provide evidence for gamification demarcating "a distinct but previously unspecified group of phenomena, namely the complex of gamefulness, gameful interaction, and gameful design, which are different from more established concepts" (p. 10). This forms the basis for a clear definition of gamification, which in simple terms, "is the use of game design elements in non-game contexts" (Deterding et al. 2010, p.10).

In other words, gamification is not simply creating a video game or board game for the sake of play. Rather, gamification is the application of game-thinking and game dynamics in *non-game* contexts to engage users, increase participation, facilitate learning, and solve problems, often through continuous and instant feedback. Game dynamics are used to motivate behavior, they create scenarios, they are bound by rules and they offer a way to progress within the game. Game mechanics are used to help players achieve goals, provide rewards and feedback. Components are built into the game design that track progress, provide quests that are rewarded by moving up levels or gaining badges and points. While you may think of these elements in the success of Angry Birds or Super Mario Brothers, they are also critical to the success of employee programs, customer loyalty, corporate training and teaching children and adults about important issues or simply inspiring them to learn.

Consider the recent hugely successful fund-raising campaign, the ALS Ice Bucket Challenge, which generated over $220 million for the fight against ALS and engaged millions of people the world over to raise awareness (ALS Association, 2015). There are many articles written about why the ALS Ice Bucket Challenge was such a huge success (e.g., Forbes, TIME, Ignite Social Media, Digiday, Fast Company and Yahoo have all written articles explaining its success). Surprisingly, none of them explain it directly in terms of gamification although some of the articles touch on aspects of it. It can be argued that one of the main reasons why the Ice Bucket Challenge was such a massive hit is because it applied game dynamics in a non-game context really well. First, it was an interesting and curious thing to watch people dump ice and cold water on themselves, which engaged viewers. Next, it made it easy and exciting to challenge and call-out one's friends in public, which increased participation. Ice Bucket Challenge also appealed to the basic human desire to compete, especially with family, friends and colleagues and not random strangers. The reward for participation was much more than unlocking a coveted badge; it involved a public display of altruism and selflessness in a video that was shared with one's entire network. And all of this was for a good cause. Of course, the aspects of altruism and social good, and the fact that it was a really simple and selfless idea may have played a bigger role but the application of game dynamics is undeniably a factor in its runaway success.

Gamification is now a commonly utilized strategy used across disciplines in education, environment, government, marketing, web and mobile app design, journalism and newsgathering, social good, work and health. Researchers in all of these fields are working toward bettering our understanding of how game dynamics can be used in non-game contexts to produce desired outcomes. However, the research on gamification is in its nascent years, emerging from diverse fields and with an extraordinary range of purposes. The overall mission of this edited volume is to bring multiple disciplines together in order to first, expose gamification researchers from one field the work of others in unrelated areas; second, enhance the understanding of gamification across these disciplines; third, use that increased understanding to lead to interesting research ideas and collaborations among otherwise unrelated fields; and finally, to help advance our understanding of gamification and its application across disciplines. This collection brings together academic and industry minds from a variety of fields all connected by an interest in understanding the role of game dynamics in non-game contexts or, simply, the concept of gamification.

ORGANIZATION OF THE BOOK

The edited volume helps guide our understanding of gamification from a number of research perspectives. They reflect five categories of gamification research including the importance of game design, gamification in business, gamification in education, social change, health and self-tracking, and the gamification of journalism. Although each chapter can stand on its own, collectively the chapters provide a comprehensive view of contemporary research in gamification.

1. DESIGNING SUCCESSFUL GAMIFICATION

The volume begins with a focus on the design of games and what elements of gamification distinguish it from traditional gaming and poorly designed gamification. In Chapter 1, Nathan Hulsey explores the study of gamification from the lens of game studies and ludology. By doing so, he expands on the definition and conceptual history of gamification. He then discusses the controversial nature of history of game study and how gamification is well suited to that debate. What are the differences among gamification, serious games and traditional concepts of games and play? Hulsey provides some answers to that question in his chapter.

The next three chapters dig into the importance of game design and how that design impacts engagement and outcomes. William Upchurch and Susan Wildermuth, for example, provide a comprehensive review of what both academic and industry experts consider essential elements and functions of successful games in Chapter 2. They identify fourteen essential elements—chance, control, creativity, completion, spectacle, status, strategy, unification, rules, narrative, recognition, collaboration, escapism, and enjoyment—that all gamification designers and developers will want to consider as they consider gamification.

These elements are further explored in Chapter 3 when Selcen Ozturkcan and Sercan Sengun focus on the role of rewards and incentives as motivations in gamification. Their chapter took the concepts of regulatory focus and fit along with risk, reward and punishment and the balance of loss and gain to explore the motivations of players via an experiment that featured a fictional gamified competition. Does punishment or loss trump reward in game challenges? Their result may surprise you.

In Chapter 4, Yowei Kang extends the exploration of game design and game player experience with the use of rhetoric. Kang's chapter reviews the development of a user experience scale, *Hybrid Interactive Rhetorical Engagement (H.I.R.E)*, to better understand user experience (UX), arguing that persuasion plays an important role in that experience.

2. GAMIFICATION AND BUSINESS

The second section of the book dives into the use of games in business. Perhaps the most widely covered use of gamification in contemporary media is in the promise and peril of gamification in the workplace and in marketing. In 2012, Gartner predicted, "By 2016, gamification will be an essential element for brands and retailers to drive customer marketing and loyalty" (Gartner, 2012). And, while enterprise gamification ranked as the top contender at the peak of the Gartner Hype Cycle for Emerging Technologies in 2013 (Gartner, August 2013), it had fallen to the middle of the technologies in the downward cycle of the trough of disillusionment by 2014 (Gartner, July 2014). Will it survive that trough, ultimately reaching mass adoption or Gartner's "Plateau of Productivity" (Gartner, 2014)? The following chapters provide innovative insights into the role of gamification in market research and in human resource management.

Chapter 5 is guided both by existing literature and original research exploring the use of gamification in market survey research. Kartik Pashupati and Pushkala Raman begin with a comprehensive overview of the existing research outlining the challenges of digital data collections methods including online surveys and follow that with a discussion of how gamification may be the solution to these challenges. To test this hypothesis, Pashupati and Raman report on their own experimental research that compares traditional text-based online survey methods to a gamified version of the same survey. They conclude that gamification, when done right, has potential to improve the survey-taking experience for respondents and increase the response rates and quality of the data collected by marketing professionals.

The following two chapters look specifically at the use of gamification in human resource (HR) practices. Jared Ferrell, Jacqueline Carpenter, Daly Vaughn, Nickki Dudley and Scott Goodman, researchers and consultants at SHAKER begin Chapter 6 with their study of the use of games and game elements in HR. They review the key motivational theories that explain the effectiveness of gamifying HR processes. They conclude with a proposed set of best practices in gamification for HR managers and organizational leaders. They touch on the use of games in recruitment, selection, training and performance management in the workplace. Chapter 7 builds on this theme as Michael Armstrong, Richard Landers and Andrew Collmus look at and report on the same four elements of human resource management where gamification has been successful. They conclude with recommendations on how game thinking can be used to benefit organizations from an HR perspective.

3. GAMIFICATION OF EDUCATION

Educators have long been considered pioneers in the realm of gamification. As education continues to experience challenges and change, educators have turned to games to seek creative ways to inspire and motivate their students. This section of the volume includes two chapters that explore how games may achieve this task from a better understanding of the theoretical foundations of game design. The section concludes with original research that challenges the practical applications of games in the classroom.

The section begins with Zeynep Tanes' review of the role of behaviorism, cognitivism and constructivism in game based learning via video games. In Chapter 8 Tanes offers students, academics, game designers, policy makers and industry professionals a comparative and explanatory review of major learning theories and how they should be considered in the effective use of video games as an educational tool. In Chapter 9, Michael Hanus and Carlos Cruz further analyze the theoretical approaches that may guide game-based learning. Their thorough review of the theoretical literature across disciplines aims to give researchers and educators a better understanding of benefits of gamification in the classroom and the importance of sound design to achieve that success.

In Chapter 10, which concludes this section, Darcy Osheim extends the conversation regarding effective use of games in the classroom and their potential impact on student engagement and learning. Osheim takes the reader to school, reporting on the use of World of Warcraft to examine and re-imagine pedagogy in the traditional college classroom, concluding "gamification must consist of high-choice, low-risk engagements in a clearly structured environment."

4. SOCIAL CHANGE AND HEALTH TRACKING THROUGH GAMIFICATION

Although Games for Change has been around since 2004, in 2010 Jane McGonigal placed the international spotlight on the use of games to enact social change in her TED talk and subsequently in her New York Times bestseller, *Reality is Broken* (2011). Since then, games have found a solid strategic place among change makers as games such as protein folding game "Foldit" and SimCityEDU have garnered international audiences and the attention and respect of industry and funding leaders as well as researchers and educators. As access and technology continue to improve and give these games even greater potential, what research is being done to aid this movement? The three chapters included here provide some insight.

In Chapter 11, Marty Kearns and Meredith Wise, of Netcentric Campaigns provide a foundational study of the most successful advocacy networks and their use of games as well as a proposed framework from which to design advocacy-related multiplayer games. Jolene Fisher's chapter outlines her research of games for social change with a specific exploration of the international development industry. In Chapter 12, Fisher provides an historical review of both the successful and not-so-successful use of digital games in international development and challenges the notion of gamification as a passing trend rather than a meaningful and sustainable tool for the field.

Another highly touted area of gamification as it relates to the human condition and health has been in recent advancements in the quantified or gamified self movement. Chapter 13 explores the "gamified self" as DiGregorio and Gangadharbatla identify the factors that influence the acceptance and use of self-tracking technologies via an online survey using Technology Acceptance Model (TAM) as a theoretical framework. Their results indicate that perceptions of ease of use and enjoyment of self-tracking tools are less influential than perceptions of usefulness in the ultimate acceptance and use of such tools.

5. GAMIFICATION AND JOURNALISM

The book concludes with a look into the growing trend of gamification and journalism. While "immersive journalism" such as Nonny de la Pena's groundbreaking stories, *Hunger in Los Angeles* and *Project Syria* take readers on a journey into an immersive 3D story, it is not a game. Social virtual worlds provide interesting new platforms to engage audiences in storytelling and social engagement and are fruitful environments for study. However, when they do not incorporate the game elements discussed throughout the chapters of this book, they are social and learning places rather than a game space. Still, we have seen traditional journalists use game platforms to engage readers in fascinating ways as will be seen in the final two chapters.

In Chapter 14, Bartosz Wojdynski examines the use of games and quizzes in journalism. Bartosz reviews changes in journalism audience engagement and consumption and the use of games and quizzes in that environment. He then also offers recommendations of best practices of online news games and quizzes including identity quizzes, knowledge quizzes, simulations and topical play. Bartosz concludes with a call for additional research to continue to understand the changing nature of the relationship between audiences and the news. Raul Ferrer Conill and Michael Karlsson additionally dive into the gamification of journalism. In Chapter 15, the authors engage readers with their systematic review of the literature that explores the tension between the professional and commercial interests of journalism, i.e. the reader vs. the consumer and how gamification may or may not be an appropriate strategy for bridging that divide. They also shed light on the way gamification is currently being used in journalism and how it may engage audiences in ways that has the potential to improve both democratic process and civic engagement.

Overall, this edited volume is the much-needed compilation of research from both academic and industry minds in the area of gamification from business, education, health and social change, and journalism. That said, research on gamification is still in its infancy with its applications undoubtedly expanding to many other areas like government and environment that were not covered in the current volume. Although not a comprehensive volume on gamification research—given the pace with which the field itself is growing—the current volume is unique in that it brings together research from several disparate fields that seldom communicate with one another. By using the common theme of gamification, the current volume accomplishes several things: first, gamification researchers from one field (say, education) are now exposed to research in other areas (say, marketing); second, such an exposure to research in a different field should certainly enhance one's own understanding and application of gamification; and third, an increased understanding should lead to interesting research ideas and even possible collaborations among researchers from unrelated fields. For example, research in the area of gamification of health such as chapter 13, which investigates the factors that influence self-tracking technology acceptance has tremendous practical implications for researchers and professionals in the area of marketing looking to better understand (and change) consumer behavior. Similarly, the chapters on gamification of marketing research (chapter 5) and human resource processes (chapter 6) provide theoretical and practical implications for researchers interested in gamification of education. If gamification of surveys leads to increased response rates then perhaps the same technique can be employed in educational settings when the objective is increased participation in classroom or online discussions. These are examples of precisely the type of cross-pollination of research we expect will result from our edited volume.

Harsha Gangadharbatla
University of Colorado Boulder, USA

Donna Z. Davis
University of Oregon, USA

REFERENCES

Applying Lessons from 20 Years of Hype Cycles to Your Own Innovation and Forecasting Strategies. (2014, September 16). *Gartner*. Retrieved from https://www.gartner.com/doc/2847417?srcId=1-3132930191#-58610447

Caillois, R. (1961). *Man, Play and Games* (M. Barash, Trans.). New York: Free Press.

Deterding, S., Dixon, D., Khaled, R., & Nacke, L. (2011, September). From game design elements to gamefulness: defining gamification. *Proceedings of the 15th International Academic MindTrek Conference: Envisioning Future Media Environments* (pp. 9-15). ACM. doi:10.1145/2181037.2181040

Fink, E., Saine, U., & Saine, T. (1968). The Oasis of Happiness: Toward an Ontology of Play. *Yale French Studies*, (41): 19–30. doi:10.2307/2929663

Huizinga, J. (1950). Homo Ludens: A Study of the Play-Element. In *Culture*. Boston: Beacon Press.

Impact of the Ice Bucket Challenge. (2015). *ALS Association*. Retrieved from http://www.alsa.org/news/archive/impact-of-ice-bucket-challenge.html

McGonigal, J. (2011). *Reality is Broken: Why Games make us better and how they can change the world*. New York: Penguin.

Murray, H.J.R. (1913). *A History of Chess*. Benjamin Press (originally published by Oxford University Press).

Paharia, R. (2010). Who coined the term "gamification"? *Quora*. Retrieved from http://goo.gl/CvcMs

Piccione, P. (1980). In Search of the Meaning of Senet. *Archaeology*, (July/August): 55–58. Retrieved online from http://www.gamesmuseum.uwaterloo.ca/Archives/Piccione/index.html

Size of the online gaming market from 2003 to 2015 (in billion U.S. dollars). (2015). *Statistica.com*. Retrieved from http://www.statista.com/statistics/270728/market-volume-of-online-gaming-worldwide/

Spariosu, M. (1989). *Dionysus Reborn*. Ithaca, N.Y.: Cornell University Press.

Acknowledgment

The editors would like to acknowledge the help of all the people involved in this project and, more specifically, to the authors and reviewers that took part in the review process. Without their support, this book would not have become a reality.

First, the editors would like to thank each one of the authors for their contributions. Our sincere gratitude goes to the chapter's authors who contributed their time and expertise to this book.

Second, the editors wish to acknowledge the valuable contributions of the reviewers regarding the improvement of quality, coherence, and content presentation of chapters. Most of the authors also served as referees; we highly appreciate their double task.

Harsha Gangadharbatla
University of Colorado Boulder, USA

Donna Z. Davis
University of Oregon, USA

Section 1
Designing Successful Gamification

Chapter 1
Ambiguous Play:
Towards a Broader Concept of Gamification

Nathan Hulsey
North Carolina State University, USA

ABSTRACT

This chapter is a critical-conceptual introduction to the topic of gamification from the standpoint of game studies (the study of games) and ludology (the study of play). A secondary task is to move the definition and conceptual history of gamification away from essentialist notions of play and games and towards a more nuanced understanding of gamification as a philosophy of design with situational outcomes. By examining the controversy surrounding gamification as a complex history of concepts, the chapter aims to give the reader an overview of how gamification aligns with or deviates from various definitions of games and play. Gamification can be controversial when using traditional ludological concepts largely because traditional ludology is pre-digital, and does not account for the current technological and cultural shifts driving gaming and gamification. Finally, the chapter ends with the suggestion that the current cultural turn in game studies provides a way to analyze gamification as an example of the "gaming of culture."

INTRODUCTION

This chapter, in part, serves as a conceptual introduction to the study of Gamification from the standpoint of Game Studies and Ludology. Particularly, I focus on how gamification can be controversial when using traditional approaches to the study of play commonly referred to as ludology. By examining gamification's conceptual controversy as a history of ideas, I also aim to give the reader an overview of how gamification aligns itself with or deviates from 'standard' definitions of games and play. Gamification has been controversial since its inception, often clashing with proponents of the so-called "serious games" movement (Ruffino, 2014). The supposed conflict of interest between serious games and gamification prompted Ian Bogost, a prominent scholar, game designer and serious games proponent, to call it "bullshit" (Bogost, 2011). Gamification has been linked with governmentality (Schrape, 2014), behaviorism (Ruffino, 2014) and, according to Bogost (2011), a complete perversion of play. The lit-

DOI: 10.4018/978-1-4666-8651-9.ch001

Copyright © 2016, IGI Global. Copying or distributing in print or electronic forms without written permission of IGI Global is prohibited.

erature on gamification, scholarly or otherwise, represents a major split between utopian and dystopian interpretations of gaming. This chapter hopes to conceptually and ontologically 'ground' gamification as a set of practices that have no overriding ethical code.

First, I begin with a brief definition of gamification as it stands today, in which it is primarily utilized as a tool for marketing and consumer surveillance (Whitson, 2013). Next, I will examine ludological currents in a variety of scholarly fields from historical standpoint, including in-depth analyses of the definitions of play and games put forth by ludologists such as Johan Huizinga (1950), Roger Callois (1961), Mihai Spariosu (1989) and Eugene Fink (1968). I then contrast these definitions of play and games against the concept of "life-as-play" put forth by practitioners and scholars, particularly Alan Watts (1995), James P. Carse (1989) and Charles A. Coonradt (2007). I will explore the controversy associated with gamification, while avoiding dystopian and utopian takes on Gamification and related practices (Bogost, 2011; McGonigal, 2011). I suggest that the primary reason that gamification is often separated from gaming is the inability of traditional ludological theory to deal with the technologically-driven convergence of life, leisure and labor. This chapter does not propose a 'new' definition of gamification. Rather, it proposes that the current definition creates controversy because of the way play and games have been treated in Western thought, largely due to the supposition that play is inherently ethical. However, any 'ethic' of play is ambiguous. Presenting arguments for or against gamification based on faulty ethics-based assumptions only serves to obscure gamification's ontological status. Second, I will consider contradictory definitions of games and play put forth by tertiary ludologists such as Jean Baudrillard (1979, 1981b, 1998a) and Lewis Mumford (1934). Finally, I will propose that Gamification's unstable position as both game and anti-game rests in ambivalent discursive frameworks surrounding "play" and "fun." I suggest that the Gamification produces examples of "ambiguous play" (Sutton-Smith, 1997), in which play is reimagined as a set of situational practices rooted in notions of power and control. Reimagining play as an ambiguous act moves towards an inclusive and complex notion of play that invites a more nuanced view of gamification as it stands currently. Gamification is not necessarily a question of "game culture" but rather an example of "the gaming of culture" (Boellstorff, 2006), where game thinking permeates wired culture in the 21st Century. In conclusion, I make the call for a nuanced position regarding what gaming and gamification can tell us about games and play.

SITUATING GAMIFICATION

While no expansive critical histories of gamification have been produced, most general histories of the so-called "trend" begin with the inception of the term. Some exceptions include Raczkowski (2014), who examines the history of point-based economies and flow in gamification and Fuchs (2014), who offers an explorations gamification's history in terms of different fields of practice such as music, magic and art. Both authors reiterate the need to historicize gamification. Starting scholarly inquiry with the term "gamification" is the root of most arguments surrounding gamification. Any time a novel technology is introduced, the first scholarly reactions to the "new" technology or technique are often diametrically opposed between utopian and dystopian notions (Carey, 1989). As I stated in the introduction, gamification is not exempt from this controversy. However, to construct gamification as a viable academic and professional concept, we must utilize the conceptual histories to produce a fair and useful conceptualization of gamification *beyond* business, education or marketing. I argue a good place to start is ludology, or the study of play. Ludology a continuous undercurrent in sociology, anthropology and other life/social sciences centered on exploring the social, cultural, biological, historical and metaphysical aspects of play in humans. Ludologists may not have coined the term "gamification," but they were the first to propose the *concept* of gamification. The concept of using games to influence and transform non-ludic practices and systems is, ostensibly, as old as play itself.

Defining Gamification

Before we explore a conceptual history of gamification, I will first provide a working definition. Gamification, according to many noted practitioners and scholars, is a method augmenting non-ludic systems with game dynamics to provide intrinsic motivation for loyalty, labor, learning and consumption (Chapin, 2011; Comer, 2012; Danforth, 2011; Delo, 2012; Deterding, 2012; Fuchs, 2012; Kim, 2012; Liyakasa, 2012c; McGonigal, 2011; Shaer, 2012; Swan, 2012; Zicherman & Cunningham, 2011; Zuk, 2012). While this definition is straightforward and simple, it also leaves much to be desired. Simply tacking game mechanics onto an existing set of practices isn't always useful (Zicherman & Linder, 2010). Gamification, in a word, is *situational*. Because of this I would like to add some definitional modifications for the purposes of this chapter. First, gamification is a set of diverse practices rather than a clear or discernable methodology. For example, gamification proponent Yu-Kai Chou's (2013) method for studying gamified design, called "Octalysis," makes use of multiple nodes (eight, to be exact) that represent many sets of game mechanics. These sets, arranged in an octagon, are accounted for within a gamified application. Each of the eight nodes are divided into different sets of strategies for manipulating engagement and motivation—strategies for creating meaning, accomplishment, cooperation, competition, scarcity and other motivational techniques. These game mechanics, or perhaps 'tricks of the trade,' are not viewed as mutually exclusive. . Interestingly, Chou (2013) distinguishes between "black hat" and "white hat" gamification, pointing out that the ways in which game dynamics are used serve a variety of purposes. "Black hat" gamification, like black hat hacking, disrupts systems. In gamification, black hat practices are strategies used to support the dark, competitive and compulsion-based side of play (Chou, 2013). "White hat" gamification, like white hat hacking, seeks to reinforce and protect a system. White hat strategies often involve cooperative play and positive reinforcement (Chou, 2013). Chou (2013) maintains that there is any number of approaches to gamifying something, and each one is situational.

Even at the practitioner level the seemingly simple definition of gamification becomes surprisingly complex, with a variety of approaches and outcomes embedded in the term. As such, I will utilize my own, slightly modified, definition for the purposes of this chapter: *gamification is a design philosophy centered around transferring game mechanics[1]—and, by extension game logics[2]—into traditionally non-ludic environments*. By centering gamification as an open-ended design philosophy rather than a specific, all-inclusive concept we can be more sensitive to the historical, ontological and social implications of pursuing gamification as a diverse set of ludic techniques[3] that can work towards a variety of ends. Using this definition of gamification, focus shifts away from the essentialist ethical assumptions about the 'nature' of gamification. Rather, by situating gamification as a set of meta-approaches to design, I suggest that gamified practices are situational—they are based in the actual design and use of individual applications (e.g. what game mechanics are or are not present). This also avoids sweeping generalizations and embraces the complexity of play. As we will see over the course of this chapter, games and play have historically been classified according to a diverse number of characteristics, many completely at odds with one another. Extricating a fair, rigorous and working concept of gamification through a conceptual history to fit an (appropriately) broad definition of gamification is the primary goal for this chapter.

Gamification and Ludology

The notion that play and other, supposedly non-ludic individual pursuits (such as shopping, budgeting, social networking, matriculating, and working) and non-ludic fields of practice (like economics, warfare, politics and statecraft) are ontologically opposed has been covered, and subsequently debunked, by many ludologists and modern game theorists (Baudrillard, 1979, 1998a; Boellstorff, 2006; Consalvo, 2009; Dyer-Witheford & de Peuter, 2009; Huizinga, 1950; Malaby, 2007; M. Montola, Stenros, & Waern, 2009; Steinkuehler, 2006; T.L. Taylor, 2006, 2009; T. L. Taylor & Kolko, 2003). As we will see, ludology can be a contradictory course of study with different iterations. While ludology is currently most active in the field of game studies, ludological currents occur in a variety of academic fields. These fields range from biology to philosophy to geography to sociology—possibly the result of play's universality as an evolutionary reference point (Bateson, 1956; Sutton-Smith, 1997). In the fields of ecology and biology play is largely considered ubiquitous in mammals and corvids: it is a pursuit in learning, socialization, communication and rearing young (Bateson, 1956; Brown & Vaughan, 2009). At the most basic bodily level, play serves a major social purpose in almost every social aspect of intelligent life—it involves the transmission and sharpening of instinct, making it necessary for socialization and life itself (Brown & Vaughan, 2009). In advanced social structures, play is a lifelong, rather than juvenile, pursuit promoting social cohesion; it is an aggression/stress reducer in social situations (Brown & Vaughan, 2009; Sutton-Smith, 1997). It also promotes exploration, skill-building and cross-species communication (Brown & Vaughan, 2009). Play is pre-lingual, and key to social and—in the case of humans, apes (Bower, 2013; Limber, 1977), corvids (Diamond & Bond, 2003) and cetaceans (Kuczaj & Highfill, 2005)—basic cultural, technological and linguistic development.

However, biological interpretations of play (and by extension, games) also represent biological and social uncertainty. Gregory Bateson (1956), a biologist, suggests that play is a paradox because it is and is not what it seems to be. The playful "nip" of an animal at play is a both a bite and not a bite; it "connotes a bite but not what a bite connotes" (Sutton-Smith, 1997). Robert Fagen (1981), an animal play theorist, states: "The most irritating feature of play is not the perceptual incoherence, as such, but rather that play taunts us with its inaccessibility. We feel that something is behind it all, but we do not know, or have *forgotten how to see it*" (as cited in Sutton-Smith, 1997, p.2, emphasis mine). Similarly, sociological and philosophical applications of ludology also question the nature of play.

In the field of sociology, Huizinga (1950) has perhaps been the most-mentioned ludologists, largely because of his concept of the magic circle. Huizinga (1950) discusses play as something happening outside ordinary life. Huizinga's (1950) version of play, and by extension, games, is a type of ritual activity that emerges through rules that are largely separate from everyday reality. Huizinga (1950) states that play and games constitute a "free activity standing quite consciously outside 'ordinary' life as being 'not serious,' but at the same time absorbing the players intensely and utterly" (p. 13). Huizinga (1950) was also interested in understanding how play, ensconced in the ritual space of games, is both an outlet for culture and a key component in cultural circulation. Oddly, for Huizinga (1950), games and play are also activities connected with no material interests. They entail actions from which no profit can be gained. They also proceed within their own proper boundaries of time and space according to fixed rules and in an orderly manner. Huizinga's (1950) primary thesis is that play is a primogenitor of culture, and games are its vehicle. The order created in the ritual nature of games is a sort of laboratory for cultural pursuits ranging from law to sexuality to art. The magic circle has been a misunderstood term (Consalvo, 2009; Harviainen, 2012). Primarily, the magic circle is often cited as proof that games are somehow separated from reality and must be disconnected from non-ludic spaces. Even more troubling is the suggestion that the magic circle is actually a metaphor for "virtual" or "synthetic" worlds that run parallel to our own "real" spaces (Castronova, 2005). One reason for the misunderstanding is that Huizinga (1950) is occasionally unclear; while he associates games and gameplay with social and cultural activities, one of his key assumptions about games is that no profit can truly be gained from them. Games and play, for Huizinga (1950), entail actions that are, at the onset of a game, contextual only to the rules of play. Games also proceed in an orderly manner within rule-oriented, situational boundaries outside of quotidian time and space[4]. However, this does not mean that play is self-contained. If we think about Gamification, it is not the actual game mechanics that are profitable—rather it is the *information* and *activity* generated from gameplay that generates capital. Huizinga's (1950) primary thesis is that play is a primogenitor of culture, a mode of *transmission*, and games are its vehicle. The order created through the ritual nature of games is a sort of laboratory for cultural pursuits ranging from law to economics to art and beyond. Huizinga's (1950) argument is not one that precludes a bounded space, but one that suggests all culture is a realm of networked spaces, of topographies, and play inhabits and influences many spaces at the same time. Huizinga's primary goal is not to identify play as a set of practices existing within culture or to define games a inhabiting their own cultural milieu; rather, he attempts to examine how "all aspects of culture bears resemblance to play and games" (Huizinga, 1950). Games imply a cultural cycle—they are containers, or spaces of germination, for cultural possibility. Huizinga assumed that play was contained in a "magic circle" created by games—however, games themselves circulate freely in the liminal spaces between leisure and labor. The magic circle has different temporal constraints, spatial boundaries and sets of rules than quotidian spaces. Huizinga (1950) points out that the activities within the magic circle are (eventually) carried over into "real life." In other words, play is a form a cultural learning that is only superficially separated from everyday pursuits.

Huizinga (1950) was one of the first ludologists to specifically explore play as a mode of cultural transmission, and also one of the first to suggest, alongside Marcel Mauss[5] (2000) and Georges Bataille[6] (1991), that games, gifts and playful exchanges are a precursor to primitive economic systems, and thus advanced systems of language and writing. These conclusions make Huizinga a primary ludologist who saw games as a mode of cultural and technological transmission and play as a sort of 'cultural energy' directed and shaped by gameplay. Finally, Huizinga was one of the first to examine competitive play as precursor to the formation of a modern capitalist culture. Life and play are inherently linked for Huizinga both are driven by free, democratic and voluntary competition based on a set of contractual rules.

Roger Callois (1961) builds on Huizinga's (1950) work, primarily disagreeing on Huizinga's focus on competitive play. Occasionally, Caillois is accused of conflating play with "escapism" (Calleja, 2010). However, he offered multiple suggestions (rather than caveats) on possibilities for defining play and games. Caillois, like Huizinga, believed that play was not merely "escapist;" rather, play is socially embedded in (and necessary to) culture. Also like Huizinga, Caillois feared games and play could easily be manipulated or institutionalized.

Caillois (1961) primarily analyzes different aspects of play in various cultures and then create a "comprehensive review" of different play forms[7]. Caillois notes that there is considerable difficulty in defining play without first categorizing it. His conclusion is that play is characterized through six core characteristics: it is never forced; it is separate from everyday activities; it occupies its own time and space; its results cannot be pre-determined and thus requires special initiative from the player; it is ultimately not tied to capital in that creates no wealth and it has a definite "end" and "beginning"; it is a-cultural in that play is produced through rules that suspend normative laws and behaviors; and finally, play involves a process of imagination that allows players to players confirm the imagined realities it produces (Caillois, 1961). Caillois was primarily interested in games and play as social forces that exist alongside everyday activities while also providing a distinct, positive social influence.

Interestingly, Caillois (1961) is highly critical of any games that involved chance, which he associated with gambling and compulsion. Games of chance are "all games that are based on a decision independent of the player, an outcome over which he has no control, and in which winning is the result of fate rather than triumphing over an adversary" (17). In games of chance, Caillois claims "the player is entirely passive: he does not deploy his resources, skill, muscles, intelligence. All he need do is await, in hope and trembling, the cast of the die" (17). Chance "negates work, patience, experience, qualifications… It seems an insolent and sovereign insult to merit" (Caillois, 1961; p. 17). These observations are compelling primarily because, if we take Caillois literally, all computer games are essentially games of chance. While digital games were unheard of and computers were in their nascent stage when Caillois (1961) was writing, games of chance are constructed as games in which there is any agency other than human dictating rules or outcomes. Caillois' definition of play requires human actors engaged in solitary games that require raw imagination, cooperative games that require players to help one another or adversarial games in which wits and strategy prevail. In order for "healthy" play to occur, games must bring human players together in a ritual pact. Games where resources or mechanics are generated impartially by a non-human system are games in which chance plays a key role. These games are, according to Caillois, compulsory in nature—they lead to undesirable situations in which the game masters often the player, as opposed to the other way around.

This holds some key implications for the conceptual reception of gamification: if we look at gamification as a process that seeks to add gaming mechanics to non-gaming systems for the purpose of "inviting" or "driving" engagement, it becomes highly suspect under Caillois' (1961) and Huizinga's (1950) notions of play and games. Because gamification is primarily used to monitor and influence behavior within environments, it often involves simulation and chance. Also, gamified applications and services often have positive reinforcement through points and rewards with real-world value, making gamified play "for profit." Gamified applications often reinforce "normal" or "desired" behaviors and outcomes rather than disrupting them—many of these applications rely heavily of chance-based games and positive/negative reinforcement (e.g. white and black hat gamification). Still, gamification is largely about "fun" and inspiring "playfulness" in everyday situations (Zicherman & Linder, 2010) while also providing "loyalty-oriented" tools to the organization that seeks to benefit from it (Zicherman & Cunningham, 2011). So there seem to be some elements of gamification that fit the bill for traditional games (fun and playfulness) while also disrupting the idea that play is "free" or separate from more quotidian sectors of life like economics and government.

While early sociological explorations of play suggest that it is a positive, natural pursuit of freedom and exploration through games and gameplay, historiographic explorations of play suggest that it is rooted in more primal, dangerous drives. Mihai Spariosu (Spariosu, 1989) noted play's possible dark side in his comparative analysis on historical writings about ludic activity. Spariosu suggests that play is not at all a "free" or harmless event. Play can be many things at once: Appollionian play is sportive, skillful and mastery-oriented while Dionysian play is illusionary, labyrinthine, dangerous and sexual (Spariosu, 1989). Like Bataille (1950) and Mauss (2000), Spariosu states that play can be a form of self-abandonment and excess as well as a socially constructive activity.

Similar to Spariosu (1989), philosopher Eugene Fink (1968) explores play as a metaphysical activity with a wide range of possible outcomes. Fink (1974) contended that play was unfairly devalued in metaphysical tradition, and maintained that to understand the world as a ontological concept, play must first be interrogated (Elden, 2008). For Fink (1974), play is cosmological force that is not necessarily human in nature; rather, is both the cosmos and a symbol of the cosmos—it produces and realizes ontological difference (Elden, 2008). Fink (1968) states:

the mode of play is that of spontaneous act, of vital impulse. Play is, as it were, existence centered in itself. The motivation of play does not coincide with that of other human activity. All other activity…is a means to the final end (telos) of man, namely his ultimate happiness. For the adult, however, play is a strange oasis, an enchanted rest-spot…Play interrupts the continuity and purposive structure of our lives; it remains at a distance from our usual mode of existence. But while seeming to be unrelated to our normal life, it relates to it in every meaningful way (p.20-22).

Play, in an illusory manner, produces the world around us. It also produces the objects that we interact with every day. Play is like a mirror or a shadow of a larger concept; it allows humans the ability to don and discard a variety of social, spiritual and material possibilities. For Fink (1968), "play always has to do with play objects. The play-thing alone is enough to assure us that play does not take place in pure subjectivity without any reference to the concrete world around us" (p.27). Illusion and reality, the world and the world we perceive, are all processes of interplay and interpolation—all play produces a "play world" that mirrors and affects what is only perceived as "the real" (Fink et al., 1968).

Similar to Huizinga's (1950) thesis, play and games are spaces of possibility for both Fink (1968) and Spariosu (1989). However Fink (1968, 1974) takes Huizinga's conceptualizations on play and life one step forward: play is not only the primary wellspring culture, it is also a "basic existential phenomenon" which is "just as primordial and autonomous as death, love, work, and struggle for power" (p.22). "We play at being serious," Fink (1968) postulates, "we play truth, we play reality, we play work and struggle, we play love and death and we even play play itself" (p.22). For Fink, play is the polarity of two extreme modes of existence—the clear 'Apollonian' moment of self-determination and the dark 'Dionysian' moment of panic and self-abandonment. Both are procreative of the world as humans perceive it.

Ludological currents in biology, philosophy and sociology acknowledge that games and play are vital parts of—and a necessary precursor to—cultural activity. Interestingly, play is also linked to early economic systems, particularly the potlatch style of exchange linked with the eventual development of capitalism, the persistence of a "general economy" of waste, and the creation exchange-based communities and gift economies (Bataille, 1991; Baudrillard, 1998a, 1998b, 2005; Esposito, 2011; Huizinga, 1950; Mauss, 2000). At the same time, play and games are often thought of as ritualistically separated from a "real" or "non-synthetic" commodity-based economy (Castronova, 2005). Games and play tap into a more primal economy comprised of reciprocal gifts, honor and a sense of protocol (Mauss, 2000). For traditional ludologists, play is a riotous and mercurial force that is contained and directed by the contractual, ritualistic rules of the game. At the same time, play is also construed as easily manipulated (and possibly dangerous) because gameplay eventually seeps its way into the general cultural milieu.

In short, the relationship between games and play is complex. Compulsion, profitability and abuse are considered deal-breakers when it comes to play. However, gameplay is also inextricably linked to social structures that *do* thrive on profit. For example, the link between games and modern capitalism is so strong that evolutionary economists claim games (and the drive to play them) are a major force in steering the current era of capitalism (Metcalfe, 2014). Yet, Huizinga (1950) argues that games do not directly contribute to economics or law; they inform, or perhaps preclude, economic or governmental activity. As we move into modern definitions of gamification, the caveat that games and play must be 'free' pursuits—ideologically divested of cold, hard capital—often serves as evidence against gamification as a viable set of ludic practices (Bogost, 2011). This viewpoint echoes Huizinga (1950) and Caillois (1961): a game for profit is no longer a game. At the same time, it is the very exploratory freedom promised by gameplay that excites proponents of gamification (McGonigal, 2011). In this viewpoint, "the play's the thing" that drives gamification, not games ("The play's the thing," 2011). Gamification aims for behavioral results. After all, it is playful behaviors that produce the 'results' necessary for the service or application to continue. In a more positive interpretation of gamification, both Apollonian and Dionysian play serve the interests of a more creative, open and stress-free life—we owe it to ourselves and our employers to *enjoy* the labor of life.

Currently, positive interpretations of gamification claim it provides a potential release from the perils of unrewarded drudgery (McGonigal, 2011). Games are perceived as the final collapse between the (imaginary) line separating leisure from labor (Baudrillard, 1991; Calleja, 2010; Coonradt, 2007). In short, "modern" gamification is an exercise in convergence: ubiquitous computing, surveillance, big data and networked play often defy past definitions of "games" and gaming offered by traditional ludologists (de Souza e Silva, 2006; Hulsey & Reeves, 2014; M. Montola et al., 2009; Whitson, 2013). For example Thorhauge (2013) questions the efficacy of construing the rules of a digital game as identical to the rules of non-digital games like those studied by pre-digital ludologists. Similarly, Tulloch (2014) maintains that "rather than operating through restriction, rules construct the possibility of the game, producing the game world and norms of play practice…rules should not be understood in opposition to player agency, but rather as a contributor to, and product of it" (p. 1). In other words, play and games are as malleable as their historical context—they are, after all, produced by the players who play them. Rules, and by extent, games, are not ethically or procedurally set in stone—rather, play and games are what the collective "we" make of them. Thus, many modern conceptualizations of gamification characterize it as part of a playful world: play (and gamification) contributes to an increasing diversity of, hopefully playful, outcomes primarily centered around work and everyday life.

The "Infinite Game:" Gamification and Work-As-Play

Alan Watts (1995), a well-known Zen philosopher, is perhaps the first popular scholar to ever mention the core concept behind modern gamification in the early 1970s. In a series of lectures entitled "Work as Play," Watts (1995) states that making everything a game, or "playing through" all aspects of life, is the key to conquering the fear of death. By "playing through" life, everyday tasks, love, work and even dying become secondhand illusions to the process of becoming (Watts, 1995). Play brings focus back to the moment—because games are, by nature, a momentary pursuit. Work-as-play is the processes of subordinating all other processes behind the guise of play, sublimating the order of all things into a game, and finally producing a type of reality in which production and consumption are mirror images of one another.

Similarly, in the 1980's, religious philosopher James P. Carse (1987) also toyed with the concept of 'life-as-play.' Carse noted that play revolves around two different world-making technologies: finite and infinite games. Finite games are games that take place in a space—they are contests of power, ritual and governance. They are also voluntary, and cannot be undertaken if compulsory (Carse, 1987). Infinite games, on the other hand, are games of life. They are games in which the only rules that exist are rules that ensure the continuation of the play (Carse, 1987). While finite games can be seen a pursuits linked to distinct spatial and temporal boundaries, infinite games are games that transcend both space and time—infinite games play *with* boundaries. Carse maintains these two types of games demarcate the boundaries between the world of the social (finite games) and the realm of metaphysical truth (infinite games). Carse states, "the rules of an infinite game must change in the course of play. The rules are changed when the players of an infinite game agree that the play is imperiled by a finite outcome…The rules of an infinite game are changed to prevent anyone from winning the game and to bring as many persons as possible into the play" (p.9). Thus, finite games are interested in self-contained logistic outcomes and infinite games involve raw generativity.

What play 'generates' in an infinite game is open to question. Play behaviors associated with gamification serve several purposes—gamified play is generative of everything that can be recorded via gameplay and utilized for a purpose 'outside' the context of the game dynamics (Whitson, 2013). This "anything" is basically the data of everyday life: shopping, socialization, fitness, surveillance and mobility all fall under the purview of gamification (Hulsey & Reeves, 2014; Whitson, 2013). The "boundary play" (Nippert-Eng, 2005) between things that 'are' or 'are not' a game is most apparent in how gamification is transforming the labor and consumer markets with playful, everyday applications (Austin, 2014; Byrne, 2012; Deterding, 2012; Environment, 2012; Liyakasa, 2012a, 2012b; Myron, 2012; Scofidio, 2012). Behind these varied transformations is the idea that almost anything—including 'things' formerly cloistered off from the concept of play—can be made more game-like with the right design choices and technology (Zicherman & Cunningham, 2011). This viewpoint is in contrast with proposition that games cannot be associated with productive or profitable labor.

For example, the *concept* of work-as-play may have been explored popularly by Watts (1995) in his lectures and television show during the 1970's; however, *practical* applications of work-as-play gained traction during the managerial revolution of the 1980's. Leisure studies scholars note that this revolution ended the idea that leisure is a matter of having more "free time"—instead, as the globalized economy became more computerized work became "24/7"—almost inseparable from everyday life (Gray, 2007). Charles A. Coonradt (2007) proposed in 1984 that games may serve as a better personal framework for conducting business. Deemed the "grandfather of Gamification" by *Forbes* magazine (Krogue, 2012), Coonradt points out that recreational games provided better motivation and feedback, stable rules of play and efficient scorekeeping than traditional managerial methods, stating "in recreation participants feel they have a higher degree of choice…Part of the reason for liking a recreational activity is the freedom you have in doing it" (p.150-51). In the years since the 1984 publication of Coonradt's *The Game of Work*, scholars have noted a ludic managerial turn. For example, Costea, Crump, and Holm (2005), identify a "Dionysian turn" in the way the play is deployed in a typically "adult" workplace. Costea et al (2005) point out that "play emerges as a managerial resource because it has an affinity with the increased weight placed upon 'work' as a site for the pursuit of collective and individual 'wellness' and happiness as key dimensions of self-assertion" (p.140). In other words, the biological and cultural trajectories of play in the workplace have combined—the authors state that the social manifestation of play embodies a confluence between an "entitlement to happiness" and a "duty to be happy" as a form of both managerial and biological form of self-work (Costea et al., 2005).

The distinction between freedom and compulsion in play, labor and life perforates the conceptual history of gamification. This (in)distinction has only been exacerbated by the recent, rapid advances information technologies(Colman, 2012). While Coonradt (2007) was proposing games as a set of personal solutions for increasing productivity in the workplace and mitigating stress, recent technological trends have catapulted the idea that game logics can work as a collective solution to productivity and motivational issues in both client-facing and internal business operations into the mainstream (Byrne, 2012; Kim, 2012; Nicholson, 2012). Adding game mechanics to non-gaming systems has been lauded as an answer to increasing workplace frustration and consumer loyalty issues (McGonigal, 2011; Zicherman & Cunningham, 2011; Zicherman & Linder, 2010); it has also been decried as an opaque set of practices aimed at manipulation and surveillance (Bogost, 2011; Whitson, 2013). Either way, the concept of work-as-play seeks to marry the processes of consumption and production into a manageable, play-oriented economic, cultural and social cycle.

Gamification and Digital Technology

Far from Watts' (1995) idealist conception of work-as-play as way of personal exploration and becoming and Coonradt's (1997) notion of using games to free oneself from the compulsory nature of labor, the digital iteration of gamification has largely been proposed as a business/lifestyle solution. Gamification is often cast as a technologically-driven set of design practices; it is also, supposedly, a "new" or emerging concept (Deterding, 2012; Fuchs, 2012; Liyakasa, 2012a; Mosca, 2012). The current visibility of gamification comes on the heels of advertising through social media games (Clavio, Kraft, & Pedersen, 2009). Social media games, such as *Farmville*, exposed a new brand of consumer provisionally called the "cyber-farmer," an ideal consumer whose loyalty could be bought with virtual goods rather than expensive real-world loyalty rewards (Luscombe, 2009) and led to development of "advergaming," or free, digital games that showcased a product, location or service using persuasive elements such as avatar customization driven by a "harvesting" mechanic (Bailey, Wise, & Bolls, 2009; Choi & Lee, 2012). Advergaming also had internal uses for the workplace—by attaching points and rewards to daily tasks employers sought new ways to manage production and consumption within the workplace (Byrne, 2012; Liyakasa, 2012c). However, advergaming had inconclusive results in promoting consumer action; it only produced affective responses to products and brands rather than driving any cognitive or behavioral outcomes (Sukoco & Wu, 2011; van Reijmersdal, Rozendaal, & Buijzen, 2012). Two key aspects for this failure to produce consistent action was 1) the fact that users were playing the games online at a home or public computer terminal and 2) the advergames themselves were self-contained systems—they only produced motivational results within the context of the game and its rules (van Reijmersdal et al., 2012). If the game ended, so did the spike in engagement and retention.

To produce reliable results, marketers assumed that game dynamics nested in advergames needed to be divorced from the idea of "a game." Games are, by most standards, self-contained worlds with their own timelines and sets or rules. If producing and consuming are 24/7 pursuits that rely on maintaining interest, efficiency and overall motivation, then the idea of a single game would be insufficient to fulfill the dictum of work-as-play. Game dynamics must be set free from their ritualistic bubble and directly injected into everyday life. The affective nature of gaming must be extrinsic, tied to real-time physical and economic events, and the mechanics and the logics behind the gamified design must be continuous. The smart phone and tablet computer provided the platform to test out a mode of attaching game dynamics to everyday behaviors and locations while ensuring the gamified system was always present (Keats, 2011). Trade journals noted that the mobile revolution would usher in a new era of customer interaction and workplace management (Clavio et al., 2009; Keats, 2011; Naughton, 2003; Qin, Rau, & Salvendy, 2009; Rizzo, 2008; Sennott, 2005). Industry blogs asserted that "what yesterday's science called Human Computer Interaction is today's art of playing" (Gopaladesikan, 2012). If gamification is intended to make everyday life more fun and profitable in terms of engagement, then it is a philosophy of design directly aimed at the continuation of play in its generative form—play becomes a productive state of being that permeates not just labor, but all aspect of life[8].

Carse (1987) and Fink (1968, 1974), in their own respective times and ways, iterate the ideal notion of play-as-life. Gamification, when deployed through networked technologies, holds many resemblances to Carse's infinite game. However, unlike Carse's infinite and emancipatory games, gamification is largely about motivating and promoting certain behaviors while also discouraging and silencing others. This is largely accomplished through the design of the gamified application in question (Fuchs, 2012; Zicherman & Cunningham, 2011). It is true that gamification's rules only exist to extend play 'infinitely'—here meaning as long as play is profitable (Campbell, 2011; Zicherman & Linder, 2010); however, gamification's boundary play is aimed at concealing the compulsory nature of labor rather than eradicating it. Furthermore, the aims of gamification are solidly tied to finite material and social outcomes. Thus, gamification lands squarely on the side of Fink's world of illusion and shadows. From a metaphysical standpoint, gamification's infinite game mirrors Dionysian self-abandonment: it does not replace or supersede work or life, it simply aims at persuading players to momentarily forget.

The distinction between choice and compulsion perforates the recent history, and controversy, surrounding Gamification. While Coonradt (2007) and Watts (1995) proposed personal solutions to increasing productivity in the workplace and mitigating stress, recent technological trends have catapulted the idea that game thinking can work as a collective solution to productivity and motivational issues in both client-facing and internal business operations into the mainstream (Byrne, 2012; Kim, 2012; Nicholson, 2012). Adding game dynamics to non-gaming systems has been lauded as an answer to increasing workplace frustration and consumer loyalty issues (McGonigal, 2011; Zicherman & Cunningham, 2011; Zicherman & Linder, 2010) and decried as an opaque set of practices aimed at manipulation and surveillance (Bogost, 2011; Whitson, 2013). Part of this debate that has plagued gamification over the past few years seems to be rooted in how scholars and practitioners conceptually define "play" and "games." Unfortunately, technological advances have left many older interpretations of game-related concepts like cheating (Kücklich, 2009), rules (Tulloch, 2014) and gameplay (Dovey & Kennedy, 2006) lacking. Simon (2006) sums up the cultural turn in game studies neatly:

We should describe and analyze the myriad forms of sociality manifest in digital games and how these forms affect our understandings of self and collectivity in a world increasingly dominated by computer-mediated interaction. We should continue to theorize the relationship between technology, culture, social interaction, and subjectivity but also more carefully consider the role of games and play in a world often defined only in terms of relations of work and stress (p. 64)

Gamification, then, is not conceptually separate from games or play. Rather it can be construed as one of the "myriad forms" Simon (2006) refers to in the context of digital games. While traditional ludological definitions help to provide a solid history of ideas from which to examine gamification, it has also created conceptual haziness in determining how gamification is related to more widely studied forms of digital games.

AMBIGUOUS PLAY AND THE GAMING OF CULTURE

Pressing social and technological issues have led to a greater awareness that games and play exist as practices embedded in material culture[9]. Games and gaming work "simultaneously as central nodes in the organization of contemporary leisure culture, computer-mediated interaction, visual culture, and information societies" (Simon, 2006, p. 64). When examined alongside these particular loci of concerns, gamification no longer represents a black box marketing methodology aimed at behavioral modification and surveillance or a metaphysical and ethical quandary. Rather, gamification, games and gaming represent "critical locations for understanding the role of digital technologies in mediating and constituting the social interaction and organization of subjects in late modern information societies" (Simon, 2006, p. 66). While the link between technology, play and games is largely absent from the historical and theoretical work of primary ludologists, another, more ambiguous view of games and play may help to rectify the supposed dissonance between play as a free activity and play as a force to be harnessed for profit.

Tertiary Ludology: Play, Culture and Technology

It is valuable to note that while Carse (1987), Huizinga (1950) and Caillois (1961) all primarily link play and games with *positive* elements of cultural production and notions of free will, other theorists did not take the same path. Tertiary ludologists are scholars that do not focus solely on games and play; instead, the examine play as a part of much larger processes. For example, Lewis Mumford (1934), in *Technics and Civilization*, links the evolution of games with the creation of a "technical society." Jean Baudrillard (1981b, 1998c) also frequently used the metaphor of games and gaming to illuminate consumerism and simulation theory. Like Fink (1968, 1974) both authors were somewhat hesitant to extol ludic activity as a whitewashed pursuit, metaphysical or otherwise. Baudrillard (1981) and Mumford (1934) can both considered "tertiary ludologists" because their interest in games is often nested in much larger, and occasionally sinister, social trends. These tertiary ludologists pitted notions of games and play against economics, mechanization and warfare, something that should be noted as we move towards examining gamification.

Mumford (1934) felt that games operate as an "agents of mechanization" that reverse Mumford's (1934) romanticized "eotechnic" age. As games become more technical, they present an illusion that "fair play" is an obtainable ideal. For instance, technology has often been seen as the great leveler, and advances in technology are often accompanied with the caveat that they will create a more equal society (Cary, 1989). Mumford (1934) argues that in reality "win at any cost" becomes the standard operating procedure in a fully technicized society. Winning, in this case, is obtaining more time and resources for leisure by making more powerful machines. He maintains that mechanized parts such as wheels, gears and levers, are really just "buckets and shovels dressed up for adults" (Mumford, 1934; p. 101) and that games and play are infinitely caught between "consumptive pull and productive drive" (p. 102). Civilization's advance towards "complete mechanization" is closely intertwined with the desire for leisure, namely the desire to save time and increase efficiency. What is efficient in a game is also efficient in real life, especially if real-life is altered to follow the set of rules as the game.

Thus, leisure activities spawn technologies that focus on producing more leisure by automating labor. Formerly non-practical objects, like toys and models made of moving parts, eventually become larger and more powerful. Mumford (1934) notes that the gyroscope was originally a toy before it became a stabilization device. Also, carriages existed in the miniature before they became widely used (Mumford,

1934). For Mumford, mechanization begins with the maximization of sensual pleasure and "life itself." Unfortunately, mechanization ends in a hellish arena where the brutality of real-life is inseparable from the games it was based on (Mumford, 1934). In seeking a maximal, luxurious balance between leisure, play and work, mechanization leads to an "upthrust in barbarism, aided by the very forces and interests which originally had been directed towards the ...perfection of human nature" (Mumford, 1934; p.154). This barbarism originates partly from the luxury of play transforming into a form a bloodlust. Mumford states that modern play consists of spectacle and "mass-sport." Consequently, play has degenerated into the worship of the productive "bitch-goddess," a goddess who values generativity above all else (Mumford, 1934). He states "Sport, then, in this mechanized society, is no longer a mere game empty of any rewards other than playing: it is a profitable business...and the technique of mass-sport infects other activities: scientific expeditions and geographic explorations are conducted in the manner of a speed-stunt..." (Mumford, 1934; p. 307). Mumford envisions games as precursors to a situation where the *desire* for leisure results in leisure and labor becoming indistinguishable. His take on games and play is premeditative of the later writings of Jean Baudrillard (Baudrillard, 1981b, 1998a), who links games with simulation.

For Baudrillard, gaming and play is an ambivalent experience that suffuses the modern condition of being human (Coulter, 2007; Crogan, 2007). Similar to Fink's (1968) illusory world and Huizinga's (1950) space of social possibility, Baudrillard (1981) saw games as an exercise in the eradication of reality; perhaps more accurately, the increasing importance of games to simulation is a sign that reality is already eradicated. Play, for Baudrillard, is an act of *seduction,* or a complicity with generating and living within an illusion, a world in which simulation has already triumphed (Galloway, 2007). Seduction is the ultimate metaphysical *tromp d'oeil*—a type of charade in which appearances move beyond the stable categories of production or consumption (Baudrillard, 1991). Baudrillard (1991) states "all appearances conspire to combat meaning, to uproot meaning, whether intentional or not, and to convert it into a game" (p.153). He continues, "We seduce with weakness, never with strong powers and strong signs. In seduction we enact this weakness, and through it seduction derives its power...Seduction makes use of weakness, makes a game of it, with its own rules" (p.165). For Baudrillard, the advent of the information age is also the advent of appearances and signs—seduction is the type of force complicit with technologies of appearance and inscription (i.e. writing, art, screens, lenses and mirrors). Baudrillard (1981b) maintains that proliferation of technological objects and their related codes is based on the assumption that nature as we can perceive it is mechanistic and capable of being reproduced. In other words, technology improves upon nature on insomuch as nature itself is technological (Lane, 2008). Technology acts as a compensatory mode of being in a world that is increasingly automated; any naturalistic relationship between human actors and the world has been fractured by the transferal of human desire and agency to a system of replicable objects and processes. In turn, the human subject no longer embodies a natural sense of 'being in the world'. Rather, the world is populated by simulacra—objects, signs and representations that human subjects are eventually dominated by.

The seduced human subject is adrift in a simulative environment that replaces, or at worst obliterates, any notion of reality as a stable concept (Baudrillard, 1981b). Seduction and games are primarily simulative processes sustained by a myriad of technical networks; seduction serves to manipulate and direct the desires of humans while games sustain the seductive process. Baudrillard (1991) maintains that seduction is essentially a mechanic embedded in "a game of simulation" that is being played. This game is not one that someone chooses to play, rather the game of seduction "plays itself" and human actors are caught up in it; as such, Baudrillard viewed life and game as a mutated category, in which they infinitely refer to each other (Galloway, 2007). For Galloway (2007), a Baudrillardian approach to games implies that "what we recognize as games (digital or otherwise) are merely old order distractions from the real game or perhaps the game of the real" (Simon, 2007, p. 356). "The virtual is emphatically not the gamic for Baudrillard," Galloway (2007) writes, "it is this world that is the game" (p.378). Games and play are an order of "psychic complicity" with simulation, a complicity that finds its roots in the seductive system of objects (Galloway, 2007). Games and play here are indicative of a technological imbroglio, one born of rampant computerization and the rapid diffusion of media technologies throughout the developed world: they are indicative a technologized world, rather than being mere parts. As such, they behave as harbingers of a self-generating, object-infused irreality—a "precession of simulacra" (Baudrillard, 1981b).

Mumford (1934) and Baudrillard (1981) present a line of reasoning that postulates games and play are seductive forces that serve to direct and manipulate human agency. Games are materialistic, political, metaphysical and often not what they seem. Gaming is an ambivalent act that also leads to diverse consequences directly linked to economic, technological and social issues at large. Seduction is the promise of simulation; that technologically supported leisure leads to more leisure, and that more leisure ensures more technology. For both Baudrillard and Mumford, what ensues is a society in which all meaningful references to labor or leisure collapse, resulting in a world that resembles a game at all times. Labor and leisure become meaningless symbols, replaced by consumer-driven games of chance and luxury. From this standpoint, gamification is the epitome of a game: It supplants and mimics ludic protocol in manner that presupposes consumerism and desire are "naturally" occurring, teleological processes in an increasingly mechanized, simulated society.

A layman's definition of both games and play might situate them as fun, harmless, ebullient systems—they rise and fall in an ebb-flow cycle that dovetails with a set of fantastical ritual and material spaces. This supposition upholds the insistence that humans determine the rules, and that rules are agreed upon through a ritualistic pact that has no bearing on 'reality.' However, Huizinga (1950) and Caillois (1961) both noted that games, while existing in a specific categorical space, are actually conjoined to social and material processes. Fink (1968) and Carse (1987) postulated that play and games are primogenitors of metaphysical experience and, in the works of Mumford (1934) and Baudrillard (1981), games are a force that can be culturally harnessed and directed towards a variety of means and ends, including social and technological control. In the case of Baudrillard and Mumford, the 'pact' inherent in games is inherently social and technological. Mumford's obsession with games as "mass blood sport" and toys as miniature precursors to weapons—as well as Baudrillard's (2005) assertion that economics are merely games played for the rich—identify both as being concerned with the relations between games and dangerous or disruptive technologies. For Baudrillard (1994), games are complicit with simulation, consumption and seduction and for Mumford play-objects such as toys are inherently tied to teleological material processes. As such, games and play can create variety of unpleasant results. Each author's approach is illuminating because it provides a background for why gamification is considered by scholars as existent within a black and white gaming universe: games either represent an ethical fault line where a "game" stops short of control and exploitation or games present the natural and welcome expansion of play by presuming that control is always a starting point. What is important here is that, after some examination, ludology's take on both games and play is largely ambiguous; both can be used as tools for freedom or regulation, for stability or disruption and for leisure or labor. Gamification and games, then, are practices rooted in variable cultural outcomes rather than essences with a derivative set of encoded ethics.

Ambiguous Play

Play is such a diffuse concept its discursive boundaries seem to infuse everything from warfare to lovemaking to religion. Perhaps, then, it is best to focus on the ambiguity of play in the context of how it alters the discursive environments where it takes place. Play always seems to occupy a position that implies some sort of power or action is needed to activate, regulate and direct it. The need to direct or define play as a clearly defined set of activities is largely linked to the rhetorical framing of what play entails. Sutton-Smith (1997) points that play is often seen as existing between two diametric poles: progress and chaos. Ensconced within these two polarities are several subsets of discursive statements made about play, two of which are particularly relevant to the idea of play in the context of both gaming and gamification: *play as progress* and *play as power*.

The first discursive framework is play as progress; Sutton-Smith (1997) points out that progressive play is a biological approach, one that has, until recently, implied "the notion that animals and children, but not adults, adapt and develop through their play" (p. 9). This belief in play as progress is something of a scientific ideal, and it is often rooted in the epistemology of both biologists and educators. Play is a currency in children and animals that can be used to culturally imbue certain favorable aspects through the application of ludic rules and procedure. Sutton-Smith (1997) states that "most educators over the past two hundred years seem to have so needed to represent playful imitation as a form of children's socialization and moral, social, and cognitive growth that they have seen play as being primarily about development rather than enjoyment" (p. 10). What is interesting here is that this educational view of play is beginning to be transferred to behavioral analysis of adults, especially in the workplace (Costea, Crump and Holm, 2005). For example, in the research done at the National Institute For Play (NIFP) under Stuart Brown (2009) and the psychological research of Mihaly Csikszentmihalyi (1990), both scholars approach play as a biological and psychic necessity for the continues growth and health of adult human beings. What is important here is the change in conditionalities that allows play as progress to find itself applied to what have traditionally been considered non-ludic subjects and spaces. In the case of Csikszentmihayi, play is a rabbit-hole to the realm of flow—a timeless space where mastery is the key to joy. For Brown and Vaughn (2009), mastery in the mind is the key to bodily health. Both of these authors assume that play is a golden horizon to be sought out in the drudgery of day-to-day living; it is a key to biological wellness and mindful joy. Play, in these cases, is seen as a lifelong undertaking and part of the duty of every person to live a "good life."

Play as power is the second discursive framework play inhabits. Sutton-Smith (1997) points out that play as power is inherent in games of competition--games pitting a human player against fate, chance, destiny and "will of the gods." Play as power advocates "collectively held community values rather than individual experiences," and as a rule it denotes that play is way to make things more real, rather less so (Sutton-Smith, 1997). He states, "The rhetoric of play as power is about the use of play as the representation of conflict and as a way to fortify the status of those who control the play or are its heroes" (p.10). What is interesting in that the view of play-as-power has its roots psychological literature about excess energy, similar to Bataille's accursed share—play is a primitive mode of enacting a death drive; it is not necessarily a good or bad thing, but a way a transmitting power as catharsis or fulfillment (Schiller, 1965; Sutton-Smith, 1997). Play as power also links back to two key play theorists: Huizinga (1950) and Mihail Sparisou (1989). Huizinga viewed play as a catalyst for culture—the excess energy of play was redirected into spheres such as law, war, art and even scholarship (scholars do, in fact, compete with each other by "playing" with ideas and concepts). These connections between play and society are "morphological parallelisms" in which the mastery of games is a catalyst in the formation of social hierarchies through the formation of *communitas* (Sutton-Smith, 1997). Interestingly, recent thinkers in biopolitics (see Esposito, 2011) have also pointed out that the potlatch style of playful excess is key in the formation and regulation of community—the reciprocity of play is the glue that allows communities form (Campbell, 2006). However, Sparisou (1989) maintains that the ties that bind are also the ties that can dissolve. Sparisou contends that play is as much about disorder as it is about order. In this manner, play and games act as disruptive agents just as much as they can be ordering principles. In short, "there are two conflicting rhetorics about the play: One that says it is positive, as a mode of cultural origination, humanization, catharsis, or socialization, and another that says it is a site for power seeking, domination, and hegemony, or disorder, inversion, and resistance" (Sutton-Smith, 1997, p.81-82). The unifying thread between power and progress is the question of ambiguity. That is to say, play is inexorably linked to the environments in which it occurs: It directs and is directed towards a number of possibilities. However, each possibility is tied to the concept of power and progress.

Gamification and the Gaming of Culture

Power and progress are both at play in almost all iterations of games in the 21st Century (Dyer-Witheford & de Peuter, 2009; Galloway, 2006). Boellstorff (2006) states "many games, and other forms of interactive media…that are less clearly game like, are taking on cultural forms in their own right… These cultures cannot be reduced to the platform, that is, the rules and programming encoded in the game engine" (p. 33). Gaming, and by extension gamification, encompasses the meanings created through cultural engagement with games. This implies that engagement shapes understandings of how gaming, and the subject position of "a player," relies not just on the presence of games or formal rules, but also the active interpretation of what gaming entails as a living, active set of practices (T.L. Taylor, 2009). Pivotal, here, is the approximation that gameplay is both historically and materially rooted—there is no definite truth as to what 'games,' 'gaming' or 'gamification' entail outside of the time and place where they manifest.

For example, Malaby (2007) suggests that games are "dynamic and recursive" in that they reproduce their form over time and space, but also encode within themselves the patent for change. Key here is that games, as cultural objects, embed the desire for control alongside the possibility for alternate, appropriated meanings. Malaby suggests that on the surface, games are a series of processes based on *contrived contingencies*; outcomes that, theoretically, can be contained and constricted through the rules of play (or perhaps, the rules *in* play) but also rely on open-endedness and subjective interpretation. "Contingencies" represent "that which could have been otherwise" (Malaby, 2006, p. 106). Like Huizinga (1950) suggests, games are germination spaces for perpetual cultural recalibration that operate through a series of external relationships. Games contain, according to Malaby, the "fundamental quality of multilayered contingency that allows them both to mimic and constitute everyday experience (p. 107)." "Contrived" suggests that games are both ordered and disordered. Unlike bureaucratic rules and regulations, the contingencies created through ludic processes are not aimed to "reduce unpredictability across cases" (Malaby, 2006, p. 105). Rather, ludic processes "are about contriving and calibrating multiple contingencies to produce a mix of predictable and unpredictable outcomes" (Malaby, 2006, p. 106). This implies that games, from the standpoint of intent, encourage exploration and pathfinding as much as they require a player to abide by rules. Games embody a fluid system of control that relies as much on innovation as it does compliance. Malaby claims:

...the contrivance of these sources of unpredictability is achieved through various modes of control... these modes of control additionally include the architectural (encompassing the gamut of relatively non-negotiable and concrete constraints, from physical layout and landscape to the implicit code of online games), the cultural (the set of practices and expectations that are often implicit and taken for granted), and the economic (the familiar constraints of the market in all its forms). Games are distinctive in their achievement of a generative balance between the open-endedness of contingencies and the reproducibility of conditions for action (p.106).

One key aspect of open-ended approach to game contingencies is that games promote multiple configurations across social and technological matrices. The multiplicity of outcomes and interpretations that games produce are subject to varied, culturally shared, meanings that are consistently renegotiated in the realm of practice. Thus, games and gamification are sets of practice-based contingencies occupying wide ecology of meanings.

For example, Molesworth and Denegri-Knott (2007) examine how gaming, and constructing meanings through play, is an act of consumption. However, rather than accumulating, hording and territorializing resources, gaming operates through complex, liminal activities that occupy a culturally productive position that tethers the practical activity of using goods with a malleable digital sandbox. Meaning-making in game culture blurs the lines between producer and consumer, occupying a liminal space that encourages change, performativity and imagination (Molesworth & Denegri-Knott, 2007). Players adopt a "doing with" attitude—actively embodying both regulative, ritual-based contingencies—and a chaotic, imaginative "acting out" that link possibilities with the practical function of world-making (Molesworth & Denegri-Knott, 2007). This dynamism between consumption and production, the small and grand narratives of cultural performativity, accentuate both Malaby (2006) and Boellstorff's (2006) claims that games may underline a shift in the processes through which culture is coded and decoded in the digital age. Boellstorff states that "most persons who participate in games and other interactive media...play more than one game...We are seeing the emergence of cultures of gaming on a range of spatial scales—some local, some national or regional, some global—shaped by a range of factors from language spoken to quality of Internet connection" (p. 33). The decentering of gaming as a ritual practice set apart from more serious social processes has resulted in a growing interest in the "gaming of culture." Boelstorff maintains that "As [gaming] gains in significance, [it] increasingly affects the whole panoply of interactive media...Gaming also shapes physical-world activities in unexpected ways, including the lives of those who do not play games or participate in interactive media" (p.33). The gaming of culture is perhaps similar to what Baudrillard (1979, 1981) envisioned when he proposed that seduction and gaming were part and parcel to the (de)programming of reality, simulative or no.

Gamification, then, challenges some of the more traditional conceptualizations of games and play. However, if we take a more nuanced view of gamification as contextually situational, then we find that cultural definitions put forwards by recent game studies scholarship can ease the dialectic tensions embedded in the current debate on gamification. Gamification is not a game, true. Rather, it is indicative of a larger cultural shift, a Dionysian turn, in how play is viewed in an increasingly technologized society. It is a collection of design practices that serve playful, practical and even dangerous rationales. *Gamification does not necessarily present a different set of concerns than games; rather, it warps how play operates, and by extension destabilizes past definitions of what play and games actually entail.* Gamification is about motivating players to perform behaviors not typically associated with the "free," "harmless," or "ritual" play as defined by Huizinga (1950) and Caillois (1961). Gamification's form of gameplay operates closer to the murky side of play—the ambiguous, Baudrillardian contract: Gamified play is seductive as much as it is ludic. It is consumerist, controlling, connective and panoptic. It is also fun, innovative and profitable. Different combinations of design choices, technology and modes of deployment serve to meet each of these conditions. Accepting gamification as a sign that the historical conditions of play are shifting and examining it without essentialist or secondary judgments ensures that the study of gamification remains theoretically and conceptually nimble for future research and practice.

CONCLUSION AND RESEARCH DIRECTIONS

Exploring the ethical and conceptual debate over Gamification and related practices requires that the concept be historicized properly and ludology, which informs a wide spectrum of inquiry into gaming and its cultural impact (Chee Siang Ang, Zaphiris, & Wilson, 2010; Markus Montola, 2012) is a great place to start. However, technological and practical realities call for a more nuanced approach. Games have traditionally been defined as finite sets of rules and rituals that interact with culture, but remain somewhat separate by nature (Huizinga, 1950; Salen & Zimmerman, 2003). Games also produce definite behaviors in the form of play, which is often characterized by ludologists as a "free" activity that does not share clear ties with so-called "serious" pursuits in the fields of law, economics and politics (Caillois, 1961; Huizinga, 1950). This historical definition has led to criticism or outright dismissal of gamification (Bogost, 2011). However, there is a hidden history to the study of games and play that support more ethically complex definitions. Tertiary ludologists, social and anthropological scholars who address games and play extensively in their work, often show a more conflicted standpoint: games and play are naturally embedded in our social fields (Bourdieu, 1993; Calhoun, 2000), historically drive processes of mechanization and managerialism (Mumford, 1934) and contribute to an increasingly blurred line between leisure and labor (Baudrillard, 1981a, 1998a; Galloway, 2007). These viewpoints contradict the idea that games and play are, by definition, fun, free and finite. Rather, ludic pursuits are situational and ambivalent: according to Sparisou (1989), play can encompass both order, chaos, constriction *and* freedom.

Building on this line of thought, I contend that studying Gamification's complexity rests on viewing play as a set of complex discursive frameworks rather than ethically white-washed fun. Play is ambiguous and it invites players to enter into an ambiguous state of being. Sutton-Smith (1997) points out that "there are two conflicting rhetorics about the play: one that says it is positive, as a mode of cultural origination, humanization, catharsis, or socialization, and another that says it is a site for power seeking, domination, and hegemony, or disorder, inversion, and resistance" (p.81-82). Problematizing the question of play opens up a new debate, one that expands the mindset that games operate along a clear set of ethical boundaries. Play can be resituated as a question of progress and power (Sutton-Smith, 1997) whiles games serve as a medium. Gamification, which relies as much on fun as it does notions of profitability and control, clearly straddles both contentions. A grey-zone of ambiguous play raises questions about how scholars should proceed in unraveling emerging notions of what games entail and how we should direct our attention in defining and studying them over the course of time.

By resituating play as a question of progress and power, we can move beyond the debate over whether Gamification results in a game or a perversion. Rather, the concept of ambiguous play draws attention to the problematic notion that all game-related activities (such as gamification) belong to a mutually exclusive "game culture" (Boellstorff, 2006). Gamification and ambiguous play demand that we view play and games as situational, with a multitude of possible outcomes and contingencies. This situational approach draws attention to what Boellstorff (2006) calls "the gaming of culture." Gamification brings to light a transitional point in the study of games; it forces scholars and practitioners from a finite concept of games to the "infinite game" (Carse, 1987), where the rules only exist to perpetuate the continuance of ambiguous play.

REFERENCES

Austin, D. (2014). The Gamification of Energy Conservation Retrieved from http://www.dzone.com/articles/gamification-energy

Bailey, R., Wise, K., & Bolls, P. (2009). How Avatar Customizability Affects Children's Arousal and Subjective Presence During Junk Food–Sponsored Online Video Games. *Cyberpsychology & Behavior*, *12*(3), 277–283. doi:10.1089/cpb.2008.0292 PMID:19445632

Bataille, G. (1991). The Accursed Share: an Essay on General Economy: Vol. 1. *Consumption*. Cambridge: Zone Books.

Bateson, G. (1956). The message, "This is play. In B. Schaffner (Ed.), *Group processes*. New York: Josiah Macy.

Baudrillard, J. (1979). *Seduction*. Montreal: New World Perspective.

Baudrillard, J. (1981a). Hypermarket and Hypercommodity (S. F. Glaser, Trans.) Simulacra and Simulation (pp. 75-78). Ann Arbor: University of Michigan Press.

Baudrillard, J. (1981b). The Precession of Simulacra (S. F. Glaser, Trans.) Simulacra and Simulation (pp. 1-42). Ann Arbor: University of Michigan Press.

Baudrillard, J. (1991). *Seduction* (B. Singer, Trans.). New York: St. Martin's Press.

Baudrillard, J. (1998a). *The Drama of Leisure or the Impossibility of Wasting One's Time The Consumer Society: Myths and Structures* (pp. 151–158). Thousand Oaks: Sage.

Baudrillard, J. (1998b). *The Social Logic of Consumption The Consumer Society: Myths and Structures* (pp. 49–68). Thousand Oaks: Sage.

Baudrillard, J. (1998c). *Towards a Theory of Consumption The Consumer Society: Myths and Structures* (pp. 69–86). Thousand Oaks: Sage.

Baudrillard, J. (2005). *The System of Objects* (J. Benedict, Trans.). London: Verso.

Boellstorff, T. (2006). A Ludicrous Discipline? Ethnography and Game Studies. *Games and Culture*, *1*(1), 29–35. doi:10.1177/1555412005281620

Bogost, I. (2011). Gamification is Bullshit. Retrieved from http://kotaku.com/5829210/gamification-is-bullshit

Bourdieu, P. (1993). *The field of cultural production: Essays on art and literature*. Boston: Polity Press.

Bower, B. (2013). Life: Chimps play fair when it counts: Critics question extent to which apes cooperate. *Science News, 183*(3), 16–16. doi:10.1002/scin.5591830316

Brown, S., & Vaughan, C. (2009). *Play: how it shapes the brain, opens the imagination and invigorates the soul*. New York: Avery.

Byrne, T. (2012). The evolving digital workplace. *KM World, 21*(9), 12–14.

Caillois, R. (1961). *Man, Play and Games* (M. Barash, Trans.). New York: Free Press.

Calhoun, C. (2000). Pierre Bourdieu. In G. Ritzer (Ed.), *The Blackwell Companion to Major Sociological Theorists* (pp. 696–730). Malden: Blackwell.

Calleja, G. (2010). Digital Games and Escapism. *Games and Culture, 5*(4), 335–353. doi:10.1177/1555412009360412

Campbell, M. (2011). The audacious plan to make the world into a game. *New Scientist, 209*(2794), 2.

Carey, J. (1989). *Communication as Culture*. New York: Routledge.

Carse, J. P. (1987). *Finite and Infinite Games: A Vision of Life as Play and Possibility*. New York: Ballantine.

Cary, J. W. (1989). *Mass Communication and Cultural Studies Communication as Culture: Essays on Media and Society* (pp. 37–68). Boston: Unwin Hyman.

Castronova, E. (2005). *Synthetic Worlds: The Business and Culture of Online Games*. Chicago: Chicago University Press.

Chapin, A. (2011). The Future is a Videogame. *Canadian Business, 84*(4), 46–48.

Choi, Y. K., & Lee, J.-G. (2012). The Persuasive Effects of Character Presence and Product Type on Responses to Advergames. *Cyberpsychology, Behavior, and Social Networking, 15*(9), 503–506. doi:10.1089/cyber.2012.0012 PMID:22897431

Clavio, G., Kraft, P. M., & Pedersen, P. M. (2009). Communicating with consumers through video games: An analysis of brand development within the video gaming segment of the sports industry. *International Journal of Sports Marketing & Sponsorship, 10*(2), 143–156.

Colman, F. J. (2012). Play as an Affective Field for Activating Subjectivity: Notes on The Machinic Unconscious. *Deleuze Studies, 6*(2), 250–264. doi:10.3366/dls.2012.0061

Comer, B. (2012). Gamification GROWS UP. *Pharmaceutical Executive, 32*(6), 30–35.

Consalvo, M. (2009). There is No Magic Circle. *Games and Culture, 4*(4), 408–417. doi:10.1177/1555412009343575

Coonradt, C. A. (2007). The Game of Work: How to Enjoy Work as Much as Play [Kindle ed.]. Salt Lake City: Gibbs Smith.

Costea, B., Crump, N., & Holm, J. (2005). Dionysus at Work? The Ethos of Play and the Ethos of Management. *Culture and Organization, 11*(2), 139–151. doi:10.1080/14759550500091069

Couldry, N. (2000). *Inside Culture: Re-imagining the Method of Cultural Studies*. Tousand Oaks, CA: Sage.

Coulter, G. (2007). Jean Baudrillard and the Definitive Ambivalence of Gaming. *Games and Culture*, *2*(4), 358–365. doi:10.1177/1555412007309530

Crogan, P. (2007). Remembering (Forgetting) Baudrillard. *Games and Culture*, *2*(4), 405–413. doi:10.1177/1555412007309531

Csikszentmihaly, M. (1990). *Flow: The Psychology of Optimal Experience*. New York: Harper & Row.

Danforth, L. (2011). Gamification and Libraries. *Library Journal*, *136*(3), 84–84.

de Souza e Silva, A.de Souza e Silva. (2006). From Cyber to Hybrid: Mobile Technologies as Interfaces of Hybrid Spaces. *Space and Culture*, *9*(3), 261–278. doi:10.1177/1206331206289022

Delo, C. (2012). What is gamification, and how can I make it useful for my brand? *Advertising Age*, *83*(9), 58–58.

Deterding, S. (2012). Gamification: designing for motivation. *interactions*, *19*(4), 14-17. doi: 10.1145/2212877.2212883

Diamond, J., & Bond, A. B. (2003). A Comparative Analysis of Social Play in Birds. *Behaviour*, *140*(8), 1091–1115. doi:10.1163/156853903322589650

Dovey, J., & Kennedy, H. W. (2006). *Game Cultures: Computer Games as New Media*. New York: Open University Press.

Dyer-Witheford, N., & de Peuter, G. (2009). *Games of Empire: Capitalism and Video Games*. Minneapolis: University of Minnesota Press.

Elden, S. (2008). Eugene Fink and the question of the world. *Parrhesia*, *5*, 48–59.

Environment, B. t. (2012). Gamification Revolutionizes Consumer Recycling Incentives. *Business & the Environment*, *23*, 10-11.

Esposito, R. (2011). *Immunitas: The Protection and Negation of Life*. Cambridge: Polity.

Fagen, R. (1981). *Animal play behavior*. New York: Aldine.

Fink, E., Saine, U., & Saine, T. (1968). The Oasis of Happiness: Toward an Ontology of Play. *Yale French Studies*, (41): 19–30. doi:10.2307/2929663

Foucault, M., & Blasius, M. (1993). About the Beginnings of the Hermenuetics of the Self: Two Lectures at Dartmouth. *Political Theory*, *21*(2), 198–227. doi:10.1177/0090591793021002004

Fuchs, M. (2012). Ludic interfaces. Driver and product of gamification. *GAME Journal of Game Studies*, *1*(1).

Galloway, A. R. (2007). Radical Illusion (A Game Against). *Games and Culture*, *2*(4), 376–391. doi:10.1177/1555412007309532

Gopaladesikan, S. (2012). Gamification: Envisioning a New Tomorrow. *Forward Thinking*, from http://weplay.co/gamification-envisioning-a-new-tomorrow/

Gray, C. B. (2007). *Philosophy of Man at Recreation and Leisure*. New York: Peter Lang.

Gregory, C. A. (1997). *Savage money: the anthropology and politics of commodity exchange*. Amsterdam: Harwood Academic.

Harviainen, J. T. (2012). Ritualistic Games, Boundary Control, and Information Uncertainty. *Simulation & Gaming*, *43*(4), 506–527. doi:10.1177/1046878111435395

Huizinga, J. (1950). Homo Ludens: A Study of the Play-Element. In *Culture*. Boston: Beacon Press.

Hulsey, N., & Reeves, J. (2014). The Gift that Keeps on Giving: Google, Ingress, and the Gift of Surveillance. *Surveillance & Society*, *12*(3), 389–400.

Keats, A. (2011). Loyalty is the greatest value of location-based marketing. *PRWeek (U.S.)*, *14*(12), 26–26.

Kim, B. (2012). Harnessing the power of game dynamics. *College & Research Libraries News*, *73*(8), 465–469.

Krogue, K. (2012). 5 gamification rules from the grandfather of gamification. Retrieved from http://www.forbes.com/sites/kenkrogue/2012/09/18/5-gamification-rules-from-the-grandfather-of-gamification/

Kücklich, J. (2009). A Techno-Semiotic Approach to Cheating in Computer Games: Or How I Learned to Stop Worrying and Love the Machine. *Games and Culture*, *4*(2), 158–169. doi:10.1177/1555412008325486

Kuczaj, S. A., & Highfill, L. E. (2005). Dolphin play: Evidence for cooperation and culture? *Behavioral and Brain Sciences*, *28*(05), 705–706. doi:10.1017/S0140525X05370129

Lane, R. J. (2008). *Jean Baudrillard* (2nd ed.). New York: Routledge.

Lefebvre, H. (1991). *The Production of Space* (D. Nicholson-Smith, Trans.). Malden, MA: Blackwell-Wiley.

Limber, J. (1977). Language in child and chimp? *The American Psychologist*, *32*(4), 280–295. doi:10.1037/0003-066X.32.4.280

Liyakasa, K. (2012a). *GAME ON!*. CRM Magazine, 28–32.

Liyakasa, K. (2012b). *Serious About Gamification*. CRM Magazine, 33–33.

Liyakasa, K. (2012c). Turning Business into Pleasure. *CRM Magazine*, *16*(3), 14–14.

Luscombe, B. (2009). Zynga harvests the cyberfarmer. *Time*, *174*(21), 59–60. PMID:19891392

Malaby, T. M. (2007). Beyond Play: A New Approach to Games. *Games and Culture*, *2*(2), 95–113. doi:10.1177/1555412007299434

Marx, K. (1997). The German Ideology [extract]. In D. McLennan (Ed.), *Karl Marx--Selected Writings*. Oxford: Oxford University Press.

Massey, D. (1992). Politics and space/time. *New Left Review*, *196*, 65–84.

Mauss, M. (2000). *The Gift: The Form and Reason for Exchange in Archaic Societies*. New York: W.W. Norton & Co.

McGonigal, J. (2011). *Reality is Broken: Why games make us better and how they can change the world*. New York: Penguin.

Metcalfe, S. (2014). Capitalism and evolution. *Journal of Evolutionary Economics, 24*(1), 11–34. doi:10.1007/s00191-013-0307-7

Molesworth, M., & Denegri-Knott, J. (2007). Digital Play and the Actualization of the Consumer Imagination. *Games and Culture, 2*(2), 114–133. doi:10.1177/1555412006298209

Montola, M. (2012). Social Constructionism and Ludology: Implications for the Study of Games. *Simulation & Gaming, 43*(3), 300–320. doi:10.1177/1046878111422111

Montola, M., Stenros, J., & Waern, A. (2009). *Pervasive games: experiences on the boundary between life and play*. Burlington: Morgan Kaufman Publishers.

Mosca, I. (2012). +10! Gamification and deGamification. *GAME Journal of Game Studies, 1*(1).

Mumford, L. (1934). *Technics and Civilization*. New York: Harcourt Brace & Company.

Myron, D. (2012). *Going Against the Grain with Gamification and NLU*. CRM Magazine, 2.

Naughton, K. (2003). PIXELS to PAVEMENT. *Newsweek, 141*(10), 46.

Nicholson, S. (2012). *A User-Centered Theoretical Framework for Meaningful Gamification*. Proceedings of Games+Learning+Society 8.0. Madison, WI.

Nippert-Eng, C. (2005). Boundary Play. *Space and Culture, 8*(3), 302–324. doi:10.1177/1206331205277351

Qin, G., Rau, P.-L. P., & Salvendy, G. (2009). Perception of interactivity: affects of four key variables in mobile advertising. *International Journal of Human-Computer Interaction, 25*(6), 479–505. doi:10.1080/10447310902963936

Rizzo, S. (2008). The promise of cell phones: from people power to technological nanny. *Convergence (London), 14*(2), 135–143. doi:10.1177/1354856507087940

Salen, K., & Zimmerman, E. (2003). *Rules of Play*. Cambridge: MIT Press.

Schell, J. (2010). *Visions of the Gameocolypse*. Proceedings of Gameification Summit. San Francisco, CA.

Scofidio, B. (2012). Get Serious About Gamification. *Corporate Meetings & Incentives, 31*(7), 2.

Sennott, S. (2005). Gaming the Ad. *Newsweek, 145*(5), E2-E2.

Shaer, M. (2012). Game of Life. *Polar Science, 280*(2), 54–77.

Sicart, M. (2008). Defining Game Mechanics. *Game Studies, 8*(2). Retrieved from http://gamestudies.org/0802/articles/sicart

Simon, B. (2007). What if Baudrillard was a Gamer?: Introduction to a Special Section on Baudrillard and Game Studies. *Games and Culture, 2*(4), 355–357. doi:10.1177/1555412007309535

Spariosu, M. (1989). *Dionysus Reborn*. Ithaca, N.Y.: Cornell University Press.

Steinkuehler, C. A. (2006). The Mangle of Play. *Games and Culture, 1*(3), 199–213. doi:10.1177/1555412006290440

Sukoco, B. M., & Wu, W.-Y. (2011). The effects of advergames on consumer telepresence and attitudes: A comparison of products with search and experience attributes. *Expert Systems with Applications, 38*(6), 7396–7406. doi:10.1016/j.eswa.2010.12.085

Sutton-Smith, B. (1997). *The Ambiguity of Play*. Cambridge: Harvard University Press.

Swan, C. (2012). Gamification: A new way to shape behavior. *Communication World, 29*(3), 13–14.

Taylor, T. L. (2006). *Play Between Worlds: Exploring online game culture*. Cambridge: MIT Press.

Taylor, T. L. (2009). The Assemblage of Play. *Games and Culture, 4*(4), 331–339. doi:10.1177/1555412009343576

Taylor, T. L., & Kolko, B. E. (2003). Boundary Spaces: Majestic and the uncertain status of knowledge, community and self in a digital age. *Information Communication and Society, 6*(4), 497–522. doi:10.1080/1369118032000163231

The play's the thing. (2011). *Economist, 401*(8763), 10-11.

Thorhauge, A. M. (2013). The Rules of the Game—The Rules of the Player. *Games and Culture, 8*(6), 371–391. doi:10.1177/1555412013493497

Tulloch, R. (2014). The Construction of Play: Rules, Restrictions, and the Repressive Hypothesis. *Games and Culture, 9*(5), 335–350. doi:10.1177/1555412014542807

van Benthem, J. (2003). Logic Games are Complete for Game Logics. *Studia Logica, 75*(2), 183–203. doi:10.1023/A:1027306910434

van Reijmersdal, E. A., Rozendaal, E., & Buijzen, M. (2012). Effects of Prominence, Involvement, and Persuasion Knowledge on Children's Cognitive and Affective Responses to Advergames. *Journal of Interactive Marketing, 26*(1), 33–42. doi:10.1016/j.intmar.2011.04.005

Watts, A. (1995). Work as Play. In M. A. Watts (Ed.), *The Essential Alan Watts*. London: Celectial Arts.

Whitson, J. R. (2013). Gaming the Quantified Self. *Surveillance & Society, 11*(1/2), 163–176.

Williams, R. (1989). Culture is Ordinary. In B. Highmore (Ed.), *The Everyday Life Reader* (pp. 91–100). New York: Routledge.

Zaphiris, P., & Wilson, S.Chee Siang Ang. (2010). Computer Games and Sociocultural Play: An Activity Theoretical Perspective. *Games and Culture, 5*(4), 354–380. doi:10.1177/1555412009360411

Zicherman, G., & Cunningham, C. (2011). *Gamification by design: implementing game mechanics in web and mobile apps*. New York: O'Reilly Media.

Zicherman, G., & Linder, J. (2010). *Game-based marketing: inspire customer loyalty through rewards, challenges and contests*. New Jersey: Wiley.

Zuk, R. (2012). Get in the game: How communicators can leverage gamification. *Public Relations Tactics, 19*(2), 7.

KEY TERMS AND DEFINITIONS

Contingencies: The wide array cultural, social and technological possibilities opened up by through game mechanics and logics.

Game Logics: Intended outcomes for a game (or gamified application). For example, health-related gamified applications may have a certain heart rate as a logic served by game mechanics that involve movement.

Game Mechanics: Specific tactics and rules as they pertain to games and game design. For example, progressively harder levels are a common game mechanic.

Game Studies: The study of games across disciplines.

Gameplay: The cultural and technological performance of play in the context of games and gaming.

Gamespace: The rule-bound space in which the complex relationship between player, technology and game unfolds.

Gamification: Design practices that seek to embed game logics and mechanics into non-ludic environments and applications. Gamification also represents a philosophy of design that prizes intrinsic, motivated play as a profitable or useful resource.

Ludology: The study of play across disciplines.

ENDNOTES

[1]   Game mechanics are the specific architectural qualities of game design—the formal or structural components that constitutes rule systems, constraints and pathways (Sicart, 2008).

[2]   Game logics encode the outcomes of player choices through algorithmic sequences and represent the rationale for the end-state of actions produced in the game system (van Benthem, 2003).

[3]   Foucault (1993) identifies techniques as technological modes of dispersing or implementing power. He states, ""One can distinguish three major types of technique: the techniques that permit one to produce, to transform, to manipulate things; the techniques that permit one to use sign systems; and finally, the techniques that permit one to determine the conduct of individuals, to impose certain ends or objectives. That is to say, techniques of production, techniques of signification or communication, and techniques of domination" (Foucault, 1993; p. 203).

[4]   The web of relations between the space where a game is played, the technologies through which gameplay is mediated and the actions of players is commonly referred to as "gamespace" (Dovey & Kennedy, 2006).

[5]   Mauss (2000), in 1925, proposed that the ritualistic exchange of gifts, often in the form of games, magical rites or festivals, serves as a precursor to modern economics. His primary thesis is that gifts are never "free;" rather they require reciprocity, an honor-based or spiritual bonding between then giver and the recipient (Mauss, 2000). This reciprocity serves as the cornerstone for developing a community. His ideas set up the primary distinction between a "gift economy" and "a commodity economy" (Gregory, 1997).

[6]   Bataille (1950) believed that the playful exchange of gifts reverses the productive drive embedded in capitalism. Excess energy in the "general economy" is burned off in the form of games, festivals, luxury, magic, sacrifice and general waste (Bataille, 1950).

7   Caillois' (1961) forms of play are: Agon, or competition (chess); Alea, or chance (poker); Mimicry, or mimesis (role playing games), and Ilinx, or vertigo, in the sense of altering perception (roller coasters; virtual reality). It is also important to note that these forms are not mutually exclusive.

8   For example, game designer Jessie Schell's (2010) concept of the "Gameocolypse" suggests that anything that involves an action, conscious or unconscious, from waking through sleeping, can be gamified.

9   Material culture, here, refers to a distinct approach to cultural activity that emphasizes culture as a practical activity (Marx, 1997). In other words, culture is not stable history of ideas or meta-narratives but rather a diverse collection of practices embedded in everyday activities (Lefebvre, 1991). Materialism holds that all cultural processes are, to some degree, material processes (Williams, 1989). They involve actual constraints that are the result of heterogeneous times and spaces (Massey, 1992). The ability to engage in cultural production is based on a wide array of problems and conditions: who is allowed to communicate; how are people communicating; what technologies are available to whom; how and why are these technologies available? This short list of issues does not do justice to the wide array of approaches and problems embedded in a materialist approach to culture. However, they serve as groundwork for examining what many would claim is the primary goal in a cultural approach: examining the relationship between power and cultural production (Couldry, 2000).

Chapter 2
"A Spoonful of Game Design Makes the Work-Out More Fun":
Essential Game Design Elements for Use in Gamified Applications

William R. Upchurch
University of Pittsburgh, USA

Susan M. Wildermuth
University of Wisconsin Whitewater, USA

ABSTRACT

Gamification is the concept of infusing elements of gameplay (competition, incentives, story/narrative, collaboration, problem-solving, etc.) into non-game activities in order to make those activities more compelling. Recently, game designers have begun stressing the need for greater "maturity" in the field of gamification with greater focus on the importance of designing applications for optimal user experience. One hurdle to achieving maturity in the field is the fact that even gamification experts question "What exactly are the essential elements of gameplay that optimize user engagement and enjoyment?" Thus, the goal of the current chapter is to provide a comprehensive listing of the elements of gameplay that are essential to user engagement, and to provide examples of how each of those elements has been applied successfully in game design in the past. The chapter reviews 14 essential gameplay elements including: chance, control, creativity, completion, spectacle, status, strategy, unification, rules, narrative, recognition, collaboration, escapism, and enjoyment.

INTRODUCTION

The newest buzz word being tossed around from such diverse groups as marketing professionals, university deans, seasoned politicians, military leaders, and even grassroots activists, is "gamification." Gamification is the concept of infusing elements of gameplay (competition, incentives, story/narrative, collaboration, problem-solving, etc.) into non-game activities in order to make those activities more

DOI: 10.4018/978-1-4666-8651-9.ch002

compelling. The concept of gamification is nothing new. For example, advertising has long used elements of play to attract customers, from the free toys in Cracker Jack boxes beginning in 1912, to the riddles on the Burma Shave signs in the 1930s. What is new is the term itself (the word gamification was first coined in 2002, but did not really catch on until much later in the decade), and the associated systematic study of and application of the individual elements of game design in non-game contexts in order to increase motivation, engagement, positive emotional expression, and social connections among users or consumers.

Gamification has become the "next big thing" in many fields, indicated by the monetary resources being poured into gamified applications in a variety of contexts. For example, in 2012, Badgeville secured $25 million in funding for gamification platform creation, and according to Gartner's research, 70% of firms on the Forbes Global 2000 list will use at least one gamified application in 2014 (Nelson, 2013). Despite the hype and popularity of gamification as a concept, some argue that current approaches to gamification are poorly executed. This perspective argues that in the rush to "jump on the bandwagon," bad gamification has become the norm. Rather than focusing on narrative, problem-solving, collaboration and other true gameplay elements that lead to user interest, motivation, and engagement (but are quite complicated to design, implement, and assess), designers have simply added badges, points, and leaderboards to a task or experience and then called it gamified. Experts are arguing that there is a need for greater "maturity" in the field of gamification with greater focus on the importance of designing for optimal user experience (Fitz-Walter, 2013). Academic studies of gamification efforts have yielded mixed results based on both psychological and behavior-based outcomes (Hamari, Koivisto, & Sarsa, 2014).

One hurdle to achieving maturity in the field is that even gamification experts raise the question, "What exactly are the essential elements of gameplay that optimize user engagement and enjoyment?" (Deterding, Dixon, Khaled, & Nacke, 2011). There have been multiple scholarly attempts to locate, analyze, and describe the basic components of gaming in general (Eskelinen, 2001; McCormick, 2013; Nelson, 2013). Additionally, as early as the 1980's, scholars have worked to derive heuristics from games in order to apply those heuristics in other contexts and increase the enjoyment of other experiences (Dickey, 2007). This work has given rise to studies detailing specific design features of games that afford player enjoyment – including challenge, narrative, goals, and chance. An obvious matter of interest is to what degree these elements can be effectively transferred to the design of gamified systems. One important step toward "maturity" in the field of gamification is a well-developed understanding of such elements. This understanding will allow designers greater ability to identify potential gameplay elements as well as match the right elements with the right setting to maximize the likelihood that their use in a gamified application will be effective.

In sum, a deep understanding of the relationship between the needs of the gamification project and the appropriate choice of game elements to apply is what allows for the development of the best applications (Deterding, Dixon, Khaled, & Nacke, 2011). Additionally, it is an understanding of the pivotal moments and events in the evolution of gameplay that gives designers the knowledge necessary to best apply the gamification process to other aspects of human life in the present. Thus, the goal of the current chapter is to provide a comprehensive listing of the elements of gameplay that experts agree are essential to user engagement, to define and discuss how each element functions, and to provide examples of how each of those elements has been applied successfully to game design in the past. This chapter identifies fourteen essential gameplay elements, stemming from both scholarly work and practice in the field: chance, control, creativity, completion, spectacle, status, strategy, unification, rules, narrative, recognition, collaboration, escapism, and enjoyment.

CHANCE

Chance, or luck, is an essential ingredient of many forms of gameplay. Randomness is often placed in opposition to skill, but it can in fact introduce elements of skill, such as risk management, into a game. In this way it increases the variety of gameplay possible and broadens the range of competition. It also creates uncertainty of outcomes at both decision points within the game and in terms of the overall winners and losers. For many players, uncertain outcomes increase the long-term enjoyment of games (Burgun, 2014), as well as their re-playability (Lagel, 2010). Games of chance rely on their unpredictable nature, and players who enjoy them find that randomness increases their sense of challenge (Jamison, 2014). Some games, such as bingo, use randomization tools to achieve the element of chance, while others rely on the unpredictable actions of other players or the ebb and flow of changes in the player themselves (muscle fatigue, lack of concentration, etc.).

The amount of chance in a game must be calibrated to the type of game, the expectations of players, and the context in which the game takes place. The latter is particularly important for gamification efforts, because a great deal of randomness in an organizational context may actually contradict the goals of those efforts by reducing motivation, morale, and fun. Randomness needs restraint so that players who get more skilled can gain more success and are not unfairly defeated by things outside their control. But regardless of how it is achieved or implemented, some chance is essential to gameplay.

One enduring example of the popularity of chance in games is the historical resilience of the lottery concept. As early as 205 and 187 BC there are records of the Han Dynasty using keno to raise funds for major government projects such as the Great Wall of China. Additionally, King James I used a lottery to raise money to finance an English settlement in Jamestown, Virginia (Shelley, 1989). Although lotteries are games of pure chance, their presentation has evolved to evoke more addictive gameplay elements such as control and strategy; for example, the selection of favorite number combinations and the escalation of rewards that gives the illusion of meaningful cost-benefit analysis in the purchase of tickets. The element of chance in lotteries can ironically give players a greater sense of control, as the "even odds" of each ticket being a winner can feel fairer than attempts to accumulate wealth in more standard ways. Certainly there are ways to increase your odds of winning (buy more tickets, etc.), but for any one ticket, each person has the exact same chance of winning as any other participant in the lottery game. Likewise, each player faces the same chance of losing.

Chance can also mirror or produce the excitement of risk, which makes games more compelling and encourages repeat play. It is utilized in video games such as World of Warcraft to add excitement to some of the repetitive tasks necessary to gain levels. Every time a player kills a monster there is a chance that monster will drop a treasure chest, and each chest contains random items, some of which may be very valuable while others are mundane or disappointing. If the player is lucky and things go his or her way, the spoils enhance their character's effectiveness. In sum, chance can be a powerful tool when applied appropriately. Well-designed gamification applications can allow for players to randomly "luck out" or have to "try again" in order to keep the application interesting. The effects of chance on the overall outcome of a game should be carefully monitored, however, so that it does not contravene the overall goals of its application.

CONTROL

As noted above, while chance can be a factor in enjoyable gaming, good gameplay is not completely random. Another essential element of gameplay is control. The previous section briefly touched on the relationship between randomness and control in satisfying games, and this section will further elaborate on that concept. Control is at its core about player choice, and just as in games the first choice players must make in gamified applications is the choice to play at all. This taps into research demonstrating that the ability to have even a minimal level of control over ourselves, our surroundings, or even others makes us feel important, free, and safe (Wanenchak, 2014). People expect games to replicate the cause-and-effect pattern that helps them feel comfortable in their everyday lives (Lagel, 2010). Thus, players highly value control in the games they play. They tend to judge the quality of a game according to whether or not meaningful choices are available through which they can control how the game progresses, or how their character progresses within the game (Wanenchak, 2014).

The massive success of certain video games and genres in the 1990's illustrates the importance of control in gameplay. Wolfenstein 3D, released in 1992, was a huge success based partially on an innovative user input experience. The game provided players with a vanishing point perspective on the playing environment, which was mediated by player input. Through their onscreen avatar, players could negotiate a world that had similar physical rules to those of real life. This greatly increased the ability players had to control the movements of their avatars as players now more naturally understood the spatial reality the characters operated within (Bryce & Rutter, 2002). Up to that point, most games that attempted realistic physics were vehicle-based, such as flight, car, and tank simulators, rather than representing the bodily experience now referred to as telepresence. Telepresence is a powerful way to link the narrative fictions of a game world with actions taken in the real world (McGonigal, 2003). In another example, id Software released the source code for their game Doom to the public. This enabled players to modify the game to suit their own tastes, and allowed for customizability of the game controls. The ability for the user to create custom levels and otherwise modify the game gave users unprecedented control over gameplay. Such control was an enormously popular element of the game that helped Doom get ranked as the fifth best video game of all time in 1996 (Bryce & Rutter, 2002). As a final example of the value of player control, in 1997 Quake II allowed the application of "skins" on characters, thus permitting gamers to customize existing characters and alter their appearance. Mods (or game modifications) like those pioneered by Doom and Quake II are now common in video gaming and account for much of the popularity of video games. The ability to alter characters, environment and texts means that the gamer can become a producer of the game in addition to being a consumer of the game. Players enjoy the ability to have control over a game's setting, characters, or physical rules (Bryce & Rutter, 2002). Because control is an essential element to gameplay, when designing a gamified application, it is important to consider how much and what kind of control your application will grant to the user.

CREATIVITY

The ability to innovate and create is an essential element of gameplay. While play is not limited to humans, many argue that it is the human propensity to transform play into creation that sets humans apart. This perspective argues that it is play that drives curiosity, invention, experimentation, wonder, research—essentially, all human learning and growth (Eigen & Winkler, 1981). It was essentially through play—through curiosity and the search for knowledge—that man discovered fire, invented tools, and evolved to form civilizations. Thus, within a good game, it is important for gamers to have opportunities for exploration and manipulation in order to construct knowledge and experience the gratification of creation (Dickey, 2007). Exploration is one of the key aspects of popular 4X computer games (eXplore, eXpand, eXploit, eXterminate) such as Master of Orion, Civilization, and SimCity. A quick look at history from the Age of Discovery to Manifest Destiny to the Apollo Moon landing demonstrates the human propensity for exploration and adventure, and the creative improvisation necessary to survive them. However, in the modern world there are fewer opportunities for exploring new physical worlds and discovering new landscapes, flora and fauna, and even people. Games can grant people the ability to explore virtual worlds, and to do so safely and as an avocation rather than a career.

To illustrate the importance of exploration and creativity in game design, one simply has to look to the popularity and longevity of games that involve designing and building. Legos are one of the most popular toys of all time and their primary design fosters and supports creative play. It is no surprise that the wildly popular video game Minecraft has an aesthetic combining virtual worlds and Legos. Video games that allow players the ability customize characters, to design worlds, and to create story lines either through mods or through gameplay design are extremely popular. And people who play these games get quite vested in their creations. Players mourn the loss of characters they have created, save virtual environments so they can apply them in other gameplay, and get upset when characters or environments they have created are harmed or destroyed by other players for purposes other than fairly advancing gameplay.

The value of creativity in game design also extends beyond the typical contexts for gaming. For example, the US Navy launched a massively multiplayer video game to generate ideas for fighting piracy in the Horn of Africa; the idea behind the game was to encourage creativity among military and civilian strategists and develop new techniques for military interventions that might otherwise not have emerged (Dickey, 2007). Great games foster creativity and self-expression, and thus, so should great gamified applications.

COMPETITION

By many accounts, competition is what sets games apart from general play. It is the ability to identify a winner that makes something a game rather than simply an activity, diversion, or amusement (Roberts, Arth, & Bush, 1959). Competition is a contest for access to or obtainment of key resources. Those resources might include food, goods, mates, territory, prestige, recognition, social status, money, or power; in games, they might be points, artifacts (such as bonus cards or additional game pieces), status, or simply the thrill of victory.

Historically, competitive games have been seen as a way to allow us to experience those rewards while simultaneously channeling the potentially harmful innate human need for competition, violence, and domination into more productive or entertaining pastimes than war or brawling (Jewell, Moti, & Coates, 2002). Giving rein to one's need for competition in the "real world" can be costly to humans on many levels, including lives lost to war, physical injuries, damaged psychological well beings, and increased feelings of aggression and stress. Thus, recreational competition through games is beneficial because it provides an outlet for our innate competitiveness in a less costly way. Whether tabletop games, parlor games, sports, video games, or the Olympics (an intermittent global proxy war that provides a safe outlet for national pride), recreational gaming provides humans with a way to compete and to gain the physical, chemical, and social benefits of winning without incurring extreme physical, emotional, and cultural costs.

Because gamification can bring the rewards for gameplay into the real world, it complicates definitions that hinge on declaring winners within the bounds of the rules of a particular game. Using the traditional definition of competition as a stand-alone benchmark for identifying successful games also oversimplifies the concept, envisioning it merely as a struggle between two or more parties for victory in a game. There are zero sum games that must always identify a winner and a loser, but as competition comes into contact with one or more of the other elements outlined in this chapter, it becomes clear that competition can take many forms. Solo video games such as the massively popular Katamari Damacy, in which a player races against time to collect enough objects to rebuild the universe, and cooperative board games such as Pandemic, which pits one or more players against the board itself, offer models of competitive gaming that go beyond antagonistic win/lose conditions.

Additionally, the tale of Timmy, Johnny, and Spike is an excellent illustration of how other elements can change the nature of competition even for different players in the same game. Timmy, Johnny, and Spike are three psychographic profiles used by the designers and developers of the collectible card game Magic: the Gathering (Rosewater, 2002a). They emerged from the research and development team's interactions with players and the realization that their audience was split between those who wanted to win at any cost and those who valued other aspects of the gameplay, such as enjoyment or creativity. The online test used to identify one's own profile included statements such as "I enjoy making money from a game" (Spike), "I enjoy winning in creative ways" (Johnny), and "I enjoy smashing my opponents" (Timmy). According to Mark Rosewater, head designer for Magic, "Timmy likes to win big, Johnny likes to win in innovative ways, [and] Spike cares more about the quantity of wins than the quality" (Rosewater, 2002b). Winning is a goal for each of these player types because the game is only resolved through the elimination of one's opponents, but winning in and of itself is the primary goal only for Spike. The other two kinds of players were excited by creativity and spectacle, and sought to infuse their victories with these other elements. The genius of Magic's design is that it does not simply provide a structure for determining a competitive outcome, but it recognizes that competitive satisfaction comes in many forms.

Competition is also not limited to particular instances of gameplay. While tournament gaming, both in video and tabletop games, has exploded in popularity over the past two decades, it is only one of the many ways game players compete. This once again points to the complexity of the idea of competition in relation to other gameplay elements. For example, a popular board gaming website, Boardgamegeek, allows players to track and publicize the size of their game collection, the number of times they have played particular games, and the sheer amount of gaming they do on a monthly basis. Gamers can then acquire status through having played a certain game thousands of times or collecting a roomful of games, much like video gamers pursue badges, achievements, and leaderboard positions. The competitive spirit can also be found in the headlines for online quizzes that appear in social media feeds. These often take the form of a challenge, such as "Only 6% of people can complete this task." Known as linkbait because of the strong psychological appeals they use to encourage clicks, these headlines tap into people's competitive nature without specifying an opponent or even a victory condition. Because competition is biological, it is an important and pleasurable part of gameplay that must be considered when designing gamified applications.

SPECTACLE

Spectacle or entertainment value is another important element of gameplay. The emphasis of spectacle in entertainment is on performances that elicit intense and instantaneous visual pleasure, and the use of image and action that will excite, astound, horrify, or astonish the audience. In numerous blockbusting popular entertainment successes, it is not character development, social discourse, or exemplary storytelling that is the focus of the film, play, or concert. Rather, it is the size, frequency, intensity, and breath-taking excitement of the spectacle being enacted before one's eyes that generates the high number of viewers (Byce & Rutter, 2002). In one scholarly study, researchers found that games with spectacular sounds and visuals were highly stimulating to people who played them (Amory, Naicker, Vincent, and Adams, 1999). The increasing sophistication of graphics, narrative, and game play has created conditions that allow the gamer to feel a part of the unfolding and increasingly spectacular narrative of game play (Bryce & Rutter, 2002). As a consequence, in the gaming industry there is a constant need for innovative games with better graphics, better music, and better controls—games with new realms, or new laws, or even totally new types of games in order to continue adding to the hype and spectacle.

Spectacle in gaming has its roots in early empires when a few very wealthy people sought to maintain control over masses of impoverished people. Providing spectacular entertainment for the masses was one way that rulers distracted subjects from resentment over unequal living conditions. For example, chariot races and gladiatorial combat in Rome were always more prevalent during times of economic strife. The Roman Coliseum has space for 50,000 spectators to view various spectacles (Kyle, 2007). While physical sporting matches were popular, the Roman culture also promoted death as a sport. Executions, gladiator contests, beasts versus men battles, and live reenactments of great battles were all popular public events that Roman citizens flocked to by the thousands (Cowles, 2011). These events were billed as entertainment, so the bloodier and gorier the better, because the greater the spectacle, the larger the crowds. The Olympic games are another example of the value of the spectacular. From Greece to Sochi, the games are as much about putting on a spectacular show that demonstrates the wealth, power, and prestige of the host nation as it is about the athletes (Simon, 2014). Additionally, network television coverage has turned football from a sport into a spectacle. From the need for a half-time show, to the commentator arguments, to the ratings and prices of Superbowl ads, the NFL organization recognizes and promotes the televising of football as spectacle (Pierce, 2013).

A more modern example of the importance of spectacle in gameplay is the video game. With the advent of software that can render compelling 3D environments, the "look" of a game is now very important to the player. Many of the most popular games are highly realistic and filled with vibrant color, extensive detail, excellent audio, and often, sensationally graphic images of blood, guts, and gore. The focus in video game development is on improving the graphics engines so that characters' hair, clothes, and body parts can sway, move, or bounce. When you shoot people in modern games they now realistically recoil and splatter blood. The audio is enhanced too so that the sound of the shot, as well as the muzzle flash, and even the recoil of the weapon all feel real. The game Quake is an excellent example of the value of spectacle in games. Quake's main two attractions are extreme, realistic violence and high speed action. We all enjoy watching a good show and games that provide us with attractive visual spectacle are very popular. When creating gamified applications it may also be important to consider the value of spectacle.

STATUS

Another essential element of gameplay is the acquisition and demonstration of status or prestige. One reason that people enjoy playing games is because games provide players with access to status through skilled performance within a specific game, or because access to certain games is an indication of pre-existing status to others. The values that drive status in gaming mirror those of the broader culture: perceived exclusivity, quality, and social benefits (Vigneron & Johnson, 1999). These values come into play when games are used as markers of social class. Sports such as horse racing, tennis, polo, yachting, and hawking have all been used at various times in history to denote wealth and privilege, as they required time and financial investment available only to the upper classes. The wealthy also use skill at such games to reinforce class distinctions. In addition to certain games being used as markers of status, in cultures that value particular games, success at such games can confer status on previously low-status individuals. For example, in modern sports culture, the ability to perform very well at a professional sport such as baseball, basketball, hockey, football, golf, or soccer results in that player receiving high levels of wealth, fame, and status, regardless of the player's race, gender, education level or previous economic class.

Beyond professional sports (which are so pervasive in many cultures that even if you don't follow a golf, you still know who Tiger Woods is, for example), status in gaming is primarily recognized within the community at the heart of the activity. Thus, attempts to transfer or recognize status across communities may encounter dissonance. For example, gaming communities often fracture into even smaller groups dedicated to a certain genre, style, or technology. A successful video game tournament player might be a minor celebrity at video game conventions such as Pax Prime or Gamescom, but be virtually unknown at tabletop conventions like Gencon. Even then, a Magic: the Gathering champion might be unknown if she showed up at a board gaming event at Gencon. It is therefore important to understand the cultural context within which a particular game-based status is valued when considering how to incorporate the acquisition of status into a gamified application.

Broader cultural status can sometimes be imported into gaming communities as well, because it brings a sense of prestige to the hobby as well as game players in general. This can be seen by the rise in celebrities who identify themselves as gamers, and the close attention paid by gamers to which celebrities play which games. For example, the death of Robin Williams was met with an unusual level of attention in tabletop gaming circles because Williams avidly played the Warhammer 40k miniatures game, making him in the words of many, "one of our tribe." Videos of Vin Diesel talking about his Dungeons & Dragons characters on mainstream talk shows routinely make rounds on social media, and Wil Wheaton's celebrity status has increased over the past decade as he has capitalized on his lifelong love of games to build a geek-oriented brand around his writing, acting, and producing. Professional poker players and athletes have also lent star power to the gaming industry in recent years. Like many poker pros, David Williams got his start on the Magic: the Gathering tournament circuit and translated those skills to a successful poker career. Things came full circle when Williams invested heavily in the launch of a tournament card game called The Spoils, along with Magic pro Jon Finkel. According to Scott Dodson, CEO of Spoils publisher, Tenacious Games, "It's very meaningful to the player community to have these people involved" (Dietrich, 2007). Similarly, high profile video and tabletop game industry professionals, fantasy authors, and comic artists flocked to working at baseball star Curt Schilling's 38 Studios based partially on the belief that his celebrity and wealth would translate into a successful game company. It is clear that including high status members of a cultural group such as CEOs and athletes can help increase buy-in and lend credibility to gamification projects even if these people are status-neutral within the game itself.

Status is also conferred by demonstration of insider knowledge or early access to games. The Pathfinder tabletop roleplaying game rocketed to the top of the field after conducting the largest public beta test in tabletop gaming history. This experience carried over to the development of the Pathfinder Online MMO, in partnership with MMO developer Goblinworks. In addition to hewing to typical online gaming alpha and beta tests, Goblinworks crowdfunded development of the game through two successful Kickstarter campaigns. The Pathfinder business and development teams understood the power of various forms of status to drive early interest in the new game. According to Ryan Dancey, CEO of Goblinworks, the company "spent a lot of time promoting, highlighting, and reinforcing the people in our community who make an effort to help other people by creating how-to guides, or answering questions, or organizing [out of game activities]" (R. Dancey, personal communication, August 18, 2014). Interaction with Goblinworks employees is an important part of the feedback loop that Dancey says players enjoy, and status-based hierarchies within the community help foster a sense of shared commitment and fun.

Kickstarter has changed the way that some companies approach status-giving promotions within the gaming industry. There is a long tradition of rewarding dedicated fans with promotional items, distributed via contests, conventions, or pre-order packages in retail stores. But now, fans that support game projects via crowdsourcing are able to choose from a wide array of status-giving promotional items only available to those with the most knowledge and commitment. Pathfinder Online awarded backers at certain levels with both in-game and out-of-game rewards, including tiered icons on their message boards, in-game real estate, and a "secret salute" animation only available to a select few players. "It is obvious from watching people talk that if you have one of those goblins, the community listens to what you say more than people who don't," Dancey says. Although recent research has suggested that things like badges and leaderboards have been poorly implemented in gamification programs, they are still highly valuable in creating a sense of status within a community when handled well.

STRATEGY/PROBLEM SOLVING

The need to think strategically and problem solve is an essential element of gameplay. Inherent in many highly successful games is the element of a puzzle to be solved. Whether it is figuring out the proper deployment of roles in an MMO raiding party or deciding the distribution of resources in a Euro-style board game, good strategy is essential to achieving success at the game. Strategic thinking involves pulling together information and knowledge from various past experiences or research, adding in innovative ideas of your own, and then applying that knowledge in creative ways to a new situation in order to solve a problem. In gaming, the end results of a good strategy typically tie into one or more of the other gameplay elements—success, perhaps through victory, creation, completion, or recognition. Strategic thinking as a form of play mirrors the human desire to optimize life by controlling for variables, evaluating options, and working toward goals perceived to be most beneficial based on available data. Many individuals so enjoy the mental challenge and personal reward of solving a complex puzzle that they pursue occupations or hobbies with a central goal of problem solving. For example, strategic thinking and problem solving can be found in the work of public health agencies such as the Centers for Disease Control and Prevention and the World Health Organization. The various tasks undertaken by these groups – identification, documentation, understanding, and area control – resemble the problem-solving tactics and strategic requirements found in various games. For medical researchers, engineers, doctors, mathematicians, detectives, and many others, their occupations involve strategic problem solving. Others pursue hobbies, including playing strategy or puzzle games, in order to satisfy their need for engaging in creative problem solving.

Strategy games emerged from the military tradition of using various kinds of war games to train officers and soldiers, analyze past battles, and prepare for future conflicts by anticipating deployments, tactics, and outcomes. The earliest war games were abstract games focusing on territorial control – a predecessor to Go called Wei Hai was played as far back as 3000 BCE – and included chess and its ancestor, the Indian game of Chaturanga (Smith, 2010). The use of sand tables to position and maneuver objects representing battle units dates as far back as the Roman Empire, and the practice would continue to be used widely into the 20th century. Perhaps the most famous of these war games is Kriegsspiel. Designed by a Prussian military chief under Otto von Bismarck, Kriegsspiel resembles modern wargames for its use of a grid system, representative miniatures, and terrain. It was used to train Prussian officers and was credited with aiding Prussian military dominance throughout the 19th century. Board games are still used to train the military, and there are dozens of contract and military employees with secret clearance whose job is to create and modify board (and computer) games for this purpose. War games and simulations have evolved with technology as well. For example, the U.S. Army created a video game called America's Army, which began as a marketing and recruitment tool but has since expanded to a range of "virtual soldiering" applications. The game is a first-person shooter utilizing the Unreal Engine, though it strives to present a more realistic combat experience than most commercial video games. Additionally, although powerful computer software is now used to run predictive scenarios in video games for training, board games are also still used to nurture the critical and creative thinking needed in military offensives.

Strategy games involving war and colonization are extremely popular, but problem solving is also the basis for another popular category of games known as puzzle games. Tetris, released in 1985, was the first blockbuster puzzle video game, launching a genre that includes more recent hits such as Bejewelled and Candy Crush Saga. In fact, Tetris has sold more than 170 million copies, making it the best-selling video game of all time (Johnson, 2009). Myst, another puzzle game that added elements of exploration and narrative was the best-selling PC game of the 1990's (Robinson, 2013). Myst is the ultimate puzzle game-- you can't die, you can't shoot anyone, and you have to read a bunch of books in the game in order to solve the puzzles. Problem solving and the use of strategy are also essential elements in 4X computer games referred to earlier. Finally, problem solving and a balance between strategic and tactical play form the core mechanics of many of the most popular Euro-style board games. Many incorporate a lot of the principles of war games – area control, resource management, etc., but some board games have also adopted the play structures of puzzle games. This has opened the door to immersive and interesting single-player options, and has also lead to what board game enthusiasts refer to as "multiplayer solitaire" when problem solving forms the core challenge of a multiplayer board game. People gain a sense of accomplishment from solving a puzzle. Thus, when designing gamified applications for non-game contexts, including puzzle or problem solving elements may be valuable.

UNIFICATION

Many successful games provide a social function, granting the ability to bond and identify with others through gameplay. Research has long demonstrated that playing table top games creates a sense of community among the players and allows for social bonding (Bowman, 2010). Additionally, fan culture for professional sports is an excellent example of the unification function of gameplay. A shared passion for a particular sport or game provides people with a shared vocabulary, a common topic of conversation, and a national or regional loyalty. A shared love of a sport or a shared fandom brings people together. In this way, games provide a common ground for people from different states, ethnicities, religions, or classes to connect (Duggan, 2013). Perhaps the ultimate expression of this is the meteoric rise of fantasy sports in the past two decades. Fantasy sports, which are a gamified version of spectatorship, provide an excellent model for successful gamification.

Additionally, good games provide people with a way to socialize in a safe context (lower risk) than face to face settings might. This makes gameplay very attractive to people, who, for a variety of reasons, may not be as comfortable interacting in certain face to face contexts, or who are just highly social folks in all contexts. According to Bartle (1996), gamers come in four different types, one of which is the socializer. Socializers are interested in people; for this type of gamer, the game is merely a backdrop, a common ground where things happen to players. For the socializer, inter-player relationships are important. They value empathizing, sympathizing, joking, entertaining, listening, and even merely observing as people play (Twitch.tv, a website where people watch other people play video games, was recently acquired by Amazon for $970 million, and as of early 2014 was responsible for the fourth-largest share of internet traffic). While playing the game is fun to these users, the most fulfilling aspect of gameplay is getting to *know* people, to understand them, to form lasting friendships, and to see them grow.

The idea that games unify people around shared values is nothing new. In early American colonial times, colonist saw gameplay as a way to promote and support puritan values of family and hard work. Additionally, in the 1950's and in the 1990's there were extensive public service campaigns designed to promote playing games as a family. The organizations behind these campaigns saw family game time as a way to create a strong family unit and promote "family values." The idea was, "the family that plays together, stays together" (Davis, 2014). Research has found that parents who play games with their kids do have better relationships with those children (and the children have better moods, higher grades, and less behavior problems than their comparable peers) (Davis, 2014). The huge popularity of Magic the Gathering and Pokemon trading card games in the 1990's is additional evidence of the value of the unification function of games. Young people of various genders, races, economic classes, education levels, and backgrounds shared a common passion for Pikachu.

In sum, creating community is an important part of successful gaming. Good games, and by extension, good gamified applications will foster social interaction and build community by rewarding players for interacting with others, putting channels in place for easy communication with other players, accounting for multiple friends spheres (Facebook, Snapchat, etc.), and giving players a sense of being part of a larger community (Davis, 2014).

RULES

Another essential element of gameplay is that of rules. Games operate in a world of structure and logic, such that one can "master the game" with skill and practice. Humans like patterns and the human brain is attracted to logical sets and combinations in any form. Thus, the rules that structure games add to the pleasure of gaming because well-structured, logical puzzles or mysteries are something human brains enjoy and do well (Dickey, 2006). Games have rules to facilitate these logical patterns. Without rules, games wouldn't be much fun. Rules encourage fairness and safely; they make things that are chaotic or dangerous safer; they breed creativity. Rules decrease the ability of other players to cheat without consequences, and their presence helps teach the value of structured interactions (Sonmez, 2011). Finally, rules help establish boundaries and provide a context for players to construct casual patterns; in short, they help define the boundaries of a game (Dickey, 2007). For all these reasons, good games have logical rules that can be learned and taught to others.

Rules are a necessary part of every game. The creation of various rules in sports and gaming allowed us to advance beyond hitting each other with sticks (Bucholz, 2013). The necessity for rules and structure in recreational sports grew during the industrial revolution, in part because leisure time became more regimented as work took on the artificial temporal boundaries of the time clock. Similarly, in the late 1800s sports leagues began to form, and people began to see organized sports as a serious pastime rather than a mere diversion. Rules took on additional importance as shared regulations were essential to ensure that teams could compete fairly. To heighten competition, it was important that games were not random, but had a structure that could be learned, mastered, and adjudicated. This limited the likelihood of player burnout and heightened competition between equally or similarly skilled teams and players. Games should be challenging, but the learning and mastery time for each level of the game should be proportional to the complexity of the task and the skill of the player. In any case, some logical structure to the game is essential for both regular game play and for gamified applications as well.

NARRATIVE/STORY

An essential element to successful games is the role of narrative or story. Storytelling is one of the oldest and most fundamental human activities. The ability to recount our experiences and use imagination to experiment and explore the world without taking physical risks is an evolutionary trait that humanity shares across cultures. Recounting and creating narratives are ways to educate our children, entertain others, and preserve ourselves for future generations. Humans tell stories through words, music, art, dance, films, and also games (Parker, 2009). Games often incorporate all the basic elements of storytelling, including the eternal human emotions that are played over and over again in stories across all media and all cultures—love, family, threat, danger, adventure, mortality, and death, to name a few. We find these same stories played out in tabletop games such as Dungeons & Dragons and MMORPGs all the time, from the heroic slaying of a dragon to expressions of real-world grief and solidarity represented by avatar-attended memorial services for players who have died. On the surface, narrative may seem to simply make games more fun, but narratives also help engage players in the other elements of the game (Wanenchak, 2014).

From "choose your own adventure" games to the huge success of the Oregon Trail game for children, it is easy to find many powerful examples of the importance of story within a game. For example, the creation of roleplaying games (RPGs) such as Dungeons & Dragons highlighted the importance of the story and narrative in gameplay. In RPGs, gamers make up their own complex story lines that then shift and expand as the action of the game commences. Players in RPGs frequently seek to create a satisfying storyline for their character rather than successfully complete adventures (Zagal, Rick, His, 2006). More recently, roleplaying and the importance of story have extended to video games through the creation of MMORPGs and open-ended virtual environments such as Second Life. Most MMORPGs have a very loose over-arching narrative and one central conflict, similar to the basic narrative found in stories as old as Greek tragedies and as modern as film genres (Dickey, 2007). Thanks to creations such as Choose Your Own Adventure books, RPGs, MMORPGs, and video games, we are no longer passive observers in the stories we encounter. As a result, narrative is increasingly valued as an essential component to a good game and to a good gamified application (Howitt, 2014).

RECOGNITION/ACKNOWLEDGEMENT

Recognition and reward are important motivations for playing games. Each of the elements discussed in this chapter offers rewards that appeal to certain types of players, so this section will address the psychological characteristics of reward structures themselves. The earliest computer games were intrinsically rewarding because they demonstrated access to and mastery of complex computer systems, which were relatively rare. Home and commercial video games introduced elements such as the high score, a competitive leaderboard that granted a player public recognition for skillful gameplay. Activision pioneered interactive rewards in the early 1980's by offering prizes to players that achieved benchmarks on certain games produced for the Atari 2600. For example, scoring one hundred thousand points on the Laser Blast cartridge netted the player a "Commander: Federation of Laser Blasters" patch, while scoring one million points caused every graphic element on the screen to turn into an exclamation point, a photograph of which got the player a "1,000,000 stripe." Nintendo created a global community through their house magazine, *Nintendo Power*, which featured letters, photographs, and stories about fans alongside articles about the latest games. The magazine also ran stories about celebrities who played Nintendo games to feed interest from the fan community, a form of implicit celebrity endorsement that lent status to the hobby just as it does today. Tabletop gaming has extrinsic rewards built in to the hobby because tabletop games are played with physical products, which can range from cheaply made components to luxury goods. Many publishers go even further by offering exclusive rewards for early buyers and convention goers. Often these rewards find their way to Ebay and fetch premium prices.

Digital technologies have distilled the reward structures for playing games down to their essence, triggering many critics to argue that some digital games, especially in the social space, are nothing more than aesthetically pleasing Skinner boxes (Bogost, 2010). A Skinner box is the colloquial name for the operant conditioning chamber associated with behavioral psychologist B. F. Skinner and his experiments into the links between rewards, punishment, and behavior. The classic example of a Skinner box is one in which a rat or pigeon presses a lever and is either distributed a food pellet or not. Game designer and theorist Ian Bogost created a game called Cow Clicker that satirized social games like FarmVille, exposing the operant conditioning built into the game design and arguing that such designs have reversed the traditional relationship by placing players in service to the games. Still others have argued that while there are traces of behavior economics and behavioral psychology to be found in social games, these elements are only one aspect of the games and thus should not be considered Skinner boxes (Lewis, Wardrip-Fruin, & Whitehead, 2012). Either way, these games are incredibly successful and highly instructive to gamification experts looking to understand the limits and character of reward-driven behavior.

Behavioral conditioning and rewards are built into many customer loyalty programs – essentially gamified marketing – in place today. For example, Nike+ partnered with iPod to create the Nike Fuel program, which uses iPods to track movement and exercise in order to monitor and monetize consumers' daily activities. Daily statistics are uploaded to the Nike+ website, where they are used to visualize a community of people around the globe that are dedicated to movement as life. The promotional video for Nike Fuel explains the belief system behind the technology,

Our minds, our bodies, and our experience all tell us that movement is life, and that the more we move, the more we live...Life doesn't come with convenient ways of measuring movement, so we developed one. Nike Fuel...uniquely designed to measure the movement of the entire human body, or the entire human race. (Nike, 2014)

The World Wide Web and other digital technologies have created a space for the public reporting of private activities, and Nike has taken it a step further by providing a technology that turns our bodily functions into data to be scrutinized by the world. Thus, it is also a space in which to gain recognition for having the right body or the right attitude. Other customer loyalty programs utilize email or texting to provide rewards at carefully determined intervals, drawing from the vast knowledge of behavioral psychology employed by slot machine designers in order to maximize transactions. Whether rewards are private or public, it is clear that they have a powerful effect on human behavior and the motivation to repeatedly return to a game.

COLLABORATION

Games that allow people to work together harness the gameplay element of collaboration. The vast majority of games played all over the world are collaborative (Zagal, Rick, and Hsi, 2006). In gaming, social connections are often necessary for completing tasks that require collaboration. In multiplayer games, for example, the positions and actions of the other players constantly affect each other so collaboration is essential (Eskelinen, 2001). Collaborative games teach us to work together, to play by the same rules and to respect the same values. In fully collaborative games, all players work together as a team, sharing the payoffs and outcomes. Games allow us a sense of giving back to the team or gaming community through good play and smart choices and give us an opportunity to socialize with others (McGonigal, 2012). Collaboration is paramount to building a strong gaming community, although this is often expressed outside the rules or object of the games themselves (such as working together to hold a competitive league together).

There are many examples of cooperative game mechanisms within popular games. Roleplaying games are a highly successful genre of collaborative games. In a roleplaying game the team works together to accomplish an adventure. In MMORPGs like World of Warcraft, the shared experience is also often the focus. The collaboration and the crowdsourcing possible in MMORPGs can enhance the enjoyment of the problem solving and puzzle pieces of a game, because it allows for more complex puzzles as well as those requiring simultaneous, coordinated actions to solve.

Doom was the earliest first person shooter game to support multiplayer options via local area network (LAN) or modem connections. This allowed for competition against real human opponents, but also for collaboration with other players (Bryce & Rutter, 2002). Most MMORPGs, likewise, are social environments in which players communicate, collaborate, plan, strategize, and socialize with other players. Players form contacts and develop relationships of trust based on their characters' actions and players' skill. Chat tools allow players to request help, strategize, and assist others. Studies of multi-user dungeons (MUDs) and 3D virtual worlds note the importance of collaboration because collaboration allows for the emergence of peers and appreciative audiences (Dickey, 2007). MUDs offer players a shared virtual experience and a platform for collaboration (McCormick, 2013). Already more than 50 U.S. government agencies use games to crowdsource ideas for everything from enhancing arms control transparency to mapping dark matter, and Volkswagen did a collaborative crowdsourcing game project in China to design a new car (McCormick, 2013). For many people, collaboration and collective intelligence has become a norm, not just in gaming, but in life. Thus, the emergent social value placed on collaboration should be reflected in gamified projects.

ESCAPISM

Many games offer experiences that go beyond the everyday lives of their players; this is the core of escapism. While a game can only ever be a part of the lived reality of its players, its mechanics, narrative, controls, and aesthetics can immerse players in an enhanced or altered version of the real world, or in another world entirely. Games can also provide a structure for imagining oneself as a different kind of person: stronger, smarter, richer, faster, or not even a human at all. In this way gaming can resemble acting, as players inhabit the minds and bodies of characters doing things they cannot do in "real life." Escapism does not have to be the focus of a game in order to be an important element in its success. Even in action-oriented games like Prince of Persia or Tomb Raider, the personality and backstory of the main characters matters. Story-based computer RPGs like Final Fantasy rely on escapism to establish an emotional connection that keeps players coming back for more, and escapism provides extra-mechanical rewards for completing tasks such as rebuilding a city or defeating a villain. It is this emotional connection that defines escapism: players know the story behind Mario's tireless efforts to navigate the bizarre worlds on which he finds himself, but few imagine themselves in those worlds or really care what happens to Mario or Princess Peach. According to Darrell Hardy, lead designer of the My Little Pony collectible card game, escapism functions by "giving what you're doing a context beyond the reality of it…beyond the abstract, beyond the mechanics, you become immersed in the fiction of the game" (D. Hardy, personal communication, August 16, 2014). Game designers have found many ways to achieve this, and innovation in escapism and immersion can be more important than mechanics in determining the success of a game.

For example, roleplaying games allow players to imagine themselves as fantastic characters using enhanced abilities to complete quests. Dungeons & Dragons and Final Fantasy are two of the most popular roleplaying games, but the genre has spawned thousands of games in which players escape into different identities as part of the gameplay experience. Massively multiplayer online roleplaying games (MMOs) like World of Warcraft have combined elements of action-oriented video games with the immersion of an RPG to disrupt the gaming field and launch a billion-dollar category that continues to be a major source of innovation and revenue for publishers. The fiction of a game does not have to rely on pure fantasy or alien environments to draw on escapism. In the Grand Theft Auto (GTA) series, for example, players control a character moving through a facsimile of the world in which they live. The difference is that in GTA players are rewarded for being anti-social, and for performing acts that are prohibited or sanctioned by society. This represents an escape from social norms rather than a physical environment or body, and is the type of escapism typically used to fuel moral panics about the links between games and criminal acts, character deficiencies, and physical or emotional problems. While some argue such escapism is problematic, others see GTA and games like it as simple fantasy which allows people to safely break the rules of reality and experience thrills that would bring fines, imprisonment, or worse if performed in real life. In any case, the ability to step outside of ourselves and "pretend" for a while is enjoyable for many, and thus, may be a valuable element when designing games for non-game contexts.

ENJOYMENT

The last, but perhaps most important element of gameplay is play itself. Play at its core is a voluntary activity that is intrinsically motivating. Game theorists and philosophers including Johan Huizinga, James P. Carse, and Bernard Suits have all emphasized the voluntary aspect of play and its connection to freedom. Play is the freedom within the constraints of rules, an expression of creativity or fantasy within the spatial and temporal structures of a game. It has even been said that play is a primary way that humans learn (Amory, Naicker, Vincent, and Adams, 1999). Games need to be enjoyable in order for the player to play. Fun is a critical aspect of game design, and enjoyment is often the only metric for a game's success. This is especially true for gamified applications, because time spent playing the game must be balanced against the everyday responsibilities that are being ignored in its favor.

The enjoyment and fun that comes from a game often comes from the positive emotions generated by play. Playing and having fun trigger the release of endorphins which promote a sense of well-being and release pain. The positive effects of play are so powerful that clinical trials have demonstrated that playing games can outperform pharmaceuticals for treating mild to moderate depression and anxiety (McGonigal, 2012). McGonigal's (2011) thesis in her book, *Reality is Broken*, is that structuring reality in the mode of games can have positive psychological and social effects. Additionally, play allows us to learn, to create, and to feel challenged. Play can make people smarter, more creative, and more strongly connected to others. Being a successful game player often means learning how to work together with others, to follow agreed upon rules, and to socialize appropriately. To play well and to keep others interested in playing with you, you must be able to see the world from the other player's point of view and demonstrate empathy (Nauert, 2009).

Humans have a history of playing games. Playing games together enabled hunter-gatherer cultures to develop a cooperative style of life, and to overcome their innate tendencies toward aggression and dominance (Nauert, 2009). Additionally, there is a long history of using elements of gameplay to motivate people and to make work seem more enjoyable. Workplace incentive programs, in-house team competitions, and corporate contests all attest to the popularity of Mary Poppin's spoonful of sugar philosophy (Fitz-Walter, 2013). In the gaming world, the importance of enjoyable, fun game play is highlighted by the fact that the casual gamer is now the biggest portion of the gaming market. This niche is filled with people who do not normally play elaborate games or purchase game platforms, but people who, when they have a few free minutes, pull out their phones to play Candy Crush. Casual gaming is less about the graphics, the story, or the connection to others and is more about the sheer enjoyment of a few minutes of play. In 2008, more than half of all the apps sold by Apple were mobile games. Many are puzzle games, such as *Bejeweled* or *Diner Dash*, while others are games with a more relaxed pace and open-ended play. One of the most popular casual games is FarmVille, which at its peak had more than 80 million active users worldwide (Chiang, 2010). Casual games do not require a large investment in time and energy and the play is often more free form, expressive, and improvisational than in more complex games. In the case of such games, people are not looking for complex challenge, spectacle, escapism, or competition, they are simply seeking a few minutes of enjoyment. This desire to play is the central reason theorists argue that gamification works. People are motivated to seek the feelings of pleasure that come from play in all contexts.

CONCLUSION

Gamification brings elements of game design into non-game contexts, which is a process rife with the potential to transform a wide variety of organizations and services. From innovative public health campaigns, to crowd sourced solutions for environmental problems, to creative ways to enhance customer loyalty-- the applications for gamification are endless. However, as Deterding, et al. (2011) noted, if gamification is to be implemented well, one must understand how it is distinct from related concepts such as serious games, toys, and playful design. In her 2011 book, *Reality Is Broken: Why Games Make Us Better and How They Can Change the World*, Jane McGonigal introduced the idea of "gamefulness" as a complement to playfulness, focusing on the elements of interaction and structure that differentiate games from play. What these exact elements are, however, is contested. This chapter has explained fourteen important elements of gamefulness that experts have used to describe games, as well as offered historical and contemporary accounts of how those elements have been both used by game designers and experienced by players. The elements discussed include chance, control, creativity, completion, spectacle, status, strategy, unification, rules, narrative, recognition, collaboration, escapism, and enjoyment. In order to successfully utilize these elements of game design in non-game contexts, organizations that want to capitalize on gamification must be able to identify, understand, and utilize these elements well.

In order to do so, an organization pursuing gamification should ask a series of questions. For example, "Who is the target audience for this gamified experience?" While demographic data is important to answer this question, it is also helpful to clearly articulate the needs, wants, and passions of the target group. An additional question might be, "What specific actions do we want to incentivize with a gamified experience?" Knowing this allows an organization to be able to create measurable goals and to gather the necessary data to know if they have met those goals. A third question might be, "How does my audience currently choose to interact with existing games?" Knowing what choices a target audience currently makes in gaming can help an organization ensure that any gamified application is attractive to that audience. A final question could be, "Why do you want to gamify?" Does the organization want to crowdsource a problem, to enhance customer loyalty, to provide information or services in a playful manner, to enhance brand recognition, or to educate the public, for example?

In essence, knowing the answers to questions such as these, as well as knowing the various elements essential to designing successful games that are discussed in this chapter, and then carefully choosing to incorporate those elements that best meet their goals, is what will ultimately enable organizations to excel at future gamification projects.

REFERENCES

Amory, A., Naicker, K., Vincent, J., & Adams, C. (1999). The use of computer games as an educational tool: Identification of appropriate game types and game elements. *British Journal of Educational Technology, 30*(4), 311–321. doi:10.1111/1467-8535.00121

Bartle, R. (1996). Hearts, Clubs, Diamonds, Spades: Players Who suit MUDs. Retrieved from http://www.mud.co.uk/richard/hcds.html

Bogost, I. (2010). Cow clicker: The making of an obsession. Retrieved from http://bogost.com/writing/blog/cow_clicker_1/

Bowman, S. L. (2010). *The functions of role-playing games: How participants create community, solve problems and explore identity*. McFarland.

Bryce, J., & Rutter, J. (2002). Spectacle of the Deathmatch: Character and narrative in first person shooters. In G. King & T. Krzywinska (Eds.), *ScreenPlay: Cinema/videogames/interfaces* (pp. 66–80). Wallflower Press.

Bucholz, C. (2013, May 23). Four important rule changes that make every game more fun. www.cracked.com/blog/4-important-rule-changes-that-make-every-game-more-fun/

Burgun, K. (2014). What makes a game? *Gamasutra: The art and business of making games*. www.gamasutra.com/view/features/167418/what_makes_a_game?

Chiang, O. (2010, October 15). FarmVille Players Down 25% since Peak, Now Below 60 Million. *Forbes*. Retrieved from http://www.forbes.com/sites/oliverchiang/2010/10/15/farmville-players-down-25-since-peak-now-below-60-million/

Cowles, L. (2011). The spectacle of bloodshed in Roman society. *Constructing the Past, 12*(1).

Davis, J. (2014, April 15). Tabletop strategy games still popular, create a sense of community. *The Beacon News*. Retrieved from http://stingydungeon1921.wordpress.com/2014/04/11/tabletop-strategy-games-still-popular-create-sense-of-community/

Deterding, S., Sicart, M., Nacke, L., O'Hara, K., & Dixon, D. (2011). *Gamification: Using game design elements in non-gaming contexts. CHI'11 Extended Abstracts on Human Factors in Computing Systems, 2425-2428*. New York, New York: ACM.

Dickey, M. (2007). Game design and learning: A conjectural analysis of how massively multiple online role-playing games (MMORPGs) foster intrinsic motivation. *Educational Technology Research and Development, 55*(3), 253–273. doi:10.1007/s11423-006-9004-7

Dietrich, H. (2007). Wizards veterans conjure new trading card company. *Puget Sound Business Journal*. Retrieved from http://www.bizjournals.com/seattle/stories/2007/03/19/story9.html?page=all

Duggan, R. (2013, September 19). Sporting events bring people together and create a sense of community for fans of all teams. *Washington County Enterprise and Pilot Tribune online*. Retrieved from http://m.enterprisepub.com/dakotacountystar/opinion/columns/sporting-events-bring-people-together-and-create-a-sense-of/article_25ccc47c-2158-11e3-a2f9-0019bb30f31a.html?mode=jqm

Eigen, M., & Winkler, R. (1981). *Laws of the Game: How the principles of nature govern chance*. New York, New York: Random House.

Eskelinen, M. (2001). Towards computer game studies. *Proceedings of SIGGRAPH*.

Fitz-Walter, Z. (2013). *A brief history of gamification*. Retrieved from http://zefcan.com/2013/01/a-brief-history-of-Gamification/

Hamari, J., Koivisto, J., & Sarsa, H. (2014, January 6-9). Does Gamification Work? – A Literature Review of Empirical Studies on Gamification. *Proceedings of the 47th Hawaii International Conference on System Sciences*. Hawaii, USA. doi:10.1109/HICSS.2014.377

Howitt, G. (2014, February 21). Writing video games: can narrative be as important as gameplay? *The Guardian*. Retrieved from http://www.theguardian.com/culture/australia-culture-blog/2014/feb/21/writing-video-games-can-narrative-be-as-important-as-gameplay

Jamieson, D. (2014). *A look at luck in game design. Tuts+ Game Development article*. Retrieved from http://gamedevelopment.tutsplus.com/articles/a-look-at-luck-in-game-design--gamedev-14195

Jewell, R. T., Moti, A., & Coates, D. (2012). A brief history of violence and aggression in spectator sports. In R.T. Jewell (Ed.), Violence and Aggression in Sporting Contests (pp. 11–26). Springer New York. doi:10.1007/978-1-4419-6630-8

Johnson, B. (2009, June 1). How Tetris conquered the world, block by block. *The Guardian*. Retrieved from http://www.theguardian.com/technology/gamesblog/2009/jun/02/tetris-25anniversary-alexey-pajitnov

Kyle, D. (2007). *Sport and Spectacle in the Ancient World*. Malden, MA: Blackwell.

Lagel, E. (2010, August 27). Randomness in games . . . why? *Gamasutra*. Retrieved from www.gamasutra.com/blogs/EricLagel/20100827/Randomness-in-games-why.php

Lewis, C., Wardrip-Fruin, N., & Whitehead, J. (2012). Motivational game design patterns of 'ville games. *Proceedings of the International Conference on the Foundations of Digital Games* (pp. 172-179). ACM. doi:10.1145/2282338.2282373

McCormick, T. (2013, June 24). Gamification: A short history. *Foreignpolicy.com*. Retrieved from http://foreignpolicy.com/2013/06/24/gamification-a-short-history/

McGonigal, J. (2003). A real little game: The performance of belief in pervasive play. *Level Up*. Retrieved from http://www.avantgame.com/MCGONIGAL%20A%20Real%20Little%20Game%20DiGRA%202003.pdf

McGonigal, J. (2011). *Reality is broken: Why games make us better and how they can change the world*. Penguin.

McGonigal, J. (2012, October 15). How might video games be good for us? *Big Questions Online*. www.bigquestionsonlin.com/content/how-might-video-games-be-good-us

Nauert, R. (2009). Leisure Play is important for human collaboration. PsychCentral. Retrieved from http://psychcentral.com/news/2009/04/17/leisure-play-is-important-for-human-collaboration/5398.html

Nelson, E. (2013, October 16). *Gamification.* Opening remarks for the Education Technology Innovation Summit. Retrieved from www.youtube.com/watch?v=F6iBcvRuiQI

Nike+. (2014). Nike. Retrieved from https://secure-nikeplus.nike.com/plus/

Pierce, D. (2013, November 25). Any given Sunday: Inside the chaos and spectacle of the NFL on Fox. *The Verge.* Retrieved from http://www.theverge.com/2013/11/25/5141600/any-given-sunday-the-chaos-and-spectacle-of-nfl-on-fox

Roberts, J. M., Arth, M. J., & Bush, R. R. (1959). Games in Culture. American Anthropologist, *61(4),* 597–605.

Robinson, J. (2013, November 13). Creators of Myst hope for come-back with new fan-funded game. *NW News Network.* Retrieved from http://nwnewsnetwork.org/post/creators-myst-hope-comeback-new-fan-funded-game

Rosewater, M. (2002a, March 11). Our three favorite players: Timmy, Johnny, and Spike. *Wizards of the Coast.* Retrieved from http://archive.wizards.com/Magic/Magazine/Article.aspx?x=mtgcom/daily/mr11

Rosewater, M. (2002b, March 11). Our three favorite players: Timmy, Johnny, and Spike. *Wizards of the Coast.* Retrieved from http://archive.wizards.com/Magic/Magazine/Article.aspx?x=mtgcom/daily/mr11b

Shelley, R. (1989). *The Lottery Encyclopedia.* Austin, TX: Byron Publishing Services.

Simon, S. (2014, February 8). What a week in Sochi, Russia! *Weekend Edition - National Public Radio.*

Smith, R. (2010). The long history of gaming in military training. *Simulation & Gaming, 41*(1), 6–19. doi:10.1177/1046878109334330

Sonmez, J. (2011, April 13). Why Rules Rule. Elegant Code blog. *Elegantcode.com.* Retrieved from Elegantcode.com/2011/04/13/why-rules-rule/

Vigneron, F., & Johnson, L. W. (1999). A review and a conceptual framework of prestige-seeking consumer behavior. *Academy of Marketing Science Review, 1999(1).* Retrieved from http://www.academia.edu/4793340/Vigneron_and_Johnson_A_Review_and_a_Conceptual_Framework_of_Prestige_A_Review_and_a_Conceptual_Framework_of_Prestige-Seeking_Consumer_Behavior

Wanenchak, S. (2014, January 27). Player vs. Game: Design, narrative, and power. *The Society Pages – Cyborgology.* Retrieved from http://thesocietypages.org/cyborgology/2014/01/27/player-vs-game-design-narrative-and-power/

Whitson, J. (2010). FCJ-106 rule making and rule breaking: Game development and the governance of emergent behavior. *The Fiberculture Journal, 16.* Retrieved from http://sixteen.fibreculturejournal.org/rule-making-and-rule-breaking-game-development-and-the-governance-of-emergent-behaviour/

Zagal, J., Rick, J., & His, I. (2006). Collaborative games: Lessons learned from board games. *Simulation & Games, 37*(1), 24–40. doi:10.1177/1046878105282279

KEY TERMS AND DEFINITIONS

Game Design Elements: Factors related to how the game is conceptualized, designed, and created. These elements include factors such as: what are the rules of play, what does the game environment look like, how do you win at the game, and so on.

Gamification: The concept of infusing elements of gameplay (competition, incentives, story/narrative, collaboration, problem-solving, etc.) into non-game activities in order to make those activities more compelling.

Gamified: When a non-game activity such as shopping or voting has elements of game-play infused into it in order to motivate people to complete the activity.

Magic Circle: The imaginary or invented space that all players enter when playing a game, in which they agree to a set of rules that may be unfamiliar or contradictory to social norms and logical behavior. For example, all basketball players agree that a normal basket is worth two points, and Monopoly players agree to roll two six-sided dice to determine where to move their pieces.

MODs: Is the alteration of the program code of a video game in order to make it operate in a manner different from its original version.

Skinner Box: An operant conditioning chamber, attributed to behavioral psychologist B. F. Skinner, in which an animal interacts with one or more levers or buttons that distribute rewards at controlled intervals.

Skins: Software programs that change the physical look of a particular digital character.

Chapter 3
Gaining Reward vs. Avoiding Loss:
When Does Gamification Stop Being Fun?

Selcen Ozturkcan
Istanbul Bilgi University, Turkey

Sercan Şengün
Istanbul Bilgi University, Turkey

ABSTRACT

This chapter enhances the dyadic gain-loss concept by presenting findings of a research project on uncovering whether the efficiency component of gamification could be better attained by balancing a shift from gain to loss, or completely avoiding it altogether. The gamification of any system requires a good selection and balance of game design elements to make the overall experience fun, as well as gaming emotions to keep it intrinsically rewarding. However, if not designed properly, participators of a gamified system that expect the prospect of gaining rewards, may ultimately realize a shift of engagement from gain to avoiding losses any earned status, badge, experience, or popularity often defined within the periphery of the gamified system. Findings reveal changing levels of motivation within different participatory foci, where loss avoidance (punishment scenarios) generates more motivation than the prospect of gaining rewards.

INTRODUCTION

In February 2014, the town of Gukeng in Taiwan announced a campaign in which the residents of the town could collect cigarette butts from the streets and exchange 100 cigarette butts for a boiled egg from the municipality (Chung, 2014). By the end of April, the resident had already turned in around 700,000 cigarette butts in exchange for almost 7,000 eggs as a reward. The residents seemingly were so happy with the opportunity to gain free eggs for minor labor, the prospect of losing this merit pushed them into loss avoidance. After a while the residents of the town started cheating by collecting cigarette butts

DOI: 10.4018/978-1-4666-8651-9.ch003

from the neighboring towns, and as a result the municipality had to intervene and the gamified system was deteriorated.

In a research study highlighted by Poverty Action Lab, an experiment concerning hairdressers in Zambia tried to pinpoint the conditions under which the hairdressers would be more motivated to sell female condoms to their customers (Ashraf, Bandiera & Kelsey, 2014). It has been suggested that instead of monetary rewards, the hairdressers were found to be more motivated by a non-monetary incentive that consisted of a star badge reward which could be put up inside their shops. Similarly, the World Bank's *World Development Report 2015* suggests that rewards, particularly social and status rewards, can help shape behaviors, and these whole processes are slated as applications of gamification (Rafiq, 2014).

Gamification is often associated with utilizing gaming structures that include reward and incentive designs inside task systems that seem to be inherently unrewarding and low motivated. These systems may range from marketing campaigns that require consumer participation to learning, from HR trainings to boosting efficiency in a work place, from encouraging the use of a certain product to better management of online communities, from changing behaviors to social causes.

In the following sections, gamification is conceptualized with different definitions. Game system related challenges and rewards are framed to explain and understand the gamers' motivations. Then, a summary of the concepts of regulatory focus and regulatory fit was given to comprehend gaining reward and avoiding loss within gamification. This is followed by a fictional gamified competition experimentation. Via randomized block design, subjects are manipulated for reward, punishment and a balanced competition environment, which later also involves the presence of cheaters. The main finding of the research revealed changing levels of motivation within different participatory foci. It was found that the loss avoidance (punishment scenarios) generated more motivation than the prospect of gaining rewards. The balanced approaches, on the other hand, generated significantly lower motivations than both rewards and punishments.

BACKGROUND

Approaches to Gamification

The idea of gamification draws both positive and negative feedback from researchers and professionals. It involves a range of applications from commercial (e.g. FourSquare[1]) to humanitarian, including the discovery of protein algorithms in an online scientific game (Khatib, Cooper, Tyka, Xu, Makedon, Popovic, & Baker, 2011).

Jane McGonigal, in her TED talk (2010) and her following book (2011), claims that applying gaming structures into everyday problem solving could contribute to changing the world for the better. Accordingly, with gaming as a problem solving activity in which millions participate willingly on a daily basis, serious humanitarian issues could be transformed into gaming structures for which the said crowd would volunteer for resolution. For example, UNICEF's TAP Project[2] involves a gamified app to help or draw attention to water sanitation issues suffered by children around the world. TAP Project involves, gamers restraining themselves from touching their phones for 10 minutes a day, and if they fail they must donate 1 USD to help provide clean water to underprivileged geographies lacking it. Similarly, the "Half the Sky" mobile game developed by USAID, as a part of the Half the Sky Movement[3], aims to address oppression against women. Particularly, *Family Choices* and *9-Minutes* mobile games aim to educate young girls about family, marriage, education, family planning and pregnancy[4] (Fox, 2012). On an individual level, Nike+[5] provides a popular gamification example for motivating runners (Bernandin, Kemp-Robertson, Stewart, Cheng, Wan, Rossiter, & Fukawa, 2008) by allocating a virtual race. The Nike sponsored free app is not only praised for motivating individuals for higher sports engagement to improve their health, but also for its big data to be utilized for constructing improved health policies (Tegtmeyer, 2007).

Engagement plays a critical role for any gamification applications to be successful in providing information that leads to a social benefit. The stress level a gamer is exposed to during engagement presents a defining threshold for engagement. Gaming structures should hence involve *eustress* (Selye, 1964) or "good stress", which is the *"stress between too much or too little, an optimal level of stress"* (Fevre, Matheny, & Kolt, 2003, p. 726). Similarly, Zichermann and Linder (2010) underline the marketing applications of gamification, and confirm McGonigal (2010) in suggesting participation to be voluntary in gamified systems. For instance, utilization of rewards, badges, levels, missions and achievements to enhance gamers' experiences of persuasion, motivation and manipulation (Zichermann & Linder, 2010) is exemplified in PINK, Victoria's Secret's gamified app. In this social app, Pink Points collected by users via participation in promotion and freebie hunt are then used as discounts. Interestingly, Victoria's Secret's sales growth in May 2014 is attributed to PINK (L Brands, 2014).

Despite all the popularity gamification received, Bogost (2011a) believes "it takes games--a mysterious, magical, powerful medium that has captured the attention of millions of people--and it makes them accessible in the context of contemporary business" and opposes the concept of gamification. In response, Zichermann (2011) argues that "this [approach] overlooks all the good that gamification does, and has the potential to do more of." Moreover, gaming itself has also received similar critiques; e.g., Dibbell's concept of ludocapitalism underlines the relationship between gamers' efforts and their translation into the real world currency – a process which reverberates a form of capitalism (2006). In addition, Dyer-Witheford and Peuter's (2009) investigation of ludocapitalistic practices in Second Life[6] reveals that "[the game] recapitulates patterns of online shopping, social networking, and digital labor crucial to global capitalism" (p. 14). Similarly, Kücklich claims that by producing tools for gamers to create in-game commodities (such as maps, models, in-game items, graphics, etc.) while keeping those commodities under the ownership of the production companies through EULAs[7] and digital agreements, the gamers' leisure time and efforts are being converted into commodities for the industry via playbour (Kücklich, 2005, 2009). Furthermore, Goggin concludes that twork and play, formerly thought to be stable distinct entities, are now blurring together to form new hybrid structures (Goggin, 2011). Within these structures "work" is not the only domain where commodities are produced, but leisure itself is also turning into a commoditized experience. Recently, Watson presents a connective critique (Watson, 2013) in his response to a research question in Media Commons. He agrees that the concept of gamification weakens the concept of games, since "a game is about the unexpected, [gamification] is about the expected." Despite this, he defines gamification as "a sleazy kind of behavioral control", which partially refutes its use in marketing or business applications.

As a conclusion, critiques to gamification mostly focus on the business (and eventually the capitalist) scene's adoption of the application, and its possible results of abusive transformation of voluntary leisure into free labor and commodity for corporate agendas. However, this perspective provides an incomplete picture. Firstly, the gamer acquires a theoretical gain from the trade in question – which may be in the form of fun, gratification, social status and experience, if not financial or physical, though projected as "free" labor. Secondly, an undefined trade takes place between the gamified system and its participant. The user's participation is voluntary, but their labor is not entirely free. The trade may seem to be unfair because the rewards offered are mostly virtual; however, it should be noted that leisure is also a virtual commodity. As a result, the main question that needs to be addressed is whether the design of the gamified system is satisfactory. In cases of poor gamified systems, intrinsic psychological gains can be below the value or worthless, not allowing gamers to have good leisure in return for their voluntary participation. When the gamified system is designed effectively and in an immersive way, allowing gamers to accumulate gains inside the system, participants would refrain from losing in the long run. This in turn may result in excessive participation to avoid the loss of these gains, in which case the activity of participating itself may cease to be fun or intrinsically rewarding.

Emerging addictive and compulsive gaming research on "massively multiplayer online" (MMO) gaming analyses players creation of and investment in virtual characters or locations for long periods of time, which leads them to behave on the borders of addictive and compulsive behavior to protect their investments (Wan & Chiou, 2006a, 2006b; Rooij, Schoenmakers, Eijnden, & Mheen, 2009; Lu & Wang, 2008; Collins, Freeman, & Chamarro-Premuzic, 2012; Liu & Peng, 2009). These behaviors may very well translate into gamified systems and convert players into grief systems. This study aims to elaborate on foci of design points that could prevent this transformation and highlight requirements for good gamification designs.

Deepening the Definition of Gamification

The widespread accepted definition of gamification involves *"the use of game design elements in non-game contexts"* (Deterding, Dixon, Khaled, & Nacke, 2011). In addition, Groh (2012) identifies four components within this definition, which are namely (i) *game*, (ii) *element*, (iii) *design,* and (iv) *non-game contexts*. The following sub-sections are devoted to each of these components and their relative comparison with other theoretical approaches.

i. Game

Plato defines the two basic game forms as *ludus* and *paidia*. Ludus is the *"pre-existing rules that players agree to observe; these rules specify a goal and the allowed means to attain that goal"* (Herman, Jahn, & Ryan, 2005). Paidia, on the other hand, provides the opposite of ludus. It is a free form of play with no rules or goals. In this aspect, gamification seems to be mostly achievable by ludus formations and very little by paidia, which is also referred to as *gameful* (Lucero, Karapanos, Arrasvuori, & Korhonen, 2014).

ii. Element

Game elements involve various approaches. *Points, badges and leaderboards* (PBL) are often employed in gaming structures (Werbach & Hunter, 2012). However, adding these elements to non-engaging and weak content is critiqued as similar to efforts of *"flavouring in cough syrup"* (Trippenbach, 2013). Recent research by Hamari, Koivisto and Sarsa (2014) reviews empirical gamification research and concludes that the motivational affordance elements for gamification are *points, leaderboards, achievements / badges, levels, story / theme, clear goals, feedback, rewards, progress* and *challenge*.

iii. Design

Psychological and engagement based frameworks, which create motivation to play, keep playing and increase emotional gain (i.e., fun) from the overall system, are often utilized.

iv. Non-Game Context

Finally, the non-game context is where playing seems inherently unlikely or contradicting. Social applications that address humanitarian issues are viable examples, for instance. The *serious games*, in which *"models of great ideas can be recaptured by simulations"* (Abt, 1987) are advanced to contemporary digital games, video games and applications (Michael & Chen, 2005). As a result, gamification is more often seen applied in contexts of education, training and information.

Discussion on game heuristics provides that the inherently *ludic* components construct clearer gamification premises. However, many *paidic* elements linger between the borders of gamified systems. As a result, gamified systems constitute a moving target, where perfect formulation of a gamified system is still inconclusive. On the other hand, there seems to be no formula to determine how few or how many elements should be employed before a system could be accepted as gamified. A suggested approach proposed by Robinson and Bellotti includes six major categories of context (2013); (1) a general framing which outlines the content and cause of the system, (2) general rules and performance framing by which the user constitutes the idea of a good performance, (3) social features that allow users to interact with others, (4) incentives, (5) resources and constraints which levels the players' chances and (6) feedback and status information that report players' performance during the process. Nevertheless, it still seems possible for the context to be minimal, even when the listed elements are satiated. Accordingly, the research reported in the analysis section of this study employs a gamified system as minimal as possible.

If one is to assess reputation, ranks and levels in game context, it seems that these entities require sustainable approaches. Reeves and Read (2009, 2010) point out that the reputations need to be accessible and broadcasted for successful engagement. Unlike the online reputations in systems like eBay, where online reputations may affect the outcome of electronic trades and carry value other than intrinsic motivation, in-game reputations are mostly about social gains. Jakobsson and Taylor (2003) compare reputation in online gaming with mafia practices such as trust, honor, silence, favors and family and *"the deep connections, the social rituals, the insider / outsider status, the exchange of favors, and the general reliance on others that resonates."* Therefore, gamers would have reluctance towards actions that might result in loss of hard earned reputation, and even grief upon realization of the loss.

Similar to the reputation, virtual currencies create real markets and economies too. Reeves and Read (2009) report behavior of users of virtual currencies to be similar to their real currency using behavior. Hence, literature on losing money and its findings are applicable to virtual currencies, particularly the constant fear of losing money even when the odds are significantly positive (Thaler & Johnson, 1990) and the fear of losing money stimulating aversive behavior (Delgado, Labouliere, & Phelps, 2006). Much like reputation loss, currency (virtual or real) loss is a factor degrading the gaming experience.

As per the time pressure, it is documented that not doing anything in game-time, or not doing things fast enough, has its consequences (Juul, 2004). Therefore, excessive use of punitive time may easily elevate eustress to stress.

Peer pressure is also reported as many online gamers demonstrate serious fears of letting others (in their teams or guilds) down, greater than the fear of actually failing inside the game (Taylor & Taylor, 2009). Guilds (player organizations) of online games are identified as pressuring their members to spend more time online (Seay, Jerome, Lee, & Kraut, 2004). Competition, teams and communication inside gaming structures are origins of peer pressure (Reeves & Read, 2010).

Lastly, a *game layer* that covers the real world is argued to emerge by Priebatsch (2010). Since the year 2000, a new social layer stemming from the rise of the digital social platforms onto the real world has been identified. Xu lists four mechanics that the new game layers are operational with: (1) appointment, (2) influence & status, (3) progression and (4) communal discovery (Xu, 2011). It should be noted that Priebatsch critizes the game layer in its power to have anyone do anything (Priebatsch, 2012). Gamification can indeed be employed to induce positive behavior change, such as fighting against obesity (Baranowski & Frankel, 2011), driving sustainability and environmental ideas for corporate employees (Stevens, 2013), and preventing substance abuse and relationship violence (Schoech, Boyas, Black, & Nada, 2013).

Frameworks for Motivation and Fun

This study focuses on simpler systems for the purpose of gain/loss analysis, which are constructed from the components of motivation to play (engagement), motivation to keep playing (continuation) and emotions felt during play (fun).

The pleasure principle in play has been highlighted in the development of psychology. Wälder (1933), quotes Bühler's theories of *functional pleasure* that results from performance during play and *gratification pleasure* that results from success during play. Similarly, Freud suggests that pleasure is a form of economics where the individual is trying to balance unpleasurable tension by avoiding it or producing pleasure (2003). Therefore, individuals participating in a gamified systems would be expected to avoid unpleasurable tension, and try to succeed towards pleasure.

Salen & Zimmerman (2004) introduce the concept of *play as pleasure,* and conclude that "*the carefully crafted arc of rewards and punishments that draws players into games and keep them playing connects pleasure to profitability*". This pleasure is defined under particular actions such as *concentration* the games provide and the *excitement* of winning – all related to the "*physical, emotional, psychological, or ideological sensations*" (Salen & Zimmerman, 2004). A complete gain vs loss perspective needs to consider the antonym of pleasure, frustration. Gain leads to pleasure upon rewards, while struggle to prevent loss of earned rewards and status lead to frustration

Gaming experiences provide some emotional arousals via the "*internal sensations that occur in relationship to pursuing a goal*" (Lazzaro, 2009). The more emotions felt during gaming, the more intense engagement is experienced. XEODesign's research on observations of facial gestures, body language and verbal comments has identified gamers' emotions as: *fear (threat of harm), surprise (sudden change), disgust, naches / kvell (pride for a child/mentee), fiero (triumph over adversity), schadenfreude (gloating over the misfortune of a rival) and wonder (odds against overwhelming improbability)* (Lazzaro, 2004). Gamification designs that exclude these situational emotions should be researched in terms of their implications on perceiving the balance in between gain and loss. Particularly, *naches* provides an interesting topic. *Naches* is referred to as the pleasure or pride a participator feels via his/her virtual presence in the gaming system. It is inclusive of all reputational symbols earned via accumulated rewards, badges, achievements, levels, and ranks. In game designs where the participants' virtual presence fades with time, incentives for the player diminish consecutively. When game design allows for further rewards upon continuing engagement, skills required for elevated challenges might also create a barrier. In both cases, gamers start experiencing an avoidance period.

Leading emotion is a key element in good gamification design. However, an engaging game system would need more than just one led emotion. Various player types would demand different emotional leads (Ryan, Rigby, & Przybylski, 2006). The four major player types commonly referred to in video games, known as *hard fun, easy fun, altered states,* and *people factor,* could be translated to gamified systems for better design. Hard fun players are known for playing to beat the game and see how good they are, while easy fun players are often interested in exploration, adventure, story and characters. On the other hand, altered states players usually want to clear their minds from daily issues and/or avoid boredom, while people factor players are generally interested in the interaction with other players. Similarly, Bartle categorizes online players as *Killers, Achievers, Socializers and Explorers* (Bartle, 1996, 2004). *Killers* want to be strongest among players, while *Socializers* want to bind with other players. *Explorers* want to discover the virtual game world content, while *Achievers* want to finish (consume) the quests and goals within the game content. On another note, Yee (2006) reports main game engagement reasons as *creating relationships* (interacting with other players), *immersion* (identifying with game content and experiencing the game world) and *achievement* (becoming powerful and beating the game content).

Fun, though known as the ultimate purpose of play, is not a homogeneous emotion, but a combination of many emotions. Fun can be felt upon a range of activities from beating others to exploring the options. Therefore, there is no one fits all model to serve for the various gamers. Here, *regulatory focus* provides a good fit for award and punishment based motivational factors with its gain and loss perspective. Moreover, a gamified experience involves a deep cognitive absorption also known as the *flow state,* which occurs under certain conditions (Table 1). Flow is defined as the "*activities in which there is a match between high challenge and high skills*", and activities undertaken during flow state often lead to happiness (Csikszentmihalyi, 1997).

A gamified system design that has a harmonious flow state should also consider differing learning curve and challenge levels of the target player segment. Moreover, self-determination theory (SDT) suggests intrinsic motivation as the core motivation for sports and play (Frederick & Ryan, 1995), and underlines factors of *autonomy, competence* and *relatedness* as influential. Game play is often voluntary, which is an *autonomous* state. However, an engagement with a gamified system that allows for high levels of freedom is likely to raise the sense of autonomy. For example, non-controlling instructions, replay options and different possible outcomes are likely to lead to more autonomy. Challenging players optimally and giving positive feedback usually creates *competence. Relatedness* is experienced when one feels (s)he is connected with others (Ryan & Deci, 2001). Accordingly, discussion forums, scoreboards, and multi-player structures are some alternatives to enhance relatedness.

Attention, Relevance, Confidence and Satisfaction (ARCS for short) are key elements that provide and upkeep motivation (Keller, 1984). Attention consists of (i) perceptual arousal related with surprise and uncertainty; (ii) inquiry arousal related with challenge or problem solving, and (iii) variability. As a gamer becomes more familiar with a gaming structure, perceptual arousal diminishes independent of the inquiry arousal and variability. Moreover, clear goal definition in gamification provides relevance upon motive matching and familiarity. In addition, the gamer's confidence is related with awareness of performance requirements and success opportunities, and autonomy to exert personal control over his/her own performance. Lastly, satisfaction involves intrinsic and extrinsic rewards that lead to motivation (Keller, 1987), as well as equity based on the standardization of evaluation. Particularly, lack of standard-

Table 1. The conditions of Flow State (Csikszentmihalyi, 1997) applied to game structures

Clear goals	The player instantly understands what his goal is and what he must do to achieve it. For every gamified system there can be a certain anxiety period before when the player learns what to do and how to do it. Easing this period with tutorials and/or clear interaction designs may result in a faster transition into the flow state.
Immediate feedback	The player can instantly see and understand the results of his actions. The player also understands if he is doing well or not.
Challenges matching skills	The player needs to climb a learning curve that keeps challenging him as the game progresses. Challenges too high or too low for the skill level of the player will both frustrate him equally.
Deep concentration	The task at hand encourages attention.
A feeling of control	The player needs to feel in control throughout the entire game experience. Unjustifiably hard to learn or hard to execute actions will break the experience.
The sense of time is altered	The player loses track of time or time seems to pass with rapidity.
The activity is intrinsically rewarding	The experience is worth engaging in for its own sake. The game awards you for progressing through with the experience.

ized evaluation in gamified systems that may contain cheaters is of special interest. Finally, Pintrich and Schrauben (1992) stress the link between motivational beliefs and cognitive engagement in education.

Gain vs. Loss

Regulatory focus literature suggests that risk aversion relevant mental accounting within the domains of gains and losses may create anomalies in behaviors (Kahneman & Tversky, 1984). These behaviors may be effected by experiences, objectivity and hedonistic approaches. Crowe and Higgins propose two types of focus in such behaviors; promotion and prevention (1997). *Promotion focus* revolves around participation and accomplishment, while *prevention focus* is inclined to safety and security. Promotion focus inside gamification would ease joining the gamified system and participating in risks, yet would also expect gains as overall results. Prevention focus, on the other hand, would practice loss aversion. In another study Higgins ties the promotion/prevention foci to the basic dichotomy of pleasure and pain (1998). Similarly, research on video gamers indicates that negative messages are significantly effective for promotion-focused players in preventing them from becoming addicted to the games; meanwhile, positive messages influence prevention-focused players significantly in leading them to become addicted (Ho, Putthiwanit, & Lin, 2011).

Loss aversion oriented individuals are reported to perform better in virtual reality in comparison to numeric or categorical data (Bateman, Day, Jones, & Jude, 2009). Therefore, virtual reality can moderate loss aversion behavior. Gamified systems on the other hand offer a kind of reality simulations. Therefore, gamified systems may induce moderation of loss aversion behavior. Moreover,) propose regulatory foci influential on creativity, promotion and prevention focus effecting creativity positively and negatively, respectively. Gamification design usually includes creative problem solving and embracing challenges (Ronald & Jens, 2001). Accordingly, gamers with promotion focus would be expected to create solutions and/or shortcuts (sometimes bypassing rules) while prevention focus gamers would play it safe. In addition, regulatory focus is also researched in the domain of self-regulation in relation to consumer psychology and goal orientation (Freitas, Liberman, & Higgins, 2002; Higgins, 2002). It has been suggested that prevention focus individuals fare better under conditions where they have to resist temptation.

Regulator fit suggests that if the orientation of the action at hand and the regulatory state of the participator fit together, the process becomes enjoyable (Freitas & Higgins, 2002). Further research associates regulatory fit with motivational strength during goal pursuit and tests promotion and prevention foci subjects under vigilance/eagerness conditions (Spiegel, Grant-Pillow, & Higgins, 2004). It is found that promotion focus individuals perform better under awarding systems while prevention focus individuals perform better under punishing conditions.

When the concepts of regulatory focus and fit are applied to gamified systems, several propositions emerge. Gamification systems are inherently promotion focused, highlighting participation and accomplishments. Moreover, gamified systems are not endless and could hardly be designed for endless winning and providing endless content as a result. Instead they employ diminishing accumulated resources, which in turn triggers prevention focus. When participants who have entered the system with promotion focus start to feel the presence of prevention focus, the regulatory fit begins to get damaged. It could also be argued that although this may push some participants out of the system at hand, it may also revert the participants' state of focus into a prevention one and create a reconnection of prevention fit.

Cheating

Disrupting acts performed by gamers to sabotage other gamers in massively multiplayer games are known as grief play (Foo & Koivisto, 2004). Subsequent research offers various motivations and management of grief play (Foo, 2008). When promotion focus gamers are trapped inside a system with prevention focus (or vice versa) and are unmotivated to adjust the state of their participatory focus, it seems likely that they will demonstrate disrupting behaviors such as grief play and cheating.

Yan and Randell (2005) developed a taxonomy of cheating inside gaming structures to identify fifteen different levels of cheating. In their search for ultimate pleasure, *"many players cheat in games to 'play God' or have fun, without necessarily wanting to get ahead or defeat another human player"* (Consalvo, 2005). Evidently cheating doesn't seem like an action that could always be associated with disruption of the game experience, but also found as part of it. Research on cheating in Foursquare, renown as a popular gamification application, revealed that *"[cheating pervades] the spatial, temporal and social boundaries of play"* and *"has the potential to affect the real world in unexpected ways"* (Glas, 2013). Lastly, *"sham, counterfeit incentives"* offered in corporate gamification has little value compared with the participation required, therefore cheating could be considered as a two-way and justified reaction (Bogost, 2011b).

RESEARCH

To test the propositions that have been identified within this chapter, an experimental research was designed. The main focus of the research was to initially explore individuals' motivations to engage with gamified systems within the framework of regulatory focus. Additionally, deriving results from past data and theories, the research also focused on two additional constructs; the motivation to keep playing (continuance) and the positive feelings the overall experience provided to the participant. Depending on the past research, it was seemingly beneficial to understand the differences of a reward gaining gamified system, a loss avoidance gamified system and a reward-loss balanced gamified system, which in turn are

Table 2. Between-subjects factors

		Value Label	N
Test type Regulatory Focus	1	Award	63
	2	Punishment	45
	3	Balanced	62
Test type Cheater Presence	0	No Cheat	96
	1	Cheat	74

crucial for gamification designers for the purpose of better design and business. Additionally, the effects of cheaters' presence were also explored with regard to various regulatory foci.

Methodology

The research study involved randomized block design experimentation (3x2). Subjects were manipulated with three regulatory focus conditions (reward, punishment and balanced), by two conditions of no-cheater's presence, and cheater's presence. The analysis included 170 subjects in total (Table 2). Subjects were chosen from voluntary graduate and post-graduate student participants with the aim of representing bread earner individuals' responses to gamified approaches.

The research scenario involved a competition included in a photography course (available also in appendix). Within this competition, a photography assignment was expected from the participants each week and the delivered assignments were marked with awarding, punishing and balanced approaches. Moreover, each week a scoreboard of the resulting marks were announced in awarding, punishing and balanced terms.

The subject of photography was chosen to reflect a non-mandatory situation, which was not inherently non-motivating, while the concepts of assignments, competition and scoreboards were utilized as frameworks to reflect structured conceptualization of gamification. Since it has been established that a correct amount of gamification elements to form a gamified system was still inconclusive, the research scenario was designed as clear and understandable as possible and the gamification aspect was built mostly on scoreboard rivalry. It seems agreeable that the research scenario may not be considered as a "heavy" or "hardcore" gamified system, but more of a "casual" one, which could indicate potential for future research. The scenarios were given to each subject, including differences depending on the test condition, and their attitudes towards the scenario were gathered using a 5-point Likert type scale (Likert, 1932).

Results

First of all, the results of manipulation checks indicate that the manipulations were useful for stimulating the intended conditions (Table 3). Upon reading the scenarios the participants were able to differentiate responses between awarding and punishing systems as motivating/awarding and dissuasive situations. However, comprehension of a gamified system also induced an expectancy of arduous conditions. While rewarding scenarios proved to be highly motiving, punishment scenarios were not reported that powerful in punishing. This finding confirms the stance that gamified systems inherently create an expectancy of

Table 3. One-sample statistics

	N	Mean	Std. Deviation	Std. Error Mean
The announced lists are motivating. *(Manipulation asked only to Award and Balanced themes)*	134	1.79	.694	.060
The announced lists are dissuasive. *(Manipulation asked only to Punishment and Balanced themes)*	118	2.88	1.118	.103
The marking system is awarding. *(Manipulation asked only to Award and Balanced themes)*	135	2.07	.821	.071
The marking system is dissuasive. *(Manipulation asked only to Punishment and Balanced themes)*	119	2.92	1.161	.106
The final reward of the competition is motivating.	187	1.53	.690	.050
The doubt of the cheaters created hesitations about the competition. *(Manipulation asked only to Cheat themes)*	90	1.82	.696	.073
15 weeks seems like a tiring competition period.	187	2.31	1.042	.076

challenge. Overall, these results lead to the belief that the participatory foci of the scenarios were clear to the participants. Subjects reported the final prize of the competition to be adequate and the period of the competition acceptable. Subjects, all in all, concluded that the gamified scenario was inherently worth participating in. The introductions of cheaters to the gamified system was also comprehended as a factor that affected the answers to certain questions.

The main dependent variable of the research which was the motivation to play under various participatory focus and two other independent variables (motivation to keep playing and emotions) were tested with 2, 2, and 3 items, respectively. Factor analysis confirmed three factors, explaining 64,2% of total variance in the data set (Table 4). These factors match the intended model of one dependent variable (motivation towards the gamified system) and two independent variables of emotion towards the gamified system and continuance intention within the gamified system (motivation to keep playing).

The main aim of this research was to create an analysis of regulatory focus within gamification. Within the general group, the scoreboards seemed as a strong motivation element to participate within the competition independent from the reward or punishment based system. Even the punishment condition did not lead a participant to deter, since fairness was established via similar conditions for all participants. Interestingly, presence of cheaters was not received as an inhibiting element to participate, to keep play, and overall to enjoy the gamified system. Perhaps uncertainty on the density of the cheating might have generated toleration towards cheaters, not disturbing the justice perception of the competition. However, further results by comparison of means (Figure 1) indicated that the presence of cheaters had effected the motivation between groups, but was overall a less motivating factor compared to having a gamified environment with no cheaters at all. Consequently, presence of cheating within the gamified system only marginally effected motivation to play.

In terms of regulatory foci, findings indicate significant differences between groups. The possible contentment of punishment groups was also reverberated within the regulatory foci. Regardless of the effects of cheaters' presence, the group subject to the punishment condition seemed more motivated than the group subject to the reward condition, who seemed more motivated than balanced design conditions. This result is surprising and unexpected. The most important finding of this study underlines the punishment condition as the most effective in motivation to keep playing. First of all, it should be suggested

Table 4. Rotated component matrix[a]

		Component		
		1	**2**	**3**
The announced lists are motivating for me to participate in the competition.	Motivation to play	.863	.056	-.002
The teacher's marking system is motivating for me.	Motivation to play	.748	.121	.126
I would be happy to be within the best competitors.	Emotions	.169	.749	-.096
I would be thrilled to be in competition with the other competitors.	Emotions	.453	.664	.266
I feel free to take the photos I want.	Emotions	-.078	.658	.081
Even if there is the doubt of cheaters, I would still go on.	Motivation to keep playing	-.100	.054	.869
If I am not among the winners for the beginning weeks, I would still go on.	Motivation to keep playing	.355	.042	.705
Extraction Method: Principal Component Analysis. Rotation Method: Varimax with Kaiser Normalization.[a]				
a. Rotation converged in 4 iterations.				

Figure 1. Comparison of means

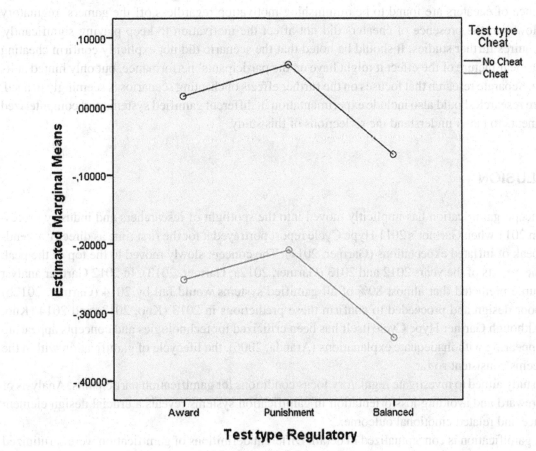

59

that balanced systems are recognized as perplexing by the participants and generate low motivation. Seemingly, the participants would rather be involved with systems which are exclusively rewarding or punishing, but felt confused by mixed or balanced approaches. Therefore, it can be proposed that the regulatory foci operate best in polarity and through a consistent approach within gamification. Secondly, it has been displayed that gamified systems are inherently competitive and some forms of challenge are expected by participants engaged with them. It could be argued that punishing systems were perceived as more challenging and more competitive than rewarding systems, which could explain the difference between motivations.

FUTURE RESEARCH DIRECTIONS

Our findings present an interesting case, as to revealing a greater motivational effect of punishment related loss avoidance regulatory focus in comparison to award related gaining rewards regulatory focus. It has also been found that both groups displayed positive emotions towards the experience. It should be noted this study prioritized theory development over generalizability. Hence, experimental research conveyed involved subjects in a fictional scenario. Findings represent attitudes rather than behavioral reactions. Thus, findings need to be tested with future research in field experiments for improved generalizability. Additionally, balanced approaches were found to be the least motivating scenarios in all cases.

Presence of cheaters are found to be diminishing motivation regardless off the gamers' regulatory focus. However, the presence of cheaters did not affect the motivation to keep playing significantly, which requires further studies. It should be noted that the scenario did not explicitly confirm cheating or draw a clear picture of the effect it might have on the participants' performance, but only hinted at its presence. Separate research that focuses on the further effects of cheating scenarios is seemingly in need.

Future research should also include experimentation in different gamified systems and computerized environments to better understand the reflections of this study.

CONCLUSION

As a concept, gamification has implicitly moved into the spotlight of researchers and industry professionals in 2011 when Gartner's 2011 Hype Cycle report portrayed it for the first time as directly ascending the peak of inflated expectations (Gartner, 2011). The concept slowly moved to the top of the peak within the reports of the years 2012 and 2013 (Gartner, 2012a; Gartner, 2013). In 2012 Gartner analyst Brian Burke predicted that almost 80% of all gamified systems would fail by 2014 (Gartner, 2012b) due to poor design and proceeded to confirm these predictions in 2013 (Kuo, 2013) and 2014 (Kuo, 2014). Although Gartner Hype Cycle itself has been criticized for technologies and concepts appearing and disappearing with inadequate explanations (Aranda, 2006), the lifecycle of gamification within the report seems consistent so far.

This study aimed to investigate regulatory focus conditions for gamification participants. Analysis of gaining reward and avoiding loss orientation in gamification systems reveals a crucial design element experience and related emotional outcome.

First, gamification is conceptualized in detail. Different definitions of gamification were scrutinized to understand the components that construct the process. Accordingly, game system related challenges and rewards referred to in literature of psychological and behavioral models are framed to explain and understand the gamers' motivations. Underlined gaming emotions indicate that the much sought fun element is a combination of different emotions. It is concluded that gamers' positive emotions do not always pair with fun solely.

Second, a summary of the concepts of regulatory focus and regulatory fit were given to comprehend gaining reward and avoiding loss within gamification. Moreover, disrupting behaviors might result from the lack of these foci and fits.

Third, an experimental research is undertaken. A fictional gamified competition was devised, which involved randomized block design experimentation. Subjects were given scenarios which represent awarding, punishing and balanced environments. Presence of cheaters with a control group is also introduced as an additional condition to the three environments. The main aim of the research was to explore if motivation to play changes upon different regulatory focus conditioned in gamification. Additionally, the motivation to keep playing and the positive emotions felt throughout the gaming experience were also measured. It has been found that the presence of cheaters led to different levels of motivation. However, the presence of cheaters is not found to have a major role on the motivation to play and keep playing, and induced positive emotions. This result requires further research.

The main finding of the research unpacked changing levels of motivation within different participatory foci. It was found that loss avoidance (the punishment scenarios) generated more motivation than the prospect of gaining rewards. The balanced approaches, on the other hand, generated significantly lower motivations than both rewards and punishments. It could be proposed that balanced approaches might have confused the participants and they felt uncomfortable with inconsistent systems (be it punishing or awarding). This is suggested as an important finding. The gamified systems need consistency in terms of their regulatory approaches to succeed.

Additionally, the higher motivation detected in the punishment based gamified system could be related with challenge expectancy. Since the fictional competition scenario was only mildly challenging and used simple gamification terms, it could be concluded that constantly rewarding scenarios were found "too easy" or "not worthy to compete". Likewise, the general attitude towards punishing systems may indicate that they were not challenging enough.

The overall findings present an interesting case which points out that challenge and loss avoidance still generate a higher motivator for gamified systems than the prospect of rewards. The study did not identify a loss of positive feelings or a loss in the motivation to continue to play within punishing systems. Results need further confirmation inside a live gamified scenario, since it is seemingly in conflict with previous propositions which suggest that long time gamified processes might degrade into negative experiences.

As a last remark, when does gamification stop being fun? Well, it doesn't!

REFERENCES

Abt, C. C. (1987). *Serious games*. Boston, MA: University Press of America.

Aranda, J. (2006, October 22). Cheap shots at the Gartner Hype Cycle. *Catenary*. Retrieved from http://catenary.wordpress.com/2006/10/22/cheap-shots-at-the-gartner-hype-curve/

Ashraf, N., Bandiera, O., & Jack, B.K. (2014). No margin, no mission? A field experiment on incentives for public service delivery. *Journal of Public Economics*, *120*, 1–17. doi:10.1016/j.jpubeco.2014.06.014

Baranowski, T., & Frankel, L. (2012). Let's get technical! Gaming and technology for weight control and health promotion in children. *Childhood Obesity*, 8(1), 34–37. PMID:22799477

Bartle, R. A. (1996). Hearts, clubs, diamonds, spades: Players who suit MUDs. *Journal of MUD Research*, 1(1). Retrieved from http://mud.co.uk/richard/hcds.htm

Bartle, R. A. (2004). *Designing virtual worlds*. San Francisco, CA: New Riders Publishing.

Bateman, I. J., Day, B. H., Jones, A. P., & Jude, S. (2009). Reducing gain–loss asymmetry: A virtual reality choice experiment valuing land use change. *Journal of Environmental Economics and Management*, 58(1), 106–118. doi:10.1016/j.jeem.2008.05.003

Bernandin, T., Kemp-Robertson, P., Stewart, D. W., Cheng, Y., Wan, H., Rossiter, J. R., & Fukawa, N. (2008). Envisioning the future of advertising creativity research: Alternative perspectives. *Journal of Advertising*, 37(4), 131–150. doi:10.2753/JOA0091-3367370411

Bogost, I. (2011a, August 9). Gamification is bullshit. *The Atlantic*. Retrieved from http://www.theatlantic.com/technology/archive/2011/08/gamification-is-bullshit/243338/

Bogost, I. (2011b, May 3). Persuasive games: Exploitationware. *Gamasutra*. Retrieved from http://www.gamasutra.com/view/feature/6366/persuasive_games_exploitationware.php

Brands, L. (2014, May 7). May sales report podcast. *LB.com*. Retrieved from http://www.lb.com/investors/financial_information/sales_earnings.aspx

Chung, J. (2014, June 20). Gukeng runs out of eggs in cigarette butts battle. *Taipei Times*. Retrieved from http://www.taipeitimes.com/News/taiwan/archives/2014/06/20/2003593232

Collins, E., Freeman, J., & Chamarro-Premuzic, T. (2012). Personality traits associated with problematic and non-problematic massively multiplayer online role playing game use. *Personality and Individual Differences*, 52(2), 133–138. doi:10.1016/j.paid.2011.09.015

Consalvo, M. (2005). Rule sets, cheating, and magic circles: Studying games and ethics. *International Review of Information Ethics*, 4(2), 7–12.

Crowe, E., & Higgins, E. T. (1997). Regulatory focus and strategic inclinations: Promotion and prevention in decision-making. *Organizational Behavior and Human Decision Processes*, 69(2), 117–132. doi:10.1006/obhd.1996.2675

Csikszentmihalyi, M. (1997). *Finding flow*. New York, NY: Basic Books.

Delgado, M. R., Labouliere, C. D., & Phelps, E. A. (2006). Fear of losing money? Aversive conditioning with secondary reinforcers. *Social Cognitive and Affective Neuroscience*, 1(3), 250–259. doi:10.1093/scan/nsl025 PMID:17332848

Deterding, S., Dixon, D., Khaled, R., & Nacke, L. (2011). From game design elements to gamefulness: Defining "gamification". In A. Lugmayr, H. Franssila, C. Safran, & I. Hammouda (Eds.) *Proceedings of the 15th International Academic MindTrek Conference: Envisioning future media environments* (pp. 9-15). New York, NY: ACM.

Dibbell, J. (2006). *Play money: Or, how I quit my day job and made millions trading virtual loot*. New York, NY: Basic Books.

Dyer-Witheford, N., & De Peuter, G. (2009). *Games of empire: Global capitalism and video games*. Minneapolis, MN: University of Minnesota Press.

Le Fevre, M., Matheny, J., & Kolt, G. S. (2003). Eustress, distress, and interpretation in occupational stress. *Journal of Managerial Psychology, 18*(7), 726–744. doi:10.1108/02683940310502412

Foo, C. Y. (2008). *Grief play management: A qualitative study of grief play management in MMORPGs*. Saarbrücken, Germany: VDM Verlag.

Foo, C. Y., & Koivisto, E. M. I. (2004). Defining grief play in MMORPGs: Players and developer perceptions. In R. Nakatsu, M. Billinghurst, & G. Yu (Eds.), *Proceedings of the 2004 ACM SIGCHI International Conference on Advances in Computer Entertainment Technology* (pp. 245-250). New York, NY: ACM.

Fox, Z. (2012, May 31). Best-selling book turns into mobile game for women in developing countries. *Mashable*. Retrieved from http://mashable.com/2012/05/31/half-the-sky-movement-game/

Frederick, C. M., & Ryan, R. M. (1995). Self-determination in sport: A review using cognitive evaluation theory. *International Journal of Sport Psychology, 26*, 5–23.

Freitas, A. L., & Higgins, E. T. (2002). Enjoying goal-directed action: The role of regulatory fit. *Psychological Science, 13*(1), 1–6. doi:10.1111/1467-9280.00401 PMID:11892772

Freitas, A. L., Liberman, N., & Higgins, E. T. (2002). Regulatory fit and resisting temptation during goal pursuit. *Journal of Experimental Social Psychology, 38*(3), 291–298. doi:10.1006/jesp.2001.1504

Freud, S. (2003). *Beyond the pleasure principle and other writings* (J. Reddick, Trans.) (Original work published 1920). London: Penguin Books.

Gartner (2011, August 10). Gartner's 2011 hype cycle special report evaluates the maturity of 1,900 technologies. *Gartner.com*. Retrieved from http://www.gartner.com/newsroom/id/1763814

Gartner (2012a, August 16). Gartner's 2012 hype cycle for emerging technologies identifies "tipping point" technologies that will unlock long-awaited technology scenarios. *Gartner.com*. Retrieved from http://www.gartner.com/newsroom/id/2124315

Gartner (2012b, November 27). Gartner says by 2014, 80 percent of current gamified applications will fail to meet business objectives primarily due to poor design. *Gartner.com*. Retrieved from http://www.gartner.com/newsroom/id/2251015

Gartner (2013, August 19). Gartner's 2013 hype cycle for emerging technologies maps out evolving relationship between humans and machines. *Gartner.com*. Retrieved from http://www.gartner.com/newsroom/id/2575515

Glas, R. (2013). Breaking reality: Exploring pervasive cheating in Foursquare. *Transactions of the Digital Games Research Association, 1*(1). Retrieved from http://todigra.org/index.php/todigra/article/view/4

Goggin, J. (2011). Playbour, farming and labour. *Ephemera: Theory and Politics in Organization, 11*(4), 357–368.

Groh, F. (2012). Gamification: State of the art definition and utilization. In N. Asaj, B. Könings, M. Poguntke, F. Schaub, B. Wiedersheim, & M. Weber (Eds.), RTMI '12 - Proceedings of the 4th Seminar on Research Trends in Media Informatics (pp. 39–46). Retrieved from http://vts.uni-ulm.de/query/longview.meta.asp?document_id=7866

Hamari, J., Koivisto, J., & Sarsa, H. (2014). Does gamification work? A literature review of empirical studies on gamification. In R. H. Sprague (Ed.), System Sciences (HICSS), 2014 47th Hawaii International Conference Proceedings (pp. 3025–3034). IEEE; Retrieved from http://ieeexplore.ieee.org/xpl/mostRecentIssue.jsp?reload=true&punumber=6751593 doi:10.1109/HICSS.2014.377

Herman, D., Jahn, M., & Ryan, M. (2005). Narrative, games and play. In D. Herman, M. Jahn, & M. Ryan (Eds.), *Routledge Encyclopedia of Narrative Theory*. London: Routledge.

Higgins, E. T. (1998). Promotion and prevention: Regulatory focus as a motivational principle. *Advances in Experimental Social Psychology*, *30*, 1–46. doi:10.1016/S0065-2601(08)60381-0

Higgins, E. T. (2002). How self-regulation creates distinct values: The case of promotion and prevention decision making. *Journal of Consumer Psychology*, *12*(3), 177–191. doi:10.1207/S15327663JCP1203_01

Ho, S., Putthiwanit, C., & Chia-Ying, L. (2011). May I continue or should I stop? The effects of regulatory focus and message framings on video game players' self-control. *International Journal of Business and Social Science*, *2*(12), 194–200.

Jakobsson, M., & Taylor, T. L. (2003). The Sopranos meets EverQuest: Social networking in massively multiplayer online games. In *Proceedings of the 2003 Digital Arts and Culture (DAC) Conference.* (pp.81-90). Melbourne: RMIT School of Applied Communication.

Juul, J. (2004, July 9). Introduction to game time. *ElectronicBookReview.com*. Retrieved from http://www.electronicbookreview.com/thread/firstperson/teleport

Kahneman, D., & Tversky, A. (1984). Choices, values, and frames. *The American Psychologist*, *39*(4), 341–350. doi:10.1037/0003-066X.39.4.341

Keller, J. M. (1984). The use of the ARCS model of motivation in teacher training. *Aspects of Educational Technology*, *17*, 140–145.

Keller, J.M. (1987). The systematic process of motivational design. *Performance + Instruction, 26*(9-10), 1-8.

Khatib, F., Cooper, S., Tyka, M. D., Xu, K., Makedon, I., & Popovic, Z. et al. (2011). Algorithm discovery by protein folding game players. *Proceedings of the National Academy of Sciences of the United States of America*, *108*(47), 18949–18953. doi:10.1073/pnas.1115898108 PMID:22065763

Kücklich, J. (2005). Precarious playbour: Modders and the digital games industry. *The Fibreculture Journal, 1*(5). Retrieved from http://five.fibreculturejournal.org/fcj-025-precarious-playbour-modders-and-the-digital-games-industry/

Kücklich, J. (2009). Virtual worlds and their discontents: Precarious sovereignty, govermentality, and the ideaology of play. *Games and Culture*, *4*(4), 340–352. doi:10.1177/1555412009343571

Kuo, I. (2013, December 18). Gartner: 80% of poorly designed gamification initiatives still on track to fail by 2014. *Gamification.co.* Retrieved from http://www.gamification.co/2013/12/18/gartner-bad-gamification-initiatives-still-fail-2014/

Kuo, I. (2014, February 3). Gartner's latest gamification research for 2014 with Brian Burke. *Gamification.co.* Retrieved from http://www.gamification.co/2014/02/03/gartners-gamification-research-2014-brian-burke/

Lazzaro, N. (2004, March 8). Why we play games: Four keys to more emotion without story. *XeoDesign.com.* Retrieved from http://xeodesign.com/xeodesign_whyweplaygames.pdf

Lazzaro, N. (2009). Understading emotions. In C. Bateman & R. Bartle (Eds.), *Beyond Game Design: Nine Steps Towards Creating Better Videogames* (pp. 3–47). Hampshire: Cengage Learning.

Likert, R. (1932). A technique for the measurement of attitudes. *Archives de Psychologie, 1*(55), 140.

Liu, M., & Peng, W. (2009). Cognitive and psychological predictors of the negative outcomes associated with playing MMOGs (massively multiplayer online games). *Computers in Human Behavior, 25*(6), 1306–1311. doi:10.1016/j.chb.2009.06.002

Lu, H., & Wang, S. (2008). The role of internet addiction in online game royalty: An exploratory study. *Internet Research, 18*(5), 499–519. doi:10.1108/10662240810912756

Lucero, A., Karapanos, E., Arrasvuori, J., & Korhonen, H. (2014). Playful or gameful? Creating delightful UX. *Interactions (New York, N.Y.), 21*(3), 34–39. doi:10.1145/2590973

McGonigal, J. (2010, February). Gaming can make a better world. *TED.* Retrieved from http://www.ted.com/talks/jane_mcgonigal_gaming_can_make_a_better_world

McGonigal, J. (2011). *Reality is broken.* London: Jonathan Cape.

Michael, D. R., & Chen, S. L. (2005). *Serious games: Games that educate, train and inform.* Cincinnati, OH: Muska & Lipman Publishing.

Pintrich, P. R., & Schrauben, B. (1992). Students' motivational beliefs and their cognitive engagement in classroom academic tasks. In D. H. Schunk & J. L. Meece (Eds.), *Student Perceptions in the Classroom* (pp. 149–183). London: Routledge.

Priebatsch, S. (2010, July). The game layer on top of the world. *TED.* http://www.ted.com/talks/seth_priebatsch_the_game_layer_on_top_of_the_world

Priebatsch, S. (2012, August). When the game means freedom. *CNN.* Retrieved from http://edition.cnn.com/interactive/2012/08/tech/gaming.series/prison.html

Rafiq, S. (2014, June 26). Gamification of thrones. *World Bank Blog.* Retrieved from http://blogs.worldbank.org/developmenttalk/gamification-thrones

Reeves, B., & Read, J. L. (2009). *Total engagement: How games and virtual worlds are changing the way people work and businesses compete.* Boston, MA: Harvard Business Publishing.

Reeves, B., & Read, J. L. (2010, April 27). Ten ingredients of great games. *ASTD.org*. Retrieved from http://www.astd.org/Publications/Newsletters/ASTD-Links/ASTD-Links-Articles/2010/04/Ten-Ingredients-of-Great-Games

Robinson, D., & Bellotti, V. (2013). A preliminary taxonomy of gamification elements for varying anticipated commitment. *Proceedings of ACM CHI 2013 Workshop on Designing Gamification: Creating Gameful and Playful Experiences*. Retrieved from http://gamification-research.org/wp-content/uploads/2013/03/Robinson_Bellotti.pdf

Ronald, F., & Jens, F. (2001). The effects of promotion and prevention cues on creativity. *Journal of Personality and Social Psychology*, *81*(6), 1001–1013. doi:10.1037/0022-3514.81.6.1001 PMID:11761303

Rooij, A. J., & van, . (2009). Compulsive internet use: The role of online gaming and other internet applications. *The Journal of Adolescent Health*, *47*(1), 51–57. doi:10.1016/j.jadohealth.2009.12.021 PMID:20547292

Ryan, R. M., & Deci, E. L. (2001). On happiness and human potentials: A review of research on hedonic and eudaimonic well-being. In S. Fiske (Ed.), *Annual Review of Psychology 52* (pp. 141–166). Palo Alto, CA: Annual Reviews, Inc. doi:10.1146/annurev.psych.52.1.141

Ryan, R. M., Rigby, C. S., & Przybylski, A. K. (2006). Motivational pull of video games: A self-determination theory approach. *Motivation and Emotion*, *30*(4), 347–365. doi:10.1007/s11031-006-9051-8

Salen, K., & Zimmerman, E. (2004). *Rules of play: Game design fundamentals*. Cambridge, MA: The MIT Press.

Schoech, D., Boyas, J. F., Black, B. M., & Nada, E. (2013). Gamification for behavior change: Lessons from developing a social, multiuser, web-tablet based prevention same for youths. *Journal of Technology in Human Services*, *31*(3), 197–217. doi:10.1080/15228835.2013.812512

Seay, A. F., Jerome, W. J., Lee, K. S., & Kraut, R. E. (2004). Project massive: A study of online gaming communities. In E. Dykstra-Erickson, & M. Tscheligi (Eds.) *Proceedings of CHI EA '04 Extended Abstracts on Human Factors in Computing Systems* (pp. 1421-1424). New York, NY: ACM. doi:10.1145/985921.986080

Selye, H. (1964). *From dream to discovery*. New York, NY: McGraw-Hill.

Spiegel, S., Grant-Pillow, H., & Higgins, E. T. (2004). How regulatory fit enhances motivational strength during goal pursuit. *European Journal of Social Psychology*, *34*(1), 39–54. doi:10.1002/ejsp.180

Stevens, S. H. (2013). How gamification and behavior science can drive social change one employee at a time. In A. Marcus (Ed.) *Design, User Experience, and Usability. Health, Learning, Playing, Cultural, and Cross-Cultural User Experience. Proceedings of Second International Conference, DUXU 2013* (pp. 597-601). New York, NY: Springer. doi:10.1007/978-3-642-39241-2_65

Taylor, J., & Taylor, J. (2009). A content analysis of interviews with players of massively multiplayer online role-play games (MMORPGs): Motivating factors and the impact on relationships. *Online Communities and Social Computing*, *5621*, 613–621. doi:10.1007/978-3-642-02774-1_66

Tegtmeyer, K. (2007). Data, data, data – but how to keep track of it all. *American Journal of Lifestyle Medicine, 1*(2), 144–145. doi:10.1177/1559827606297324

Thaler, R. H., & Johnson, E. J. (1990). Gambling with the house money and trying to break even: The effects of prior outcomes on risky choice. *Management Science, 36*(6), 643–660. doi:10.1287/mnsc.36.6.643

Trippenbach, P. (2013, April 17). Kill it with fire: Why gamification sucks and game dynamics rule. *Trippenbach.com.* Retrieved from http://trippenbach.com/2013/04/17/kill-it-with-fire-gamification-sucks-game-dynamics/

Wälder, R. (1933). The psychoanalytic theory of play. *The Psychoanalytic Quarterly, 2,* 208–224.

Wan, C., & Chiou, W. (2006a). Why are adolescents addicted to online gaming? An interview study in Taiwan. *Cyberpsychology & Behavior, 9*(6), 762–766. doi:10.1089/cpb.2006.9.762 PMID:17201603

Wan, C., & Chiou, W. (2006b). Psychological motives and online games addiction: A test of flow theory and humanistic needs theory for Taiwanese adolescents. *Cyberpsychology & Behavior, 9*(3), 317–324. doi:10.1089/cpb.2006.9.317 PMID:16780399

Watson, J. (2013, September 21). Gamification: Don't say it, don't do it, just stop. *Media Commons.* Retrieved from http://mediacommons.futureofthebook.org/question/how-does-gamification-affect-learning/response/gamification-dont-say-it-dont-do-it-just-sto

Werbach, K., & Hunter, D. (2012). *For the win: How game thinking can revolutionize your business.* Wharton, PA: Digital Press.

Xu, Y. (2011, April). Literature review on web application gamification and analytics. *CSDL Technical Report 11-05.* Retrieved from http://csdl.ics.hawaii.edu/techreports/11-05/11-05.pdf

Yan, J., & Randell, B. (2005). A systematic classification of cheating in online games. *Proceedings of 4th ACM SIGCOMM Workshop on Network and System Support for Games.* (pp. 1-9). New York, NY: ACM. doi:10.1145/1103599.1103606

Yee, N. (2006). The psychology of MMORPGs: Emotional investment, motivations, relationship formation, and problematic usage. In R. Schroeder & A. Axelsson (Eds.), *Avatars at Work and Play: Collaboration and Interaction in Shared Virtual Environments* (pp. 187–207). London: Springer-Verlan. doi:10.1007/1-4020-3898-4_9

Zichermann, G. (2011, August 23). Gamification is here to stay (and it's not bullshit). *Kotaku.* Retrieved from http://kotaku.com/5833631/gamification-is-here-to-stay-and-its-not-bullshit

Zichermann, G., & Linder, J. (2010). *Game-based marketing: Inspire customer loyalty through rewards, challenges, and contests.* New York, NY: John Wiley & Sons.

KEY TERMS AND DEFINITIONS

Achievements: Achievements are awards for reaching certain targets inside gamified systems. They are often used as synonymous with *Badges*, however there seem to be slight nuances. Achievements often result from accumulated success (such as "win 100 games"), while badges often represent one shot events (such as "win a game with 100 points"). However this distinction is hardly mandatory and both terms are used interchangeably.

Autonomy: Autonomy is the feeling of being in control, whether this feeling is justified or unfounded. However note that if the founding of this feeling was actually virtual, this might surface eventually and shatter the perception.

Badges: Please see *Achievements*.

Cheating: Cheating in gamified systems has various connotations. They may range from technical interventions, indecency, lack of social authenticity, etc.

Competence: Competence is the feeling of having the abilities to accomplish the task at hand, whether this feeling is justified or unfounded. However note that if the founding of this feeling was actually virtual, this might surface eventually and shatter the perception.

Digital Reputation: Participation in a digital social system, such as social media sites, online games, social mobile applications, etc., creates a digital self that represents the user, which is generally called an avatar. Through the actions taken inside the system, the avatar eventually builds a digital reputation that might convey persona, skills, manners and ethical implications as to the owner of the avatar.

Eustress: Eustress is the optimal balance of stress for a person, such that when this limit is traversed the negative effects of stress begin to surface.

Flow State: Flow state is the ideal balance between skills and challenges inside an activity. If the participant of the activity has little skills yet the challenges before it are too high, this creates an anxiety. If the participant of the activity is highly skilled yet the challenges before it are too easy, this creates a boredom. The flow state represents an ideal path balancing the skills and challenges.

Gamification: Gamification is the utilization of gaming structures that include reward and incentive designs, inside task systems that seem to be inherently unrewarding and low motivated. Gamification can have possible applications in various fields such as marketing, solution of social problems, engagement, and education, to name a few.

Grief Play: Grief play is the disrupting actions taken by a player inside a gamified system, which aim to diminish the enjoyment of other players. It has been suggested that grief players have come to a point inside a gamified system where they can only enjoy the game by disrupting others.

Ludocapitalism: Ludocapitalism covers the processes in which virtual currencies of gamified systems transform into real world currencies, such as physical rewards and money. This possibility in turn, initiates capitalist practices inside these virtual gamified systems.

Playbour: Playbour is the transformation of the efforts of players or participants inside a gamified system for the benefit of the owners or creators of the gamified system. A valid example is DIY (do-it-yourself) tools supplied with some digital games, which encourage players to build their own content which then becomes a commodity of the production company.

Regulatory Fit: Please see *Regulatory Focus*.

Regulatory Focus: The states of promotion or prevention foci. Promotion focus revolves around participation and accomplishment, while prevention focus is inclined to safety and security. If these states of the individuals fit with the focus of the system they are in, this creates a fit which is called the *Regulatory Fit*.

Relatedness: Relatedness is the feeling of being in contact with others. This feeling encompasses the cases in which a person feels the task at hand is important or spending time on it is justified because others are also doing so.

ENDNOTES

[1]   FourSquare http://www.foursquare.com

[2]   UNICEF Tap Project http://www.unicefusa.org/mission/survival/water/tap-project

[3]   Half the Sky Movement is inspired by the same name book by Nick Kristof and Sherly WuDunn. More information is available at http://www.halftheskymovement.org/

[4]   In *Family Choices,* the players take on the role of Anu (in India) or Mercy (in Kenya) and see the outcome of life choices concerning family and education, within their countries. In *9-Minutes,* the nine months of pregnancy is played out in nine minutes and in each layer information about how to keep both mother and baby healthy is given. More information is avaliable on USAID's website http://www.usaid.gov/halfthesky/mobile-games

[5]   Nike+ http://nikeplus.com

[6]   Second Life is an online virtual life simulation/game, in which players discover the virtual world, socialize and interact with other players, and can create virtual goods and build virtual spaces. The game was developed by Linden Research and released in 2003. More information available at http://secondlife.com/

[7]   End User License Agreement.

APPENDIX: THE SURVEY SCENARIO

Your photography course which you have finished is running a contest. For the contest, participants will need to take photos of buildings in Istanbul which are over 75 years old, and prepare a report that covers the history of that building.

Each week your teacher collects the reports and marks them.

- **For awarding theme**: Each week your teacher collects the reports, marks them and provides bonus marks for the extra number of photos and extra information details.
- **For punishing theme**: Each week your teacher collects the reports, and reduces points for missing information and unsatisfying photos.
- **For balanced theme**: Each week your teacher collects the reports and reduces points for each information and unsatisfying photos, while awarding bonus points for extra information and striking photos.

Additionally your teacher announces the results.

- **For awarding theme:** Additionally your teacher announces the top students each week on the competition's website and awards the first place winner with a star.
- **For punishing theme:** Additionally your teacher announces the worst students each week on the competition's website.
- **For balanced theme:** Additionally your teacher announces the complete list of marks each week on the competition's websites.

After 15 weeks, the winners will be sent on a photo-safari to Africa.

- **Non-cheat:** -
- **Cheat:** It has been brought to your attention that some of your class mates are cheating by hiring a professional photographer.

Please select the option that expresses your view: (These questions were provided on a 5-scale, 1. I completely agree, 2. I agree, 3. No idea, 4. I disagree, 5. I completely disagree)

a.   The announced lists are motivating for me to participate in the competition.
b.   The teachers marking system are motivating for me.
c.   If I am not among the winners in the first weeks, I would still go on.
d.   Even if there is the doubt of cheaters, I would still go on. (**Asked only to Cheat themes**)
e.   I feel free to take the photos I want.
f.   I would be thrilled to be in the competition with the other competitors.
g.   I would be happy to be within the best competitors.
h.   The announced lists are motivating. (**Asked only to Awarding and Balanced themes**)
i.   The announced lists are dissuasive. (**Asked only to Punishing and Balanced themes**)
j.   The marking system is awarding. (**Asked only to Awarding and Balanced themes**)

k.   The marking system is dissuasive. **(Asked only to Punishing and Balanced themes)**
l.   The final reward of the competition is motivating.
m.   The doubt of the cheaters created hesitations about the competition. **(Asked only to Cheat themes)**
n.   The 15 weeks sound like a tiring competition period.

Chapter 4
Development of the "Hybrid Interactive Rhetorical Engagement" (H.I.R.E.) Scale:
Implications for Digital Gamification Research

Yowei Kang
Kainan University, Taiwan

ABSTRACT

Digital game is an essential part of digital creative industries around the world. This chapter aims to develop H.I.R.E. scales that can be used to explain and understand users' responses to digital creative contents. Although multiple methodologies have been used to study gameplayers' experiences and interactions with different genres of digital games that lead to their gamifications, this chapter is based on a rhetorical theoretical tradition by arguing that gameplay interactions are a rhetorical process in which players interact with game designers as well as other players in the same guild through a series of persuasive manipulations. H.I.R.E. scales are developed to explain how gameplayers have different experiences when playing a digital game that contributes to their gamifications. Because digital game is an important branch of contemporary digital creative industry, the development of the H.I.R.E. scales will help researchers and practitioners to study and develop better digital games and other digital creative contents.

INTRODUCTION

A strong economic rationale supports the growing importance of digital games in society, warranting growing intellectual interests in this emerging topic. The apparent result of such economic and scholarly attention is also due to an exponential growth in the number of digital gamers and the fast expansion of the industry in the past few years. According to industry facts published by Entertainment Software Association (henceforth, ESA) (2014), consumers spent $21.53 billion on video games, accessories,

DOI: 10.4018/978-1-4666-8651-9.ch004

and hardware. According to the marketing research firm, the NDP Group, the computer and video game industry generated $21 billion in sales (cited in the Entertainment Software Association, 2014). A recent ESA report also estimated that the computer and video game industry in the U.S. added $6.2 billion to the U.S. Gross Domestic Product (GDP), compared with $4.9 billion in 2011 (Entertainment Software Association, 2011; Siwek, 2014). The computer and video game industry has continued to contribute disproportionally to the overall U.S. economy and GDP in spite of recent economic recession (Entertainment Software Association, 2011, 2014). The total sales of the industry have grown from $10.1 billion in 2009 to $15.4 billion in 2013 (Siwek, 2014).

Exponential developments of the digital game industry have generated enthusiasm among scholars from diverse disciplines to explore this phenomenon (Raessens & Goldstein, 2005; Wolf & Perron, 2003). Social science scholars have often examined unanticipated media effects of digital gameplay; topics include violent and aggressive behaviors among players (Baldaro, Tuozzi, Codispotic, & Montebarocci, 2004; Chambers & Ascione, 1987), addiction to digital games (Chuang, 2006), gendered gameplay behavior (Hussain & Griffiths, 2008), adoption of new game technologies (Chang, Lee, & Kim, 2006), and methodological implications for studying digital games (Boellstorff, Nardi, Pearce, & Taylor, 2012). In the area of digital game rhetorical research where the book chapter was situated for the discussion of scale development, research topics included interactive narratives (Crogan, 2003; Frasca, 2003; Juul, 2005; Neitzel, 2005), identity (Filiciak, 2003; Turkle, 1984, 2001) and learning (Gee, 2004; Prensky, 2005). Wolf and Perron (2003) claimed that digital games have become "the hottest and most volatile field of study within new media theory" (p.1).

The popularity of digital games have led marketers and educators to make the best of users' desire for achievement, self-expression, and competition into developing strategies that are capable of engaging and educating consumers for a variety of intended tasks (Hamari & Eranti, 2011; Hamari, Koivisto, & Sarsa, 2014; Reeve & Read, 2009; Swallow, 2012). As a result, a more comprehensive term, gamification, has been developed to address users' desire for achievement, education, entertainment, and stimulation through the use of game design elements, instead of full-fledge games, in non-game contexts (Deterding, Sicart, Nacke, O'Hara, & Dixon, 2011a; Morschheuser, Rivera-Pelayo, Mazarakis, & Zacharias, 2014). Gamification has been defined as "the application of game elements and digital game design techniques to non-game problems, such as business and social impact challenges" (Werbach, 2014, https://www.coursera.org/course/gamification). In other words, gamificiation involves the "development of enhancing (non-game) services with game mechanics" (Hamari & Eranti, 2011, http://www.quilageo.com/wp-content/uploads/2013/07/Framework-for-Designing-Eval-11307.59151.pdf). For example, in a business context, Swallow (2012) described how the help desk software company, *Freshdesk*, launched its gamified help desk product, *Freshdesk Arcade*, which rewards agents with points and rewards when completing customer support tasks. U.S. Army also developed its *American's Army* gamification systems for mall exhibits and public events for recruitment purposes (Stanley, 2014). Various metrics and frameworks have been developed to assess gamification (Hamari & Eranti, 2011), and psychological and behavioral outcomes (Hamari, Kovisto, & Sarsa, 2014). To summarize, Deterding et al. (2011a) defined gamification as "an informal umbrella term for the use of video game elements in non-gaming systems to improve user experience (UX) and user engagement" (http://gamification-research.org/wp-content/uploads/2011/04/01-Deterding-Sicart-Nacke-OHara-Dixon.pdf).

Popular digital games such as Massively Multiplayer Online Role-Playing Games (MMORPGs, MMOs, MMOGs) have attracted much attention from game researchers (Chuang, 2006; Steinkuehler & Williams, 2006). The design principles and interaction patterns in MMORPGs often demand thousands of gamers role-playing and collaborating simultaneously in a graphical and 3-D environment (Filiciak, 2003; Hussain & Griffiths, 2008). Popular MMORPGs include *Ultima Online*, *EverQuest*, *World of Warcarft*, and *Second Life*. With the advent of the Internet, digital games such as MMORPGs increasingly depend on networking technologies to link global gamers to collaborate with others to complete some tasks. The task-oriented and strategy-guided nature of advanced digital game applications such as MMORPGs has transformed digital games into potentially gamification practices for serious purposes. In other words, recent developments of MMORPGs are likely to bridge the gap between leisure and serious games for a variety of applications in non-game contexts. In this book chapter, the author posits that MMORPGs as an advanced digital game application should be treated as a gamified system. This position also concurs with Hamari and Eranti (2011) who have argued that games can be considered as gamified systems to accomplish some common objectives for applications in non-game contexts.

Derived from past digital game research and its applications in educational contexts (Gee, 2007a, 2007b), well-developed gamified systems are expected to generate positive outcomes. However, while human-computer interaction (henceforth, HCI) research has extensively examined the use of game design and game elements in non-game contexts (Deterding et al., 2011), theory-based measurements derived from the persuasive manipulations between gamified systems and their users to assess the effects of gamification on user experience is lacking. Therefore, in this book chapter, the author proposes a newly-developed theoretical concept, hybrid interactive rhetorical engagements (henceforth, H.I.R.E.) (Kang, 2011) to study gamification through the analysis of user experience in digital games and other gamified systems and applications. As a concept originally developed to study MMORPGs (Kang, 2011) from a rhetorical theoretical perspective, H.I.R.E. can be broadly defined as what users will experience and feel from a sequence of persuasive interactions and interplays of textual, aural, visual, and kinetic design elements when interacting with digital contents in both game and non-game contexts.

Objectives of This Chapter

This book chapter aims to develop H.I.R.E. scales to measure and assess user experience in gamified systems and applications. The H.I.R.E. scales will enable the developers of gamified systems and applications to better assess the processes and their effects at various development phases and for future system improvements. In particular, the author discusses gamification from the context of digital games because they can be considered as alternative gamified systems/applications which have been well-studied and widely-used. The author reasons that user experience (UX) in digital games resembles that in gamified systems and applications. Therefore, through H.I.R.E. scales, gamification researchers and practitioners can explain, analyze, and assess digital games and other gamified systems/applications to better understand their effects.

BACKGROUND

Gamification research often includes the study of "adoption, institution, and ubiquity" of digital games (Deterding, Dixon, Khaled, & Nacke, 2011b, https://www.cs.auckland.ac.nz/courses/compsci747s2c/lectures/paul/definition-deterding.pdf). Recently, scholars have begun to examine a more serious side of digital games such as their power to engage and educate gameplayers (Deterding et al., 2011a). This has led to the application of game design in non-game contexts (Deterding et al., 2011b). Therefore, the author reasons that advanced gamified systems such as MMORPGs are extremely task-oriented and demand a high level of cognitive and motor skills among players, similarly expected among users of gamified systems.

This chapter takes a rhetorical theoretical stance by arguing that what gamers have experienced during MMORPG gameplay is equivalent to user experience in more serious gamified systems and applications. The author further posits that a successful gamified system and application should imitate the immersive, engaging, and collaborative processes as seen in most MMORPG gaming sessions. In other words, the author characterizes such user experience in MMORPGs as a gamification phenomenon. Deriving from digital game literature, the author argues that the study of digital games will help develop H.I.R.E. scales that can be useful for not only digital game research, but also for gamification research and applications.

Kang (2011) argues that digital game environment is equivalent to a virtual rhetorical situation when H.I.R.E. is created, maintained, and developed when all gamers take part in responding to the rhetorical situation. MMORPGs are designed to create a gaming space where gamers can collaborate and negotiate with other players to co-create an engaging user experience in a mythical world with chosen identities (Kang, 2011). MMORPGs are designed to enable gamers to interact with other players using avatars, metaphors, concepts, and tools from the virtual medieval period. What is created in the virtual world is equivalent to the concept of game as "designed experience" (Squire, 2006) in which a wide range of human practices is conducted by gamers to "actively inhabit those worlds of rules and texts and render them meaningful" (Steinkuehler, 2006, p.97). MMORPG gamers are required to select or create their own avatar characters designed by game developers. Interactions among gamers, though dependent on tasks, missions, and circumstances, are still scripted and pre-determined. The author argues that the interaction processes bear much resemblance to those found in any gamified system and application.

MAIN FOCUS OF THE CHAPTER

This chapter aims to develop H.I.R.E. scales to study digital games and other gamified systems/applications from a rhetorical perspective because current digital game studies have often centered on the following areas: 1) game design (Prensky, 2005; Raynauld, 2005; Salen & Zimmerman, 2005); 2) aesthetic and reception of gamers (Calvert, 2005; Holmes & Pellegrini, 2005; Gunter, 2005; Griffiths, 2000); 3) cultural (Bryce & Rutter, 2005; Edwards, 2004; Klabbers, 2003; Richard & Zaremba, 2005; Turkle, 2011) and social issues (Goldstein, 2005; Griffiths & Davies, 2005; Schleiner, 2001; Rushkoff, 2005). Despite the comprehensive coverage of these research areas, failure to address the rhetorical perspective of digital game gamification research left a void in the current literature.

This chapter aims to study digital games from a rhetorical perspective and is important to our understanding of this emerging phenomenon. The author argues that user experience in digital games should be properly assessed as an important area of gamification research. First, unlike traditional stand-alone digital games, gamers' multimodal interactions constitute a major portion of their user experience in games. Collaborations among gamers rely on whether they are able to effectively persuade each other to complete a task to advance to another game hierarchy. Failure to communicate and persuade other gamers from the same guild is bound to generate incoherent, frustrating, and often dissatisfied user experience in digital games. Secondly, a compartmented approach to study digital game as gamified systems and applications, while generating useful insights into game design, users' reception, or even macro-level social and cultural issues, only provided limited understanding of how gamers interact and persuade each other online.

The concept of H.I.R.E. was originally developed to understand user experience with persuasive manipulation in digital games (Kang, 2011). Because digital games can be considered as one type of gamified systems (Hamari & Eranti, 2011), the author thus reasons that the same H.I.R.E. concept can be extended to study gamification in non-game contexts (such as business and education applications) because these involve similar persuasive processes. Theoretically, while H.I.R.E. is situated within the rhetorical tradition that examines various rhetorical elements (e.g., aural, visual, textual, and kinetic) and their roles in persuasion, this concept can be used to examine similar persuasive processes in entertaining, educating, and informing gamers—a process that bears a lot of resemblances to the concept of gamification. These rhetorical elements can be viewed as design elements in gamified systems and applications, so a similar gamification process can be accomplished to create more engaging and persuasive applications and systems. H.I.R.E. is particularly useful because contemporary gamified systems and applications are full of fluidity and exchangeability of persuasive roles among game designers/system designers (rhetors) and gamers/users (audiences) in creating persuasive interactions in the gaming space where rhetorical actions and events are situated. Rhetorically, playing digital games can be equated with the involvement in creation, delivery, and comprehension of symbolic acts (Klabbers, 2003). Gamers try to make sense of symbols, icons, characters, scenes created by game designers, but at the same time they also want to understand what other gamers say and act. To explain user experience in digital games further as a gamification phenomenon, the author further reasons when gamers enter into a digital game by adapting themselves to structural and aesthetic design elements within the game, they learn the narratives from game designers, as well as other gamers, and transform and construct their own identities through the adoption of online avatars. Such experience is what Klabbers (2003) characterizes as, "engaging in embodied experience" (p.1). From the perspectives of gamification research, designers of gamified systems also employ non-game elements to attract, engage, and educate users to accomplish their intended objectives.

The main focus of this book chapter is to develop H.I.R.E. scales to help gamification researchers and practitioners to assess what makes persuasive gamified systems and applications and how to assess their persuasive effects at various phases of development. H.I.R.E. refers to the examination of user experience when taking part in any digital contents to accomplish outcomes as a result of gamification. The following discussions help explain the conceptualization of H.I.R.E. and the development of H.I.R.E. scales.

Issues, Controversies, Problems

"Hybrid" refers to the multimedia capacities which gamified systems and applications can provide by offering their users aural, visual, textual, kinetic elements-. When interacting with gamified systems such as MMORPGs, gamers/users constantly exchange textual and aural messages to collaborate on completing their tasks during gameplay (Juul, 2005; Vorderer & Bryant, 2006). Visual elements are also enriched with broadband connection and blue-ray PS3 game devices in the context of digital games. Devices such as mouse, joystick, and even virtual reality glove enable gamers to physically move their avatars in the virtual gaming environment. Real-time voice chat/communication is also possible through utilities such as *Ventrilo*, *MorphVox*, and *Xfire*. These technological advancements provide players enriched and intensive user experience with amified systems and applications, including MMORPGs.

"Interactivity" as a dimension of the H.I.R.E. concept refers to another key attribute of digital gamified systems in the marketplace. Interactivity is viewed as an important part of the gameplay (O'Brien & Toms, 2007) in MMORPGs and user experience with any gamified system and application Although interactivity is a term with several different meanings (Kiousis, 2002), in the context of digital games, it refers to the process that a gamer can modify, based on the context and characters involved, the state and happening in a digital game by some action through an interface (Grodal, 2003). By extension, the same concept can be applied to explain the process that a user can also modify digital contents through interactions with any gamified system and application. Interactivity embedded in digital game devices and gaming environments allow gamers to conduct real-time communication, modify gaming spaces, and navigate the digital game environment (Ryan, 1999). Similarly, modern gamified systems and applications that are network- and computer-based share the same interactivity attribute as seen in digital games. For example, a gamer can explore and respond to the gaming environment by interacting with the game interface, type in chats to converse with other gamers, and enjoy the pleasure of terminating an enemy by similar motor actions. Many gamified systems and applications have been designed with the intention to encourage interactions with users in mind to create the intended outcomes ranging from better learning results, more satisfied customers, and highly engaged users.

Another H.I.R.E. dimension, "engagements," can refer to a psychological state that gamers and users will experience with digital game and other gamified systems and applications that explain the reason and the result that gamers and users want to interact with them (O'Brien & Toms, 2007). In the context of digital games, the level of engagement that gamers can experience in these environments cannot be understated because it constitutes an important part of their gamification.

In the context of digital games, engagement can also be defined as a psychological concept that refers to how and whether gamers are satisfied with their experience in digital games (O'Brien & Toms, 2007). As such, rhetorical engagement can be defined as the interpretive, sympathetic, and interactive engagement with all game design elements that gamers are exposed to that have the purposes of educating, informing, entertaining, and persuading them (Tavinor, 2005). Furthermore, the concept can be extended to examine interactive rhetorical engagements with other gamers during gameplay or interactions with any gamified system and application in a non-game context. For example, how users of the Samsung's gamified website, *Nation*, can be studied using the same engagement concept. Users of this gamified application are encouraged to take part in product reviews, promotional video watching, and Q&A discussion to be rewarded with badges and progress in different levels of achievements (Stanley, 2014)—similar to what are rewarded to gamers of MMORPGs to generate customer engagement. Such experience can be said to be similar to hearing a speech, reading a novel, or watching a movie that can persuade, excite, or inspire the audience. Unlike the latter conventional rhetorical discourses, gamers and users of many gamified system and application can take the role of the characters and have a more embodied hybrid interactive rhetorical experience. In other words, MMORPGs enable gamers to become an active rhetor to create rhetorical discourses to persuade other gamers to follow a strategy, to create plots unique to each gameplay session, and to experience the twists and turns as gamers co-write an adventure and fantasy novel similar to J.R.R. Tolkiens' *The Lord of the Rings*.

On the basis of discussions above, H.I.R.E. is a useful analytical concept derived from rhetorical theories to describe what gamers experience playing MMORPGs. Given that many gamified systems employ game design elements in non-game contexts, H.I.R.E. is also beneficial to study the process of gamification as demonstrated in online persuasive interactions vital to gamers' satisfying gameplay/

user experience. Furthermore, because the study of H.I.R.E. investigates MMORPG user experience beyond the persuasive intents of game designers (rhetors), the concept of H.I.R.E. aims to capture the multiplicity of user experience in digital games by examining the role of participating gamers (audiences) and their fluid role as rhetors during gameplay to accomplish the serious purposes of many gamified systems and applications. Similar to what gamers will experience in digital games, the author argues that users of many gamified systems and applications are likely to experience rhetorical engagements that are also derived from a series of persuasive events made possible by the interactivity, immersion, interconnectivity, and role-playing functions

SOLUTIONS AND RECOMMENDATIONS

Using H.I.R.E. to Analyze World of Warcraft Gaming Session

In this chapter, the author used one representative MMORPG gaming session as an example from a total amount of 120 sessions that the author participated in three guilds as a player in *World of Warcraft* over a period of three years. Each gaming session ranges from three GB to four GB in terms of file size, and ranges from 8 minutes to 14 minutes. The 3-year data collection period leads to a large amount of MMORPGs gameplay data recorded by Fraps captured videos. Fraps, abbreviated from frame per second, is "a universal Windows application that can be used with games using *DirectX* or *OpenGL* graphic technology" (Fraps). Among many tasks and functions Fraps performs, the author employed Fraps' screen capture and real-time video capture functions to capture high quality graphics, audio, and video clips (Fraps). To capture real-time gaming session clips, Fraps can "capture audio and video up to 2560x1600 with custom frame rates from 10 to 120 frames per second" (Fraps).

The representative gaming session used to demonstrate how H.I.R.E. can be used to analyze user experience in MMORPG gaming sessions as rhetorical entities is a battle with *Lady Deathwhisper*, who is the second in command in the *Icecrown Citadel*. During the time of the author's participation as a gamer-researcher, a good rapport was established with the guild members to facilitate the process of capturing representative gaming sessions. In this gaming session, the raid leader began by arranging each raid member in different strategic positions, so the raid can be ready for the upcoming battle with the arch-enemy, *Lady Deathwhisper*. The raid leader used aural commands to assign each guild member to either the right, left, or back positions. For example, aural interactivity was done by saying "Bodi going on the left," "Xander going on the back with RhhockeyBoy," "Character A is assigned to the right flank..... are assigned to the left flank. ...... are assigned to the back of the room." Other gamers immediately provided aural feedback to clarify what to do after hearing the commands. These exchanges of aural interactivities demonstrated a sequence of persuasive expressions initiated by the raid leader. Even though the voice commands tended to be brief and succinct, they were persuasive because all identified raid members (such as *Bodi*, *Xander*, or *RhhockeyBoy*) all acted accordingly. These gamers demonstrated their kinetic responses after being persuaded by the raid leader. In other words, the aural interactivity initiated by the raid leader led to the persuasion of the raid members to respond by using kinetic interactivities (as demonstrated by the movement of avatars). The strategic positioning of each raid member was an important step because the leader needs to prepare every player by counting down before the raid began.

The multimodal interactivities were not merely employed by interactions between the raid leader and gamers. Other raid members were found to employ textual and aural interactivities to communicate with each other, so their gaming experience can be greatly enhanced. These multimodal interactivities were noteworthy rhetorical interactions as seen in any MMORPG gaming session. For the fight with *Lady Deathwhisper*, the raid members had to kill the allies showing up on the left flank, right flank, and in the back close to the gate quickly and efficiently during the phase one. After the allies were terminated successfully, all *DPS* raid members needed to switch back to *Lady Deathwhisper* as soon as possible, so her *mana* shield was going to disappear and then went into the next phase of the fight. Also, *Damage per Second* (*DPS*) of the raid members played an important role during the complete period of the fight. The game was designed to contain the gameplay rule that, the higher amount of *DPS* a raid group had, the sooner a task can be done. The raid leader arranged the positions according to their classes and *DPS* attributes (melee and ranged) evenly to the left and right to make sure the time limitation was met.

Lady Deathwhisper is a Non-Player Character (NPC) and a virtual representation of various in-game design elements created by the designers of *World of Warcraft* to make the *Icecrown Citadel* raid dungeon persuasive. *Lady Deathwhisper* is an in-game character equipped with multimodal interactive capabilities to make the raid in the game convincing and entertaining. For example, *Lady Deathwhisper* often threatens the gamers with her aural and textual interactivities during the raid. She voices her anger by saying "What is this disturbance? You dare trespass on this hallowed ground. This shall be your final resting place…." In addition, her threats are presented in the textual area in red fonts at the left bottom of the screen. The use of the term, "hallowed ground", intends to present a sense of medieval atmosphere and carries the same meaning as a sacred ground blessed by priests, druids, and shamans. *Lady Deathwhisper* is programmed to cast a *Death and Decay* spell, which is a green puddle on the ground and deals damage to players who stand in it. When *Lady Deathwhisper* continues to present her rhetorical manipulations either through aural, visual, or kinetic interactivities by voicing her threats, waving her magic power, and casting her green puddle spell visually, all gamers have to respond by either moving their avatars (i.e., kinetic interactivity), and discussing their strategies that will lead to more kinetic interactivities among these gamers, so they can avoid being terminated. In response, these gamers reacted promptly to make the gameplay enjoyable and engaging. At the beginning of this gaming session, the raid leader rearranged the gamers to a new strategic position. The raid leader also used aural commands to persuade selected gamers to respond by moving their avatars. Once this was done, *Lady Deathwhisper* voices another round of embedded aural interactivity. In response, the raid leader solicited the help of a caster, so the raid can be successful. During this raid, numerous interactivities were observed on the screen near the end of the session. Visually engaging images were shown when the gamers attack *Lady Deathwhisper*. Textual interactivities (such as "Out of Range" and "Dominate the Mind of Nugemage") that recorded spontaneous gamer actions were also presented to let the gamers know their status in the game.

These embedded in-game design elements are persuasive manipulations produced by the game designers (as rhetors) to make *Lady Deathwhisper* a persuasive character with her magical power. Her programmed behaviors are rhetorical in nature because they intend to persuade and invite multimodal interactivities from these gamers. Adding these visual effects (or visual interactivities) is game designers' persuasive tool to make *World of Warcraft* more engaging and entertaining. The battle with *Lady Deathwhisper* involves textual, aural, visual, and kinetic interactivities used by the gamers to interact with each other, game characters, and in-game interface. All these rhetorical manipulations enable the gamers to become fully immersed within the game environment and the characters in their pursuit of highly engaging intensive rhetorical experience. The experience is rhetorical in nature, in that all gamers constantly employ multimodal interactive expressions and practices to persuade other gamers and the in-game design elements. For example, *Lady Deathwhisper's* voice was heard by all raid members along with the textual representations of what she says. The raid leader coordinated through aural and textual commands to persuade all members and ensure all raid members work synergistically to defeat *Lady Deathwhisper*. The guild leader's persuasion was effective because he clearly recommended what should be done to make a successful raid.

The analysis of user experience in a *World of Warcraft* gaming session laid the foundation for the author to extend the concept of H.I.R.E. to examine similar user experience in other gamified systems and applications. In other words, H.I.R.E. enables digital gamification researchers to examine user experience in and interactions with gamified systems and applications as persuasive manipulations. Although a thorough analysis of aural, visual, textual, and kinetic interactive components help researchers to understand what constitutes user experience in gamified systems and applications, it does not address why users are persuaded when interacting with the systems. In other word, the captured gaming session helps account for the persuasive interactions by which gamers rely on multimodal interactivities to be immersed in the game, so optimal engagements can be achieved through the gamification process. However, without effective persuasion, a MMORPG is not likely to maintain a high level of interest among many gamers. Furthermore, because playing *World of Warcraft* is made up of constant collaborations among gamers, the author thus argues that the collaborative process in itself involves persuasive interactions that prompt other players to adapt their motoric, cognitive, and emotional states to different gaming sessions.

Davidson (2003), in *The Rhetoric of GamePlay*, equates these in-game multimodal design elements with "rhetorical elements that serve the purpose of conveying the game's techniques and rules enabling play" (11). Many design elements of gamified systems and applications have lent their technical characteristics to "the rhetoric of game" and the subsequent "rhetoric of gameplay" (to use Davidson's terms). Like any other rhetorical interaction among rhetors and audiences to accomplish persuasive goals and to seek for maximum gamification, MMORPG gameplays follow the same process so online interactivities can be completed through a set of agreed rules that contribute to the common objectives of the raid team (Lindley). Users' interactions with gamified systems and applications are analogous to gamers' experience in many digital games. The process is also similar to the stasis theory in rhetoric that Aristotle states that the invention process in rhetoric involves the identification, comprehension, and assessment of facts, which leads to the proposal of plan of actions. In the context of digital games, the structural features of digital games demonstrate game designers' rhetorical manipulation to persuade gamers as part of the gamification process when designers attempt to integrate these game design principles and elements into creating gamified systems and applications. Despite being fully aware of the make-believe world experienced in *World of Warcraft* gamers are persuaded to take part in these gameplay sessions with other players to seek entertainment and gratifications. Users of these gamified systems and applications need to be persuaded to engage in similar activities, so designers' intended objectives can be accomplished. When gamification designers include selected game design principles and elements into creating gamified systems and applications, their actions are similar to what game designers are doing. Thus, scholars like Ian Bogost (2007) and Janet Murray (2006) refer to these types of embedded rhetorical expressions, executions, and practices as "procedural rhetoric" in which rules of gameplay constitute an important part of gamer experience as manipulated by digital game designers. For example, when gamers adopt the avatar of a healer (class), they are given the capabilities to cast spells, heal other wounded gamers, and bolster the spirits of other gamers, according to the embedded gameplay rules for this avatar class. In persuasive gamified systems and applications, users can obtain similar experience when they interact with many design elements to feel entertained, be educated, and become engaged in the process to generate behavioral changes (Burke, 2013). For example, users of Nike+platform need to engage with this gamified system, so they can change their workout habit to another level (Burke, 2013). Students who are using Khan Academy's gamified system for educational purposes also need to understand how the system is designed to make the best use of the gamified systems and applications.

The concept of H.I.R.E. provides digital game researchers to better understand user experience in gamified systems and applications as a process of persuasive interactions and to offer an analytical tool to evaluate why one gamified system and application is more engaging and entertaining than the other. H.I.R.E. is thus a useful analytical concept to explain what makes one gamification application more effective and persuasive than the others. Theoretically, H.I.R.E. provides a close theoretical linkage to dominant rhetorical scholars like Kenneth Burke (1965, 1966, 1969), in explaining the persuasive process and outcome. According to Burke (1966) in *The Language as Symbolic Action*, any purposeful use of symbols can be considered as one type of symbolic action. The symbolic action is not limited to language and literature, but also includes magic, ritual, religion, and history as stated in Burke's books, *Permanence and Change* and *Attitudes toward History*. As such, Walz (2004) contends gameplay is also a symbolic action among participating agents because persuasive manipulations exist in that rhetorical situation. Walz's discussions of gameplay can be extended to understand user experience in many gamified systems and applications.

To extend from Burke's argument in *A Rhetoric of Motives* (1969), designers of gamified systems and applications need to solicit the multimodal interactive responses from users as their symbolic actions in the gamification process. In the context of MMORPGs such as *World of Warcraft*, this digital game has to be designed "as a symbolic means of inducing cooperation in beings that by nature respond to symbols" (p.43). Walz (2004) maintains gameplay is "a rhetorical performance between player(s) and game design, a symbolic action that takes place amongst agents" (p.186). Analogous to what is experienced by gamers, users of gamified systems and applications also go through the same interaction process with design elements that are designed to generate users' attitude and behavioral changes. Just like the aural, visual, textual, and kinetic interactivities that constitute an essential part of gamers' experience, these multimodal design elements are likely to generate user experience within these gamified systems and applications. The discussion above shows that a skillful manipulation of these design elements in many gamified systems and applications can lead to most gratifying user experience. The analysis above also demonstrates how H.I.R.E. can provide an analytic tool to understand gamification.

Measuring H.I.R.E. for Gamification Research

The inclusion of H.I.R.E. will certainly pose great challenges to digital gamification scholars in terms of what to study and how things work to create user experience in digital games and other gamified systems and applications. For example, van den Hoogen, IJsselsteijn, and de Kort (2008) observes digital game researchers are often faced with developing "a coherent and fine-grained set of methods and tools that enable the measurement of entertainment experience in a sensitive, reliable and valid manner" (p.11). These problems are likely to attribute to the difficulty in defining what user experience is in digital games and what methodological approaches are appropriate to study them. As such, in terms of methodological implications, the study of gameplay experience is often problematic in digital gamification research because of the number and types of persuasive manipulations and representations needed to work together to create different experiential representations that can later be recorded and analyzed. In other words, the study of gameplay experience cannot merely depend on the analyses of textual (such as game narratives or plots), visual (such as the gaming environment), and aural (such as background or embedded sound effects) interactivities. These rhetorical manipulations are only some of the many essential parts in constituting user experience in digital games.

To measure H.I.R.E., the author relies on past empirical studies to examine user experience in digital games (Calvillo-Gámez, Cairns, & Cox, 2011; Zagal, Chan, & Zhang, 2010). Calvillo-Gámez et al.'s *Core Elements of the Gaming Experience Questionnaire (CEGEQ)* (2011) in particular provides very useful foundation to develop similar scales to assess H.I.R.E. for digital gamification research. Although *CEGEQ* offers an objective measurement of user experience in digital games, the statements are designed for studying digital games (Calvillo-Gámez, Cairns, & Cox, 2009). The author thus proposes to revise *CEGEQ* to better study gamification phenomena. On the basis of the 38-item scales, the author has developed H.I.R.E. scales to capture the persuasive aspect of user experience in gamified systems and applications (See Table 1 below). These H.I.R.E. statements will be used to ask participants to respond, after interacting with the selected gamified system and application, by indicating their agreements through five-point Likert scale with 1 representing "strongly disagree," 2 representing "disagree," 3 representing neutral, 4 representing "agree," and 5 representing "strongly agree." Participants' quantitative assessment scores can be analyzed through various descriptive or inferential statistical procedures to assess the persuasive effectiveness of these gamification practices.

FUTURE RESEARCH DIRECTIONS

A rhetorical study of user experience in gamified systems and applications will be an important component of gamification research and will have significant theoretical and methodological implications. First, the exploration of user experience will discover new data that can be analyzed in empirical gamification research. Despite the breadth of gamification research as an interdisciplinary academic endeavor, the foci of conventional approaches seem mostly on the process of the causes and outcomes of gamifications (Hamari et al., 2014). Secondly, because the creation of user experience in digital games is based on a close collaboration between game designers and gamers, between gamers' interactions with in-game design elements, there exists a constant modification of their roles in the persuasive process. Using the same analogy, the author reasons that interactions with gamified systems and applications are likely to be similar to user experience in digital games.

Past gamification research has been based on psychological approaches to understand the process and outcome of gamification (See Hamari et al., 2014 for literature review). The chapter focuses on persuasion as an important part of gamification because users of gamified systems and applications have to take part in the interactions and become responsive to designers' persuasive manipulations to accomplish gamification objectives. As such, persuasive interactions with gamifeid systems and applications are generative and situational. Thus, questions arise as to whether these new modes of persuasive manipulations should be included as a new domain of gamification research. Furthermore, this book chapter hopes to generate continuous discussions to explore how rhetorical theories can be instrumental to gamification research.

Table 1. H.I.R.E. Scales for gamified systems and applications

Calvillo-Gámez et al.'s CEGEQ Scales	H.I.R.E. Scales for Gamification	Scales Corresponding to Various H.I.R.E. Dimensions
I enjoyed playing the game.	I enjoyed using the [name of the gamified system and application].	Scale measuring engagement
I was frustrated at the end of the game.	I was frustrated at the end of using [name of the gamified system and application].	Scale measuring engagement
I was frustrated whilst playing the game.	I was frustrated while using the [name of the gamified system and application].	Scale measuring engagement
I liked the game.	I found the [name of the gamified system and application] engaging.	Scale measuring engagement
I would play this game again.	I would use the [name of the gamified system and application] again.	Scale measuring engagement
I was in control of the game.	I was in control of the [name of the gamified system and application].	Scale measuring interactivity
The controllers responded as I expected.	I interacted with design elements as I expected.	Scale measuring interactivity
I remember the actions the controllers performed.	I remember the actions the designers of the [name of the gamified system and application] performed.	Scale measuring interactivity
I was able to see on the screen everything I needed during the game.	I was able to see on the screen everything I needed during the interaction with the [name of the gamified system and application].	Scale measuring design elements (textual interactivity)
The point of view of the game that I had spoiled my gaming.	===== (not applicable)	
I liked the way the game looked.	I liked the way the [name of the gamified system and application] looked.	Scale measuring design elements (visual interactivity)
The graphics of the game were plain.	The graphics of the [name of the gamified system and application] were plain.	Scale measuring design elements (visual interactivity)
I do not like this type of game.	I do not like this type of the [name of the gamified system and application].	Scale measuring engagement
I like to spend a lot of time playing this game.	I like to spend a lot of time interacting with the [name of the gamified system and application].	Scale measuring engagement
I got bored playing this time.	I got bored interacting with the [name of the gamified system and application] this time.	Scale measuring engagement
I usually do not choose this type of game.	I usually do not choose this type of the [name of the gamified system and application].	Scale measuring engagement
I did not have a strategy to win the game.	I did not have a strategy to win the [name of the gamified system and application].	Scale measuring engagement
The game kept constantly motivating me to keep playing.	The [name of the gamified system and application] kept engaging me to keep interacting.	Scale measuring engagement
I felt what was happening in the game was my own doing.	I felt what was happening in the [name of the gamified system and application] was my own doing.	Scale measuring persuasion
I challenged myself even if the game did not require it.	I challenged myself even if the (gamified) system did not require it.	Scale measuring persuasion
I played with my own rules.	I interacted with the [name of the gamified system and application] my own rules.	Scale measuring persuasion

continued on following page

Table 1. Continued

Calvillo-Gámez et al.'s CEGEQ Scales	H.I.R.E. Scales for Gamification	Scales Corresponding to Various H.I.R.E. Dimensions
I felt guilt for the actions in the game.	===== (not applicable)	
I knew how to manipulate the game to move forward.	I knew how to manipulate the [name of the gamified system and application].to move forward.	Scale measuring persuasion
The graphics were appropriate for the type of game.	The graphics were appropriate for the type of [name of the gamified system and application].	Scale measuring design element (visual interactivity)
The sound effects of the game were appropriate.	The sound effects of the [name of the gamified system and application] were appropriate.	Scale measuring design element (aural interactivity)
	The characters of the the [name of the gamified system and application] were appropriate.	Scale measuring design element (kinetic interactivity(
I did not like the music of the game.	I did not like the music of the [name of the gamified system and application].	Scale measuring design element (aural interactivity)
The graphics of the game were related to the scenario.	The graphics of the [name of the gamified system and application] related to the scenario.	Scale measuring design element (visual interactivity)
The graphics and sound effects of the game were related.	The graphics and sound effects of the (gamified) system were related.	Scale measuring design element (visual and aural interactivity)
The sound of the game affected the way I was playing.	The sound of the [name of the gamified system and application] affected the way I was interacting.	Scale measuring i design element (aural interactivity)
	The text entry of the [name of the gamified system and application] affected the way I was interacting.	Scale measuring design element (textual interactivity)
	The graphics of the [name of the gamified system and application] affected the way I was interacting.	Scale measuring design element (visual interactivity)
	Being able to manipulate interface of the [name of the gamified system and application] affected the way I was (gamified) system.	Scale measuring design element (kinetic interactivity)
The game was unfair.	===== (not applicable)	
I understand the rules of the game.	I understand the rules of the [name of the gamified system and application].	Scale measuring design element
The game was challenging.	The [name of the gamified system and application] was challenging.	Scale measuring engagement
The game was difficult.	The [name of the gamified system and application] was difficult when users did not collaborate.	Scale measuring game engagement
The scenario of the game was interesting.	The scenario of the [name of the gamified system and application] was interesting.	Scale measuring design element
I did not like the scenario of the game.	I did not like the scenario of the [name of the gamified system and application].	Scale measuring design element
I knew all the actions that could be performed in the game.	I knew all the actions and procedures to be performed in the [name of the gamified system and application].	Scale measuring persuasion

The study of user experience in digital games as a result of their encounters with persuasive discourses during gameplay is the area worthy of gamification scholars' attention. Insights from digital game research will be helpful to better understand user experience and interaction in gamified systems and applications. The experience includes the interactions with other users, with ample design elements by designers, and numerous persuasive acts by all participants. Through these interactions, new research data are generated to better understand various issues related to the gamification process. Playing digital games such as *World of Warcraft* is rhetorical in nature because the process involves constant practices and expressions of persuasion by designers, and among other system users themselves. Design elements are embedded in gamified systems and applications as the rhetorical manipulations of the designers, so users can be persuaded to take part in these systems. On the other hand, users can opt to interact with the gamified system and other users by formulating strategies, so they can complete a task successfully to seek for maximum gamification. The study of user experience with gamified systems and applications helps gamification scholars focus on the persuasive nature of experiential rhetoric as demonstrated in H.I.R.E. during their encounters with different persuasive rhetorical manipulations in any gamified system and application.

A potential area in the gamification study is to examine the collaborative process by which users/gamers work together to complete a task, so the objectives of gamificiation can be achieved. As experienced by many MMORPG gamers during gameplay, their intensive rhetorical encounters with numerous rhetorical manipulations constitute one of the most gratifying social experiences all gamers enjoy. Persuasive gamified systems and applications are also expected to accomplish the same outcome in terms of modifying users' attitude, knowledge, purchase intention, and behavior (Burke, 2013). Game researchers like T.L. Taylor (2003) agree MMORPG gamers "actively engaged in creating the game worlds they inhibit" (p. 155). Gamers are not "producers" of the imagined virtual world, but they are actively involved in creating multimodal rhetorical expressions and practices through the use of in-game rhetorical devices to persuade other gamers. This same process and outcome should be expected in any persuasive gamified systems/applications and the study of these variables is likely to become a fruitful area of gamification research, in addition to the study of people's motivation and gamification behaviors.

CONCLUSION

In conclusion, digital game researchers often complain of "theoretical imperialism" within games research. Game scholars often question the indiscriminating adoption of methods, analytical tools, and interpretive approaches developed for other media texts and not applicable to studying game rhetorics. As Aarseth (2003) concurs with this lack of theories and methods in game research, these concerns reflect the problems among game researchers, in that instead of treating the new phenomena carefully, and as objects of a study for which no methodology yet exists, frequently games "are analyzed willy-nilly, with tools that happen to be at hand, such as film theory or narratology" (1). Gamification as an emerging area of research faces similar theoretical and methodological challenges as seen in digital game research. Therefore, the objectives of this book chapter aim to propose the concept of H.I.R.E. and its quantitative assessment tools to help gamification scholars to better investigate this important area of gamification research. With this emerging focus on the experience of gamers in general, and their H.I.R.E. in particular, this book chapter intends to provide a preliminary understanding of this important area of gamification study to explore in the future.

Implications

Previous digital game researchers often focus on digital games as narratives by examining the structure and interpretation of game narratives. For example, Kerr (2006) summarizes contemporary game scholars often adopt one of the three approaches to study game narratives: 1) a classical, formalist, and narrow approach; 2) a historically-located and cultural post-structuralist approach; 3) rejection of the narrative theories. The limitations of these approaches are clear because user experience in digital games as a manifestation of persuasive interactions goes far beyond texts and narratives. Similarly, to better study the practices of gamification in various contexts (such as customer engagement, employee training and education, personal development, innovation management, health and wellness, sustainability, etc.) (Burke, 2013), the author therefore argues that H.I.R.E. offers a useful conceptual and analytical tool for gamification scholars study user experiences with many gamified systems and applications

Secondly, the author argues that the process of interacting with digital games such as *World of Warcraft* is analogous to interactions with any gamified system and application. The concept of H.I.R.E. and its derived measurement help gamification scholars to the interaction process as a rhetorical process that involves both structural design components (no matter whether they are audio, visual, kinetic, or textual) and stand-alone structural components. Connections between these elements should be examined to see how their synergetic integration leads to positive user experience in any gamified system and application. As such, H.I.R.E. offers a useful analytical tool to uncover the interconnectivity among these persuasive interactions. What gamers have experienced from playing digital games is influenced not only by these rhetor-centric in-game design components, but also by social, economic, cultural, and psychological aspects of gamers that become parts of gamer experience during gameplay (Humphreys, 2003; Yee, 2006). Humphreys (2003) claims user experience in digital games is derived from "a complex interplay between the rules and affordances of a game, the user's offline context, and the online social world created with other players" (p.79). In this book chapter, the author reasons when users interact with a gamified system, it creates their own user experience once they are given the tools embedded in any gamified system and application to respond to numerous rhetorical manipulations. To further extend this line of thinking, the generation and maintenance of rhetorical engagement with the gamified systems and applications are not completely controlled by designers; instead, interactions with existing designers' rhetorical devices, and most importantly with other users lead to these processes to create persuasive interactions and ultimately gratifying user experience in digital games as similarly felt by many users of many gamified system and application.

Thirdly, H.I.R.E., developed from the line of rhetorical research, offers a potentially powerful analytical tool to examine the persuasive interactions critical to understanding gamification. H.I.R.E. is comprehensive to cover all key characteristics of gamified systems and applications such as MMORPGs. At the same time, H.I.R.E. examines one important aspect of user experience; that is, being persuaded to interact with the design elements and with other users' symbolic action. Because of gamified systems and applications constantly change due to the interactions and manipulations of users using symbols to persuade and convince other users, the rhetorical approach of gamified systems and applications as H.I.R.E. intends to investigate will help advance gamification theories by examining the persuasive manipulations during gameplay as an important component of gamification.

REFERENCES

Aarseth, E. J. (2003). Cybertext: Perspectives on ergodic literature. Baltimore, M.D.: Johns Hopkins University Press.

Boellstorff, T., Nardi, B., Pearce, C., & Taylor, T. L. (2012). *Ethnography and virtual worlds: A handbook of method*. Princeton, N.J.: Princeton University Press.

Bogost, I. (2007, July). *Persuasive games: The expressive power of videogames*. Cambridge, M.A.: The MIT Press.

Bryce, J., & Rutter, J. (2005). Gendered gaming in gendered space. In J. Raessens & J. Goldstein (Eds.), *Handbook of computer game studies* (pp. 301-310). Cambridge, M.A.: The MIT Press.

Burke, B. (2013, January 21). The gamification of business. *Forbes.com*. Retrieved from http://www.forbes.com/sites/gartnergroup/2013/01/21/the-gamification-of-business/

Burke, K. (1965). *Permanence and change: An anatomy of purpose* (2nd ed.). Indianapolis, I.N.: The Bobbs-Merrill Company, Inc.

Burke, K. (1966). *Language as symbolic action: Essays on life, literature, and method*. Berkeley, C.A.: The University of California Press.

Burke, K. (1969). *A rhetoric of motives*. Berkeley, C.A.: The University of California Press.

Burrill, D. A. (2005). Out of the box: Performance, drama, and interactive software. *Modern Drama*, *48*(3), 492–512. doi:10.3138/md.48.3.492

Calvert, S. L. (2005). Cognitive effects of video games. In J. Raessens & J. Goldstein (Eds.), *Handbook of computer game studies* (pp. 125-131). Cambridge, M.A.: The MIT Press.

Calvillo-Gámez, E. H., Cairns, P., & Cox, A. L. (2009, September). *Assessing the core elements of the gaming experience*. Retrieved from http://www.eduardocalvillogamez.info/2009/09/assessing-core-elements-of-gaming.html

Calvillo-Gámez, E. H., Cairns, P., & Cox, A. L. (2011). Assessing the core elements of the gaming experience. In R. Bernhaupt (Ed.), *Evaluating user experience in games: Concepts and methods* (pp. 41–71). London: Springer.

Chambers, J. H., & Ascione, F. R. (1987, December). The effects of prosocial and aggressive videogames on children's donating and helping. *The Journal of Genetic Psychology*, *148*(4), 499–505. doi:10.1080/00221325.1987.10532488 PMID:3437274

Chang, B.-H., Lee, S.-E., & Kim, B.-S. (2006, April). Exploring factors affecting the adoption and continuance of online games among college students in South Korea: Integrating uses and gratification and diffusion of innovation approaches. *New Media & Society*, *8*(2), 295–319. doi:10.1177/1461444806059888

Chuang, Y.-C. (2006). Massively multiplayer online role-playing game-induced seizures: A neglected health problem in internet addiction. *Cyberpsychology & Behavior*, *9*(4), 451–456. doi:10.1089/cpb.2006.9.451 PMID:16901249

Crogan, P. (2003). Gametime: History, narrative, and temporality in combat flight simulator 2. In M. J. P. Wolf & B. Perron (Eds.), *The video game theory reader* (pp. 275–301). New York, N.Y.: Routledge.

Davidson, D. (2003, August). *Games and rhetoric: A rhetorical look at gameplay, the IGDA ivory tower column.* Paper presented at the International Game Developers Association (IGDA), San Jose, CA.

Deterding, S., Dixon, D., Khaled, R., & Nacke, L. (2011b, September 28-30). *From game design elements to gamefulness: Defining "gamification."* Paper presented at the MindTrek '11, Tampere, Finland. Retrieved from https://www.cs.auckland.ac.nz/courses/compsci747s2c/lectures/paul/definition-deterding.pdf

Deterding, S., Sicart, M., Nacke, L., O'Hara, K., & Dixon, D. (2011a, May 7-12). *Gamification: Using game design elements in non-gaming contexts.* Paper presented at the CHI 2011, Vancouver, BC, Canada. Retrieved from http://gamification-research.org/wp-content/uploads/2011/04/01-Deterding-Sicart-Nacke-OHara-Dixon.pdf

Edwards, J. L. (2004). Echoes of Camelot: How images construct cultural memory through rhetorical framing. In C. A. Hill & M. Helmers (Eds.), *Defining visual rhetorics* (pp. 179–194). Mahwah, N.J.: Lawrence Erlbaum Associates, Publishers.

Entertainment Software Association. (2011). *Video game and the economy.* Washington, D.C.: Entertainment Software Association, 2011. Retrieved from http://www.theesa.com/gamesindailylife/economy.pdf

Entertainment Software Association (2014). *Industry facts: Sales and genre data.*

Filiciak, M. (2003). Hyperidentities: Postmodern identity patterns in massively multiplayer online role-playing games. In M. J. P. Wolf & B. Perron (Eds.), *The video game theory reader* (pp. 87–102). New York, N.Y.: Routledge.

Frasca, G. (1998). Ludology meets narratology: Similitude and differences between (video)games and narrative.

Gee, J. P. (2004). *What video games have to teach us about learning and literacy.* New York, N.Y.: Palgrave Macmillan.

Gee, J. P. (2007a). *What video games have to teach us about learning and literacy* (Rev. and updated ed.). New York: Palgrave Macmillan.

Gee, J. P. (2007b). *Good video games + good learning: Collected essays on video games, learning and literacy.* New York: Peter Lang.

Goldstein, J. (2005). Violent video games. In J. Raessens & J. Goldstein (Eds.), Handbook of computer game studies (pp. 341-357). Cambridge, M.A.: The MIT Press.

Griffiths, M., & Davies, M. N. O. (2005). Does video game addiction exist? In J. Raessens & J. Goldstein (Eds.), *Handbook of computer game studies* (pp. 359-369). Cambridge, M.A.: The MIT Press.

Grodal, T. (2003). Stories for eye, ear, and muscles: Video games, media, and embodied experiences. In M. J. P. Wolf & B. Perron (Eds.), *The video game theory reader* (pp. 129–155). New York, N.Y.: Routledge.

Gunter, B. (2005). Psychological effects of video games. In J. Raessens & J. Goldstein (Eds.), *Handbook of computer game studies* (pp. 145-160). Cambridge, M.A.: The MIT Press.

Hamari, J., & Eranti, V. (2011, September 14-17). *Framework for designing and evaluating game achievements*. Paper presented at the Proceedings of DiGRA 2011 Conference: Think Design Play, Hilversum, Netherlands. Retrieved from http://www.quilageo.com/wp-content/uploads/2013/07/Framework-for-Designing-Eval-11307.59151.pdf

Hamari, J., Koivisto, J., & Sarsa, H. (2014, January 6-9). *Does gamification work? A literature review of empirical studies on gamification*. Paper presented at The 47th Hawaii International Conference on System Sciences, Hawaii, USA. doi:10.1109/HICSS.2014.377

Humphreys, S. (2003). Online multi-user games. *Australian Journal of Communication, 30*(1), 79–91.

Juul, J. (2005). Games telling stories? In J. Raessens & J. Goldstein (Eds.), *Handbook of computer game studies* (pp. 219-226). Cambridge, M.A.: The MIT Press.

Kang, Y. W. (2011). *Hybrid interactive rhetoric engagements in Massively Multiplayer Online Role-Playing Games (MMORPGs): Examining the role of rhetors and audiences in generative rhetorical discourses*. [Dissertation]. The University of Texas at El Paso, 2011.

Kiousis, S. (2002). Interactivity: A concept explication. *New Media & Society, 4*(3), 355–383. doi:10.1177/146144480200400303

Klabbers, J. H. G. (2003, November 4-6). *The gaming landscape: A taxonomy for classifying games and simulations*. Paper presented at the LEVEL UP: Digital Games Research Conference, University of Utrecht, The Netherlands.

Morschheuser, B. S., Rivera-Pelayo, V., Mazarakis, A., & Zacharias, V. (2014). Interaction and reflection with quantified self and gamification: An experimental study. *Journal of Literacy and Technology, 15*(2), 136–156.

Murray, J. H. (2006). Toward a cultural theory of gaming: Digital games and the co-evolution of media, mind, and culture. *Popular Communication, 4*(3), 185–202. doi:10.1207/s15405710pc0403_3

Nardi, B. (2010). *My life as a night elf priest: An anthropological account of world of warcraft*. Ann Arbor, M.I.: University of Michigan Press.

O'Brien, H. L., & Toms, E. G. (2007). What is user engagement? A conceptual framework for defining user engagement with technology. *Journal of the American Society for Information Science and Technology, 59*(6), 938–955. doi:10.1002/asi.20801

Pickering, A. (1995). *The mangle of practice: Time, agency, & science*. Chicago, I.L.: The University of Chicago Press.

Prensky, M. (2005). Computer games and learning: Digital game-based learning. In J. Raessens & J. Goldstein (Eds.), *Handbook of computer game studies* (pp. 97-122). Cambridge, M.A.: The MIT Press.

Raessens, J., & Goldstein, J. (2005). Introduction. In J. Raessens & J. Goldstein (Eds.), *Handbook of computer game studies* (pp. xi-xvii). Cambridge, M.A.: The MIT Press.

Raynauld, L. (2005). Click reading: Screenwriting and screen-reading practices in film and multimedia fictions. In J. Raessens & J. Goldstein (Eds.), *Handbook of computer game studies* (pp. 81-95). Cambridge, M.A.: The MIT Press.

Rushkoff, D. (2005). Renaissance now! The gamers' perspective. In J. Raessens & J. Goldstein (Eds.), *Handbook of computer game studies* (pp. 415-421). Cambridge, M.A.: The MIT Press.

Ryan, M.-L. (1999). Immersion vs. interactivity: Virtual reality and literary theory. *SubStance, 28*(2), 110–137. doi:10.1353/sub.1999.0015

Schleiner, A.-M. (2001, June). Does Lara Croft wear fake polygons? Gender and gender-role subversion in computer adventure games. *Leonardo, 34*(3), 221–226. doi:10.1162/002409401750286976

Siwek, S. E. (2014). *Video games in the 21st century: The 2014 report.* Washington, D.C.: The Entertainment Software Association.

Stanley, R. (2014, March 24). Top 25 best examples of gamification in business, *ClickPedia: A Click-Software Blog.* Retrieved from http://blogs.clicksoftware.com/clickipedia/top-25-best-examples-of-gamification-in-business/

Steinkuehler, C. (2006, July). The mangle of play. *Games and Culture, 1*(3), 199–213. doi:10.1177/1555412006290440

Steinkuehler, C. A., & Williams, D. (2006). Where everybody knows your (screen) name: Online games as "third place". *Journal of Computer-Mediated Communication, 11*(4), 885–909. doi:10.1111/j.1083-6101.2006.00300.x

Swallow, E. (2012, September 18). Can gamification make customer support fun? *Forbes.* Retrieved from http://www.forbes.com/fdc/welcome_mjx.shtml

Tavinor, G. (2005). Videogames and interactive fiction. *Philosophy and Literature, 29*(1), 24–40. doi:10.1353/phl.2005.0015

Taylor, T. L. (2003). Multiple pleasures: Women and online gaming. *Convergence, 9*(1), 21–46.

The Entertainment Software Association. (n. d.). Retrieved from http://www.theesa.com/facts/salesand-genre.asp

Turkle, S. (1984). *The second self: Computers and the human spirit.* New York, N.Y.: Simon and Schuster.

Turkle, S. (2011). *Alone together: Why we expect more from technology and less from each other.* New York, N.Y.: Basic Books.

Walz, S. P. (2004). Delightful identification & persuasion: Toward an analytical and applied rhetoric of digital games. *Works and Days, 22*(1&2), 185–200.

Williams, D. (2005, December). Bridging the methodological divide in game research. *Simulation & Gaming, 36*(4), 1–17. doi:10.1177/1046878105282275

Williams, D., Caplan, S., & Xiong, L. (2005). Can you hear me now? The impact of voice in an online gaming community. *Human Communication Research, 33*(4), 427–449. doi:10.1111/j.1468-2958.2007.00306.x

Yee, N. (2006, January). The labor of fun: How video games blur the boundaries of work and play. *Games and Culture, 1*(1), 68–71. doi:10.1177/1555412005281819

Zagal, J., Chan, S. S., & Zhang, J. (2011). *Measuring flow experience of computer game players.* Paper presented at the AMCIS 2010 Proceedings (pp. 137). Retrieved from http://aisel.aisnet.org/amcis2010/137

ADDITIONAL READING

Bolter, J. D., & Grusin, R. (2000). *Remediation: Understanding new media*. Cambridge, M.A.: The MIT Press.

Cai, X. (2005, February). An experimental examination of the computer's time displacement effects. *New Media & Society*, *7*(1), 8–21. doi:10.1177/1461444805049139

Dibbell, J. (1998). *My tiny life: Crime and passion in a virtual world*. New York: Owl Books.

Donath, J. (1999). Identity and deception in the virtual community. In M. Smith & P. Kollack (Eds.), *Communities in Cyberspace*. London: Routledge; http://smg.media.mit.edu/people/judith/Identity/IdentityDeception.html

Elverdam, C., & Aarseth, E. (2007, January). Game classification and game design: Construction through critical analysis. *Games and Culture*, *2*(1), 3–22. doi:10.1177/1555412006286892

Friedman, T. (1995). Making sense of software: Computer games and interactive textuality. In S. Jones (Ed.), Cybersociety: Computer-mediated communication and community. Thousand Oaks, C.A.: Sage.

Fuller, M., & Jenkins, H. (1995). Nintendo and new world travel writing: A dialogue. In Jones, S. (Ed.), Cybersociety: Computer-mediated communication and community (pp. 73-89). Thousands Oaks, C.A.: Sage.

Helmes, R. M., & Pellegrini, A. D. (2005). Children's social behavior during video game play. In Raessens, J., & Goldstein, J. (Eds.), *Handbook of Computer Game Studies* (pp. 133-144). Cambridge, M.A.: The MIT Press.

Hussan, Z., & Griffiths, M. D. (2008). Gender swapping and socializing in cyberspace: An exploratory study. *Cyberpsychology & Behavior*, *11*(1), 47–53. doi:10.1089/cpb.2007.0020 PMID:18275312

Jansz, J., & Martens, L. (2005, June). Gaming at a LAN event: The social context of playing video games. *New Media & Society*, *7*(3), 333–355. doi:10.1177/1461444805052280

McBirney, K. (2004, December). Nested selves, networked communities: A case study of diablo ii: Lord of destruction as an agent of cultural change. *Journal of American Culture*, *4*(4), 415–421. doi:10.1111/j.1542-734X.2004.00146.x

Miklaucic, S. (2001). Virtual real(i)ty: Simcity and the production of urban cyberspace, Association of Internet Researchers. Minneapolis, M.N.

Mikula, M. (2003, March). Gender and videogames: The political valency of Lara Croft. *Continuum (Perth)*, *17*(1), 79–87. doi:10.1080/1030431022000049038

Nielsen, R. P. (1996). *The politics of ethics: Methods for acting, learning, and sometimes fighting with others in addressing ethics problems in organizational life*. New York: Oxford University Press.

Okorafor, N., & Davenport, L. (2001, August). Virtual women: Replacing the real, *The Association for Education in Journalism and Mass Communication*. Washington, D.C.

Peña, J., & Hancock, J. T. (2006, February). An analysis of socio-emotional and task communication in online multimedia video games. *Communication Research*, *33*(1), 92–109. doi:10.1177/0093650205283103

Reeves, B., & Read, J. L. (2009). Total engagement: Using games and virtual worlds to change the way people work and businesses compete. Cambridge, M.A.: Harvard Business Press.

Richard, B., & Zaremba, J. (2005). Gaming with grrls: Looking for sheroes in computer games. In J. Raessens & J. Goldstein (Eds.), *Handbook of computer game studies* (pp. 283-300). Cambridge, M.A.: The MIT Press.

Salen, K., & Zimmerman, E. (2005). Game design and meaningful play. In J. Raessens & J. Goldstein (Eds.), *Handbook of computer game studies* (pp. 59-79). Cambridge, M.A.: The MIT Press.

Steinkuehler, C. A., & Williams, D. (2006). Where everybody knows your (screen) name: Online games as "third place". *Journal of Computer-Mediated Communication*, *11*(4), 885–909. doi:10.1111/j.1083-6101.2006.00300.x

Turkle, S. (1984). *The second self: Computers and the human spirit*. New York, N.Y.: Simon and Schuster.

Yates, S. J., & Littleton, K. (1999, December). Understanding computer game cultures: A situated approach. *Information Communication and Society*, *2*(4), 566–583. doi:10.1080/136911899359556

KEY TERMS AND DEFINITIONS

Digital Creative Industry: A term that refers to a wide range of economic activities on the basis of knowledge and information generation through digital media platforms. Creative economic activities range from advertising, architecture, art, design, fashion, digital game, and media contents.

Hybrid Interactive Rhetorical Engagements (H.I.R.E): The examination of gameplay experiences when gamers take part in any digital game. H.I.R.E. refers to a state of engaging and interactive gameplay experiences when interacting with other gamers in MMORPGs. H.I.R.E. refers to a state of engaging and interactive gameplay experiences when interacting with other gamers in MMORPGs.

Hybrid: Referring to the multimedia capacities which advanced game technologies can provide by offering their users aural, visual, textual, kinetic elements during gameplay.

Interactivity: A key attribute of digital games and is viewed as an important part of the engagements gameplay experience.

Massively Multiplayer Online Role-Playing Games (MMORPGs): Any computer network-mediated games where thousands of gamers are role-playing simultaneously in a graphical and 3-D environment. Popular MMORPGs include *Ultima Online*, *EverQuest*, *World of Warcraft*, and *Second Life*.

Rhetorical Engagements: Referring to a series of rhetorical events made possible by the interactivity, immersion, interconnectivity, and role-playing functions abundant in MMORPGs. Furthermore, engagements with the digital game and other gamers are also the results of continuous persuasive exchanges during gameplay.

Section 2
Gamification and Business

Chapter 5
Gamification in Market Research:
Promises, Results, and Limitations

Kartik Pashupati
Research Now, USA

Pushkala Raman
Texas Woman's University, USA

ABSTRACT

This chapter presents an overview of gamification in the domain of market research, with a specific focus on digital data collection methods, such as online surveys. The problems faced by the market research industry are outlined, followed by a discussion of why gamification has been offered as a possible way to overcome some of these challenges. The literature on gamification is reviewed, with a focus on results from empirical studies investigating the impact of gamification on outcome variables such as data quality and respondent engagement. Finally, the authors present results from an original study conducted in 2013, comparing differences between a conventional (text-dominant) survey and a gamified version of the same survey.

INTRODUCTION: THE EMERGENCE OF DIGITAL DATA COLLECTION

Steve Jobs famously said that he never relied on market research, because "people don't know what they want until you show them" (Isaacson 2011). In spite of this oft-quoted (and controversial) dictum, organizations spent more than $39 billion on market research worldwide in 2012. The greatest share of this expenditure came from Europe (40%), followed by North America (37%) and Asia Pacific (16%). Together, Latin America and Africa together accounted for just 6% of global market research spending (ESOMAR 2013). While exact figures are not available, it is safe to say that survey research probably accounted for the largest proportion of research expenditure.

With the widespread diffusion of the Internet, online surveys have become the dominant form of quantitative data collection for marketing research. Correspondingly, face-to-face interviews and phone

DOI: 10.4018/978-1-4666-8651-9.ch005

surveys have declined in importance, although these techniques still remain important in order to ensure inclusion of target segments that are not online for a variety of reasons (e.g. low socio-economic status, remote geographic location, or low Internet penetration in emergent economies). However, in both mature and emerging markets, it is becoming increasingly more difficult to obtain representative samples using telephone surveys – due in large part to low or declining use of landline phones, coupled with the use of unlisted numbers and call screening devices. In the United States, for example, the Pew Research Center reports that several response metrics for phone surveys – such as contact rates, cooperation rates, and response rates – have declined drastically between 1997 and 2012 (Pew Research Center 2012; Shepard 2012).

Online surveys offer many benefits over other forms of data collection, such as the ability to implement complex logic, the ability to present audio and visual stimuli, and the ability to randomize the order of questions, among others. In addition to these benefits, the creation of online panels in many countries has made it possible for marketers to field multi-country surveys in a matter of weeks, rather than months, as was required with older methodologies.

THE CHALLENGES OF ENGAGING SURVEY PARTICIPANTS

Unlike other forms of data collection, such as face-to-face or telephone interviews, most online and mobile surveys tend to be self-administered. Self-administered surveys have many advantages – including the ability to administer surveys asynchronously, and the reduction of social desirability bias in answers – but they also present challenges in terms of how to keep participants engaged in the data collection process. A skilled interviewer can find ways to encourage people to stay interested in a survey, probe for additional information, and extract answers to open-ended questions. Even if the research topic is not very interesting – or the survey is very long -- the very presence of the interviewer might help to reduce the temptation among respondents to abandon the survey.

With the growing popularity of online surveys, "researchers have raised concerns about the effects of long, onerous, poorly designed and simply dull surveys" (Downes-Le Guin, Baker, Mechling & Ruyle 2012). A report by the National Science Foundation (NSF) raises concerns that the validity – and indeed the very future – of survey research may be endangered, due to *declining response rates,* accompanied by rising costs (NSF 2011).

Besides declining response rates, market researchers are also concerned about *declining attention spans* among survey takers. For example, the Advertising Research Foundation (ARF) launched the Foundations of Quality (FoQ) initiative in 2007, with the mission of investigating key concerns in online research. Among other topics, the ARF FoQ 1.0 underlined the need to study the effects of *respondent motivations and engagement* on survey results (ARF 2012).

These concerns about declining attention spans are compounded by the fact that *mobile devices* have increasingly supplanted traditional personal computers (PCs) and laptops as the favored means of accessing the Internet (O'Toole 2014). Surveys that are designed for traditional PCs are not always user-friendly on mobile devices. If respondents take surveys designed for a traditional PC on a mobile device – and these surveys are not optimized for mobile – this will probably result in higher abandonment rates for surveys, and consequently higher costs, not to mention concerns about response bias (i.e., are respondents who complete surveys – especially longer ones -- somehow different from those who abandon them?).

SUB-OPTIMAL BEHAVIORS AMONG SURVEY RESPONDENTS

Thomas (2014) notes that people have been concerned about low-quality responses since the early days of survey research. However, the proliferation of online surveys – and their increasing length – has accentuated concerns about the quality of data collected from respondents. Specifically, researchers are concerned that lazy, tired or disinterested respondents might end up giving responses that are unusable or, in the worst case, misleading. For example, if several disengaged respondents mindlessly assign a rating of 7 (say) on a 10-point attitude scale, this might lead researchers to believe that overall attitudes are more positive (or negative) than the underlying reality.

Krosnick (1991) used the term "satisficing" to describe the tendency for survey respondents to lose interest and become distracted or impatient as they work their way through a survey, putting increasingly less cognitive effort into answering questions. Examples of satisficing behaviors include stylistic responding (Baumgartner & Steenkamp 2001; Pashupati, Courtright & Pettit 2013; Pashupati, Courtright, Pettit & Knowles 2013; Puleston & Eggers 2012), more frequent selection of "don't know" responses, non-differentiation in rating scales and random responding (Downes-Le Guin et al. 2012). Several experimental studies suggest that there is an inverse relationship between questionnaire length and respondent engagement: as questionnaire grows longer, there is a greater likelihood that respondents will engage in satisficing behaviors, or even abandon the survey altogether (Galesic & Bosnjak 2009; Lugtigheid & Rathod 2005).

Thomas (2014) notes that survey researchers commonly use three indicators of sub-optimal responses, namely speeding, grid non-differentiation, and failure of compliance traps. These terms are defined below:

1. *Speeding* refers to a situation where a respondent rushes through a survey without expending much cognitive effort in processing the content of the questions. Several studies in the literature suggest that speeding is highly correlated to other forms of sub-optimal responding (see, for example, Puleston & Eggers 2012).

2. *Grid non-differentiation* (also known as straight-lining) refers to a situation where a respondent gives the exact same response to a battery of questions (most commonly laid out in the form of a grid, hence the name). Extreme responding, acquiescent responding, and midpoint responding are specific cases of grid non-differentiation.

3. *Compliance trap failure:* Market research practitioners use various types of red herring or trap questions to detect respondents who might be lying, or not paying attention. One example of a trap question is to ask respondents for their date of birth at the beginning of a survey, and then ask for their age at the end of the survey. A mismatch between the two numbers indicates mendacity or inattention. Another commonly used trap question is to insert a question in the middle of a grid, asking respondents to "Mark a 2 here to continue the survey" (Miller & Baker-Prewitt 2009).

The indicators identified above pertain mainly to sub-optimal responses to *closed-ended* survey questions. However, one of the main limitations plaguing self-administered online surveys is the fact that it is very difficult to convince even sincere survey respondents to provide thoughtful responses to *open-ended* questions. Most online surveys are designed such that respondents cannot advance to the next question without filling in at least some responses in the open-end text box. However, sub-optimal respondents tend to circumvent this technicality by typing random (gibberish) characters (in the worst case), or by providing very laconic responses, which fail to provide the deeper insight sought by the researcher.

GAMIFICATION: CHARACTERISTICS AND BENEFITS

In order to minimize sub-optimal responding, researchers have proposed that respondent engagement should be increased, by making surveys more lively and interactive. Several practitioners argue that creating game-like elements environments in surveys will improve respondent satisfaction with surveys, while reducing non-response error and abandonment rates (Adamou 2011; Puleston 2011, 2012; Sleep & Puleston 2011). This has also led to efforts to define gamification and identify its elements. Ziechermann & Cunningham (2011) define gamification as "the use of game thinking and game mechanics to engage users and solve problems." Based on the work of Schell (2008) and McGonigal (2011), Downes-Le Guin et. al (2012) have identified five basic elements of game mechanics:

1. A back story
2. A game-like aesthetic
3. Rules for play and advancement
4. A challenge
5. Rewards

Puleston (2012a) recognizes that the use of all of these game elements may not always be practical in market research. Instead, he recommends that market researchers should apply creative thinking to the design of surveys in order to keep surveys more interesting. Puleston and his colleagues provide the following suggestions for introducing game elements into survey design without necessarily having to design an elaborate game-style interface:

1. *Question Style:* Questions should be framed in a way that makes respondents want to answer them. Survey participants should be encouraged to use their imagination through personalization, role playing and the use of invented scenarios. For example, instead of asking "What is your favorite color?" ask "If you were to paint your bedroom in one of these colors, which would you choose?" Instead of asking "What are your favorite types of music," one could ask, "Imagine you owned your own radio station and could play any music you liked. Which of these artists would you place on your play list?"
2. *Rules:* Rules can be used to transform almost any task into a game. Examples of rules include applying word limits to open-ended questions, such as "describe yourself using only 7 words," and applying selection limits, such as "If you were able to keep only 3 items in your wardrobe, which would they be?" Puleston (2012b) reports that the application of the "word limit rule" resulted in an increase in both the answering rate for an open-ended question (85% answered the regular version versus 98% for the gamified version), as well as in the number of descriptors used by survey participants (2.4 descriptors for the regular version versus 4.5 descriptors for the gamified version).
3. *Competition and Reward:* Even ordinary questions can have an element of competition added to them, such as "What are your favorite restaurants? List as many as you can in 60 seconds." A reward mechanism can also be built in to the survey, such as awarding points for guessing the most popular answers.
4. *Interactive Elements:* Puleston suggests that simply replacing words with images and graphics where possible can result in better participation rates. However, this suggestion might be more difficult to implement if surveys are being administered on a smartphone or mobile device.

Figure 1. A conceptual model of the benefits of gamification

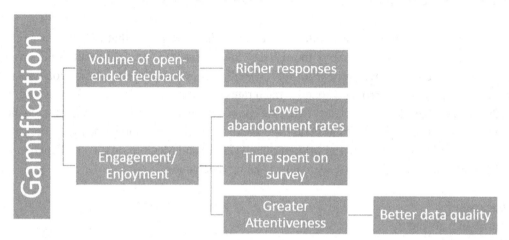

The highlights from the foregoing discussion can be summarized in the conceptual model presented in Figure 1. This model is intended to be illustrative, rather than comprehensive. Researchers such as Koenig-Lewis, Marquet & Palmer (2013) have identified several additional variables that might mediate or moderate the impact of gamification on survey responses -- and ultimately on data quality. For closed-ended questions, data quality is operationally measured in terms of *minimizing* the sub-optimal behaviors identified previously, namely, straight-lining, speeding and trap question failure. For open-ended questions, data quality is measured simply in terms of a greater volume of responses (i.e., a higher word count, more thought units, fewer gibberish responses).

EMPIRICAL EVIDENCE

There is something intuitively appealing about the use of game-like approaches as a means of stimulating greater interest among survey participants. Yet, empirical investigation into the links between gamification and market research outcomes is somewhat scarce. In recent years, studies by Downes-Le Guin et. al (2012) and Koenig-Lewis et al. (2013) have tried to fill this gap.

Downes-Le Guin and his associates (2012) conducted an experimental study, wherein the same survey was administered using four different styles, which they describe as follows:

1. *Text Only.* This presentation style that typically uses no images at all. Images are included only if intrinsic to the content of the survey, such as images of a product packaging in a package test. Most commonly, questions are presented in the form of black text on a white background. Radio buttons, check boxes and grids are widely used.
2. *Decoratively Visual.* This presentation style uses visual elements (graphics, images, color) that are not intrinsic to the study content, questions or responses. Graphics and colors are used only to provide "visual stimulation," e.g. colored backgrounds, or colored bars separating question wording from response options.
3. *Functionally Visual.* This presentation style uses visual and motion elements, integrated into the way that questions and responses are presented. For example, check boxes and radio buttons are

replaced by slider bars; drag-and-drop boxes replace grids; and images are used to exemplify, augment or replace text response categories.

4. *Gamified.* This presentation style uses various qualities common in most games such as rules, barriers, missions, progress indicators, and rewards. Sometimes, the entire survey may become game-like, or only certain sections may be recast as game-like. The game may directly relate to the survey content or may exist as a method of increasing respondent engagement independent of the survey content. Downes Le-Guin et al. used a software company to design a game for the experiment. A narrative was provided to immerse participants in a fictional online world. Players first chose avatars, which were then allowed to advance through fantasy worlds as they answered survey questions.

Downes-Le Guin et al. (2012) conducted an online survey using 12,289 respondents recruited from the Research Now online panel. Respondents were randomly assigned to one of the four styles of survey. The dependent variables in the study were (1) survey completion rate; (2) actual time taken to complete the survey; (3) perceived time taken to complete the survey; (4) self-reported interest and enjoyment; (4) rate of engagement trap failures, using three different measures (namely, inconsistent responding, failure to follow response instructions, and straight-lining of two or more grids). The researchers found that, while functionally visual and gamified treatments produced higher respondent satisfaction scores, there were no real differences in responding patterns or engagement measures.

Koenig-Lewis et al. (2013) conducted an experimental study using a similar design. Survey participants were assigned to either a text-only or gamified version of the same online survey. The gamified condition included elements such as visuals and imagery, competitive elements, and a fantasy framework that sent participants on mini-quests, ultimately tying the completion of the survey to a reward. Nine hypotheses were proposed, based on the literature on engagement theory, and motivations for survey participation. These hypotheses and results are summarized in Figure 2.

CAN GAMIFICATION WORK FOR COMPLEX SURVEYS?

In recent years, marketers have been drawn to the use of discrete choice methods (e.g., conjoint analysis, choice based conjoint, and Max-Diff) due to their superior ability to predict consumer preferences in a forced-choice situation. The increasing availability of software solutions (such as Sawtooth Software) has made it possible for marketers to use such techniques to aid marketing decision-making. On the downside, the operational execution of conjoint-analytic studies requires respondents to engage in repetitive – and potentially tedious – evaluations of many alternative permutations of product bundles. A single choice-based conjoint (CBC) exercise can take 10-15 minutes to complete.

Kaul, Narang & Shant (2014) conducted a study to investigate whether gamification could be implemented in a complex survey environment, such as the CBC module provided by Sawtooth Software. The objective of the study was to see if the use of gamification could reduce tedium, and improve respondent satisfaction with a CBC study. Kaul and his associates conducted a field experiment to compare the results of four different types of conjoint studies in two countries (the US and India). The four studies were (1) non-gamified CBC; (2) non-gamified adaptive CBC; (3) gamified conjoint with time constraint;

Figure 2. Results reported by Koenig-Lewis, et al. (2013)

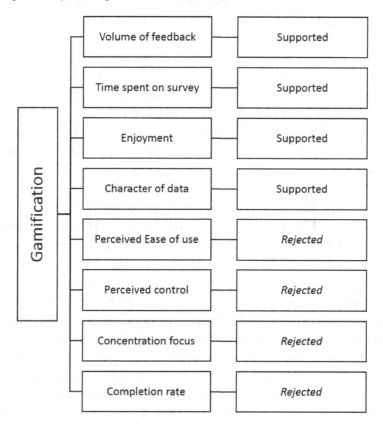

(4) gamified conjoint with no time constraint. The gamified environment allowed respondents to select an avatar for the survey. Respondents were instructed that they would be given the opportunity to acts as users and investors in a low-cost tablet computer. The avatar was then presented with a series of product bundles (as in any conjoint exercise). Respondents were asked to "hire" or "fire" each of the product bundles presented to them. Progress in the survey was rewarded with clothing accessories, such as a hat and sunglasses. Respondents who successfully completed the entire CBC exercise were rewarded by being "appointed" as new the Chief Information Officer (CIO) of the fictional company. Screen shots from this gamified conjoint exercise are shown in Figure 3.

Kaul et al. report that in the US, the gamified conjoint produced significantly higher scores on measures of respondent satisfaction, enjoyment of the survey, and ease of understanding. While there were no differences in overall model fit across the four conditions, the non-timed gamified conjoint exercise produced slightly higher levels of holdout accuracy. The results in India were not as consistent, partly due to the fact that lower Internet access speeds in India probably slowed down access to the gamified conjoint, thereby reducing respondent enjoyment. These results underline a very practical issue, namely, that advocates of gamification need to be cognizant of external factors that might adversely affect respondent attitudes toward gamified environments – such as slow loading of graphics due to Internet access speeds, and potential battery life issues on mobile devices.

Figure 3. Screen shot from a gamified conjoint exercise

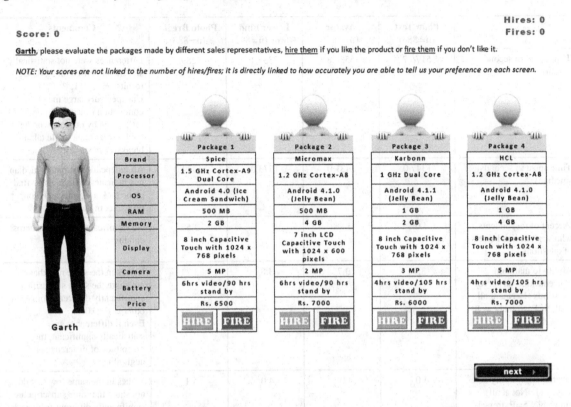

RESULTS FROM ORIGINAL RESEARCH: THE COLLEGE EXPERIENCES SURVEY

In this section, we present the results of a primary research project designed to replicate and extend previous work, and therefore increase our understanding of the impact of gamification in survey research. In the fourth quarter of 2013, Greenwald & Associates, and a team from Research Now collaborated on a study aimed at collecting data from current college students and recent college graduates. The objectives of the survey were to measure several different aspects of the participants' student life experiences, and to measure their reactions to a concept for an interactive online tool designed to match prospective students with colleges, based on the personalities of prospective students, as well as a list of features sought by them.

Design

Data were collected from a sample of 3,547 participants, drawn from the panels maintained by Research Now. Respondents were randomly assigned to one of four experimental conditions, described below. (See Table 1 for counts of the number of respondents in each condition.)

1. *Text only.* Respondents were presented with standard text-based survey questions. Multi-item questions were presented in the form of a grid, with statements in rows and response options (such as ratings) in columns.

Table 1. Results from the collegiate experiences survey

	Plain Text (n=885)	Avatar (n=887)	Letter Find Game (n=892)	Photo Breaks (n=883)	Comments
Time spent in seconds (mean)	5176.7	5538.8	7335.1	8289.3	Differences were not statistically significant, based on ANOVA results (F=1.211; P>0.3). Unexpectedly large mean completion times might be influenced by outliers who left the browser open while taking breaks from survey.
Time spent in seconds (median)	1347.0	1431.0	1573.0	1329.0	An independent samples median test indicates that the letter-find game took a significantly longer time to complete.
Percent of respondents who straight-lined 3 sets of questions	4.0%	3.8%	3.3%	3.5%	No significant differences across conditions.
Ability to maintain concentration on survey questions (1=Not at all well; 5=Extremely well)	3.7_a	3.7_a	3.8_b	$3.7_{a,b}$	Values in the same row that do not share the same subscript are significantly different from each other at P<0.05. Even if differences are statistically significant, the magnitude of differences is negligible.
Overall enjoyability of survey (1=Not at all enjoyable; 5=Extremely enjoyable)	$4.0_{a,b}$	$4.0_{a,b}$	4.0_a	4.1_b	Values in the same row that do not share the same subscript are significantly different from each other at P<0.05. Even if differences are statistically significant, the magnitude of differences is negligible.
Control variables (scores on 14 personality and attitude variables were compared to see if there were differences across methods due to measurement artifacts)					There were no significant differences in mean scores for any of the 14 variables.

2. *Letter find game.* In order to build respondent engagement, respondents were told they would participate in a "letter hunt" game. At the end of each sub-section of the survey, respondents were asked to look for mentions of a letter either in the question text or the responses. For example, the question text or response options might say "You just found an I," or "Here's an X for you." When respondents found a letter, they had to type it in into a space provided at the bottom of the screen. At the end of the survey, respondents who had found all letters would "unscramble" them to complete the game.

3. *Photo breaks.* This was not a "gamified" condition, but rather, an effort to visually relieve tedium among participants. Randomly selected stock photographs were shown in between blocks of standard text questions. At the beginning of the survey, participants were told, "This survey will be most

helpful if you read and answer each question carefully. To help you, we'll be giving you "visual breaks" by presenting a few photos along the way. So enjoy them, and then give your best attention again to the survey questions." Each photo was presented on a separate screen with the caption "Enjoy your photo breaks! Here's the [first] one." Images included photographs of skateboarder Tony Hawke, a whimsical image of a chicken, and scenic landscapes featuring a botanical garden and a sunset.

4.   *Avatar.* In an attempt to build engagement through interactivity, respondents in this condition were given the edition to select an avatar, who would then guide them through the rest of the survey. At the beginning, respondents received the instruction, "Just for fun, please choose one of the avatars below to accompany you through the survey!" Participants could select any one avatar from several static images. The avatar images were taken from stock illustrations, and included both male and female characters. Examples of avatar images included cartoon depictions of Santa Claus, male and female cartoons dressed in business or casual attire, cartoons of an older male in a white lab coat, and photorealistic illustrations of a woman in a formal business suit.

As this study was part of a project conducted for a commercial client with budget and time constraints, the researchers were not able to include a custom programmed game (unlike Downes Le-Guin, et al. 2012). These constraints also limited the number of dependent variables that could be tested. Similarly, all of the variables listed in Figure 2 could not be included for testing in this study.

Results

Data from the four survey conditions were examined to see if there were any significant differences with respect to: (1) total time spent on the survey; (2) the amount of straight-lining of responses (Thomas (2014) calls this behavior "egregious non-differentiation"); (3) self-reported concentration ability; (4) self-reported overall survey enjoyment. The results of the study are summarized in Table 1. The only substantial difference across the four survey types was with respect to the median time spent. Participants who received the "letter find game" version spent 1573 seconds (26.2 minutes) completing the survey, compared with shorter times for participants who received the other three versions. (As noted in Table 1, a comparison of medians is more appropriate than comparing means, as means were probably skewed toward higher numbers by outliers who walked away from the computer in between segments of the survey. After deleting outliers, the trimmed mean time across all four conditions was 1781 seconds (29.7 minutes), versus the overall mean of 6585 seconds (109.7 minutes).)

The finding that "gamification" made no difference to the data in terms of straight-lining is consistent with the results reported by Downes Le-Guin, et al. (2012). The letter-find game caused respondents to spend more time with the survey, which is consistent with the results reported by Koenig-Lewis, et al. (2013). Unlike the findings reported in previous research, there were no significant differences in overall enjoyability of the survey. It should be noted that the overall mean scores for survey enjoyability were 4.0 or higher on a 5-point scale, which indicates that the respondents who completed the survey enjoyed the survey greatly. This result could be an outcome of the topic of the survey, i.e., that respondents found it very interesting to take a survey about their college experiences. One may get different results with surveys about less involving subjects -- such as consumer packaged goods (a highly researched product category).

In sum, the results reported here underline the fact that there is limited empirical support for the beneficial effects of gamification. This finding may be counter-intuitive, especially for proponents of gamification, but it is in line with the research comparing survey participants' preferences for plain text versus rich media surveys. Miller (2009) conducted a study wherein respondents were offered a choice between a plain text survey and a rich media version of the same survey. Out of a total sample of more than 1600 respondents, 400 were forced into a rich media version, 400 were forced into a plain text version, and 800 were allowed to choose their survey environment. Among respondents who had a choice, an overwhelming 74% chose the plain text version of the survey over the rich media option. Respondents in the 18-24 age group were slightly more likely to choose rich media, but there were no statistically significant differences across other demographic groups. Miller concluded that while demographics were not a good predictor of rich media preferences, personality variables might be better predictors. He found that respondents who chose rich media had significantly higher scores for non-conformity ("I like to do things that are unconventional"), risk-taking, and technology adoption. This finding underlines the need for future researchers to investigate the impact of personality traits on gamification preferences.

CONCLUSION

In theory, gamification has the potential to improve the survey-taking experience for participants, and to yield better response rates and better data quality for market researchers and decision makers. The experimental studies reported here and elsewhere demonstrate that it is possible to introduce game-like elements and make surveys more creative without having to invest heavily in creating advanced gaming environments. The empirical studies in the literature — including the original research reported in this chapter — offer only limited support for the benefits of gamification. However, this could be due partly to the use of inappropriate dependent variables in examining the effects of gamification. Most studies in the literature – including ours – use conventional measures of data quality, such as straight-lining and trap question failure. The use of these measures is guided by the current state of thinking about the operationalization of the construct of data quality. Alternative measures of respondent engagement and data quality might reveal greater support for the benefits of gamification. The topic of finding a better definition and operationalization of data quality is an important one for future researchers, not only in the domain of gamification, but in the larger domain of marketing research in general. Due to the widespread use of opt-in panels, many market researchers sometimes tend to take survey respondents for granted, and forget the importance of engaging and retaining their attention. Increased consumer engagement –whether through gamification or other means—is critical in order to produce better data, and ultimately, to guide better marketing decisions.

ACKNOWLEDGMENT

We would like to thank Greenwald & Associates (especially, Ruth Helman, Research Director, and Linda Naiditch, former Assistant Vice President) for agreeing to share key results from the College Experiences Survey. We also thank Rajat Narang and his colleagues from Absolutdata for permission to let us use screen shots from the Gamijoint study.

REFERENCES

Adamou, B. (2011). The Future of Research Through Gaming. Paper presented at the 2011 CASRO Online Research Conference. Retrieved from http://www.casro.org/?page=2011ORC&hhSearchTerms=%22adamou%22&#rescol_765745

Adamou, B. (2014). Research Games as a methodology: The impact of online ResearchGames and game components upon participant engagement and future ResearchGame participation. Proceedings of the 2013 Association of Survey Computing Conference.

Research Quality Council Launches Largest ARF Research Initiative Ever. (2012). Advertising Research Foundation. Retrieved from http://www.thearf.org/orqc-initiative.php

Baumgartner, H., & Steenkamp, J. E. M. (2001). Response Styles in Marketing Research: A Cross-National Investigation. *JMR, Journal of Marketing Research, 38*(2), 143–156. doi:10.1509/jmkr.38.2.143.18840

Downes Le-Guin, T., Baker, R., Mechling, J., & Ruyle, E. (2012). Myths and realities of respondent engagement in online surveys. *International Journal of Market Research, 54*(5), 613–633. doi:10.2501/IJMR-54-5-613-633

ESOMAR. (2013). *Global Market Research 2013*. Amsterdam: ESOMAR (the European Society for Opinion and Market Research). Retrieved from http://www.esomar.org

Galesic, M., & Bosnjak, M. (2009). Effects of questionnaire length on participation and indicators of response quality in a web survey. *Public Opinion Quarterly, 73*(2), 349–360. doi:10.1093/poq/nfp031

Isaacson, W. (2011). *Steve Jobs*. New York: Simon and Schuster.

Kaul, A. Narang, R. & Shant,M. (2014). Gamijoint: Improving Conjoint Through Gamification. Paper presented at the 2014 CASRO Digital Research Conference, San Antonio, TX. Retrieved from http://c.ymcdn.com/sites/www.casro.org/resource/collection/F0F10496-BE87-48E8-8746-521D403EE4A2/Paper_-_Anil_Kaul_and_Rajat_Narang_-_AbsolutData_Analytics.pdf

Koenig-Lewis, N., Marquet, M., & Palmer, A. (2013). The effects of gamification on market research engagement and response. Paper presented at the Academy of Marketing conference. Retrieved from http://marketing.conference-services.net/resources/327/3554/pdf/AM2013_0291_paper.pdf

Krosnick, J. A. (1991). Response strategies for coping with the cognitive demands of attitude measures in surveys. *Applied Cognitive Psychology, 5*(3), 213–236. doi:10.1002/acp.2350050305

Lugtigheid, A. & Rathod, S. (2005). *Questionnaire Length and Response Quality: Myth or Reality?* Stamford CT: Survey Sampling International.

McGonigal, J. (2011). *Reality Is Broken: Why Games Make Us Better and How They Can Change the World*. New York, NY: Penguin Press.

Miller, C. (2009) Respondent technology preferences in surveys: plain text versus rich media. Paper presented at the CASRO Technology Conference, New York.

Miller, J., & Baker-Prewitt, J. (2009). Beyond 'Trapping' the Undesirable Panelist: The Use of Red Herrings to Reduce Satisficing. Paper presented at the 2009 CASRO Panel Quality Conference. Retrieved from http://www.burke.com/library/conference/beyond%20trapping%20the%20undesirable%20panelist_final.pdf

Surveys: Tracking Opinion. Special Report. (2011). National Science Foundation. Retrieved from http://www.nsf.gov/news/special_reports/survey/index.jsp?id=question

O'Toole, J. (2014, February 28). Mobile apps overtake PC Internet usage in U.S. *CNN Money online*. Retrieved from http://money.cnn.com/2014/02/28/technology/mobile/mobile-apps-internet/

Pashupati, K., Courtright, M. & Pettit, A. (2013, March 7-8). Battle Of The Scales: Examining Respondent Scale Usage across 10 Countries. Paper presented at the 2013 CASRO Online Research Conference, San Francisco.

Assessing the Representativeness of Public Opinion Surveys. (2012). *Pew Research Center*. Retrieved from http://www.people-press.org/2012/05/15/assessing-the-representativeness-of-public-opinion-surveys/

Puleston, J. (2011). *Market Research Game Theory*. Bellevue, WA: Global Market Insight, Inc.

Puleston, J. (2012). What It Is and What It Is Not: 8 Things Everyone is Asking about Gamification. Retrieved from http://www.lightspeedresearchblog.com/data-quality/what-it-is-and-what-it-is-not-8-things-everyone-is-asking-about-gamification/

Puleston, J., & Eggers, M. (2012). Dimensions of Online Survey Data Quality: What Really Matters? [White paper]. *GMI-Lightspeed Research*. Retrieved from http://www.gmi-mr.com/uploads/file/PDFs/gmi_formatted_whitepaper_DimensionsWhatReallyMatters.pdf

Schell, J. (2008). *The Art of Game Design: A Book of Lenses*. Burlington, MA: Elsevier.

Shepard, S. (2012, August 6). Sorry, Wrong Number. *National Journal*. Retrieved from http://www.nationaljournal.com/magazine/who-responds-to-telephone-polls-anymore-20120719

Sleep, D., & Puleston, J. (2011). *Measuring the Value of Respondent Engagement: Summary of Research Findings*. Bellevue, WA: Global Market Insight, Inc.

Thomas, R. K. (2014). Fast and Furious… or Much Ado About Nothing? Sub-Optimal Respondent Behavior and Data Quality. *Journal of Advertising Research*, *54*(1), 17–31. doi:10.2501/JAR-54-1-017-031

Zichermann, G., & Cunningham, C. (2011). *Gamification by Design*. Sebastopol, CA: O'Reilly Media.

KEY TERMS AND DEFINITIONS

Acquiescence Response Style: The tendency to answer toward the positive end of a scale. This is also referred to as yea-saying behavior.

Extreme Response Style: The tendency to answer toward the extreme points of a scale.

Gamification: The use of game thinking and game mechanics to engage users and solve problems.

Midpoint Response Style: The tendency to answer toward the middle points of a scale.

Response Style/Stylistic Responding: A survey participant's tendency to systematically respond to questionnaire items regardless of the content.

Satisficing or Sub-Optimal Responding: A term to describe multiple behaviors exhibited by survey takers, wherein they do not exert the full cognitive effort required to provide high quality data.

Speeding: A form of satisficing behavior where a survey participant tries to finish a survey as quickly as possible, without much attention to the actual content of the question.

Straight-Lining: Also known as non-differentiation, this term refers to a form of satisficing behavior where a survey participant gives the exact same response to a battery of questions. Straight-lining behavior is motivated by the participant's desire to progress quickly through the survey, rather than provide thoughtful and well-considered answers.

Survey Abandonment Rate: The percentage of respondents who started a survey, but did not complete the survey despite being qualified to participate. Invitees who did not qualify for the survey (e.g., because they did not meet certain criteria) should not be included in the calculation of the abandonment rate.

Survey Response Rate: In traditional survey research, response rate is defined as (the ratio or percentage of) the number of completed survey responses, divided by the number of total survey invitations sent out. Some researchers define response rate as the number of survey invitations that were opened (rather than completed), divided by the total number of survey invitations sent out.

Trap Question: Any form of survey question whose main purpose is to identify untruthful or inattentive respondents. Examples include the use of fake brands embedded in a list of real ones, and questions with instructions to "Mark 2 here" in a multi-item scale.

Chapter 6
Gamification of Human Resource Processes

Jared Z. Ferrell
SHAKER, USA

Jacqueline E. Carpenter
SHAKER, USA

E. Daly Vaughn
SHAKER, USA

Nikki M. Dudley
SHAKER, USA

Scott A. Goodman
SHAKER, USA

ABSTRACT

Gamification promises to deliver more motivating, engaging, and, ultimately, effective human resource (HR) processes. The following chapter presents an overview of key motivational theories supporting the potential effectiveness of gamifying HR processes. Key motivational theories underpinning the success of gamification include Need Satisfaction Theories, Operant Conditioning, Flow, and Goal Setting Theory. After providing a theoretical framework supporting the effectiveness of gamification, emphasis will shift to an examination of key game elements used to improve four large categories of HR processes: recruitment, selection, training, and performance management. Case studies will be leveraged to provide real-world examples of organizations using gamification to improve HR initiatives. Finally, the chapter will cover key considerations and best practices that should be followed when developing and implementing gamified HR initiatives.

DOI: 10.4018/978-1-4666-8651-9.ch006

INTRODUCTION

Imagine exploring a company's career site and being lured into a virtual multi-media adventure where you race against the clock to reach a dream job interview. Along the journey numerous obstacles force you to make choices, such as wearing your ink-stained lucky shirt, risking punctuality by washing it, or donning an obnoxiously colored scarf to hide the stain. Reckitt Benckiser, a multinational consumer goods company, developed such a game-like recruiting experience which they refer to as a character profile test, that invites users to "play [the] interactive experience to reveal who [they] really are." The recruiting application, termed Insanely Driven, does not contain any content overtly describing the job or company. Instead, users are invited on an adventure and provided with choices to drive their own experience. A series of videos presenting a first-person view of the bizarre virtual world, a progress bar indicating how far into the experience the user has travelled, periodic feedback on time left to the deadline, and a storyline that puts responsibility for advancing on the user's shoulders are all game elements serving to enhance user motivation to follow through to the end. Upon completion of the experience, the user is provided feedback about what their choices 'say' about their personality and potential fit with the company.

The mere existence of this gamified recruitment application serves as a differentiating feature showcasing Reckitt Benckiser's brand, and also highlights the growing trend of gamified applications in employment contexts. A recent estimate by Gartner (2011), suggests 70% of Global 2000 organizations will employ at least one gamified application in 2014. In addition, industry experts anticipate gamification spending will grow by more than 1,100% in a four year period from $242 million in 2012 to roughly $2.8 billion by 2016 (Burmeister, 2014).

The primary goals of this chapter are threefold: (1) to provide a theoretical basis for gamification in human resource (HR) practices, (2) to highlight case studies and other practical implementations of key game elements across several HR processes, and (3) to offer best practice considerations for HR managers and organizational leaders proposing or implementing gamified processes. This chapter will focus on the HR processes of recruitment, selection, training, and performance management. For each HR area, commonly integrated game elements will be presented, along with examples of gamified interventions from an HR perspective.

While gamification is increasingly referenced, requested, and implemented within organizations as part of HR practices, there still exists a lack of uniformity and clarity surrounding a universal definition. Deterding and colleagues' (2011) broad definition of gamification, is widely cited; however, this definition fails to fully clarify what should or should not be considered gamification in the realm of HR processes. For example, providing visible rewards for superior performance is a widely cited game element, but this does not help clearly differentiate 21st century HR processes from those of Taylor and Scientific Management (1914). The current chapter narrows the focus on gamification to the definition leveraged by Dominguez and colleagues (2013), such that gamification is defined as "incorporating game elements into a non-gaming software application to increase user experience and engagement" (p. 381). This allows for a more concrete, uniform explanation of what constitutes a gamified HR initiative.

Why Gamify?

As gamification promises to enhance the user experience and increase user engagement, it should come as no surprise that HR contexts have become fertile launching grounds for gamified applications. Many may consider traditional HR functions as the inherent antithesis of fun and engaging contexts. This image has not been lost in Hollywood or in popular culture, as evidenced by the prototypical HR portrayals in the Sunday comics, sitcoms, and movies (Toby Flenderson, anyone?). Over the last few decades, new technologies have spurred an accelerated shift away from the old HR processes and into more innovative and engaging activities for candidates and employees. Gamified applications represent a promising next step in the technological advancement of HR systems and processes.

The reason organizations are so eager to improve engagement in HR processes is intuitive. Across disciplines, research and strategic thinking indicates that talent and human capital are a company's most important competitive advantage (Ployhart & Moliterno, 2011). Engaged candidates are likely more eager to join an organization, thus improving the organization's pool of well-qualified candidates. Providing more engaging onboarding and development applications will boost initiative and motivation to complete critical training modules. Finally, improved performance management capabilities can enhance employee productivity, as well as provide leaders with a better understanding of critical performance gaps.

Even though there has been a recent surge of gamified approaches and applications, the research literature is lagging behind in its understanding of the theoretical basis of gamification and the mechanisms by which it works (Landers, Bauer, Callan, & Armstrong, 2014). The field of psychology provides a lens for explaining and understanding the ways gamification facilitates these highly sought after effects. Before discussing common elements of gamified HR applications, a brief review of theoretical foundations explaining the motivational effects of gamification is provided next.

THEORETICAL EXPLANATIONS OF GAMIFICATION SUCCESSES IN HR

In order to effectively integrate gamification into HR systems, practitioners need to understand its theoretical basis. This chapter draws heavily upon psychological research and theory to provide its foundational underpinnings. In particular, research and theory from the area of industrial-organizational (I/O) psychology is drawn upon to create a much needed theoretical framework to ground future gamification research. I/O psychology involves the application and study of psychological principles to better understand organizations and work processes. The application of psychology to work has been incorporated since the early stages of the field of psychology's formal existence. Applications to workplaces and organizations appeared in early 20th century utilizations, with interesting examples and case studies such as the rise of selection testing beginning in 1917 for uses during World War I and II and the Hawthorne Effect studies carried out in the 1920s and 30s in an electric factory (Levy, 2012). Most theoretical conceptualizations suggest that gamification impacts engagement, learning, and behaviors through a number of psychological mechanisms (Landers et al., 2014). A discussion of four categories of motivational theories offering insight into the psychology behind gamification is presented next. Each brief theory overview is accompanied by a description about how the theories guide the success of gamified initiatives.

Need Satisfaction Theories

The first category of psychological theories that can help explain the motivational pull of game elements are need satisfaction theories, including Maslow's Hierarchy of Needs and Self-Determination Theory. Need satisfaction theories assert that people seek out and continue to engage in activities that satisfy specific psychological needs. Maslow's Hierarchy of Needs identifies basic human needs, each of which must be met in order to feel fulfilled or complete (Maslow, 1970). Maslow's needs hierarchy includes physiological (basic needs like food, water, sleep, shelter), security (the need to feel emotionally and economically secure), belongingness (the need to be part of and accepted by a group), esteem (the need to feel valued for one's contribution to the group), and self-actualization needs (the need for achieving something, making a difference). Pink (2011) expanded on Maslow's hierarchy, asserting that the self-actualization level consists of three primary motivational factors including purpose (the need to feel engaged in a meaningful activity that will have an effect), autonomy (the need to feel free to make one's own choices), and mastery (the need to feel one is improving and contributing to important objectives). Aside from physiological and security needs, carefully implemented gamified interventions may be successful in satisfying many psychological needs.

Self-Determination Theory (SDT; Ryan & Deci, 2000) is another need satisfaction theory that can help illuminate the psychological processes underlying increased motivation through gamified interventions. According to SDT, behaviors that provide inherent satisfaction are intrinsically motivating, whereas behaviors that are intended to reach desired end states or avoid undesirable states are extrinsically motivated. Said another way, intrinsic rewards are driven by need satisfaction whereas extrinsic rewards are driven by the environment (Ryan & Deci, 2000).

Within SDT, sub-theories (e.g., Cognitive Evaluation Theory, Deci & Ryan, 1985; Basic Psychological Need Theory, Deci & Ryan, 2000) specify fundamental psychological needs that drive intrinsic motivation and underlie psychological well-being. These fundamental needs include autonomy (sense of willingness or volition), competence (sense of efficacy and the need to feel challenged), and relatedness (sense of social connectedness). Research has shown that those who are intrinsically motivated tend to enjoy an activity more, are more creative, have greater cognitive flexibility, process information at a deeper level, and have greater psychological and physical health benefits than those not intrinsically motivated (Przybylski, Rigby, & Ryan, 2010). In contrast, when one is extrinsically motivated, they are driven to complete a task to achieve some other outcome (e.g., a promotion) or to avoid an outcome (e.g., punishment). Both intrinsic and extrinsic motivators can be powerful incentives that drive specific behaviors.

Gamified applications may influence behavior via both intrinsic and extrinsic motivators, depending on the specific game elements incorporated in the application, as well as the motivations of the person completing the gamified application. Badges, points, and levels are commonly implemented to facilitate and enhance participant motivation. The accumulation of these virtual tokens and level advancements may serve as intrinsic motivation by signifying competence in a given task or area. The prevalence of applications employing badges and encouraging badge collections and displays (e.g., social media websites such as Foursquare), suggests that the accumulation process is, in itself, enjoyable. Public display of badges may also tap into needs for relatedness as they allow users to identify similar and/or complementary attributes of others and provide a common ground for making social connections (Przybylski et al., 2010). These same game elements could also serve as extrinsic motivation in some instances. As an example, users hoping to achieve extrinsic rewards such as new career opportunities may desire to accumulate more publicly displayed badges or points assuming that this will enhance their ability to differentiate themselves from other prospective job candidates.

Game elements that provide the opportunity to satisfy needs for autonomy, competence, and relatedness should also enhance intrinsic motivation (Landers et al., 2014). Feelings of autonomy may be increased by affording choice over tasks and goals, providing flexibility in the strategies and actions an individual may take, and providing informational rather than prescriptive feedback. Autonomy may also be enhanced by having non-controlling instructions, such as encouraging an individual to explore a task rather than providing step-by-step commands (Ryan, Rigby, & Przybylski, 2006). Game elements that put the user in control, or give such an illusion, within an experience, may be useful for enhancing intrinsic motivation through satisfaction of autonomy needs. Avatars, a game element that allows people to represent themselves within virtual worlds are said to have a positive impact through allowing optimization of the self (Reeves & Read, 2009). Avatars enable users to customize toward a range of personal preferences and can be combined with other game elements, such as a narrative context, to bring awareness to the self and give users the feeling that they are driving the experience.

The need for competence may be met through gamified applications that provide opportunities to learn new skills at an optimally challenging level and receive feedback. Game elements that provide an indication of proficiency or achievement relative to a goal or referent other, such as progress bars, completion badges, level advancement, leaderboards, and error notification may be implemented to achieve

Table 1. Game element framework

	Game Element	Description	Recruitment	Selection	Training	Performance Management
Environmental Elements	Avatars	Allow self-representation within online programs. Help increase user engagement.	X	X	X	
	3-D Environment	Provide an immersive feel during activities, and also facilitate integration of multiple game elements.	X	X	X	
	Narrative Context	Provide a purpose and structure that can increase excitement and attention, while also improving memory.	X	X	X	X
	Competition	Impacts motivation in certain individuals, thus increasing engagement and drive to improve performance.			X	X
	Time Pressure	Increases arousal and engagement in employees as long as set at a resonably difficult level.	X	X	X	
Feedback Elements	Progress Bars	Provide feedback regarding progress within activities. Can also show performance progress over time to increase motivation.	X	X	X	X
	Badges	Provide immediate feedback for accomplishments that employees can then display, providing extrinsic motivation.	X	X	X	X
	Points	Immediate feedback that can be used to shape behavior within specific activities, or at a broader level.	X		X	X
	Levels	Feedback showing a person's accomplishments relative to prespecified goals. Helps indicate critical advancements in skills or knowledge.	X	X	X	X
	Leaderboards	Instill competition by making performance more transparent. Feedback's manifestation of competition.			X	X
	Error Notification	Provides real-time feedback to strengthen the link between an action and its consequence to improve learning.		X	X	X
Note. X indicates game elements easily translate to the HR process.						

satisfaction of competence needs. Alternatively, these elements may elicit powerful extrinsic motivators, such as the desire for increased rewards, recognition, and the potential for monetary gain. Relatedness needs may be satisfied within a gamified context to the extent that the game elements encourage or require social connectivity or interaction (Przybylski et al., 2010). Any of the game elements mentioned previously and in Table 1 could be implemented in a (semi) public context to encourage interaction and contribute to relatedness need fulfillment.

Operant Conditioning

Operant conditioning, one of the earliest and most well-known theories of learning, is often cited as a theoretical foundation for gamification (Landers et al., 2014). The theory of operant conditioning describes how individuals make associations between a particular behavior and a consequence or outcome. Operant conditioning occurs in a three-phase process. First there is a stimulus or event, next a behavioral response, and third a consequence or outcome that follows based on the behavioral response (Skinner, 1948, 1953). In operant conditioning, outcomes are either reinforcements, intended to increase the behavior they follow, or punishments, intended to decrease the behavior they follow.

Reinforcers can be used to affect behavior through a process called shaping. Shaping involves reinforcing approximate desired responses to a stimulus or event in an effort to increase the likelihood of the targeted response (Skinner, 1958). In the beginning, individuals are reinforced for easy tasks, and gradually they must perform more and more difficult tasks in order to receive reinforcement. This gradual adjustment of the behaviors required for reinforcement enables the shaping of the behavior so that over time the desired behavior is achieved (Skinner, 1958). The principles of operant conditioning, specifically the administration of conditioned reinforcers, lend themselves well to gamified contexts (Antin & Churchill, 2011). Conditioned reinforcers are stimuli that have reinforcement properties through their association with a primary reinforcer, such as a basic human need or life necessity (e.g. food, water, safety).

Conditioned reinforcers within gamified contexts can take many forms including points on a scoreboard or leaderboard, badges representing virtual wealth, and level advancement within a virtual environment (Landers et al., 2014). As an example, a badge acquired either by completing an action, mastering a particular skill, or demonstrating a required level of knowledge may encourage users to maintain or continue the behaviors that resulted in receiving the badge. Manipulation of the type and frequency of reinforcer allocation can further assist in shaping or guiding users toward a desired behavior.

Flow Theory

Flow theory emerged from an attempt by the psychologist, Mihaly Csikszentmihályi, to describe happiness. Csikszentmihályi (1990) found that people's happiest moments are those in which they are voluntarily trying to accomplish something challenging for which they have the right skill match to do so. This state is what Csikszentmihályi (1990) called flow. Described another way, flow is a state of deep absorption in an intrinsically enjoyable task. When someone is in flow, they are fully engaged and even lose track of time and self—nothing else matters (Csikszentmihályi, 1990). Often people refer to this as 'being in the zone'.

When someone is in a flow state, they experience three things simultaneously: interest, concentration, and enjoyment (Csikszentmihályi, 1997). Interest means just that—that the individual finds the task interesting. Interest is critical to flow because it sets the foundation for intrinsic motivation and learning. When a person is in flow, this means the person is in a deep state of concentration and completely absorbed in the task at hand. Enjoyment means the task is satisfying, often providing a sense of creative accomplishment. While enjoyment is critical, it may be realized only in retrospect since all concentration is on the task itself for the duration of task performance (Csikszentmihályi, 1997).

As Garris, Ahlers, and Driskell (2002) explain, flow provides insight into the feelings of enjoyment and engagement that game users experience. Csikszentmihályi and LeFevre (1989) found that people reported being happiest in non-work flow and least happy in work non-flow (Csikszentmihályi & LeFevre, 1989). Reeves and Read (2009) propose that games are a way in which we can bring more flow to the workplace. As such, gamification may be a great opportunity to help facilitate flow at work.

Reeves and Read (2009) describe several features of a flow state, which may be facilitated and enhanced by implementing particular game elements within traditionally non-game contexts in which a flow state is desired. For example, game elements such as progress bars and leaderboards can serve as clear indications of goals and reduce ambiguity—a key feature of flow states. Allocation of badges, points or virtual tokens, level advancement and error notification can each be implemented as immediate task feedback to assist the user in entering or maintaining flow. Additionally, elements such as the use of avatars, narrative context, and 3-D environments can help create an immersive environment, which may assist with the exclusion of distractions—a key feature of a flow state. Gamification efforts should also consider and account for balance between skill and challenge such that gamified HR applications can accommodate varied skill levels of applicants or employees.

Research has shown workers who are in flow are happier, satisfied, more productive, more creative and more relaxed (Csikszentmihályi & LeFevre, 1989). As such, it makes sense for organizations to learn as much as they can about flow and ways they can facilitate it within the contexts of HR systems.

Goal Setting Theory

Goal setting theory has an extensive research history, dating back to the 1960s (Locke, 1968). At its core, goal-setting theory contends that goals impact action directly and indirectly. Goals directly motivate action by steering attention and effort toward goal-relevant activities and away from goal-irrelevant activities, and by increasing effort and persistence. Goals indirectly impact action through the use of task strategies or self-regulatory processes. As people strive to figure out the optimal way to achieve a goal, they employ task-relevant knowledge and strategies as well as self-regulatory behaviors to manage efforts toward the goal. Goal difficulty is an important factor in goal setting theory. Research has documented that specific, difficult, yet attainable goals are more likely to lead to higher levels of performance than 'do your best' goals (Fishbein & Ajzen, 1975; Locke & Latham, 2002). The relationship between goal difficulty and task performance remains linear and positive as long as the person is committed to achieving the goal, has the ability to meet the goal, and does not have conflicting goals. Research also suggests that adding proximal goals on the route to more distal ones tends to increase self-efficacy, and belief that the more distal goal is attainable (Latham & Seijts, 1999).

There are four primary ways in which the principles of goal setting theory can be useful for designing gamified applications: setting goals, increasing self-efficacy, providing feedback, and ensuring attention. Gamified applications already incorporate goal setting and reward for goal attainment to motivate behavior. Often, goals are set for the user of gamified HR applications with attainment of badges, points, or virtual goods serving as the desired end state or as rewards for other accomplishments within the gamified context (Landers et al., 2014). The concepts of levels and level advancement also serve as externally set goals that can motivate action. Gamification can influence individuals to set goals by providing options and avenues for people to work toward personally relevant or chosen end states. Implementing variety with a game element is a simple way to accomplish this in a typically non-game context. For example, Hsu and colleagues (2013) found that people enjoyed and were motivated by having a diversity of badge types available to obtain. This suggests that a variety of goals might be helpful in creating the optimal gamified application.

In addition, goal-setting theory provides insight into how to increase goal commitment, including increasing goal importance and self-efficacy. Enhanced goal commitment may be particularly relevant for gamified HR contexts if there's a danger of users failing to perceive goals within the gamified environment as legitimate. The goal-setting research suggests making the commitment public to others or posting the achievement of goals (e.g., badges) or having the individual's supervisor assign the goal (creating demand characteristics) as options for increasing goal commitment. Steps could also be taken to increase self-efficacy, such as ensuring adequate training in the gamified experience or having the individual's supervisor express confidence in the individual's ability to achieve the goal (Locke & Latham, 2002).

Incorporating feedback into gamified systems will also help drive performance, as long as that feedback doesn't decrease motivation or self-efficacy. Progress bars that track an individual's progress toward goals are the simplest form of feedback commonly used in gamified HR applications.

Given that people have a limited pool of attentional resources that can be devoted to on-task, off-task, and self-regulatory strategies, gamified applications should be structured and implemented such that game design elements don't pull necessary attentional resources off task.

Summary of Theoretical Foundation

The aforementioned theories provide insight into how and why gamification efforts enhance engagement, motivation, and psychological well-being. Several themes emerge across theories, such as the need to integrate gamification elements with regard for key motivational needs (e.g. autonomy, competence, and relatedness). The importance of setting goals and providing feedback is also clear, yet these need to be chosen and delivered in a way that enhances rather than deters motivation. Finally, end results must be considered. It is critical to align gamification goals with organizational goals to ensure that game elements drive the intended behaviors.

With the foundation of some key psychological theories underlying the effects of gamified initiatives, the next sections elaborate upon the definitions of specific game elements found in gamification research and within gamified HR systems. Following the description of game elements, specific examples from various HR contexts will be discussed.

GAMIFICATION IN HR SYSTEMS

Game Elements

In order to discuss specific instances of gamification in HR contexts, a review of some key gamification elements is provided in the table below. While not intended to be an exhaustive list, these descriptions provide a quickly accessible reference to some of the most common game elements found within HR systems.

As seen in Table 1, specific game elements are grouped into two broad categories: environment and feedback. Environmental components, such as avatars and narrative storytelling, develop the context of gamified initiatives, while feedback components, such as progress bars and badges, points, and levels, show performance and progression during the experiences. Many of the environmental game elements facilitate engagement and motivation during a gamified experience or application. Feedback elements may impact engagement during progression through the experience, but these elements will also help shape learning and transfer of behaviors outside of the gamified application.

Applying Game Elements to HR

There is ample opportunity for implementing game elements within organizational HR functions. It is the goal of this chapter to discuss some of these gamified solutions as they apply to four major areas of HR: recruitment, selection, training, and performance management. Examples of actual gamified HR initiatives will be leveraged to exemplify how different game elements can be applied to these four HR functions to improve engagement, motivation, well-being, and performance. The examples described herein were either accessed and researched via publicly available resources or garnered from SHAKER's proprietary content and client engagements.

Recruitment

Recruitment, as defined by Rynes (1991), "encompasses all organizational practices and decisions that affect either the number, or type, of individuals who are willing to apply for or accept a given vacancy" (p. 429), making it the foundational HR function that determines the breadth and depth of talent available to an organization. Historically, recruitment sources included employee referrals, newspaper or radio advertisements, employment agencies, and "walk-in" applications (Barber, 1998). While many organizations continue to engage these sources to advertise vacancies, corporate websites, internet job boards, and social media outlets now dominate the recruitment landscape (Dineen & Soltis, 2010). These sources provide ample opportunity for organizations to introduce gamified technology and interventions in the pursuit of human capital.

Successful recruitment efforts at the organization level are typically measured in relation to both candidate volume and applicant quality. At an individual level, recruitment efforts are typically targeted at enhancing organizational attraction and enticing job seekers to engage further with the company, usually via an invitation to apply for a job. The objective of recent applications of game elements in recruitment contexts is to facilitate and encourage job seekers to learn about companies and vacancies through web and social media outlets (Callan, Bauer, & Landers, 2014). Presumably relying on principles of operant conditioning, the assumption is that encouragement of extensive investigation and engagement with the company's content will encourage qualified applicants to apply for employment and/or spread the word about job opportunities with the company (DuVernet & Popp, 2014). Some organizations are aiming to accomplish this goal by introducing gamified elements to their recruitment media to serve as reinforcement for investigating and learning about the organization. For example, an organization may invite a job seeker to create a profile within which they can acquire and display badges, receive points or virtual tokens as a reward for viewing a certain number of pages or pieces of content, or offer progress and level completion feedback as job seekers navigate 3-D renderings of corporate headquarters. If the candidate is periodically awarded points, badges, or tokens viewing portions of a web site, without knowing when the next reward will occur, referred to as a variable ratio reward schedule, the candidate is theoretically more likely to continue with the desired behavior of exploring the site in an effort to trigger the next set of reinforcers.

Providing realistic job previews (RJPs) within a recruitment, and often selection, context is another key tool relied upon by organizations as a way to inform, engage, and refine a pool of potential applicants. The industrial-organizational (I/O) psychology literature speaks broadly to the idea that the more real an RJP, the more likely it will positively affect applicant attraction and reduce post-hire attrition. Research on recruitment content also indicates that the volume of information provided to job seekers and the media richness of the content correlates positively with decisions to pursue employment and with overall perceptions of the organization (Barber & Roehline, 1993; Cable & Yu, 2006; De Geode, Van Vianen, and Klehe, 2011). Decades of RJP and work sample research suggests that moving away from a one-way presentation of descriptive information and toward an interactive experience is more effective for encouraging accurate self-insight, enhancing commitment and satisfaction, reducing voluntary turnover, and providing a more enjoyable learning experience (Colarelli, 1984; Dineen & Soltis, 2011; Downs, Farr & Colbeck, 1978; Ilies & Robertson, 1989; Schmitt, Ford, & Stults 1986).

HR practitioners have turned toward gamified recruitment solutions as a means of enhancing the RJP experience and to provide information to job seekers in a more engaging manner. Building narrative context around the provision of job and company culture information is one way that organizations are introducing a more game-like feel to the traditionally static delivery of facts and figures.

Across the healthcare, retail, finance, and public sector industries, assessment developers, such as SHAKER, have implemented both stand-alone and assessment-integrated RJP components that guide job seekers through a day-in-the-life experience, rather than presenting static pages of information. Narrative context in the form of employee testimonials and character descriptions allow job seekers to learn about the demands of the role, company culture, benefits, and opportunities offered, and presumably provides the immersive context shown to enhance engagement and motivation (Reeves & Read, 2009). This type of gamified recruitment solution allows companies extensive flexibility with content, information volume, and media richness (e.g., the inclusion of imagery, music, video, etc.).

Red Bull's 'A Day in the Life of Red Bull Musketeers' website is a prime example of how narrative context can be combined with video, graphic, and text content to engage job seekers and entice them to navigate through substantial amounts of information during a short period of time (Red Bull, n.d.). The website allows users to scroll and advance the clock to follow the main character through his previous 24 hours in order to discover the meaning behind a text message that awoke him at 6:30 a.m. Along the way, the user has the option to learn more via brief videos corresponding with the timeline, reading short passages describing key features of the job, and clicking around the screen to reveal facts and figures relevant to the role they're exploring. Although the website doesn't actually offer a set of information customized to the user based on any user actions, the narrative and self-paced progress elements offer users a self-driven game-like feel, allowing the user to feel as if they're autonomously moving through this virtual plane of information, a key component of the need satisfaction theories, such as SDT (Deci & Ryan, 2000). Based on research regarding applicant engagement and organizational attraction, it may be assumed that users would be less likely to absorb as much information and interact with the content as extensively had all this information about the job duties, employee testimonials, desired characteristics, and company culture been presented in one long video or a series of paragraphs, without the storyline or progress bar (Cable & Yu, 2006). The presentation of the content itself also serves as a signal about Red Bull's values and culture, demonstrating its commitment to a full brand experience, quality, and fun (Connelly, Certo, Ireland, & Reutzel, 2011; Spence, 1973).

While the Red Bull Day In the Life website focuses on describing a particular role within the company, other gamified recruitment applications aim to convey information and facilitate development of general knowledge about an organization's culture and/or broad specialty areas of operation within the organization, as opposed to focusing on specific roles. For example, Deloitte, a large, multinational professional services firm, offers a comprehensive set of gamified recruitment applications that provide both a general company overview and a tool for deeper investigation of career fit for job seekers. Deloitte's virtual office tour features a 3-D environment in which users freely navigate one of three offices located in China. The storyline suggests that it's the user's first day of work and the user is invited to explore the office, setting the stage for virtual interactions with new coworkers and launching the user on a mission to find tokens around the office that represent key features of the company culture. This free exploration methodology provides autonomy to users, a key driver of need satisfaction theories of motivation (Deci & Ryan, 2000). Users can monitor their progress and review the tokens they've already collected at any time. For job seekers who want to learn more, Deloitte also offers a 'Find Your Fit' tool wherein users choose a specialty area and answer questions about how they would handle certain situations. The content of these items may characterize it as a situational judgment test, but the experience feels less like an assessment and more like a game due to the game-like elements embedded in the application. For example, with each answer, the user learns more about the business unit they chose and what is expected of someone in that role. If they answer the item "correctly," they receive a star. The more stars collected for a particular business unit, the better presumed fit. In this case, any or all of the psychological theories reviewed above may be operating to influence job seeker behavior and motivate users to remain engaged with the experience.

HR practitioners have also implemented game elements in the form of gamified job simulations in efforts to connect with potential applicants. In 2011, Marriott International, Inc. launched My Marriott Hotel™, a set of social media games that the company hoped would generate interest in hospitality careers among millennials. In one version of the game, users are invited to manage a hotel restaurant kitchen. The gamer is responsible for managing a budget to buy equipment and ingredients, hire employees, and receive points for happy customers and turning a profit. This is arguably the most traditionally "game-like" application reviewed in this chapter thus far, and the inclusion of several game features is what distinguishes this application from others; My Marriott Hotel™ features avatars that users choose to represent themselves as the manager, time pressure to complete tasks, points for successful execution, status bars indicating the overall health and prosperity of the hotel area being managed, and a clear progression through levels of complexity.

On the surface, Marriott's gamification endeavor seems aligned with their general recruiting goal of exposing millennials to the opportunities available in the hospitality industry. The application as a whole, and its existence on a social media platform, likely opened up a new avenue for Marriott to present themselves to and engage with potential applicants, leveraging the relatedness needs of job seekers (Deci & Ryan, 2000). Within the application, the game-like elements serve to keep users engaged with the experience and allow for dissemination of information about the demands and challenges of the hotel management roles, disguised as instructional pieces of the game. Overall, the use of avatars, leaderboards, and level advancements is likely to lead to a flow state for job-seekers who become immersed in this game-like recruitment effort (Csikszentmihályi, 1997). Points and level advancements also serve as feedback that can tie back into the goal setting theory of motivation (Locke & Latham, 2002). While it's unknown whether the application assisted Marriott in achieving any specific recruiting goals pertaining to volume or quality, within a month of launching the application, Marriott reported that their

Facebook site, where the My Marriott Hotel game was hosted, had over 270,000 page views and over 12,000 active users (Marriott, 2011).

An increasing presence of gamified recruitment applications within social media platforms is expected to coincide with the boom of gamified HR initiatives in general. Reckitt Benckiser's Insanely Driven experience, Deloitte's virtual office tour and Find My Fit tool, Red Bull's Day in the Life website, and Marriott's My Marriott Hotel games all present the opportunity to share results, feedback, or invite others to participate via social media sites. As recruiting efforts continue to revolve around social media, gamified elements such as badges that display personality or work style attributes, proficiency and scores on simulated recruiting games, and feedback about potential fit with company cultures or roles are likely to become prominent features on popular social media sites.

The recruitment revolution within social media platforms and the implementation of gamified elements in this context is equally likely to be driven by third-party job matching entities, such as Knack and LinkedIn, as they are by organizations looking to recruit talent. As this trend progresses, websites related to recruitment and job search processes will likely see increased utilization of game elements such as badges, avatars, social competition, and leaderboards. What have yet to be seen are the consequences of gamification in recruitment contexts relative to recruitment goals. That is, the existence of gamified recruitment applications does not guarantee the success of such applications for attaining superior recruitment outcomes.

In a recent publication, Landers and colleagues (2014) speculated on the instrumentality of gamified interventions. Recruiting contexts may be somewhat difficult environments to implement gamified elements that motivate via operant conditioning principles because the primary reinforcer for a job seeker is distal (e.g., an eventual job offer) and intangible (e.g., identification and/or feelings of fit with the organization).

Deterding et al. (2011) and others caution that the mechanisms of gamified interventions must be aligned with desired goals and end states in order to be effective. Much of the research currently available on gamification is based on gamified learning contexts. Although the goal of implementing gamified elements in recruitment contexts may be to assist job seekers in learning about the organization or job, this doesn't mean that the mechanism of the gamified intervention is supporting this goal at a psychological level. If facilitating learning about the organization is the objective, then knowledge should be measured to confirm that the intervention is operating as intended (Landers, et al. 2014). Learning about the company, job, or one's potential fit for either appears to be the goal of each gamified recruiting application reviewed above.

Since recruitment provides the foundation for a potential extended relationship between an individual and organization, companies should take caution to ensure that the expectations, image, and messages sent via their gamified recruitment context align with what the candidate will encounter throughout selection and employment contexts. Depending on the sophistication and complexity of the gamified interventions, the introduction of badges and/or tokens of achievement and completion during early phases of recruitment may establish unrealistic expectations about a candidate's chances of being hired for an actual open position at the company. Additionally, a highly engaging, feedback-rich initial interaction with the company may set expectations for an equally feedback-rich selection process, which has been shown as the exception rather than the norm (Burnett et al., 2014).

Although a specific example of such a gamified intervention has not been reviewed herein, gamification of recruitment in the form of public display of badges and leaderboards may be on the horizon. Such recruitment platforms that encourage competition among job seekers or public display of virtual tokens, badges, or fit profiles may inadvertently introduce a type of gamified punishment that could discourage potential candidates rather than help organizations attract them. As implied by Landers and colleagues (2014), some individuals, and perhaps entire cohorts on average (e.g., older workers), may be averse to gamification and especially competitive gamified environments.

As the worlds of recruiting and assessment become increasingly technology-centric, engaging, and interactive, the lines between what constitutes a strictly recruiting versus a personnel selection process continue to blur. Many of the gamified applications described above allow prospective candidates to learn more about the organization, but the organization also has the opportunity to gather data about user behavior during the recruitment activities. Similarly, employers and practitioners have recognized that, not only do organizations select applicants, prospective candidates also use the application and assessment process to determine whether the organization is a place where they desire to work (Carpenter & Doverspike, 2014, Rynes, 1991). While recognizing this trend, the next section will expound upon examples of gamification applied to activities primarily purposed for use in personnel selection activities.

Personnel Selection

Personnel selection, henceforth referred to as selection, focuses primarily on examining a set of knowledge, skills, abilities, or other characteristics (KSAOs) of an individual that relate to certain performance outcomes or job activities of interest to organizations (Guion, 2011). Selection researchers and practitioners are acutely interested in developing and evaluating variables that will reliably predict key organizational performance outcomes.

Within HR and I/O psychology, personnel selection is one of the more established specialties (Ryan & Ployhart, 2014). In stark contrast, the nascent area of study relating to gamification in selection contexts provides ample opportunity for researchers, but has still received relatively little empirical investigation to date. Continuous advances in technology have led to the recent and ever-expanding adaptation and integration of gamification elements into selection contexts (Ryan & Ployhart, 2014). The study of the application of gamification in selection, however, continues to lag behind practitioner adoption (Landers et al., 2014; Ryan & Ployhart, 2014). As such, Ryan & Ployhart (2014) implore investigators to turn their attention to these areas, or run the risk of being marginalized in the space by technology-focused and gaming development firms.

Before describing specific game elements that have been applied to selection assessments, a brief overview of validity will help guide the discussion. There are three forms of validity often cited as methods of supporting the legal defensibility of selection assessments. The three types of validity are construct validity, criterion validity, and content validity. Construct validity refers to whether or not the selection tool measures some underlying construct, such as personality characteristics or mechanical comprehension (Binning & Barrett, 1989). Criterion validity describes the extent to which a selection tool can predict some relevant criteria for organizations, generally measures of job performance (SIOP, 2003). Content validity is the extent to which the content of an assessment mirrors the content of the job (Van Iddekinge & Ployhart, 2008).

While construct validity, criterion validity, and content validity are important from a legal defensibility standpoint, more narrow forms of validity evidence (e.g., face validity and predictive validity) have been identified and become pertinent in examining applicant reactions to gamified selection initiatives (Smither, Reilly, Millsap, Pearlman, & Stoffey, 1993). Face validity examines the extent to which applicants believe a selection procedure appears related to the job, while predictive validity assess applicants' beliefs that the selection procedure will predict future job performance (Smither et al., 1993).

Researchers and practitioners have pointed out unique factors about selection that impact the deployment of gamified solutions (DuVernet & Popp, 2014; Handler et al., 2014, May). For instance, selection contexts are focused on measuring skills or characteristics, while other HR processes are concerned with correcting behavior or motivating employees. Moreover, repeated practice may be counterproductive for the purposes of selection contexts, as the primary desire is to measure differences in relevant KSAOs, rather than bringing all candidates up to a standard level of proficiency following repeated practice opportunities. These unique factors inherent in assessment contexts put some constraints on the degree to which certain game elements found in other HR functions, such as training, can be applied to selection contexts.

Recent research has reported survey results evidencing that some social media platforms with gamified elements such as LinkedIn are being used by recruiters and hiring managers not only for recruitment purposes, but also in making selection decisions (Brown & Vaughn, 2011; Davison, Maraist, & Bing, 2011; Kluemper & Rosen, 2009). Many questions still remain, however, as to whether the gamified elements that a prospective candidate displays on his or her profile (e.g., number of skill endorsements from peers, publicly displayed honors & awards, certifications) affect ultimate job offer outcomes.

Despite the constraints unique to selection contexts, many HR consulting firms have recently begun leveraging gamification alongside traditional behavioral science principles in ways that are disrupting the traditional assessment space (Gonsalves, 2011; Rampbell, 2014). These organizations continue to find innovative ways to integrate game elements such as narrative context, avatars, 3-D environments, and time pressure into selection assessments. Additionally, some assessment developers are using game elements to provide feedback to candidates in a variety of ways including progress bars, badges, levels, and error notification.

SHAKER, an HR consulting firm, recently developed two gamified assessments for logistic associate roles at a Fortune 500 retail organization. In one simulated freight loading exercise, candidates are presented with a narrative relating the importance of safely and efficiently loading store freight. The candidates are then directed to view brief training on the exercise, including a demonstration of the task they are asked to perform. Following the additional instructions and demonstration, candidates load freight in a simulated on-screen environment according to pre-established rules dictating the optimal piece to load in the back of a truck dock. The particular task or item that the candidate is currently completing, as well as the total numbers of items in this experience, is provided on the top right of each screen to provide feedback to the candidate about his/her progress. As the assessment experience progresses, the task becomes increasingly challenging and complex. The freight loading exercise is intended to measure several constructs, including spatial reasoning ability and accuracy; speed and efficiency; and ability to follow directions and procedures.

Another game element leveraged within this exercise is the use of two levels, in which the first level involves picking only the next box to load, whereas the second level involves optimally filling the remainder of the empty space in the back of the simulated truck bed without violating the stacking rules provided in the instructions. Rapid, instantaneous feedback is provided to the candidate in level two, as when a loading error is made, the box automatically animates back to the pallet on the left side of the screen, and the candidate must use a different box size or placement in the truck dock to continue. The fun and ease of use factor is further enhanced by aesthetic design and platform considerations (Palmer, Lunceford, & Patton, 2012).

Within the second gamified simulation developed for this organization's logistics associate roles, a computer-based simulation mimics the same tasks that the logistics associates currently perform - filling an inventory order efficiently and accurately. Candidates are presented with inventory information emerging from a virtual label printer. They are required to use information presented on the left side of the screen, and match the inventory numbers with the merchandise presented on shelves on the right side of the screen. Once the candidate identifies a match, he or she must drag and drop the appropriate quantity of each product into the box. Sound effects and text strategically positioned near the box provide instantaneous feedback to inform the candidate that a product was successfully added.

The candidate fills a number of orders during the experience, and as with the load store freight exercise, this simulation becomes progressively more difficult as the candidate completes each task and advances through multiple levels. Throughout the exercise, the candidate must attend to a distractor task where they must monitor a virtual battery indicator for the label printer. The candidate must click a "Change Battery" button when the indicator light turns red, and then return to the order filling exercise. This exercise also consists of two levels. The order filling simulation is utilized as a method to capture several constructs important to success in the role. These constructs include efficiency and accuracy in matching numbers, accurate counting of merchandise, and multitasking skill.

Both of these gamified assessment experiences were found to link with the organization's key competencies, functional competencies, and core KSAOs. Taken together, these two experiences demonstrate a high degree of content-related validity evidence, as well as face validity to candidates, as they were built to reflect the requirements of the logistics roles as seen during job observation activities and extensively documented by a job analysis of these roles. The progressively increasing difficulty and instantaneous feedback in the assessment experiences are likely to increase motivation to complete the exercise through the motivational mechanisms of flow (Reeves & Read, 2009) and/or those described in goal setting theory (Locke & Latham, 2002).

In a different example, assessment developer, Knack, has leveraged gamification to measure constructs such as perceptiveness, creativity, and quick-thinking, to predict performance across a broad range of job families (Dormehl, 2014). In one of Knack's gamified offerings, Wasabi Waiter, candidates play the role of waiter and chef, and proceed through a narrative context which involves assisting customers. The candidates take orders and prepare dishes according to customers' facial expressions and other environmental cues. Throughout the experience, prospective candidates are provided a strong storyline and put into the position of a sushi chef. However, job relevance to particular jobs may feel less face valid to candidates than what might be developed for a single organization and role.

While gamification's emerging presence in selection contexts holds significant promise for ushering in an era of fun and engaging assessments, there are still some concerns that must be addressed before organizations are likely to feel fully comfortable implementing these tools. For example, the extent to which candidates will view game-like assessments as having high face validity, or measuring the KSAOs required to be successful in certain roles (e.g., managerial roles) is unclear. Concerns have also begun to surface surrounding the construct validity of heavily gamified assessments, regarding the possibility that some gamified assessments measure computer skill or video game experience instead of job or organizationally relevant competencies.

In implementing a gamified selection tool, the constructs assessed need to be studied and researched with due diligence regarding the degree to which they demonstrate construct validity. As with any selection tool, gamified applications used in personnel selection must be developed on the basis of an adequately performed job analysis and with the intent of capturing job relevant KSAOs (AERA, 1999; SIOP, 2003). Having the technology alone is not sufficient justification for the development and/or deployment of a gamified tool (Callan et al., 2014).

Aside from concerns surrounding the presence or absence of different forms of validity, gamified selection procedures are also susceptible to unique issues not encountered in traditional selection batteries. Humorous, yet concerning anecdotal examples can be found in the archives of assessment vendor technical support databases. For example, it is not unheard of for candidates to request an opportunity to retake sections of gamified assessments because their children thought the system was a game and completed it when they stepped away from the computer. This is a concern that would be less prevalent in proctored selection assessments, but with the general trend toward unproctored web-based assessments, it is an issue that is likely to increase in the future (Tippins, 2009).

Game elements that engender overt competition among candidates for employment have also been cited for their potential to result in negative consequences for organizations (Callan et al., 2014). Callan and colleagues (2014) discussed a fictitious example of a selection procedure which actively encourages applicants to compete with one another to gain points as they proceed through a battery of various measures. The candidates in this scenario also have the ability to monitor their relative standing on a leaderboard throughout the assessment process. The authors noted several risks and limitations associated with this gamified initiative. The first potential problem is that if candidates are concerned about maximizing their scores on a leaderboard, this does not necessarily motivate and reinforce desired responses (i.e., accurate and truthful responses). While impression management and faking are accepted limitations in the world of personnel selection, particularly within the non-cognitive measures, overtly and explicitly reinforcing this behavior is likely to have a detrimental impact on assessment validities (Callan et al., 2014; Hough & Johnson, 2013).

Training

As job complexity increases, training and onboarding programs will remain essential initiatives in helping organizations shape a competitive workforce (Salas & Cannon-Bowers, 2001). Training is viewed as extremely critical, in fact, that in 2012 alone, organizations in the United States spent an estimated $164.2 billion on employee training programs (American Society for Training and Development, 2013). Organizations have collectively made this astonishingly large investment under the assumption that training programs will improve the performance of their employees, positively impacting their bottom line (Salas & Cannon-Bowers, 2001). To the contrary, many studies have shown that knowledge and behaviors taught during training do not always transfer back to the job, thus failing to improve organizational performance (Goldstein & Ford, 2002; Salas, Cannon-Bowers, Rhodenizer, & Bowers, 1999).

One hindrance to the potential effectiveness of training program is a lack of employee motivation to complete them. In order for training programs to exert intended influence on employee, and ultimately organizational, performance, employees must remain motivated and engaged enough follow through and complete the entire training (Goldstein & Ford, 2002).

As mentioned in the introduction to this chapter, and echoed in other reviews of gamification in HR practices (e.g., DuVernet & Popp, 2014), training is the area of human resources most naturally lending itself to gamification, and gamification offers the promise of resolving the motivational and engagement issues that have long plagued training and onboarding programs. This is partially due to the relative ease of applying gaming elements to training programs, the widespread acceptance of e-learning, and the need for employees to remain motivated and engaged through the duration of training programs.

Kirkpatrick's (1959) model for evaluating training effectiveness describes four criteria of successful training programs. These criteria pertain to user reactions to the experience, knowledge/skill acquisition, behavioral outcomes or training transfer, and organizational level outcomes. Interested readers should reference Kirkpatrick's work for further context regarding what constitutes an effective training experience. Game elements can impact all four of Kirkpatrick's evaluation criteria, as described below.

Given gamification's status as a relatively new phenomenon, there is a paucity of empirical research on its effectiveness in organizational practice. Empirical studies on gamification in educational and other learning contexts, however, provide a suitable research base can be leveraged to guide best practices in organizational learning contexts. In fact, games themselves have been researched in training or learning contexts since as far back as the early 1980s (e.g., Malone, 1981). While the distinction has been made between games and gamification, research on both games and gamification can be leveraged to support gamified initiatives in organizations.

Nearly all of the common game elements discussed in gamification research can, and have been applied in one way or another to training and onboarding programs (Kapp, Blair, & Wesch, 2014; Landers & Callan, 2011). Indeed, avatars, levels, badges, points, leaderboards, progress bars, instantaneous feedback, and narrative context, can be seamlessly applied to a wide variety of training environments. Moreover, game elements can often complement one another to further improve the likelihood of employees remaining engaged throughout longer training cycles. Some examples of different ways to leverage these elements will now be described with the goal of offering increased clarity regarding the suitability of gamified solutions to improve training programs.

Avatars are among game elements most commonly mentioned when discussing gamification. Avatars allow for self-representation in virtual worlds, a feature that can be leveraged to improve engagement in e-learning modules. E-learning modules have become commonplace in organizational training contexts due to the flexibility they offer to both organizations and employees. Avatars are often leveraged to impact employee motivation and engagement, as opposed to the learning itself. Allowing trainees to customize their avatars is one tactic that can be leveraged to get trainees personally invested in training programs. This can be especially effective for programs that otherwise may experience significant employee attrition as the training proceeds. Supporting this notion, empirical studies have shown that avatars increase trainee time spent on tasks (Lim & Reeves, 2010). Avatars are one of the key mechanisms described by Reeves and Read (2009) in creating a flow state during different gamified initiatives.

While avatars can initially provide motivation to complete training modules, their biggest impact may lie in their ability to facilitate the inclusion of many other game elements, including 3-D environments, badges, levels, and points (Reeves & Read, 2009). Once an avatar has been created and placed into the context of a virtual world designed for training, these other elements naturally follow suit, further improving the likelihood of training programs having the desired impact on employees and organizations, through initiation of a flow state.

Three-dimensional environments, coupled with avatars, can provide an immersive and engaging training experience in which employees can acquire new skills or knowledge. The line between gamified training experiences and serious games or simulations is one that is easily blurred in both popular media and academic circles. As the focus here is on the former, fully immersive serious games and battle simulations used by the army are beyond the scope of this chapter. The good news here is that 3-D environments in more traditionally defined gamified solutions, while still costly, do fall within realistic budgets of many HR departments. In addition to helping create an immersive flow state, 3-D worlds can also satisfy the need for autonomy if they allow employees to freely explore the environment.

Badges, levels, and points all fall under the broad umbrella of feedback, a critical ingredient in effective training solutions. Immediate feedback can play an integral role in an employee's ability to understand the desired actions or behaviors training programs are designed to convey. When feedback is separated from actions during training, learning becomes significantly more difficult (Paharia, 2013). During gamified e-learning experiences, the feedback an employee receives can be nearly instantaneous, thus more effectively shaping that employees behavior and improving the learning that occurs during specific modules. Properly leveraged points, badges, levels, and other feedback can be used to encourage employees to continue to pursue desired paths of action, while discouraging the continuation of less desired patterns of thoughts or behaviors. As mentioned earlier, feedback truly can tie to any of the major motivational theories introduced in the beginning of this chapter.

Badges, levels, and points are all forms of rewards that can continue to engage employees during training modules. These rewards also directly facilitate the learning of critical knowledge and skills. This innate desire to collect and display badges affords organizations the ability to leverage badges to improve employee engagement and motivation to an extent not normally realized through more traditional training programs. Improved engagement and motivation then impacts organizational results, because employees who are more engaged will spend more time, and proceed further in training programs. These employees should, in theory, acquire significantly more information than employees who are less engaged or motivated during training modules.

Badges also afford organizations the ability to seamlessly integrate them into training programs in such a way that employees do not initially know the required steps to earn them. This can be beneficial in two ways. First, it keeps these gamified solutions more interesting, as employees will have to work harder to find these hidden badges. It also forces employees to figure out desired actions through a more experimental process (Paharia, 2013). This ties directly into the theory of error management training, which has emerged as a method of improving training effectiveness through providing trainees the opportunity to more actively explore training material and make mistakes along the way (Keith & Frese, 2005). This allows trainees to gain a deeper understanding of the associations between actions and outcomes, control negative emotions traditionally associated with making errors, as well as to improve the overall complexity of the mental models developed during training (Mathieu, Heffner, Goodwin, Salas, & Cannon-Bowers, 2000). More complex or sophisticated mental models allow trainees to then better understand how to handle unexpected resistance that can occur once employees leave the safe confines of a training module and return to the less structured work environment, where other factors are likely to impact the effectiveness of certain actions.

In 2008, the consulting firm Deloitte partnered with Badgeville to build a training program called the Deloitte Leadership Academy. This leadership academy integrated numerous training modules for employees to complete. Included within this gamified initiative were narrative context, badges, and leaderboards. As a testament to the engaging nature of gamified solutions, an employee at Deloitte completed all of the modules, a task that was estimated to take twelve months, in merely six months (Kapp et al., 2014).

In another successful example of gamified training, a solution was leveraged to improve participation in an employee onboarding procedure (Garg, 2014). The solution was developed by MindTickle, and allowed the organization to integrate pre-existing training materials into a gamified framework. This framework included game elements such as narrative context, badges, points, and leaderboards to improve engagement and motivation among new hires to participate in the onboarding program and learn more about the organization. This onboarding solution led the organization to realize benefits in both the completion rates for the onboarding socialization activities, as well as through the employees' overwhelmingly positive reactions to the activities (Garg, 2014).

A final example of feedback's role in shaping employee behavior is a safety training module providing points and other positive encouragement when an employee exhibits safe behaviors within a virtual module, while providing immediate developmental feedback when the employee exhibits behaviors that would be considered safety risks. These follow-ups could be presented in a variety of ways, including visual demonstrations of why the behavior was unsafe, or directions for the employee to go back and reference a specific portion of the training module to better understand why the proposed behavior was risky. The benefits from programs such as these can be significant. For example, Pep Boys ultimately saw a reduction of safety incidents by 45% after implementing a gamified safety training solution (Kapp, 2014).

Performance Management

Performance management involves the study of methods to improve performance at work (DeNisi & Smith, 2014). The Office of Personnel Management (OPM) defines performance management as the "systematic process by which an agency involves its employees, as individuals and members of a group, in improving organizational effectiveness in the accomplishment of agency mission and goals" (OPM, 2014). OPM goes on to define performance management as consisting of various activities such as planning work and setting expectations; monitoring performance on an ongoing basis; developing learning capacity; providing periodic ratings of performance; and offering rewards and incentives for good performance.

Within the domain of I/O psychology, the application of performance management systems have traditionally drawn upon a broad array of well studied motivational theories, spanning from the goal setting theory (Locke & Latham, 1990, 2002), goal orientation theory (Dweck, 1986; VandeWalle, 1997, 2003), and social cognitive theory (Bandura, 1982, 1997; Stajkovic & Luthans, 1998), to name a few.

In addition to workplace motivation theories, much of the research and application within the area of performance management has been focused on examining how employee performance is measured, evaluated, and appraised. Performance appraisal tools, commonly considered important as administrative or developmental guides in managing individual performance, serve a critical role in coupling an employee's performance to the goals and outcomes desired by the organization (Ayers, 2013).

Advocates of gamification in performance management processes argue that gamified interventions will allow for incumbents to create more community and ownership of expertise, allow for openly recognizing each others' achievements and accomplishments, and increase motivation and engagement (Cook, 2013). Gamification elements that appeal to needs for relatedness and help foster social interaction may indeed facilitate these results, but peer-reviewed empirical evidence is currently limited.

Further, Kennedy (2014) postulated that incorporating gamification elements could enhance lawyers' motivation to accomplish goals and tasks, particularly those that are traditionally tedious, cumbersome, or tend to go unfinished through leveraging of a flow state to increase engagement. Within this context, the author postulated that gamification elements such as points and badges, leaderboards, and narrative context could be employed to inspire timely completion of training and onboarding, timekeeping, and billing and collections tasks.

Microsoft provides an example of an organization embracing gamification in performance management functions. Ongoing gamification efforts at Microsoft, referred to as "productivity games," help increase work team engagement, participation, and productivity during voluntary quality assurance and testing efforts such as "Communicate Hope" and "Windows Language Quality Game" (Smith, n.d.). Smith provided that all types of work tasks are not equally suitable for applications of productivity games.

Based on a body of research conducted in the area of productivity game applications at Microsoft, Smith reported productivity games as most effective in expanding one's skills within a role, or using the rote skills that one already possesses to carry out the core organizational citizenship behaviors, or OCBs (Organ, 1988).

Within the Communicate Hope productivity game, Microsoft was able to motivate and entice participants to engage in beta testing a version of software in exchange for earning points for tasks and activities completed. Drawing on altruistic motivations, the points accumulated by Microsoft employees were put toward sponsored disaster relief funds at the conclusion of the project. In addition to the humanitarian benefit, the initiative generated much higher participation rates than found in prior beta testing. Further, reactions and feedback from employees participating in the productivity game were overwhelmingly positive (e.g., 97% of participants reported they would participate in the beta program again as opposed to pre-productivity beta program benchmarks of between 50-75%).

In Microsoft's utilization of the Windows Language Quality Game, the leaders of test and quality assurance again incorporated game elements into one of the more tedious and cumbersome tasks available at the large technology company (Chiang, 2010; Smith, n.d.). In this implementation of what Microsoft refers to as productivity games, incumbents working at Microsoft from nations across the world competed with one another to earn high scores while reviewing beta versions of operating systems delivered in localized languages (Chiang, 2010). The addition of game elements resulted in a faster and more effective way of inspiring participation in a tedious and arduous task, and brought an element of fun to an otherwise more mundane OCB (Smith, n.d.). As a result, Microsoft employees voluntarily reviewed and quality tested potential language issues in the employees' native languages resulting in 36 languages being quality tested in a one month time window with an impressive breadth and depth of coverage.

In another organizational application, Accenture, a management consulting, technology, and outsourcing company, incorporated gamification elements to increase and enhance desired workplace behaviors. The program uses operant conditioning to encourage collaboration and sharing across its global network through tracking 30 activities associated with three key behaviors. Each activity is assigned a point value. Excelling in collaborative behaviors results in an employee receiving monetary rewards, "shoutouts" in internal communications, badges on custom displayed profile pages, and other rewards. Through this program, Leeson (2013) reported observing group-level improvements in organizational metrics indicative of collaboration.

Palmer et al. (2012) described the performance management software utilized by Facebook (Rypple, subsequently acquired by SalesForce.com) that is used to complete internal reviews and for communications. The performance management application, referred to as enterprise gamification, allows incumbents to receive recognition from coworkers (e.g., in the form of badges), create and compete in challenges, and have insight into the projects on which others are currently working.

One gamification intervention intended to spur collaboration and interconnectedness among work colleagues is being facilitated by a small startup, WooBoard, which specializes in a software application that tracks effort and praise in a manner that is visible to the entire workforce (Gardiner, 2014). Through the application, employees can send and receive "woos" for a job well done, and recognize individuals receiving the most "woos" as "wooer of the week." This ties back into the relatedness need of the need satisfaction theories, more specifically SDT (Deci & Ryan, 2000).

Callan and colleagues (2014) presented additional fictitious case study examples of inappropriately applied or underutilized gamification within the domain of performance management. In one instance, the authors detail an example of an organization struggling to have managers complete subordinate performance appraisals on time and with enough detail to facilitate improved performance. The gamified intervention awarded points to managers for timeliness and level of detail they provided in appraisals. Point totals would then be then tracked and published. Awarding points based on submission length may indirectly reward wordy submissions of poor substantive value over more concisely written, well articulated reviews. Callan and colleagues (2014) also noted limitations associated with efficiency, resource intensiveness, and subjectivity associated with having human resources personnel provide qualitative coding of responses. The researchers call for special care to be taken to ensure that the reward or incentive system does not place undue emphasis on the speed of manager evaluations at the expense of quality. Lastly, these authors note a lack of known empirical or judicial precedent or support in the use of gamification in the sensitive area of performance appraisal incentive systems, and caution about the use of such a system from a risk mitigation perspective.

In addition to the aforementioned cautions, to achieve success implementing gamification into the performance management process, it is essential that organizational goals and strategic plans align with the intervention or application of the gamified processes. This recommendation is not unique to the use of gamification, but is critical in the development of any system intended for use in performance management (Ayers, 2013).

Practitioners should be mindful that gamification of performance management system conveys, whether implicitly or explicitly, information about what the organization values. If not careful, users may construe that other behaviors are not valued. For example, if an organization implements a competitive gaming element around individual sales, it is important that incentives are also implemented to rewards quality of service, accuracy, and following appropriate policies and procedures if these are valued by the organization (Callan et al., 2014).

Considerations regarding whether gamified performance management systems would generally align with the culture and climate of an organization should also be examined. At present, not all companies and industry sectors may react well to even the best thought out, strategically communicated, and deployed gamified interventions. Gamification advocates have suggested this solution is well suited for millennials who desire more immediate feedback, are computer-savvy, and may bore easily and disengage if presented with more traditional performance monitoring and incentive interventions in the workplace (Ankeny, 2013; Burmeister, 2014). Considerations and research targeted toward addressing whether the organizational climate for a technology-infused performance management system would be valuable. In addition, reactions by employees to the specific gaming elements should be given thoughtful consideration. For example, implementing a semi-public leaderboard within an organization's internal social networking site may inadvertently have negative motivational consequences for those employees consistently finding themselves toward the bottom of the leaderboard (Callan et al., 2014). Repeated negative feedback could lead to a reduction in effort, downwardly revised goals, and other unintentional negative consequences (Mikulincer, 1988, 1989).

CONSIDERATIONS AND BEST PRACTICE RECOMMENDATIONS

Now that the motivational theories and examples of gamified HR solutions have been discussed, it will be beneficial to cover considerations and best practices for organizational leaders anticipating a foray into the world of gamified HR solutions. As alluded to above, gamified applications are not necessarily a silver bullet. However, well thought out gamified applications have the potential to positively impact a broad range of organizational issues. Conversely, haphazardly implementing gamified solutions will not magically rectify problems facing an underperforming or disengaged workforce. In fact, Gartner has estimated that 80% of gamified interventions in organizations will fail to meet their business objectives due to poor design (Gartner, 2012). This makes it critical to calibrate expectations and provide guidance to better understand if gamified applications are appropriate for specific organizational contexts.

The most important caveat facing gamified HR applications in organizations relates to the initial intention driving implementation of a gamified solution. Gamification for gamification's sake is not an effective course of action for organizations, as creating a solution misaligned with the organization's goals can actually do more harm than good.

Gamification has reached that rarified air in the archives of organizational buzzwords that few initiatives will ever reach. This popularity breeds two critical implications. First, popular media will tout the potential benefits of gamification, enticing organizational leaders to turn toward gamification as a solution to a variety of organizational issues. HR practitioners and organizational leaders should take caution in evaluating the content of the ensuing media storm and rely upon gamification and HR literature, such as that which is cited within this chapter, to inform decisions about when and how to best introduce game elements in HR systems.

The most important step in a proper gamified implementation is to align the solution with key business objectives. This necessitates conducting a proper needs analysis to understand what objectives organizations are trying to accomplish with the proposed gamified solution. A thorough needs analysis will help prevent an organization from investing large sums of money in a misaligned initiative. Aligning a gamified solution with the needs of the organization requires an evaluation of intentions for improvements at the organizational level and also in designing specific game elements. As described earlier, game elements, such as badges, can reinforce behaviors; however, organizations need to ensure they are leveraging such game elements to reinforce the intended behaviors, attitudes, or knowledge.

Another caveat that resonates across all four HR process categories above deals with understanding the demographics of the group the gamified solution is designed to impact. Certain demographic issues could lead to a gamified initiative falling short of its potential, or in more severe cases, the potential for operational, or even legal repercussions. One example of a potential demographic concern for organizations deals with gender and competition. Croson and Gneezy (2009) found that women are less likely to prefer engaging in competitive situations. Thus, if the gamified solution rewards competitive individuals, the organization needs to ensure that competition is aligned with key business outcomes to help mitigate potential for negative backlash stemming from the gamified solution.

Demographic concerns regarding age and generational cohorts may also arise. While gamified solutions may be embraced by younger applicants who were raised on video games, the experience may be completely different for older workers, which could lead to a disengaged subgroup within an organization's population. Adding unfamiliar, and potentially time-consuming, tasks to work processes, could lead to high levels of frustration among this less technologically-savvy cohort.

Based on the potential for performance and reaction differences to emerge among various demographics within organizations, including legally protected classes, decision makers would be well served to survey the legal landscape surrounding the processes in which a gamified solution would focus. As a function of living in a litigious society, HR departments must always be cautious implementing high-stakes processes, including those that may impact employment, promotions, or compensation. This further necessitates ensuring that the gamified solution under consideration links to a specific business objective.

If the potential exists for age, gender, or ethnic group differences to emerge on one of these high-stakes processes, then the only way to build a case for legal defensibility will be through proving business necessity. This means first showing that the gamified process is a valid recruitment, selection, training, or performance management tool. Once the validity has been established, then the impetus is on the organization to further demonstrate that an equally valid option that would exhibit lower levels of adverse impact does not exist. Ultimately, the defensibility of any gamified process will hinge on those two factors. This again speaks to the criticality of properly aligning the proposed gamification initiative, and documenting the validity and utility of the solution upon implementation.

Gauging the organizational culture is another critical step in designing and implementing a gamified solution as certain organizational cultures may be inherently more receptive to gamified HR solutions. In receptive cultures, it may be acceptable to implement extensive gamified solutions. Conversely, in less receptive organizations, implementation of gamified processes will need to be handled with more finesse. In these organizations, the decision makers may be wise to start with more focused gamified initiatives. This situation is one where the more likely path to success is one paved with small wins, as opposed to one big swing for the fence (Amabile & Kramer, 2011; Bryson, 1988). A few low risk successes with gamification can help build support within an organization for larger-scale changes. Starting smaller is also a good way to determine what works and what does not work within an organization.

Cost is another key factor to evaluate when considering gamified solutions. As with any other technologically-driven solution, gamification comes at a cost. Top-tier, fully customized gamified solutions can easily set an organization back hundreds of thousands, or even millions of dollars. While not every organization will require such a media-rich solution, cost is likely to be a significant constraint for many organizations looking to gamify. Moreover, a poorly designed gamified solution can actually do more harm than good. For example, a lengthy, clunky, avatar-based selection tool may turn candidates away from an organization rather than increase organizational attraction. As a best practice, organizations should seriously consider the quality of the solutions falling within their budget to better decide if gamification is an undertaking worth pursuing.

Mechanisms of motivation can also serve as important caveats for organizations to heed when considering a gamified solution. While game mechanics such as badges, points, and leaderboards can serve as powerful motivators of behavior, they should be implemented with caution. As mentioned above, rewards increase the likelihood of a person performing the rewarded behavior, but this mechanism is only helpful if the rewarded behavior is directly tied to a desired outcome. Callan and colleagues (2014) brought this to the forefront in depicting a hypothetical gamified recruitment solution, where an organization rewarded candidates for clicking on links to learn information within a recruitment webpage. This reward reinforces clicking on different aspects of the recruitment website, but does not necessarily reinforce actual learning of the key information about the company to help decide if one is a good fit.

Ultimately, the success of any HR initiative will depend on the buy in and attitudes of all constituents involved. That is, having management and leadership repeatedly reinforce the links between gamified applications and strategic organizational goals is the most likely way to ensure that employees have knowledge of and understand how participating in gamified initiatives aligns with an organization's priorities (Ayers, 2013; Gabris & Ihrke, 2000; Rodgers, Hunter, & Rogers, 1995). Further, prior research has suggested that strengthening employee alignment is associated with positive work attitudes, employee performance outcomes, retention, and engagement (Kristof-Brown & Stevens, 2001; Mone & London, 2014).

CONCLUSION

While there are critical considerations to undertake before going all-in on gamification, the potential benefits that can be realized with properly implemented solutions still outweigh the risks for many organizations. The majority of the case studies provided in this chapter show examples of organizations that waded into the unknown territory of gamification and were able to experience great returns.

As mentioned in the previous section, implementing gamified solutions does come with risks. The best an organization can do is to gather the information necessary to make informed decisions and minimize these risks. The information provided throughout this chapter is intended to help decision makers understand the steps that should be taken to help improve the likelihood of success if they choose to gamify an HR process.

Another point to consider here is that all organizations are different. What works in one organization may not work in another, even if they seem similar on the surface. This is why it truly becomes incumbent on decision makers to leverage the expertise they have regarding potential facilitators and derailers of gamification success within their organization, as opposed to blindly copying a process that worked well in a similar organization.

The increased prevalence of gamification in HR processes is an exciting trend for practitioners and researchers alike. This is still a relatively untapped domain in terms of empirical studies examining which game elements are more or less likely to positively impact different HR processes. To date, much of what has been introduced into organizations is based on research in other domains, leaving significant room for improvement of these methodologies to those interested in advancing the science behind this trend. The proposed links to motivational theories provided in this chapter should serve as a strong starting point for researchers seeking to take initiative and begin investigating gamification's impact on organizational processes. An increase in methodologically rigorous examinations of these proposed links between game elements and motivational theories will provide a stronger, and much needed, theoretical framework that will better define the situations in which inclusion of specific game elements are likely to have their most positive impact on HR processes. As evidenced by the numerous examples provided here, it is not likely that a single motivational theory will explain the effectiveness of all gamified initiatives. Instead, it is likely that the various theories of motivation will complement each other in explaining ways to improve engagement in HR processes when game elements have been added to the mix.

REFERENCES

Amabile, T., & Kramer, S. (2011). *The progress principle: Using small wins to ignite joy, engagement, and creativity at work*. Harvard Business Press.

American Educational Research Association. (1999). *Standards for educational and psychological testing*. Washington, D.C.: Author.

Ankeny, J. (2013). Playing for keeps. *Entrepreneur, 41*(9), 62–64.

Antin, J., & Churchill, E. F. (2011). Badges in social media: A social psychological perspective. Proceedings from CHI 2011 gamification workshop, Vancouver, BC, Canada. ACM.

Ayers, R. S. (2013). Building goal alignment in federal agencies' performance appraisal programs. *Public Personnel Management, 42*(4), 495–520. doi:10.1177/0091026013496077

Bandura, A. (1982). Self-efficacy mechanism in human agency. *The American Psychologist, 37*(2), 122–147. doi:10.1037/0003-066X.37.2.122

Bandura, A. (1997). *Self-efficacy: The exercise of control.* New York, NY: W H Freeman/Times Books/ Henry Holt & Co.

Barber, A. E. (1998). *Recruiting employees: Individual and organizational perspectives.* Thousand Oaks, CA, US: Sage Publications, Inc.

Barber, A. E., & Roehling, M. V. (1993). Job postings and the decision to interview: A verbal protocol analysis. *The Journal of Applied Psychology, 78*(5), 845–856. doi:10.1037/0021-9010.78.5.845

Binning, J. F., & Barrett, G. V. (1989). Validity of personnel decisions: A conceptual analysis of the inferential and evidential bases. *The Journal of Applied Psychology, 74*(3), 478–494. doi:10.1037/0021-9010.74.3.478

Brown, V. R., & Vaughn, E. (2011). The writing on the (Facebook) wall: The use of social networking sites in hiring decisions. *Journal of Business and Psychology, 26*(2), 219–225. doi:10.1007/s10869-011-9221-x

Bryson, J. (1988). Strategic planning: Big wins and small wins. *Public Money & Management, 8*(3), 11–15. doi:10.1080/09540968809387483

Burmeister, B. (2014). Befriend the trend: Gaming goes to work. *Finweek, 1/2/2014,* 7.

Burnett, M., Clayton, P., Crispin, G., Dingee, K., Gotkin, B., & Hudson, C. … Tice, D. (2014). *Candidate Experience 2013.* Retrieved from http://nam.thecandidateexperienceawards.org/2013-cande-results/

Cable, D. M., & Yu, K. Y. T. (2006). Managing job seekers' organizational image beliefs: The role of media richness and media credibility. *The Journal of Applied Psychology, 91*(4), 828–840. doi:10.1037/0021-9010.91.4.828 PMID:16834508

Callan, R. C., Bauer, K. N., & Landers, R. N. (2014). How to avoid the dark side of gamification: Ten business scenarios and their unintended consequences. In T. Reiners & L. Wood (Eds.), *Gamification in Education and Business.* New York, NY: Springer.

Carpenter, J. E., & Doverspike, D. (2014, May). *Altering images during selection: Assessment content matters.* Poster session presented at the meeting of the Society for Industrial and Organizational Psychologists, Honolulu, HI.

Chiang, O. (2010). When playing video games at work makes dollars and sense. *Forbes.* Retrieved from http://www.forbes.com/2010/08/09/microsoft-workplace-training-technology-videogames.html

Colarelli, S. M. (1984). Methods of communication and mediating processes in realistic job previews. *The Journal of Applied Psychology, 69*(4), 633–642. doi:10.1037/0021-9010.69.4.633

Connelly, B. L., Certo, S. T., Ireland, R. D., & Reutzel, C. R. (2011). Signaling theory: A review and assessment. *Journal of Management, 37*(1), 39–67. doi:10.1177/0149206310388419

Cook, W. (2013). Five reasons you can't ignore gamification. *Incentive, 187*, 22-23. Retrieved from http://www.incentivemag.com/Incentive-Programs/Non-Sales/Articles/5-Reasons-You-Can-t-Ignore-Gamification/

Croson, R., & Gneezy, U. (2009). Gender differences in preferences. *Journal of Economic Literature, 47*(2), 448–474. doi:10.1257/jel.47.2.448

Csikszentmihályi, M. (1990). The domain of creativity. In M. A. Runco & R. S. Albert (Eds.), *Theories of creativity* (pp. 190–212). Thousand Oaks, CA, US: Sage Publications, Inc.

Csikszentmihályi, M. (1997). *Finding flow: The psychology of engagement with everyday life*. New York, NY, US: Basic Books.

Csikszentmihályi, M., & LeFevre, J. (1989). Optimal experience in work and leisure. *Journal of Personality and Social Psychology, 56*(5), 815–822. doi:10.1037/0022-3514.56.5.815 PMID:2724069

Davison, H., Maraist, C., & Bing, M. N. (2011). Friend or foe? The promise and pitfalls of using social networking sites for HR decisions. *Journal of Business and Psychology, 26*(2), 153–159. doi:10.1007/s10869-011-9215-8

De Geode, M. E. E., Van Vianen, A. E. M., & Klehe, U.-C. (2011). Attracting applicants on the web: PO fit, industry culture stereotypes, and website design. *International Journal of Selection and Assessment, 19*(1), 51–61. doi:10.1111/j.1468-2389.2010.00534.x

Deci, E. L., & Ryan, R. M. (1985). The general causality orientations scale: Self-determination in personality. *Journal of Research in Personality, 19*(2), 109–134. doi:10.1016/0092-6566(85)90023-6

Deci, E. L., & Ryan, R. M. (2000). The 'what' and 'why' of goal pursuits: Human needs and the self-determination of behavior. *Psychological Inquiry, 11*(4), 227–268. doi:10.1207/S15327965PLI1104_01

Deloitte (2014). *Virtual Tour - Life at Deloitte*. Retrieved from http://mycareer.deloitte.com/cn/en/life-at-deloitte/virtual-tour

DeNisi, A., & Smith, C. E. (2014). Performance appraisal, performance management, and firm-level performance: A review, a proposed model, and new directions for future research. *The Academy of Management Annals, 8*(1), 127–179. doi:10.1080/19416520.2014.873178

Deterding, S., Dixon, D., Khaled, R., & Nacke, L. (2011). From game design elements to gamefulness: Defining "gamification". Proceedings from MindTrek '11. *Proceedings of the 15th International Academic MindTrek Conference: Envisioning future media environments*. Tampere, Finland. ACM. doi:10.1145/2181037.2181040

Deterding, S., Sicart, M., Nacke, L., O'Hara, K., & Dixon, D. (2011, May). Gamification: Using game-design elements in non-gaming contexts. In CHI'11 Extended Abstracts on Human Factors in Computing Systems (pp. 2425-2428). ACM. doi:10.1145/1979742.1979575

Dineen, B. R., & Soltis, S. M. (2011). Recruitment: A review of research and emerging directions. In S. Zedeck (Ed.), APA handbook of industrial and organizational psychology: Vol. 2. *Selecting and developing members for the organization* (pp. 43–66). Washington, DC, US: American Psychological Association; doi:10.1037/12170-002

Domínguez, A., Saenz-de-Navarrete, J., de-Marcos, L., Fernández-Sanz, L., Pagés, C., & Martínez-Herráiz, J.-J. (2013). Gamifying learning experiences: Practical implications and outcomes. *Computers & Education*, *63*, 380–392. doi:10.1016/j.compedu.2012.12.020

Dormehl, L. (2014, May 26). Your web presence just picked your next job. *Wired*. Retrieved from http://www.wired.co.uk/magazine/archive/2014/05/features/web-presence-employment

Downs, S., Farr, R. M., & Colbeck, L. (1978). Self-appraisal: A convergence of selection and guidance. *Journal of Occupational Psychology*, *51*(3), 271–278. doi:10.1111/j.2044-8325.1978.tb00423.x

DuVernet, A. M., & Popp, E. (2014). Practitioners' forum: Gamification of workplace practices. *The Industrial-Organizational psychologist*, *52*(1), 39–44.

Dweck, C. S. (1986). Motivational processes affecting learning. *The American Psychologist*, *41*(10), 1040–1048. doi:10.1037/0003-066X.41.10.1040

Fishbein, M., & Ajzen, I. (1975). *Belief, attitude, intention, and behavior: An introduction to theory and research*. Reading, MA: Addison-Wesley.

Gabris, G. T., & Ihrke, D. M. (2000). Improving employee acceptance towards performance appraisal and merit pay systems: The role of leadership credibility. *Review of Public Personnel Administration*, *20*(1), 41–68. doi:10.1177/0734371X0002000104

Gardiner, B. (2014, March). Gamification the new game changer? How enterprise gamification is enhancing innovation, change management, and collaboration. *CIO*. Retrieved from http://www.cio.com.au/article/539654/gamification_new_game_changer_/

Garg, M. (2014). Structural gamification for onboarding employees. In *K. M. Kapp, L. Blair & R. Mesch's The Gamification of Learning and Instruction Fieldbook: Ideas into Practice*. John Wiley & Sons.

Garris, R., Ahlers, R., & Driskell, J. E. (2002). Games, motivation, and learning: A research and practice model. *Simulation & Gaming*, *33*(4), 441–467. doi:10.1177/1046878102238607

Gartner Predicts Over 70 Percent of Global 2000 Organisations Will Have at Least One Gamified Application by 2014. (2011). Gartner, Inc. Retrieved from http://www.gartner.com/newsroom/id/1844115

Gartner Says by 2014, 80 Percent of Current Gamified Applications Will Fail to Meet Business Objectives Primarily Due to Poor Design. (2012). Gartner, Inc. Retrieved from http://www.gartner.com/newsroom/id/2251015

Goldstein, I. L., & Ford, J. K. (2002). *Training in organizations: Needs assessment, development, and evaluation* (4th ed.). Belmont, CA, US: Wadsworth/Thomson Learning.

Gonsalves, A. (2011, September 29). Shaker Consulting culls weak job seekers with online games. *Bloomberg*. Retrieved from http://www.bloomberg.com/news/2011-09-26/shaker-consulting-culls-weak-job-seekers-with-online-games.html

Guion, R. M. (2011). *Assessment, measurement, and prediction for personnel decisions* (2nd ed.). New York, NY, US: Routledge/Taylor & Francis Group.

Handler, C., Popp, E., Brodbeck, C. C., Geimer, J., Kubisiak, C., Moye, N., et al. (2014, May). *Challenges and innovations of using game-like assessments in selection.* Proceedings of the Society for Industrial and Organizational Psychologists, Honolulu, HI.

Hough, L. M., & Johnson, J. W. (2013). Use and importance of personality variables in work settings. In N. W. Schmitt, S. Highhouse, & I. B. Weiner (Eds.), Handbook of psychology: Vol. 12. *Industrial and organizational psychology* (2nd ed., pp. 211–243). Hoboken, NJ, US: John Wiley & Sons Inc.

Hsu, S., Chang, J., & Lee, C. (2013). Designing attractive gamification features for collaborative storytelling websites. *Cyberpsychology, Behavior, and Social Networking, 16*(6), 428–435. doi:10.1089/cyber.2012.0492 PMID:23438264

Iles, P. A., & Robertson, I. T. (1989). The impact of personnel selection procedures on candidates. In P. Herriot (Ed.), *Assessment and selection in organizations* (pp. 257–271). Chichester, UK: John Wiley & Sons.

Kapp, K. M. (2012). *The gamification of learning and instruction: game-based methods and strategies for training and education.* John Wiley & Sons.

Kapp, K. M. (2014, Spring). What L&D professionals need to know about gamification. *Training Industry Magazine,* 16-19. Retrieved from [REMOVED HYPERLINK FIELD]http://www.nxtbook.com/nxtbooks/trainingindustry/tiq_2014spring/

Kapp, K. M., Blair, L., & Mesch, R. (2013). *The Gamification of Learning and Instruction Fieldbook: Ideas Into Practice.* John Wiley & Sons.

Keith, N., & Frese, M. (2005). Self-Regulation in Error Management Training: Emotion Control and Metacognition as Mediators of Performance Effects. *The Journal of Applied Psychology, 90*(4), 677–691. doi:10.1037/0021-9010.90.4.677 PMID:16060786

Kennedy, D. (2014). What can 'gamification' do for lawyers? *ABA Journal.* Retrieved online: http://www.abajournal.com/magazine/article/what_can_gamification_do_for_lawyers/

Kirkpatrick, D. L. (1959). Techniques for evaluating training programs. *Journal of ASTD, 11,* 1–13.

Kluemper, D. H., & Rosen, P. A. (2009). Future employment selection methods: Evaluating social networking web sites. *Journal of Managerial Psychology, 24*(6), 567–580. doi:10.1108/02683940910974134

Kristof-Brown, A. L., & Stevens, C. K. (2001). Goal congruence in project teams: Does the fit between members' personal mastery and performance goals matter? *The Journal of Applied Psychology, 86*(6), 1083–1095. doi:10.1037/0021-9010.86.6.1083 PMID:11768052

Landers, R. N., Bauer, K. N., Callan, R. C., & Armstrong, M. B. (2014). Psychological theory and the gamification of learning. In T. Reiners & L. Wood (Eds.), *Gamification in Education and Business.* New York, NY: Springer.

Landers, R. N., & Callan, R. C. (2011) Casual social games as serious games: The psychology of gamification in undergraduate education and employment training. In M. Ma, A. Oikonomou & L.C. Jain (Eds.), Serious Games and Edutainment Applications (pp. 399-423). Springer.

Latham, G. P., & Seijts, G. H. (1999). The effects of proximal and distal goals on performance on a moderately complex task. *Journal of Organizational Behavior, 20*(4), 421–429. doi:10.1002/(SICI)1099-1379(199907)20:4<421::AID-JOB896>3.0.CO;2-#

Leeson, C. (2013). Driving KM behaviors and adoption through gamification. *KM World, 22*, 10-11; 20.

Levy, P. E. (2012). *Industrial organizational psychology: Understanding the workplace* (4th ed.). New York, NY: Worth Publishers.

Lim, S., & Reeves, B. (2010). Computer agents versus avatars: Responses to interactive game characters controlled by a computer or other player. *International Journal of Human-Computer Studies, 68*(1-2), 57–68. doi:10.1016/j.ijhcs.2009.09.008

Locke, E. A. (1968). Effects of knowledge of results, feedback in relation to standards, and goals on reaction-time performance. *The American Journal of Psychology, 81*(4), 566–574. doi:10.2307/1421061 PMID:5760037

Locke, E. A., & Latham, G. P. (1990). *A theory of goal setting and task performance*. Englewood Cliffs, NJ: Prentice-Hall.

Locke, E. A., & Latham, G. P. (2002). Building a practically useful theory of goal setting and task motivation: A 35-year odyssey. *The American Psychologist, 57*(9), 705–717. doi:10.1037/0003-066X.57.9.705 PMID:12237980

Malone, T. W. (1981). Toward a theory of intrinsically motivating instruction. *Cognitive Science, 5*(4), 333–369. doi:10.1207/s15516709cog0504_2

My Marriott Hotel™ opens its doors on Facebook: Marriott uses social media gaming to help attract tens of thousands of employees. (2011). *Marriott International, Inc.* Retrieved from http://news.marriott.com/2011/06/my-marriott-hotel-opens-its-doors-on-facebook.html

Maslow, A. H. (1970). *Motivation and Personality*. New York: Harper & Row.

Mathieu, J. E., Heffner, T. S., Goodwin, G. F., Salas, E., & Cannon-Bowers, J. (2000). The influence of shared mental models on team process and performance. *The Journal of Applied Psychology, 85*(2), 273–283. doi:10.1037/0021-9010.85.2.273 PMID:10783543

Mikulincer, M. (1988). Reactance and helplessness following exposure to unsolvable problems: The effects of attributional style. *Journal of Personality and Social Psychology, 54*(4), 679–686. doi:10.1037/0022-3514.54.4.679 PMID:3367284

Mikulincer, M. (1989). Cognitive interference and learned helplessness: The effects of off-task cognitions on performance following unsolvable problems. *Journal of Personality and Social Psychology, 57*(1), 129–135. doi:10.1037/0022-3514.57.1.129

Mone, E. M., & London, M. (2014). *Employee engagement through effective performance management: A practical guide for managers*. New York, NY: Routledge.

Performance Management: Overview & History. (2014). *Office of Personnel Management*. Retrieved from http://www.opm.gov/policy-data-oversight/performance-management/overview-history/

Organ, D. W. (1988). *Organizational citizenship behavior: The good soldier syndrome*. Lexington, MA, England: Lexington Books/D. C. Heath and Com.

Paharia, R. (2013). *Loyalty 3.0: How to Revolutionize Customer and Employee Engagement with Big Data and Gamification*. McGraw Hill Professional.

Palmer, D., Lunceford, S., & Patton, A. J. (2012). The engagement economy: How gamification is reshaping businesses. *Deloitte Review*, *11*, 51–69.

Paradise, A., & Patel, L. (2013). *State of the Industry: ASTD's Annual Review of Trends in Workplace Learning and Performance*. Alexandria, VA: ASTD.

Pink, D. (2011). *Drive: the surprising truth about what motivates us*. New York, NY: Penguin Group, Inc.

Ployhart, R. E., & Moliterno, T. P. (2011). Emergence of the human capital resource: A multilevel model. *Academy of Management Review*, *36*(1), 127–150. doi:10.5465/AMR.2011.55662569

Przybylski, A. K., Rigby, C., & Ryan, R. M. (2010). A motivational model of video game engagement. *Review of General Psychology*, *14*(2), 154–166. doi:10.1037/a0019440

Rampell, C. (2014, January 26). Your next job application could involve a video game. *The New York Times*. Retrieved from http://www.nytimes.com/2014/01/26/magazine/your-next-job-application-could-involve-a-video-game.html?_r=2

Insanely driven: Reckitt Benckiser. (n. d.). *Reckitt Benckiser*. Retrieved from http://insanelydriven.archive.lessrain.co.uk/

Red Bull Musketeers: Red Bull. (n. d.). *Red Bull*. Retrieved from http://www.redbullusa.com/cs/Satellite/en_US/Red-Bull-Musketeers/001243067960808

Reeves, B., & Read, J. L. (2009). *Total engagement: Using games and virtual worlds to change the way people work and businesses compete*. New York, NY: Harvard Business School Press Books.

Rodgers, R., Hunter, J. E., & Rogers, D. L. (1993). Influence of top management commitment on management program success. *The Journal of Applied Psychology*, *78*(1), 151–155. doi:10.1037/0021-9010.78.1.151

Ryan, A., & Ployhart, R. E. (2014). A century of selection. *Annual Review of Psychology*, *65*(1), 693–717. doi:10.1146/annurev-psych-010213-115134 PMID:24050188

Ryan, R. M., & Deci, E. L. (2000). Self-determination theory and the facilitation of intrinsic motivation, social development, and well-being. *The American Psychologist*, *55*(1), 68–78. doi:10.1037/0003-066X.55.1.68 PMID:11392867

Ryan, R. M., Rigby, C., & Przybylski, A. (2006). The motivational pull of video games: A self-determination theory approach. *Motivation and Emotion*, *30*(4), 347–363. doi:10.1007/s11031-006-9051-8

Rynes, S. L. (1991). Recruitment, job choice, and post-hire consequences: A call for new research directions. In M. D. Dunnette & L. M. Hough (Eds.), *Handbook of industrial and organizational psychology* (2nd ed., Vol. 2, pp. 399–444). Palo Alto, CA, US: Consulting Psychologists Press.

Salas, E., & Cannon-Bowers, J. (2001). The science of training: A decade of progress. *Annual Review of Psychology*, *52*(1), 471–499. doi:10.1146/annurev.psych.52.1.471 PMID:11148314

Salas, E., Cannon-Bowers, J., Rhodenizer, L., & Bowers, C. A. (1999). In G. R. Ferris (Ed.), *Training in organizations: Myths, misconceptions, and mistaken assumptions* (pp. 123–161). US: Elsevier Science/JAI Press.

Schmitt, N., Ford, J. K., & Stults, D. M. (1986). Changes in self-perceived ability as a function of performance in an assessment center. *Journal of Occupational Psychology*, *59*(4), 327–335. doi:10.1111/j.2044-8325.1986.tb00233.x

Skinner, B. F. (1948). 'Superstition' in the pigeon. *Journal of Experimental Psychology*, *38*(2), 168–172. doi:10.1037/h0055873 PMID:18913665

Skinner, B. F. (1953). *Science and human behavior*. Oxford, England: Macmillan.

Skinner, B. F. (1958). Teaching machines. *Science*, *128*(3330), 969–977. doi:10.1126/science.128.3330.969 PMID:13592277

Smith, R. (n.d.). *The future of work is play: Global shifts suggest rise in productivity games*. Retrieved from http://www.42projects.org/docs/The_Future_of_Work_is_Play.pdf

Smither, J. W., Reilly, R. R., Millsap, R. E., Pearlman, K., & Stoffey, R. W. (1993). Applicant reactions to selection procedures. *Personnel Psychology*, *46*(1), 49–76. doi:10.1111/j.1744-6570.1993.tb00867.x

Principles for the validation and use of personnel selection procedures (4th ed.). (2003). *Society for Industrial and Organizational Psychology, Inc.* Bowling Green, OH: Society for Industrial Organizational Psychology. Retrieved from http://www.siop.org/_principles/principles.pdf

Spence, M. (1973). Job market signaling. *The Quarterly Journal of Economics*, *87*(3), 355–374. doi:10.2307/1882010

Stajkovic, A. D., & Luthans, F. (1998). Social cognitive theory and self-efficacy: Going beyond traditional motivational and behavioral approaches. *Organizational Dynamics*, *26*(4), 62–74. doi:10.1016/S0090-2616(98)90006-7

Taylor, F. W. (1914). Scientific management. *The Sociological Review*, *7*(3), 266–269. doi:10.1111/j.1467-954X.1914.tb02387.x

Tippins, N. (2009). Internet alternatives to traditional proctored testing: Where are we now? *Industrial and Organizational Psychology*, *2*(1), 2. doi: 1754-9426/09

Van Iddekinge, C. H., & Ployhart, R. E. (2008). Developments in the criterion-related validation of selection procedures: A critical review and recommendations for practice. *Personnel Psychology*, *61*(4), 871–925. doi:10.1111/j.1744-6570.2008.00133.x

VandeWalle, D. (1997). Development and validation of a work domain goal orientation instrument. *Educational and Psychological Measurement*, *57*(6), 995–1015. doi:10.1177/0013164497057006009

VandeWalle, D. (2003). A goal orientation model of feedback seeking behavior. *Human Resource Management Review*, *13*(4), 581–604. doi:10.1016/j.hrmr.2003.11.004

ADDITIONAL READING

Arthur, W. Jr, & Villado, A. J. (2008). The importance of distinguishing between constructs and methods when comparing predictors in personnel selection research and practice. *The Journal of Applied Psychology*, *93*(2), 435–442. doi:10.1037/0021-9010.93.2.435 PMID:18361642

Starner, T. (2014, May 7). The recruiting game. *Human Resource Executive Online*. Retrieved from: http://www.hreonline.com/HRE/view/story.jhtml?id=534357046

KEY TERMS AND DEFINITIONS

Flow: The state of optimal engagement said to exist when a person is voluntarily engaged in a task where demands are set at an optimal level for a person's skills. During flow states, people can lose track of time, as they become wrapped up in the task initiating the flow state.

Goal-Setting Theory: Motivational theory stating that goals both directly and indirectly impact action by steering activities towards goal-relevant activities and away from goal-irrelevant activities.

Maslow's Hierarchy of Needs: A need satisfaction theory claiming that there are 5 levels of needs (physiological, security, belongingness, esteem, and self-actualization) arranged in a hierarchy, such that the needs must be met in order, ranging from physiological to self-actualization.

Need Satisfaction Theories: A group of motivational theories proposing that motivation stems from a desire to satisfy certain physical or psychological needs.

Operant Conditioning: A theory of learning popularized by B.F. Skinner focused on behavioral changes, or learning, resulting as function of the consequences of actions.

Performance Management: The process of rating the performance of employees in an organization, with the goal of either developing employees or making key personnel decisions.

Personnel Selection: The process of leveraging different assessment formats to determine the likeli hood that a candidate will be successful if chosen to fill a job vacancy.

Recruitment: Organizational processes aimed at attracting a number of high-quality individuals to apply for vacancies within an organization.

Self-Determination Theory: Need satisfaction theory focusing on the differences between needs that are intrinsically or extrinsically motivating. Self-Determination Theory claims that intrinsic rewards are driven by need satisfaction, whereas extrinsic rewards are more environmentally driven.

Chapter 7
Gamifying Recruitment, Selection, Training, and Performance Management:
Game–Thinking in Human Resource Management

Michael B. Armstrong
Old Dominion University, USA

Richard N. Landers
Old Dominion University, USA

Andrew B. Collmus
Old Dominion University, USA

ABSTRACT

Game-thinking is beginning to appear in a wide variety of non-game contexts, including organizational support settings like human resource management (HRM). The purpose of this chapter is two-fold: 1) to explore the opportunities for game-thinking via gamification and serious games in HRM based on current and previous HRM literature and 2) to identify future research areas at the intersection of game-thinking and HRM. Prevailing HRM theories will be applied to the use of game-thinking in different sub-fields of HRM, including recruitment, selection, training, and performance management.

INTRODUCTION

Game-thinking is beginning to appear in a wide variety of non-game contexts. Game-thinking has been described as an umbrella term encompassing gamification, serious games, game-inspired design, and play that can be used to solve some sort of problem (Marczewski, 2014). For the purposes of this chapter, the two major forms of game-thinking are gamification, defined as the use of game elements in non-game

DOI: 10.4018/978-1-4666-8651-9.ch007

contexts (Deterding, Sicart, Nacke, O'Hara, & Dixon, 2011) and serious games, defined as games used for a primary goal other than entertainment (Michael & Chen, 2005). Gartner Inc. (2011) predicted that by 2014, 70 percent of Global 2000 organizations would have at least one gamified application and that by 2014, 80 percent of all gamified applications would fail (Gartner Inc., 2012). Considering the rising trend in gamified applications and the stakes at hand for businesses, organizations, and government, it is crucial to research game-thinking in organizational contexts.

Gamification has often been used in marketing (see, e.g., Sarner, 2013) and sales (see, e.g., Chapman, 2014). For example, online advertisements in the past decade and beyond employed simple point-and-click games (e.g. clicking a moving target on screen) to push marketing content onto consumers. The field of sales appears to be the simplest field to gamify, as many sales teams have employed points and leaderboard game mechanics to inspire competition among salespersons (e.g., Bunchball, 2013). Although these areas may see the most ubiquitous gamification, serious games and game elements can also be used in organizational support settings – namely, human resource management (HRM; DuVernet & Popp, 2014). Recent reports by organizations studying and applying HRM theory have identified gamification as a top trend in the field (Munson, 2013; Society for Human Resource Management, 2014), with research beginning to appear at professional conferences in the past two years (Landers, 2013; Bauer, Callan, Cavanaugh & Landers, 2014; Callan, Bauer, Armstrong, & Landers, 2014; Chow & Chapman, 2014; Geimer & O'Shea, 2014; Kubisiak, Stewart, Thornbury, & Moye, 2014; Popp, 2014; Sydell & Brodbeck, 2014).

The purpose of this chapter is two-fold: 1) to explore the opportunities for gamification and serious games in HRM based on current and previous HRM literature and 2) to identify future research areas at the intersection of game-thinking and HRM. Prevailing HRM theories will be applied to the use of game-thinking in different sub-fields of HRM. Empirical research will be considered when available, although the current empirical literature on gamification is sparse (Hamari, Koivisto, & Sarsa, 2014). Where empirical studies of game-thinking in HRM are absent, case studies of organizations using serious games and game elements will be discussed.

An important consideration in the gamification of HRM is to identify which game elements might be applied to non-game contexts whether individually or in combination up to a complete serious game. Bedwell, Pavlas, Heyne, Lazzara, and Salas (2012) developed a taxonomy of game elements used in learning contexts. These elements are broad in scope, incorporating larger more detailed taxonomies of game elements within it (Wilson et al., 2009). Although these taxonomies were developed with serious games in mind, the elements can be applied to gamified contexts broadly. By understanding what elements can be applied to HRM contexts, game-thinking can be better leveraged to improve HRM outcomes. The game elements identified by Bedwell and colleagues and referenced by this chapter include action language, assessment, conflict/challenge, control, environment, game fiction, human interaction, immersion, and rules/goals.

This chapter will explore four major areas of HRM where serious games and gamification have already seen some success. These areas include recruitment, selection, training, and performance management. The first of these areas, recruitment, is defined as "those organizational activities that (1) influence the number and/or types of applicants who apply for a position and/or (2) affect whether a job offer is accepted" (Breaugh, 1992, p. 4). In the second area, selection, organizations provide psychological assessments to applicants in order to use their scores to predict later job performance and thus aid in hiring decisions. Such assessments might include tests of cognitive ability, assessments of personality, work samples, interviews, application blanks, and more. The third area, training, is defined as "activities leading to the acquisition of knowledge, skills, and attitudes relevant to an immediate or upcoming job or role" (Kraiger & Culbertson, 2013, p. 244). Such activities might include an educational course, job shadowing a current employee, or on-the-job training under close supervision. Once training is complete and an employee is working within the organization, performance levels must be maintained in order to reach organizational outcomes (e.g. product quotas, financial objectives, etc.). The final area, performance management, is defined as "a continuous process of identifying, measuring, and developing the performance of individuals and teams and aligning performance with the strategic goals of the organization" (Aguinis, 2009, p. 2). It includes identifying what good performance is for a given job, consistently assessing employees on that criterion, and ensuring that employees are maintaining a specified level of performance.

Game-thinking can be used within each of these four areas of HRM to benefit organizations. Within recruitment, serious games can portray different aspects of the recruiting organization to potential applicants by immersing them within the organization, persuading them to apply or accept a job offer. Game-like assessments can be utilized within selection systems to identify the best applicants for the job. Gamified training can challenge new hires to learn more during training, benefitting both the employee and the organization in the long term. Gamification also can be applied to everyday work performance, motivating employees to higher qualities and quantities of work output. For example, performance leaderboards combine elements of conflict/challenge, assessment, and rules/goals to motivate employees (Landers & Landers, 2014). Each of these applications is addressed more in-depth in the remainder of this chapter.

RECRUITMENT

Current Research

Game-thinking can be applied to the context of employee recruitment through two processes. First, game-thinking can be applied to the process of finding the best "fit" between applicants and hiring organizations. Generally, if organizations are more attractive to potential applicants, those organizations will receive more applications for jobs. Also, if organizations are more attractive to applicants, those applicants might be more likely to accept a position with that organization if offered. Second, game-thinking can be applied to the recruitment process itself. Serious games and gamified applications can be used to relay information among job seekers about available positions.

Gamification of Applicant Fit

Serious games and gamified applications can be used to help job applicants determine their person-organization fit (Cable & Judge, 1996; Kristof, 1996; O'Reilly, Chatman, & Caldwell, 1991) with the recruiting organization. Organizations present an image of themselves to potential applicants hoping that applicants will see the organization as a desirable place to work, matching or exceeding their expectations for an employer. This can be accomplished in two major ways.

First, organizations might try to enhance person-organization fit by applying the attraction-selection-attrition framework (Schneider, 1987). Individuals seeking employment are generally attracted to organizations that represent similar beliefs, personalities, and behaviors to their own. Similarly, organizational recruiters are attracted to recruits similar to the people within their organization. Ideally, when this attraction is mutual, recruits are invited to apply to an organization. Gamified applications and recruiting techniques might be leveraged to make an organization more attractive, thus drawing more job applicants to an organization. For example, Deloitte China utilized game elements to enhance its organizational attractiveness to potential applicants during a recent recruiting campaign (Ordioni, 2013). Company offices in Beijing, Hong Kong, and Shanghai were virtually rendered, allowing job seekers to explore different aspects of jobs in the company. Users took part in a virtual tour of the organization, which utilized the game elements of immersion, environment, and control. Job seekers were immersed in a virtual version of the offices, able to navigate to different rooms, floors, and buildings. This virtual tour provided the environment of a Deloitte China office to any job seeker with a computer and Internet access. Users were given control over how to tour the organization. Job seekers could explore every aspect of the company available (e.g. reception, office environment, training), or they could focus their attention on a specific department (e.g. finance) or location (e.g. Shanghai). Additionally, the application included a challenge element to find "Green Dots" throughout the company, representing different benefits and opportunities available to employees in the company (e.g. development opportunities, career flexibility). The Deloitte China Virtual Tour campaign has received over 32,000 visitors since its inception (Deloitte, 2014).

Although this framework appears advantageous to the organization, there are potential negative consequences. Organizations might enhance their attractiveness to potential applicants with serious games or game elements to such an extent that potential applicants are misinformed about the true nature of the organization. For example, a serious recruiting game might demonstrate that an organization is environmentally conscious when in reality it is not. If an applicant desires to work for an environmentally conscious organization, they may be attracted to this organization, apply, and be selected. The organization has accomplished its goal with the recruitment game, but the new hire will soon realize that the organization is not environmentally friendly, thus increasing the probability of attrition (Schneider, 1987). The employee might leave the organization to which he or she is no longer attracted in order to join a more attractive one (Hamori, 2010; Darnold & Rynes, 2013).

Second, organizations might try to enhance person-organization fit by providing a realistic job preview (Wanous, 1973) within the context of a serious game. One example is America's Army (2014), a game developed by the U.S. Army to recruit young Americans by previewing the more exciting aspects of the soldier experience, while simultaneously demonstrating Army career opportunities and benefits. Players might perceive themselves as a good fit for the U.S. Army based upon their success in the serious game. To the extent that gameplay skills represent real-life social skills, this approach will invite a more qualified applicant pool than previously available.

Gamification of the Recruitment Process

Game-thinking also may be employed to enhance the recruitment process itself. Making recruitment processes more game-like or into complete serious games can motivate employees to recruit new applicants or involve potential applicants in the workings of the recruiting organization. These objectives are accomplished through gamified employee referral systems and through competitions among potential applicants.

Gamification can be employed to improve employee referral systems. For example, software developer Herd Wisdom created a mobile application to gamify the employee referral system by awarding points and prizes to employees for recruiting new applicants (Herd Wisdom, 2013). Points are earned by employees for various behaviors (e.g., updating a user profile, sharing job postings) within the application. Earning points through this system then increases employees' chances of winning giveaway contests within the recruiting company (e.g., a tablet computer might be awarded every month to a participating employee, with more participation points translating into more chances of winning). This form of gamification aims to motivate employees to put forth more effort into the recruitment process, improving the applicant pool by increasing the number of applicants.

The recruitment process also can be gamified through the use of competition. Competitions can include elements of challenge or conflict, as well as human interaction when players are competing against other people. For example, the U.S. Department of Homeland Security hosted a competition for high school student computer hackers in order to meet its estimated computer security employee needs (Perlroth, 2013). The competition was designed to excite young hackers about working in the government sector, hopefully for the Department of Homeland Security. The competition was divided into stages, allowing the best participants to progress through each stage, concluding with prize money for the top contenders. As the competition occurred, live-updating leaderboards tracked participant points. Points were earned for tasks such as cracking passwords, flagging security vulnerabilities, and more. Over 700 high school students participated in the earliest stage of the competition, and the 40 highest-scoring students progressed to more advanced stages, which also involved increasingly realistic government computer security issues. The competition and the associated prize money presumably motivated potential job applicants to participate. In the process, students learned more about the government sector of computer security and the recruiting organization.

Future Research

Future research on game-thinking in recruitment should examine how different serious games and game elements can increase or decrease organizational attractiveness. The element challenge/conflict might be used in a serious recruitment game to attract competitive applicants to the organization. However, some applicants might dislike games with challenge/conflict elements that are too difficult. Research should examine the interaction between the individual differences of potential applicants (e.g. attitudes toward challenges/conflicts) and game elements used in recruiting. Future research also should explore how serious games and game elements can portray truthful or false representations of recruiting organizations. For example, researchers might examine how the element immersion can be used to immerse potential applicants in either realistic or positively exaggerated virtual versions of the organization.

Additionally, the effectiveness of gamified recruitment processes should be examined and evaluated. Gamified employee referral systems might be more or less effective with different combinations of game elements. Further, different operationalizations of the same element might have different effects on employee recruitment. For example, the element assessment might be used in an employee referral system in several different ways. Employees may receive points according to the number and quality of referrals they provide. Alternatively, employees might earn badges for completing certain referral goals. A third form might be a progress bar, displaying how much progress has been made toward reaching an individual or organization-wide referral goal. When testing the effectiveness of different forms, care should be taken to isolate the effects of other elements or variables (e.g. the effect of points as an assessment itself might be confounded by the effect of competition among employees). Research should also investigate whether gamified recruitment is more or less effective than traditional recruiting methods. Chow (2014) found that standard online recruitment material led to better recruitment outcomes than gamified recruitment material. Future studies are necessary to confirm or disconfirm this effect.

Finally, models of gamified recruitment should be developed and tested. One such model has been developed by Chow and Chapman (2013), who examined the effects of gamification on recruit attitudes and affect toward organizations. The model proposed that affect and attitudes influenced overall attitudes toward the recruiting organization over time, which then influenced applicant attraction to the organization. Such models should be expanded to include other known predictors of recruitment outcomes, such as attraction to an organization and likelihood of accepting a job offer. Other models of gamified recruitment should consider person-organization fit in its various forms (Kristof, 1996) and how to maximize these outcomes with serious games and game elements.

SELECTION

Current Research

Selection research has traditionally focused on the validity of selection predictors and methods, and in the U.S., attempted to find a balance between adversely impacting protected classes (Equal Employment Opportunity Commission, 1978) and effectively predicting job performance while maintaining positive reactions to the selection process itself. Game-thinking can impact all three of these areas. By adding game elements, fairness perceptions of selection assessments might be generally improved over traditional methods (i.e. personality tests, online surveys, etc.). In regards to test validity, serious games and gamified assessments might provide new insight into the prediction of job performance.

Gamification of Applicant Reactions to Selection

Applicants who perceive selection systems as unfair react negatively to those systems, and these effects can persist after hiring. Specifically, application processes that are perceived as unfair can result in increased test anxiety and decreased test motivation (Hausknect, Day & Thomas, 2004), possibly skewing the results of assessments used in selection. The perceptions of unfair selection systems are described by organizational justice theory. This theory states that the distribution of rewards (distributive justice, e.g., which of the applicants received a job offer) and the procedures by which that distribution occurred (procedural justice, e.g., how job offers to applicants were determined) drive the overall fairness perceptions of applicants. When fairness perceptions are poor, a variety of negative selection-related outcomes for the organization are more probable, including decreased applicant self-efficacy and self-esteem, decreased organizational attractiveness, decreased job offer acceptance, and eventually decreased job satisfaction, decreased performance, and increased turnover. Exceptionally poor fairness perceptions may even increase the probability of litigation against the organization (Bauer, Truxillo, Sanchez, Craig, Ferrera, & Campion, 2001).

Applicant reactions to the use of new technologies in selection, including serious games and gamification, are driven by these perceptions. Recent research on the impact of new technologies in selection have found procedural justice perceptions to mediate the relationship between technology usage and applicant reaction outcomes (i.e., test-taking motivation, organizational attraction, intentions toward the organization; Bauer et al., 2006; Weisheimer & Giordano, 2013). However, computer experience emerged as a key moderator of this relationship, revealing a stronger relationship between procedural justice perceptions and outcomes among those with greater experience with computers. Experience with technology also appears to be generally important when considering reactions to technology more broadly. For example, people are more likely to react positively to the idea of gamification when they have previous gaming experience and positive attitudes toward serious games (Landers & Armstrong, in press). Conversely, those with little or no experience with games may view the use of serious games in a high-stakes context as inherently unfair. Even those with game experience may view the use of serious games and gamification in a high-stakes context like selection as unfair if the serious game or gamification is poorly designed or executed. Perceptions that a game is unfair or unwinnable may create perceptions that the overall selection process is unfair, even if game performance validly predicts job performance. If such perceptions vary by protected class membership, such games may even invite litigation.

The use of game-thinking to improve applicant reactions often involves the deployment of a complete serious game for maximum positive impact upon reactions. One example of this is *Insanely Driven* (less rain, 2014; http://insanelydriven.archive.lessrain.co.uk/), an interactive selection game in which each job applicant is placed into a series of unusual situations and asked to make a variety of decisions. The situations differ widely from content typically expected in any hiring process, requiring decisions regarding stained shirts and aliens, among others. At the conclusion of the game, a personality profile is produced based upon those responses. At a minimum, *Insanely Driven* is a highly memorable selection experience. Although data are not yet available on the success of this system in improving applicant reactions, the game has attracted a fair amount of media coverage.

Gamification of Assessment

In addition to improving applicant reactions to selection systems, game-thinking may be used as a replacement or supplement to traditional performance assessments. Ideally, serious games or gamified assessments would improve the quality of information about job candidates obtained during the selection process. For example, performance on a serious assessment game might be used to assess knowledge, skills, abilities, and other characteristics of job candidates. Such individual differences can already be assessed with psychological tests to effectively predict job performance (Schmidt & Hunter, 1998). However, serious games might be used to obtain higher quality data in one of two ways. First, serious game performance may be more difficult for test-takers to fake in an effort to maximize their chances to be hired. Second, serious games may be better able to elicit behaviors than traditional questionnaire-based assessments.

Response distortion on non-cognitive measures has long been a concern in the hiring process (Ones & Viswesvaran, 1998). When a test outcome is high-stakes, such as during the job application process, many test-takers distort their responses in a variety of intentional and unintentional ways. Some test-takers create a social desirability bias (Ganster, Hennessey & Luthans, 1983) when they unintentionally inflate their responses from their true scores in order to present themselves in a socially desirable fashion. Other test-takers engage in intentional distortion, such as blatant extreme responding, in which test-takers respond only with extreme answers in a purposeful attempt to inflate their scores (Landers, Sackett & Tuzinski, 2011). Gamification of the assessment process may reduce the magnitude of both effects because desirable behaviors within the serious game may be less obvious to players. For example, personality traits might be assessed indirectly via gameplay behaviors, such behaviors may be less susceptible to social desirability bias, and due to the ambiguous nature of their measurement, may also be more difficult for test-takers to manipulate purposefully.

Serious games may also elicit job-relevant behavior more readily than is possible with questionnaires. Non-cognitive survey-based hiring measures (e.g. personality surveys, interest inventories) ask that job applicants reflect upon themselves and respond based upon their judgment about their own capabilities. Several efforts to minimize the effects of inaccuracy introduced by this reflection while maintaining the otherwise strong psychometric properties of surveys have been made, most notably the use of situational judgment tests (Landy, 2007), which require test-takers to predict their future behavior rather than reflect upon their existing psychological traits and states. Serious games as assessment tools may show similar benefits. Specifically, past behavior is generally considered the best predictor of future behavior (Ajzen, 1991). By eliciting job-relevant behavior within the context of a serious game, better prediction of future work behavior may be possible than by using survey-based measures alone. Consulting company PDRI employed a gamified simulation to assess candidates on learning agility, the willingness and ability to learn from experience, in addition to self-report measures (Kubisiak et al., 2014). Willingness to learn was assessed via self-report surveys, while ability to learn was assessed via simulation. Different phases of the fictional simulation tested participants on their perception of facts, comprehension of rules, recognition of patterns, and more while solving a mystery (i.e. game fiction element combined with a challenge/goal element) about a stolen rare coin. Game-like assessments like PDRI's simulation can be used to observe and measure valuable predictor constructs like learning agility in a selection context where survey methodology may not suffice.

With either approach to gamifying assessment, minimization of negative reactions and maximization of beneficial psychometric properties is needed for legal defensibility and maximum utility. This is best ensured through the processes described by the various seminal documents on test validation, including those produced by the Equal Employment Opportunity Commission (1978), the Society for Industrial and Organizational Psychology (2003) and the joint efforts of the American Educational Research Association, American Psychological Association, and National Council on Measurement in Education (1999). These guidelines, commonly cited in selection cases within the U.S. legal system, provide specific guidelines for the creation of psychometrically valid assessment tools. Specifically, tests must be reliable, valid, and fair.

Reliable tests show high consistency of measurement, and reliability is necessary to establish validity. This is of particular concern in the context of the gamification of assessment, because serious games should produce similar scores for applicants regardless of their past experience (or lack thereof) with the game. For example, the number of times a person completes a personality measure should not affect their personality score. In contrast, a person's score from an assessment game may increase as they increase their experience with the game, which decreases the reliability of the scores (Cronbach, 1951) obtained from it, confounding observed scores with game experience. Serious game designers must be careful to ensure that game skill does not influence the scores obtained from the game. If applicants can increase their scores with repeated play, those with the greatest game skill or those willing to play the game many times, either of which may correlate with protected class membership (e.g., applicant sex), will ultimately be hired, increasing litigation risk.

A test must also be valid, measuring only the constructs it is intended to measure and predicting job performance adequately. Valid prediction is necessary for legal defensibility; if the test scores do not predict job performance and do correlate with protected class membership, there is a high risk of litigation. This is also difficult in the serious assessment game context, because most serious games are intended to elicit a wide range of highly complex skills. Whereas a psychological measure can be designed to assess a single personality trait, designing serious games to measure a single construct may be more difficult

147

and is contrary to the typical game design process, which emphasizes a variety of interesting tasks to maximize player engagement (Schell, 2008). In this way, the reliability and validity of serious selection games may be at odds with the entertainment value provided by such games.

Finally, serious assessment games should be fair. A common concern in the legal systems of many countries is adverse impact, the unintentional discrimination against members of groups within protected classes (see Equal Employment Opportunity Commission, 1978). In the U.S., this most typically involves race, sex, religion, national origin, color, disability status, and age. If a test results in lower scores for one group within these categories versus another (e.g. within sex, males versus females), it demonstrates adverse impact. This adverse impact may or may not be legal, depending upon the legal system of the nation within which it is used. Of particular concern in serious assessment games is the use of first-person shooters, in which males on average have greater interest and experience than females (Jansz & Tanis, 2007). If such a game were used in the selection process, it is probable that female applicants would perform more poorly on those games due not to lower standing on target individual constructs, but instead due to less game experience. Such differences must be investigated before serious assessment games can be safely used in many countries.

Future Research

The gamification of applicant reactions, that is, the use of game elements to improve reactions, has been explored somewhat, but this research is not typically called "gamification." For example, the use of progress bars to track progression through a survey does not appear to increase response rates but may reduce test-taker anxiety (Singh, Taneja & Mangalaraj, 2009). In the study of situational judgment tests, branching has been used to provide later question prompts in direct response to applicant responses to earlier question prompts (Lievens, Peeters, & Schollaert, 2007). For example, in a situational judgment test about managerial skill, a test-taker asked to resolve a conflict between a male and a female coworker in an early question might be asked later questions based upon that response. This mimics the element "game fiction," or "narrative," commonly used in gamification efforts (see, e.g., Nicholson, 2013). Future research in the gamification of reactions must consider which game elements are likely to elicit which effects on reactions, isolating these effects, and measuring them carefully. An integration of Hausknecht and colleagues' (2004) theory of applicant reactions along with theories of meaningful game elements (see, e.g., Landers, 2014; Landers & Landers, 2014) is needed as a next step.

Current research on the use of complete, developed serious games in selection is in its infancy. The basic psychometric properties of effective serious selection games and the design process to ensure favorable properties have not been established. Future research should target each of the major psychometric properties of serious games and the game development process necessary to establish this. A research program should entail investigations of reliability, validity, and fairness.

First, the reliability of scores obtained from serious games must be established. Core to measurement theory is that a construct representing an individual characteristic of interest drives behavior within an assessment (Nunnally, 1978). If the construct does not change, scores obtained to measure that construct through a serious game should not change either. This indicates a need for both over-time examinations of scores obtained from video games (i.e., that scores stay the same from play session to play session to ensure test-retest reliability) as well as within-game examinations (i.e., that scores are similar between exercises focusing upon the same construct in order to assess internal consistency reliability).

Second, the validity of scores obtained from serious games must be established. Even if reliability can be demonstrated, whatever is measured via serious games must be the construct intended to be measured when designing the game. This has been a critical problem in several selection-related literatures, notably interviews (Salgado & Moscoso, 2002), assessment centers (Arthur, Woehr & Maldegen, 2000), and situational judgment tests (Cabrera & Nguyen, 2001). In each of these literatures, a selection technique was found not to assess the constructs it was originally intended to measure, which is contrary to the guidelines of the Equal Employment Opportunity Commission, the Society for Industrial and Organizational Psychology, the American Educational Research Association, the American Psychological Association, and the National Council on Measurement in Education, as described earlier. No documented design process is in place to ensure that a developed serious game actually measures what it is intended to measure, which makes this a high priority for future research.

Third, the adverse impact of scores obtained from serious games must be investigated. A variety of demographic differences have been found in the popularity of games, broadly (Greenberg, Sherry, Lachlan, Lucas & Holmstrom, 2010). It is unknown if these preferences and varying experience levels with various game types affect the success of serious games in providing accurate measurement, making this a high priority for future research as well. Any investigations of reliability and validity would benefit from inclusion of demographics measures for this investigation, especially gender and prior experience with games.

TRAINING

Current Research

The study of serious games in learning contexts has existed for several decades (see, e.g., Malone, 1981). Because of the successes in utilizing serious games for learning, game-thinking is poised to have a substantial impact on learning outcomes in workplace training. In the field of training, game-thinking has been applied to both improving overall training effectiveness and to improving motivation during training. Game-thinking in training can have an impact on learning and organizational outcomes. Game-thinking also can serve as a motivational tool, increasing training completion rates and trainee motivation to learn.

Gamification of Training Effectiveness

Those attempting to gamify training effectiveness intend to improve trainee reactions to learning, knowledge and skill increases, behavioral change, and organizational return (Kirkpatrick, 1976). Research in this domain is generally concerned with research on serious games. It is important to note that such games are not always digital; serious games have been used to support learning for decades, long before video games even existed as a major form of entertainment (Keys & Wolfe, 1990). This research area is primarily within the educational domain rather than within human resource management. However, effectiveness in the educational domain typically focuses upon the affective reactions to students and learning as the ultimate outcomes of instruction, whereas behavioral change and return on investment are actually the ultimate focus for organizations (Burke & Hutchins, 2007). This distinction is critical.

In the human resources context, this distinction implies additional points of failure for a gaming-driven training program that do not exist in education because the ultimate effect on behavior is not typically considered in education. To illustrate this, Landers and Callan (2012) proposed a technology-enhanced training effectiveness model (TETEM), demonstrating that poor trainee attitudes toward new technologies, low trainee experience with training technologies, and poor organizational climate for training technologies can reduce reactions to training, learning from training, behavioral transfer from training, and organizational return on investment, even if the technology itself has been implemented effectively. In the present context, this means that a well-designed serious game can still fail to produce desired training outcomes if trainees are not properly motivated to engage with that game.

Landers and Armstrong (in press) tested a portion of this model in the gamification context by asking potential learners how they would feel about gamified instruction in comparison to traditional PowerPoint-based instruction, finding that those with low video game experience and poor attitudes toward game-based learning still preferred PowerPoint to serious games. Despite this, overall reactions to training were still greater for gamified training, implying that although some individuals are likely to be disadvantaged by gamification in comparison to traditional training designs, overall reactions will still be stronger when serious games are used. Effects upon other organizational training effectiveness outcomes, like transfer and return, were not examined.

Even when the training context is ideal, there is little consensus on what specific game elements or game designs actually support learning (Bedwell et al., 2012; Guillen-Nieto & Aleson-Carbonelli, 2012). A common approach in designing serious games is to create an experience in which desired skills are demonstrated through gameplay. When the game-version of skill demonstration is nearly identical to the real-life skill upon which it is modeled, these are sometimes called "simulation games". A major drive of the difficulties defining games or what makes them successful stems from the extreme complexity surrounding game design, which can involve thousands of people, from graphic designers, writers, and level designers through a variety of directors, managers, and producers (Schell, 2008).

As described in the introduction to this chapter, Bedwell and colleagues (2012) developed a taxonomy of game elements used in learning contexts. Although this is not an exhaustive list of game elements, it is an exhaustive list of game elements typically used to influence learning, making it a prime starting point to understand what about games can improve training effectiveness. Unfortunately, research in this domain is just beginning, and conclusions about which of these elements are most important are not yet available.

Gamification of Training Motivation

Similar to approaches taken by those gamifying applicant reactions, the gamification of training motivation is intended to improve completion rates and trainee motivation to learn rather than to actually deliver instruction. Of all types of gamification, this is probably the best explored because of the simplicity of its deployment and the popularity of the approach among educators. Such efforts do not require the extreme resource investment of serious games. For example, Nicholson (2013) describes the gamification of a classroom by integrating game fiction (i.e., adding a story to course progress), leaderboards, and achievements into a classroom. These additions required no additional monetary expenses, although they did require somewhat more planning time.

Landers, Bauer, Callan, and Armstrong (2015) comprehensively reviewed psychological theories of motivation to identify which theories were most promising to describe the effects of gamifying training motivation. In doing so, they identified five major theoretical motivational frameworks that might apply: the theory of gamified learning, classic learning theories, expectancy theory, goal-setting theory, and self-determination theory.

First, the authors identified the theory of gamified learning (Landers, 2014; Landers & Landers, 2014), the only psychological theory focusing upon gamified learning. This theory, targeted at gamification efforts where individual game elements are extracted and applied to support learning, proposes that game elements affect training outcomes through one or two mechanisms. First, gamification may be used to influence a mediating behavior or attitude, which is in turn theorized to affect learning. For example, in Landers and Landers' (2014) empirical test of this theory, a leaderboard was used to increase the amount of time learners spent engaging with a project, and that amount of time in turn increased learning outcomes. Second, gamification may be used to strengthen the relationship between instructional design and learning outcomes. For example, game fiction might be used to increase learner engagement, which should make existing course material more effective in increasing training outcomes. Critically, in both of these approaches, gamification is not intended to itself teach the learner anything; instead, it is used to support existing instructional material.

Second, the authors identified the classic learning theories of Skinner (1948) related to operant conditioning, where consequences are used to shape behavior. When a stimulus event occurs followed by a behavioral response, subsequent consequences will alter the frequency of the behavioral response in the future. When the consequences are desirable, they are referred to as rewards. When the consequences are undesirable, they are referred to as punishments. In the context of gamification, rewards are far more common than punishments. Often, recognition of accomplishments, such as using leaderboards, points, or badges, is used to reward target behaviors (Anderson, Huttenlocher, Kleinberg, & Leskovec, 2013; Denny, 2013; Fitz-Walter, Tjondronegoro, & Wyeth, 2011). Conditioning offers a powerful framework by which to influence behavior, but is limited to relatively narrow, very well-defined behaviors. When target behaviors are more complex, such as learning, conditioning brings many unintended negative consequences (Lee & Hammer, 2011).

Third, the authors identified Vroom's (1964) expectancy theory, which describes motivation as the mathematical product of expectancy (the belief that behavior will lead to an outcome), instrumentality (the belief that the outcome will lead to an event of value), and valence (the amount of value of that final event). Because Vroom's theory is multiplicative, it suggests that a near-zero value for any of these three components results in zero ultimate motivation. In the context of gamified learning, expectancy theory can be used to understand why some gamified rewards lead to greater behavioral change than others. For example, if scoring highly on a leaderboard is not a valuable accomplishment to a learner, its low valence is unlikely to trigger the learner to alter their behavior. Deloitte gamified an online executive training program by including rewards, rankings, and leaderboards to increase the valence of the training program (Badgeville, 2014). The executives' beliefs regarding the effectiveness and organizational benefits of the trainings did not change, but the reward value for completing these objectives did change, which motivated them to complete the training. Expectancy theory might work through other constructs as well. For example, if a trainee does not expect that playing a serious game will prepare him or her to perform workplace duties, low expectancy may cause the trainee to exert less effort in training.

Fourth, the authors identified Locke's (1968) goal-setting theory, which describes motivation as the iterative process of reducing the discrepancy between a person's goals and their actual behaviors, a process called self-regulation. When gamification is used to set goals for learners, the learners are motivated to reduce the discrepancy between the goals set for them and their actual behavior, although this varies among learners based upon their goal commitment. Goal-setting theory is one of the most powerful and flexible motivational theories in modern industrial/organizational psychology, providing a great deal of predictive power in its description of which goals people will pursue and why. In general, specific, measurable, attainable, realistic, and time-bound (SMART) goals are the most effective at encouraging goal attainment (Doran, 1981). A variety of other mediators and moderators are also proposed in the context of goal-setting theory, which adds to its predictive power. In the context of gamification, goal-setting theory provides a great deal of guidance on what type of goals might be embedded within game-based learning to maximize learner motivation to achieve them. Such goals represent the element "rules/goals," which is often at the core of games, describing the necessary conditions to "win" at a given game.

Fifth and finally, the authors identified Deci and Ryan's (1985; 2000) self-determination theory, which characterizes motivation as driven by both intrinsic and extrinsic rewards. Intrinsic motivation is characterized by satisfaction of a person's needs to be competent, autonomous, and to feel related to those around them. People feel driven to behave in ways that meet these needs. All other motivators are extrinsic in nature, caused by rational or emotional evaluation of desired outcomes and explicit decisions to pursue those outcomes. Typically, extrinsic rewards involve some of the processes involved in intrinsic motivation (external regulation, introjection, identification, and integration), but not all. Without intrinsic or extrinsic motivators, a person is said to be amotivated. Neither intrinsic motivation nor extrinsic motivation is necessarily stronger or "better" in any objective sense (Deci, Koestner & Ryan, 2001), and new evidence suggests that the two are complimentary (Cerasoli, Nicklin & Ford, 2014). Intrinsic motivation is considered by many to be the theoretical cornerstone of engaging people through games and gamification (Malone, 1981; Ryan, Rigby, & Przybylski, 2006; Przybylski, Rigby & Ryan, 2010; Aparicio, Gutiérrez Vela, González Sánchez, & Isla Montes, 2012; Gears & Braun, 2013), although gamification is often associated more strongly with extrinsic motivation.

Future Research

The gamification of training effectiveness and motivation is at a turning point. Serious games research has matured and is beginning to turn away from the case study approach toward an approach more consistent with modern social scientific methods (Bedwell et al., 2012). This shift is needed to improve the consistency of successes using serious games and should continue. Further investigations, however, must better explore which particular elements of games are linked to training outcomes of interest and why. By determining which elements of games are most closely tied to learning, those elements can be better extracted for application without the overhead of a complete serious game development process. For example, a training designer might randomly assign half of his or her trainees to experience game fiction in their training program and the other half to experience that training program in its original unmodified format. In this way, game fiction can be linked causally to differences in outcomes between the two groups in a way that is impossible with a correlational or case study design.

Future research on the gamification of training effectiveness might continue through popular training effectiveness models (e.g., Kirkpatrick, 1976), but ought to also consider models that consider the impact of technology explicitly (e.g., TETEM, Landers & Callan, 2012; Landers & Armstrong, in press). Such models should be tested with game-based training interventions and revised accordingly in order to best measure the effectiveness of game-thinking in training. While doing so, researchers should additionally consider the impact of game elements in a variety of learning contexts and based upon a variety of learning theories.

Future research on the gamification of training motivation might continue through any of the motivational theories described in this chapter. Research should specifically explore motivational theories of learning involving game-thinking (e.g., theory of gamified learning, Landers, 2014; Landers & Landers, 2014). Such models of gamified learning should be tested and revised in order to best measure the effects of game-thinking on training motivation. Recent advances in self-determination theory are particularly relevant, as the optimal balance between intrinsic motivators and external incentives has not yet been identified.

PERFORMANCE MANAGEMENT

Current Research

Job performance is determined by a number of factors including individual ability and motivation to perform. Effective performance management systems seek to maximize employee motivation toward the completion of organizational goals and objectives. Game-thinking provides a set of tools that can be utilized in order to enhance the motivational component of job performance, to bring employee behaviors more in alignment with the expectations of the organization. This can be accomplished through many of the same motivational theories impacting learning that were discussed in the training section of this chapter.

Gamification of Job Performance

The gamification of everyday job performance has the greatest potential for benefitting from game-thinking, as the variety of current existing jobs allows for an unfathomable number of gamified processes. The idea that everyday on-the-job tasks could be made fun and gamelike appeals to both employees and employers. Essential to the study of performance management is Campbell, McCloy, Oppler, & Sager's (1993) Job Performance model, which can be applied to gamify job performance. The model posits that declarative knowledge, procedural knowledge, and motivation are all antecedents of task performance, contextual performance, and adaptive performance. Each type of performance is a function of the interaction between the antecedents: declarative knowledge (i.e., an understanding of facts and requirements for the job), procedural knowledge and skill (i.e., the ability to apply declarative knowledge in the job context), and motivation. Because Campbell and colleagues' theory is multiplicative, it suggests that a near-zero value on any of these antecedents results in zero overall performance.

In order to capitalize on the motivational affordances of game-thinking, gamified performance management should focus on employee motivation. In Campbell and colleagues' (1993) theory, motivation consists of three multiplied components of choice: the choice to exert effort or not, the level of effort to exert, and the persistence of exerted effort. For example, an employee seeking to improve her organization's internal communication decides to enhance the communication software on all company computers by updating three computers per day. Thus, she has three choices via the components of motivation: the choice to exert effort toward improving internal communication, the choice of level of effort to put forth (updating software on three computers per day), and the choice of how long to persist in her efforts (until all computers have been updated). These three components provide her overall level of motivation to improve internal communication. Similar to the broader theory, the three components of motivation are multiplicative, that is, a change in any of these decisions would result in a change to her overall motivation.

Game-thinking can be applied to motivate employees to exert effort, reach higher levels of effort, and continue their effort for longer amounts of time. In the previous example, the organization could increase employees' willingness to update computers by introducing a competitive points and rewards system. This system would motivate additional employees to work toward updating the computers, that is, those who enjoy competition (Bedwell et al., 2012), the prospect of a reward (Landers & Landers, 2014), or the social benefits of playing games (Koivisto & Hamari, 2014). The unpredictability and challenge of human competition could inspire some employees to update more computers at once or to spend more time working on the updates, thus increasing their level of effort, persistence of effort, or both.

Gamification of Motivation to Perform

Motivational theories provide direction as to how motivation might be altered in order to maximize job performance. The motivational theories described earlier in the gamification of training motivation section can be similarly applied in the gamification of motivation to perform. Specifically, expectancy theory, goal-setting theory, and self-determination theory provide the greatest potential value to increasing motivation to perform.

As discussed in the gamification of training motivation, expectancy theory describes motivation as the mathematical product of expectancy (the belief that behavior will lead to an outcome), instrumentality (the belief that the outcome will lead to an event of value), and valence (the amount of value of that final event). In the context of gamified performance, expectancy theory can be used to demonstrate how serious game behaviors will lead to desirable performance outcomes, how those outcomes will be rewarded, and how valuable those rewards are to the employee.

Each of the three components of expectancy theory already exists within a work environment; therefore at a minimum, gamified performance initiatives should increase at least one component while maintaining the other components. In a recent white paper, performance management consulting firm CallidusCloud (House, 2012) notes that cash prizes are not effective for changing employee behavior, and that run-off contests effectively increase performance only for the duration of the contest. Their solution was to offer a variety of short- and long-term challenges, goals, and contests covering a wide range of employee behaviors. To ensure employees were motivated to achieve these gamified work goals, CallidusCloud recommended providing gift cards or goods from leisure, retail, restaurants, and other local businesses. By offering a wide range of rewards, their gamified performance management system aims to motivate all employees, while taking into consideration their diverse range of desires and lifestyles.

Goal-setting theory states that goals help individuals direct their efforts, increase the persistence of those efforts, and act as a catalyst for strategic thinking (Locke, Shaw, Saari, & Latham, 1981; Locke & Latham, 2002). As mentioned earlier in the chapter, the SMART acronym is an easy way to remember the general conditions necessary for creating effective goals. When setting productivity goals for employees, it is important to ensure that goal attainment does not preclude other important organizational functions (Wright, George, Farnsworth, & McMahan, 1993).

Game-thinking often involves goal-setting, making the interaction between these two concepts a promising area for research and practice. For example, by assigning a range of point values to various work tasks, an organization may clarify each task's relative importance while maintaining a balance between the tasks employees choose to complete. Effective gamification can help create optimal conditions for goal-setting by outlining specific goals and providing quick, accurate feedback. When LiveOps, a customer service call-center, gamified the workplace, the company initiated a system of points and badges to reward the completion of important tasks (e.g., customer service objectives, optional training classes) and created a leaderboard designed to provide instantaneous feedback. As a result, LiveOps' sales performance increased by 10% and the average call time decreased by 15% (Bunchball, 2013). The LiveOps application of game-thinking to performance management created clear goals that were specific, measurable, attainable, realistic, and time-bound (i.e., SMART goals). In line with goal-setting theory and current gamification research, game-thinking intended to increase performance should have a pre-determined ending point to avoid extinction effects (Koivisto & Hamari, 2014). Serious performance games will be most effective when employees know exactly how and when the game will end, so they may plan their efforts accordingly.

Self-determination theory, which distinguishes intrinsic and extrinsic motivation (Gagné & Deci, 2005), also provides mechanisms for the success of game-thinking. In 2008, Pew Research Center reported that 53% of adults age 18 and older played video games (Lenhart, Jones, & Macgill, 2008). More recent data collected by the Entertainment Software Association (2014) indicate that 59% of Americans play video games, 71% of all gamers are over the age of 18, and 48% of gamers are female. Because many working-age Americans choose to play video games in their free time, gamified work tasks may be intrinsically motivating to a large portion of employees. Employees who are not intrinsically motivated by games may still reap performance benefits from extrinsic motivators inherent to games. These motivators include rewards for specific behavior, increases in self-esteem from goal completion, positive or negative performance feedback, and social pressures. Because a sense of autonomy is important to motivation (Deci & Ryan, 1985; 2000), employees desiring to continue performing their job without the inclusion of game elements should be allowed to do so without consequence. One reason for LiveOps' success in gamifying call-center performance was that the game was optional. This made the choice to play this game more meaningful (i.e., motivational) for the 80% of agents who played (Bunchball, 2013), while allowing the remaining employees to continue performing their tasks without losing autonomy or feeling coerced.

Future Research

Future research should focus on how real work performance can be gamified, making it more motivating to employees while still accomplishing workplace objectives. Different game elements and combinations of elements should be applied to different work tasks and contexts to determine where game-thinking can be incorporated. Next, these game elements should be manipulated to determine which elements are most effective at motivating job performance. Organizations will then be able to use this information to improve productivity via gamified performance.

Additionally, future research on game-thinking in performance management should focus on employee demographic information. These studies will yield insights into which industries, organizations, and employees are likely to benefit from the inclusion of game-thinking. In a study of a gamified exercise application, Koivisto and Hamari (2014) found a difference in perceived ease of using the application among different ages, such that older users found the application more difficult to use. This study also found a difference among genders, such that women valued the social aspects of gamification more so than men did. Further research is needed in assessing how game-thinking affects employees in different industries, education levels, socioeconomic status, etc.

Practitioners need to exercise caution when implementing game-thinking to performance management. Specifically, gamified solutions must directly reward and motivate the specific behaviors desired by management, while ensuring that the level of focus on these tasks does not impede completion of other important aspects of the job. Kerr (1995) described multiple examples of organizations rewarding the wrong behavior and thus receiving an undesirable outcome. Examples include an organization with the goal of long-term growth, but rewarding quarterly sales; a basketball team with the goal of teamwork, but rewarding the highest scoring player; and a manufacturer with the goal of creating a quality product, but rewarding faster shipping. Game objectives and rules should be carefully designed such that they will not deter from the work that is to be completed.

CONCLUSION

Through this review of research trends, several themes in the gamification of HRM arise. First, empirical research seems to be directed towards the question "Does gamification work?" (Hamari et al., 2014) rather than, "Why or how does gamification work?" These questions inquire as to the broad use of gamification more so than the specific use of it in HRM. Kappen & Nacke (2013) developed a comprehensive theoretical model of gamification effectiveness, which may be applied to the HRM contexts of training and performance management in assessing motivation. Models of game-thinking effectiveness still require further testing in order to determine the antecedents of motivating serious games and game elements. A second theme arising from this review is the focus on the gamification of learning/training, the gamification of performance management focusing on the field of sales, and the gamification of assessment for selection purposes. Given the literature on serious games in learning, game-thinking in employee training has a developed theoretical and empirical basis for support. The extraction and application of game elements to learning has begun and should continue to increase (see, e.g., Landers, 2014; Landers & Landers, 2014). The gamification of sales appears to be the most common form of gamification in a business setting. This is presumably because the most basic game mechanics (i.e. points, badges, and leaderboards) can be applied easily to a sales context without much thought or planning. It will take more imagination and creativity to gamify more complex areas of HRM such as selection, which is the newest burgeoning area of applying game-thinking in organizational contexts (Geimer & O'Shea, 2014; Kubisiak et al., 2014). A final theme recognized from this review is the ubiquity of points, leaderboards, and badges. They may be the easiest mechanics to apply initially, layering over almost any context, but do not necessarily improve metrics, engagement, or efficiency (Hamari, 2013; Montola, Nummenmaa, Lucero, Boberg, & Korhonen, 2009). However, recent evidence suggests that points, levels, and leaderboards do not harm intrinsic motivation, contrary to popular belief (Mekler, Brühlmann, Opwis, & Tuch, 2013).

Research on game-thinking should focus on the extraction and application of individual game elements and combinations of game elements in non-game contexts (e.g., Landers & Callan, 2011), specifically in organizational support settings such as HRM. Several frameworks and taxonomies of game elements have been developed (Malone, 1981; Hunicke, LeBlanc, & Zubek, 2004; King, Delfabbro, & Griffiths, 2010; Bedwell et al., 2012; Robinson & Bellotti, 2013) and used in gamified contexts (Geimer & O'Shea, 2014; Landers, 2014; Landers & Landers, 2014). Game elements include the likes of conflict/challenge, level of user control, game fiction/fantasy, and human interaction among others. The extraction of game elements to gamify non-game processes in HRM is where research can progress most efficiently. The overhead associated with digital serious game development naturally limits the speed of research progress in this area due to limited research resources, but modern gamification is less limited. Game elements can be adopted at little or zero cost for rigorous empirical testing. Once specific elements are identified and validated as effective tools, researchers and practitioners alike will better understand why game elements are effective and how they can be applied to recruit, assess, and engage employees. Future research of game-thinking within each major area of HRM is necessary for the successful progression of its application. Within recruitment, research should explore how serious games and game elements affect organizational attractiveness. Within selection, future research should focus on the validation and fairness of serious games and game-like assessments. Additionally, research should explore the use of game elements to improve applicant reactions. Future research in the gamification of training should test game-thinking within the context of training effectiveness models and models of motivation. Finally, in the context of performance management, research should explore how different types of work and performance can be gamified, considering demographic differences that may impact gamified performance outcomes.

In applying game-thinking to HRM, several limitations must be considered. Unrealistic expectations of serious workplace games may prevent effective applications from being adopted. When digital serious games are adopted, they may adversely affect different demographics within the workplace. For example, Koivisto & Hamari (2014) noted an effect of age on perceived ease of use of a digital gamified exercise service such that as age increased, perceived ease of using the system decreased. Furthermore, games may demonstrate gender differences (Jansz & Tanis, 2007). Future research should investigate how individual demographic differences affect the relationship between game-thinking and learning or performance outcomes. Further, game-thinking may mislead potential job applicants. Highly enjoyable games may be excellent tools at attracting applicants, but do not guarantee that the applicants will remain in their position or with the organization for very long. Thought should be given in planning gamified recruitment efforts such that game-thinking does not mislead potential applicants. However, even if game-thinking is applied truthfully, applicant perceptions can still lead to potential litigation against the organization. Applicants perceiving serious selection games or game-like assessments as unfair or irrelevant to the job may complain when they are not selected for a job. Game-thinking in selection should ensure that assessments are reliable, valid, and fair. In training, poor trainee attitudes and lack of previous experience with games might hinder their receptivity to game-based training (Landers & Armstrong, in press).

As in any research context, sound theoretical models and methodology should be employed. Empirical research should be the basis for theory, as theory should be the basis for future research. Quantitative experimental methods should be used whenever possible, as they are objective and more easily replicable than qualitative and subjective measures. A focus on quantitative, experimental data will enable compilations of the average effects of gamification in HRM in the future (i.e. meta-analyses).

Overall, the future of gamification in HRM looks both bright and bleak. Although industries applying serious games and game elements to their HRM practices may reject game-thinking due to the failed application of mechanics such as points, leaderboards, and badges, research interest in game-thinking is quickly accelerating. The breadth of questions remaining to answer is vast. The definition of a game or even the definition of "fun," is a complex concept to grasp, debated among scholars for several decades (Jesper, 2003). After agreeing upon definitions and taxonomies of game elements, game types, player types, and more, the field of applied game-thinking still needs to determine how to best combine these characteristics in order to achieve specific objectives in the realm of HRM. Applied game-thinking and research in HRM has seen some success thus far, but its true potential might not yet be realized.

REFERENCES

Aguinis, H. (2009). *Performance Management* (2nd ed.). Upper Saddle River, NJ: Pearson Prentice Hall.

Ajzen, I. (1991). The theory of planned behavior. *Organizational Behavior and Human Decision Processes, 50*(2), 179–211. doi:10.1016/0749-5978(91)90020-T

America's Army. (2014). Retrieved from https://www.americasarmy.com/assets/americas_army_backgrounder.doc

Anderson, A., Huttenlocher, D., Kleinberg, J., & Leskovec, J. (2013, May). Steering user behavior with badges. *Proceedings of the 22nd International Conference on World Wide Web*, Rio de Janeiro, Brazil, 95-106.

Aparicio, A. F., Gutiérrez Vela, F. L., González Sánchez, J. L., & Isla Montes, J. L. (2012, October 1-2). Analysis and application of gamification. *Proceedings of Interaccion 2012*, Elche, Alicante, Spain.

Arthur, W., Woehr, D. J., & Maldegen, R. (2000). Convergent and discriminant validity of assessment center dimensions: A conceptual and empirical reexamination of the assessment center construct-related validity paradox. *Journal of Management, 26*, 813–835.

Badgeville. (2014). Deloitte augments their leadership development program. *Case Study*: Deloitte Leadership Academy. Retrieved from http://badgeville.com/customer/case-study/deloitte

Bauer, K. N., Callan, R. C., Cavanaugh, K. J., & Landers, R. N. (2014, May). *The application of goal-setting theory to gamification*. Poster presented at the 29th Annual Conference of the Society for Industrial and Organizational Psychology, Honolulu, HI.

Bauer, T. N., Truxillo, D. M., Sanchez, R., Craig, J., Ferrera, P., & Campion, M. A. (2001). Development of the Selection Procedural Justice Scale (SPJS). *Personnel Psychology, 54*(2), 387–419. doi:10.1111/j.1744-6570.2001.tb00097.x

Bauer, T. N., Truxillo, D. M., Tucker, J. S., Weathers, V., Bertolino, M., Erdogan, B., & Campion, M. A. (2006). Selection in the information age: The impact of privacy concerns and computer experience on applicant reactions. *Journal of Management, 32*(5), 601–621. doi:10.1177/0149206306289829

Bedwell, W. L., Pavlas, D., Heyne, K., Lazzara, E. H., & Salas, E. (2012). Toward a taxonomy linking game attributes to learning: An empirical study. *Simulation & Gaming: An Interdisciplinary Journal, 43*(6), 729–760. doi:10.1177/1046878112439444

Breaugh, J. A. (1992). *Recruitment: Science and practice*. Boston, MA: PWS-Kent.

Bunchball. (2013). It's no game: Gamification is transforming the call center. Bunchball White Paper. Retrieved from http://www.bunchball.com/resources/its-no-game-gamification-transforming-call-center

Burke, L. A., & Hutchins, H. M. (2007). Training transfer: An integrative literature review. *Human Resource Development Review, 6*(3), 263–296. doi:10.1177/1534484307303035

Cable, D. M., & Judge, T. A. (1996). Person-organization fit, job choice decisions, and organizational entry. *Organizational Behavior and Human Decision Processes, 67*(3), 294–311. doi:10.1006/obhd.1996.0081

Cabrera, M. A. M., & Nguyen, N. T. (2001). Situational judgment tests: A review of practice and constructs assessed. *International Journal of Selection and Assessment, 9*(1-2), 103–113. doi:10.1111/1468-2389.00167

Callan, R. C., Bauer, K. N., Armstrong, M. B., & Landers, R. N. (2014, May). *Gamification in psychology: A review of theory and potential pitfalls*. Poster presented at the 29th Annual Conference of the Society for Industrial and Organizational Psychology, Honolulu, HI.

Campbell, J., McCloy, R., Oppler, S., & Sager, C. (1993). A theory of performance. Personnel Selection in Organizations, (1983).

Cerasoli, C. P., Nicklin, J. M., & Ford, M. T. (2014). Intrinsic motivation and extrinsic incentives jointly predict performance: A 40-year meta-analysis. *Psychological Bulletin, 140*(4), 980–1008. doi:10.1037/a0035661 PMID:24491020

Chapman, L. (2014, June 4). Ambition Solutions raises $2M for new ways to gamify sales. *The Wall Street Journal*. Retrieved from http://blogs.wsj.com/venturecapital/2014/06/04/ambition-systems-raises-2m-for-new-ways-to-gamify-sales/

Chow, S., & Chapman, D. (2013, October). Gamifying the employee recruitment process. In Proceedings of Gamification '13, Stratford, ON, Canada. doi:10.1145/2583008.2583022

Chow, S., & Chapman, D. (2014, May). *A novel approach to employee recruitment: Gamification*. Poster presented at the 29th Annual Conference of the Society for Industrial and Organizational Psychology, Honolulu, HI.

Cronbach, L. J. (1951). Coefficient alpha and the internal structure of tests. *Psychometrika, 16*(3), 297–334. doi:10.1007/BF02310555

Darnold, T. C., & Rynes, S. L. (2013). *Recruitment and job choice research: Same as it ever was?* (pp. 104–142). In I. B. Weiner (Ed.), Handbook of Psychology (2nd ed). New York: Wiley.

Deci, E. L., Koestner, R., & Ryan, R. M. (2001). Extrinsic rewards and intrinsic motivation in education: Reconsidered once again. *Review of Educational Research, 71*(1), 1–27. doi:10.3102/00346543071001001

Deci, E. L., & Ryan, R. M. (1985). *Intrinsic motivation and self-determination in human behavior*. Springer. doi:10.1007/978-1-4899-2271-7

Deci, E. L., & Ryan, R. M. (2000). The "what" and "why" of goal pursuits: Human needs and the self-determination of behavior. *Psychological Inquiry, 11*(4), 227–268. doi:10.1207/S15327965PLI1104_01

Deloitte China Virtual Tour [Internet website application]. (2014). Deloitte. Retrieved from http://workatdeloitte.cn/virtualtour/

Denny, P. (2013, May). The effect of virtual achievements on student engagement. *Proceedings of CHI 2013: Changing Perspectives* (pp. 763-772), Paris, France. doi:10.1145/2470654.2470763

Deterding, S., Sicart, M., Nacke, L., O'Hara, K., & Dixon, D. (2011). Gamification: Toward a definition. *Proceedings of the CHI 2011 Gamification Workshop*, Vancouver, BC, Canada.

Doran, G. T. (1981). There's a S.M.A.R.T. way to write management's goals and objectives. *Management Review*, *70*, 35–36.

DuVernet, A. M., & Popp, E. (2014). Gamification of workplace practices. *The Industrial-Organizational Psychologist*, *52*, 39–44.

Entertainment Software Association. (2014). Essential facts about the computer and video game industry: Sales, demographic and usage data [Annual report]. Retrieved from http://www.theesa.com/facts/pdfs/esa_ef_2014.pdf

Equal Employment Opportunity Commission. (1978). Uniform guidelines on employee selection procedures. *Federal Register*, *43*(166), 38295–38309.

Fitz-Walter, Z., Tjondronegoro, D., & Wyeth, P. (2011, November) Orientation passport: Using gamification to engage university students. *Proceedings of the 23rd Australian Computer-Human Interaction Conference*, Canberra, Australia, 122-125. doi:10.1145/2071536.2071554

Gagné, M., & Deci, E. (2005). Self-Determination Theory and work motivation. *Journal of Organizational Behavior*, *362*, 331–362.

Ganster, D. C., Hennessey, H. W., & Luthans, F. (1983). Social desirability response effects: Three alternative models. *Academy of Management Journal*, *26*(2), 321–331. doi:10.2307/255979

Gartner, Inc. (2012, November 27). *Gartner says by 2014, 80 percent of current gamified applications will fail to meet business objectives primarily due to poor design*. Retrieved from http://www.gartner.com/newsroom/id/2251015

Gartner, Inc. (2011, November 9). *Gartner predicts over 70 percent of Global 2000 organisations will have at least one gamified application by 2014*. Retrieved from http://www.gartner.com/newsroom/id/1844115

Gears, D., & Braun, K. (2013, April). Gamification in business: Designing motivating solutions to problem situations. *Proceedings of the CHI 2013 Designing Gamification Workshop*, Paris, France.

Geimer, J. L., & O'Shea, P. G. (2014). Design considerations to maximize the utility of gamification for selection. In *E. C. Popp* (Chair), *Challenges and innovations of using game-like assessments in selection*. Proceedings of the 29th Annual Conference of the Society for Industrial and Organizational Psychology, Honolulu, HI.

Greenberg, B. S., Sherry, J., Lachlan, K., Lucas, K., & Holmstrom, A. (2010). Orientations to video games among gender and age groups. *Simulation & Gaming*, *41*(2), 238–259. doi:10.1177/1046878108319930

Guillen-Nieto, V., & Aleson-Carbonell, M. (2012). Serious games and learning effectiveness: The case of *It's a Deal! Computers & Education*, *58*(1), 435–448. doi:10.1016/j.compedu.2011.07.015

Hamari, J. (2013). Transforming homo economicus into homo ludens: A field experiment on gamification in a utilitarian peer-to-peer trading service. *Electronic Commerce Research and Applications*, *12*(4), 236–245. doi:10.1016/j.elerap.2013.01.004

Hamari, J., Koivisto, J., & Sarsa, H. (2014). Does gamification work? -- A literature review of empirical studies on gamification. Proceedings of the *2014 47th Hawaii International Conference on System Sciences.*

Hamori, M. (2010). Who gets headhunted—and who gets ahead? The impact of search firms on executive careers. *The Academy of Management Perspectives, 24,* 46–59.

Hausknecht, J., Day, D. V., & Thomas, S. C. (2004). Applicant reactions to selection procedures: An updated model and meta-analysis. *Personnel Psychology, 57*(3), 639–683. doi:10.1111/j.1744-6570.2004.00003.x

Herd Wisdom. (2013, May 22). Gamifying recruitment: Increase interest and results. Retrieved from http://www.herdwisdom.com/blog/gamifying-recruitment-increase-interest-and-results/

House, G. (2012) *Engage or die: Gamify your sales process.* Pleasanton, CA: Retrieved from http://www.calliduscloud.com/wp-content/uploads/2012/09/callidus_gamification_whitepaper_v12.pdf?utm_source=mysalesgame&utm_medium=CTA2&utm_campaign=whitepaper

Hunicke, R., LeBlanc, M., & Zubek, R. (2004) MDA: A formal approach to game design and game research. *Proceedings of the Association for the Advancement of Artificial Intelligence 2004 Work Shop on Challenges in Game Artificial Intelligence,* 1-5.

Jansz, J., & Tanis, M. (2007). Appeal of playing online first person shooter games. *Cyberpsychology & Behavior, 10*(1), 133–136. doi:10.1089/cpb.2006.9981 PMID:17305460

Jesper, J. (2003). The game, the player, the world: Looking for a heart of gameness. In M. Copier & J. Raseens (Eds.), *Level Up: Digital Games Research Conference Proceedings, Utrecht, Netherlands,* 30-45. Retrieved from http://www.jesperjuul.net/text/gameplayerworld/

Kappen, D. L., & Nacke, L. E. (2013, October). The kaleidoscope of effective gamification: Deconstructing gamification in business applications. Proceedings of Gamification '13, Stratford, ON, Canada. doi:10.1145/2583008.2583029

Kerr, S. (1995). An academy classic. On the folly of rewarding A, while hoping for B. *The Academy of Management Perspectives, 9*(1), 7–14. doi:10.5465/AME.1995.9503133466

Keys, B., & Wolfe, J. (1990). The role of management games and simulations in education and research. *Journal of Management, 16*(2), 306–336. doi:10.1177/014920639001600205

King, D., Delfabbo, P., & Griffiths, M. (2010). Video game structural characteristics: A new psychological taxonomy. *International Journal of Mental Health and Addiction, 8*(1), 90–106. doi:10.1007/s11469-009-9206-4

Kirkpatrick, D. L. (1976). Evaluation. In R. L. Craig (Ed.), *Training and development handbook: A guide to human resource development* (pp. 301–319). New York: McGraw-Hill.

Koivisto, J., & Hamari, J. (2014). Demographical differences in perceived benefits from gamification. *Computers in Human Behavior, 35,* 179–188. doi:10.1016/j.chb.2014.03.007

Kraiger, K., & Culbertson, S. S. (2013). In I. B. Weiner (Ed.), *Understanding and facilitating learning: Advancements in training and development* (2nd ed., pp. 244–261). Handbook of Psychology New York: Wiley.

Kristof, A. L. (1996). Person-organization fit: An integrative review of its conceptualizations, measurement, and implications. *Personnel Psychology, 49*(1), 1–49. doi:10.1111/j.1744-6570.1996.tb01790.x

Kubisiak, C., Stewart, R., Thornbury, E., & Moye, N. (2014, May). Development of PDRI's learning agility simulation. In *E. C. Popp* (Chair), *Challenges and innovations of using game-like assessments in selection.* Symposium presented at the 29th Annual Conference of the Society for Industrial and Organizational Psychology, Honolulu, HI.

Landers, R. N. (2013, April). Gamification: A new approach to serious games in training. In M.A. Lodato (Chair), R.C. Brusso (Co-Chair), & R. Wisher (Discussant), *I-O's role in emerging training technologies.* Symposium presented at the 28th Annual Conference of the Society for Industrial and Organizational Psychology, Houston, TX.

Landers, R. N. (2014). Developing a theory of gamified learning: Linking serious games and gamification of learning. *Simulation & Gaming.*

Landers, R. N., & Armstrong, M. B. (in Press). Enhancing instructional outcomes with gamification: An empirical test of the Technology-Enhanced Training Effectiveness Model [Unpublished manuscript, submitted for publication].

Landers, R. N., Bauer, K. N., Callan, R. C., & Armstrong, M. B. (2015). Psychological theory and the gamification of learning. In T. Reiners & L. Wood (Eds.), *Gamification in Education and Business* (pp. 553–568). Cham, Switzerland: Springer. doi:10.1007/978-3-319-10208-5_9

Landers, R. N., & Callan, R. C. (2011). Casual social games as serious games: The psychology of gamification in undergraduate education and employee training. In M. Ma, A. Oikonomou, & L. C. Jain (Eds.), *Serious Games and Edutainment Applications* (pp. 399–424). Surrey, UK: Springer. doi:10.1007/978-1-4471-2161-9_20

Landers, R. N., & Callan, R. C. (2012). Training evaluation in virtual worlds: Development of a model. *Journal of Virtual Worlds Research, 5*(3), 1–20.

Landers, R. N., & Landers, A. K. (2014). An empirical test of the Theory of Gamified Learning: The effect of leaderboards on time-on-task and academic performance. *Simulation & Gaming.*

Landers, R. N., Sackett, P. R., & Tuzinski, K. A. (2011). Retesting after initial failure, coaching rumors, and warnings against faking in online personality measures for selection. *The Journal of Applied Psychology, 96*(1), 202–210. doi:10.1037/a0020375 PMID:20718510

Landy, F. J. (2007). The validation of personnel decisions in the twenty first century: Back to the future. In S. M. McPhail (Ed.), *Alternate validation strategies: Developing and leveraging existing validity evidence* (pp. 409–426). San Francisco: Jossey-Bass.

Lee, J. J., & Hammer, J. (2011). Gamification in education: What, how, why bother? *Academic Exchange Quarterly, 15,* 1–5.

Lenhart, A., Jones, S., & Macgill, A. R. (2008). *Pew Internet Project data memo.* Pew Research Center. Retrieved from http://www.pewinternet.org/files/old-media//Files/Reports/2008/PIP_Adult_gaming_memo.pdf.pdf less rain. (2014). *Insanely driven.* Retrieved from http://insanelydriven.archive.lessrain.co.uk/

Lievens, F., Peeters, H., & Schollaert, E. (2007). Situational judgment tests: A review of recent research. *International Journal of Selection and Assessment, 37,* 426–441.

Locke, E. A. (1968). Toward a theory of task motivation and incentives. *Organizational Behavior and Human Performance, 3*(2), 157–189. doi:10.1016/0030-5073(68)90004-4

Locke, E. A., & Latham, G. P. (2002). Building a practically useful theory of goal setting and task motivation: A 35-year odyssey. *The American Psychologist, 57*(9), 705–717. doi:10.1037/0003-066X.57.9.705 PMID:12237980

Locke, E. A., Shaw, K. N., Saari, L. M., & Latham, G. P. (1981). Goal setting and task performance: 1969–1980. *Psychological Bulletin, 90*(1), 125–152. doi:10.1037/0033-2909.90.1.125

Malone, T. W. (1981). Toward a theory of intrinsically motivating instruction. *Cognitive Science, 4*(4), 333–369. doi:10.1207/s15516709cog0504_2

Marczewski, A. (2014, November 20). Is it gamification if....? Retrieved from http://www.gamified.co.uk/2014/11/20/gamification/

Mekler, E. D., Brühlmann, F., Opwis, K., & Tuch, A. N. (2013, October). Do points, levels and leaderboards harm intrinsic motivation? An empirical analysis of common gamification elements. Proceedings of Gamification '13, Stratford, ON, Canada. doi:10.1145/2583008.2583017

Michael, D., & Chen, S. (2005). *Serious games: Games that educate, train, and inform.* Boston, MA: Thomson Course Technology.

Montola, M., Nummenmaa, T., Lucero, A., Boberg, M., & Korhonen, H. (2009, September). Applying game achievement systems to enhance user experience in a photo sharing service. *Proceedings of the 13th International MindTrek Conference: Everyday Life in the Ubiquitous Era* (pp. 94-97), *Tampere, Finland.* doi:10.1145/1621841.1621859

Munson, L. (2013, December 31). New year, new workplace! SIOP announces the top 10 workplace trends for 2014. Retrieved from https://www.siop.org/article_view.aspx?article=1203

Nicholson, S. (2013). *Exploring gamification techniques for classroom management.* Paper presented at Games+Learning+Society 9.0, Madison, WI.

Nunnally, J. C. (1978). *Psychometric theory* (2nd ed.). New York: McGraw-Hill.

O'Reilly, C. A. III, Chatman, J., & Caldwell, D. F. (1991). People and organizational culture: A profile comparison approach to assessing person-organization fit. *Academy of Management Journal, 34*(3), 487–516. doi:10.2307/256404

Ones, D. S., & Viswesvaran, C. (1998). The effects of social desirability and faking on personality and integrity assessment for personnel selection. *Human Performance, 11*(2-3), 245–269. doi:10.1080/08959285.1998.9668033

Ordioni, J. (2013, April 26). Game on for employee gamification. *ERE Daily.* Retrieved from http://www.ere.net/2013/04/26/game-on-for- employee-gamification/

Perlroth, N. (2013, March 24). Luring young Web warriors is priority. It's also a game. *The New York Times*. Retrieved from http://www.nytimes.com/2013/03/25/technology/united-states-wants-to-attract-hackers-to-public-sector.html

Popp, E. (2014, May). Addressing practical challenges in developing game-like assessments. In *E. C. Popp* (Chair) & *C. Handler* (Discussant), *Challenges and innovations of using game-like assessments in selection*. Symposium presented at the 29th Annual Conference of the Society for Industrial and Organizational Psychology, Honolulu, HI.

Przybylski, A. K., Rigby, C. S., & Ryan, R. M. (2010). A motivational model of video game engagement. *Review of General Psychology*, *14*(2), 154–166. doi:10.1037/a0019440

Robinson, D., & Bellotti, V. (2013). A preliminary taxonomy of gamification elements for varying anticipated commitment. *Proceedings of the CHI 2013 Designing Gamification Workshop*, Paris, France.

Ryan, R. M., Rigby, C. S., & Przybylski, A. (2006). The motivational pull of video games: A self-determination theory approach. *Motivation and Emotion*, *30*(4), 347–363. doi:10.1007/s11031-006-9051-8

Salgado, J. F., & Moscoso, S. (2002). Comprehensive meta-analysis of the construct validity of the employment interview. *European Journal of Work and Organizational Psychology*, *11*(3), 299–324. doi:10.1080/13594320244000184

Sarner, A. (2013, September 13). Why game based marketing is relevant for anyone – who markets anything. Retrieved from http://blogs.gartner.com/adam-sarner/2013/09/13/why-game-based-marketing-is-relevant-for-anyone-who-markets-anything/

Schell, J. (2008). *The art of game design*. Burlington, MA: Morgan Kaufman.

Schmidt, F. L., & Hunter, J. E. (1998). The validity and utility of selection methods in personnel psychology: Practical and theoretical implications of 85 years of research findings. *Psychological Bulletin*, *124*(2), 262–274. doi:10.1037/0033-2909.124.2.262

Schneider, B. (1987). The people make the place. *Personnel Psychology*, *40*(3), 437–453. doi:10.1111/j.1744-6570.1987.tb00609.x

Singh, A., Taneja, A., & Mangalaraj, G. (2009). Creating online surveys: Some wisdom from the trenches tutorial. *IEEE Transactions on Professional Communication*, *52*(2), 197–212. doi:10.1109/TPC.2009.2017986

Skinner, B. F. (1948). 'Superstition' in the pigeon. *Journal of Experimental Psychology*, *38*(2), 168–172. doi:10.1037/h0055873 PMID:18913665

Society for Human Resource Management. (2014, January 22). Future insights: The top trends for 2014 according to SHRM's HR subject matter expert panels. Retrieved from http://www.shrm.org/Research/FutureWorkplaceTrends/Documents/13-0724%202014%20Panel%20Trends%20Report%20v4.pdf

Society for Industrial and Organizational Psychology. (2003). *Principles for the validation and use of personnel selection procedures*. Retrieved from http://www.siop.org/_principles/principles.pdf

Sydell, E., & Brodbeck, C. (2014, May). The predictive power of game-like assessments compared to traditional tests. In *E. C. Popp* (Chair) & C. Handler (Discussant), *Challenges and innovations of using game-like assessments in selection*. Symposium presented at the 29th Annual Conference of the Society for Industrial and Organizational Psychology, Honolulu, HI.

The standards for educational and psychological testing. (1999American Educational Research Association, American Psychological Association, & National Council on Measurement in Education. Washington, DC: AERA Publications.

Vroom, V. H. (1964). *Work and motivation*. New York: Wiley.

Wanous, J. P. (1973). Effects of a realistic job preview on job acceptance, job attitudes, and job survival. *The Journal of Applied Psychology*, *58*(3), 327–332. doi:10.1037/h0036305

Weisheimer, A., & Giordano, G. (2013). Perceptions of truthfulness and communication anxiety in online employment interviews. *Drake Management Review*, *3*, 48–56.

Wilson, K. A., Bedwell, W. L., Lazzara, E. H., Burke, C. S., & Estock, J. L. et al. (2009). Relationships between game attributes and learning outcomes. *Simulation & Gaming*, *40*(2), 217–266. doi:10.1177/1046878108321866

Wright, P. M., George, J. M., Farnsworth, S. R., & McMahan, G. C. (1993). Productivity and extra-role behavior: The effects of goals and incentives on spontaneous helping. *The Journal of Applied Psychology*, *78*(3), 374–381. doi:10.1037/0021-9010.78.3.374

KEY WORDS AND DEFINITIONS

Gamification: The use of game elements in non-game contexts.

Performance Management: A continuous process of identifying, measuring, and developing the performance of individuals and teams and aligning performance with the strategic goals of the organization.

Recruitment: Organizational activities that influence the number and/or types of applicants who apply for a position and/or affect whether a job offer is accepted.

Selection: The administration of psychological assessments to job applicants in order to predict later job performance from assessment scores and thus aid in hiring decisions.

Serious Game: Games used for a primary goal other than entertainment.

Training: Activities leading to the acquisition of knowledge, skills, and attitudes relevant to an immediate or upcoming job or role.

Section 3
Gamification of Education

Chapter 8
Three Perspectives on Video Game Learning:
Behaviorism, Cognitivism, and Constructivism

Zeynep Tanes
Duquesne University

ABSTRACT

Video games and gamified applications have been used for various purposes including helping businesses (in commercial marketing), or helping the individual, community or society (in social marketing). Video games are systems with rules, play structures, and narratives; while gamified applications utilize game elements, mechanics, and ways of thinking to generate meaningful, playful and fun experiences. Both video games and gamified applications require a learning process including learning to play, and learning through the game. This chapter advocates that learning is an inherent component of video games and gamified applications. The main purpose of this chapter is to examine the concept of 'game learning' from three major theoretical positions, namely Behaviorism, Cognitivism, and Constructivism. In doing so, this chapter first explains, compares, and contrasts these three positions, then elaborates on how learning takes place in specific games designed for commercial and social marketing with the lens of these three positions.

INTRODUCTION

As a classical definition, Salen and Zimmerman (2004) describe a game as "a system in which players engage in an artificial conflict, defined by rules, that result in a quantifiable outcome" (p.80). When games are digitalized, they provide immediate but narrow interactivity, manipulate information, allow automated complex systems and networked communications (Salen & Zimmerman, 2004). Based on this definition, video games are simplified and rule based digital worlds, which allow individuals to grasp a simplified version of a phenomenon fully through interactivity and engagement. Furthermore, games not only physically but also emotionally engage players through interaction (Kapp, 2012). Malaby (2007)

DOI: 10.4018/978-1-4666-8651-9.ch008

further suggests that games are not all about rules, conflict, and outcomes, and should not be separated from the process of play that allows players to "become" through interpretation of the game. In these and many ways, video games are transformative devices that allow individuals to not only learn to play the game, but also learn the game content through playing the game (Ang, Avni & Zaphiris, 2008).

Literature demonstrates an expanding scope of video games used in commercial and social marketing such as entertainment and serious games (Kotler & Lee, 2008; Lucas & Sherry, 2004; Susi, Johannesson, Backlund, 2007). Not only video games, but also gamified applications have been created for entertainment as well as serious purposes (Groh, 2012). Such gamified applications (either digital or not) derive from a more recent concept of "gamification" defined as "the use of game design elements in non-game contexts" (Deterding, Dixon, Khaled, Nacke, 2011, 9) to generate joy, satisfaction and added value to the experience (Deterding, 2014; Huotari & Hamari, 2012). For the player, each type of game and application satisfies a different kind of need they seek from their media engagement. For the developer, the games and gamified applications can be designed for commercial or social gains, leading to attitudinal and behavioral changes either profiting the company or the individual (and ultimately the society as a whole) respectively. It must, however be noted that in any category of game and gamified application, players engage in a learning process that is inherent to gameplay.

Gaming in general and video games in particular have been increasingly recognized as valuable tools for teaching and learning (Egenfeldt-Nielsen, 2006; Federation of American Scientists, 2006; Greenfield, 1984; Lieberman, 2006; Randel, Morris, Wetzel, & Whitehill, 1992; Simoes, Redondo & Vilas, 2013; Shaffer, Squire & Gee, 2004). Scholars suggest that video games are good learning tools for various reasons, including a heightened level of engagement, adoptability to the learner, and reinforcement of the content, due to their unique appeals that challenge players in observation and problem solving while demanding a set of cognitive skills from players (Leach & Sugarman, 2005; Lieberman, 2006). Moreover, if gamification is well integrated into the curriculum, the experience can create favorable outcomes (Simoes, Redondo & Vilas, 2013). All in all, gaming (video games or gamified applications) and learning are inherently connected.

Ertmer and Newby (1993) argue that three main theoretical positions, namely behaviorism, cognitivism, and constructivism dominate the scholarship examining learning. Educators use these theoretical positions to determine how they will structure their instructional designs, and which techniques they will incorporate in those designs. All three of these positions build on each other; yet differ in terms of their perspectives on how learning occurs, which factors influence learning (environmental, personality, cognitive, and situational factors), how memory functions, how transfer of knowledge form one context to another works, as well as what types of learning take place (Ertmer & Newby, 1993).

Behaviorist, cognitivist, and constructivist approaches complement each other in explaining learning from video games and gamified applications. From the behaviorist perspective learning from video games is primarily accidental, where the player inadvertently clicks on the screen to receive some positive or negative reinforcement to modify behavior. With this approach, games and gamified applications simply integrate game elements and mechanics to influence behavior. From the cognitivist perspective learning from video games is a cognitive investment. The player makes observations and conducts hypothesis testing throughout the game that modifies not only their behavior, but also the strategies they employ to achieve specific results. With this approach, games and gamified applications integrate not only game elements and mechanics, but also gaming principles, heuristics, and processes to generate a game-like thinking, and as a result, changes in attitudes and behavior (see Groh, 2012; Kapp, 2012). From the constructivist framework, learning from video games is an interpretive and social phenomenon that results from the player's interaction with others, with the system, and with the texts. The meaning making process that players go through allows them to learn, and modify not only their behavior and strategy, but also their ways of interpretation. With this approach, games and gamified applications utilize game models and design methods to allow players to become active participants of the experience and consequently influence interpretations, perceptions and behavior (see Deterding, 2014; Groh, 2012; Huotari & Hamari, 2012; Malaby, 2007).

With the understanding that learning is an inherent component of video games, the purpose of this chapter is to provide an overview of how behaviorist, cognitivist and constructivist perspectives explain the ways in which learning occurs during video game play across various categories of games. In doing so, this chapter will first explain these three positions and then explain, compare and contrast how learning takes place in games designed for commercial and social marketing with the lens of these three positions.

This chapter will provide guidance in applying major learning theories to the concept of video games in a comparative and explanatory manner that can be helpful for students, academics, and industry professionals. This chapter aims to contribute to the body of knowledge in video games and gamification by bringing the concepts of learning through games in relation to games for commercial and social good. Examining how learning occurs during video game play across various game categories would also allow scholars, game designers, policy makers, and business practitioners to better utilize video games in various campaigns as effective message transmission tools.

BACKGROUND

Video and computer games have gradually increased as a major past time for people of all ages. A 2008 study showed that, 97% of American teenagers between the ages of 12-17 played video games on various platforms, and 80% of them played five or more different game genres continuously (Lenhart et al, 2008). The same year, the amount of time Americans of all ages spent daily playing video games was 17.8 minutes, which is gradually increasing each year and is estimated to reach 28.3 minutes daily by 2018 (Statista, 2014a), as individuals spend more time playing games and 47 to 48% less time watching TV or movies (ESA, 2014). According to the Entertainment Software Association (ESA, 2014), 59% of Americans of all ages played video games across various platforms this year, while the average age of a game player is 31. Furthermore, the gender gap in game playing seems to have diminished as the gender ratio is 52% males to 48% females (ESA, 2014).

Such player statistics reflect themselves globally as rapidly increasing sales of video games. As total consumer spending on games industry was $21.53 billion in 2013 (ESA, 2014), the global revenue of video games was $78.9 billion, which is predicted to rise up to over $111 billion by 2015 (Statista, 2014b). Although many genres of games were popular among players, the best-selling video and computer games in 2013 were action (32%) and casual (28%) games respectively (ESA, 2014).

Defining Video Games

According to a classic definition of Salen and Zimmerman (2004) a game is a system, where players enter into a rule based "magic circle" that allows them to explore rules and structures while they interact with the system to obtain quantifiable outcomes. Furthermore, a game engages players within its simplified mini-world, which allows players to experience its narrative in a playful manner (Salen & Zimmerman, 2004). The interaction with this simplified version of a more complex reality allows the player to fully grasp the content covered within the narrative of that world. Juul (2003) extends this definition by including how players put forth effort in order to achieve an emotionally valuable outcome, and how the consequences of actions in the game are optional and negotiable. Juul's definition of a game emphasizes the quantification of outcomes of interactions, which makes games more engaging for players due to tangible outcomes achieved during gameplay. Furthermore, the concepts of "emotionally valuable outcome" and "negotiable consequence" are important additions to the definition, since these concepts evoke a sensation of safety in players that encourages replay and multiple rehearsals of game content (Lieberman, 2006).

Recently Kapp (2012) summarizes game as a process where "a player gets caught up in playing a game because the instant feedback and constant interaction are related to the challenge of the game, which is defined by the rules, which all work within the system to provoke an emotional reaction and, finally, result in a quantifiable outcome within an abstract version if a larger system" (p.9). According to this definition, games generate an intrinsic motivation for engagement particularly due to the elements embedded into the game.

When games are digitalized, they take on certain features that make them unique. As Salen and Zimmerman (2004) explain, first of all, digital games provide immediate but narrow interactivity, where specific actions of players are responded to immediately by the game system, but the scope of this interaction is limited to decisions, skills, and the imagination of game designers. Second, digitalized games manipulate information as they reveal and hide information throughout the gameplay, and players have to follow the game's path to reveal the information needed to proceed. Third, digital games are automated complex systems, which respond to players based on pre-determined, algorithm based, complicated codes that provide a consistent interaction in comparison to a human opponent. Finally, digital games allow for networked communications where players can interact with each other regardless of their physical location. All these features Salen and Zimmerman (2004) point out make digitalized games more consistent and predictable (unless players use cheats or hack the game system) compared to non-digital games that depend on humans following (or not following or bending) the written or negotiated game rules and structures.

According to Ang, Avni, & Zaphiris (2008), rules, play and narratives are the three major, common components of digital and non-digital games. As the scholars explain, *rules* are operational structures that determine what players need to do to proceed and consequently win the game; *play* is actions and reactions that players need to perform to achieve player-set or game-determined goals; and *narrative* is the symbolic structure of the game including happenings, worlds, and characters that create a coherent story. The crafty combination of meaningful rules, play, and narratives make the game a cohesive system.

More recent definitions propose that all games are systems, and require voluntary involvement of players, while only some games contain rules, goals, and uncertain outcomes that generate hedonic pleasure, suspense, and playfulness (Huotari & Hamari, 2012, p.18). Malaby (2007) challenges the classic definition of games as safe and separable domains that provide pleasure. He proposes a constructive approach to the definition of gaming, suggesting that "a game is a semibounded and socially legitimate domain of contrived contingency that generates interpretable outcomes" (p.96). All in all, such recent definitions acknowledge the active role and interpretive power of the player as they experience the game throughout their interaction.

Interaction with the system of a game demands various sets of cognitive skills from players. Players need to consistently pay attention to the game and make observations throughout their interaction with the game to understand how the system operates (Apperley, 2006). In other words, interacting with the game requires players to learn the rules and make sense of the game's narrative to be able to determine how to play it, and to interpret it. Furthermore, the playful elements within the game (such as emotionally valuable outcomes and negotiable consequence as explained earlier) generate motivation in players to exert greater cognitive effort (Lieberman, 2006). Consequently, due to required and motivational cognitive effort put into the game, the game is the ideal learning platform.

Categorization of Video Games

Video games can be categorized in various ways. For instance, similar to other media, video games can be categorized into genres based on "types of interactions that are available in the game" (Apperley, 2006, p.10). According to Lucas and Sherry's factor analysis (2004), video game genres can be categorized into three groups, namely traditional games, physical enactment games, and imagination games. They argue that *traditional games* are composed of genres of arcade, card-dice, quiz/trivia, puzzle, classic board, and platform; *physical enactment games* integrate genres of fighting, first person shooter, sports, racing; and finally *imagination games* are composed of genres of action, adventure, fantasy role playing, simulations, strategy. Lucas and Sherry (2004) argue that while traditional games require low levels of mental rotation skills, physical enactment and imagination games demand high mental rotation skills. Additionally, it can be argued that physical enactment games require relatively lower levels of strategy building and contain higher levels of violence, yet they stimulate arousal and require quick decision making and strong reflexes; while imagination games require higher levels of critical thinking and strategy building. It should however be noted that games can belong to more than one genre depending on the interactions allowed in the game.

In addition to the genre, literature on video game research suggests a broad scope of video game categorizations including entertainment games and serious games with relevant categories of edutainment games, educational games, training games, simulations, and advergames (Susi, Johannesson, Backlund, 2007). These categories of games commonly integrate gaming characteristics such as rules, play structures, and narrative with emotionally valuable outcomes and negotiable consequence, and they can integrate any game genre explained in the paragraph above. However, these game categories have differences in terms of their design purpose and the needs that they gratify for the player.

An *entertainment game* would have the major purpose of allowing the player to gratify various needs of media consumption, while allowing them to enjoy an intense experience. General media consumption gratifications sought by individuals include passing time, companionship, escapism, cognition, arousal, and relaxation (Greenberg, Sherry, Lachlan, Lucas, & Holmstrom, 2010). Research suggest that the unique needs gratified by playing games include competition, challenge, social interaction, diversion, fantasy, and arousal, as well as the need for attractive graphics, game realism, and the need to feel better about self (Lucas & Sherry, 2004; Sherry, Lucas, Greenberg, & Lachlan, 2006). Entertainment games are generally developed and marketed for targeted masses, and have a broad scope.

A *serious game* is not necessarily the opposite of an entertainment game. In fact, a serious game should be able to keep the player entertained. Susi, Johannesson, and Backlund (2007) define serious games as "digital games used for purposes other than mere entertainment" (p.1), expressing that for a game to be serious, it should have a specific purpose and contribute to the player's wellbeing. A serious game would contribute to the player's well-being by providing opportunities for skills building, knowledge acquisition, and targeted problem solving, as well as by introducing different perspectives to lead to attitude, motivation, and behavior change (Susi, Johannesson, & Backlund, 2007; Wouters, van der Spek, & van Oostendorp, 2009). In terms of the needs gratified, the difference between entertainment and serious games is that serious games would be designed particularly to gratify the need for cognition, either to satisfy curiosity or lead to knowledge and perspective gain. Serious games are developed to address a need, and are typically not as immensely marketed. However, according to Susi, Johannesson and Backlund (2007), their R&D funding and market is gradually expanding.

Serious games have been widely used in education due to their focus on cognitive development. However, not all serious games may be educational. An *educational game* would also have the major purpose of gratifying the particular need for cognition, and should lead to a change in knowledge. As Gradler (2004) describes, what distinguishes an educational game from other types of serious games is "the opportunity to apply subject matter knowledge in a new context." (p.576). In other words, an educational game should allow the player to practice current knowledge and use it in context, assess knowledge discrepancy, or build new knowledge through interaction with the game (Gredler, 2004). An educational game is even more targeted due to its specific learning objectives, and is typically used for training and learning purposes for appropriate audiences.

In addition to education and training, serious games can be used for marketing as well due to their influence on attitudinal and behavioral change (Susi, Johannesson, & Backlund, 2007; Wouters, van der Spek, & van Oostendorp, 2009). An *advergame* is a custom game, where the sponsoring brand's intended message is integrated into the gameplay in an entertaining way (Gross, 2010; Moore, 2006). Compared to prior forms of product placement in media, advergames require greater levels of attention and cognitive involvement, making them potentially highly effective (Gross, 2010). Advergames overlap more with the needs gratified by entertainment games for the player, while the developer intends to integrate cognitive outcomes throughout gameplay. Similar to educational games, advergames are highly targeted due to their specific attitudinal or behavioral objectives. They are typically used for marketing purposes on targeted audiences, and are commonly disseminated via online company sources.

Both entertainment and serious games can be utilized for commercial or social marketing purposes. Kotler and Lee (2008) explain that both commercial and social marketing aim to generate changes in the targeted audience in terms of beliefs, attitudes, and behaviors; yet the ultimate goal of social marketing is to lead to a behavioral change to benefit the individual, community, or society as a whole rather than a specific company. Building on Kotler and Lee's distinction of commercial and social marketing (2008), games utilized for commercial marketing would serve the purpose of profiting a company in financial, or reputational gains, whereas games utilized for social marketing would ultimately profit the society by disseminating cognizant actions, and awareness of issues, and knowledge gain.

Gamification and Gamified Applications

Compared to games, gamification is a relatively new concept which has gained attention from both scholars and various industries, and has been adopted in both commercial and social marketing efforts including the contexts of finance, management, health, education, and even news media (Groh, 2012). In its broad definition, gamification is "the application of a game layer on top of the world" (Priebatsch, 2010, npg) or "the use of game design elements in non-game contexts" (Deterding, et. al., 2011, p.2). As Groh (2012, p.40) summarizes, gamified applications integrate game interface design patterns (i.e. badges and levels), game mechanics (i.e. time and resource constraints), game design principles and heuristics (i.e. clear goals), game models (i.e. challenge, curiosity), and game design methods (i.e. playtesting) into non-game contexts.

Many applications of gamification integrate various game elements to have players perform certain tasks. However, a successful gamification application goes beyond simple integration of game elements, and provides enjoyment and sense of satisfaction to players, while holding designers as well as players accountable for facilitating a good life (Deterding, 2014). Huotari and Hamari (2012) also suggest that gamification goes beyond application of game elements, and define gamification as "a process of enhancing a service with affordances for gameful experiences in order to support user's overall value creation" (p.19). This definition addresses the critiques of perceiving gamification as simple adoption of game elements, and acknowledges gamification as valuable experiences of a process (Ferrara, 2013).

Gamification in the commercial marketing and business context is an attempt to increase engagement, involvement, and consequently attitude and behavior change among management, employees, and customers through an integrated utilization of game design with loyalty programs and behavioral economics (Zichermann & Linder, 2013). In order to generate the desired level of engagement at a sustainable level, game mechanics such as points, rewards, achievement badges, and leaderboards are creatively and meaningfully integrated into a planned process of corporate strategy (Zichermann & Linder, 2013). However, as discussed above, gamification is not only about simple integration of game elements. Furthermore, applications of gamification -may it be a frequent flyer program, or workplace improvement initiative, or an advergame- should give the player autonomy (participation should remain voluntary, not mandatory), should have situational norms of conduct (players should be cognizant of the enjoyment of others, not just himself or herself), and allow avoidance of embarrassment (players should be able to modify their behavior) to ensure that the experience generates intrinsic motivation (Deterding, 2014; Ferrara, 2013; Kapp, 2012).

Gamification in the social marketing and educational context has been wide spread. Scholars argue that serious games (games designed with purposes other than mere entertainment) are examples of gamification (Groh, 2012; Kapp, 2012). Kapp (2012) uses a broad definition for gamification, "the delivery of content … using game-based thinking and mechanics… to engage people, motivate action, promote learning, and solve problems" (p.17). According to Kapp (2012), both serious games and gamified applications (such as IBM's INNOV8 for business process management training, or the Army's massive multiplayer online war game for training against Somali pirates) utilize intrinsic goals with extrinsic rewards and elements, where the final outcome is communicated both in the game and outside the game. Similar to any gamified application, the use of gamification in the educational or advocacy contexts should maintain intrinsic motivation and focus on the experience more so than what game elements are integrated (Deterding, 2014). Furthermore, gamified applications of serious games should have clear learning objectives (Burton, Moore & Magliaro, 2004; Hannafin & Hooper, 1993) closely connected to the embedded game elements, mechanics, principles, and models.

All in all, games and gamified applications are now used in various aspects of life, including in commercial and social marketing. Whichever way games are categorized, players engage in a learning process to be able to play any type of game. In the section that follows, learning via video games will be explained in more detail.

Learning from Video Games and Gamified Applications

Learning is defined as a directed and enduring change in the behavior, attitude or beliefs of an individual, after practice or a certain experience (Burton, Moore & Magliaro, 2004; Ertmer & Newby, 1993). Regardless of the medium format, effective learning takes place with the aid of well-designed strategies that are cohesively presented to generate a meaningful experience (Hannafin & Hooper, 1993). From this perspective, well designed video games and successful gamification may lead to better learning outcomes compared to poorly designed classroom instructions.

From an educational stand point, games are "competitive exercises in which the objective is to win and players must apply subject matter or other relevant knowledge in an effort to advance in the exercise to win" (Gredler, 2004, p.571). However, a game does not have to be designed as an educational game for learning to take place. Ang, Avni and Zaphiris (2008) argue that when interacting with video games, two types of learning takes place: learning to play games, and learning through games. Both types of learning are important and valuable and interdependent, but they yield different types of thinking and learning processes. When digital games are defined in an educational context, they become "transformative devices" (Amory, 2007, p. 71) that utilize rules, play and narratives to cause enduring changes in attitudes, beliefs and behaviors in a pre-determined direction due to interaction with the game system and content.

The use of games, followed by simulations and video games for educational purposes has been endorsed since the 1950's (Gredler, 2004). Over the past four decades, scholars from various disciplines have identified that playing educational and conventional video games lead to positive learning outcomes (Lieberman, 2001, 2006; Subrahmanyam & Greenfield, 1994; Subrahmanyam, Greenfield, & Kraunt 2001) and video games were deemed effective instructional tools (Egenfeldt-Nielsen, 2006; Federation of American Scientists, 2006; Greenfield, 1984; Kirriemuir & McFarlane, 2004; Peng, 2009; Randel, Morris, Wetzel, & Whitehill, 1992; Shaffer, Squire & Gee, 2004). Over the years, games and gamified applications have been used in education to allow players to practice or review already existing knowledge, identify discrepancies between what they already know and what they should know, or to help them build new knowledge (Gredler, 2004).

Various aspects influence the effectiveness of video games in learning. For instance, games and simulations have the ability to transport players into another environment with the right learning context, and require them to proactively control that environment, which makes the learning process highly engaging (Gredler, 2004). According to Leach & Sugarman (2005), video games are good learning tools because they not only engage individuals in learning, but also allow them to review and reinforce the learning material, address different learning styles, provide immediate feedback, provide an opportunity to interact with the instructors and with other students, and keep instruction lively. Additionally, adoption of appropriate game elements in learning contexts (successful gamification) yield similar positive learning outcomes (Simoes, Redondo, & Vilas, 2013).

Games have unique characteristics that generate a constructive competition, while requiring players to follow game rules and learn necessary materials to advance in the game (Gredler, 2004). Lieberman (2006) summarizes the appeals of video games as challenging goals, curiosity that the game stimulates, control over actions, and fantasy themes within the game. She further argues that characteristics such as authenticity of sensory cues, as well as the required problem solving, competition, collaboration and skills building during gameplay demand a different set of cognitive skills from the players. The combination of these characteristics makes the gameplay experience rewarding despite the cognitive investment required, and consecutive learning throughout gameplay.

Theoretical Frameworks

When determining their instructional designs and techniques, educators utilize the frameworks of three main theoretical positions, namely behaviorism, cognitivism and constructivism (Ertmer & Newby, 1993; Hannafin & Hooper, 1993). Although all three of these frameworks complement each other in improving instructional design, they differ in terms of their considerations of the role of the learner, the nature of learning, and the generality of learning (Burton, Moore & Magliaro, 2004; Hannafin & Hooper, 1993), as well as on the process of how learning occurs; the types of learning; the environmental, personality, cognitive, and situational factors that influence the process of learning; the ways in which memory functions; and how knowledge is transferred across contexts (Ertmer & Newby, 1993).

In a nutshell, the behaviorist perspective considers learning to be primarily accidental, as a result of observing a stimulus-response-reinforcement cycle. The cognitivist perspective considers learning as a cognitive investment, as a result of deliberate hypothesis testing and schema building. The constructivist perspective considers learning to be an interpretive and social phenomenon, as a result of various levels of interactions that generate meanings. All three of these perspectives explain various aspects of how learning takes place in video games in a complementary manner. In the section that follows, each of these major theoretical frameworks will be examined in relation to video games, with examples from various types of games.

Behaviorist Perspective

The behaviorist perspective on learning focuses on the learning environment as a means to provide appropriate stimuli to create a desired response (Dickey, 2005). Although learning is stimulated by the external environment, behaviorism explains that the individual learns from a trial and error method of active engagement (Burton, Moore & Magliaro, 2004). From this perspective, learning does not require development of complex cognitive strategies; however, the learner is required to make causal associations between the stimulus, their response, and the reinforcement or punishment they receive from the environment (Hannafin & Hooper, 1993). As one of the earlier approaches to learning applied on both animals and humans, behaviorism focuses on a basic form of learning, predominantly examining the role of external stimuli directly influencing the behavior, rather than how the stimuli are processed internally.

Theories from the behaviorist perspective commonly examine changes in the individual's observable and measurable behaviors. For instance, according to Skinner (1968), learning derives from the active behaviors of the individuals such as actions, engagements, and experiences. Skinner's *operant (instrumental) conditioning theory* suggest that learning occurs when specific responses are followed by positive outcomes or negative consequences that provide satisfaction or aversion respectively. Positive outcomes such as rewards (i.e. praising) would positively reinforce the behavior, whereas avoidance of undesirable stimuli (i.e. stopping scolding) would negatively reinforce the behavior. When a specific desirable behavior is positively or negatively reinforced, it tends to be repeated. On the other hand, negative consequences such as positive punishments (i.e. assigning extra work) or negative punishments (i.e. taking away privileges) would generate aversion to the behavior. When a specific undesirable behavior is followed by a punishment, it tends to be suppressed (Burton, Moore & Magliaro, 2004; Hannafin & Hooper, 1993; Kirsch, Lynn, Vigorito, & Miller, 2004; Lovata, 1987).

Other than the *operant learning* approach explained above, the behaviorist perspective also examines respondent learning and observational learning approaches (Burton, Moore & Magliaro, 2004). *Respondent learning* focuses on shaping emotional, physiological, and involuntary reactions such as instincts or reflexes. This approach utilizes establishment of natural connections such as the one between food and salivation combined with the practice of proximity and repetition as studied by Pavlov. Although effective, this form of learning is incidental. *Observational learning* focuses on not only external stimuli, but also on personal determinants shaping behaviors. In other words, the stimulus-response-reinforcement cycle can also be derived from observing behaviors of others and the consequences of others' actions. Bandura (1977) in his social learning theory suggests that such vicarious learning from role models allows individuals to make informed decisions to perform actions with desirable consequences and avoid actions with undesirable consequences. This approach utilizes more complex connections such as the one between appreciation and a valued person.

All three of the behaviorist approaches recognize that learning can be transferred to similar contexts, making learning enduring (Hannafin & Hooper, 1993). Although such transfer of knowledge is context specific, behaviorism acknowledges that individuals adapt to the changes in the environment through the similar process of trial and error as they apply their prior knowledge of consequences of their trials to minimize error. Such transfer allows discovery of patterns and consequently making learning easier over time (Burton, Moore & Magliaro, 2004).

Video Game Learning from the Behaviorist Perspective

Considering the levels of learning involved during gameplay according to Ang, Avni, and Zaphiris (2008), behaviorist theories explain the process when the player is dealing with *learning to play the game* instead of *learning through the game*, since the first process is relevant to behaviors, and the second is relevant to meanings. As explained previously, games are cohesive systems with the components of rules, play, and narrative (Ang, Avni, & Zaphiris, 2008, Salen & Zimmerman, 2005), where all components of the system need to be comprehended to achieve meaningful play. From the behaviorist perspective, learning to play the game, particularly the game rules and play structure are learned through trial and error, whereas learning through the game requires the player to go beyond behavioral structures and grasp the content, namely its narrative and meanings. Therefore, learning through the behaviorist approach best fits for genres of games that do not incorporate complex narratives, such as some traditional/casual games (i.e. arcade, or platform games) or physical enactment games (i.e. shooters, or racing games).

Learning from video games can be explained with various aspects of behaviorist theories, particularly with concepts such as objectives, and punishment and reward mechanisms. Smith and Ragan in their definition of behaviorism, point out Spencer's and Davies' concept of "behavioral objectives," which are currently used to create "learning objectives" in instructional designs (2005, p.26). In order to be able to assess learning, it is necessary to have clearly established learning objectives that are communicated to learners so that they strive to achieve them (Burton, Moore & Magliaro, 2004). Such learning objectives should be plausible and meaningful, and should be tied to realistic reward and punishment mechanisms for players to infer causal relationships. For learning to be effective, the rewards and punishments should be frequently repeated, consistent, fair, and valuable for learners (Hannafin & Hooper, 1993).

A realistic and meaningful punishment and reward mechanism is an essential element in successful video games (Loftus & Loftus, 1983; Salen & Zimmerman, 2004) and is the primary source of learning according to the behaviorist approach. Therefore, designers of video games and gamified applications should utilize well-balanced game design patterns and mechanics (Groh, 2012), including points, leaderboards, challenges, and above all, a meaningful feedback mechanism to directly influence behavior. The learning process from this approach is the same for games designed for commercial or social marketing purposes. In the paragraphs that follow, the behaviorist perspective on learning will be explained using three video games as examples.

Probably the best example to explain the way behaviorism works in video game learning, particularly respondent learning, would be with a series of advergames that were designed for Friskies cat food products (Games for Cats, 2012). These games were designed to be downloaded on the cat owners' iPads (available on the App Store for free), and to be played by either the cat, or by the owner and cat competing against each other. For instance, in *Party Mix-up* game, the cat plays solo to catch virtual treats made by Friskies. The owner needs to tap on start to allow the cat to play, and the cat follows a floating treat on the screen to catch it. As soon as the cat catches the treat, it multiplies into many treats floating on the iPad screen. The cat's behavior of catching the treat followed by increased number of treats is the reward mechanism that positively reinforces the cat to keep playing with greater involvement and at an increasing pace. By observing the changes in the treat followed by the catching behavior, the cat learns to direct its hunting instinct on the treats floating on the screen. Another game, *You vs. Cat,* resembles air hockey games, where the cat plays against a human. The human tries to get the game pieces (including treats and cans of Friskies cat food) into the goal located at the bottom of the screen that is protected by the cat. The human gets 10 points for each goal. The cat needs to catch these moving pieces before they go into the goal. When the cat catches these pieces, they explode and the cat gets 10 points. The cat's behavior of catching the treats triggers an interaction, as the human shoots the next game piece functioning as reinforcement for the cat to keep playing the game. As the site reports, cats are ahead of humans by 37,000,000 points to 25,000,000 (Games for Cats, 2012), demonstrating the little need for complex cognitive skills to play certain games that can be explained by the behaviorist approach.

Although games played by animals is a unique example of how behaviorism explains video game learning, humans learn to play games through the similar process of reward and punishment with the addition of the concept of goals, or desirable outcomes. In fact, behaviorism perceives that the principles governing simple and complex behavioral learning are the same (Burton, Moore & Magliaro, 2004). Particular games for entertainment such as casual games and platform games (rather than strategy and adventure games) utilize the behaviorist approach to learning (particularly operant learning) through observation of behaviors in relation to reward and punishment to reach a particular goal. For instance, many versions of the *Mario Bros.* and *Super Mario Bros.* platform games available on various consoles including PC, Game Boy, Nintendo Wii and DS requires the player to go through an area safely to complete levels of the game (Super Mario Wiki, 2014). While playing *Mario Bros.*, the player is rewarded with coins when he or she walks the game character through the coins floating on the screen. In a more exploratory component of the version that requires trial and error, the player is rewarded with coins every time he or she throws a Koopa (turtle) shell onto a treasure chest. These rewards, positively reinforces the player's behavior to change their ways on the board to collect the coins that can be turned into better in-game benefits. On the other hand, the player is negatively punished with cost of health and eventually life every time he or she runs into a Piranha Plant. With this punishment and reward mechanism, the player develops behaviors of seeking turtle shells and avoiding the dangers on the platform to achieve the desirable outcome. Furthermore, as discussed earlier the behaviorist approach promotes effective transfer of learned knowledge to similar settings (Hannafin & Hooper, 1993). Since the friends and foes as well as the structure of the game have been consistent across various versions of the *Mario Bros.* games over the years, players can transfer their knowledge of satisfactory or aversive behaviors across versions of the game to achieve their goals easier. This allows players to progress faster in each version of the game, making the play experience more satisfying.

The similar process of learning to play the game through the reward and punishment system to achieve a goal is effective in serious games as well, more prominently on certain genres of games. Among such educational video games, *Re-Mission* is a first person shooter designed with a team initiated by Hope Lab. The release of the original game in 2006 was followed by the online games and mobile app, *Re-Mission 2: Nanobot's Revenge* that allows young patients to virtually fight cancer (Hope Lab, 2014). The original game has motivated young cancer patients between ages of 13 to 29 to follow their treatment by providing them a sense of control over the bacteria and cancer cells (Kato, Cole, Bradlyn, & Pollock, 2008). In the game, the player takes on the role of the heroine, Roxxi, to fight the cancer in a body. The player is rewarded for shooting the lymphoma cells with medicine guns, as their destruction leads to completion of missions. As players observe that cancerous cells are destroyed by the actions of Roxxi, they are more likely to repeat the shooting behavior to continue playing the game as a result of a (para)-social learning experience. Furthermore, as research shows, such learned game behavior has transferred to real life, as patients were more likely to follow treatment to destroy the cancer cells in real life (Liberman in Prensky, 2006).

Critique of the Behaviorist Perspective

The behaviorist perspective has been criticized based on a couple of issues that it entails (Johansson & Gardenfors, 2005; Winn, 2004). First of all, the behaviorist perspective ignores the internal mechanisms of the learner throughout the process of learning by focusing particularly on the external stimuli. Second, the behaviorist perspective focuses too much on consequences (punishment and reward) and ignores the role of language and meanings in learning. Consequently, this approach cannot fully explain the process of learning through the game. Third, although Bandura (1977) connects the role of others in the environment with the stimulus-response-consequence cycle of the behaviorist perspective, the approach focuses too much on the individual and ignores the role of collaborative learning. Finally, behaviorism puts too much emphasis on reinforcement. In doing so, the perspective emphasizes the role of extrinsic motivation more than the role of intrinsic motivation for learning, although Skinner (1968) acknowledges that individuals attribute values to the external stimuli and the consequences. All in all, the behaviorist perspective alone only partially explains the process of learning in video games, and other approaches should be incorporated to fully understand this phenomenon.

Cognitivist Perspective

The cognitivist perspective on learning examines the mental representations and mental processes of the individual in relation to how the learner processes external stimuli (Winn, 2004). While the behaviorist perspective examines the external factors, the cognitivist perspective on learning additionally examines the internal motivation process of the player and the schema that the game design promotes (Dickey, 2005). With that, the cognitivist perspective complements the behaviorist perspective in explaining the learning process. Although the analogy has been criticized (Winn, 2004), with the cognitivist perspective, the mind of the player is seen as a computer's central processor where the information is represented by symbols and those symbols are means to process information (Hannafin & Hooper, 1993; Johansson & Gardenfors, 2005).

Theories from the cognitivist perspective commonly examine how the individual processes the information they receive to generate durable mental representations (Hannafin & Hooper, 1993; Winn, 2004). For instance, from the *information processing theory*'s standpoint, learning is defined as a series of transformations of information within the brain. This theory analyzes how information received from the environment is encoded and selectively moved to working (short term) memory and how that information is later transferred to long term memory (Hannafin & Hooper, 1993). The information moved to long term memory forms schemata. These schemata or scripts function as pathways to process new information and consequently as frameworks for future knowledge gain (Hannafin & Hooper, 1993). Put differently, according to the information processing theory individuals develop beliefs to solve a specific problem in certain ways due to learned scripts that develop over time based on external factors and internal processes. It should however be noted that these scripts may also hinder rather than facilitate learning. A person who believes strongly against a certain method of solving a problem will not be influenced the same way a person who believes the method does solve problems.

Information processing theory also emphasizes the importance of the meaningfulness of information in order for it to be deeply processed and transferred to long term memory (Hannafin & Hooper, 1993; Smith & Ragan, 2005). According to Gagne's theory of instruction, there are nine events of instruction: Gaining attention, activating the existing schema, encoding and retrieving cues, providing meaningful organization to ensure semantic encoding, making the student active to ensure feedback and reinforcement, and giving opportunities for rehearsal. All of these events cumulatively lead to enduring learning, since they make it easier to move the information to long term memory.

The cognitivist perspective builds on the behaviorist perspective in terms of making the connection between the external and internal processes influencing thoughts and behaviors. For instance, the cognitivist perspective expands on the vicarious learning process. The vicarious learning phenomenon has been explained by *social learning theory*, which argues that individuals learn by observing others individuals' behaviors, attitudes, and outcomes of those behaviors (Bandura, 1977, 1986; Miller, 2005; Pajares, 2002). Although the early development of this theory focuses on behaviorism, after the theory was developed further, it was changed into *social cognitive theory* and the concept and role of cognition and environment were added. With social cognitive theory, the individual triangulates between personal factors (cognitive, affective and biological events), environmental factors, and behavior in the learning process (Bandura, 1986; Pajares, 2009). In that, the individual exerts cognitive effort to determine his or her future behaviors based on these personal, environmental and past behavioral factors.

Video Game Learning from the Cognitivist Perspective

As discussed earlier, while learning to play video games requires utilization of the behaviorist approaches through a reward and punishment system, learning through the game requires utilization of the cognitivist approaches through processing of information. With that, while games with less prominent narratives are best explained by the behaviorist approach, games with more elaborate narrative (such as adventure games) or those that require more complex play structures (such as strategy games) are best explained by cognitivist approaches. Designers of video games and gamified applications should utilize not only game elements and mechanics, but also gaming principles, heuristics, and processes such as meaningful goals and rules (Groh, 2012) to generate game-like thinking (Kapp, 2012), and consequently lead to changes in attitudes and behavior. In the section that follows, learning from video games will be explained from the lens of cognitivist approaches with examples.

In addition to learning from consequences of their own actions via punishment and reinforcement, video games require players to process game information cognitively through hypothesis testing. For instance, *Age of Empires* (Ensemble Studios, 1997) is a strategy game, which requires the player to advance over time to build the strongest empire. Depending on the game, the player can choose a more defensive, trade and civic advancement oriented strategy to victory (i.e. build a wonder and survive until time runs out), or employ a more aggressive strategy to conquer land through developed armies to win the game. One way to advance in the game is building walls for protection against enemy attacks. Since protection with walls around a city allows the player to gather gold, wood and food required for advancement in the game, the player will tend to build walls. The player's building of walls results in more resources and a prosperous empire (reward), while not building walls leads to attacks by enemy troops and premature defeat (punishment). This causal relationship is learned through trial and error and association of causal relationships between wall building and increasing resources according to the behaviorist approach. However, gameplay dynamics in a strategy game are not as straight forward as that. The player needs to go beyond single observation, and engage in hypothesis testing to realize that walls work better on a highland map, but not on an island map; or circumstances change when the other civilization is set to be an enemy rather than a neutral civilization when played in difficult mode. From the cognitivist approach, the player processes the information that the game provides in different circumstances. As a combination of observed consequences of his or her actions, and processing of situational factors, the player tests different strategies each time, considering the map, the nature of the enemies, and available resources.

When information processing theory is applied to video games, learning occurs through development of certain scripts or schemata about how to behave in specific situations. Viewing pro-social content on TV would lead to development of relevant scripts. Pro-social scenes in video games when played the next time provide cues for using existing scripts. For example, when the individual plays a game that promotes pro-social behavior, such as helping other farmers in Facebook's real time farm simulation game *Farmville* (Zynga, 2009), he or she might not only use previously learned scripts, but also further develop scripts for cooperation, as the game encourages players to help each other in providing resources or help with each other's crops.

Learning from an educational game, such as *Monkey Tales* (Larian Studios & die Keure, 2010) can also be explained by the information processing theory of the cognitivist approach. *Monkey Tales* aims to help primary school students to practice their math skills in an enjoyable way, while adapting to the player's skill level in each time-sensitive mini-game challenge. As an educational game defined by Gradler (2004), *Monkey Tales* incorporates learning objectives and requires the player to use his or her math knowledge in order to proceed in the game. From the information processing theory of the cognitivist approach, the player would have already learned schemata of how to solve a math problem from school. During the game, the player would exert cognitive effort to utilize his or her prior schema of solving a math problem and use it in the game context to be able to proceed in the game. This process allows the player to practice and develop new pathways to utilize existing knowledge in different contexts. Such practice of knowledge in return transfers back to the contexts outside the game. A previous study with 2nd graders has in fact found that playing the game led to higher levels of enjoyment as well as increased accuracy on math tests outside the game context compared to paper exercises and a control group (Nunes Castellar, Van Looy, Szmalec, de Marez, 2014).

The information processing theory of the cognitivist approach also explains learning occupational schemas. With appropriate game design, players can be immersed into the expert systems of *epistemic games* where they learn the schemas of a doctor, a lawyer or a soldier (Shaffer, Squire, & Gee, 2004; Shaffer, 2005). In an epistemic game, the player is provided with a room for rehearsal to remember his or her existing schemas, apply them in the given context, and receive feedback. With epistemic games, the player learns the cognitive schema of a doctor or soldier through hands on experience, and with an opportunity that may not be available in real life. For instance, *SimCity* (Wright, 1993) is an open-ended urban management simulation game that allows the player to take on the role of a mayor. In *SimCity*, the goal of the player is to manage a city successfully by balancing the budget and city services while keeping the citizens happy. Previous research has shown that practicing to be the mayor allowed players to learn the cognitive schema of a mayor, as players have learned about urban planning, as well as various economic and environmental concepts as they were practicing to be mayors (Kirriemuir & McFarlane, 2004; Tanes & Cemalcılar, 2010).

From the perspective of social cognitive theory, video games also give players an opportunity for vicarious learning by observing actions of their avatars, or visual representations in the game (Peng, 2006). Such vicarious learning allows the player to triangulate between personal experiences, game feedback, and behavior carried out by the game character controlled by the player and leads to learning. For instance in an adventure game, *Return to Mysterious Island* (Kheops Studio, 2004), the player controls the game character, Mina, to help her survive through a revisit to the mysterious island from Jules Verne's novel. The player directs Mina to utilize survival skills, including application of some physics and chemistry knowledge. Mina needs to pick certain items, combine them and make tools. When the player observes Mina make ropes out of coconut shells, he or she would learn that coconuts are not only for eating, but also for making a strong rope to climb a tree. In order to learn from this experience, the learner cognitively processes the consequences of the game characters' behaviors, the game's feedback of progress in the game, and his or her perceptions of the uses of coconuts. This leads the player to think creatively with other items on the island, and thus survive.

Another example of vicarious learning through the lens of social cognitive theory is an iPhone and iPad advergame, *The Scarecrow* for Chipotle Mexican Grill Inc. (Moonbot Studios, 2013) which integrates a platform game with a mild narrative. *The Scarecrow* aims to engage the player while conveying Chipotle Mexican Grill's (2014) message of "cultivating a better world" that represents the company's image. Throughout the game, the player directs the scarecrow on a series of missions to bring back good quality food that is sustainably produced. The player witnesses the unconventional practices of the current food industry and identifies with the game character to change that dystopia. The player vicariously experiences the difficulties as well as benefits of using high quality, fresh produce through the experiences of the scarecrow, which leads to changes in perceptions and attitudes towards processed food. From a social cognitive perspective, such perceptual changes are the personal factors, combined with game feedback and play experience may determine future behaviors in real life.

Critique of the Cognitivist Perspective

The cognitivist perspective has been criticized as reductionist in the analogy that humans process information like a computer, and the information learned is nothing more than symbols and algorithms (Winn,

2004). This critique highlights that the relationship between the mental and physical world as well as the individuals selective attentions should be acknowledged. Additionally, the cognitivist perspective of learning has been criticized as focusing too much on the cognition and underestimating the social, cultural and various other environmental influences on the learning process (Johansson & Gardenfors, 2005; Winn, 2004). For instance, the cognitivist approach does not focus enough on the formation of schemata in different situations. All in all, the cognitivist approach alone again falls short on explaining the whole process of learning in video games, and another approach should also be considered to better explain video game learning.

Constructivist Perspective

Among the three major perspectives of learning, namely behaviorism, cognitivism and constructivism, the latest perspective is gaining significant attention from instructional communication scholars (Allen, 2005; Almala, 2006; Benbunan-Fich & Arbaugh, 2006; Ertmer & Newby, 1993; Ruey, 2010). In particular, the concepts of *contextually situated learning* and *active learning* have been frequently discussed within the constructivist perspective (Bryceson, 2005; Huang, 2002; Ruey, 2010), and have strongly influenced contemporary instructional design strategies.

The constructivist perspective builds on the behaviorist and cognitivist approaches in explaining the nature, structure, and consequences of learning. According to the constructivist perspective, knowledge is subjective (Driscoll, 2000; Miller, 2005) and is rationally constructed based on the learner's experiences with previous events, the environment and the context (Ang, Avni, & Zaphiris, 2008; Ertmer & Newby, 1993; Smith & Ragan, 2005). The learner continuously interprets meanings in relation to their cumulative history of experiences (Ertmer & Newby, 1993). During the process of subjective interpretation, the learner acquires complex learning materials, as he or she situates tasks in real life settings in relation to real life examples, uses cognitive apprenticeship, learns collaboratively, and practices social negotiation through discussions and engagement (Ertmer & Newby, 1993).

Different traditions within the constructivist perspective, namely individual constructivism, social constructivism, cognitive constructivism, and contextualism commonly support the perspective that learning requires the active engagement of the learner in relation to multiple contexts and creation of meanings within those contexts. In order to make connections, knowledge should be situated in meaningful and realistic (rational) experiences.

According to *individual constructivism,* learning is an end result of personal interpretations of knowledge, information, and experiences. Individuals recreate knowledge based on their experiences with their environment. Learning depends on factors such as the number of learners, the nature of the task and the content of the learning material (Smith & Ragan, 2005).

Social constructivism argues that learning is an end-result of collaborative action among many learners (Smith & Ragan, 2005). The meaning is embodied in the social dynamics of the group, where multi-level meanings are negotiated and created as a collective action (Ang, Avni, & Zaphiris, 2008). Discussion, negotiation, restriction, collaborative agreement and understanding define the nature of learning from the social constructivist perspective. Vygotsky (1960-1981 in Johansson and Gardenfors, 2005) recognizes that learning is a social function and reasoning and problem solving cannot be separated from the social context. Vygotsky's approach to learning emphasizes this notion of social element, in other words, the importance of the learners' interaction with each other.

Cognitive constructivism argues that learning requires cognitive effort, and is a result of the accommodation, assimilation, and equilibration process as defined by Piaget (Ang, Avni, & Zaphiris, 2008). Based on cognitive constructivism, individuals learn by applying logic and reasoning for hypothesis testing. For that, learners observe, reflect upon and infer rules, and consequently make sense of the world.

According to the *contextualizm* tradition in the constructivist philosophy, learning should be situated in realistic settings or "contexts" that help learners derive meanings (Smith & Ragan, 2005). Learners engage in authentic learning when they strive to solve problems that are designed within realistic, meaningful situations and learning environments. Such learning environments, for instance virtual environments or simulations, allow learners to be in situated cognitions. Situated cognition refers to thinking in connection to contexts that can be experienced in the real world setting (Gee, 2007).

The common assumption across all traditions of constructivism is that learning requires active engagement of the learner in the meaning making process. Therefore, the constructivist approach emphasizes the role of the individual as an engaged component of the learning process. However, expanding on behaviorism and cognitivism, constructivism recognizes not only the role of external factors and internal cognitive processes, but also the contextual factors that allow individuals to learn, make sense and relate to the acquired information.

Video Game Learning from the Constructivist Perspective

Among the two levels of learning involved during gameplay (Ang, Avni, & Zaphiris, 2008), constructivist theories, in particular, explain *learning through the game*, since the process is relevant to interpretation of meanings. Since learning through the game requires the player to go beyond behavioral structures and grasp the content, namely its narrative and meanings, learning through the constructivist approach best fits for genres of games that incorporate complex narratives, such as strategy, role plating, and adventure games in addition to multi-player games.

The constructivist perspective focuses on the player's relation to the game environment and social elements that the design should integrate (Dickey, 2005). Video games provide many opportunities for the player to relate. For instance, with video games the player can experience interaction with another learner through the computer, with the computer system, and with the text (Jones, 2003; Livingstone, 2002). In online gaming communities as well as virtual learning environments, the player interacts with other players and learns from their experiences. In single-player video games, the player interacts with the computer and learns from this interaction with the system. Moreover, the player interacts with the text in some of the online and offline games, and manipulates information on the game space.

From the constructivist perspective, designers of video games and gamified applications should utilize game models (such that player experiences facilitate satisfaction of the need for curiosity, diversion, and social interaction) and design methods (for instance playtesting and player-centric design) in game development (Groh, 2012). This would allow players to become active and valuable participants of meaningful experience (Deterding, 2014; Huotari & Hamari, 2012; Malaby, 2007), and consequently influence interpretations, perceptions and behavior.

From the constructivist perspective, video games and gamified applications are ideal for learning because they demand higher level cognitive engagement (cognitive constructivism), enable multi-level interactivity for collaboration and negotiation (social constructivism), facilitate meaning-making through active learning (individual constructivism) and allow contextually situated learning (contextualism). Each of these reasons is explained below with examples from various categories of games.

Cognitive Engagement

Based on cognitive constructivist tradition, learning requires cognitive processing, while video games demand a high level of cognitive processing from the player. Game play requires pattern recognition and making sense of the rules, a loop of decision making and action, immediate feedback, as well as a sense of enjoyment due to mastery skills (Brown, 2006). Scholars further suggest that video games require parallel processing of information in the individual's mind instead of sequential processing (Gee, 2007; Greenfield, 1984; Prensky, 2006). While sequential processing allows the learner to make inferences out of orderly information, parallel processing requires the learner to rapidly connect seemingly unrelated information in order to make sense of the environment. Consequently, parallel processing requires a different, if not more demanding cognitive effort from the learner.

Lieberman (2006) points out that the learner is not only required, but also motivated to be cognitively engaged while playing games. As games have their own logic and rules, and the player needs to recognize patterns in order to complete a game, the player learns the embedded rules along the way. The player invests time and effort into the game to be able to play the game. This time and effort is even more than they put in reading the material, yet more rewarding due to the interaction and feedback that the player receives from the game. As a result of this satisfactory investment, the experience that is rewarded by communication of quantified outcomes becomes more valuable to the player (Juul, 2003). Lieberman (2006) argues that the mental effort the player puts into the game leads to better learning as well as retention.

From the cognitive constructivist standpoint, the player makes sense of his or her efforts in relation to the game rules and engages in a meaningful gameplay experience, which in turn results in meaning making and learning. For instance, an action adventure game on Wii Console, *Disaster: Day of Crisis* (Monolith Soft, 2007) challenges the player to take on the role of a trained rescue team member (Ray) to overcome consequences of various natural disasters including earthquake, fire, tsunami, volcano eruption, flood, and hurricane, while fighting against an underground Special Forces unit (SURGE). The player must identify hazards, determine appropriate ways to help survivors, and practice triage, CPR, and first aid on wounded civilians. The game increases awareness of risks relevant to natural disasters such as falling debris, smoke, and dust that might incapacitate an individual, while allowing them to practice search and rescue skills. The main character in the game engages in unreasonably brave actions throughout the story, which remind the player that he or she is playing a game, and needs to figure out the patterns of this game to get out of trouble. From the cognitive constructivist approach, the player would apply their existing knowledge of natural disaster response and first aid into the game context, learn from the experiences of the game character, combine pieces of information scattered throughout the game narrative, and consequently acquire new knowledge of possible hazards and survival strategies during natural disasters. Unlike behaviorist and cognitivist approaches, the constructivist approach acknowledges the players' ability to identify the context of the game from reality. The player would critically reflect on what he or she can do in a similar real life context, for instance, sign up for search and rescue trainings, but not engage in unrealistic bravery as the game character does.

Interactivity for Collaboration and Social Negotiation

Video games facilitate learning because they provide multi-level interactivity. With video games, the player can experience interaction with another player through the computer, with the computer system, and with the text (Jones, 2003; Livingstone, 2002). From the social constructivist tradition, interacting with others during game play is essential for learning. Hence, the player's relation to the game environment and other gamers are essential aspects of video game design (Dickey, 2005). Furthermore, social play is another important factor in gaming, even if the game is not played on-line with random strangers. A study by Kahne, Middaugh, and Evans (2008) showed that 49% of teenagers are social players and 77% of those social players play in the presence of others such as friends or family members. Even if it is a single-player game, during social play, the player makes sense of the game content, rules and system as a result of his or her direct interaction with the game, as well as from the communication he or she has about the game with a friend or family member. Interaction with others during gameplay allows players to discuss and negotiate meanings and lead to learning that could not have been achieved from other types of gameplay.

During gameplay, learners experience "the world in different ways, forming new affiliations and preparation for future learning" (Gee, 2007, p. 24). A good video game is designed to encourage active and critical participation of the learners in contextually bound meaning creation. Gee (2007) argues that such meaning-creation can best be achieved with a social mind. The meaning making process through the social mind is facilitated in affinity groups -communities of practices- where members support each other in terms of information and practical issues (Gee, 2007; Lave & Wenger, 1991). With that, affinity groups create the social mind. Gee argues that the players think in terms of patterns and tend to recognize patterns. However, the recognition of these patterns is restricted by cultural workings that are affected by previous experiences. For those who gather around a video game, when they create "affinity groups," they also create a culture that forms the understanding of the knowledge that is created within that specific domain (Gee, 2007). So, learning from video games is inherently social. The learners have an insider's perspective and actively influence the context, where meaning is created.

In massively multiplayer online games (MMO's, MMOG's or MMORPG's) such as *World of Warcraft* (Blizzard Entertainment, 2004), the player develops his or her game character (avatar) in terms of skills and abilities throughout a series of gameplays and quests in realms. Throughout the game, the player interacts with not only non-player characters in the virtual space, but also with other players. Moreover, the player can join guilds, which can provide competitive advantage in the game. Although the game can be played solo, more complex quests require team-play, and consequently the ability to collectively strategize, negotiate, collaborate, and act as a team. From the perspective of social constructivism, through this interaction the player learns not only game tricks from his or her fellow team members, but also develops a different perspective on the understanding, identification and resolution of issues in the game context. In other words, interaction with others in the game allows the player to construct a broader set of meanings that leads to learning.

Active Learning

Active learning refers to being engaged with the learning content by taking a participatory role. Such active participation is related to higher levels of comprehension and critical thinking skills (Leach & Sugarman, 2005). In the article *Seven Principles for Good Practice in Undergraduate Education*, Chickering and Gamson (1987) explain that students must talk and write about what they are learning and relate it to the past and present. The authors further argue that having hands-on experience through work experience ensures active learning.

Instead of the teacher systematically designing learning instructions, in a video game the designer establishes rules and the underlying systems before the application of the learning materials. Instead of the teacher, the game provides cues, participation, reinforcement, and feedback to the player. Moreover, the video game allows the student to learn at his or her pace, and interact with the material individually, and yet creates a feeling that he or she is being evaluated on a standard basis, or based upon some previous players who have gone through the game and achieved high scores.

From the individual contructivist tradition, video games are a good fit for learning because of the active participation they offer to the learner (Brown, 2006). Active learning is the first learning principle built in video games (Gee, 2007). Video games create opportunities for meaning-making through such active participation, since the player constantly makes and manages meanings throughout the game-play (Turner, 2006). Furthermore, instead of reading about phenomena from textbooks, learners experience them first hand through their interaction with the game system or with other players (Shaffer, Squire, & Gee, 2004).

The interactive nature of video games allows learners to have this hands-on experience in a safe environment since the consequences of their actions do not have serious implications (Juul, 2003). Video games engage the learner so much that they learn "to be something" by taking over the role of for instance an EMT, in addition to "learn about something" such as triage (Brown, 2006, p. 19). Moreover, video games allow an informal type of learning that becomes a "reflective practicum" (Brown, 2006, p. 23), where the player practices a task (triage for instance) without the threat or making grave mistakes.

Active learning is an important phenomenon especially in simulation games (Lieberman, 2006). Simulations are simplified systems of real life, where the complexity of real life is reduced to predictable rules (Salen & Zimmerman, 2004). For instance, a flight simulation game, *Microsoft Flight* (Microsoft Studios, 2012) allows the player to cruse over cities flying various types of aircrafts. Since each aircraft is different, their reaction to the environment varies in the game as they would in the real world. For instance, the game responds differently during ascent versus descent due to difference in air resistance. Yet, such resistance is consistent every time the player restarts the game after a crash, making it easier to learn the association between air resistance and required action in a safe environment.

With active learning during simulations, players not only learn about the patterns, but also can relate their knowledge to real life situations. In that, simulation games utilize active learning in order to help players contextually situate meaning and transfer knowledge from one domain (virtual) to the other (real). For instance, in addition to the *America's Army* game utilized in recruitment and training of active soldiers (Susi, Johannesson & Backlund, 2007), the US Navy utilizes simulation games to reliably assess officers' competencies based on behavioral and cognitive algorithms, and determine what they need to learn (Office of Naval Research, 2014). Within this simulation game environment, the Navy allows officers to take over multiple roles on a destroyer which require them to "organize personnel, manage resources, follow established protocols and coordinate containment actions across multiple events" (Office of Naval Research, 2014, npg). This virtual environment challenges officers to understand the causes and potential consequences of various situations such as fire and flood; use appropriate communication channels; and make appropriate decision to alleviate the situation in a realistic yet safe virtual environment. The use of this game for educational purposes better allow officers to not only practice but also transfer their knowledge to real life settings during active combat.

Contextually Situated Learning

When learning is contextually situated, instructions are "anchored" in problem based contexts "that are realistic to learners and common to everyday applications of knowledge" (Smith & Ragan, 2005, p.20).

From the contextualism tradition of the constructivist perspective, Gee (2007) points out that human learning is not about simply taking in the information presented to them; rather learning is situated in a material, social and cultural world. Gee also expresses that video games contain built-in learning principles that allow the players to situate meanings within specific contexts and domains. With the "situated meaning principle" (p.105), Gee points out that the meanings of signs are situated in embodied experiences- in contexts.

Constructivists and situated learning theorists argue that human behavior is bounded by context (Squire, 2002). Shaffer, Squire and Gee also argue that the power of video games in learning come from their ability to develop "situated understandings" (2004, p. 5). This context related situation allows the transfer of knowledge acquired from one context to another, between levels, among sequels or even among genres, and hopefully between game and real life (Squire, 2002). Due to this transfer and exposure to multiple contexts, the learner is exposed to even more complex concepts and systems. As learning becomes challenging, it becomes more attractive.

Prensky (2006) points out that knowing the terms related to a subject matter does not necessarily mean knowing the concepts, and that current schooling does not engage students enough to fully grasp concepts. However with video games, the player can situate meanings and make connections between concepts, much better than reading about them, because video games give learners situations that they actively engage (Lieberman, 2006). With that, video games not only give examples of situations, but allow the learners to interact with that situation, modify the dynamics of this situation and examine the consequences of their actions within any given situation.

The constructivist perspective also highlights the role of meaningfulness in learning (Smith & Ragan, 2005). A video game's meaningfulness is related to its ability to successfully mimic complex realities to allow players to make connections with real life situations as well as their existing knowledge and expectations. A video game is meaningful if there is consistency within its "magic circle" (Salen & Zimmerman, 2004, p. 93), where all the rules that govern the game form a unifying context. For instance, *The Elder Scrolls IV: Oblivion* (available on PC, Xbox360, mobile, and PS3) is an action role-playing game that follows an open ended storyline with a character of the player's choice (Bethesda Game Studios, 2006). The player needs to go through a series of quests helping non player characters, and getting useful items or money as rewards as well as skills points when the mission is accomplished. Although the game takes place in imaginary lands with magic, potions, poisons, and mythical creatures and races, the characters and interactions overlap with those of everyday humans. The character can be customized in terms of not only demographics, but also in birth sign, skills, and attributes, which influence gameplay. Similar to real life characters, the game character needs to sleep, heal, advance his or her skills, and develop strategies to get out of trouble. For instance, the player needs to read faces to understand if their negotiation strategies are working. Puzzles that the player needs to solve are targeted attempts to help proceed in the game. All in all, throughout the gameplay the player combines real life knowledge and perceptions of relationships in understanding the rules, structures, and story of the game that takes place in imaginary lands. Through this process of cross transfer of knowledge and with the help of realistic and meaningful game design, the game makes sense within its magic circle, or its context. Consequently, the player develops relational and strategy building skills with the meaning making process throughout his or her game interaction.

DISCUSSION: FUTURE RESEARCH DIRECTIONS

There is a growing body of high quality research about the process and outcomes of both entertainment and serious video game play. Recent studies utilize various theories including social cognitive theory, flow theory, actor-network theory, theory of reasoned action, and self-determination theory. Despite the growing body of theory driven research, few studies focus on how and why learning takes place in video games. Therefore, there is still a need for empirical research to examine how and why learning takes place during gameplay. Such research can derive from the three major theoretical frameworks discussed in this chapter. Below are some recommendations for future research that would utilize behaviorist, cognitivist, and constructivist approaches in empirical examination.

1. Need for research from behaviorist approach

The behaviorist approach focuses on a basic form of learning in terms of changes in behavior as a result of the game's reward and punishment mechanics. Although previous research has examined how the players' skills overlap with the demands of the game, and how the game's reward system reinforces behaviors, there is a need for empirical research that manipulates games to assess how game stimuli work on the player. Future research can focus specifically on the reward and punishment system of games by manipulating games and various elements of gamified applications across experimental conditions to detect differences in behavioral learning during gameplay.

2. Need for research from cognitivist approach

Most of the research on video games has been conducted from the perspective of the cognitivist approach. Earlier studies have focused on cognitive engagement during gameplay, as well as cognitive skills acquired as a result of gameplay. Future research should test how messages, ideas and concepts are learned throughout gameplay in relation to the formation on schemata in the long run. Furthermore, future research can particularly examine what specific game elements, mechanics, principles and heuristics generate the greatest cognitive engagement in gamified applications.

3. Need for research from constructivist approach

There is a growing body of literature from the constructivist perspective, especially focused on multiplayer online games and interactions between players in identity formation and negotiation. However, there is still a further need for empirical research from various disciplines to test how collaborative learning, contextually situated learning and active learning takes place in video games, where the game environment is manipulated to test its influence on the learning and meaning making process. Moreover, there is still room for examining the player's meaning making process in single-player games with the constructivist perspective, focusing on the player-game system interaction. Finally, there is need for more research on how participants contribute to the value making process in gamified applications.

CONCLUSION

The purpose of this chapter was to emphasize that learning is an inherent component of any type of video game and gamified application. With this understanding, the behaviorist, cognitivist and constructivist perspectives were used to explain how, why, and what type of learning occurs during video game play. In doing so, this chapter explained, compared, and contrasted these three positions, then provided examples of specific games and applications designed for commercial and social marketing with the lens of these three positions. Furthermore, concepts of cognitive engagement, social negotiation, active learning and contextually situated learning were further explained in relation to video games, since recent literature highlights the importance of these concepts.

In summary, from the behaviorist perspective, learning from video games is primarily accidental as a result of the game feedback to player's behaviors of trial and error. The player needs to make the causal inference for learning to take place. Learning emerges from the player's interaction with the game rules while discovering how to play it. The gamification efforts from this approach would utilize game elements and mechanics such as badges, points, leaderboards, and challenges to generate an engaging stimulus-response mechanism. From the cognitivist perspective, learning from video games is a cognitive investment. The player makes observations, and conducts hypothesis testing throughout the game. The player needs to go beyond making causal inferences, and develop schemas and inferences for learning to take place. Learning emerges from the player's interaction with the game rules, play structure, and narrative. The gamification efforts from this approach would utilize design principles and heuristics such as meaningful goals and rules to cognitively engage the player and allow them to develop various strategies. From the constructivist perspective, learning from video games is not only a social phenomenon that results from the player's interaction with others, with the system and with the texts, but also an active meaning-making process that is a result of gameplay. The cognitively demanding, active meaning making process of gameplay allows an individual to learn. Learning emerges from the player's interaction with the rule based system of the game, interaction with other learners, and interaction with the narrative content. The player situates phenomena in the game's context, and is actively engaged in the meaning-making process. The gamification efforts from this approach would utilize game models such that player experiences facilitate satisfaction of the need for curiosity, diversion, and social interaction; and design methods such as play-centric approaches to allow players enjoy a meaningful experience.

Although there is a growing research emphasis on both entertainment and serious video games, most of the current research focuses on whether or not cognitive, affective, and behavioral change is taking place. There is still a great need for empirical research from various disciplines examining how and why learning occurs throughout video game play with a solid theoretical focus. Although this chapter attempted to provide guidance in applying major learning theories to the concept of video games in a comparative and explanatory manner, such guidance would be more concrete with empirical research evidence. Examining how learning occurs during video game play across various game categories may allow scholars, instructors, game designers, policy makers, and business practitioners to utilize video games and gamified applications more efficiently in their work.

REFERENCES

Age of Empires [computer software]. (1997 Ensemble Studios. Microsoft.

Allen, K. (2005). Online learning: Constructivism and conversation as an approach to learning. *Innovations in Education and Teaching International, 42*(3), 247–256. doi:10.1080/01587910500167985

Almala, A. H. (2006). Applying the principles of constructivism to a quality e-learning environment. *Distance Learning, 3,* 33–40.

Amory, A. (2007). Game object model version II: A theoretical framework for educational game development. *Educational Technology Research and Development, 55*(1), 51–77. doi:10.1007/s11423-006-9001-x

Ang, C. S., Avni, E., & Zaphiris, P. (2008). Linking pedagogical theory of computer games to their usability. *International Journal on E-Learning, 7,* 533–558.

Apperley, T. H. (2006). Genre and game studies: Toward a critical approach to video game genres. *Simulation & Gaming, 37*(1), 6–23. doi:10.1177/1046878105282278

Bandura, A. (1977). *Social learning theory.* New Jersey: Prentice Hall.

Bandura, A. (1986). *Social foundations of thought and action: A social cognitive theory.* Englewood Cliffs, NJ: Prentice-Hall.

Benbunan-Fich, R., & Arbaugh, J. B. (2006). Separating the effects of knowledge construction and group collaboration in learning outcomes of web-based courses. *Information & Management, 43*(6), 778–793. doi:10.1016/j.im.2005.09.001

The Elder Scrolls IV: Oblivion. [computer software]. (2006). Bethesda Game Studios, 2K Games.

Brown, J. S. (2006). New learning environments for the 21st century: Exploring the edge. *Change, 38*(5), 18–24. doi:10.3200/CHNG.38.5.18-24

Bryceson, K. (2007). The online learning environment—A new model using social constructivism and the concept of 'Ba' as a theoretical framework. *Learning Environments Research, 10*(3), 189–206. doi:10.1007/s10984-007-9028-x

Burton, J. K., Moore, D. M., & Magliaro, S. G. (2004). Behaviorism and instructional technology. In D. H. Jonasses (Ed.), *Handbook of Research on Educational Communications and Technology* (2nd ed.). Mahwah, NJ: Lawrence Erlbaum Associates.

Chickering, A. W., & Gamson, Z. F. (1987). Seven principles for good practice in undergraduate education. *AAHE Bulletin, 39,* 3–7.

Chipotle Mexican Grill. (2014). Food with integrity. *Chipotle.* Retrieved from https://www.chipotle.com/en-us/fwi/fwi.aspx

Deterding, S. (2014). Eudaimonic design, or six invitations to rethink gamification. In S. Fizek, M. Fuchs, P. Ruffino & N. Schrape (Eds.), *Rethinking Gamification.* Lüneburg, Germany: Meson Press. Retrieved from http://projects.digital-cultures.net/meson-press/files/2014/06/9783957960016-rethinking-gamification.pdf

Deterding, S., Dixon, D., Khaled, R., & Nacke, L. (2011, September 28-30). From game design elements to gamefulness: Defining "gamification". *Proceedings of the 15th International Academic MindTrek Conference*, Tampere, Finland. Retrieved from https://www.cs.auckland.ac.nz/courses/compsci747s2c/lectures/paul/definition-deterding.pdf

Dickey, M. (2006). Game design narrative for learning: Appropriating adventure game design narrative devices and techniques for the design of interactive learning environments. *Educational Technology Research and Development, 54*(3), 245–263. doi:10.1007/s11423-006-8806-y

Disaster: Day of Crisis [Software]. (2007Monolith Soft. Nintendo.

Driscoll, M. P. (2000). *Psychology of learning for instruction*. Boston: Allyn & Bacon.

Egenfeldt-Nielsen, S. (2006). Overview of research on the educational use of video games. *Digital Kompatense, 1*, 184–213.

Essential facts about the computer and video game industry. (2014). Entertainment Software Association. Retrieved from http://www.theesa.com/facts/pdfs/esa_ef_2014.pdf

Ertmer, P. A., & Newby, T. J. (1993). Behaviorism, cognitivism, constructivism: Comparing critical features from an instructional design perspective. *Performance Improvement Quarterly, 6*(4), 50–72. doi:10.1111/j.1937-8327.1993.tb00605.x

Farmville. [Online Application]. (2009). Zynga. Facebook

Federation of American Scientists. (2006). Harnessing the power of video games for learning. Retrieved from http://www.fas.org/gamesummit/Resources/Summit%20on%20Educational%20Games.pdf

Ferrara, J. (2013). Games for persuasion: Argumentation, procedurality, and the lie of gamification. *Games and Culture, 8*(4), 289–304. doi:10.1177/1555412013496891

Games for Cats. (2012). *Nestle Purina Petcare Company*. Retrieved from http://gamesforcats.com/

Gee, J. P. (2007). *What video games have to teach us about learning and literacy*. New York: Palgrave Macmillan.

Greenberg, B. S., Sherry, J., Lachlan, K., Lucas, K., & Holmstrom, A. (2010). Orientations to video games among gender and age groups. *Simulation & Gaming, 41*(2), 238–259. doi:10.1177/1046878108319930

Greenfield, P. M. (1984). *Mind and media: The effects of television, video games and computers*. Cambridge, MA: Harvard University Press.

Groh, F. (2012, February 14). Gamification: State of the art definition and utilization. In N. Asaj, B. Konings, M. Poguntke, F. Schaub, B. Wiedersheim & M. Weber (Eds.), *Proceedings of the 4th Seminar on Research Trends in Media Informatics*. Ulm University, Germany. Retrieved from http://vts.uni-ulm.de/docs/2012/7866/vts_7866_11380.pdf

Gross, M. L. (2010). Advergames and the effects of game-product congruity. *Computers in Human Behavior, 26*(6), 1259–1265. doi:10.1016/j.chb.2010.03.034

Hannafin, M. J., & Hooper, S. R. (1993). Learning principles. In M. J. Fleming & W. H. Levie (Eds.), *Instructional Message Design: Principles from the Behavioral and Cognitive Sciences* (2nd ed.). Englewood Cliffs, NJ: Educational Technologies Publications.

Hope Lab. (2014). Innovative solutions. *Hope Lab.* Retrieved from http://www.hopelab.org/innovative-solutions/

Huang, H.-M. (2002). Toward constructivism for adult learners in online learning environments. *British Journal of Educational Technology*, *33*(1), 27–37. doi:10.1111/1467-8535.00236

Huotari, K., & Hamari, J. (2012, October 3-5). Defining gamification - A service marketing perspective. *MindTrek*, 17-22. *Proceedings of the 16th International Academic MindTrek Conference*, Tampere, Finland. Retrieved from http://www.hubscher.org/roland/courses/hf765/readings/p17-huotari.pdf

Johansson, P., & Gardenfors, P. (2005). Introduction to cognition, education, and communication technology. In P. Gardenfors & P. Johansson (Eds.), *Cognition, education and communication technology*. London: Lawrence Erlbaum Associates.

Jones, S. (Ed.). (2003). *Encyclopedia of new media*. Thousand Oaks: Sage. doi:10.4135/9781412950657

Juul, J. (2003, November). *The game, the player, the world: Looking for a heart of gameness*. Paper presented at the Level Up: Digital Games Research Conference. Retrieved from http://www.jesperjuul.net/text/gameplayerworld/

Kahne, J., Middaugh, E., & Evans, C. (2008). *The civic potential of video games*: CERG and MacArthur Foundation. Retrieved from http://www.civicsurvey.org/sites/default/files/publications/Civic_Pot_Video_Games.pdf

Kapp, K. (2012). *The gamification of learning and instruction: Game-based methods and strategies for training and education*. San Francisco, CA: Pfeifer.

Kato, P. M., Cole, S. W., Bradlyn, A. S., & Pollock, B. H. (2008). A video game improves behavioral outcomes in adolescents and young adults with cancer: A randomized trial. *Pediatrics*, *122*(2), e305–e317. doi:10.1542/peds.2007-3134 PMID:18676516

Kheops Studio. (2004). *Return to Mysterious Island* [computer software]. The Adventure Company.

Kirriemuir, J., & McFarlane, A. (2004). Literature review on games and learning. (Report No. 8). *NESTA*. Retrieved from http://archive.futurelab.org.uk/resources/documents/lit_reviews/Games_Review.pdf

Kirsch, I., Lynn, S. J., Vigorito, M., & Miller, R. R. (2004). The role of cognition in classical and operant conditioning. *Journal of Clinical Psychology*, *60*(4), 369–392. doi:10.1002/jclp.10251 PMID:15022268

Kotler, P., & Lee, N. R. (2008). *Social marketing: Influencing behaviors for good* (3rd ed.). Thousand Oaks: Sage.

Lave, J., & Wenger, E. (1991). *Situated learning: Legitimate peripheral participation*. Cambridge, UK: Cambridge University Press. doi:10.1017/CBO9780511815355

Leach, G. J., & Sugarman, T. S. (2005). Play to win! Using games in library instruction to enhance student learning. *Research Strategies*, *20*(3), 191–203. doi:10.1016/j.resstr.2006.05.002

Lieberman, D. A. (2001). Management of chronic pediatric diseases with interactive health games: Theory and research findings. *The Journal of Ambulatory Care Management, 24*(1), 26–38. doi:10.1097/00004479-200101000-00004 PMID:11189794

Lieberman, D. A. (2006). What can we learn from playing interactive games? In P. Vorderer & J. Bryant (Eds.), *Playing video games: Motives, responses, and consequences*. Mahvah, New Jersey: Lawrence Erlbaum Associates.

Livingstone, S. (2002). *Young people and new media*. London: Sage.

Loftus, G., & Loftus, F. (1983). *Mind at play: The psychology of video games*. New York: Basic Books.

Lovata, L. M. (1987). Behavioral theories relating to the design of information systems. *Management Information Systems Quarterly, 11*(2), 147–149. doi:10.2307/249354

Lucas, K., & Sherry, J. L. (2004). Sex differences in video game play: A communication-based explanation. *Communication Research, 31*(5), 499–523. doi:10.1177/0093650204267930

Malaby, T. (2007). Beyond play: A new approach to games. *Games and Culture, 2*(2), 95–113. doi:10.1177/1555412007299434

Microsoft Flight [computer software]. (2012Microsoft Studios. Microsoft.

Miller, K. (2005). *Communication theories, perspectives, processes and context* (2nd ed.). New York: McGraw-Hill.

Monkey Tales [computer software]. (2010 Larian Studios & die Keure. Larian Studios.

The Scarecrow. [Software]. (2013). Moonbot Studios. Chipotle Mexican Grill Inc. Retrieved from http://www.scarecrowgame.com/index.html

Moore, E. S. (2006). It's child's play: Advergaming and the online marketing of food to children. *Kaiser Family Foundation Report*. Retrieved from http://kaiserfamilyfoundation.files.wordpress.com/2013/01/7536.pdf

Nunes Castellar, E., Van Looy, J., Szmalec, A., & de Marez, L. (2014). Improving arithmetic skills through gameplay: Assessment of the effectiveness of an educational game in terms of cognitive and affective learning outcomes. *Information Sciences, 264*, 19–31. doi:10.1016/j.ins.2013.09.030

Office of Naval Research. (2014). Game-based training and education. *U.S. Navy*. Fact sheet. Retrieved from http://www.onr.navy.mil/en/Media-Center/Fact-Sheets/Game-Based-Training.aspx

Pajares, F. (2002). Overview of social cognitive theory and of self-efficacy. Retrieved from http://www.emory.edu/EDUCATION/mfp/eff.html

Peng, W. (2006). *Using a computer game to promote a healthy life style to college students*. [Doctoral dissertation]. University of Southern California, Los Angeles, CA.

Peng, W. (2009). Design and evaluation of a computer game to promote a healthy diet for young adults. *Health Communication, 24*(2), 115–127. doi:10.1080/10410230802676490 PMID:19280455

Prensky, M. (2006). *Don't bother me mom- I'm learning*. St. Paul, MN: Paragon House.

Priebatsch, S. (2010). The game layer on top of the world. *TED*. Retrieved from http://www.ted.com/ talks/seth_priebatsch_the_game_layer_on_top_of_the_world.html

Randel, J. M., Morris, B. A., Wetzel, C. D., & Whitehill, B. V. (1992). The effectiveness of games for educational purposes: A review of recent research. *Simulation & Gaming*, *23*(3), 261–276. doi:10.1177/1046878192233001

Ruey, S. (2010). A case study of constructivist instructional strategies for adult online learning. *British Journal of Educational Technology*, *41*(5), 706–720. doi:10.1111/j.1467-8535.2009.00965.x

Salen, K., & Zimmerman, E. (2004). *Rules of play*. Cambridge: MIT Press.

Shaffer, D. W. (2005). Epistemic frames for epistemic games. *Computers & Education*, *43*, 223–234.

Shaffer, D. W., Squire, K. R., & Gee, J. P. (2004). Video games and the future of learning. Retrieved from http://www.academiccolab.org/resources/gappspaper1.pdf

Sherry, J. L., Lucas, K., Greenberg, B., & Lachlan, K. (2006). Video game uses and gratifications as predictors of use and game preference. In P. Vorderer & J. Bryant (Eds.), *Playing computer games: Motives, responses, and consequences* (pp. 213–224). Mahwah, NJ: Lawrence Erlbaum.

Simoes, J., Redondo, R. D., & Vilas, A. F. (2013). A social gamification framework for a K-6 learning platform. *Computers in Human Behavior*, *29*(2), 345–353. doi:10.1016/j.chb.2012.06.007

Skinner, B. F. (1968). *The technology of teaching*. Englewood Cliffs, NJ: Prentice-Hall.

Smith, P. L., & Ragan, T. J. (2005). *Instructional design* (3rd ed.). Hoboken, NJ: Wiley.

Squire, K. R. (2002). Cultural framing of computer / video games. *The International Journal of Computer Game Research, 2*. Retrieved from http://gamestudies.org/0102/squire/

Statista, daily time spent playing video games per capita in the United States in 2008, 2013 and 2018 (in minutes). (2014a). *Statista*. Retrieved from http://www.statista.com/statistics/186960/time-spent-with-videogames-in-the-us-since-2002/

Statista, global video games revenue from 2012 to 2015 (in billion U.S. dollars). (2014b). *Statista*. Retrieved from http://www.statista.com/statistics/237187/global-video-games-revenue/

Subrahmanyam, K., & Greenfield, P. (1994). Effect of video game practice on spatial skills in girls and boys. *Journal of Applied Developmental Psychology*, *15*(1), 13–32. doi:10.1016/0193-3973(94)90004-3

Subrahmanyam, K., Greenfield, P., Kraut, R., & Gross, E. (2001). The impact of computer use on children's and adolescent's development. *Applied Developmental Psychology*, *22*(1), 7–30. doi:10.1016/S0193-3973(00)00063-0

Super Mario Wiki. (2014, July 30). Retrieved from http://www.mariowiki.com/Main_Page

Susi, T., Johannesson, M., & Backlund, P. (2007). *Serious games: An overview* [Technical Report HS-IKI -TR-07-001). School of Humanities and Informatics University of Skövde, Sweden. Retrieved July 8, 2014, from http://www.diva-portal.org/smash/get/diva2:2416/FULLTEXT01.pdf

Tanes, Z., & Cemalcılar, Z. (2010). Learning from SimCity: An empirical study of Turkish adolescents. *Journal of Adolescence*, *33*(5), 731–739. doi:10.1016/j.adolescence.2009.10.007 PMID:19931157

Turner, J. S. (2006). Book reviews. *The Quarterly Journal of Speech*, *92*, 109–112.

Winn, W. (2004). Cognitive perspective in psychology. In D. H. Jonasses (Ed.), *Handbook of Research on Educational Communications and Technology* (2nd ed.). Mahwah, NJ: Lawrence Erlbaum Associates.

World of Warcraft [computer software]. (2004). Blizzard Entertainment.

Wouters, P., van der Spek, E. D., & van Oostendorp, H. (2009). Current practices in serious game research: A review from a learning outcomes perspective. In T. Connolly, M. Stansfield, & L. Boyle (Eds.), *Games-Based Learning Advancements for Multi-Sensory Human Computer Interfaces: Techniques and Effective Practices*. Hershey, PA: IGI Global. doi:10.4018/978-1-60566-360-9.ch014

Wright, W. (1993). *SimCity 2000* [computer software]. Maxis.

Zichermann, G., & Linder, J. (2013). *The Gamification revolution: How leaders leverage game mechanics to crush the competition*. New York: McGraw Hill.

KEY TERMS AND DEFINITIONS

Advergames: A form of serious games. Games that transmit a message for a business or organization, while gratifying various needs of media consumption for the player.

Behaviorism: Pedagogical approach that focuses on the role of external stimuli in determining learned behavior.

Cognitivism: Pedagogical approach that focuses on the role of external factors, cognitive processes, and mental representations of information in learning.

Constructivism: Pedagogical approach that focuses on the role of external, individual, and contextual factors in how humans generate meanings throughout the process of learning.

Educational Games: A form of serious games. Games that satisfy the need for cognition where specific learning objectives are fulfilled by players using their knowledge in context.

Entertainment Games: Games that were designed for entertainment purposes. Games that satisfy various needs of video game media consumption including passing time, companionship, escapism, cognition, arousal, relaxation, competition, challenge, social interaction, diversion, and fantasy.

Serious Games: Games that were designed for more than mere entertainment purposes. Games that satisfy particularly the need for cognition which would lead to cognitive, affective, and behavioral change in players through game interaction.

Chapter 9
Leveling up the Classroom:
A Theoretical Approach to Education Gamification

Michael D. Hanus
The Ohio State University, United States

Carlos Cruz
The Ohio State University, United States

ABSTRACT

Gamification continues to grow in popularity, and has significant application to education and student motivation. Because gamification is a large, encompassing concept it may be best to assess its effects by breaking down its composite features and assessing the positive and negative effects of these features. This chapter takes features including immediate feedback, use of narrative, tailored challenges, and displays of progress, and discusses popular current theories in communication and psychology to discuss the potential benefits and drawbacks of each feature, placing a focus on student motivation, comparison, and self-perception. This moves to discuss practical ways to best employ gamification features, and discusses the impact of digital technology on gamification in the classroom and should be useful for researchers interested in the topic and for teachers considering how to best gamify their classrooms.

INTRODUCTION

In a gamified classroom, students can go on quests instead of do homework. They can gain experience points instead of grades, and they can pick anonymous avatars and usernames to represent their progress on a leaderboard with their peers. They can work with, or compete against, their classmates in a system that is set up to pull them out of the traditional classroom narrative of going to class, listening to lectures, and taking tests and putting them into something that feels new, interesting, and makes them motivated to learn.

Gamification is the process of taking mechanics and features traditionally used in games and applying them to traditionally non-gaming contexts (Deterding, Sicart, Nacke, O'Hara, & Dixon, 2011).

DOI: 10.4018/978-1-4666-8651-9.ch009

Educators have become increasingly interested in bringing game elements to the classroom in the hopes of shaking up the traditional style and making things more interesting. The interest in gamification is growing. Gamification is appealing beyond the classroom, as 50% of companies are predicted to gamify at least one aspect of their workplace by 2015 (Gartner, 2011). Jane McGonigal, in her book *Reality is Broken*, writes extensively about the benefits of using gamification to harness the motivation, attention, and energy of large groups of people to create lasting and positive change.

On the surface, gamification is appealing. We know students like games, because they play them on their phones, computers, and consoles for tens of thousands of collective hours each year, and their popularity continues to increase year by year as gaming shifts upwards in entertainment dominance, recently surpassing the movie industry (Chatfield, 2009). For some reason, games have the ability to capture our interest for long periods of time. If we could make students as interested in their homework as they are in games, we would create lifelong learners.

Much has been written extolling the benefits of gamification (Cronk, 2012; Hellwege & Robertson, 2012; McGonigal, 2011; Muntean, 2011). It has great potential. Unfortunately, due to the recent and speedy movement towards gamification its effects have yet to be fully explored, and the mechanisms behind the positive benefits for gamification have yet to be academically isolated and studied. There are a variety of theories from psychology, communication, human-computer interaction, and evolutionary biology that we can draw from to better understand the effects of gamification. Using these as theoretical backgrounds can give a strong start to research on gamification, and can go a long way towards better understanding how gamification can help or hinder the learning process. This chapter is an attempt to collate a variety of theories from a variety of fields that explain the mechanisms behind gamification. These are theories and concepts that have extensive bodies of research to support and develop them, and our goal with the chapter is not to go into a detailed examination of any particular theory or concept. Instead, this will present an overview of these relevant theories and how they might be used to give researchers a lens to understand the benefits of gamification and offer teachers tools to better design gamification systems in the classroom.

Chapter Overview

We will begin with a discussion of commonly used features that are borrowed from games and used to gamify classrooms. Then we will examine theories that explain why these features may be beneficial, and suggest effective ways to use these features in a gamified classroom. First, we will look into research on need satisfaction using self-determination theory and the benefits of games, and shift into a discussion on intrinsic and extrinsic motivation and how reward systems often used in gamification affect motivation. Next, we will examine how badges, avatars, methods of self-representation, and visual displays of achievement can affect individual self-perception and shape identity through warranting and signaling theory. Following that, we will discuss the effects of engagement and transportation into narratives, and how being able to absorb students into a story surrounding their learning can make them more interested. Then we will examine how theories revolving around cooperation, competition, and social comparison can be useful for understanding how gamification works when we pit students together or against each other. Finally, we will spend some time examining how gamification in virtual classrooms (or worlds) might be done, and how students' understanding of their presence in that world can positively affect their learning. These theories are very different, but taken together they should help paint a broad picture of all the key aspects of gamification, and should offer potential researchers or game designers areas to explore.

Before moving on, it is important to note some clarification of terms. *Gamification* refers to using any game elements in a non-game setting (Deterding et al., 2011). Though many examples we will use come from video games, many board games or other types of games feature similar systems of engagement and fun. Video games are especially relevant to this conversation, as the digital affordances they bring offer special considerations and benefits to the gamified classroom. As such, many of our examples will discuss features from video games. We would recommend that a teacher interested in gamifying a class should at least consider a digital component in order to take full advantage of these affordances. It should also be noted that though the concept of gamification is relatively recent, educators have been using games in their classroom for centuries to try to get students motivated to learn. So we will be referring to gamification as a more modern, holistic approach to making the entire setting—from desk arrangement to syllabi—a game. Before discussing different theories that can be applied to gamification, it is important to first discuss what we know about the features gamified classrooms frequently borrow from games.

BACKGROUND

Teachers commonly employ games in the classroom (Kapp, 2012), but only recently have teachers begun exploring the possibility of making the class itself a game, complete with a narrative, rewards, and social interaction. For example, Mr. Gonzalez gamified his 6th grade science classroom into the World of Sciencecraft (2012). Students were grouped by desks into "guilds" where they went on quests to explore science topics. Students could gain achievements by completing their requirements and submitting them to the "king" and each lesson was transformed with fantasy language; students met the "character" Mt. Saint Helens, and went on a quest to find evidence if she would erupt. If the students completed the appropriate task, they could earn the Volcano badge, which they could display on their personal classroom blog.

Mr. Gonzalez's classroom mirrors the game World of Warcraft, where players can go on quests, join guilds, and gain achievements. Modern students are growing up in an age of interactive media and video games, so modeling a classroom as a game may be appealing and motivating to them (Glover, 2013). Using games in education has a variety of benefits, and there are several game design mechanics that have been shown to be successful in educational environments (Stott & Neustaedter, 2012). First, games typically have the option to allow the player to restart and play again. This allows mistakes to be fixed, and does not make failure permanent. This allows students to experiment and explore without the fear of failure, which can lead to increased engagement with material (Lee & Hammer, 2011). In addition, some teachers have experimented with gradeless classrooms, with the thought that grades place too much emphasis on a final product instead of a gradual learning process.

Second, games (particularly video games) excel at giving immediate and focused feedback. If a player bumps into an enemy, or eats a poisoned apple in a game, their character is harmed. Players can quickly learn to adapt and change their behavior based on that feedback. Despite their best efforts, teachers can often only evaluate and give feedback to one student at a time, and often feedback on assignments is handed back days after the assignment has been completed. By incorporating digital learning into the classroom, teachers allow for immediate feedback for the whole class that is tailored to each individual student (Kapp, 2012).

Games are also particularly good at tailoring their challenges to each individual player. If a player struggles in an area, the game will not progress until the player has sufficient mastery. Some digital games are even able to adapt challenges to players' particular playing tastes and better differentiate between player personalities. Teachers, like video games, often present information to their students in categories of steadily increasing difficulty, a process known as scaffolded instruction. However, teachers can be limited by teaching to the entire class; they must balance concerns of curriculum progress with how to keep the advanced students interested and the struggling students from falling behind. This can lead to instructing to the average of the class in the hopes that the lesson is tailored to the most individuals. Video games can scaffold instruction on a player-by-player basis, continually challenging the advanced students with new material and being patient with struggling students until they also achieve mastery (Beed, Hawkins, & Roller, 1991).

Games often construct narrative contexts around essentially mundane tasks. At its basic level, defeating an enemy in World of Warcraft involves using the keyboard to walk to the enemy, clicking on that enemy, and then clicking an "attack" skill until the enemy is defeated. If we told players to press these keys in the same sequence facing a blank screen, they would quickly lose interest. But because the players are playing a specific character surrounded by an attractive world and given a purpose to defeat that enemy, players remain engaged. By placing their tasks within a narrative, engagement and motivation increase (Clark & Rossiter, 2008). Teachers may be able to benefit from creating new narratives around tasks, rather than emphasizing learning for learning's sake. For example, it may be more effective to help wandering state capital names find their home, rather than require that students memorize all 50.

Games are also exceptionally good at showing players' progress and achievements (Camilleri, Busuttil, & Montebello, 2011; Kapp, 2012). Video games often show leaderboards where players can view their progress and skill in comparison to others. Other games often show progress directly through the gamer's character. For example, as one progresses through the game *Skyrim* the player's character gains increasingly ornate and powerful weapons and armor. Both Xbox and Playstation consoles feature reward systems that exist to collate a player's progress across all the different games that they play, and players can view and compare their progress with others. Being able to see displays of progress in a game can give players a sense of identity and concrete success that they can show to others. In a traditional classroom, progress can sometimes be hard to see; students have to wait for their grades or report cards.

Freedom to fail, immediate feedback, tailored challenges, engaging narratives, and displays of progress are some of many mechanics games typically use that may be effective in facilitating engagement and motivation in the classroom. The limited studies that have looked at gamification tend to look at it on a holistic level, rather than studying each individual mechanic (Bellotti et al., 2013; Charles, Charles, McNeill, Bustard, & Black, 2010; Hamari, 2013). Each of these studies includes or excludes leaderboards, badges, narratives, and other mechanics in a different way, and thus it is hard to draw conclusions about gamification. Instead, it should be most beneficial to begin examining gamification on the level of individual mechanics and features, to better understand what is effective and what is not. For the rest of this chapter, we will break down these individual game features and explore the theoretical mechanisms behind why they may or may not be effective. First we will examine the theories that discuss the effects of giving rewards such as points, badges, achievements, gold, or experience, on student motivation.

THEORIES AND CONCEPTS TO APPLY TO FEATURES OF GAMIFICATION

Need Fulfillment and Motivation

At its core, gamification is an attempt to motivate students to better engage with, pay attention to, and stay interested in their education. It is a fine goal to find creative ways to make information stick with uninterested students, but if we can get students truly interested in a subject or in their own learning then we can create learners for life. As such, it is important to understand motivation. There are two types of motivation: intrinsic (i.e., internal) and extrinsic (i.e., external; Deci & Ryan 1987, 2000). *Intrinsic motivation* is the ideal, and occurs when an individual wants to engage in a behavior. *Extrinsic motivation* occurs when an individual engages in a behavior due to some external force (e.g., peer pressure). Individuals who are intrinsically motivated to do a task stick with it longer and care about it more. If we can get students to be intrinsically motivated to learn, then they will be more motivated to study, engage with the material, and be more likely to stay interested for longer periods of time than someone extrinsically motivated. Unfortunately, traditional education systems offer a lot of extrinsic motivation: students are encouraged to study in order to get into college, to appease their parents, to avoid failure, and to receive good grades.

There are some theories that can help us understand why students are motivated to play games, or are not motivated to study or pay attention in the classroom. Self-determination theory is an excellent lens for studying the benefits of gamification because it identifies concrete concepts to target when designing a gamified course and offers a robust set of research that show the positive effects of fulfilling these needs (Deci & Ryan, 1985, 1987, 2000). Self-determination theory posits that there are three basic psychological needs: autonomy, competence, and relatedness. Successful fulfillment of these needs results in positive outcomes, such as increases in self-esteem, intrinsic motivation, and enjoyment. Video games have been shown to be very effective in fulfilling the three basic needs (Przybylski, Rigby, & Ryan, 2010; Przybylski, Weinstein, Ryan, & Rigby, 2009; Sheldon & Filak, 2008); one study found that satisfaction of self-determination theory needs accounted for 51% of the variance in self-reported enjoyment in video game playing (Tamborini et al., 2011).

For students to feel autonomous, they would need to feel that their behaviors stem from an "internal locus" of desires (Deci & Ryan, 2000). In other words, people feel autonomous when the actions they commit are done because they want to do them, rather than any external force requiring them to be done. If students believe that they are learning because they enjoy the subject matter and want to learn more, their need for autonomy will be fulfilled. If those students believe they are learning because their parents want them to get good grades, or they are afraid of failing and being removed from their group of friends, they will not feel autonomous. According to self-determination theory, we assess why we do things as either supporting or controlling of our autonomy. Rewards, threats, deadlines, evaluations and surveillance are all controlling factors that affect autonomy negatively, while situations that encourage personal choice and offer positive feedback are seen as supporting and affect autonomy positively. Games offer players a large amount of decisions to make, from choosing which tunnel to explore, to choosing the "good" or "bad" narrative path, to moment-to-moment choices such as where to hide, which item to use or where to go next. These are choices offered to the player, and the player is not pressured by an outside force to decide. Because players are free to make their own choices, games should strongly boost feelings of autonomy.

The need for competence concerns the need to control our outcomes and achieve mastery over tasks (Deci & Ryan, 2000). In order to feel competent, we need to see evidence that what we are doing has an effect on a given task, and see evidence that we are getting better, or mastering, a task. Giving someone a video game controller that only works half the time will remove their feelings of competence; only half the time their actions are having an effect. Likewise, making tasks too difficult or not showing proper progression undermines our need for competence. Games can give points when an attack is successful or remove a life when an attack is unsuccessful. Games can give feedback visually, through audio, and haptically through the player's controller. The constant feedback coupled with a player's successful progression through a game's narrative ought to result in fulfillment of a need to feel competent.

Finally, relatedness concerns our psychological need to connect with others (Deci & Ryan, 2000). When we have opportunities to connect, interact with, care for and be cared for by others, our need for relatedness is satisfied. We often seek out opportunities to be with others, and when those advances are refused, our needs are not satisfied. Gamification often works towards facilitating the need to relate to others by pooling students together, having them work with others, and reciprocate interactions. It should be noted that relatedness and autonomy are not two ends of a spectrum; feeling autonomous is not the same as feeling individualistic. If we follow our internal desires to connect with others we are satisfying our needs for autonomy and relatedness. Games can be social experiences, especially when played with others. Players can cooperate with one another to achieve a goal or compete in a safe, arbitrated environment. Many games foster large communities within and outside the game environment, and some games allow thousands of players to band together to play and socialize. Connecting with other players through games ought to foster feelings of relatedness.

Self-determination theory offers an excellent theoretical lens to view the benefits of gamification and offers good advice towards creating better gamified experiences in the classroom. First, it gives suggestions as to what really motivates students to act. If we can create experiences that give students choices, make them feel competent, and connect them with others we might have a better chance at motivating them. Teachers can look to lesson plans and think about how each need is fulfilled: give students options of assignments for autonomy, give them immediate feedback in many forms for competence, and group them together for relatedness. Second, self-determination theory offers concrete ways to empirically test different forms of gamification. Researchers can look at the effects of creating games that emphasize one need over the others.

Motivation and Rewards

Almost inevitably, discussions of gamification in the classroom include discussions of proper ways to reward students to increase their motivation. It is important to look at the research concerning intrinsic motivation, extrinsic motivation, and rewards when applied to gamification. This is an area to step carefully; proper use of rewards can increase intrinsic motivation, while improper use can result in a drop of intrinsic motivation all together. As discussed above, self-determination theory suggests that there are three basic psychological needs that should be present in order to facilitate intrinsic motivation. It also suggests that external factors can lead toward increases in extrinsic motivation, something less desired in the classroom. Many researchers have studied what happens to intrinsic motivation when rewards are present. The above may suggest that it is a straightforward process; rewards are external factors given to an individual to do a task, and as such they should facilitate extrinsic and not intrinsic motivation. Logically, we should not give rewards if our goal is intrinsic motivation.

In reality, the effect of rewards on motivation is much more nuanced. Cognitive evaluation theory, a subset of self-determination theory, was created to explain how external events such as rewards affect motivation (Deci & Ryan, 1985). Cognitive evaluation theory suggests that whenever we are given a reward for doing a task, we make an internal assessment that decides whether that reward makes us feel competent and whether it makes us feel autonomous. If a reward is seen as an affirmation of our competence and control over the task, we will have increased intrinsic motivation. If a reward makes us feel powerless and incompetent, we will have less intrinsic motivation to continue the behavior. This interpretation can change between people, or between situations; the same reward accompanied by controlling or positive tones of voice could elicit different attributions. Therefore, careful consideration should be taken when deciding how to give rewards for student behaviors.

A substantial body of research has examined the effects of giving rewards for a task one is already interested in doing. If we take students who love to read and give them rewards for reading, what will happen? The overjustification effect suggests that giving rewards for doing behaviors one is already motivated do to (i.e., finds inherently interesting) will decrease motivation to engage in that behavior over time (Lepper, Green, & Nisbett, 1973). Imagine an athlete who sets out to play basketball because of a love for the game. The athlete gains skill, and eventually lands a job to play professionally. The overjustification effect predicts that the money that now comes with playing basketball for a career could change the athlete's motivations for playing basketball from intrinsic reasons (i.e., the love of the game) to extrinsic reasons (i.e., doing it for the money). Bill Russell, a former basketball star, said: "I remember that the game lost some of its magical qualities for me once I thought seriously about playing for a living." The overjustification effect shows that once this change in attribution occurs, removal of the extrinsic reward results in a lack of desire to continue playing.

Considerable debate has emerged over the effects of rewards on intrinsic motivation. One group of meta-analyses on rewards and motivation found that rewards have little to no effect on intrinsic motivation (Cameron & Pierce, 1994; Cameron, Banko & Pierce, 2001, Cameron, 2001). This work suggests that at worst, giving rewards for tasks has no effect on intrinsic motivation, and there is some evidence that giving rewards for tasks actually increases intrinsic motivation. However, other authors have suggested that rewards affect motivation depending on how initially interesting the task is. For initially interesting tasks, the research is conclusive: external rewards tend to decrease intrinsic motivation (Deci, Koestner, & Ryan 1999; Deci, Koestner, & Ryan, 2001; Deci, Ryan, & Koestner, 2001). Whether or not a reward decreases intrinsic motivation depends whether the individual is initially interested in the task, the reward is given for completing the task, the reward is tangible, and individuals expect the reward (Lepper, Green, & Nisbett, 1973; Tang & Hall, 1995).

According to this research, giving rewards to students who are already interested in a subject or learning could undermine their intrinsic motivation. To date, many efforts at gamification involve the use of rewards to motivate behavior. These rewards can come in many different types, from giving out coupons, achievements, points, experience, money, gold stars, new equipment for a character, or badges. The research indicates that rewards can be effective tools to get individuals motivated in tasks they find boring. The rewards give those bored individuals something to think about instead of the boring task. But much care should be taken when giving those same rewards to individuals who are already interested in a task. Rewards should be designed and given in such a way that emphasizes the individual's autonomy and competence. Teachers should focus on giving verbal praise over more tangible rewards, and should take care to give rewards only when the student has earned it and will view it as supportive of autonomy and competence.

Indicators of Progress and Effects on Identity and Self-Perception

Warranting Theory

In gamified systems, rewards often come in the form of badges. These are certificates of achievement that a player can earn by completing specific tasks. Often, the badges are displayed for others to see. Badges can be an effective way to provide students feedback so long as the badges are perceived as affirming one's competence as opposed to attempting to control one's behavior. These badges display important information: to the earner, the badges display records of achievement. To others, the badges can display information about the expertise or accomplishments of the earner.

Warranting theory is commonly used to discuss how we display and interpret signals from others in online profiles, and may help to shed some light on how students may interact with gamified systems, in particular badges, to create and form impressions of others. Warranting theory (Walther & Parks, 2002) posits that when it comes to putting information about oneself online, individuals can either be extremely different from their online presentation or there could be little to no difference between the presentation and the individual. Scholars (DeAndrea, 2014; Walther & Parks, 2002) have proposed that when we want to know the truth about someone based on their online profile, we look for cues that that person cannot control or manipulate.

According to DeAndrea (2014), people seek out warranting cues that provide insight into how we perceive online information about others. For example, individuals should grant more weight to badges and leaderboards attesting that a student is particularly proficient at math as opposed to a student claiming extraordinary math skills. It is incredibly easy for a student to make any but it is far more difficult for students to be ranked high on a leaderboard if they did not excel at a particular task. Previous work on warranting theory (DeAndrea, 2014) argues that perceivers of information may assign different weights to information contingent on their judgments of the information's manipulability and control by the audience it refers to. Thus, warranting theory would predict that students would grant more weight to badges in the when compared to claims by other students, because the badges cannot be faked or manipulated.

Scholars interested in warranting theory have argued that there are three types of information (Tong, Van Der Heide, Langwell, & Walther, 2008). Self-generated information is provided by the target in question, such as a proud boast about one's artistic abilities. Other-generated information comes from individuals other than the target, such as a peer stating that one is the best artist in the class. Finally, system-generated information refers to information that is produced automatically by a particular system. In the classroom, system-generated information would exist predominantly in the form of badges and leaderboards. Early research has found evidence that individuals use system-generated information to make judgments on a variety of characteristics including social attractiveness (Tong et al., 2008), communal orientation (Utz, 2010) and credibility (Westerman, Spence, & Van Der Heide, 2012). Future work may examine if and how students use system-generated information to make judgments in the classroom setting. Those designing a gamified system should note that students may place the most value on status cues that come from the system.

Warranting theory provides a unique lens through which we can understand the appeal of gamification processes. In the classroom, much like all other settings, individuals have a desire to present themselves in the best possible light. Warranting theory suggests that students may be able to use a gamified system that utilizes leaderboards or badges in order to make a judgment about other students' abilities, rather than simply to the student at his or her word. Jakobsson (2011) has argued that gaming profiles represent "player dossiers" capable of providing an individual with a wealth of information from which individuals can make judgments of a particular player. This verification process can happen in any environment that includes elements of profiles, leaderboards, and badges as key components of a gamification system.

In the gamified context, the system-generated badge is the most difficult piece of information to fabricate and thus should be weighed more heavily when evaluating Clark's claim of artistic ability. Warranting theory has the potential to serve as a great aid in understanding how individuals make sense of badges in a variety of contexts. While the example of badges was discussed primarily in judging artistic ability, warranting theory provides individuals with a way to understand badges as a form of both capital and evidence in particular communities. Badges can be used as a way to form groups based on complementary skills instead of preexisting friendships. Moreover, a badge can strongly reinforce the claim made by a particular individual.

As mentioned previously, warranting theory is capable of providing insight into both impression formation and impression management processes. Warranting theory (Walther & Parks, 2002) also proposes that individuals may perform certain behaviors in order to convince the viewer that the presentation is authentic .Individuals can use elements of gamification systems in order to provide evidence for claims that were made to other individuals. For example, a student may seek out a particularly difficult badge in the classroom as a way of indicating a high degree of ability or a particular skill. Warranting theory can shed some light on how certain components of the gamification experience, primarily visual feedback, can aid both senders and receivers of information across a variety of contexts.

Signaling Theory

Where warranting theory discusses how badges might be trusted to give information about someone, signaling theory discusses the types of information that can be given through a badge. Signaling theory proposes that senders and receivers of information perform cost and benefit analyses in order to determine the reliability associated with a signal. Signaling theory delineates three types of signals. An assessment signal (Donath, 2007) is inherently reliable as it requires the possession of a particular trait or characteristic in order to perform a behavior. For example, running a 40 yard dash in 4 seconds is a great indicator of an ability to run fast. There are very few ways an individual can fake an ability to run fast or an ability to lift heavy objects. A strategic signal indicates the possession of a resource primarily by wasting that resource. Zahavi (1975) highlighted that gazelles tend to jump up and down upon seeing a predator as opposed to fleeing immediately. The jumping up and down is supposed to serve as a signal to predators that they have both additional speed and energy resources to spare. Strategic signals are not limited to the animal kingdom as individuals frequently spend a great deal of money on rare products in order to flaunt their wealth to other individuals. Finally, conventional signals (Donath, 2007) do not have a single interpretation, as what is classified as a conventional signal is largely the product of the norms and rules associated with a particular domain. For example, a commonly mentioned conventional signal in online environments is an individual's age. Whether an individual enters an accurate age largely stems from the norms associated with a particular website. On some websites, individuals may be encouraged to play with various aspects of their identity while other websites rely entirely on the honesty of their consumers.

In attempting to understand gamification in online environments, signaling theory would need to understand how badges are interpreted by individuals in a given community. It may be the case that badges would be classified as assessment signals as they demonstrate proof that an individual is capable of performing a particular behavior such as beating a hidden boss. As stated previously, an assessment signal is considered to be inherently reliable. However, others may argue that badges are not indicators of the possession of a particular trait and instead would argue that interpretation may differ among different communities. This latter perspective on the influence of badges closely resembles the idea of conventional signals. Understanding how individuals perform cost-benefit analyses using different gamification systems will certainly aid understanding on how visual feedback processes affect the behavior of both senders and receivers.

Applying both warranting theory and signaling theory in the classroom is an intuitive process as both theories focus on the production and interpretation of information. Under a gamified system, the information cues that are likely to be produced and interpreted by members of the classroom are badges. Badges provide students with information that is largely free from manipulation and that may be considered an inherently reliable indicator of some skill. It is important in implementing badges to ensure that some badges can be earned by all members of the classroom. Both of these theories provide insight as to how these cues may be interpreted but a lack of badges may be interpreted negatively by the class. The emphasis on system generated feedback found under warranting theory is important as badges are system generated pieces of information that are capable of providing the immediate feedback so few classrooms can offer.

Self-Perception Theory

As students begin a new year of school, they often find themselves in environments containing a host of people and objects for which they have no preexisting attitude. Everyone can recall the first day icebreakers designed to place both teachers and students at ease in the classroom. It is only after spending time in the classroom that individuals form attitudes regarding the structure of the course, the teacher, their fellow classmates, and all other matters educational. This is especially the case if the student is placed into a gamified classroom that is unlikely to resemble any class they have taken during their years in school. Self-perception theory puts forth the idea that doing something influences our attitudes, and can serve as a useful lens for understanding how giving students activities and actions on tasks they do not necessarily understand in a gamified environment can shift their attitudes in a positive way.

Self-perception theory (Bem, 1972) provides a perspective that allows us to understand the formation of attitudes. Traditional theories of the attitude-behavior relationship typically classify attitudes as one of the inputs associated with output that we classify as behavior. However, self-perception theory flips this relationship on its head with the claim that behavior serves as input for the formation of attitudes. In its original formulation, self-perception theory (Bem, 1972) included two postulates that helped explain this novel way of perceiving the formation of attitude development. The first postulate is that individuals become aware of their attitudes through observations of their own behavior or the particular situations in which a behavior is most likely to occur. Thus, a student that spends long periods of time looking at badge lists or attempting to earn a particularly difficult badge may infer that they really think positively of the badge system if the second postulate of self-perception theory is also true. The second postulate of self-perception theory states these processes are especially likely to unfold in situations where an individual's inner state is difficult to understand. Students with no preexisting conceptualizations of gamification or a gamified classroom are unlikely to have strong attitudes regarding this approach to education. The lack of strong attitudes allows for behavior, in this case interacting with a gamified system, to be used as a determinant of one's attitude.

Self-perception theory would predict that in this context students would infer their attitudes toward the presence of gamification systems in the classroom by observing their behavior in a manner befitting a neutral third-party observer. Students that buy into the system relatively early and spend a great deal of time learning the intricacies the system are likely to infer that time spent is directly attributable to their strong positive attitudes toward these systems.

To apply self-perception theory in the classroom, instructors should encourage students to discuss the gamified system with their classmates during the first few days of class. In order to be able to hold a conversation regarding the system, students will need to interact with it. The instructor should be careful regarding the language they use in encouraging the students as language that is perceived to be controlling may result in students attributing their interaction to the system to external forces. Instead, the instructor should attempt to foster curiosity regarding the structure of the gamified classroom. These initial interactions with the system may encourage students to invest themselves in the system throughout the class. As frequency of interactions with the system increase, students should infer that their behavior is a direct reflection of their attitude. Once the attitude is inferred, overall engagement with these systems should continue to increase.

Social Cognitive Theory

Social cognitive theory (Bandura, 1982) is capable of explaining how gamification principles may be successful in the classroom primarily due to the scope of the theory. Social cognitive theory seeks to understand a variety of factors that are likely to impact how individuals interact with gamified systems and how likely they are to continue to interact with these systems in the face of difficulties. This latter point regarding persistence in the face of difficulties is especially important as all classrooms, gamified or not, will present students with a variety of challenges throughout the year. One of the defining characteristics of video games is their ability to continue to motivate players to try again in response to suffering a defeat. Social cognitive theory may serve as a guiding post on how to structure a gamified classroom in a way that convinces students to continue on the difficult road of mastery.

Social cognitive theory (Bandura, 1982) is perhaps one of the most famous frameworks available to understand human behavior. It speculates on how we learn new behaviors, especially through observation. People learn new behaviors based on how they feel about the behavior, and how the perceive the behavior will be affected by the environment. We learn by watching others. If an individual has observed others perform a behavior he or she is likely to replicate the behavior in the future if the observed actor was rewarded the first time. In addition, individuals may replicate a behavior if the observed actor was not punished for performing a negative behavior the first time. However, observation of a behavior is not enough to ensure that a particular behavior is performed as that ignores the notion of self-efficacy. Self-efficacy (Bandura, 1982) involves an individual's perception of their ability to complete a particular behavior irrespective of their actual ability to perform the behavior. For example, people may have high self-efficacy in regards to singing in public but not all individuals are actually capable of singing in public. Understanding self-efficacy is important as work has found that self-efficacy is associated with persistence in academic endeavors (Multon, Brown, & Lent, 1991).

Social cognitive theory (Bandura, 1982) gives as a unique perspective with which to understand the appeal of gamification in the classroom. Theorists associated with SCT argue that the influences of the three previously mentioned factors are inextricably linked. However, knowing that self-efficacy is a good predictor of effort given to a particular task helps in understanding the appeal of gamification systems in the classroom. Self-efficacy has been conceptualized in a litany of ways from general self-efficacy (Bandura, 1982) to task specific self-efficacy associated with a variety of behaviors including driving (George, Clark, & Crotty, 2007) and video game playing (Lee & LaRose, 2007).

Gamified classrooms provide educators with the means to encourage cooperation among students in a variety of ways as suggested by social cognitive theory. First, a gamified classroom allows students to model the actions performed by other students used to earn particular badges. Under social cognitive theory, individuals are more likely to replicate a behavior that they witness has been rewarded thus a badge serves as a potential way to increase the likelihood that students will model ideal classroom behaviors.

The presence of a badge system may also encourage relationship formation among certain students. If a student is interested in earning a particular badge but is unable to earn the badge on their own it may prompt them to seek assistance from other student. This peer to peer relationship may take the form of a modified expert-novice relationship. Thus, the student that was initially unable to perform the behavior needed to complete a particular quest may find that with the aid of another student they are now capable of performing behaviors that they could not have imagined a few shorts weeks ago. This form of peer mentorship encouraged by gamified systems can serve to increase student's level of self-efficacy. As they see their skills continue to develop and expand, individuals will seek out higher quests to match their newfound skills. A gamified system simply by placing emphasis on social interactions allows for the development of self-efficacy in a way that most traditional classrooms do not.

For the research minded, a longitudinal study would allow educators to track both how general self-efficacy and behavior specific self-efficacy change as a function of interaction with a gamification system over time. Moreover, educators could examine how self-efficacy relates to the pursuit of goals within the confines of the classroom. This feedback would allow educators to adjust assignments on the fly if it appears that the initial tasks are perceived as too difficult for individuals with low perceived self-efficacy.

Engagement, Narrative Transportation, and Flow

Narrative Transportation

A good gamification system goes beyond implementing a few external reward systems into an environment that did not feature them. Some scholars (Bogost, 2011) have criticized the gamification movement for focusing primarily on badges. Scholars (McGonigal, 2011) have argued that using a good narrative context around the tasks is an integral component of these systems. A good story can go a long way toward increasing the benefits of a gamified classroom. Narratives are associated with the experience of transportation which research has shown results in a variety of positive outcomes.

Transportation refers to involvement in a narrative. More specifically, Green, Brock, and Kaufman (2004) define transportation as "the process of becoming fully engaged in a story." Thus an engrossing narrative can result in the experience of transportation. According to Green and Brock (2000) transportation results in changes in imagery, affect, and attentional focus. Imagery refers to being able to picture the events of the narrative. Affect refers to the narrative producing an emotional reaction in the consumer. Finally, attentional focus refers to how engrossed an individual becomes when exposed to a narrative.

Green and Brock (2000) found transportation is associated with favorable evaluations of protagonists in the narrative. Green et al. (2004) have found evidence that transported readers exhibit more story consistent attitudes when compared to individuals that reported lower levels of transportation. In addition to positive evaluations of characters and changes in attitudes, the process of transportation fosters enjoyment through multiple pathways: enjoyment through escaping the self, enjoyment through transformation, and enjoyment through connections with characters (Green et al., 2004).

The first two types of enjoyment are especially relevant to understanding how transportation might affect enjoyment of a gamification application. Narratives that allow the individual to become so immersed into the content that they forget their worries are likely to prove useful both in the workplace and in the classroom. Individuals of all ages are typically juggling a variety of roles and the accompanying expectations associated with those roles, so an activity that can help to alleviate that stress may be construed as a positive experience.

Transportation that brings about transformation is arguably the most important of the four pathways linking transportation to enjoyment. Green, Brock, and Kaufman (2004) argue that transportation into a narrative can bring about great changes in the individual as a result of exposure to new experiences. More simply, a narrative can change the way we view the world around us. In our everyday experience, we often talk about the power of a television program, book or movie. Powerful narratives can bring about great change in the individual exposed to them as research has found that narratives have been associated with beneficial health outcomes such as safe-sex intentions (Moyer-Guse & Nabi, 2010).

The third way transportation can affect an individual's enjoyment of a particular narrative is through their interaction with the characters in a story. Scholars interested in narrative persuasion have examined a variety of concepts related to the relationships individuals form with mediated characters. The term parasocial relationship (Horton & Wohl, 1956) is used to refer to relationships individuals form with mediated characters. In the original formulation of parasocial relationships, the relationships were deemed to be one-sided in nature (Horton & Wohl, 1956). However, given the development of social media that allows individuals to interact with a celebrity directly, more recent conceptualizations of parasocial relationships view interaction as existing on a continuum (Giles, 2002). These relationships with characters bolster our enjoyment of narratives.

Perhaps some of the best examples of creative narratives facilitating user engagement comes from the work of the Institute for the Future. The Institute for the Future (2014) develops games that they classify as alternate reality games (ARG). ARG's feature narratives that unfold across multiple media. Jenkins (2006) refers to storylines that traverse multiple media as examples of transmedia storytelling. More specifically, Jenkins (2006) classifies transmedia storytelling as, "the art of world-making." The story's presence on each medium adds a unique component that helps to make sense of the overall picture. An example of an ARG developed by the Institute for the Future is A World without Oil. The research team was interested in examining the variety of creative solutions individuals would devise in order to survive. These solutions could be uploaded in a variety of formats including clips, pictures and text. The best player ideas were integrated into the overall narrative of the world that unfolded over 32 days. ARG's designed by the Institute for the Future attract hundreds if not thousands of players around the game highlighting the appeal of a well-constructed narrative. Similarly, a well-developed narrative in the classroom could serve to increase experiences of transportation while reading material thus clearing the way for a host of positive outcomes. The importance of narratives as a component of a gamification system cannot be understated.

Narratives are an integral component of the ideas underlying gamification. Unfortunately, implementations of gamification systems often completely neglect or overlook the role of narratives in a successful gamified system. The creation of well-thought out narratives has numerous advantages for the classroom according to transportation theory. First, narratives encourage individuals to expand their horizons so perhaps a straight lecture is unable to produce the level of attitude change associated with the presence of narrative. Moyer-Guse's (2008) model of entertainment overcoming resistance argues that narratives may be particularly effective at producing attitude change as individuals are less likely to produce counterarguments in response to a persuasive message.

Narratives as part of the gamification experience provide students with an opportunity to become a part of the content creation process. As indicated earlier, individuals participating in the A World without Oil ARG were allowed to upload evidence of their contribution in a variety of different formats. The overall structure was able to adjust to user contributions on the fly. It is nice to have a narrative structure surrounding a gamified system but it is even better to be able to track how a narrative unfolds as the result of one's own contributions.

Consider the following example, an assignment built into the course that allows the class to design new characters or quests for their characters to interact with throughout the semester. The class would be able to vote on the best new character and it would be the responsibility of the teacher to integrate these unexpected characters or events into the overall class narrative. Furthermore, similar assignments would be completed throughout the semester always allowing students more control over the system and its capabilities. Students may be interested in designing new badges or quests as well to supplement the previously introduced characters. The creation of new quests provides students with new opportunities for specialization and mastery. The creation of new characters provides students with potential partners for parasocial relationships. These relationships are likely to be viewed as very enjoyable thus increasing their liking of not only the characters but by association the narrative that spawned the creation of the characters.

A narrative that involves co-creation demands much more interaction from the audience than the traditional fixed narrative. Building in a system that can deal with a variety of changes in a matter of hours is especially likely to enhance feelings of autonomy by the gameplayers. Adaptable narratives allow for the co-creation of content and meaning over the course of an entire semester. Providing students this much freedom in how a storyline unfolds is much more aligned with the viewpoint of the participatory culture (Jenkins, 2006) that stands as one of the hallmarks of our current society. Viewers no longer expect to passively view the development of a brand or company's existence. Viewers instead want to be treated as an equal when it comes to cherished properties which are something narratives in the classrooms allow for users. Narratives as part of a gamification system built from the ground up could have a multitude of positive outcomes for students across all levels.

In addition to the development of narrative flexibility through frequent class assignments, transportation into a narrative has the capability to reduce student counterarguing. Using transportation as a method of reducing opposition to information may encourage students to approach material with a more open mind than they might have without exposure to the narrative. The flexibility of a narrative as a persuasive tool in the classroom dictates that additional research should be conducted on the best methods for narrative development and implementation.

Presence

Just as one can become immersed in a story by means of transportation, one can become immersed into a place by feeling they have a sense of presence there. Presence is the idea of "being there" (Lee, 2004), where one feels that they have the ability to act within, and upon, a place apart from their physical body. This is a theory that requires the mediation of new, digital technology. Video games or video conferencing is typically discussed as ways to make someone feel present somewhere else.

This is especially true of contemporary video games and virtual worlds that feature breathtaking graphics while affording gamers ever increasing levels of interactivity and realism. Perhaps the most famous of all virtual worlds is Linden Labs' Second Life. Second Life is not a traditional game in the sense of having clearly defined objectives that increase in difficulty over time. Instead the primary purpose for Second Life is inherent in the name as it offers users the opportunity to construct a second life in the virtual world. The existence of Second Life has given educators the ability to test the effectiveness of teaching in virtual worlds.

As established previously, the concept of presence at its most fundamental level involves an experience of non-mediation. Research has found that interactions in Second Life are capable of creating the experience of cognitive, social and teaching presence (Burgess, Slate, Rojas-LeBouef, & Prairie, 2010). Other work has highlighted the ability of virtual worlds to create a sense of immersion that, "can impact the affective, empathic and motivational aspects of the experience" (Warburton, 2009, p. 421). A recent review exploring the work on augmented reality and education (Wu, Lee, Chang, & Liang, 2013) proposed that role-playing activities and simulations in augmented reality environments are likely to foster experiences of presence and engagement. Increased levels of presence during a mediated experience has also been associated with higher levels of enjoyment (Skalski, Tamborini, Shelton, Vuncher, & Lindmark, 2011).

The research indicates that providing students with an opportunity to experience presence may result in a host of positive outcomes including increased levels of engagement and enjoyment with the material. Given this work, teachers should pursue virtual worlds as a supplement to the traditional classroom; instead of reading about the Amazon, students could go on a virtual tour through the rainforest.

Flow

A separate but very important concept when it comes to understanding how individuals engage with tasks or games is the concept of a flow state. Picture a time when you were so engaged with a task that you seemed to tune everything out and you lost track of time – you would be entering a flow state (Csikszentmihalyi & Csikszentmihalyi, 1991). This occurs when an individual enters an experiential state characterized by intense, relaxed concentration, a loss of self-reflection, a strong sense of control, a loss of the sense of time, and a feeling that the activity is rewarding. A flow state can be described as being "in the zone" where the mind drifts and actions take over. Michael Jordan, arguably the most successful professional basketball player to ever live was considered to be able to enter flow states on the court with extreme ease: "When [Jordan] is 'in the zone,' he can jump with amazing ease, float through the air in gravity-defying grace, and never miss a shot" (Cheng, 2008).

There are two important situational factors that must occur in order for one to enter a flow state. Flow occurs when a task achieves an ideal balance between one's skill and the difficulty of the task. Ideally, one's skill should be very close or just below the difficulty level of the task, so the task continues to challenge but not overwhelm the individual. Any other combination will not result in a flow state; playing a game that is much too difficult for a player's skill level would result in frustration, while playing a game that is much too easy will result in boredom. A good game manages to find a sweet spot between skill and difficulty and steadily improves in difficulty as one gains more skill. Video games are particularly good at quickly adjusting on the fly to a player's skill level and present the player with tough but not-too-hard challenges.

Where transportation concerns engagement in a narrative, flow concerns engagement with a task or challenge. Good gamification systems should utilize both to get students to forget that they are learning and wrap them up in an engaging world with engaging tasks. Achieving a flow state through the ideal balance of challenge and individual skill is similar to the idea of scaffolded instruction discussed earlier, and is often sought out in the classroom. Flow is typically discussed in terms of playing games or doing activities, but it can apply to any mental or physical challenge. It is also a much more "active" concept in relation to transportation and presence; it requires very active concentration and cognition. It is a pleasing experience to enter a flow state, and considerations for good gamification design in the classroom should consider how to effectively balance task difficulty with individual skill. Teachers interested in creating a flow state in their gamified course should make sure to frequently assess the students and see if they are being sufficiently challenged, or if they find the tasks too easy.

Social Comparison, Competition, and Cooperation

A very popular technique in gamification involves using game systems to encourage students to interact, cooperate, and compete against each other. This can give students and teachers both a break from a more traditional lecture-based model of instruction. Many gamification systems attempt to utilize the advantages that come from being able to directly compare one's progress with other peers. For example, gamification systems often employ leaderboards on display for the entire class. This way it is easy to see at a glance where one stands in the system and should spur individuals towards working harder to move higher on the leaderboard. Social comparison theory discusses the benefits and drawbacks from these sorts of systems.

It is difficult to tell how good we are without comparing our ability to someone else. By nature, humans make ability judgments about the self and others via comparison, as it is difficult to make a true assessment of one's ability without a reference point (Hoorens & Van Damme, 2012). Social comparison theory predicts that individuals compare themselves to others in order to validate opinions, make judgments, and reduce uncertainty (Festinger, 1954). Ideally, individuals would socially compare with those that are equal on a desired trait, but research shows comparisons often occur with others who are worse (downward comparison) or better (upward comparison) than the one making the comparison (Major, Testa, & Bylsma, 1991). Downward comparisons have been shown to lead to feelings of superiority and positive affect (Major et al., 1991), whereas upward comparisons can evoke negative affect and lower academic self-concept (Dijkstra, Kuyper, van der Werf, Buunk, & van der Zee, 2008).

Gamification often includes the addition of a global leaderboard, where players' scores on given tasks or earned badges are displayed for all players to see. Depending on one's position, a leaderboard can offer opportunities for both upward and downward comparisons on the dimension of class performance. Although individuals high on the leaderboard may feel better and more superior, they might also feel more pressure and be more likely to choke under that pressure (Wells & Skowronski, 2012). The classroom setting naturally facilitates comparison by providing objective evaluation and constant exposure to peer performance and ability (Wells & Skowronski, 2012), and adding leaderboards ought to further provide students with a visible, objective reminder of their performance relative to others.

Compared to traditional similar methods (e.g., a sticker chart posted in a classroom), digital leaderboards have distinct affordances. Rather than only being accessible in one place, digital leaderboards can be accessed by students outside the classroom, further reinforcing their standing. Because digital leaderboards can be accessed outside of the classroom, they also allow anonymous and covert viewing.

In physical locations, there are social barriers that prohibit one from spending too much time examining a leaderboard. Online, students can spend as much time as they like checking out each individual classmate or comparing each of their achievements with others' without anyone else observing or knowing that they are engaging in such deep social comparison. Thus, given their persistence outside of the classroom and the opportunity for unhindered and covert viewing, the impact of digital leaderboards may be considerably more pervasive.

When considering gamification system design, thought should be put into how to best use social comparison to facilitate better interactions and increase motivation, rather than harm it. Leaderboards can be especially tough on individuals at the bottom. By learning their standing they can see they have a long, difficult path to climb upward and this may result in them giving up or losing motivation to continue (Garcia, Tor, & Gonzalez, 2006). Likewise, a leaderboard can put some pressure on individuals at the top as they strive to continually be at the top, which may remove some of the fun from the activity and make it feel more like work, decreasing intrinsic motivation.

Additionally, social comparison naturally leads to competition, as comparison often makes individuals aware of their lack of skill, status, or position relative to others (Garcia et al., 2006). When social comparison is made on a mutually relevant dimension (e.g., placement on the leaderboard) and made with another of equal status, competition emerges. Competition is often used as a tool in the classroom to increase motivation but findings are somewhat mixed concerning whether it is beneficial or harmful to intrinsic motivation. Some studies indicate that competition can benefit intrinsic motivation (Reeve & Deci, 1996) as individuals are motivated to push themselves in order to win. However, competition can diminish overall performance, cooperation, and problem solving, and also has a positive relationship with cheating (Orosz, Farkas, & Roland-Levy, 2013). Some studies have shown that competition decreases intrinsic motivation among children when the children are told to play to "beat the other" students (Vallerand, Gauvin, & Holliwell, 1986). Competition may also be detrimental to feelings of relatedness (Tripathi, 1992); it is hard to feel personally close or connected with that of a rival.

The negative effects of competition may depend on whether it is constructive competition or destructive competition. Constructive competition occurs when competition is a fun experience and structured in ways to achieve and grow positive interpersonal relationships where destructive competition is harmful for at least one competitor (Fülöp, 2008). Although it is currently unclear whether leaderboards facilitate constructive or destructive competition, leaderboards typically highlight a single winner. Given the easy ability to view others' progress and socially compare, leaderboards may be a form of destructive competition and may lead to negative outcomes in the classroom. Thus, care should be taken when considering implementing leaderboards as a means for social comparison and competition. If used, work to keep penalties for failure light, and emphasize friendly competition with benefits that help the whole class, rather than just one individual who wins. For example, a classroom game designed to compete to see who can collect the most information for the class wiki benefits the entire class regardless of who entered more information.

Unlike competition, cooperation is one of the most encompassing and powerful educational tools. Over 900 studies have demonstrated that cooperative beats competitive and individualistic efforts in the classroom in learning outcomes (Johnson, Johnson, & Stanne, 2000). Working together has a proven record of benefits, from academic success to decreasing racial stereotyping (Aronson, 1978). Putting students together to work toward a common goal avoids many of the potential pitfalls of gamification systems that encourage competition. It puts less emphasis on individual success or failure and pushes goals for the common good. It also gets students interacting in positive ways together and not looking at each other as rivals or someone to defeat, which ought to increase feelings of relatedness and connection to others.

Gamification and Virtual Worlds

Most of the discussion so far has concerned how to utilize different features of gamification in traditional classrooms, and how existing theories and concepts can help promote better understanding of the processes underlying gamification and the benefits it can pass on for students. This would not be complete without a brief discussion on the potential of gamifying education in virtual settings. As discussed with video game examples, interactive digital technology has some affordances not available within a traditional classroom, and these might be used to great advantage. Transformed social interaction suggests that virtual technologies enable communication in virtual environments to be modified in ways that are not feasible in the physical world (TSI; Bailenson, Beall, Loomis, Blascovich, & Turk, 2004), and is a useful framework for understanding some of the advantages that come with online digital technology.

According to Bailenson et al. (2004), virtual technologies have advantages over traditional forms of interpersonal communication in three ways: sensory capabilities, situational context, and self-representation. First, virtual technologies give users the opportunity to modify and augment their senses, gaining more information than they would be able to in regular, face-to-face interactions (Bailenson & Beall, 2006). For example, perceptions could be enhanced in a virtual classroom, allowing teachers to see students' names, grades, or other measures of comprehension or attention as they view each student's avatar. Virtual technologies could also enhance the students senses when learning. For example, a student could move an avatar in a virtual world through historical settings, seeing facts, important figures, listen to conversations and view primary documents directly in front of them.

TSI also allows for the manipulation of the context surrounding the situation (Bailenson & Beall, 2006). If a student missed an important lecture point in a virtual classroom, he or she could rewind and replay the conversation. Students having a hard time focusing in a virtual classroom could pause the lesson and step away. Alternatively, the virtual classroom itself could disappear, and students could learn about ecodiversity from within a virtual rainforest or learn about the planets while floating through the solar system. Altering elements of the context may improve desired learning outcomes.

Finally, virtual worlds allow for the manipulation of one's self-representation (Bailenson & Beall, 2006). Students can change their height, weight, or hair color in a virtual environment. They can also make changes drastically beyond possibility in the real world, such as inhabiting the body of a mythological beast. Individuals could also manipulate their appearance based on situational contexts or change them over time. The ability to alter one's self-representation maximizes the opportunity for students to present their preferred identity and act with anonymity if they desire. It helps customize the education experience to the student, allowing them to meet their individual needs.

Gamification and Digital Technology

Until now, our discussion of gamification has been focused on a traditional classroom setting. Our goal was to give examples of theory that can help guide a teacher interested in gamification to create their own courses without the aid of technology. However, we believe that technology, particularly interactive digital technology, can very much aid the gamification process. Beyond facilitating immediate feedback or making it easy to keep track of points or placement on a leaderboard, interactive technology can directly benefit students and their learning process (De Freitas, & Griffiths, 2008).

One of the benefits of interactive technology is that it allows users to become the source of content. Instead of reading information that was created by a source and distributed to the user, interactive technology allows users to create their own information, or actively be involved in the message creation process. This idea of "self-as-source" (Sundar & Nass, 2001) can have a host of benefits. Users are more engaged with material that they create, and they feel a stronger sense of identity with their own material (Sundar & Limperos, 2013). Thus, a gamified course that gives students the opportunity to interact with and create material on their own should facilitate positive engagement, user autonomy, competence, and enjoyment.

In addition, digital technology has become extremely good at letting us connect with others via social media. Social media gives users the ability to create their own content and then share it with others (McGonigal, 2007). It allows for monitoring and conversation with others, which can facilitate cooperation, social comparison, competition, or boost feelings of relatedness. Teachers can take advantage of social media to facilitate cooperation and relatedness perceptions between students in a modern way that extends outside of the classroom, which may continue when the students come back to the classroom the next day.

FUTURE RESEARCH DIRECTIONS

This chapter has discussed a variety of theories, concepts, and frameworks that help paint a better picture of the mechanisms behind gamification. It is only through understanding motivation, rewards, engagement, and identity that we can gain a clear understanding of how to best apply mechanics specific to gamification, and identify what mechanics we should steer clear from. Gamification is a relatively new concept in the literature, and the academic community is only beginning to study it. Thus, there are a number of potential areas we have identified that may benefit from greater scrutiny.

As gamification systems include visual feedback in the forms of leaderboards and badges, studies should examine how individuals process visual feedback in both the impression formation and impression management processes. Under what circumstances are individuals going to weigh components of the gamification system differently? Warranting theory provides some predictions but we need to examine whether warranting theory is upheld in evaluations of individuals in hybrid educational and game environments. Similarly, understanding how visual feedback, in particular badges, are interpreted as different types of signals and how the type of signal is important for the community remains a rather open area of research at this particular time.

Scholars must examine if there are any features that underlie narratives likely to produce a sense of presence and transportation for the viewer. Being able to explicitly identify a checklist of items associated with narratives likely to have positive effects on the viewer is exceedingly important for the development of the field going forward. It would not be a cost-effective manner of implementing gamification systems if every system required extensive testing prior to being implemented. This is not to say of course that the narratives should be completely tested prior to being dispersed, but rather that it would make sense to develop a list of structural characteristics that are important for a developing narrative. Potential characteristics important for developing a narrative include the ability of the narrative to change in response to user feedback, the existence and development of characters in the narrative over time, and the world depicted in the narrative.

Communication scholars have long shown an interest in understanding the motivations individuals have for interacting with particular mediums or particular genres of television programming. In the uses and gratifications tradition (Ruggiero, 2000), scholars are typically interested in assessing both the gratifications sought and the gratifications obtained by individuals that are currently using the item of interest. In addition, uses and gratifications theorists (see Ruggiero, 2000 for a review) would argue that individuals are more likely to use an object if there is a match between gratifications sought and gratifications obtained. This of course begs the question, what gratifications are being sought by individuals that spend the most time interacting with gamification systems?

Gamification systems can vary from simple to incredibly complex so it may be the case that individuals interacting with less complex gamification systems are seeking and obtaining different gratifications from those individuals interacting with more complex systems. These studies could be conducted both as single snapshot surveys that capture variables in a moment in time and as more longitudinal designs. We think longitudinal research is critical to developing a more thorough understanding of gamification processes as both gratifications sought and obtained may be contingent on the level of familiarity an individual has with the system. In addition, the effects of rewards on motivation or engagement may change as the reward loses potency over time.

As highlighted earlier, games are defined by the presence of a variety of features including: freedom to fail, immediate feedback, appropriate challenges, engrossing narratives and visual depictions of progress. The importance of these game defining features to the student may fluctuate over time. Perhaps individuals first interacting with the system consider the immediacy of the feedback as the most important gratification as this feedback serves as a socialization tool. After all if individuals are receiving positive feedback for performing particular behaviors they are likely to come to understand that those behaviors being rewarded are evaluated as positive by members of the community in question. Conversely, individuals that are familiar with the intricacies of the system, may seek challenge as an important gratification associated with the system. As discussed in our section on flow, individuals seek a perfect match between the difficulty of a task and their current skill level. If an individual is capable of completing all of the tasks developed as part of the gamification system within the first week then the need for this particular gratification will go unmet.

Finally, researchers must continue to examine how the presence of gamification systems impact users' levels of motivation. As the goal of these systems is to encourage user engagement, both in the classroom and the workplace, research must fully explore when features of these systems are likely to backfire. Early research on the impact of gamification on motivation is inconclusive with some research indicating the presence of a gamified system can enhance motivation (Bellotti et al., 2013) while other research has found that gamification using leaderboards, rewards, and competition harms student motivation, satisfaction, and results in lower final exam scores (Hanus & Fox, 2015). Research exploring the connection between gamification and motivation should account for a host of personal factors likely to moderate the effects of this relationship such as need for achievement (McClelland, 1961).

PRACTICAL APPLICATIONS

As gamification is in its relative infancy both as a field of study and as a practical tool, we believe it is important to discuss what educators should and should not do with their gamified systems.

First, include a variety of gameplay elements. Critics frequently lambast the gamification movement for simply throwing an external reward system onto a mundane task. Gamification is not solely coming up with funny names for badges that can be provided to individuals for performing a particular set of behaviors. Rather, gamification is the application of game elements to a non-game environment and feedback is only one component of the video game playing experience.

Also include a variety of badges that users can earn while interacting with the gamified system. As mentioned previously, badges have the capability to be used as indicators of particular skills so it is important to provide some badges that all individuals can earn. This is to ensure that some individuals do not become demotivated if they are unable to earn any badges on their profile.

Those interested in designing a gamified course should examine current gamification systems before building their own. There is certainly no shortage of gamification systems from which individuals can draw inspiration or ideas prior to developing their own system. As you are investigating gamification systems, please keep in mind that the affordances associated with the system is likely to vary. Systems should be built with the appropriate community in mind so perhaps a few features from a bevy of different systems may aid in developing a system more than simply adopting an entire system from one example.

It is very important to be careful when considering the types of rewards and feedback to give to students in the gamified course. Effort should be made to create rewards that are given only when the student has earned it, and are more complementary and verbal in nature than are tangible objects, like money or points.

A course designer should not be afraid to change things. As we saw when discussing ARG's, feedback is the single most important component of a successful gamification system. If students want to take the narrative to a place unforeseen at the outset of the class by all means let them. Fostering a sense of autonomy when interacting with gamification systems is incredibly important and experiences of autonomy should not compromised for the sole purpose of sticking to a particular script.

Focus on ways to provide visual evidence of one's progress. In addition to providing users with badges following the performance of a task, if possible allow users to design avatars that can be updated as they continue to progress throughout the storyline. Linking new items for the avatar to the performance of certain behaviors will increase the time some users spend with the system.

Gamification designers should focus on ways to make their system social in nature. As mentioned previously in our discussion on self-determination theory, scholars (Ryan & Deci, 2000) have found that activities that make individuals feel competent, autonomous, and related to other individuals are likely to be performed again. This feeling of social relatedness can manifest itself in a variety of ways in a gamified environment. Individuals can compare their performance to that of their classmates with a leaderboard function. However, individuals can also cooperate with their classmates to complete particular quests that are difficult if not impossible to complete alone. Systems built on social interactions help to establish the student as a person in the classroom as opposed to a nameless face.

It is important to not forget to include immediate feedback. Individuals in all walks of life appreciate quick feedback as this provides them with additional time to change behaviors if need be before the next time feedback is dispersed. Even if feedback cannot be designed to happen immediately after a student performs a particular task, designers should aim to minimize the amount of time between behavioral completion and feedback. In addition, create an engaging narrative around the task. Students will get more absorbed into the story and focus less on the tasks that they are doing. Using narratives can a fun way to teach important material without making students aware.

Make sure that the costs of are not entry too high. Students prefer that the difficulty of class material and tasks increase over time in order to best match their developing skills. Initial tasks should be viewed as a training area for new students thus allowing them to become familiar with this new system. In addition, there should be opportunities for incredibly difficult tasks at the end of class when it is assumed that students are now masters of the domain in question. It is important to make some of the incredibly difficult tasks optional so as to serve as an extra challenge for particularly ambitious students.

Finally, do not lose sight of the users. Gamified systems are implemented for a wide range of reasons including to increase user engagement, motivation, and brand loyalty. Administrators should make sure to survey the users of the system frequently in order to ascertain whether the system is meeting their needs. Ultimately, no gamified system can be a success if users turn away from the system due to unmet gratifications.

CONCLUSION

The process of gamification merges educational techniques and ideas from a variety of disciplines, and additional work must be conducted to test the overall effectiveness of some of these ideas. It is important to look at gamification systems as a combination of separate game features, each with their own benefits and potential drawbacks. The theories above discuss how these different features might be best implemented, as well as give some promising theoretical lenses to examine the best possible ways to use gamification in a classroom.

REFERENCES

Aronson, E. (1978). *The jigsaw classroom*. Oxford, UK: Sage.

Bailenson, J. N., & Beall, A. C. (2006). Transformed social interaction: Exploring the digital plasticity of avatars. In R. Schroeder & A.-S. Axelsson (Eds.), *Avatars at work and play: Collaboration and interaction in shared virtual environments* (pp. 1–16). New York: Springer-Verlag. doi:10.1007/1-4020-3898-4_1

Bailenson, J. N., Beall, A. C., Loomis, J., Blascovich, J., & Turk, M. (2004). Transformed social interaction: Decoupling representation from behavior and form in collaborative virtual environments. *Presence (Cambridge, Mass.), 13*(4), 428–441. doi:10.1162/1054746041944803

Bandura, A. (1982). Self-efficacy mechanism in human agency. *The American Psychologist, 37*(2), 122–147. doi:10.1037/0003-066X.37.2.122

Beed, P. L., Hawkins, E. M., & Roller, C. M. (1991). Moving learners toward independence: The power of scaffolded instruction. *The Reading Teacher, 44*, 648–655. Retrieved from http://www.reading.org/general/Publications/Journals/RT.aspx

Bellotti, F., Berta, R., De Gloria, A., Lavagnino, E., Dagnino, M. F., Antonaci, A., & Ott, M. (2013). A gamified short course for promoting entrepreneurship among ICT engineering students. Proceedings of *13th International Conference on Advanced Learning Technologies*. doi:10.1109/ICALT.2013.14

Bem, D. J. (1972). In L. Berkowitz (Ed.), *Self-perception theory* (Vol. 6, pp. 1–62). Advances in experimental social psychology San Diego, CA: Academic Press.

Bogost, I. (2011). Persuasive Games: Exploitationware. Retrieved from http://www.gamasutra.com/view/feature/134735/persuasive_games_exploitationware.php

Burgess, M. L., Slate, J. R., Rojos-LeBouef, A., & LaPrairie, K. (2010). Teaching and learning in Second Life: Using the community of inquiry (CoI) model to support online instruction with graduate students in instructional technology. *The Internet and Higher Education, 13*(1/2), 84–88. doi:10.1016/j.iheduc.2009.12.003

Cameron, J. (2001). Negative effects of reward on intrinsic motivation—a limited phenomenon: Comment on Deci, Koestner, and Ryan (2001). *Review of Educational Research, 71*(1), 29–42. doi:10.3102/00346543071001029

Cameron, J., Banko, K. M., & Pierce, W. D. (2001). Pervasive negative effects of rewards on intrinsic motivation: The myth continues. *The Behavior Analyst, 24,* 1–44. Retrieved from https://www.abainternational.org/journals/the-behavior-analyst.aspx PMID:22478353

Cameron, J., & Pierce, W. D. (1994). Reinforcement, reward, and intrinsic motivation: A meta-analysis. *Review of Educational Research, 64*(3), 363–423. doi:10.3102/00346543064003363

Camilleri, V., Busuttil, L., & Montebello, M. (2011). Social interactive learning in multiplayer games. In M. Ma, A. Oikonomou, & L. C. Jain (Eds.), *Serious games and edutainment applications* (pp. 481–501). London, England: Springer-Verlag. doi:10.1007/978-1-4471-2161-9_23

Charles, D., Charles, T., McNeill, M., Bustard, D., & Black, M. (2011). Game-based feedback for educational multi-user virtual environments. *British Journal of Educational Technology, 42*(4), 638–654. doi:10.1111/j.1467-8535.2010.01068.x

Chatfield, T. (2009, September). Videogames now outperform Hollywood movies: Titles such as Halo: ODST are drawing people away from cinemas, television, and DVDS. *The Guardian.* Retrieved from http://www.theguardian.com/technology/gamesblog/2009/sep/27/videogames-hollywood

Cheng, J. (2008). The Success Secrets of Michael Jordan. Retrieved from http://www.jordancheng.net

Clark, M. C., & Rossiter, M. (2008). Narrative learning in adulthood. *New Directions for Adult and Continuing Education, 119*(119), 61–70. doi:10.1002/ace.306

Cronk, M. (2012, June). Using gamification to increase student engagement and participation in class discussion. Proceedings of *World conference on education multimedia, hypermedia, and telecommunications* (Vol. 2012, No.1, pp. 311-315).

Csikszentmihalyi, M., & Csikzentmihaly, M. (1991). *Flow: The psychology of optimal experience.* New York: Harper Perennial.

De Freitas, S., & Griffiths, M. (2008). The onvergence of gaming practices with other media forms: What potential for learning? A review of the literature. *Learning, Media and Technology, 33*(1), 11–20. doi:10.1080/17439880701868796

DeAndrea, D. C. (2014). Advancing warranting theory. *Communication Theory, 24*(2), 186–204. doi:10.1111/comt.12033

Deci, E. L., Koestner, R., & Ryan, R. M. (1999). A meta-analytic review of experiments examining the effects of extrinsic rewards on intrinsic motivation. *Psychological Bulletin, 125*(6), 627–668. doi:10.1037/0033-2909.125.6.627 PMID:10589297

Deci, E. L., Koestner, R., & Ryan, R. M. (2001). Extrinsic rewards and intrinsic motivation in education: Reconsidered once again. *Review of Educational Research, 71*(1), 1–27. doi:10.3102/00346543071001001

Deci, E. L., & Ryan, R. M. (1985). *Intrinsic motivation and self-determination in human behavior*. New York: Plenum Press. doi:10.1007/978-1-4899-2271-7

Deci, E. L., & Ryan, R. M. (1987). The support of autonomy and the control of behavior. *Journal of Personality and Social Psychology, 53*(6), 1024–1037. doi:10.1037/0022-3514.53.6.1024 PMID:3320334

Deci, E. L., & Ryan, R. M. (2000). The ''what'' and ''why'' of goal pursuits: Human needs and the self-determination of behavior. *Psychological Inquiry, 11*(4), 227–268. doi:10.1207/S15327965PLI1104_01

Deci, E. L., Ryan, R. M., & Koestner, R. (2001). The pervasive negative effects of rewards on intrinsic motivation: Response to Cameron (2001). *Review of Educational Research, 71*(1), 43–51. doi:10.3102/00346543071001043

Deterding, S., Sicart, M., Nacke, L., O'Hara, K., & Dixon, D. (2011). Gamification: Using game-design elements in non-gaming contexts. *Proceedings of the 2011 annual conference on human factors in computing systems* (pp. 2425-2428). ACM. doi:10.1145/1979742.1979575

Dijkstra, P., Kuyper, H., van der Werf, G., Buunk, A. P., & van der Zee, Y. G. (2008). Social comparison in the classroom: A review. *Review of Educational Research, 78*(4), 828–879. doi:10.3102/0034654308321210

Domínguez, A., Saenz-de-Navarrete, J., De-Marcos, L., Fernández-Sanz, L., Pagés, C., & Martínez-Herráiz, J. J. (2013). Gamifying learning experiences: Practical implications and outcomes. *Computers & Education, 63*, 380–392. doi:10.1016/j.compedu.2012.12.020

Donath, J. (2007). Signals in social supernets. *Journal of Computer-Mediated Communication, 13*(1), 231–251. doi:10.1111/j.1083-6101.2007.00394.x

Festinger, L. (1954). A theory of social comparison processes. *Human Relations, 7*(2), 117–140. doi:10.1177/001872675400700202

Fülöp, M. (2009). Happy and unhappy competitors: What makes the difference? *Psihologijske Teme, 18*, 345–367. Retrieved from http://hrcak.srce.hr/index.php?show=clanak&id_clanak_jezik=74342

Garcia, S. M., Tor, A., & Gonzalez, R. (2006). Ranks and rivals: A theory of competition. *Personality and Social Psychology Bulletin, 32*(7), 970–982. doi:10.1177/0146167206287640 PMID:16738029

Gartner says by 2015 more than 50 percent of organizations that manage innovation processes will gamify those processes. (2011, April). Retrieved from http://www.gartner.com

George, S., Clark, M., & Crotty, M. (2007). Development of the Adelaide driving self-efficacy scale. *Clinical Rehabilitation, 21*(1), 56–61. doi:10.1177/0269215506071284 PMID:17213242

Giles, D. C. (2002). Parasocial interaction: A review of the literature and a model for future research. *Media Psychology, 4*(3), 279–205. doi:10.1207/S1532785XMEP0403_04

Gonzalez, A. (2012). Gamifying my classes. Retrieved from http://www.educatoral.com/wordpress/2012/07/16/gamifying-my-classes/

Green, M. C., & Brock, T. C. (2000). The role of transportation in the persuasiveness of public narratives. *Journal of Personality and Social Psychology, 79*(5), 701–721. doi:10.1037/0022-3514.79.5.701 PMID:11079236

Green, M. C., Brock, T. C., & Kaufman, G. F. (2004). Understanding media enjoyment: The role of transportation into narrative worlds. *Communication Theory, 14*(4), 311–327. doi:10.1111/j.1468-2885.2004. tb00317.x

Hamari, J. (2013). Transforming homo economicus into homo ludens: A field experiment on gamification in a utilitarian peer-to-peer trading service. *Electronic Commerce Research and Applications, 12*(4), 236–245. doi:10.1016/j.elerap.2013.01.004

Hanus, M. D., & Fox, J. (2015). Assessing the effects of gamification in the classroom: A longitudinal study on intrinsic motivation, social comparison, satisfaction, effort and academic performance. *Computers & Education, 80*, 152–161. doi:10.1016/j.compedu.2014.08.019

Hellwege, B., & Robertson, C. (2012, October). Entertain, engage, educate. *Proceedings of ACEC 2012*. Perth, Australia: ACEC.

Hoorens, V., & Van Damme, C. (2012). What do people infer from social comparisons? Bridges between social comparison and person perception. *Social and Personality Psychology Compass, 6*(8), 607–618. doi:10.1111/j.1751-9004.2012.00451.x

Horton, D., & Wohl, R. R. (1956). Mass communication and para-social interaction: Observations on intimacy at a distance. *Psychiatry, 19*(3), 215–229. PMID:13359569

Jakobsson, M. (2011). The achievement machine: Understanding Xbox 360 achievements in gaming practices. *Game Studies, 11*(1). Retrieved from http://gamestudies.org/1101

Jenkins, H. (2006). *Convergence culture: Where old and new media collide*. New York, NY: New York University Press.

Johnson, D. W., Johnson, R. T., & Stanne, M. B. (2000). *Cooperative learning methods: A meta-analysis*. Minneapolis: University of Minnesota.

Kapp, K. M. (2012). *The gamification of learning and instruction: game-based methods and strategies for training and education*. San Francisco, CA: Pfieffer.

Lee, D. W., & LaRose, R. (2007). A socio-cognitive model of video game usage. *Journal of Broadcasting & Electronic Media, 51*(4), 632–650. doi:10.1080/08838150701626511

Lee, J. J., & Hammer, J. (2011). Gamification in education: What, how, why bother? *Academic Exchange Quarterly, 15*(2), 146. Retrieved from http://www.rapidintellect.com/AEQweb/

Lee, K. M. (2004). Presence, explicated. *Communication Theory, 14*(1), 27–50. doi:10.1111/j.1468-2885.2004. tb00302.x

Lepper, M. R., Greene, D., & Nisbett, R. E. (1973). Undermining children's intrinsic interest with extrinsic reward: A test of the ''overjustification'' hypothesis. *Journal of Personality and Social Psychology, 28*(1), 129–137. doi:10.1037/h0035519

Major, B., Testa, M., & Bylsma, W. H. (1991). Responses to upward and downward social comparisons: The impact of esteem-relevance and perceived control in social comparison. In J. Suls & T. A. Wills (Eds.), *Contemporary Theory and Research* (pp. 237–260). Hillsdale, N.J.: Erlbaum.

McClelland, D. C. (1961). *The achieving society*. Princeton, NJ: Van Nostrand. doi:10.1037/14359-000

McGonigal, J. (2007). Why I love bees: A case study in collective intelligence gaming. In K. Salem (Ed.), *The ecology of games: Connecting youth, games, and learning* (pp. 199–227). Cambridge, MA: The MIT Press.

McGonigal, J. (2011). *Reality is broken: Why games make us better and how they can change the world*. New York, NY: Penguin.

Moyer-Gusé, E. (2008). Toward a theory of entertainment persuasion: Explaining the persuasive effects of entertainment-education messages. *Communication Theory, 18*(3), 407–425. doi:10.1111/j.1468-2885.2008.00328.x

Moyer-Gusé, E., & Nabi, R. L. (2010). Explaining the persuasive effects of narrative in an entertainment television program: Overcoming resistance to persuasion. *Human Communication Research, 36*(1), 25–51. doi:10.1111/j.1468-2958.2009.01367.x

Multon, K. D., Brown, S. D., & Lent, R. W. (1991). Relation of self-efficacy beliefs to academic outcomes: A meta-analytic investigation. *Journal of Counseling Psychology, 38*(1), 30–38. doi:10.1037/0022-0167.38.1.30

Muntean, C. I. (2011). Raising engagement in e-learning through gamification. *Proceedings of the 6th International Conference on Virtual Learning* (pp. 323-329). Retrieved from http://icvl.eu/2011/disc/icvl/documente/pdf/met/ICVL_ModelsAndMethodologies_paper42.pdf

Orosz, G., Farkas, D., & Roland-Lévy, C. (2013). Are competition and extrinsic motivation reliable predictors of academic cheating? *Frontiers in Psychology, 4*(87), 1–16. doi:10.3389/fpsyg.2013.00087 PMID:23450676

Przybylski, A. K., Rigby, C. S., & Ryan, R. M. (2010). A motivational model of video game engagement. *Review of General Psychology, 14*(2), 154–166. doi:10.1037/a0019440

Przybylski, A. K., Weinstein, N., Ryan, R. M., & Rigby, C. S. (2009). Having to versus wanting to play: Background and consequences of harmonious versus obsessive engagement in video games. *Cyberpsychology & Behavior, 12*(5), 485–492. doi:10.1089/cpb.2009.0083 PMID:19772442

Reeve, J., & Deci, E. L. (1996). Elements of the competitive situation that affect intrinsic motivation. *Personality and Social Psychology Bulletin, 22*(1), 24–33. doi:10.1177/0146167296221003

Ruggiero, T. (2000). Uses and gratifications theory in the 21st century. *Mass Communication & Society, 3*(1), 3–37. doi:10.1207/S15327825MCS0301_02

Ryan, R. M., & Deci, E. L. (2000). Self-determination theory and the facilitation of intrinsic motivation, social development, and well-being. *The American Psychologist, 55*, 68–78. doi: 10.1037110003-066X.55.1.68

Sheldon, K. M., & Filak, V. (2008). Manipulating autonomy, competence and relatedness support in a game-learning context: New evidence that all three needs matter. *The British Journal of Social Psychology*, *47*(2), 267–283. doi:10.1348/014466607X238797 PMID:17761025

Skalski, P., Tamborini, R., Shelton, A., Buncher, M., & Lindmark, P. (2011). Mapping the road to fun: Natural video game controllers, presence, and game enjoyment. *New Media & Society*, *13*(2), 224–242. doi:10.1177/1461444810370949

Stott, A., & Neustaedter, C. Analysis of gamification in education. Retrieved from http://carmster.com/clab/uploads/Main/Stott-Gamification.pdf

Sundar, S. S., & Limperos, A. M. (2013). Uses and grats 2.0: New gratifications for new media. *Journal of Broadcasting & Electronic Media*, *57*(4), 504–525. doi:10.1080/08838151.2013.845827

Sundar, S. S., & Nass, C. (2001). Conceptualizing sources in online news. *Journal of Communication*, *51*(1), 52–72. doi:10.1111/j.1460-2466.2001.tb02872.x

Tamborini, R., Grizzard, M., Bowman, N. D., Reinecke, L., Lewis, R. J., & Eden, A. (2011). Media enjoyment as need satisfaction: The contribution of hedonic and nonhedonic needs. *Journal of Communication*, *61*(6), 1025–1042. doi:10.1111/j.1460-2466.2011.01593.x

Tang, S., & Hall, V. C. (1995). The overjustification effect: A meta-analysis. *Applied Cognitive Psychology*, *9*(5), 365–404. doi:10.1002/acp.2350090502

What we do. (2014). The Institute for the Future. Retrieved from http://www.iftf.org/what-we-do/

Tong, S. T., Van Der Heide, B., Langwell, L., & Walther, J. B. (2008). Too much of a good thing? The relationship between number of friends and interpersonal impressions on Facebook. *Journal of Computer-Mediated Communication*, *13*(3), 531–549. doi:10.1111/j.1083-6101.2008.00409.x

Tripathi, K. N. (1992). Competition and intrinsic motivation. *The Journal of Social Psychology*, *132*(6), 709–715. doi:10.1080/00224545.1992.9712101

Utz, S. (2010). Show me your friends and I will tell you what type of person you are: How one's profile, number of friends, and type of friends influence impression formation on social network sites. *Journal of Computer-Mediated Communication*, *15*(2), 314–335. doi:10.1111/j.1083-6101.2010.01522.x

Vallerand, R. J., Gauvin, L. I., & Halliwell, W. R. (1986). Negative effects of competition on children's intrinsic motivation. *The Journal of Social Psychology*, *126*(5), 649–656. doi:10.1080/00224545.1986.9713638

Walther, J. B., & Parks, M. (2002). Cues filtered out, cues filtered in: Computer mediated communication and relationships. In M. L. Knapp, J. A. Daly, & G. R. Miller (Eds.), *The handbook of interpersonal communication* (3rd ed., pp. 529–563). Thousand Oaks, CA: Sage.

Walther, J. B., Van Der Heide, B., Hamel, L., & Shulman, H. C. (2009). Self-generated versus other-generated statements and impressions in computer-mediated communication: A test of warranting theory using facebook. *Communication Research*, *36*(2), 229–253. doi:10.1177/0093650208330251

Warburton, S. (2009). Second Life in higher education: Assessing the potential for and the barriers to deploying virtual worlds in learning and teaching. *British Journal of Educational Technology*, *40*(3), 414–426. doi:10.1111/j.1467-8535.2009.00952.x

Wells, B. M., & Skowronski, J. J. (2012). Evidence of choking under pressure on the PGA tour. *Basic and Applied Social Psychology*, *34*(2), 175–182. doi:10.1080/01973533.2012.655629

Westerman, D., Spence, P. R., & Van Der Heide, B. (2012). A social network as information: The effect of system generated reports of connectedness on credibility on Twitter. *Computers in Human Behavior*, *28*(1), 199–206. doi:10.1016/j.chb.2011.09.001

Wu, H.-K., Lee, S. W.-Y., Chang, H.-Y., & Liang, J.-C. (2013). Current status, opportunities and challenges of augmented reality in education. *Computers & Education*, *62*, 41–49. doi:10.1016/j.compedu.2012.10.024

Zahavi, A. (1975). Mate selection – a selection for a handicap. *Journal of Theoretical Biology*, *53*(1), 205–214. doi:10.1016/0022-5193(75)90111-3 PMID:1195756

KEY TERMS AND DEFINITIONS

Badges: A visual representation of a player's achievement—often called trophies or achievements—that are typically displayed where others can see them. For example, upon defeating 10 monsters a player might earn the Monster Slayer badge.

Feedback: The response given to a player's input, typically given by the instructor or the game.

Game Features: Traditional elements, mechanics, or rule-sets commonly found in games (e.g., keeping track of a player's points, sending players on quests, or displaying their progress on a leaderboard).

Gamification: The use of game features or mechanics in a non-game setting (e.g., a classroom).

Intrinsic Motivation: Occurs when one does a task due to internal reasons (e.g., "I want to do it"), rather than due to outside pressures (e.g., "My parents are making me").

Narrative Context: Creating a story around a task to make a task more interesting or engaging.

Rewards: A form of feedback designed to signal success for a player. Can come in many forms including points, badges, or verbal praise.

Chapter 10
Gamification of the Classroom:
Potential, Pitfalls, and Practices

Darcy Osheim
Maine Maritime Academy, USA

ABSTRACT

Students need the classroom in order to educate in a way in which they can relate, and grow bored when that does not happen. Gamification employs game mechanics, techniques, and theory in areas that traditionally are not set up to function like a game, and many instructors and administrators at the university level are eager to use gamification to encourage students to learn. However, gamification is not a generic fix to the problems found in the classroom. Instructors should gain insight on how successful games work, and gamify specific classroom functions to retain the deep learning required for subject mastery. The author employs the method of heterotopian rhetorical criticism and the methodology of autoethnography to analyze World of Warcraft and re-imagine experiences in the game through critical communication pedagogy to enact change in the traditional college classroom. A general definition emerged: Gamification must consist of high-choice, low-risk engagements in a clearly structured environment.

INTRODUCTION

Instructors find a gap between what they experienced in school in the mid to late 20th century and the experiences of students entering college in after 2012. This generation, born in the 1990s and known as the Games Generation (Prensky, 2001), Generation Me, or Generation Y, interacts so differently with the world than the generations that came before. According to the Beloit College, the class of 2016 has "always lived in cyberspace, addicted to a new generation of 'electronic narcotics'" ("The Mindset List," 2012, List number 2). Yes, these children might seem lucky, however in the United States, this influx of almost universal access to technology has marked this generation in a way the previous generations must work to understand. The technology that has always been available to the Games Generation continues to change the way humans think about the world. It is clear that if this technology has changed our lives as adults, it has almost rewired this younger generation to think differently than previous generations.

DOI: 10.4018/978-1-4666-8651-9.ch010

This change becomes apparent when viewing the classroom. Students now learn differently than students did even a generation ago. The problem is instructors use "...yesterday's education for tomorrow's [students]. Where is the programming, the genomics, the bioethics, the nanotech—the stuff of their time? It's not there. Not even once a week on Fridays" (Prensky, 2005, p. 62). Teachers of all levels of education risk losing the interest of students when the choice of curriculum falls short of student need (Cohen, 2011; Frymier & Shulman, 1994). Educators must start looking at how students learn, and why learning occurs. I employed the method of heterotopian rhetorical criticism and of autoethnography to analyze World of Warcraft and re-imagine experiences in the game through critical communication pedagogy to enact change in the traditional college classroom

Potential

Gamification is a strategy that employs game mechanics, techniques, and theory in areas that traditionally do not function like a game. The word can be traced back as early as 2004 ("Gamification," n.d.), but the concept goes back further. The boy scouts, sports, and military branches use forms of gamification, in which a person can gain a "level" or rank when successfully completing enough tasks (Geuter, 2012). Digital ranking takes shape in gamified applications (apps) like Foursquare, in which a "player" is able to earn points, badges, and "mayorships" of businesses, homes, and other points of interest by letting friends and companies know that they are "checked in". Apps like Chorewars and EpicWin help encourage people to finish daily and tedious chores (Lee & Hammer, 2011). These applications, by being simple, pervasive, and easy to use, improve mundane tasks, making them enjoyable. Applications like these serve as mini games that people can easily play anywhere.

Games are generally simple concepts that follow simple sets of rules that regulate game play. Those rules guide players to correct behavior through feedback of either success or failure. "A well-built game is, in essence, a series of short-term feedback loops, delivering assessment in small, frequent doses" (Corbett, 2010, para. 15). Unlike most institutional learning systems, "games associate learning with fun and allow for trial and error" (Cohen, 2011, p. 17). Games work because players do not fear failure. Even death is just a minor setback in the course of a game. In games, failure presents an opportunity for improvement/adjustment to player behavior. Players can make multiple attempts at a quest, fight or engagement, with low risk to the fun or motivation of the player. This low-risk failure changes learning from a short-term to a long-term endeavor in which mastery, not scores, is the end result. By adopting a gamified mindset, learning returns to its historical function, allowing students to learn through low-risk fun, which increases participation (Lui, Alexandrova, & Nakajima, 2011). The participation increases in subtle ways as the general population becomes more enthralled with all things gamified.

Games Are Work

Gamification is so rich in possibilities because gamers of all skill levels happily work hard and rely on internal motivation to complete game-like tasks. Gamers are willing to work, as long as this work challenges them in some way, because, "in a game, players (learners) will endure frustration and challenges that in other situations would cause them to give up" (Ladley, 2011, p. 3). This challenging play/work is more fun and healthier for people than entertainment (*Why we play games*, 2004), because while watching TV can be relaxing, watching large amounts stops being fun and quickly drains happiness and stamina. To best understand the hard, yet satisfying, play/work found in games, it breaks down in the following ways: high stakes/hard work, busy work, and team work (McGonigal, 2011; *Why we play games*, 2004). Perhaps the most difficult to understand is why hard work is a beneficial mechanism of games.

Players easily can find hard work in video games. A player might experience fantastic success, but she/he might also fail spectacularly. Part of what makes games fun is the challenge that a game presents to the body and mind of player in ways that are not monotonous and that are not so hard that she becomes discouraged (Jegers, 2007). A player enjoys this work when she is down to her last health bar, surrounded by enemies, relying on skill, and a little luck to get her past the zombies, monsters, or bad guys without dying. If she does die, death occurs because of overwhelming odds, but if she succeeds she becomes a goddess of gaming (McGonigal, 2011). Numerous deaths on a single quest, or slow feedback make the game too challenging and not fun, and game designers must balance quests to be challenging, without being impossible for a new player or monotonous for an experienced player (*Why we play games*, 2004). When the high stakes work becomes too overwhelming, a gamer can seek out busy work, sometimes within the same game.

Busy work keeps the mind entertained with minimal effort, even though it sounds like a bad thing. However, real busy work is meaningful and necessary. Unlike watching television, busy work still adds to happiness because busy work is easy fun. Games encourage easy and fun completion of tasks allowing for quick feedback and easy turnover (Juul, 2010). Busy work is in games like Tetris, Temple Run, Bejeweled Blitz, and Solitaire that are relaxing. These solitary efforts can help a player unwind from a team mission or quest.

School, work, and play require individuals to work together in order to succeed. In a team players contribute knowledge, collaborate, as well as socialize with others. Players play games for relaxation, fulfillment of social needs or for excitement. As many gamers can attest, unlike the "real world", "within these groupings, players can communicate easily, meet, support one another, and share resources" (Williams, 2006, p. 655). The sense of community changes how a player interacts with a game and how a game interacts with a player. People enjoy contributing to a larger cause, even if that cause works towards a mutual virtual end. EQ2 has raids in which up to 24 players work together to complete larger tasks that would be impossible to complete with a single player ("Community News," 2009 Groups learn each individual's strengths and weaknesses, as well as learn how to deal with undesirable traits. Virtual teamwork gives the satisfaction of gaming and live teamwork that is hard to find in the "real world." People are able to enter into friendly competition within a game and have that competition stay within the space of the game. When players can experience failure or success in teamwork in a low-stakes situation, they transfer the abilities and concepts of teamwork into a "real world" situation and make it enjoyable.

Gamification

Gamification encourages people to rely on internal motivation by making mundane tasks fun. While games in an everyday part of life is still a fledgling concept (Schell, 2010), gamification of life is the way much of our consumer world, especially in the United States, is heading (Lee & Hammer, 2011). Defining gamification in relation to the classroom is critical because some people outside the education research field, such as parents, politicians, and journalists, criticize the lack of change and innovation in the classroom. While becoming more inclusive for students of color, those who identify as Lesbian, Gay, Bisexual, and/or Transgender (LGBT), and those who have disabilities, school has not changed much since the 19th century. Researchers who are working to gamify the classroom are desperate for it to happen (Gee, 2007). Educators fight for a better school experience for all students based on better methods of learning, performing, and succeeding. Although many colleges are employing smart class-rooms or even virtual gamification, encompassing technology remains a privilege for only some of the student population. A majority of gaming in education research concentrates on bringing actual video games or game building software into the classroom, therefore saving money and physical resources (Corbett, 2010). Although some researchers embrace video games in the classroom, others argue that software are not the only way to change the way students learn.

Gamification of the Classroom

It is difficult to successfully define gamification through a merge the 19ᵗʰ century model of teaching and the 21ˢᵗ model of learning. However, some have had success. Lee Sheldon, a professor at Rens-selaer Polytechnic Institute and co-director of the Games and Simulation Arts and Sciences program, is part of a "small but increasingly influential group of education specialists who believe that going to school can and should be more like playing a game, which is to say it could be more participatory, more immersive and also, well, fun" (Corbett, 2010, para. 15). Sheldon uses the class, in which every part of the class performs like a game, to actively define gamification. His syllabus functions like a quest log, and instead of grades presented to the students in a typical points lost configuration, Sheldon approaches earning grades as a player earns experience points in a MMORPG (Laster, 2010). Though this is a different way of approaching the classroom, changing the function of grades is not implausible as grades are a primitive, although not often thought of, form of gamification (Lee & Hammer, 2011). This gamification of the classroom puts the power in the hands of the student, placing responsibility for his/her gaining "experience" by performing tasks within the classroom. Students no longer lose points for errors due to confusing and sometimes unknown grading systems implemented differently by each teacher, and in this gamified sense, grades might have a more internally motivating affect. Assignments are weighted differently as difficulty increases, just as players would find in a game. Group projects are worth more points, as students must put forth more effort. Unlike so many instructors, Sheldon (2010) does not require students to work in groups but rewards those who are willing to take on the difficult task of group work. Sheldon's classroom is an example of what could be possible. By implementing an inverse grading system and classroom power structure, Sheldon's model allows others to imagine and construct the future of college classrooms.

In the interest of future students' learning, a focused definition of gamification of the classroom take into consideration that Generation Me does not need actual games in the classroom to have an ideal class but needs a classroom in which "every course, every activity, every assignment, every moment of instruction and assessment would be designed by borrowing key mechanics and participation strategies" from games that successfully engage "players" on an everyday basis (McGonigal, 2011, p. 128). In an MMORPG, raiding is a constant trial and error as leaders try to find the perfect combination of skills, knowledge and luck in order to defeat the handful of bosses the raid presents. Games allow for achievable levels of difficulty, and the feeling that even if there is failure, that the failure helps the player learn for future success. To understand and master the raid can take weeks of work, more than 80 hours of trial and error, usually four to six hours at a time. Coupling this kind of commitment with a full-time job and/or a family is the point of an "epic" game; "The industry wants to create *lifelong gamers*: people who can balance their favorite games with full and active lives [emphasis in original]" (McGonigal, 2011, p. 43). This joy in failure, struggle, and extracurricular commitment that players experience in a game could be a strategy to change how students and teachers interact with a subject and each other. Most games are rooted in the model of "reflection in action" (Salen, 2008, p. 14) or what Gee calls "active learning" (2007, p. 25), which are concepts already used in the classroom. If gamification is to be a strategy to improve the classroom, instructors and researchers need to understand not only a history of classroom strategies and how gamification relates to them, but also how our communication practices helps to name what is important in the classroom.

BACKGROUND

Gamification has caught the attention of our culture. It is important to name the potential gamification shows, as a framework or strategy, in the classroom. Critical communication pedagogy, heterotopian rhetorical criticism and autoethnography creates a framework that helps researchers understand how gamification might enhance learning.

Critical Communication Pedagogy

Critical communication pedagogy (CCP) combines critical pedagogy, inspired by Paulo Freire and others, and communication education, inspired by Jo Sprague's introduction of critical pedagogy into the communication field (Fassett & Warren, 2007). As a method of study and a pedagogical practice, CCP brings education research across interdisciplinary lines and uses the communication within the subject to order, label, and urge to change. "…In our communication practices…we produce knowledge, define how identities are negotiated and maintained, and imply that power is something only the powerful possess" (Fassett & Warren, 2007, p. 45), and CCP gives the opportunity and responsibility to find meaningful moments in everyday classroom situations. CCP highlights specific moments of reflexivity in which instructors, researchers, and students are able to name a problem and postulate ways that each participate in upholding or breaking the invisible structures of the physical and ephemeral classroom that control behavior. How CCP researchers interpret or process that language determines what strategies and tactics are formed from the information.

In education research, researchers look at specific parts of the classroom experience in order to label and organize what happens. To challenge the norms of the classroom or any space, it is not about criticizing what came before, but building upon the concepts that have value (Fassett & Warren, 2007). "Critical approaches to pedagogy must, by necessity, exist in relation to traditional or conservative approaches to pedagogy; we argue that critical pedagogies are most effective as means to interrupt, to call out, and call into question the traditional" (Fassett & Warren, 2007, p. 83). Through CCP, instructors use tactics in order to call into question the traditional strategies used in the classroom. Strategies are calculated maneuvers that exist in arbitrary but normalized relationships (de Certeau, 1984). Strategies are long term overarching ideas about how to achieve a goal, while tactics are reflexive actions taken that fulfill the strategy. Each strategy highlights some relationships and aids in the understanding of the current classroom, while tactics, such as gamification give different options of how to reach the goal of concept mastery. Many of the current tactics are based in a post-positive paradigm, but as CCP examines what came before, so must this chapter.

Student Interest

One of the areas researchers work to understand is student interest. A student's interest in a subject influences joy and classroom performance. "Interest is seen as being central in determining how students select and persist in processing certain types of information in preference to others" (Weber, 2004, p. 428). A student's involvement in a task positively relates to his/her interest with the task and it is important to manipulate the curriculum to improve it.

Researchers can do this by choosing a framework, such as gamification, that speaks to the needs of both the student and instructor. Factors that affect interest, such as the relationship of the learner and instructional activities, or environment, researchers find in three dimensions of student interest: Meaningfulness, competence, and impact (Weber, Martin, & Cayanus, 2005; Weber & Patterson, 2000; Frymier & Shulman, 1994). Student interest is a way to measure if these tactics work.

As a way to increase student interest, instructors increase meaningfulness, which encourages the student to feel the importance of the task. A student perceives meaningfulness as s/he perceives the significance or relevance of the task (Frymier & Shulman, 1994, Weber et al., 2005). To experience meaningfulness, a student must consider the value attached to the task. As the feelings of value increase, so does interest (Weber & Patterson, 2000), which leads to the perceived value of task completion. Meaningfulness has also been linked to interest and empowerment, and has become "synonymous with internal motivation" (Weber & Patterson, 2000, p. 28). Internal motivation fortifies students' feelings of competence.

When students feel important and heard in the classroom, they have a greater sense of competence. The evaluation of a student's own abilities and knowledge or competence, influences how interested s/he is in the task (Weber et al., 2005; Weber & Patterson, 2000). When students feel included in the classroom, they are more likely to continue participating. This is why games increase competence. The quick feedback loop helps a player continually evaluate her skill. Spitzberg (1983) shows that competence in communication enhances and assists in skill building. Competence represents how a student feels about his/her abilities (Weber & Patterson, 2000). Students evaluate competency better when they receive frequent and specific feedback.

Along with the evaluation of skills, the impact of the task influences how the student learns. The impact of a task denotes how important and valuable the task or the completion of the task is in the classroom (Weber & Patterson, 2000), and in the larger picture of the student's life (Frymier & Shulman, 1994). Students are willing to do work that has impact on their life and education. When a task is meaningful to a student, the more internal motivation s/he has to complete that task. Belief in the positive impact of a task influences students to complete said task, feel its meaningfulness, and increase feelings of competence.

Pathways to Learner Empowerment

In order to keep student interest and treat students as whole individuals, researchers have created strategies such as cognitive and affective learning, learner empowerment, and online classroom elements. If researchers can name "in-class factors which may affect students' state motivation could help teachers design instruction to reach previously unmotivated students" (Tibbles et al., 2008, p. 394). Critical researchers strive to find alternative teaching methods to techniques such as Behavior Alteration Techniques (Sprague, 1992). When examining these techniques, teachers/researchers need to keep in mind that the decisions on "good teaching" affect student-learning experiences. Therefore, the research needs to focus on effective overarching strategies so instructors are not just gaining compliance but are really working for what is best for the entire student population in the long term. Critical scholars uphold the idea that transformative change is possible within the classroom as long as research is not done *about* or *for* instructors, but is done *with* them (Freire, 2000). The research done about instructors, while academically stimulating, lacks the personal narratives that make critical research accessible, intriguing, and transformative (Sprague, 1992). By employing cognitive learning, affective learning, learner empowerment and new ways of presenting material to engage students fully in the classroom, teachers and students experience success.

Affect learning encourages emotional connection with the teacher, classroom or subject. "The clarity with which teachers present information, their immediacy behaviors, and how they listen and react to students are intuitive, though not exhaustive ways, through which teachers potentially influence students emotions" (Titsworth et al., 2010, p. 445). Crucial to the learning process is student preparedness for class, including completion of assignments and class readings. As many teachers and students can testify, students resist assignments and frequently come to class underprepared. This is partly because students are not connected emotionally to the reading. Quizzes much of the time seem like busy work or passive aggressive "checks" to make sure students are not resisting (Johnson, 2007), and can lead to increased anxiety and actually add to the students' resistance. Because of the emotional link to student and teachers through nonverbal immediacy, students react have a heightened emotional state when immediacy techniques are used (Titsworth et al., 2010). Emotional connection to the course empowers students to go farther and deeper into course concepts.

One of the goals instructors have when employing these strategies is to empower students and help them find joy in learning. "Learner empowerment is much more than the internalization of positive attitudes or intrinsic motivation, as it includes a cognitive belief state of personal involvement and self-efficacy that ultimately results in a heightened sense of personal effectiveness among students" (Schrodt et al., 2008, p. 184). A recent paradigm shift moves instructors from teacher-centered lecture based classrooms to more learner-centered classrooms that encourages and cultivates student involvement, and promotes student success, both short and long term. Students thrive in classrooms that minimize misbehaviors and maximize the opportunity to participate because students "generally want to learn and understand course material" (Sidelinger et al., 2011, p. 346). If gamification is going to succeed, researchers need to find a game to study to see game mechanics, theory and strategy at work.

Researchers need to define gamification as a strategy through a game, in order to experience what the basis is for good gamification. While focusing on one game can be limiting long term, a single case study allows for a starting point for the discussion of gamification of the (college) classroom. World of Warcraft (WoW), a computer based game in which players "have collectively spent 5.93 million years" playing since 2004 (McGonigal, 2011, p. 52). While the popularity alone could serve as a reason to study WoW, it is important that the game be familiar to the researcher, which allows for a focused look at what happens when a player plays the game, as well as how the rhetoric might transfer to a classroom situation.

World of Warcraft

Since 1974, role-playing games have been popular on the gaming market. However, until 2004, there was not an online version that swept the world quite like World of Warcraft (WoW). With over 12 million monthly subscribers, WoW is the largest MMORPG on the market ("WoW," n.d.). Despite the number of players, there is little research on WoW in the field of communication studies. Since the game has been on the market for 10 years, it is clear that the phenomenon is widely popular, and there are no signs of it losing that popularity any time soon. WoW is a crafted world, and understanding the rhetoric behind the game can help us understand how these choices create a motivating situation. This is why I chose WoW as a site of analysis.

WoW encourages and implements role-playing as a part of the everyday game play. Players are able to "enact multiple identities" as they use avatars to complete quests, gain experience, and reputations (Gee, 2007, p. 7). After choosing how they will play, potential players must choose one of two factions (Horde or Alliance) and one of 12 races available races (6 races per faction). Players then customize or randomize the "physical" appearance, such as skin and hair color, gender, and facial features of the character, as well as the name. The character must also possess one class ability from either a Warrior, Paladin, Mage, Priest, Shaman, Druid, Monk, Death Knight or Hunter; each class has their own unique talents that make fighting or healing, solo or group work an ever evolving experience. While playing Arcadium a MMORPG, Gee (2007) observes that since the character creation process is so diverse, each character interacts with the game differently and, "the game you have played is very different from what it would have been had you built your character differently initially and throughout the game" (p. 54). The choice a player makes here determines a path on which to start.

Once a player has committed to a character, at least for a time, the game starts and a video intro familiarizes the player with the "world" of Warcraft as well as the race that the player chose. Players proceed to a starting area in which each new quest shows the player how to play the new character. The combination of race and class in the game alters the questing experience as game play changes depending on where the character originates (starting zone) and the class (special quests available only to a particular class with specialized class rewards). Movements, basic quests, spells and attacks are slowly introduced and practiced in order for the player to learn how to perform in this new virtual world. Even for advanced players, where movements and quests are familiar, learning the spells and attack capabilities are essential, as a new class is still complicated.

Each quest consists of "backstory" that explains in a narrative why the player is on the quest. Underneath the narrative, a simplified series of quest instructions joins an explanation with a clickable icon that describes the rewards, or choice of rewards received for each completed quest. Experience gained by questing will help a character/player to level her character up to level 100. Quests vary by class and race, as stated above, as well as by region. However, each quest has similarities between different realms and with different classes. This allows for rhetorical study across different role-playing races and classes of fighting.

WoW serves as the site that provides the rhetoric needed to define gamification of the classroom. The classroom today already uses tools that work to help students connect with the material, but gamification has the potential to serve a larger body of students. Though gamification is widely used as a marketing tool, researchers and instructors see the potential in its application. Combining the site of analysis with the intention of learning how gamification interacts with task completion leads to a research question:

RQ: How can heterotopic rhetorical criticism frame critical communication pedagogy to reveal structures that determine traditional student and teachers roles and highlight ways in which gamification could change that structure?

In order to answer this question, I played and experience WoW through heterotopian rhetorical criticism (HRC) lens. Using autoethnographic narratives as artifacts enable an inside look at the game, I examine my experiences in WoW through the lens of HRC as a way to talk about the rhetorical creation of both WoW and the classroom, in order to find common themes. The themes construct a definition of gamification of the classroom through three highlighted fundamentals that use themes and ideas of CCP to change how the classroom works. The definition of gamification in the classroom for the purpose of this study is informed by the heterotopian rhetoric that constructs World of Warcraft, as well as my observations and understandings of the rhetoric through a lens of autoethnography.

Autoethnography

Autoethnography is an essential component to my research process. Unlike other methods, autoethnography highlights the intimate relationship that a researcher has with the site, work or people encountered through researching. The depth to which an autoethnographer gets with the topic shows the authentic and vulnerable nature of the method. When a researcher is open and reflexive with her/his personal experience surrounding the cultural site, the reader is able to experience the culture vicariously. For this project it is especially important to use autoethnography. As kids, many of us were encouraged by our parents to share video game time with siblings or friends, but Super Mario was never as exciting as when you were playing by yourself, because a game needs to be played in order to experience it. This creates a "layered account" (Boylorn, 2008) of gameplay and my individual experience. What I experience informs not only how I interpret the rhetorical information, but also how I define gamification.

Heterotopia

According to Foucault (1986), heterotopias are constructed by six principles that define and separate them from all other types of spaces and places. Heterotopias are liminal spaces that vary from culture to culture, and but all serve to "create a space of illusion" that exposes a real space within society such as a brothel, or creates an "other" space that is sterile and unadulterated and reflects the opposite of the messy unpredictable world, like Disneyland. Heterotopias serve as a "safety valve" in which people can release cultural tensions that surround deviant behavior in an acceptable manner. These principles give researchers a common ground on which to define spaces and situations as heterotopic.

Heterotopia creates a common place from which to view two seemingly opposing spaces. Both the space of a classroom and the space of WoW perform as heterotopias because they each follow the six principles (Blair, 2009). Both have open, fluid enrollment across the world, connect people both physically and virtually, and have a specific purpose that functions in relation to culture, all within a space that exists separate from "real life" (see Table 1).

Viewing WoW and the classroom through a heterotopic lens allows a discussion about how each space is similar to the other. This highlights specific experiences and with the addition of autoethnography, defines a specific slice of what gamification means for a classroom. The space of a classroom is heterotopian by nature. As a crisis heterotopia, a privilege or sacred space used to conceal the messiness of physical, spiritual or intellectual growth, the classroom allows students to experience failure and inexperience without being subject to "real world" ridicule (Foucault, 1986). Heterotopias of crisis are almost extinct (Foucault, 1986) as what society found to be crisis before, such as menstruation, pregnancy, boarding schools, and even honeymoons, are not anymore. Therefore, crisis heterotopias are also heterotopias of deviance. As a heterotopia of deviation, in which behavior that is different from the cultural norm is expected and encouraged, the classroom gives students a space in which learning (a deviance from the

Table 1. Side by side comparison of the classroom and World of Warcraft as heterotopias

Heterotopian Principle	WoW	Classroom
Principle 1: Common in society	Anyone with internet access can play	Available around the world
Principle 2: Serves a purpose	A social place to digitally gather and play the game with others	Provides an education for those who are given permission to enter
Principle 3: Gathers conflicting spaces	Brings together both virtual worlds and connects them to our physical world	Brings together subjects into one physical or virtual space
Principle 4: Exists in a "slice of time"	Time functions differently in Wow, and revolves around quest completion rather than hours played.	Consists of 2-10 years' time. when participating in college, students are largely free from "adult life"
Principle 5: Fluidly accessible	Available to any who do not opt out by choice or circumstance, but the more people who play concurrently, the worse the server performs	Available to any who do not opt out by choice or circumstance. Limited by funding per institution
Principle 6: Functions in relation to society Principle 6 (cont.)	• Creates an "other" space in which achievement is easily measured and risk of failure is low. • Uses language that suggests that the outside world is more "real" or authentic than the experiences inside	• Creates an "other" space in which participants are groomed and practice for careers in the "outside" world. • Uses language that suggests that the outside world is more "real" or authentic than the experiences inside

norm of knowing) is not only acceptable, but is the *purpose* of the heterotopia (Foucault, 1986). Just as with WoW, the space of the classroom is "othered" when mainstream society places it outside "real" life. This results in those inside the heterotopia to balance a meaningful life for those in the mainstream while justifying their existence in the heterotopia. Students enter in an environment in which failure is expected and should be encouraged. However, low-risk is not part of the vocabulary of the classroom even if it is the basis of education. Traditionally, instructors and administrators have imposed the rhetoric that inadequacy is unacceptable, which the mainstream culture places upon the classroom. This takes away the power the classroom holds as both a crisis and deviate heterotopian space.

Similarly, WoW is also a heterotopia of deviation. In a culture in which being idle is shunned, playing a game like WoW is deviant. One of the reasons that people continue to participate in this "deviance" is because low-risk interactions in the game provide a sense of accomplishment that the real world does not provide. By reflecting this deviant heterotopia into the similar classroom heterotopia, we can see how principles of low-risk interaction in WoW might function in the classroom.

The game and the classroom embrace low-risk encounters differently. Each class will not last as long as engagements with WoW do. The game does not require the player to critically think or theorize. In order to have gamification in the classroom, assignments must provide more low-risk interactions with the material and gradually increase the risk and reward of the interactions. The instructor needs to decide which activities, assignments or engagements in the classroom teach, and which need evaluating. Teaching assignments allow students to "…engage in the task, make mistakes, get feedback, learn and have relatively few grade consequences" (Falk, 2012, p. 14), while an evaluation assignments test the knowledge or proficiency of the student. This language focuses on assignments from a student perspective. Because all assignments, whether evaluative in nature or not, teach, these labels highlight how the student feels about the interaction. Engagements that are low risk are generally not associated with evaluation, such as Johnson's (2007) out of class quizzes or homework, and traditionally place the act of teaching upon the instructor. Higher risk engagements or evaluation assignments force the student to assume more responsibility to prove her abilities. Researchers also distinguish between these types of engagements through the use of formative and summative assignments. By giving students more low-risk teaching engagements in the classroom, instructors can simulate what happens in a game.

Games are structured so that players understand what is expected of them, so the classroom should mirror this clarity. As heterotopias of compensation, both WoW and the classroom are meticulously crafted to be better in some way than the "real world." Unlike the outside world, WoW has clear and precise objectives, supported by a system that constantly feeds information to the player. The classroom performs this same function by having regimented majors, physically or psychologically constructed classrooms, and overarching university standards that order both student and teacher. In my own class, I have seen just how important this is. While I am not able to enact a fully gamified classroom, I implemented key gamification fundamentals such as low-risk assignments. My first semester teaching out of grad school, I used rough drafts as a low-risk assignment. It was easy for students to get full or close to full points. This was a teaching assignment, and meant to be a soft checkpoint for students on the way to the final draft. However, because I didn't explain this concept, many students were upset because while they did well on the rough draft, they failed the final draft. Even with a detailed rubric and a re-write available, the failing students were discouraged and angry. It is clear that students need to understand the pedagogical choices if they differ from the traditional classroom. If the classroom changes, a student need to know his responsibilities, as well as what freedom a new structure gives him. Viewed through the lens of HRC, WoW becomes a template for possibility in the classroom. This template allows us to change the structure of the classroom without compromising the quality of education.

As a heterotopia of compliance, the educational system isolates students and their choices in order to regulate skill building and learning. Students are able to choose a major, minor and/or concentration, and even some classes within those categories. These choices help guide a student to a career path, and to some passion within that path. However, strict educational regulations make it difficult to deviate from tradition. Even within the classroom, the current structure limits choice. WoW, when viewed for a re-imagining of the classroom, functions as a heterotopia of deviance as the freedom for individualization found in the game is a stark contrast from the real world. This view of these two spaces gives us the ability to use HRC to combine the ordered nature of the classroom and the freedom of choice that comes when playing WoW.

Heterotopic Rhetorical Criticism

It is easy to forget that the classroom is part of a social construct and therefore can change to meet society's changing needs. HRC introduces a practicality into the research findings because by viewing both classroom and WoW as heterotopia, we acknowledge that triumphs and achievements as well as "problems, struggles and conflicts might also exist" in the opposing space (Spicer, Alvesson, & Kärreman, 2009, p. 551). By viewing both the classroom and World of Warcraft as heterotopias, it is clear that communication not only defines space and participant, but also aids in the construction of a communal culture. HRC examines the artifacts of one heterotopic space in order to postulate the future possibilities in another. The artifacts that range from visual to textual rhetoric (narratives) from within WoW, are analyzed to explore and highlight social norms, common practices that shape it. The elements that construct WoW are then applied to the classroom as a way of rhetorically manifesting change. By that reasoning, concepts and strategies that work in one space should work in a similar space.

However, using HRC does not mean that it is necessary to superimpose WoW directly onto the classroom. Just as Foucault (1986) wrote about heterotopias reflecting reality in order to unmake reality, the rhetoric of WoW must be unmade so it may be reflected in the classroom. By comparing these two spaces, any transfer of ideas from one to the other must be, as a heterotopia of compensation, ordered and fastidious. The principles of WoW's ordered structure must be present, but they must fit into the reflected space of the classroom. By restructuring the classroom to have open and ubiquitous communication with the students, instructors can simulate a game-like atmosphere within the classroom.

I used a lens of autoethnography and HRC to analyze how the communication that constructs WoW encourages or discourages players to complete the quests. This involved examining not only the rhetoric of the quest logs (the main form of written game communication), but also experiencing and analyzing how specific mechanics in the game transfers to the classroom. By using HRC as a way to highlight the space of the classroom, it allows researchers, teachers, and students to the CCP informed tactic of gamification to explore change to the classroom environment. I propose that this particular way of viewing gamification will expand the usefulness of its application in a college classroom setting. This research process involves my presence in a paid-for-access but public online space. However, while it is considered a social space, my research strictly chronicles my own journey in game play and the rhetoric that created it. I recorded observations of my behavior and experiences in a journal and then analyzed the patterns of structure found. By playing WoW and journaling my experiences, I was able to get a different view of the game. Using HRC allowed me to view the classroom and WoW as both heterotopias of deviance and compliance, and see the space and structure of the classroom more clearly when understanding these experiences through CCP.

GAMIFICATION OF THE CLASSROOM

Pitfalls/Limitations

As exciting as it is to implement gamification in the classroom, some potential pitfalls of gamification surfaced during the research process. To highlight these limitations, I drew from the similar learning strategy of Massively Open Online Classrooms (MOOCs). MOOCs are a fledgling concept implemented in many schools in the last few years with limited success. A MOOC course generally consists of short lectures, quizzes, readings, and collaboration with others, which serves to compensate for high student to teacher ratios. It is often a no cost, no-credit course with more than 100 students per class. While not considered a strict form of gamification, MOOCs and gamified classrooms both rely on similar concepts to create student success: automated feedback (short feedback loop), accessibility (fluid access) and group collaboration (teamwork). It is possible by looking at the limitations and failings of MOOCs, we might be able to overcome the possible limitations of gamification.

Possibly the biggest limitations of gamification is its potential. The ease of reaching the younger demographic with a gamified systems means that gamification is been used by companies that want to layer this tactic over a broken strategy, resulting in meaningless interactions. MOOCs also try to eliminate the need for instructors, or at least the need for low student to teacher ratios. At San Jose State University (SJSU) one student said of MOOCs "There were no people; there was no professor. In a sense you're just learning in this void" (Westervelt, 2013, para. 20), with thousands of students enrolled in a free course, it is expected that each student could go without the attention s/he needs to experience success.

Unfortunately, this is a risk when gamifying the classroom. Administrators are looking for ways to remove the teacher from the classroom, by replacing seemingly mundane tasks with electronic or gamified components. I do not advocate a teacher-less classroom. Instructors are an important and meaningful component, especially as a gamified classroom is tested further and monitored for value. Critical thinking does not happen in a vacuum, and if we remove the direct access between student and teacher, students will leave the educational system without the skills necessary for critical thinking. Without an instructor available to mediate and create discussions, a student would miss valuable opportunities to explore important and potentially volatile subjects in a safe environment in which other students challenge her belief systems. Gamification is a tactic that shows how learning changes when the space changes, and it must be integrated into the current classroom environment, not by removing interactions with both other students and the instructor.

An instructor would have to learn how to adapt the new learning system to the current system, or create a new online system, while making sure that the grading system does not disrupt the overarching school grading structure. The extra work of creating and testing a new system can be daunting if an instructor that does not possess passion for it. MOOCs suddenly appeared in the education scene in 2012 (Pappano, 2012). Princetown, Duke, Standford, and SJSU embraced this new strategy and the technology that went along with it. However the function and success of a MOOC had not been tested enough to ensure success. Students and faculty consider MOOCs to be a disaster at SJSU. In one class "fewer than a quarter of the students… earned a passing grade" (Lewin, 2013, para. 6). Without proper testing, a more deeply gamified classroom could suffer the same fate, which would confirm the thought in many minds, "Games cannot teach". Without a way to see that the benefits of gamification outweigh the initial extra work, teachers will not implement a new system. This is why it is crucial that instructors understand the gamification fundamentals and know which ones they can implement easily for each course.

There are certain things that can only be learned by doing, testing or practicing, and through the research process I realized that one the player is used to the quest format, quest logs are largely unnecessary, unless additional information is needed, and this problem is not isolated to WoW. According to Newman and Oh, "fewer than one in 10 view even half of the material" available in a MOOC (2014, para. 6), and only 5 percent of student who enrolled in a MOOC at either Massachusetts Institute of Technology (MIT) or Harvard earned a certification of completion. A quarter of a million students in a MOOC at Harvard or MIT never engaged in the content at all (Kolowich, 2014). Similarly, students in a traditional classroom often do not read the syllabus which leads to confusion, and could affect how a gamified classroom functions. While mechanics compensate for player apathy towards reading quest logs in the game, if instructors change the way that the classroom functions, and gamify it, there are no underlying systems to ensure success in the classroom. In my classroom, rubrics are available for assignments from the first day of class, and even with review of these necessary components, students still claim to no know that something was on the rubric. The future success of gamification of the classroom rests on the success of the students who participate in it, and the clarity of the instructor's communication, in all forms, with the students. This means that educators may not be able to construct a clean and informative syllabus and expect that to be enough to implement gamification. Students still might treat a gamified classroom with the recklessness they show while playing a game, or while in a traditional classroom.

One of the greatest things about playing a game could be gamification's biggest pitfall. In WoW when a character dies, the player does not have to start the whole game over because his progress within a quest is saved along the way. This can cause the player to be reckless when fighting, because death is a small consequence. In MOOCs, the low certification rates and high failure rates are a symptom of a few things, but most importantly, when a virtual classroom loses touch with the instructor, and there are little to no consequences for mistakes, the majority of students will experience failure. Students that seem to thrive in a MOOC are not surprisingly, students who are highly motivated and highly educated (Newman & Oh, 2014). If classroom failure is reconstituted as a death (as discussed later), the students might experience the same reckless behavior. This pitfall adds to the apprehension of instructors when implementing gamification in the college classroom.

When it comes to gamification, not everyone is sure that it can work in the classroom. The current definition of gamification, while promising, is vague (Albrecht, 2012). Many people, including teachers, politicians, and parents, have decided already that games and gamification wastes time (Bogost, 2011). Teachers who are not gamers themselves are frustrated by unfamiliar learning or teaching strategies (Gee, 2007). Many see gamification as a quick fix for many companies who are eager to increase profits without changing basic operations as with MOOCs. Skeptics say that,

Gamification is easy...For the consultants and the startups, that means selling the same bullshit in book, workshop, platform, or API form over and over again, at limited incremental cost. It ticks a box. Social media strategy? Check. Games strategy? Check. (Bogost, 2011, para. 8)

For Bogost and others, gamification offers little real reward, and generally lacks substance. It seems to be missing the point of gaming and focuses instead on layering fun over a broken system (Owen's blog, 2011). "Gamified environments pacify the player in an attempt to get them to go through the mechanical motions of game mechanics" (Chorney, 2012, p. 9). In many applications, gamification has been watered down to little more than a fill-in-the-blank reward system. Websites such as Badgeville and Lithium offer companies the ability to insert their products in to pre-arranged systems that produce monetary gains for little work because these companies focus on manipulation of behavior instead of fixing how the products work in the first place (Badgeville, 2012). SJSU also used MOOC program Udacity which was implemented in a number of different classes without customization for that particular course (Lewin, 2013). The potential of the MOOC was lost in bad execution, and unmotivated students.

A limitation of this study comes from the method and methodology I used and could serve as another pitfall. While heterotopia is a widely used concept and way of viewing spaces, I crafted HRC as a method specifically for this study. Geuter (2012) uses heterotopia as way to inform his criticism of science fiction novels, but no other study has used HRC. This means that it has yet to be tested and evaluated on a larger scale. Because the methodology that informs HRC in this study is autoethnography, my experiences in the game before and during the research process, affect the conclusions I drew. While I have a deep knowledge of the game was beneficial in many ways, without a replicate study from another researcher who has little or no experience with WoW, it is unclear if that previous knowledge informed not only the experiences, but also the creation of HRC. Since past experiences may have led to assumptions about the game, thus informing HRC, it is important that this method is tested further in order to ensure future success of both HRC and gamification of the classroom. Thankfully, gamification potential outweighs the limitations.

Practices

Different experiences in the classroom and WoW highlight the different ways these spaces act as these two types of heterotopias. HRC revealed fundamentals that are essential for gamification of the classroom.

Fundamental one: a gamified classroom will have low-risk engagement in all "teaching" assignments. Fundamental two: a gamified class will use structure not only to call attention to how to do a quest, but what the benefits are of doing said quest. Fundamental three: within a gamified structure, the student must have choice in order to unite learning style and time. A classroom that accomplishes this successfully brings gamification to the students.

In WoW, quest trackers, NPC quest givers, maps, and even the mobs provide information and direct a player through the quest. Using WoW as a research site allowed me to look at it in a different light, and I experienced the leveling process as more of a collaborator and less like a player. This new role for me helped me to focus on the rhetoric of the game mechanics to see why and how players are able to complete tasks without specific directions. A lot of the structures found in WoW seem invisible when I am playing, because powerful structures are hidden from those in close proximity. As a researcher, these structures, tools, and strategies that promote participation become more prominent. While these strategies in WoW cannot transfer directly to the classroom, the structure of the classroom must clearly reinforce continual mastery building behavior.

A gamified classroom can function in one of two ways. A teacher can implement just one or a few of the actual quests or structures or s/he can change the entire structure of the class. For a gamified classroom in either part or whole, the structure must not only be tested for function and clarity, it must offer low-risk choice for the students because a lack of clarity in the classroom, whether through verbal or structural, can be detrimental (Chesebro & McCroskey, 2001). For a fully gamified classroom, online components found in a learning management system (LMS) allow instructors to give quick feedback, which mimicking game mechanics. The structure of a gamified classroom should be laid out in the syllabus with clearly marked descriptions of the student responsibilities. Students need to understand how the teacher will assess them and how assignments function.

Grading in a Gamified Classroom

One problem in school is that grades are often subjective and, if assignments are done wrong, a student receives little credit regardless of work accomplished. Thankfully, a game is objective. Unless a player abandons a quest, she gets full experience points for every one she completes. While experience for killing different mobs varies, the quest experience is consistent and measurable. Any difference from what is projected through the quest log and what is earned is a positive difference, with players killing mobs for more experience. So when gamifying the classroom, instructors should not only restructure the grading system, but completely restructure what it means to earn a grade. While the leveling system from WoW cannot be transferred exactly to the classroom, small changes will allow the classroom to benefit from it. Most quest can convert to a credit/no credit or a teaching assignment, but larger quests would become an evaluation assignment like speeches, performances, tests, or research papers. This way student participate in more teaching assignments rather than heavily weighted evaluation assignments, which in will help students interact more with the material.

In WoW characters level quickly at the start, which encourages players to continue to play. Experience needed to level at first is much less than at towards the end of leveling of the character. This allows players to get swept up into the game as they experience early success. Translating this to the classroom, grading would change from a loss function to a gain function, and students would earn points and levels quickly. This leveling system (Table 2) could be changed to suit any class material.

Table 2. Grades reimagined as a leveling system

Level	Total XP Needed	Letter Grade
Level 1	10	
Level 2	30	
Level 3	70	
Level 4	135	
Level 5	230	
Level 6	330	
Level 7	460	
Level 8	620	
Level 9	800	
Level 10	960	
Level 11	1090	
Level 12	1150	
Level 13	1300	
Level 14	1400	
Level 15	1480	C
Level 16	1560	C+
Level 17	1680	B
Level 18	1760	B+
Level 19	1880	A
Level 20	1960+	A+

Teachers could also change the point system, but in order to promote a game-like atmosphere, a low point scale will not work. Low-risk quests cannot exist when each point largely affects a student's grade. This system could be implemented in a fully online, hybrid or even traditional classroom, and gives a student more power over her grades. This power includes the freedom to stop working when the student reaches her desired level (or grade range), specific learning objectives aside. As this approach to grading is new and different for most students, the syllabus must clearly lay out what is expected of them, as well as having the instructor explain, so there is no confusion.

The Structure of Quests

Changing the language in the classroom from assignments to quests or missions not only borrows from games, but also enhances the grading system by using consistent rhetoric. While players accomplish quests, students simply do assignments; checking off meaningless boxes. In order for students to receive the quick feedback that is necessary for steady, measurable growth in the form of experience, some technology must be implemented for a fully gamified classroom. While trying to improve the student interaction with the course material, it is imperative not to add to the daily duties of an instructor. If technology were to be built to enhance gamification of assignments, a quest log might look and function something like it does in WoW.

I push the number four on the keyboard, and she performs a flying kick right at the stork. For me, the attack is executed by pushing buttons on the keyboard that correspond to Palei's skills. But for her, it is a much different story. She throws and blocks punches, and uses her staff to inflict damage, all while risking her life. While she is *performing* the tasks, I am *practicing* how to use her skills in the right combination so I can have her do the most damage in the least amount of time. Each time she gains a new skill I learn how to use it in conjunction with the other skills while completing quests, and before long each new skill is second nature.

In an assignment quest log, the "backstory" provides a sense of meaningfulness. It is crucial for students to understand why an assignment is important because meaningful tasks encourage the student to feel "…the perceived value of a task" (Weber et al., 2005, p. 72). The criteria clearly shows a student what is expected to complete the quest, and the rewards show exactly what s/he will get if completed. A quest log, like in WoW, only works with teaching quests. Most quests in WoW give both experience and some amount of in-game money. Participation points can take the place of monetary gains, rewarding students for all interaction (or participation) with the course.

The meaning of participation varies widely between classrooms. Participation points are often held over a student's head as an unknown grade at the end of the semester. A grad student of Lehigh University is suing the school because "her teacher gave her a "zero" for class participation because she complained about having to take on an extra internship" (Cavaliere, 2013, para. 7). While this case fails to recognize the student's responsibility, it is an example of an all too common occurrence. Participation is extremely subjective, and most teachers prefer an active verbal participation within the class where outgoing and unabashed students are favored as they publically perform their participation. Instructors often require students to take a quiz or write notes to ensure participation with the reading material. Some teachers make this practice more meaningful by letting students use the notes on tests and quizzes, but for some learners, reading notes are empty interactions.

By following the game model, participation is attached to every interaction. Each assignment gives participation badges as well as experience as seen in the mock up quest log. For each 10 points of experience offered, students earn one participation badge. The badges are then turned in for extensions on assignments, an extra time cushion during speeches or presentations or any other benefit a teacher might implement. This will honor the participation without discounting the importance of actually completing quests. By folding the participation badges into every point, however the student participates with the material, teachers include students of more diverse learning styles, cultural differences, and disabilities. In WoW, every small attempt at mastery contributes to overall success. Students could still earn participation points through any in class measurement the instructor wanted, as long as no student could lose points for not being verbal. This could range from giving bonus badges to those who show up to the lecture, free writing about the class, or even verbal participation, and every opportunity of engagement is a way to *gain* and not lose points.

When studying WoW, I realized I have the freedom to do whatever I want to in order to level. Either in a combination or alone, I can quest, gather/craft, and run dungeons. How I level is my choice, and I can decide what my goals and needs are. This choice is only made available because of the structure of the game. This structure provides me with an overview of what I need to know about leveling, from rewards written out in quest logs to maps showing where the mobs are. These tools serve as check points along the way to keep on track or to change plans. Guided choice in games is foundational. I can choose any character to play at any time and act in the game as I please. Within that character, I can still customize her even further as she gains levels. Each choice determines play style down the line.

Another way to honor the work that students do is to treat evaluation assignments differently. As shown earlier, evaluation assignments are larger and test a student's mastery of course content. If evaluation assignments break into a few teaching assignments (rough drafts, outlines, etc.), then students could still have the freedom to experience failure with time to recover. For example, if the annotated bibliography as an evaluation engagement is broken into components then it would be complete only when enough correct teaching quests (individual annotated bibliographies) were complete. So when a student "kills" the wrong mob, or in this case reads an unhelpful article, he would have an opportunity to still get points that count towards his overall grade, just not to that particular assignment. Gamification causes a paradigm shift from only counting what is done correctly, to include all efforts made along the way. The naming of these opportunities can be a strategic and critical move if the instructor draws attention to why specific quests or assignments are required, using departmental or institutional learning objectives (LOs) (Chesebro & McCroskey, 2001). This also eliminates student excuses for not understanding an assignment as gamification provides multiple checkpoints to change and direct behavior and performance.

Group Structure

Just like participation, group work can cause anxiety for students. Often, students do not have a specific role, and therefore ambiguous responsibility within the group. Leaders can become frustrated with the lack of contribution from the group, and the other group members might resent the leader for taking over. In a gamified situation, the classroom group dynamic gives students a chance to choose a role ahead of time. In WoW, everyone looking to join a group chooses the part they want to play and the game matches up players accordingly. Each person then has a role and everyone knows the responsibility of each role. Players go into a group with a specific function, and as long as they follow that function, then the whole group experiences success. By assigning different responsibilities to the group structure and giving the students the freedom to choose their path, the traditional group structure changes. In a gamified classroom, group work would follow a pattern, pulling from WoW's structure; each position would have incentives that appeal to the different learning styles. The roles are first come, first serve and clearly lay out the responsibility of each group member: a leader, a facilitator, and three support members.

Each group needs a leader, and to reward a person who is willing to take on the responsibility, an extra 10 percent is added to the total points available for the assignment. The leader is in charge of the entire project, and is therefore responsible for filling in and performing multiple tasks as needed. The leader would also be responsible for topic selection and other students could choose what group they were in based on the topic. The healer or group facilitator would be in charge of the management of the team by mediating the needs of the group and acting as the liaison with the instructor. The facilitator would also be responsible for the aesthetic portion of the project (visuals, editing, etc.). The three remaining roles of the group could be in charge of finding research, understanding it, and sharing it with the rest of the group. The roles could change based on the needs of the assignment and/or class and a teacher could add responsibilities to any position as is needed by the course content. With every student understanding her role in the group, she can perform her duties without fear that the group might ruin her grade.

In the game, there are checks and balances to make sure a group functions properly, and this is needed in the classroom as well. In WoW, if someone does not fulfill his responsibility another player can vote to kick him out of the group. This function could be included in the classroom through the use of student distributed participation points. Each student would work with 10 participation badges to reward good behavior in other group members. The average number of badges for each student would determine the total points earned at the end of the assignment, and if for some reason a student does not fulfill her role, the instructor can determine if the student needs to re-do her section of the assignment.

Death Structure

While the rhetoric of "death" even in a gamified setting might not appeal to students, labeling this function as a re-do would allow a student to have an opportunity to revisit his work for an edit, a re-work or even a re-imagine of the material. With only a few re-dos per student, the instructor could limit extra work, while giving the student a way to learn from the mistakes they made. Instructors would still be able to navigate exactly what a re-do looked like for the individual courses based on time and preference. Many times, students are able to get close to a higher level of mastery (such as a C+ or B+), but fall short without any chance of improvement. A re-do would take the stigma out of failure, even for evaluation quests, and hopefully set the students up to take on other challenges.

Customization

To further the low-risk atmosphere and to engage students with the material, it is important for students to have choice. Re-imagining WoW's character customization for the classroom gives students a choice in how not only their preparedness counts but also their interaction with the reading material functions in the classroom. This kind of choice mimics the skill ups in WoW by having distinct advantages and disadvantages. Each student would choose between quizzes, chapter lectures or leading discussions. Using Bloom's Taxonomy, Johnson (2007) shows a way to encourage student preparedness while not infantilizing the educational process. The five levels of involvement require students to be more deeply involved with the information, which leads to greater depth of discussions in class (Johnson, 2007). The three areas of learning that Bloom's Taxonomy stimulates are Cognition, Affect, and Psychomotor, or knowing, feeling and doing. Johnson's quiz structure implements affective learning to connect each student to the material by having each student create the questions as well as the answers.

Students who choose to do the quizzes must create their own quiz each week. Each quiz will include one question from each of the five levels of Bloom's taxonomy to ensure cognitive learning for each chapter or reading:

- *Knowledge*: Surface level questions that express/explain overall ideas from the reading.
- *Application*: A question that shows application of student's/avatar's experiences to core concepts in the reading.
- *Analysis*: A compare/contrast application of two concepts from the reading.
- *Synthesis*: A question that uses a previously discussed concept from the class to relate to the current reading.
- *Evaluation*: Students evaluate a direct quote of their choosing, and explain why they agree or disagree (Johnson, 2007).

Each question is worth two points, for a total of 10 points. One point for the construction of a question that follows one of the five levels and one point for a thoughtful and correct answer to the question. The quizzes are a high-choice, low-risk way of interacting with the readings.

A chapter lecture, while functioning like reading notes, helps students gain skills in media presentation, as well as gaining a deeper understanding of concepts. Creating a lecture takes time and effort, especially when using presentation software such as Prezi or PowerPoint. Examples, in video or picture form take time to find and apply to the software. This type of preparedness helps students to grasp the knowledge of the lesson through key self-chosen examples. Here, like the quizzes, students are not focused on coverage, but on deep comprehension on highlighted topics.

Leading a classroom discussion, while intimidating to some, is thrilling for others. Students would prepare and understand the selected chapters enough to answer questions and with the instructor's guidance, lead and facilitate the discussion in the classroom. Students would be responsible for preparing 15 questions that follow Johnson's (2007) quiz model. Each of these reading interactions not only enforce the subject matter, but give students a way to practice different skills, aligning with student's preferences or strengths. The deadlines could be determined by the instructor depending on course restrictions. When a student feels in control of her learning, whether inside or outside of the classroom, she is motivated to learn. "Learner empowerment addresses the extent to which students feel motivated and in control of their academic task, and is associated with cognitive learning and affective learning" (Kranstuber, Carr, & Hosek, 2011, p. 49). Choice not only empowers the student, but increases participation.

Deadlines

Customizable deadlines are also a way of creating an opportunity for choice in the classroom. In WoW, each time a player kills something or gathers something, s/he gains experience. However, if s/he happens to level from killing a mob and still has completed quests to turn in, it is rewarding to turn in multiple quests at the same time and rush through a level. By letting the student determine when the deadlines are or choose to turn in assignments every week, nontraditional students who work 30-40 hours a week in addition to full time classes are served as well as those students who need more structured deadlines. Students would have to decide, not which road is easiest, but which road is best for their learning style. Instructors would construct overarching deadlines as needed to meet with learning objectives or evaluation quests.

Application of Quests

Mimicking the structure in WoW, quests are reimagined to work in conjunction with the classroom or as a gamified piece in a traditional classroom. In WoW there is a type of a quest that gives a character something to protect (a totem, a person doing a ritual, etc.), and a length of time for the encounter. It functions as a speed test of the players' skill and strategy in the game. While instructors cannot attack the students to test their knowledge, this quest could become "survival quiz" in which students answer as many questions as possible in five minutes. The questions would be simple and straightforward and all true or false. This reinforces classroom ideas as well rewarding those students who are prepared. The use of true or false will help to ease student apprehension, and used in combination with the new leveling system, students would not experience punishment for a wrong answer. Special accommodations would still be made for students with registered disabilities, so each student has a chance at as many points as possible. A survival quest could also function as a way to encourage greater participation in class performance.

FUTURE RESEARCH DIRECTIONS

In order to ensure the future success of gamification, instructors need to implement tactics to make sure that they meet the students' needs. This means that not only does the instructor need to prepare the class, set up point systems to allow for a gamified classroom, and adopt current curriculum to a gamified classroom, s/he also has to test the class. In games, this is called beta-testing. Before Mists of Pandaria came out, I was part of the lucky few (hundred thousand in this case) who got to test the game, looking for bugs and other issues and reporting any problem I found. This same practice would help to ensure that any mishaps or trouble spots are taken care of before students even interact with the class. Even still, beta testing does not find all the problems. This means that during the process of gamifying the classroom in whole or in part, instructors need to put in place some system checks to allow for students express spots of confusion.

One strategy to ensure clarity is a small group instructional diagnosis (SGID). A SGID is one tool originated at the University of Washington (Clark & Redmond, 1982) and implemented at the GTA program at SJSU. Sometime during the middle of the semester, a colleague comes into the classroom and asks the students how the classroom is working, how the teacher can improve the classroom, and how each student can contribute to these improvements. This allows for students to open a conversation about the classroom and make sure that their collective needs are being met. This practice helps the teacher understand the needs of her students while there is still time correct and improve. If there was a problem with the gamified classroom, the students could let the instructor know before it affects their grades or instructor's evaluations. With students also taking responsibility, the class can grow and evolve as a community.

CONCLUSION

During the research process, I was concentrating so hard on making sure I was "researching" and journaling about my experiences, that I actually did not have fun playing WoW. Originally, I was planning on restricting my characters from the extra game mechanics like dungeons and profession (gathering). This was so I would be able to avoid replicating past experiences. In many ways, this was good, because my lack of knowledge of the Alliance quests not only caused me to get lost allowed me to feel frustration, it also led me to quests I was not expecting. I was able to keep this up for three characters, but when I leveled the fourth character, I was so burned out that after level 16, I changed my strategy. At that point I decided that if I was going to get the perspective of how a game functions, I should play it like a game.

So I just played.

Once I did, not only did I have fun, but I learned a lot about a few of the other parts of the game that I would have missed, like group interactions and gathering. More importantly, I got to experience what it felt like to play the game. Quests flowed from one to another, reminding me of what it meant to play. Gaming has a rhythm that keeps a player going and makes tasks fun to do.

Gamification does not make assignments fun all the time. It is not magic or a switch to turn on that all of a sudden makes every mundane or unappealing task the most fun activity in the world. Even games have quests or components that require patience, perseverance and some external motivation. Rather, gamification makes the process better overall. As instructors, even with this new working definition of gamification, we cannot expect one solution to be the answer for every student. The three fundamentals of gamification as it pertains to the classroom lay out a general definition; Gamification must consist of high-choice, low-risk engagements in a clearly structured environment. Gamification is by no means a guarantee for a higher GPA, but as a fledgling classroom strategy, there is potential for real and long-term change in the class, because "this *could* be a game [emphasis original]" (McGonigal, 2011, p. 34).

REFERENCES

2016 List. (2012). Retrieved from http://www.beloit.edu/mindset/2016/

About Badgeville. (2012). Badgeville. Retrieved from http://www.badgeville.com/about

Albrecht, S. C. (2012). *The game of happiness – Gamification of positive activity interventions* [Doctoral thesis]. Maastricht University, Netherlands. Retrieved from http://arno.unimaas.nl/show.cgi?fid=26239

Blair, E. (2009, March). A further education college as a heterotopia. *Research in Post-Compulsory Education*, *14*(1), 93–101. doi:10.1080/13596740902717465

Bogost, I. (2011). Gamification is bullshit. Retrieved from http://www.bogost.com/blog/gamification_is_bullshit.shtml

Boylorn, R. M. (2008, October). As seen on TV: An autoethnographic reflection on race and reality television. *Critical Studies in Media Communication*, *25*(4), 413–433. doi:10.1080/15295030802327758

Cavaliere, V. (2013, February 12). Former grad student sues Lehigh University for $1.3 million over average grade. *New York Daily News*. Retrieved from http://www.nydailynews.com/news/national/ex-student-sues-school-1-3m-grade-article-1.1261784

Chesebro, J. L., & McCroskey, J. C. (2001, January). The relationship of teacher clarity and immediacy with student state receiver apprehension, affect, and cognitive learning. *Communication Education*, *50*(1), 59–68. doi:10.1080/03634520109379232

Chorney, A. (2012). Taking the game out of gamification. *Dalhousie Journal of Interdisciplinary Management*, *8*(1), 1–14. doi:10.5931/djim.v8i1.242

Cohen, A. (2011, September-October). The gamification of education. *The Futurist*, 16–17.

Corbett, S. (2010, September 15). Learning by playing: Video games in the classroom. *The New York Times*. Retrieved from http://www.nytimes.com/2010/09/19/magazine/19video-t.html?_r=1

Corbett, S. (2010, September 15). Learning by playing: Video games in the classroom. *The New York Times*. Retrieved from http://www.nytimes.com/2010/09/19/magazine/19video-t.html?_r=2&

De Certeau, M. (1984). *The practice of everyday life*. Retrieved from http://danm.ucsc.edu/~dustin/library/de%20certeau,%20the%20practice%20of%20everyday%20life.pdf

Falk, E. (2012). *Becoming a new instructor: A guide for college adjuncts and graduate students*. New York, NY: Taylor& Francis.

Fassett, D., & Warren, J. T. (2007). *Critical communication pedagogy*. Thousand Oaks, CA: Sage.

Foucault, M., & Miskowiec, J. (1986, Spring). Des Espaces Autres. [Of Other Spaces]. *Diacritics*, *16*(1), 22–27. doi:10.2307/464648

Freire, P. (2000). Pedagogy of the oppressed (30th Anniversary ed.). New York, NY: Continuum International Publishing Group.

Frymier, A. B., & Shulman, G. M. (1994, November). *Development and testing of the learner empowerment instrument in a communication based model*. Paper presented at the Speech Communication Association annual convention, New Orleans, LA.

Gee, J. P. (2007). What video games have to teach us about learning and literacy (Revised and updated edition ed.). New York, N.Y.: Pelgrave Macmillan.

Geuter, S. (2012). Did you think gamification was a new concept? Think again! Retrieved from http://wonnova.es/2012/07/did-you-think-gamification-was-a-new-concept-think-again/

Jegers, K. (2007). Pervasive game flow: Understanding player enjoyment in pervasive gaming. *ACM Computers in Entertainment*, *5*(1), 1–11. doi:10.1145/1236224.1236238

Johnson, D. I. (2007, April). Using out-of-class quizzes to promote cognitive engagement. *Communication Teacher*, *21*(2), 35–38. doi:10.1080/17404620701529431

Kolowich, S. (2014, January 22). Completion rates aren't the best way to judge MOOCs, researchers say [Blog post]. Retrieved from http://chronicle.com/blogs/wiredcampus/completion-rates-arent-the-best-way-to-judge-moocs-researchers-say/49721

Kranstuber, H., Carr, K., & Hosek, A. M. (2012, January). "If you can dream it, you can achieve it." Parent memorable messages as indicators of college student success. *Communication Education*, *61*(1), 44–66. doi:10.1080/03634523.2011.620617

Ladley, P. (2011). Gamification, education and behavioural economics [Entire issue]. *Games: innovation in learning*. Retrieved from http://www.games-ed.co.uk/resources/Gamification-Education-and-Behavioural-Economics-v1.pdf

Laster, J. (2010, March 23). At Indiana U., a class on game design has students playing to win [Blog post]. Retrieved from http://chronicle.com/blogs/wiredcampus/at-indiana-u-a-class-on-game-design-has-students-playing-to-win/21981

Lee, J. J., & Hammer, J. (2011). Gamification in education: What, how, why bother? *Academic Exchange Quarterly*, *15*(2), 1–5.

Lewin, T. (2013, December 10). After setbacks, online courses are rethought. *New York Times*. Retrieved from http://www.nytimes.com/2013/12/11/us/after-setbacks-online-courses-are-rethought.html?_r=1&

Lui, Y., Alexandrova, T., & Nakajima, T. (2011, December). *Gamifying intelligent environment*. Paper presented at the International ACM Workshop on Ubiquitous Meta User Interfaces, Scottsdale, AZ.

McGonigal, J. (2011). *Reality is broken: Why games make us better and how they can change the world*. New York, NY: Penguin Press.

Newman, J., & Oh, S. (2014). 8 things you should know about MOOCs. Retrieved from http://chronicle. com/article/8-Things-You-Should-Know-About/146901/

Owen's blog. (2011, October 20). Why gamification misses the point. [Blog post]. Retrieved from http:// www.gurudigitalarts.com/tips/IXD/gamification

Pappano, L. (2012, November 2). The Year of the MOOC. *New York Times*. Retrieved from http://www. nytimes.com/2012/11/04/education/edlife/massive-open-online-courses-are-multiplying-at-a-rapid-pace. html?pagewanted=all&_r=0

Prensky, M. (2001). The games generations: How learners have changed. In *Digital game-based learning* (pp. 02-1-02-26). Retrieved from http://www.marcprensky.com/writing/prensky%20-%20ch2-digital%20 game-based%20learning.pdf

Prensky, M. (2005). Engage me or enrage me: What today's learners demand. *EDUCAUSE Review*, 60–64.

Schell, J. [msc81]. (2010, July 17). *Jesse Schell @ DICE2010 (Part 1)* [Video file]. Retrieved from http:// www.youtube.com/watch?v=DLwskDkDPUE

Schrodt, P., Witt, P. L., Myers, S. A., Turman, P. D., Barton, M. H., & Jernberg, K. A. (2008, April). Learner empowerment and teacher evaluations as functions of teacher power use in the college classroom. *Communication Education*, *57*(2), 180–200. doi:10.1080/03634520701840303

Sheldon, L. (2010). Syllabus [Blog post]. Retrieved from http://gamingtheclassroom.wordpress.com/ syllabus/

Sidelinger, R. J., Bolen, D. M., Frisby, B. N., & McMullen, A. L. (2011, July). When instructors misbehave: An examination of student-to-student connectedness as a mediator in the college classroom. *Communication Education*, *60*(3), 340–361. doi:10.1080/03634523.2011.554991

Spicer, A., Alvesson, M., & Kärreman, D. (2009). Critical performativity: The unfinished business of critical management studies. *Human Relations*, *62*(4), 537–560. doi:10.1177/0018726708101984

Spitzberg, B. H. (1983, July). Communication competence as knowledge, skill and impression. *Communication Education*, *32*(3), 323–329. doi:10.1080/03634528309378550

Sprague, J. (1992, April). Critical perspectives on teacher empowerment. *Communication Education*, *41*(2), 181–203. doi:10.1080/03634529209378879

Tibbles, D., Richmond, V. P., McCroskey, J. C., & Weber, K. (2008, July). Organizational orientations in an instructional setting. *Communication Education*, *57*(3), 389–407. doi:10.1080/03634520801930095

Titsworth, S., Quinlan, M. M., & Mazer, J. P. (2010, October). Emotion in teaching and learning: Development and validation of the classroom emotions scale. *Communication Education*, *59*(4), 431–452. doi:10.1080/03634521003746156

Weber, K. (2004, Fall). The relationship between student interest and teacher's use of behavior alteration techniques. *Communication Research Reports*, *21*(4), 428–436. doi:10.1080/08824090409360007

Weber, K., Martin, M. M., & Cayanus, J. L. (2005, January). Student interest: A two-study re-examination of the concept. *Communication Quarterly*, *53*(1), 71–86. doi:10.1080/01463370500055996

Weber, K., & Patterson, B. R. (2000, Winter). Student interest, empowerment and motivation. *Communication Research Reports*, *17*(1), 22–29. doi:10.1080/08824090009388747

Westervelt, E. (2013). The online education revolution drifts off course. Retrieved from http://www.npr.org/2013/12/31/258420151/the-online-education-revolution-drifts-off-course

Why we play games: Four keys to more emotion without story. (2004, March 8). *Xeodesign.com.* Retrieved from http://www.xeodesign.com/xeodesign_whyweplaygames.pdf

Williams, D. (2006). Groups and Goblins: The social and civil impact of an online game. *Journal of Broadcasting & Electronic Media*, *50*(4), 651–670. doi:10.1207/s15506878jobem5004_5

World of Warcraft. (2012, October 9). *Wikipedia.* Retrieved from http://en.wikipedia.org/wiki/World_of_Warcraft

KEY TERMS AND DEFINITIONS

Critical Communication Pedagogy: A theory/practice of intersecting education research and communication to label, order and promote change.

Gamification: The application of game mechanics, theory and/or techniques in a non-game setting.

Heterotopia: A theory by Foucault that examines "other spaces" that highlight the extremes of order and chaos in society.

Heterotopian Rhetorical Criticism: A method of study that combines Foucault's theory and rhetorical criticism and compares and contrasts two "othered" spaces in order to enact change upon one of the spaces.

High-Choice: An activity that gives creative freedom to the student while following overarching learning objectives.

Low-Risk: An activity that allows the student to experience failure without a large effect on the end grade.

Mastery: A high level of understanding of a subject, concept, or learning objective, regardless of the path that led to it.

Section 4
Social Change and Health through Gamification

Chapter 11

A Framework for Collaboration among Game Designers and Social Change Makers:
Multiplayer Missions That Matter

Marty Kearns
Netcentric Campaigns, USA

Meredith Wise
Netcentric Campaigns, USA

ABSTRACT

We live in an age of networks: transportation networks, computer networks, economic networks, research networks, energy networks, social networks, the list goes on. Each consists of nodes connected to each other to manage the production and distribution of output to network users. Two large networks that share some particularly interesting overlap are gaming networks and advocacy networks. This chapter encourages an understanding of the potential overlap of these types of networks – both of which involve many millions of users, countless hours of interaction and billions of dollars of investment – and explores the intersection and impact of games designed to matter and gamified advocacy efforts. The chapter concludes with a proposed common planning framework from the field of advocacy network building and explores how gamification may more deeply help drive advocacy and social change, while advocacy work also opens new, valuable and more meaningful interactions and ideas for game designers.

INTRODUCTION

In 2012, the election of the entire United States House of Representatives cost $1.1 billion and engaged more than 115 million people in voting. The 2012 election was the most expensive election on record and included the engagement of tens of thousands of volunteers, campaign activists and candidates working in every neighborhood in every state ("2012 Election Spending," 2012). The most expensive race for a seat in the U.S. House of Representatives was in Florida, where in that one race alone it cost more than

DOI: 10.4018/978-1-4666-8651-9.ch011

$29 million to ultimately influence and engage 331,000 voters – an approximate spending of $88 per voter (Trygstad, 2012). In any election, people are inspired (or forced) to learn about the candidates, the issues, the news and the process of voting. The dominant teams of political parties rally both new voters and experienced voters to the polls. Elections bring out a wide range of people and initiatives including professional campaign teams, lone advocates and ad hoc efforts to rally groups of people. Overall, the 2012 election was a high-stakes struggle which consisted of nearly two years' worth of effort and a billion dollars' worth of donations and expenditures, just to organize formal and ad hoc teams to win an election.

Switching fields, within the first 24 hours of its release in September 2013, *Grand Theft Auto V* sold over 11 million copies, generating an estimated $815.7 million in revenue (Lynch, 2013). By the end of the third day, the game had reached $1 billion in sales – almost equal to the total cost of the election of the entire House of Representatives in 2012. In May 2014 when Take-Two Interactive, the developer of *Grand Theft Auto V*, released their 2014 fiscal year report, the game had sold more than 33 million copies (Take-Two Interactive Software, Inc., 2014). An article published in Forbes noted that, "Assuming people paid the full $60 (an incorrect assumption, as many people probably picked it up on sale, but a useful assumption nonetheless), that means that Take-Two has sold $1.98 billion worth of *Grand Theft Auto V* (Thier, 2014)." Nearly $2 billion in sales for one game is nothing to scoff at, but it is still just a drop in the bucket compared to the overall $21.53 billion the gaming industry made in 2013 – simliar to how one candidate's election campaign is only one small part of an entire election. And, like politics, the gaming industry brings together a wide range of users of all ages – kids, teenagers and adults – as well as people from every background and walk of life. In fact, according to a recent report from the Entertainment Software Association (2014), 59 percent of Americans play some sort of video game. Interestingly, the Center for Voting and Democracy lists an identical percentage as the number of Americans who voted in the 2012 elections (Fair Vote, n.d.).

The 2012 Election Day represented a single event of many advocacy networks' focus, much the same way as one game release is a single event within the larger scope of video gaming. Both advocacy networks and gaming networks involve many millions of people, countless hours of interaction and billions of dollars of investment, and in each case, the efforts are part of a broad landscape that includes a variety of industries. There is an opportunity to look at the overlap among the aspects of advocacy networks and gaming networks. Not only is there definitely an overlap in the actual people involved with each, but at the heart of both types of networks are similar design and implementation challenges: how to attract people, engage them with your content, learn about their skills and interests and connect them with each other to work together for mutual benefit.

Gamification has already been used effectively in fields ranging from science to education and humanitarian work, but leaders in political advocacy and issue-based advocacy have largely not yet tapped into the potential power of gamifying their efforts. Given how similar political networks and gaming networks can be, this seems to be a missed opportunity. Some advocacy leaders (both political and issue-based) are beginning to explore invoking gamification strategies in their own efforts, using mechanics such as quizzes, point systems, badges, achievements and progress bars to build support and engagement for their efforts. Those working toward the gamification of advocacy are also beginning to consider sharing the broader lessons of game mechanics to the overall strategy of movement building. Likewise, the lessons from advocacy network building can be applied to game design, allowing these two fields to interact in ways that once were not thought possible.

The age of networks is not only the age of connected players but also the age of connected social movements—and in both gaming and advocacy work, the fields have been discovering ways that participants need to be connected in order to foster collaboration with others to accomplish missions. This chapter explores the cross-pollination of lessons between the ways the most successful advocacy networks are built and the ways powerful games leverage the same dynamics in building networks of players to collaborate in group play. The chapter closes with a proposed framework for creating learning opportunities and conversations that will lead to a broader adoption of the lessons of gamification for both large and small local advocacy efforts, and also help game designers benefit from the lessons of network design that help drive advocacy campaigns and social change.

BACKGROUND

Advocacy and Advocacy Networks

Advocacy Landscape

Advocacy is an intentional agitation that sparks change. It is the struggle to disrupt, improve or change the status quo through cultural, societal, economic or policy shifts. The advocacy world includes hundreds of millions of volunteers, activists, change makers, private foundations, nonprofit organizations, unions, think tanks, associations, political parties and informal grassroots movements. It includes the industries of professional communications, fundraising, organizing, management, consulting and others. Advocacy work is international, and within the U.S. it is the third biggest sector of the economy.

Consider the following overview of just the nonprofit sector in the U.S. As of 2012, there were an estimated 1.6 million nonprofits registered with the Internal Revenue Service. In that year, the nonprofit sector contributed $804.8 billion to the U.S. economy, or 5.5 percent of the total GDP. Of those, only 40 percent were required to file a financial return (618,062 organizations), but those alone reported a total revenue of more than $2 trillion (Roeger, 2012).

As large as the sector is, there is one area that all advocacy organizations struggle with at some point: engagement. There are many ways to measure engagement, but some of the most commonly used metrics are email message statistics, and include open rate, click-thru rate and response rate. The 2014 M+R Benchmarks study found that for advocacy messages, there was an overall decrease in each rate between 2012 and 2014. The steepest decline was seen in response rate, which fell to 2 percent, a decrease of 25 percent from the 2012 rate, though an overall increase in email list size counteracts some of that decline (M+R, 2014).

Advocacy Networks

Advocacy networks can be simplified into four general but distinct models, based on how an individual is attracted, inspired, organized and engaged. These basic models are: direct advocacy, grassroots advocacy, organizational advocacy and netcentric advocacy.

Direct advocacy involves an individual acting alone to influence society or government. People engaging in direct advocacy can do so in a number of ways, including writing letters to the editor, speaking at a town hall in support or opposition of an idea or policy, or by making a choice to vote or change purchasing behaviors to make a statement.

Grassroots advocacy occurs when individuals act as part of a broad but loosely organized coalition. For example, neighborhoods or other groups of people that come together in candlelight vigils to raise awareness for gun violence, organize the cleanup of a local park or promote a march or protest are all engaging in grassroots advocacy. In this type of advocacy, people in one part of the movement are inspired by those directly around them and continue to organize locally with local resources to promote change.

Organizational advocacy involves working directly through a nonprofit or established advocacy organization that generally has a governing board and centralized leadership. For example, events and initiatives organized by groups like the National Rifle Association, the Sierra Club or the AARP would be considered organizational advocacy efforts.

Finally there is netcentric advocacy, where an individual acts as part of a coordinated network. Netcentric advocacy is a hybrid of the individual determination and participation typical of direct and grassroots models, with the efficiencies and strengths of the organizational model. The networked model is becoming more possible because of the increased density of communications and connection capacity among participants, and the ability to scale those connections to meet demand. The potential for netcentric advocacy increases with each advancement in connectivity technology (web meetings, cell phones with Wi-Fi and teleconference systems, among others) and a drop in transportation costs for flights and shipping. Netcentric advocacy is the least understood and least supported model for organizing the people and resources involved in the pursuit of advocacy.

Modern advocacy movements are often designed to leverage all four models of advocacy network building, in order to engage the greatest number of supporters and have the greatest impact on their issues. However, advocacy initiatives are beginning to shift from organizationally dominated to network-based. The emerging trends in advocacy are focused on connecting people together via loose networks to drive social and policy change. We now live in a world where individual people have the capability to become the leaders of powerful advocacy networks that have the capacity to transform the world. Encouraging the success of an advocacy network means supporting each model for engagement and finding the most effective investments to empower the individuals that are driving change.

Video Games and Gaming Networks

The Gaming Industry Landscape

The gaming industry is an ever-growing powerhouse, earning $21.53 billion in 2013. By many accounts that amount is predicted to grow by many more millions in the coming years. Its audience is also surprisingly diverse. The average age of a gamer is 31 years old, a slightly higher number than many would expect, and divided almost evenly between men, who make up 52 percent of the gaming population, and women, who make up the remaining 48 percent. Currently, video gamers are playing mostly on computers and consoles, though mobile gaming is becoming more and more common, with 44 percent of gamers reporting that they play some sort of game on their smartphones (Entertainment Software Association, 2014). According to the same Entertainment Software Association report, 62 percent of gamers play games with others, either in-person or online, and a majority of gamers under 18 believe that games help them connect with their friends.

Online gaming allows players from around the world the ability to connect and play interactively. An emerging trend in the online video game world is that of eSports, competitively played video games including major titles like *League of Legends*, *Counter-Strike*, *Starcraft II* and *Dota2*, all online multiplayer games, as well as fighting games like *Street Fighter 4* and *Super Smash Brothers Melee*. These competitions are high-stakes and growing exponentially: A report from SuperData notes that in 2013, $25 million in prize money was awarded to eSports winners, a 350 percent increase over four years. *Dota2* offered the largest prize pool in eSports, giving away $2.87 million in prize money at one competition alone (Llamas, 2014).

Like the number of people who play games causally, the number of people who watch and participate in eSports is steadily growing. The same report from SuperData indicates that viewership of eSports has doubled in the past year, ending 2013 with more than 71 million viewers. One event, the *League of Legends* Season 3 World Championship, drew 32 million viewers on its own; by contrast, only 14.9 million watched the World Series and 26.3 million watched Game 7 of the NBA Finals (Llamas, 2014). These numbers indicate that audience engagement has thus far not been a problem for eSports or the gaming industry at large.

Gaming Networks

Perhaps the most obvious examples of networks within the gaming industry are the communities found among digital distribution platforms like Steam, Xbox Live and the Playstation Network. In the computer gaming world, Steam is the most widely used digital distribution platform, and as of January 2014 boasted 75 million registered users. This figure represents a three-month growth period of 15 percent (Pereira, 2014), which some attribute to the growing popularity of free-to-play games like *League of Legends*, *Dota2* and *Team Fortress 2*. Gaming consoles like Microsoft's Xbox and Sony's Playstation also host their own player networks: Xbox Live and Playstation Network, respectively. Playstation Network, as of November 2013, had 150 million registered users (Brightman, 2013), while Xbox Live claims more than 48 million members (Microsoft, Inc., 2014).

There are other examples of networks within the gaming community as well. Some forums dedicated to a specific game can be tight-knit groups where players make friends and connect with other gamers with similar interests. Many games also spawn their own in-game networks of players. For example, massive multiplayer online games (MMOGs) like *Eve Online* generally have very active, social player bases that by nature encourage relationships and connections to form between players. *Eve Online* has its own in-game economy that affects all players and because of this, many players join corporations, which in turn form alliances. Corporations and alliances both work to network players together in order to navigate the game's landscape, ensure the virtual safety of their players and assets, and gain influence in the online world that *Eve Online* players inhabit. Their emerging interactions drastically shape the landscape of the game, as everything from territory to technology and the economy evolves through this dynamic.

Regardless of the platform, members use these networks to connect with each other through chat functions, to create teams of players to navigate multiplayer games together, to share resources and experience and much more.

GAMIFICATION

Gamification is widely described as the inclusion of game mechanics or elements in non-game contexts. In non-game contexts like advocacy, this concept includes using quizzes, point systems, badges, achievements, progress bars and other game mechanics to attract and empower users in deeper ways than merely clicking "like" on Facebook or signing a petition. Previous research by Hamari, Koivisto and Sarsa (2014) has shown that gamification strategies do work. In their literature review, the majority of the studies they analyzed did yield positive effects or results.

Another interesting view of gamification comes from the work of Ferro and Walz (2013), who propose that gamification "does not have to be about making an ordinary task such as collaboration an explicit 'game' and rewarding the user with badges and achievements. Rather, incorporating game elements as part of an OSNS [online social networking service] to facilitate the flow of information than to drive it." This view of gamification also lends support to several communication-based components of Netcentric Campaigns' Seven Elements of an Advocacy Network, which will be discussed later in the chapter.

"On the internet, there is potential for this kind of adaptation to be used as part of an intranet to encourage collaboration within organizations and educational institutions – rewarding users for competence rather than compliance," Ferro and Walz conclude. It is possible that this theory can also be extended from general organizations to advocacy networks.

As a whole, gamification is not always big or virtual. Simply put, it is the application of certain elements of game design and mechanics in order to engage users. In advocacy networks, once users are engaged the goal becomes focused on connecting them to each other to enhance their experience and achieve a common goal, similar to many types of online video games.

Achievements: Unlocked

Gamification has been used successfully in many fields already, including science and social media. Take for example *Foldit*: Developed by researchers at the University of Washington's Center for Game Science and their Department of Biochemistry, *Foldit* is an online puzzle game based on the mechanics of protein folding. Players do not have to have a science degree to play the game – they fold proteins as if solving a puzzle, based on in-game tools and some general guidelines.

The highest scoring solutions proposed by players are evaluated by scientists to see whether or not there are any "real-world" implications for their creations. In addition to itself being a puzzle, *Foldit* utilizes several other gamification concepts including a score system to tell players how well their protein is folded and a high score list that shows how well a player is doing compared to others. These concepts encourage players to keep folding in hopes they will make it onto that list.

Foldit already has two highly touted successes to its name. In 2011, *Foldit* players were able to shed light on the crystal structure of the Mason-Pfizer monkey virus retroviral protease, an AIDS-causing virus found in monkeys (Khatib *et al.*, 2011). This effort only took players about three weeks, though scientists had been working on it for 15 years. Later, in 2012, players were able to completely redesign an enzyme used in Diels-Alder reactions to include 13 more amino acids and ultimately increase the enzyme's activity 18 times (Eiben *et al.*, 2012).

In addition to crowdsourced science, gamification is also being incorporated into the health and fitness world. Games like Nintendo's *Wii Fit* are revolutionizing physical activity by allowing players to see progress bars that track how well they are doing on their way to a set goal and encourage friendly competition.

Zombie, Run! is an app for iPhone and Android that immerses runners in a world where zombies have taken over. Runners become Runner 5, and using announcements like, "Zombies attacked a nearby farmhouse," and "Collect a bottle of water, a radio and a box of batteries," runners are encouraged to keep going to escape the horde. According to the game's website, over 800,000 runners currently use *Zombie, Run!* worldwide.

Social media networks were one of the first fields to gamify their user experience. Platforms like Foursquare and Untappd award users badges for accomplishments like checking in a certain number of times or having a certain number of check-ins of one type. Even information giant Wikipedia awards its editors ranks based on how long they have served and the number of edits they have made ("Wikipedia:Service Awards," n.d.).

Perhaps the first field that incorporated gamification techniques was education, a field that has been using game mechanics nearly as long as computer games have existed. Learning games such as *Reader Rabbit* and *Math Blaster* in the 1980s could be considered the beginning of the trend. In the present day, programs like DuoLingo and Livemocha continue the trend by teaching foreign language in ways that incorporate gamification concepts like progress bars and badges to show students how well they are doing.

More than just ways to teach concepts, teachers are also incorporating gamification into their classroom in other ways, for example, in the way they grade. Lee Sheldon, a professor at Indiana University, transformed his grading system into one that more closely resembles an experience points system in video games. In games, experience points are points earned by completing tasks and defeating enemies; in his classes Sheldon awards points for completing assignments, presentations and tests. Once a player has received a set number of experience points they gain a level, or in this case a student moves from one letter grade up to another (Tay, 2010). Reviews of this system suggest it is effective because this method ensures that "each assignment and each test feels rewarding, rather than disheartening (Extra Credits, 2012)."

The examples in this section range across a wide spectrum of both fields and types of mechanics used, but each shows a marked success in the implementation of gamification techniques.

Identifying Engaging Game Mechanics

With so many different types of game mechanics available with current technology, it can be difficult to decide which would effectively increase user engagement or provide the best user experience. One of the best feedback loops through which to identify engaging game elements and mechanics can be found in the various networks that spawn around both the audience and developers themselves. Many game enthusiasts share their opinions on game mechanics through writing for games journalism-based websites or making videos on YouTube. For example, YouTube personality Sequelitis focuses his videos on positive mechanics within games. On the development side, industry professionals use events like the annual Independent Games Festival to share ideas and insights with other developers. By paying attention to these thought leaders and enthusiasts, advocacy network builders could learn strategies that may help influence their work.

Because the spawning grounds for game mechanics – and thus the keys to successful gamification – come so much from a sense of creativity and art, it is just as necessary for developers and network builders to grow intimate with the communities that celebrate the depth of games as it is for them to understand the mechanics behind their success. Combining the two efforts could provide insight into future implementation of gamification strategies, as well as foresight on how to be flexible with new business models and ideas.

Intersections of Networks and Gamification

Though there is much narrative on how gamification may benefit education and science, there is not currently extensive research on how gamification may help advocacy network building and advocacy campaign initiative efforts specifically. However, there are already a number of examples of how advocacy networks and promoters of social change are effectively utilizing gamification strategies to create social or policy change. Take for instance the following examples:

The Gamification of Issue-Based Advocacy

In 2014, The Food Trust of Philadelphia, Pennsylvania, wanted to educate citizens about, and shift public attention onto, the issue of food deserts. The U.S. Department of Agriculture defines food deserts as "urban neighborhoods and rural towns without ready access to fresh, healthy, and affordable food." Many times, these communities only have access to fast food or convenience stores ("Food Deserts," n.d.).

To raise awareness of food deserts, The Food Trust worked with PreventObesity.net (an advocacy network of more than 300,000 people working to reverse the childhood obesity epidemic in the U.S.) to create a quiz that tested participants' knowledge of food deserts and the challenges they pose to millions of Americans. Three emails were sent to PreventObesity.net's list of supporters over the course of two months in early 2014, asking them to take the quiz and test their knowledge.

Because food deserts can often be a hard concept to grasp for populations who have never had to worry about food access, the quiz was extremely difficult. Even still, The Food Trust was ultimately able to engage more than 7,000 people in only three weeks.

However, the final and most successful element of this campaign was a challenge to the public to beat the director of the program's score. Such challenges are a commonly used gamification mechanism. This challenge was sent in an email with the subject line "Even I was stumped. Can you do better?," and was the third and final email of the campaign. This final email performed better than either of the two previous emails, based on its open rate and click-thru rate. The average open and click-thru rates of the first two emails, which were simply calls to action to take the quiz, were 14.97 and 1.83, respectively. When the final challenge was issued, those rates rose to 16.50 and 2.54, also respectively (Netcentric Campaigns, 2014).

Not only did this challenge add another layer of engagement to their efforts, it ultimately raised overall engagement levels by adding a mechanic that was more fun than the original ask. The success of their efforts also fueled the growth of PreventObesity.net, adding thousands of grassroots supporters to their email list.

The Gamification of Political Advocacy

Early in 2012, the idea to gamify political advocacy entered the American political scene with the first game targeted at educating voters about an incident involving a major party nominee in a presidential election. The idea for the game came from the founders of a grassroots advocacy group called Dogs Against Romney, whose mission was to educate voters about an incident involving Republican presidential candidate Mitt Romney and his family dog, an Irish Setter named Seamus (Parker, 2007). Seamus had been transported by Romney in a kennel strapped to the roof of the family station wagon, rather than inside the car with the family. The incident incensed dog lovers who quickly began to network around the Dogs Against Romney group—virally sharing the group's blog and Facebook posts. From purely grassroots beginnings, the network quickly grew to around 20,000 people by January 2012, at which point the popularity of the group caught the attention of MSNBC's Rachel Maddow, who featured Dogs Against Romney on The Rachel Maddow Show on January 12, 2012 (Maddow, 2012).

Maddow's feature of the group set off a tidal wave of news coverage that soon propelled the network to over 100,000 members on Facebook and drove over 6,000 daily readers to the group's blog. One of Dogs Against Romney's founders, Scott Crider, happened to be serving on the board of a small, Dallas-based gaming startup called Censault. The idea to create a game around the Dogs Against Romney movement was born at a board meeting that occurred soon after the group began receiving intensive media attention.

Research conducted by Censault revealed that, in early 2012, there had not yet been a game developed for the purpose of supporting a political advocacy effort in a major U.S. election. The only similar effort they uncovered at the time was a New Dehli, India-based online game called *Angry Anna*, which sought to draw attention to an ongoing anti-corruption movement in the country. *Angry Anna* had been launched in 2011 and gone viral, being played over 435,000 times worldwide (Harjani, 2011).

Encouraged by the performance of *Angry Anna*, Censault and Dogs Against Romney proceeded with the gamification of the group's advocacy message. The plan for development of the game, called *The Crate Escape: Seamus Unleashed*, was to work through the summer of 2012 and to release it on the eve of the Republican National Convention, which also happened to be National Dog Day.

Evidence of the national media's interest in the game came quickly, as word of the game's development leaked. Coverage of the game's impending release reached a crescendo when it was revealed that the internationally famous punk rock band Devo had contributed a music track to the game (Greene, 2012). Covered by media outlets ranging from Rolling Stone and Vanity Fair to major broadcast networks to gaming and entertainment websites, the stage was set for a successful release.

Efforts to develop the game for multiple platforms, combined with technical issues that frequently arise in such complex projects, caused Censualt to miss the release date goal. In fact, the Republican National Convention came and went without the game hitting the marketplace. By the time the game did finally become available two weeks later, during the Democratic National Convention, media attention had waned, leaving the fate of the game – for which there was no marketing budget – in the hands of Dogs Against Romney's more than 100,000 network members.

Despite having no advertising support, missing the optimal release date and not being available for Android devices, *The Crate Escape: Seamus Unleashed* garnered tens of thousands of iOS downloads and received strong ratings from users on iTunes. With the game's success, it became clear that politics was a field in which gamification strategies might be effective.

Games with a Purpose

Games for Change is a nonprofit organization focused on supporting and distributing social impact games that help fuel various educational and humanitarian efforts. They work to connect designers with stakeholders and investors in order to develop new, powerful games that drive social change. Through the years, they have promoted several games that have a strong social or policy change focus.

For example, *The Migrant Trail* is a single-player simulation game that examines the life of migrants and border patrol agents on the U.S.-Mexico border, with the option to play as either group. Throughout the game, users are exposed to various hardships faced by each side: For the migrants, this might involve loss of family members, hunger or injury. When playing as a border patrol agent, your goals might involve locating undocumented migrants, tending to injuries sustained by the migrants you find or consoling a family who has lost a loved one. This game, developed by Gigantic Mechanic, was a nominee in the Most Significant Impact category at the Games for Change Festival in 2014.

In 2013, developer Kognito released *Start the Talk: Underage Drinking* with support from the U.S. Department of Health and Human Services and the Substance Abuse and Mental Health Administration. *Start the Talk* is a role-playing game in which users build knowledge and skills regarding how to talk to their children about the impacts and potential harms of underage drinking, while also gaining feedback on how their word choice might influence the reception of such a conversation. This game was also a nominee in the Most Significant Impact category at the Games for Change Festival in 2014.

The winner of the Most Significant Impact category for 2014 was a game called *Mission US: A Cheyenne Odyssey,* developed by THIRTEEN. In this educational game, players assume the identity of a Northern Cheyenne Indian boy. Through the gameplay, players learn about the history of the Cheyenne Indians and the effects and consequences of the United States' westward expansion in the mid-to-late 1800s, among other things. *Mission US* currently supports 483,000 registered players and 27,000 registered teachers—a solid number of people now learning about the struggles of the Cheyenne (Games for Change, 2014).

While very different, each of these games represents the gamification of an educational or awareness-raising effort that has had a good reception in the gaming and advocacy realms. These games are all examples of how, when done well, gamification can lend support to raising awareness of an issue and are solid precursors for future initiatives.

ISSUES, CONTROVERSIES, AND PROBLEMS

Key Issues and Problems

There are at least two key problems that need to be addressed in order for game designers and advocacy leaders to be able to learn from each other. First, lessons learned by each group are not being shared. This may be partly due to the lack of a common framework through which both sides can look at the way networks emerge to build capacity and more deeply engage users. Gaming and advocacy networks leaders, while similar in what they try to accomplish (attracting users, engaging them with good content, learning about their skills and interests and connecting them with each other to work together for mutual benefit), have few opportunities for professional connection: Game industry leaders do not often attend advocacy-based conferences, and vice versa.

It may be beneficial for representatives from both types of networks to come together and discuss ideas and strategies that have and have not worked, and why that may be. It is possible that their counterparts in the other industry may have already worked out ways to combat similar issues within their own scope of work. However, with the current lack of communication between the two sides these ideas and solutions might never be shared with those in the other sector who could benefit from them.

Second, examples of the good that can come from the intersection of gaming and advocacy, and opportunities for the sharing of ideas between relevant leaders are being ignored. As mentioned in the previous section, there are already a number of successes that advocacy networks and campaigns can claim that involved gamification strategies, and the next section of this chapter will explain how many games and gaming networks are already including all of the key parts of a successful advocacy network to some extent. However, thus far there has been little to no research focused on how gamification benefits advocacy networks or campaigns, and how incorporation of network building strategies may influence a game or gaming network's success.

Additional Concerns

User Backgrounds and Preferences

As presented in several of the research articles we studied, not all users appreciate or are receptive to gamification strategies. At least one research article (Montola, 2009) found that some users expressed concerns about gamification strategies "motivating undesirable usage patterns." A paper by Antin and Churchill (2011) that cites the Montola study agrees, and also notes that, "Our own in-progress research on FourSquare indicates that most users find only some types of badges interesting or motivational."

A person's background can also influence how they perceive a newly gamified system. Users with a gaming background might be more receptive to seeing gamification techniques in a new space, and would be more familiar with the mechanics of such a system. People who regularly advocate for a cause via more traditional means might also be hesitant to adopt a new system that has not been widely tested in the advocacy space, or one with which they have no experience or are not as comfortable.

It is also important to understand people's motivations for participating in a gamified situation or campaign – everyone's will be different. Much research has been done on how and why using incentives for motivation works to attract and entertain people, and some relevant research is suggested in the "Additional Reading" section at the end of this chapter.

Finally, it is interesting to note one study that analyzed findings of several papers on games with a purpose, and found that "motivation for people to play a game was not driven by the fact that they will solve a problem, but to be entertained (Raftopoulos & Walz, 2013)." When translating this finding to gamifying advocacy networks, it becomes clear that though the purpose of most advocacy networks is, in essence, to solve a problem by promoting social and policy change, developers working to gamify an advocacy initiative must recognize that the game must first and foremost be fun, or they risk losing the interest of users.

Audience and Subject Matter

In developing a gamified initiative, research also suggests that it is important to ensure that no users feel excluded or slighted, and all experiences end on a positive note. It is also important to keep your audience in mind, especially if they may have special needs. Failure to recognize user needs can have the potential to alienate certain demographics of your target audience. An evaluation of a social network called Blues Buddies that caters to people with mild to moderate depression depicts several key lessons: "In the case of gameful design, it is necessary to reconsider current popular gamification strategies based on competition and win, public humiliation through leader boards and accumulation of points and virtual wealth... and conceive alternative design models that favor altruism (the motivation to increase others' well-being regardless of one's own), positive feelings towards oneself and positive social interaction (Rao, 2011)."

In that context, Rao touches on how a network specifically built for a target audience, in this case depressed individuals, needs certain elements involved to be successful. It may be beneficial for developers to give thought to the elements that Rao identified as being important for Blues Buddies, such as inclusion of an emphatic feedback system, the implementation of psychological and learning theories (Rao suggests techniques like mood transfer and social responsibility appeals can promote positive feelings), and considering the choice of whether to use intrinsic or extrinsic motivation techniques based on which would appeal or apply more to the target audience.

SOLUTIONS AND RECOMMENDATIONS

The Seven Elements of an Advocacy Network

One issue identified in the previous section is the lack of a common lens through which both advocacy and game industry leaders can look at the way networks build capacity and more deeply engage users. Based on research and experience with advocacy network building, Netcentric Campaigns has developed a framework to determine if an advocacy network is destined to be successful: the Seven Elements of an Advocacy Network. According to Netcentric Campaigns, if a network does not work to implement each of these Seven Elements, it ultimately will not function at full capacity ("What makes," n.d.). This proposed framework can serve to guide analysis and discussion between game industry and advocacy leaders.

Each of the Seven Elements is described below, with examples of how they work in advocacy, as well as how many games and gaming networks already utilize these components to some degree in their design. The Seven Elements include:

- Building and reinforcing *social ties*. Strong social ties create trust among network participants, allowing them to collaborate and making it easier to overcome potential strategy disagreements.
- Creating a *communications grid* where network participants begin to have conversations with one another. This grid includes a variety of communications channels for aligning work, solving issues and building identity as a group.
- Developing a *common language* that reinforces the identity of the network and allows members to more efficiently resolve conflict.
- Defining a *clear vision* to help participants understand the advantages of being a part of the network. This vision guides the network culture and helps participants focus their activities.
- Creating a system for collecting and distributing *shared resources* that allows participants to pool their skills, talents, experiences, expertise, services and funding streams. This strengthens social ties and also saves individual members of the network time and money.
- Identifying *actors* who drive the activities of the network by monitoring resources, creating messaging, outlining participant responsibilities and receiving feedback.
- Creating mechanisms to provide *feedback* on network activity, which helps leaders and other participants understand the trends, resources and needs of the entire network.

Though in normal conversation it might be easier to tease apart these elements for discussion, in reality they are dependent upon each other. One alone cannot make a network functional (like being tall doesn't make someone a good basketball player). The combination of the elements adds genuine capacity to a network. It is easiest to see how the Seven Elements work together by visualizing them as a Venn diagram. In Figure 1, the Seven Elements have been divided into three separate groups: connections, tools and leadership. When each group of elements is entirely present, the result is a fully functioning network.

Figure 1. Elements of an effective network. It is easiest to see how the Seven Elements work together by visualizing them as a Venn diagram. Here, the Elements have been divided into three separate groups: connections, tools and leadership. In this example, the representation of each group is strong, resulting in a fully-functioning network shown in the center of the Venn diagram. (© 2014, Netcentric Campaigns. Used with permission.)

Additionally, some individual practices can support multiple elements. For example a listserv may be one part of a communications grid, but it also serves to build social ties between its members. Each of the elements is presented in this section, and examples from video games and parallels in network strategy are presented.

Communications Grid

A communications grid includes the ways that participants are able to communicate in order to align work, solve issues and build identity as a group. In advocacy networks, a communications grid may include things like use of a listserv or group email address, a message board, forums or a newsletter. A strong communications system has been shown to be an essential part of maintaining a network (The Policy Project, 1999).

In the gaming community at large, there are hundreds if not thousands of forums and message boards for both specific games and more general forums such as the r/games subreddit of the popular website reddit. Both types allow users to communicate and share ideas, news and information. Many of these communities also sponsor a voice chat server via programs such as Mumble or TeamSpeak where users can talk to each other, in-game and out, to help develop a strategy while playing or get to know other members of the community. Voice chat, forum posting and personal messages make up a large part of the communications grid for these gaming networks.

Most digital distribution platforms, programs that allow players to purchase, store and launch many games from a common program such as Steam or Origin, also have built-in chat functions where users can add other users to a friends' list and communicate with them via instant message. Additionally, in some video games, and nearly all multiplayer online games in particular, one will find some sort of in-game chat function through which online users can connect with each other to strategize and keep in touch with people they meet while playing.

It is important to note that a communications grid can be comprised of multiple forms of communication, as there may not be one form that offers all the needed functionalities. For example, a communications grid may include a listserv for sharing information, an instant message program for quick contact and a forum for deeper conversations. No matter what components are used to create a communications grid, the purpose is the same: to provide a way for participants to communicate, plan and connect to other members of the group.

Social Ties

Creating and sustaining social ties is another key part of network-building. Previous research by Haythornthwaite (2002) concludes that, "ties of various strengths, with their different ranges and access to resources, fill important niches in our daily work and lives." Building social ties among network participants creates trust, allowing them to collaborate and making it easier to overcome potential strategy disagreements. In the advocacy world, organizations and networks might foster social ties by hosting events such as happy hours, webinars or other events where participants are actively meeting each other and creating relationships and connections that they might otherwise not have had access to.

Through the previously mentioned concept of forums and discussion boards, gamers are able to foster and create social ties with others. In-game, systems that allow users to automatically connect to others looking for people to play with also fall into the category of mechanics that foster social ties. Gamers might also make social ties by creating or joining competitive teams. Another common occurrence in the gaming world is LAN parties, where players physically come together and play as a group on a common local area network (a LAN), creating relationships that will be continued both online and offline.

Video game companies play a part in fostering social ties as well. Attending game conventions like PAX or the Electronic Entertainment Expo (better known as E3) gives developers the chance to connect to developers at other companies, and connect with game enthusiasts at the same time. General attendees of such conferences also have a chance to meet and connect with other enthusiasts with similar interests.

Creating social ties between all types of participants ultimately increases the knowledge a network or organization has about their audience or fellow members. The better one knows their audience, the easier it will be to create content that the majority of them enjoy.

Common Language

A report from the Marzano Center about the importance of a common language of instruction in teaching explains that "shared understanding is developed based upon a common language," an observation that also is relevant to networks (Schooling & Toth, 2013). In organizations, having a common language helps to reinforce the identity of the network. It allows employees, advocates and supporters to talk about their work in terms that are consistent across the board. Using common language also brings all parties onto the same page, ensuring that everyone understands what is meant by a certain word or phrase and how to describe certain important concepts, which can cut down on both internal and external misunderstandings and disagreements. It is also essential for organizations to develop a common language for brand management purposes, to ensure that their organization is seen as consistent and also to help foster an overall positive recognition of the group or cause.

In day-to-day conversation, especially in mobile texting and online conversation via email or a chat program, there are many commonly used acronyms like TY (thank you), BRB (be right back) and LOL (laugh out loud). Understandably, these can also be seen in the chat box of any online multiplayer game one might play. There is also language that is widely used in the gaming community in general: acronyms like GG (good game) and GLHF (good luck, have fun) and terms like "easter egg" (a reference to something unrelated within a game) or lag (a drop in frame rate)—are all terms that non-gamers might not immediately understand. Subtypes of games tend to develop their own language as well. For example, people not accustomed to online multiplayer games, even those who play other types of games, might not recognize terms like 5's (a five player versus five player game) or gank (generally, an ambush).

Creating a common language helps players or advocates feel like they are part of the group, and understanding the common language helps make it easier to communicate to teammates or supporters. Common language serves as a bridge between advocates and the general public; it is a medium both can feel free to use.

Clear Vision

Research shows that having a clear vision for an organization or movement helps all participants understand what it is that they are trying to accomplish, giving them a sense of the advantages of being a part of the network. Results from one study show that "employees who realize the importance of being aligned with the goals and objectives of the organization will increase their value by enhancing their productivity and reducing waste (Cato and Gordon, 2012)." These results support previous research, much of which Cato and Gordon cite in their paper.

Organizational and video game visions, or goals, are very similar. An organization's mission statement, for example, is what drives the day-to-day activities of the group—at the end of the day, it is what they are ultimately working toward. In video games, it is also essential for players to have a clear vision. Often, the vision is the obvious goal: beat the final boss. In many video games however, there are also smaller goals (puzzles, mini-bosses, side quests) that provide experience or items needed to keep a player's attention focused on, and ultimately help them complete, the main goal. These mini-goals along the way also provide players with what are sometimes called "win states," times when both the game and the player realize a sense of success that serves to keep players motivated. Advocacy leaders attempting to incorporate gamification strategies might do well to incorporate similar smaller goals in their overall strategy for the same purpose.

In each case, establishing the vision or goal for what you want to do, or what you want players or supporters to do, serves to keep momentum going and remind players, or advocates, what it is they are ultimately trying to accomplish.

Shared Resources

Creating a way to collect and distribute shared resources allows members of a network to pool their skills, talents, experiences, expertise, services and funding streams. This strengthens social ties through collaboration, and also saves individual members of the network time and money. For example, if an advocacy network was to share its list of supporters with another whose focus aligns closely with their own, each network could potentially grow their email lists or supporter base and save countless hours that otherwise would have been devoted to those tasks. Previous research has found that: "By encouraging shared resources and collaboration amongst nonprofit organizations and by developing community-oriented facilities, nonprofit centers achieve a number of significant benefits" (Mt. Auburn Associates, 2011).

There are quite a few ways that shared resources are utilized in the video game world as well. For example, a game designer may use code from one game in another, or they may base their game on a pre-existing physics engine, so that they do not have to spend countless hours developing such a system on their own.

In many video games, there is also the opportunity to trade items between players. In the *Borderlands* series, players have access to a "shared stash," through which they can store items to share between their different characters. Gamers playing through an MMOG such as *World of Warcraft* or *Eve Online* with a generally consistent group of players may also share money and resources between their companions for the greater good of the team. For example, if a member of the team does not have enough money to buy a weapon that they need to help defend the rest of the team, another member may chip in to help that player acquire what they need or just buy it for them outright. Additionally, groups of players also typically share expertise by building a team comprised of players that are adept at different types of play: combat, role-playing or strategy, and taking newer players under their wing to help them learn the "ins and outs" of a game, thereby sharing their experience and knowledge.

Actors

Actors are those who drive the activities of a network by monitoring resources, creating messaging, outlining participant responsibilities and receiving feedback. In organizations, actors can include foundation leaders, key spokespeople for the movement, nonprofit organizers and others. Actors are the people who keep the network running and ensure all participants feel included. They are the ones who ultimately need to be connected to ensure that a network runs as a well-oiled machine. It is also important for a pool of actors to be diverse, because a lack of differing viewpoints can lead to a lack of fresh ideas or approaches to problem-solving. Additionally, at least one study has found a link between diversity and overall organizational success (Winston, 2001).

In the gaming world at large, actors may be any of several types of people. For example, the vice president of public relations and marketing for a game company would be considered an actor because he or she helps create the messaging around the company and their game releases. Those who produce video about game content or who commentate on and those who write and report for game journalism websites could also be considered actors because of the high level of attention they draw to various games. In individual games, actors may be people such as well-known or professional video gamers (for example, Major League Gaming teams and players), as they are the "celebrities" of the video game world who drive viewership, as well as encourage others to play games both casually and professionally. Those who create Let's Play videos (where a player walks you through a game in an almost movie-like manner) and players who stream live gameplay on websites like Twitch could also be considered actors, as they also give millions of viewers across the world access to gameplay footage.

Regardless of who the person is or the type of work they do, actors are essential to a strong network because they are the leaders or key players who are encouraging others to get involved or stay focused on goals. They are the people who are most often looked up to and imitated for their motivation, knowledge and skills in moving change forward or, in the case of games, providing access to, information about or entertainment for the community.

Feedback

The final component of the Seven Elements is feedback. A study by Hattie and Timperley (2007) found that feedback is a powerful tool, noting that, "when feedback draws attention to the regulatory processes needed to engage with a task, learners' beliefs about the importance of effort and their conceptions of learning can be important moderators in the learning process," and also, "this process results in higher confidence and greater investment of effort." Feedback in the sense of an advocacy network refers to information that helps leaders and other participants understand the trends, resources and needs of the entire network. In video games, it is much the same.

Feedback for organizations may involve data collection from a campaign: How many people opened an email? How many people were reached? How did the public perceive the language used to create the campaign? All of this information and data helps organizations to understand what works, what does not and what they need to change in the future. It also helps communicate to advocates how the landscape is changing and what issues are important to their population at any given time.

In video games, feedback comes in various ways. Many video game developers release a version of the game as an "alpha" or a "beta," meaning that they allow a certain number of players to test the game for bugs and glitches before releasing the game to the broader gaming community. This player-generated feedback is essential to help developers understand where to focus their time and what needs work before the game releases. Once a game is released, feedback could include anything from compiling reviews and ratings to analyzing the general tone with which players are discussing the game.

Also, feedback can encourage designers to develop patches to existing games that fix any issues that players may encounter, though some may come too late to influence changes needed to a current game or campaign. If that is the case, feedback can still help shape and drive the development process for future ideas. For example, analyzing an advocacy campaign after its conclusion can serve to inform the direction and planning of future campaigns, help organizers understand why a campaign did well or did not, or pinpoint areas for improvement.

More Support for the Seven Elements in Game Mechanics

Extensive research has already been done on incentives as motivation. One study (Sailer, Hense, Mandl and Klevers, 2013) analyzed six motivational perspectives: trait perspective, behaviorist learning perspective, cognitive perspective, perspective of self-determination, perspective of interest and perspective of emotion. From these types of perspectives, the authors proposed hypotheses for each based on their understanding of psychology and gamification. For example:

- Players are likely to be motivated if gamification provides immediate *feedback* in the form of positive and negative reinforcement.
- Players are likely to be motivated if gamification provides a *clear and achievable goal*.
- Players are likely to be motivated if they experience the feeling of *social relatedness*.

These examples fall directly in line with several of the Seven Elements of an Advocacy Network: feedback, a clear vision and social ties, respectively.

Sharing Lessons Learned

Both advocacy network builders and the game industry could benefit from each other's knowledge of network building and creating engagement due to their previously mentioned similarities. As discussed, one current issue is the lack of communication between leaders in both areas. It is also possible that advocacy and gaming leaders do not realize how similar their goals and activities actually are. Compounding these problems is the fact that game industry leaders do not often attend advocacy-based conferences or events, and advocacy leaders do not often attend gaming conventions – at least not with the purpose of learning from others' work. Leaders from both areas should work to communicate more often, so that best practices and lessons learned are shared for the benefit of both fields.

It might also benefit game designers to spend time learning about the Seven Elements and analyzing how they are already or could be implemented into a game's design. The inclusion of any one of the Seven Elements in a deliberate, planned manner could have an effect on player perceptions and experiences with a game.

Since games are the very embodiment of gamification strategies in practice, advocacy networks should look more closely at the success or failure of games. In particular, MMOGs could provide clear examples of how best to implement various strategies because of how similar they are to typical advocacy networks: large numbers of demographically varied players all engaged at one time and working toward a common goal. Advocacy leaders should also closely examine highly successful video games to identify gamification strategies that are not currently being used in the advocacy world.

Exploring Available Technology

Attention should also be given to different forms of technology, such as ensuring mobile or tablet compatibility, and to emerging technology that has not been widely used in gamification efforts thus far.

Perhaps the most growth potential lies in mobile development. Ninety percent of U.S. adults now carry mobile phones, 58 percent of which are smart phones, and trends suggest these numbers will only rise ("Mobile Technology Fact Sheet," 2014). As proven after the 2010 earthquake in Haiti and the 2011 earthquake and tsunami in Japan, direct text messaging is a very effective way to raise money during a crisis. Within a week of the 2010 Haiti earthquake, mobile users had donated $22 million to the American Red Cross for disaster relief via text, which accounted for one-fifth of the total donations at that time (Heath, 2010). It is possible that similar mechanisms could be used to help raise money for non-crisis advocacy efforts as well.

The game industry has already latched onto the mobile market in a big way. Mobile games are the fastest-growing segment of the industry, with revenue projected to top $22 billion in 2015 (Gartner, 2013). Simple game apps are already very popular. One game, *Candy Crush*, supports 93 million players a day and is worth an estimated $7.1 billion (Smith, 2014). Other mobile games are seeing similar successes.

Some advocacy networks are already using mobile solutions to engage users, though not to the extent that the gaming industry is utilizing the available technology. In 2013, the Moving Maryland Forward Network offered a weekly text-based news quiz where users were asked to answer a true or false or multiple choice question about an issue related to their work. Their efforts saw high response rates and low numbers of users asking to unsubscribe (Netcentric Campaigns, 2013), while raising awareness for their focus areas.

Finally, satellite imaging is an example of an emerging technology that could be considered when developing gamification strategies, and has already been used in advocacy efforts worldwide. Greenpeace Innovation Lab developed a game called *Greenpeace Guardianes*, which uses satellite photos to help monitor illegal deforestation in Argentina. Players are asked to compare satellite image maps from 2008 with recent images, and flag any areas where they suspect illegal deforestation is occurring. As of March 2014, players had flagged more than 200 square miles of land as possible areas where illegal deforestation had taken place (MobLab Team, 2014).

Advocacy experts interested in gamification should look at each of these examples, as well as the numerous other successes and failures in using emerging technology in gamification, in order to learn from their experiences.

FUTURE RESEARCH DIRECTIONS

To Benefit Gaming

There has been no research to date evaluating the implementation of the Seven Elements of an Advocacy Network into video games and how they may, or may not, help increase a game's perception, success or user experience. Future research could examine the success and perceptions of a game that includes strong examples of each of the Seven Elements as compared to a game that was weak in or completely lacking one or more of them. Future research could also investigate which of the Seven Elements seems to have the greatest impact on user experience and gamers' perception of the game as a whole, as well as a game's success. This could provide game developers with an understanding of where time needs to be devoted in the development process to ensure success.

For example, *World of Warcraft* is an MMOG that has been steadily losing players. Between April and June 2014, the game lost close to 800,000 players (Makuch, 2014). Contrast that trend with multiplayer online battle arena (MOBA) games such as *League of Legends* or *Dota2*, which are becoming increasingly more popular – *League of Legends* is estimated to grow from 52 million active users in 2013 to 94 million in 2015 (Llamas, 2014). Future research could investigate why one type of game is losing players while interest is growing for another similar type, and attempt to determine if any of the players leaving *World of Warcraft* cite reasons for departure that could be mediated by implementing strategies that correspond with any of the Seven Elements.

To Benefit Advocacy Networks

Multiple studies cited in this chapter note that further research should be done on topics including the context of the gamification, user preferences and the gamification environment in general in order to better understand how each influences the success and players' perceptions of a gamification effort (Sailer, Hense, Mandl and Klevers, 2013; Hamari, Koivisto and Sarsa, 2014). We also feel that these areas would benefit from further research, as solid information on how each component interacts could lead to proven best-practices when developing a gamification strategy for an advocacy movement or network.

Future research could also examine what types of gamification strategies work best for certain types of advocacy networks or campaigns. This would provide organizers with a more solid understanding of which tactics might encourage engagement and motivation for a certain audience, and which mechanics they should avoid.

Many games already use in-game purchases as a source of revenue. *Candy Crush* earns about $800,000 per day from in-game purchases of items that help players beat a level or give them extra lives (Smith, 2014). Future research could explore how implementing such a currency system in a gamified initiative, network or campaign would benefit advocacy as a whole, as a way to fundraise and encourage supporters to make donations.

Additionally, future research should also focus on best practices of creating and implementing a gamified advocacy campaign, using data from successful games and initiatives such as Games for Change Festival winners or the Moving Maryland Forward Network's text-based quiz campaign. Thought should also be given to understanding how differences between users' backgrounds and their perceptions of gaming could play a part in their levels of participation in gamified advocacy initiatives, and future research should seek to understand how these differences could be mitigated.

Finally, the gamification of political advocacy, a fledgling industry in 2012, is likely to be more developed in 2016. As previously mentioned, 90 percent of U.S. adults now carry mobile phones, 58 percent of which are smart phones, and trends suggest these numbers will only be higher by the 2016 election cycle ("Mobile Technology Fact Sheet," 2014). After that election, research should be done on any gamified efforts and how game mechanics can influence political advocacy and elections.

CONCLUSION

In the past, advocacy tended to be structured in top-down systems. People have always advocated for change, but previously they could only reach small, often personal networks. With the rise of the internet, advocates were given new capabilities they did not have before. Suddenly people could use online networks to reach potentially millions of people. This shattered the former top-down advocacy structure and created new ad hoc network-building opportunities.

Gamification has been used in a wide variety of fields already – health and fitness, social media, science, education – with proven results. The potential to better connect advocacy and gamification is great, and there is much that game developers and designers could learn from the advocacy network building process, and vice versa, due to the similarities in the structures of gaming networks and advocacy networks.

It is important to keep in mind the Seven Elements of an Advocacy Network when connecting advocacy and gamification, as doing so has the potential to maximize success. In the game development process, designers should set aside time and effort devoted to ensuring their game incorporates each of the Seven Elements for a complete and fully immersive user experience.

If both game designers and advocates utilize the same framework in their work, it will be easier for each side to understand and learn from the other's successes or failures, and if game developers and social activists are willing to take a look at each other's systems – both of which work to connect people together for a common cause – significant advancements could be made in both fields.

ACKNOWLEDGMENT

Special thanks to Elizabeth Brotherton-Bunch for her work on the original outline of this chapter, to Scott Crider and Chris Casey for their input on the chapter's content and to Ryan Hicks for loaning us his knowledge of video games and gamification.

REFERENCES

2012 Election Spending Will Reach $6 Billion, Center for Responsive Politics Predict. (2012, October 31). Retrieved from http://www.opensecrets.org/news/2012/10/2012-election-spending-will-reach-6/

Antin, J., & Churchill, E. (2011, May). *Badges in Social Media: A Social Psychological Perspective.* Paper presented at the CHI 2011 Conference, Vancouver, BC, Canada.

Brightman, J. (2013, November 13). PlayStation Plus has seen "significant growth" says Sony [Blog]. *Gamesindustry.biz.* Retrieved from http://www.gamesindustry.biz/articles/2013-11-13-playstation-plus-has-seen-significant-growth-says-sony

Cato, S., & Gordon, J. (2012, March). Relationship of the strategic vision alignment to employee productivity and student enrollment. *Research in Higher Education Journal, 15,* 1.

Eiben, C., Siegel, J., Bale, J., Cooper, S., Khatib, F., & Shen, B. et al. (2012). Increased Diels-Alderase activity through backbone remodeling guided by Foldit players. *Nature Biotechnology, 30*(2), 190–192. Retrieved from http://www.nature.com/nbt/journal/v30/n2/full/nbt.2109.html doi:10.1038/nbt.2109 PMID:22267011

Electronic Arts Reports Q1 FY14 Financial Results [Press release]. (2013, July 23). Electronic Arts. Retrieved from http://investor.ea.com/releasedetail.cfm?ReleaseID=779751

2014 Sales, Demographic and Usage Data: Essential Facts About the Computer and Video Game Industry. (2014). Entertainment Software Association. Retrieved from http://www.theesa.com/facts/pdfs/ESA_EF_2014.pdf

Online game 'Cerberus' launching today to help relief effort in the Philippines uses VHR satellite imagery [Press Release]. (2013, November 14). European Space Imaging. Retrieved from http://www.directionsmag.com/pressreleases/online-game-cerberus-launching-today-to-help-relief-effort-in-the-philippin/367285

Extra Credits. (2012, May 13). *Extra Credits: Gamifying Education* [Video file]. Retrieved from https://www.youtube.com/watch?v=MuDLw1zIc94

Voter Turnout. (n.d.). Fair Vote, The Center for Voting and Democracy. Retrieved from http://www.fairvote.org/research-and-analysis/voter-turnout/

Ferro, L., & Walz, S. (2013, April). *Like this: How game elements in social media and collaboration are changing the flow of information.* Paper presented at the CHI 2013 Conference, Paris, France.

Food Deserts. (n.d.). *USDA.gov.* Retrieved from http://apps.ams.usda.gov/fooddeserts/fooddeserts.aspx

Play Mission US: A Cheyenne Odyssey. (2014). Games for Change. Retrieved from http://www.games-forchange.org/play/mission-us-a-cheyenne-odyssey/

Gartner Says Worldwide Video Game Market to Total $93 Billion in 2013 [Press release]. (2013, October 29). Gartner. Retrieved from http://www.gartner.com/newsroom/id/2614915

Greene, A. (2012, August 15). Song Premiere: Devo, 'Don't Roof Rack Me, Bro! (Seamus Unleashed). *Rolling Stone*. Retrieved from http://www.rollingstone.com/music/news/song-premiere-devo-dont-roof-rack-me-bro-seamus-unleashed-20120815

Hamari, J., Koivisto, J., & Sarsa, H. (2014). Does Gamification Work? -- A literature Review of Empirical Studies on Gamification. *Proceedings of the 47th Hawaii International Conference on System Sciences*. Honolulu, Hawaii. doi:10.1109/HICSS.2014.377

Harjani, P. (2011, August 29). 'Angry Anna' gains a virtual victory. *CNN Travel*. Retrieved from http://travel.cnn.com/mumbai/life/team-anna-eliminates-indias-corrupt-politicians-well-virtually-386861

Hattie, J., & Timperley, H. (2007, March). The Power of Feedback. *Review of Educational Research*, 77(1), 81–112. doi:10.3102/003465430298487

Haythornthwaite, C. (2002). Strong, Weak and Latent Ties and the Impact of New Media. *The Information Society: An International Journal.*, 18(5), 385–401. doi:10.1080/01972240290108195

Heath, T. (2010, January 19). U.S. cellphone users donate $22 million to Haiti earthquake relief via text. *Washington Post*. Retrieved from http://www.washingtonpost.com/wp-dyn/content/article/2010/01/18/AR2010011803792.html

Hense, J., & Mandl, H. (2014). Learning in or with games?: Quality criteria for digital learning games from the perspectives of learning, emotion, and motivation theory. In *Digital Systems for Open Access to Formal and Informal Learning* (pp. 181–193). Springer. doi:10.1007/978-3-319-02264-2_12

Khatib, F., & DiMaio, F., & the Foldit Contenders Group. Foldit Void Crushers Group, Cooper, S., Kazmierczyk, M., ... Baker, D. (2011). Crystal structure of a monomeric retroviral protease solved by protein folding game players. *Nature Structural & Molecular Biology*, 18(10), 1175–1177. Retrieved from http://www.nature.com/nsmb/journal/v18/n10/full/ nsmb.2119.html

Llamas, S., & Barberie, S. (2014, April). *eSports Digital Games Market Trends Brief*. SuperData. Retrieved from http://www.superdataresearch.com/blog/esports-brief/

Lynch, K. (2013, October 8). Confirmed; Grand Theft Auto 5 Breaks 6 Sales World Records. *Guinness Book of World Records*. Retrieved from http://www.guinnessworldrecords.com/news/2013/10/confirmed-grand-theft-auto-breaks-six-sales-world-records-51900/

Maddow, R. (2012, January 12). Insensitivity, gaffes dog Romney [Video file]. *NBC News*. Retrieved from http://www.nbcnews.com/video/rachel-maddow/45980205#45980205

Makuch, E. (2014, August 5). World of Warcraft Loses 800,000 Subscribers in Three Months [Blog]. Gamespot. Retrieved from http://www.gamespot.com/articles/world-of-warcraft-loses-800-000-subscribers-in-thr/1100-6421529/

Microsoft by the numbers [Infographic]. (2014). *Microsoft, Inc.* Retrieved from http://news.microsoft.com/bythenumbers/index.html

Mobile Technology Fact Sheet. (2014). *Pew Research Internet Project.* Retrieved from http://www.pewinternet.org/fact-sheets/mobile-technology-fact-sheet/

Gamers use satellites to spot deforestation: New 'Forest Guardians' game relies on crowd to monitor illegal forest destruction [Blog]. (2014, March 28). MobLab Team. Retrieved from http://www.mobilisationlab.org/gamers-use-satellites-to-spot-deforestation/

Montola, M., Nummenmaa, T., Lucero, A., Boberg, M., & Korhonen, H. (2009, September). *Applying Game Achievement Systems to Enhance User Experience in a Photo Sharing Service.* Paper presented at MindTrek 2009, Tampere, Finland. doi:10.1145/1621841.1621859

M+R. (2014). Benchmarks 2014. Retrieved from http://mrbenchmarks.com/

Mt. Auburn Associates. (2011). *Measuring Collaboration: The Benefits and Impacts of Nonprofit Centers.* Prepared for The NonprofitCenters Network. Retrieved from http://www.tides.org/fileadmin/user/ncn/Measuring_Collaboration_Executive_Summary.pdf

Netcentric Campaigns. (2013). *The Moving Maryland Forward Network | Year 2 Final Report.* Washington, DC: Casey.

Netcentric Campaigns. (2014). *PreventObesity.net Analytics February 2014.* Washington, DC: Brooks.

Parker, J. (2007, June 8). Romney Strapped Dog to Car Roof. *ABC News.* Retrieved from http://abcnews.go.com/blogs/politics/2007/06/romney-strapped/

Pereira, C. (2014, January 15). Steam tops 75 million users [Blog]. *IGN.* Retrieved from http://www.ign.com/articles/2014/01/15/steam-tops-75-million-users

Raftopoulos, M., & Walz, S. (2013, April). *Designing events as gameful and playful experiences.* Paper presented at the CHI 2013 Conference, Paris, France.

Rao, V. (2013, April). *Challenges of Implementing Gamification for Behavior Change: Lessons Learned from the Design of Blues Buddies.* Paper presented at the CHI 2013 Conference, Paris, France.

Roeger, K., Blackwood, A., & Pettijohn, S. (2010). *Nonprofit Almanac 2012.* Urban Institute Press.

Sailer, M., Hense, J., Mandl, H., & Klevers, M. (2013). Psychological Perspectives on Motivation through Gamification. *Interaction Design and Architecture(s). Journal, 19,* 28–37. Retrieved from http://www.fml.mw.tum.de/

Schooling, P., & Toth, M. (2013). *The Critical Importance of a Common Language of Instruction.* Learning Science International.

Smith, (2014, April 1). This is what Candy Crush Saga does to your brain [Blog]. *The Guardian.* Retrieved from http://www.theguardian.com/science/blog/2014/apr/01/candy-crush-saga-app-brain

Take-Two Interactive Software, Inc. Reports Record Results for Fiscal Year 2014. (2014). Take-Two Interactive Software, Inc. Retrieved from http://ir.take2games.com/phoenix.zhtml?c=86428&p=irol-newsArticle&ID=1930485&highlight=

Tay, L. (2010, May 18). Employers: Look to gaming to motivate staff. Gamer rewards could boost employee engagement. *itnews*. Retrieved from http://www.itnews.com.au/News/169862,employers-look-to-gaming-to-motivate-staff.aspx

Networking for Policy Change: An Advocacy Training Manual. (1999). The Policy Project. Retrieved from http://www.policyproject.com/pubs/AdvocacyManual.pdf

Thier, D. (2014, May 13). *Grand Theft Auto V* Has Sold Nearly $2 billion. *Forbes*. Retrieved from http://www.forbes.com/sites/davidthier/2014/05/13/grand-theft-auto-5-has-sold-nearly-2-billion-at-retail/

Trygstad, K. (2012, December 23). The Most Expensive House and Senate Races of 2012. *Forbes*. Retrieved from http://www.rollcall.com/news/the_most_expensive_house_and_senate_races_of_2012-220314-1.html?pg= 2&dczone= politics

What makes a successful advocacy network? These Seven Elements [Blog]. (n.d.). Retrieved from http://www.netcentriccampaigns.org

Wikipedia. Service Awards. (2014, October 22) In *Wikipedia*. Retrieved from http://en.wikipedia.org/wiki/Wikipedia:Service_awards

Winston, M. (2001, November). The Importance of Leadership Diversity: The Relationship between Diversity and Organizational Success in the Academic Environment. *College & Research Libraries*, *62*(6), 517–526. doi:10.5860/crl.62.6.517

ADDITIONAL READING

Arjuilla, J., & Ronfeldt, D. (2000). *Networks and Netwars: The Future of Terror, Crime, and Militancy*. RAND Corporation.

Barabasi, A.-I., & Frangos, J. (2002). *Linked: The New Science of Networks*. Perseus Books Group.

Bateman, C., & Boon, R. (2005). *21st Century Game Design*. Cengage Learning.

Benkler, Y. (2006). *The Wealth of Networks: How Social Production Transforms Markets and Freedom*. Yale University Press.

Bisnow, M. (1990). *In the Shadow of the Dome: Chronicles of a Capitol Hill Aide*. William Morrow & Co.

Bissell, T. (2010). *Extra Lives: Why Video Games Matter*. Vintage.

Bostan, B. (2009). Player Motivations: A Psychological Perspective. Computers in Entertainment Special Issue: Media Arts and Games (Part II), 7(2), Article No. 22.

Brafman, O., & Beckstrom, R. (2006). *The Starfish and the Spider: The Unstoppable Power of Leaderless Organizations*. Portfolio.

Burke, B. (2014, April 10). How Gamification Motivates the Masses. Forbes. Retrieved from http://www.forbes.com/sites/gartnergroup/2014/04/10/how-gamification-motivates-the-masses/

Fine, A. (2007). *Momentum: Igniting Social Change in the Connected Age*. Jossey-Bass.

Godin, S. (2005). *All Marketers Are Liars: The Power of Telling Authentic Stories in a Low-Trust World*. Portfolio Hardcover.

Heath, C., & Heath, D. (2007). *Made to Stick: Why Some Ideas Survive and Others Die*. Random House.

Heath, C., & Heath, D. (2010). *Switch: How to Change Things When Change Is Hard*. Crown Business.

Heibeck, T., & Pentland, A. (2010). *Honest Signals: How They Shape Our World (Bradford Books)*. The MIT Press.

Kaplancali, U., & Barbaros, B. (2013). Gaming Technologies for learning; virtual teams and leadership research in online environments. Retrieved from http://www.academia.edu/796173/Gaming_Technologies_for_learning_virtual_teams_and_leadership_research_in_online_environments

Koster, R. (2010). *Theory of Fun for Game Design*. Paraglyph Press.

Leet, R. (2013). *Message Matters: Succeeding at the Crossroads of Mission and Market*. Fieldstone Alliance.

Plenda, M. (2014, July 11). Are Multiplayer Games the Future of Education? *The Atlantic*. Retrieved from http://www.theatlantic.com/education/archive/2014/07/are-multiplayer-games-the-future-of-education/374235/2/

Rigby, B. Rock the Vote. (2008). Mobilizing Generation 2.0: A Practical Guide to Using Web 2.0: Technologies to Recruit, Organize and Engage Youth. Jossey-Bass.

Sachs, J. (2012). *Winning the Story Wars: Why Those Who Tell (and Live) the Best Stories Will Rule the Future*. Harvard Business Review Press.

Sailer, M., Hense, J., Mandl, H., & Klevers, M. (2013). Psychological Perspectives on Motivation through Gamification. Interaction Design and Architecture(s) Journal, *19*, 28–37. Retrieved from http://www.fml.mw.tum.de/

Salen Tekinbas, K., & Zimmerman, E. (2003). *Rules of Play: Game Design Fundamentals*. The MIT Press.

Seely Brown, J., Davison, L., & Hagel, J. III. (2010). *The Power of Pull: How Small Moves, Smartly Made, Can Set Big Things in Motion*. Basic Books.

Shabecoff, P. (2003). *A Fierce Green Fire: The American Environmental Movement*. Island Press.

Tapscott, D., & Williams, A. (2008). *Wikinomics: How Mass Collaboration Changes Everything*. Portfolio.

KEY TERMS AND DEFINITIONS

Advocacy Network: People connected to each other in order to work toward advocacy interests.

Advocacy Network Building: The process of attracting, connecting and supporting advocates so that they can pursue their advocacy interests more effectively.

Advocacy: A use of power or influence to cause or push policy or cultural change.

Cultural Change: A shift in social norms including perceptions around values, economics, behavior or other widely held norms.

Digital Distribution Platforms: A program that allow players to purchase, store and launch multimedia (used here to refer to distribution of video games) from a common location.

Gamification: The use of game elements in non-game contexts.

MMOG: Stands for Massive Multiplayer Online Game; an online video game that can support a large number of players simultaneously.

Policy Change: An actual change in state, local, federal or corporate rules, regulations, legislation or general guidance.

Seven Elements of an Advocacy Network: Netcentric Campaigns' framework for examining ties between individuals to understand if a network exists and if it is functioning at full capacity.

Chapter 12
Digital Development and International Aid:
Are Games Changing the World?

Jolene Fisher
University of Oregon, USA

ABSTRACT

This chapter constructs a historical overview of digital games used for international development. While the decade long use of digital games in this field has seen mixed results, a trend towards gamification has continued. The various approaches to international development taken in these games are analyzed alongside the gaming goals, platforms, and narrative structures. Broadly, this chapter argues that the field of digital development games breaks down into three categories: Developing Developers, Digital Interventions, and Critical Play. Because these games are tied to larger frameworks of development thought, they are an important part of the development discourse and should be critically analyzed, regardless of their success at the level of individual attitude and behavior change. Such an analysis presents a useful way to think about what's happening in the current development field and how the trend towards gamification may impact its future directions.

INTRODUCTION

In a 2010 Ted Talk, award winning social cause videogame designer Jane McGonigal makes a few claims about the power of digital games to change our lives. Actually, she makes a few *really big* claims – claims so big they elicit laughter from the audience – about the power of gameplay to not only change our lives, but to in fact *save* our *world*. She declares that her goal for the next decade is to "try to make it as easy to save the world in real-life as it is to save the world in online games" (McGonigal, 2010). And to do so, she argues, we need to increase our collective time spent playing online games from the current 3-billion hours per-week to a massive 21-billion hours per-week (at least). Only by doing so will we be able to change the world and survive as a species on this planet, according to her calculations. It is clear why the audience laughed. Not because her claims are a joke – to her, and many serious game

DOI: 10.4018/978-1-4666-8651-9.ch012

supporters, they certainly are not –they laughed because her world saving plan seems at once totally radical and yet completely simple: Play online games; make the world a better place. Presto. Of course, it isn't all that simple. Beyond the big question—Can video games change the world?—there are many other, perhaps less obvious, questions that need to be asked, such as who is going to make these games? Who will pay for them? Who will and will not be able to play them, and thus, who will and will not get to actively change the world? And change the world to look like whose idea of better?

Similar questions have long been asked by those involved with (both in terms of practice and critique) the international development industry, the very purpose of which is to change the world in presumably positive ways. While there is general agreement that the goal of international development is to improve the living conditions of society, what is meant by "improvement" and how it should be achieved is widely debated (Melkote & Steeves, 2001). Whatever the "improvements" are deemed to be, innovations in mass communication technology have been considered key tools in achieving them throughout the history of the development industry. Digital games are no exception: although only recently heralded by mainstream media outlets as the "next frontier" for advocacy and aid groups, digital games have already been in use as a tool for international development for almost a decade, with mixed results (Sydell, 2013). The gamification of the international development industry is already underway, but many important questions have yet to be addressed: What is the potential of digital games to change and "save the world" in an international development context? What type of development will games promote? What are the implications of gamification for the development industry at large? And what will it mean for the people whom development is meant to serve? While researchers stop to consider these questions, McGonigal, along with a slew of international development and humanitarian aid organizations, nonprofits, and video game industry stalwarts are forging ahead, making decisions and coming up with their own answers.

This chapter conceptualizes the gamification of the international development industry as a process of game design for "productive interaction," in which games are used to produce development-oriented results in a non-game context (Rughinis, 2013). Through the construction of an historical overview of digital games used for development the various approaches to international development taken in games are analyzed alongside gaming goals, platforms, and narrative structures. While technological trends certainly influence game design and implementation (and will be discussed), more important to an understanding of the gamification of international development is an analysis of how an organization's approach to development defines the various characteristics of the game it creates—Who created the game and why? How is it played? Who is it for? What should it do? And for whom should it do it? Finally, because mass communication technology has played a major (and oft critiqued) role throughout the history of international development, the chapter questions whether gamification is merely the most recent iteration of a longstanding discourse on technology as the *key* to international development, or if it presents truly new implications for the field and its future. An analysis of the themes, successes and failures of digital games used in international development is important for scholars and practitioners in a variety of disciplines, including development communication, international communication, international studies, nonprofit management, public relations, and advertising.

BACKGROUND

Mass communication technologies have been used in international development projects since the very beginnings of the field. Just as innovations in communication technologies have changed the media landscape, so have they impacted how international development projects are carried out, creating new ways for practitioners to spread development messages and inspiring new communication strategies for increasing awareness, influencing favorable attitudes, and affecting behavior change in target audiences (Singhal & Rogers, 1999). Radio, satellite television, websites, phone apps and digital games have all been taken up as tools used to reach a variety of development objectives. Understanding how each new technology is implemented is an important area of study, but more important to an analysis of the gamification of this field is an understanding of the varying conceptualizations of development built into digital games—what development should look like, how it should be done, and by whom. Just as organizations vary in their approaches to development, the games they create target different issues, highlight diverse (and potentially competing) solutions, and call on distinct actors to carry out the work of development. When game designers like McGonigal (2010) say they want to make it "as easy to save the world in real-life as it is to save the world in online games," scholars and practitioners must ask what the work and the end-product of a world saved by games would look like. In order to analyze the gamification of international development the starting point must be an analysis of term "development" itself.

Development, as it currently stands, is a difficult term to define. While most would agree it speaks to an intentional process meant to improve quality of life and create beneficial social change, a standard, contemporary definition of what beneficial change looks like, who is in the best position to enact it, how it should be done, and for whom is less clear (Escobar, 1984; Melkote & Steeves, 2001; Parpart, Rai, Staudt, 2002; Wilkins & Mody, 2001). Communication plays two important roles in the development process. Communication for development refers to the use of communication technologies and processes in strategic interventions that work to facilitate development goals (Wilkins & Mody, 2001). Just as important, however, as the role of communication technologies and processes for carrying out development—communication *for* development—is the role of communication in shaping how we conceptualize development, or communication *about* development (Escobar, 1984; Wilkins, 1999; Wilkins & Mody, 2001). The discourse around development, generated by the institutions and organizations that carry out development work as well as by media representations of development, has important implications in the framing of issues, the selection of target groups, and the defining of possible solutions (Kabeer, 1994; Wilkins, 1999). Wilkins and Mody (2001) point out that the act of defining a target group at whom a project should be aimed (often done by isolating demographic terms such as gender or ethnicity) both generates and reinforces understandings of social responsibility: "For example, when women are highlighted in projects designed to reduce fertility rates, contraception becomes reinforced as a female responsibility" (pp. 392). Reinforcing gender roles such as who is responsible for family planning or childcare is just one of the many ways the discourse *about* development influences the way development is done.

Melkote and Steeves (2001) outline three broad perspectives that have traditionally influenced both the discourse around and the work of development. These perspectives are categorized as *modernization*, which prioritizes capitalist economic development and leans on neo-classical economic theory, *critical* perspectives, which challenge the tenets of modernization and point to structural inequalities as the root of many development issues, and *liberation* or *monastic* perspectives, which emphasize the capacity of individuals to guide and define their own path to development and personal empowerment (Melkote & Steeves, 2001). Development projects using mass communication technologies have drawn on all of these perspectives. What we know as the modern development industry began post-World War II with the creation of the United Nations, the World Bank (originally the International Bank for Reconstruction and Development) and the International Monetary Fund. From an early focus on the post-war reconstruction of Europe, to a Cold War emphasis on eradicating global poverty and winning over the hearts and minds of people in the so-called Third World, to the various contemporary approaches to modernizing the Global South, development has traditionally been conceptualized as an international project directed and led by the Global North (Mody, 2002). From the outset, the use of mass communication technology was conceived of as a key tool in carrying out this project. In his foundational work *The Passing of Traditional Society*, Daniel Lerner (1958) emphasized the role of mass media—specifically radio—in promoting new attitudes and ideas to people living in traditional societies in the Middle East. Exposure to other people, places, and cultures, argued Lerner (1958), would foster the individual attitude and behavior changes necessary to ensure the transition from a traditional to modern (read: Western) society. A proponent of modernization, Lerner saw mass communication technology as a key resource in fostering the development of individualized, rational subjects in the developing world and in promoting industrialization and capitalist economic growth, the end-goal of modernization. Lerner's work had a lasting impact on the field, and, though it has many challengers, many would argue modernization continues to be the dominant perspective in the field today (Melkote & Steeves, 2001).

While the terms and goals of international development were clearly defined according to the theory of modernization early on, from the 1970s onward the discourse around what development should do, and how it should be done, would become much less so (Kabeer, 1994; Melkote & Steeves, 2001; Rogers & Hardt, 2002). Two decades after the formal beginnings of international development it became clear that little *development* had actually taken place; rather, many countries in the area referred to as the Third World were actually worse off than they were before. The development field fractured as critical voices of the 1970s questioned the tenets of modernization and the institutional, top-down approach in which Western development experts identified solutions to local problems. Alternative development approaches began to gain traction and mass communication technologies were employed to reach a variety of objectives, some based on modernization (e.g. the 1975 SITE project), others based on participatory, localized approaches (e.g. the Mahaweli Community radio project). But while each new innovation was held up as *the key* to development, actual development outcomes rarely matched up against the supposed potential of the communication technology, whether it was radio, television, or, most recently, Information Communication Technology (ICT) (Leye, 2009).

The 1990s brought not only an emphasis on alternative development approaches in the field, but also a shift in focus from broadcast media technologies to ICTs (Leye, 2009; Melkote & Steeves, 2001; Ogan et al., 2009). Supported by a discourse on the power of the Internet to democratize access to information, thereby closing the digital divide and empowering individuals, the focus on ICTs has led to a growing trend towards digitization within the development industry (Leye, 2009; Ogan et al., 2009). Like many past communication technology-based projects, a large number of ICT projects have operated on the assumption that by simply providing people in developing countries with access to ICTs their needs will be met, their individual lives will improve, and poor countries will be integrated into the global economy resulting in national development (Leye, 2009; Melkote & Steeves, 2001). However, ICT based projects have faced broad critique for continuing problematic top down, one-way information structures in the development field; for incorporating gender biases that have further entrenched existing social issues; for sustaining "knowledge monopolies" that privilege western ways of knowing; and for ignoring important local contexts and needs (Innis, 2007; Kwami, Wolf-Monteiro & Steeves, 2011; Melkote & Steeves, 2001). Despite these critiques, the popularity of ICT projects for international development has continued to grow (Ogan et al., 2009). Beyond supplying hardware to developing regions, recent projects have worked to produce development oriented software to address a variety of issues: the mobile apps

Esoko, iCow and Farmer's Friend aim to increase farmer productivity by linking farmers in Africa to agricultural information; Zimbabwe's Freedom Fone was developed to help NGOs spread important messages to rural populations; and Senegal's Jokko Initiative connects people in rural communities bringing marginalized voices into community decision making processes. These mobile suites use voice, video, email, and SMS messages to deliver informational content to aid in development projects. Beginning in 2005, a new kind of digital development came along: the use of online and mobile-phone based games. The United Nations World Food Programme game *Food Force* was the first game designed specifically for humanitarian aid (Games for Change, n.d.). Since then, digital games have been developed for use in a variety of international development capacities—from fundraising, to awareness raising, to, most recently, on-the-ground development work. Games, according to mainstream media, are sure to be the next big thing in development, and the number of games recently designed, along with the growing number of nonprofit organizations responsible for creating them, would make it seem the gamification of international development is in full swing (Sydell, 2013). But what, exactly, is the "gamification" of international development? Is it simply the most recent in a long line of communication technology innovations to be taken up and used for traditional development approaches (radio, satellite, ICT hardware, games)? Or does gamification present new implications and opportunities for the field?

The concept of gamification, defined by Deterding et al. (2011) as the use of game design elements in non-game contexts, has gained traction across a wide range of industry and social sectors, in areas as diverse as banking, organizational behavior and employee health, substance abuse prevention, and elementary school education (Bragg, 2003, 2007; Lee, 2012; Schoech, Boyas, Black & Lambert, 2013). In an educational context, games have been looked to as a way to reform traditional schooling systems across the globe, and the use of games as serious learning, assessment and behavior change tools has seen increasing interest as games are predicted to gain widespread use both inside and outside of traditional classrooms (Federation of American Scientists, 2006; Johnson, Smith, Willis, Levine & Haywood, 2011; Lee & Hammer, 2011; McClarty, Orr, Frey, Dolan, Vassileva, McVay, 2012; Schoech, Boyas, Black & Lambert, 2013; United States Department of Education, 2010; Wastiau, Kearney & Van den Berghe, 2009). The potential of digital games as educational and behavior change tools is pertinent to the development industry, which has long used mass communication technologies in its attempts to disseminate educational messages, expose people to new ideas, and facilitate behavior change at the individual level (Lerner, 1958; Melkote & Steeves, 2001; Rao, 1963; Rogers, 1976, 1973 ; Schramm, 1964; Singhal & Rogers, 1999). Although scholars have clearly pointed to the potential for learning within game environments (Gee, 2005; Shaffer, 2004), the potential for the transferability of those learned skills to other contexts outside of the game-world is less clear (Connolly, Boyle, MacArthur, Hainey & Boyle, 2012; Curtis & Lawson, 2002; Engenfeldt-Nielson, 2006, 2007; McClarty, Orr, Frey, Dolan, Vassileva, McVay, 2012; Squire, 2002, 2003). Despite much enthusiasm and positive theoretical support for games as sound learning tools, empirical support for these claims has, thus far, been mixed (Gee, 2003; Malone, 1980; McClarty, Orr, Frey, Dolan, Vassileva, McVay, 2012; McGonigal, 2010; Rosas, Nussbaum & Cumsille, 2003). Thus, the debate on whether games will prove to be effective in traditional learning contexts and/ or for broader educational and behavior change purposes, including such projects within the international development industry, remains to be seen.

As research on the effectiveness of games as tools for learning and assessment continues, a more foundational disagreement over the boundaries of gamification itself is also at play: Does the simple application of game-mechanics and game-like elements (e.g. badges, progress bars, and point systems) to a non-game context qualify as "gamification"? Or is this process merely the "pointsification" of a non-game activity (Robertson, 2010)? If so, then what does gamification actually look like? Rughinis (2013) argues that for the concept of gamification to in fact be tied to games, "it cannot consist soley of game mechanics, but it should also encourage gameplay," thus the mere application of point systems or progress bars that don't encourage actual gameplay are not part of the gamification process (p. 3). This conceptualization moves gamification away from a simple system of applied game-mechanics and instead focuses on the expected outcomes of such a system: "we understand gamification as designing technology-with-intent, and therefore intent matters" (Rughinis, 2013, p. 4). Gamification, in this context, is understood as a system of gameplay oriented towards a "productive purpose"; it is the "structuring and stimulating [of] *productive interaction* – that is, interaction that is ultimately evaluated with the productivity criteria of a non-game activity" (Rughinis, 2013 p. 4). Building on this conceptualization, this chapter argues that the gamification of the international development industry can be understood as a process of "productive purpose," in which games are used to produce development-oriented results in non-game contexts. While the individual games used might fall under the definition of "serious games," as put forward by Deterding et al. (2011), the games taken together, along with the intent of the development industry in using them, makes evident a process of gamification in which gameplay is integrated into the system as a way to conduct or *do* development: games replace traditional development projects that would previously have been carried out in a non-game context, and the gameplay structures and stimulates productive interactions, the results of which are evaluated by traditional development criteria within a non-game context.

The gamification of the development industry, then, is much more than "simple playification" or the use of "playful design" in development projects; rather, it represents a process in which gameplay is utilized with the intent of producing specific development outcomes (Deterding, 2011; Nicholson, 2012; Rughinis, 2013). The purpose of this chapter is to understand what those intended development outcomes are, where they come from, and what they mean for the development industry at large. The work of Bogost (2011) becomes pertinent here as it points to the need for a critical examination of the ideological frames used within games. Beyond text-based narratives, games, argues Bogost (2006), express rhetoric in their rules; they operate according to a "procedural rhetoric" that can be used to either reinforce or contest the ideological frames represented in them (Bogost, 2006). An analysis, then, of the ideological framing of development in digital games as well as the procedural rhetoric used in them is important not only from the perspective of gamification scholarship, but also as a continued critique of the broader international development industry (Escobar, 1984-85; Wilkins, 1999). Historically, mass communication technologies have been used to facilitate myriad approaches to development; they are taken up as tools, the parameters of their use set by an organization's understanding of the best approach to development. It remains to be seen if digital games can in fact have the kind of broad, world changing impact scholars such as Gee (2003, 2005) and McGonigal (2010) hope for. But, if and when they can, it would be, at best, naïve to assume they will be used to create a sort of world saving development utopia beyond the problematic approaches and biases of the international development industry to date. Thus it is necessary to analyze digital games not only in terms of their effectiveness as educational and behavior change tools—they must also be understood and analyzed within a broader context of development discourse and practice in which certain strategies (and certain groups of people) are privileged. To do so, this chapter categorizes 29 digital development games (see Table 1) and closely analyzes examples from each category in order to highlight the various approaches to development taken up within individual games. Looking at these games categorically, as well as alongside one another, it becomes clear how the gamification of the field works to define both how development is talked about and how development is done.

Table 1.

Name	Organization/Funder	Developer	Year	Platform	Category
Food Force	UNWFP	Konami	2005	PC	DD
3rd World Farmer	Arcade Town/NeoDelight	3rd World Farmer Team	2005	Web	CP
Water Game	Tearfund Youth (UK), EU Funding		2005	Web	DD
Darfur is Dying	Reebok Human Rights Foundation	interFUEL, LLC	2006	Web	DD
Ayiti:The Cost of Life	Microsoft/UNICEF	Global Kids, GameLab	2006	Web	DD
Global Kids - Second Life	Global Kids' Online Leadership Program	Linden Lab	2006	Web	DD
Free Rice	UNWFP/sponsors	John Breen	2007	Web	DD
Race Against Global Poverty	Department for International Development	Department for International Development	2008	Web; CD	DD
Heifer Village: Nepal	Heifer International	Beaconfire, Forgefx	2008	Web	DD
Karma Tycoon	JP Morgan Chase		2008	Web	DD
Pamoja Mtaani	Warner Bros./US Government/PEPFAR	Virtual Heroes	2008	PC	DI
MILLEE	MacArthur Foundation, Microsoft, National Science Foundation, Qualcomm, Verizon	Matthew Kam and Team	2009	Mobile Phone	DI
Urgent EVOKE	World Bank Institute	Jane McGonigal	2010	Web	DI
Raise the Village	New Charity Era	New Charity Era; Intersog	2010	iPhone app	DD
Wildfire		Implication	2010	Web	DD
Inside the Haiti Earthquake	Canadian Media Fund, Bell New Media Fund, TVO	PTV Productions, Inc.	2010	Web	DD
Sweet Seeds for Haiti		Zygna	2010	Web	DD
Food Force Facebook	UNWFP	Konami	2011	Facebook	DD
Moraba	UN Women Southern Africa	Afroes	2011	Mobile Phone	DI/L
WeTopia	Mattel, Clorox, Save the Children, buildOn	Sojo Studios	2011	Facebook	DD
The Invisible Hand: The Challenge for a Fair World		TiconBlu, Koala Games, RTM	2011	Web	CP
9 Minutes	Half the Sky/USAID	Mudlark/E-Line Media	2012	Mobile Phone	DI
Worm Attack!	Half the Sky/USAID	Mudlark/E-Line Media	2012	Mobile Phone	DI
Family Values	Half the Sky/USAID	Mudlark/E-Line Media	2012	Mobile Phone	DI
Half the Sky Movement: The Game	Half the Sky/Ford Foundation/Zygna.org	Frima Studio, Show of Force, Games for Change	2012	Facebook	DD
Block by Block & Minecraft	UN	Majong	2012	Web	DI/L
Haki 1: Shield and Defend		Afroes	2012	Mobile Phone	CP
Sidekick Cycle	World Bicycle Relief	GGI; It Matters Games	2013	iPhone app	DD
Haki 2: Chaguo Ni Lako		Afroes	2013	Mobile Phone	CP

DEVELOPMENT GONE DIGITAL

What Games Tell Us about the State of International Development

Video games have been used by international development organizations since 2005. From downloadable PC games played in classrooms to the newest versions designed to work on popular social media platforms such as Facebook, the development industry has spent almost a decade adapting and redesigning games for its cause. While the earliest games focused on raising awareness about development and humanitarian aid issues by targeting students in the so-called developed world, social cause games have evolved over time to include mechanisms for direct-donations; they've embedded real-world-impact features into game play; and, most recently, they've become part of on-the-ground development work in the Global South. The almost decade-long trend of gamification in development has facilitated the rise of non-profits focused on facilitating the creation and distribution of social cause games, a growing web of conferences, awards, and funding for these games, and new relationships between the development industry and the for-profit gaming sector. The creation of social cause games for international development has seen steady support from within the industry, but an important question remains: Are development focused digital games merely the most recent technological packaging for mainstream, modernization development projects? Or do they have the potential to be something new and innovative in the field? The rest of this chapter analyzes specific games in order to understand where and how games have worked or failed, and what their use means for the future of international development. By breaking these games into three categories it becomes clear that the way development is conceptualized within an organization influences both the objectives within the game and the real-world impact the game is meant to have. Digital games as a new technological platform do not in-and-of themselves present a revolutionary approach to international development; rather the way development is conceptualized in the game reinforces or subverts the dominant approaches to development already at play in the world.

Three Approaches: Developing Developers, Digital Interventions, Critical Play

Looking over the types of digital development games produced in the last decade, three broad categories emerge. These categories will be referred to as *Developing Developers*, *Digital Interventions,* and *Critical Play*. The first, *Developing Developers (DD)*, is used to describe games that present a primarily Western audience with development issues situated in the Global South. While their specific projects vary, the purpose of these games is to construct for players an understanding of development—what it should look like and how it should be done—as well as to call on them as actors in the development process, both within the game and beyond.

The second category, *Digital Interventions (DI)*, describes games that are intended for use as on-the-ground development interventions. They target individuals living in the Global South using digital formats as a new avenue for carrying out health, education, and skill based projects. These games can stand-alone or be included as part of larger strategic intervention packages.

Finally, *Critical Play (CP)* refers to games that address structural inequalities as the root cause of underdevelopment and ask players to challenge local and global power structures through game play. These games are often made independently of large international development institutions, or are produced by local companies for a local audience. (See Table 1 for a complete listing of games.)

The strategy of incorporating educational and change-related development messages into entertaining media content has been established as a useful practice in the field (Melkote & Steeves, 2001; Singhal & Rogers, 1999, 2002; Singhal et al., 2004). Klimmt (2009) posits that the unique characteristics of digital games, including multimodality, interactivity, game narrative, social/multiplayer use, and the specific frame of play situations, provide possibilities for engagement that go beyond traditional media, positioning games as potentially effective platforms for carrying educational messages and affecting social change at an individual level. Of course, it is noted that a number of variables must be at play for games to successfully impact social and behavioral change, and there is certainly no guarantee that any one game, or any one gameplay situation, will affect the intended change (Klimmt, 2009). Nevertheless, the potential for the entertaining properties of games to be exploited for use in serious games for social change has generated many supporters for the cause across a variety of fields. The type of social change these games work towards, however, varies depending on the type of development project they're integrated into and the role they are given. These games, then, are tied to larger frameworks of development thought, and, regardless of their success at the level of individual behavior change, they are an important part of the discourse that asks us to imagine development and its goals in particular ways. Analyzing these games categorically presents a useful way to think about what's happening in the current development field and how gamification may impact its future directions.

Developing Developers: Half the Sky and Women in Development

Just by playing the game, you are working to change the world! (Michelle Byrd, former Games for Change co-president, speaking about the Half the Sky Movement: The Game)

In 2005, the United Nations World Food Programme (WFP), along with Japanese game design company KONAMI, launched *Food Force*, the first humanitarian video game to explore the issue of global hunger. Available as a free download, the game was designed for play on a PC and was aimed at children aged 8-13. By 2007, the game, which takes players on six different emergency aid missions that address hunger crises on a fictitious island, had been downloaded over five million times; the game was considered a hit (WFP, 2007, 2011; UN Video Game Sweeps, 2011). *Food Force* put players on a team of emergency aid workers and asked them to take on realistic WFP challenges such as piloting helicopters as part of reconnaissance missions, air-dropping food to remote villages, and delivering truckloads of food through areas dotted with minefields (Video Game Sweeps, 2007). According to John Powell, the WFP Deputy Executive Director for Fundraising and Communications at the time of the game's release, the goal of *Food Force* was to "help children become better global citizens—now and in the future" (Video Games Sweeps, 2007). While it was eventually downloaded over six million times and played by approximately 10 million people, the game's popularity and the flurry of media attention died down after the first two years (WFP, 2011; UN Video Game Sweeps, 2007).

In an attempt to recapture the excitement, the WFP and KONAMI jumped on the growing popularity of social media games like *FarmVille* and created a 2011 *Food Force* update for Facebook. By making use of social media platforms, the WFP was able to integrate "real-world impact" into an online game, allowing players to provide "real meals to hungry children around the globe," by directing real money spent by players to purchase virtual, in-game goods like crops and farming equipment directly to its school meals projects (Online Game 'Food Force', 2011). In the updated *Food Force* players weren't just acting out WFP's work—they were making it happen in the real world. It was one of the first, but it's certainly not the only game that asks players to actively join in on the development process. Through game narrative and/or built in digital-to-real-world actions, *DD* games ask individuals in the Global North to take an active role in ensuring the development of people in the Global South. *Food Force* asks gamers to play out the role of a development practitioner, with the hope that their identification with the WFP in the game will inspire them to support the organization's projects in the non-digital world (Food Force 2005, 2011). Other *DD* games ask players to step into the shoes of a character in the Global South and, after experiencing the difficulties of the situation, take steps to address the development issues they see the character facing (Darfur is Dying, 2006; Raise the Village, 2010; Half the Sky Movement: The Game, 2013) Some use unrelated entertainment games to generate sponsored or individual donations for development organizations (Free Rice, 2007; Sidekick Cycle, 2013). What all of these games have in common is an approach to development based on material aid from individuals in the Global North.

Through their representations of development, these games work as part of a discourse that constructs an understanding of the development project itself—what it looks like, who is in charge of enacting it, what its goals are—as well as an image of who is in need of it. This discourse plays an important role in constructing popular understandings not only of international development, but also of the social power relations between the people involved—namely those in the Global North (the development actors) and those in the Global South (at whom development is aimed) (Cameron & Haanstra, 2008). The way this relationship is presented in *DD* games has the potential to reinforce or challenge dominant representations of the Global South, often referred to as the 'Third World,' as well as existing global political and economic power relations between the North and South (Cameron & Haanstra, 2008). Games, as part of a larger development discourse, have important implications for the way development is understood by a mainstream audience, the type of development projects that are supported and potentially the direction in which the development industry moves. A closer look at a current game makes this argument clearer.

Join the global movement to empower women and girls... Play a groundbreaking game and make a real-world impact (The Half the Sky Movement: The Game Trailer)

The Half the Sky Movement: The Game (HTSMG) launched on Facebook in March of 2013. After four months, the game (which claims to be the first social media game with direct virtual to real-world donations and social action opportunities) reached one million players, and mainstream media outlets were hailing video games as the new frontier for activism and social change (Sydell, 2013).

Based on the best-selling book "Half the Sky: Turning Oppression into Opportunity for Women Worldwide" by journalists Nicholas Kristof and Sheryl WuDunn, the Half the Sky Movement (HTSM) is a multi-donor, multi-media initiative that seeks to "ignite the change needed to put an end to the oppression of women and girls worldwide" (Half the sky, 2013). Along with the Facebook game, the HTSM has developed a suite of educational material including a documentary, three websites, various classroom resources and three mobile phone based development games (to be discussed in a later section). The Facebook game, much like its predecessors *Food Force* (UN, 2005) and *Darfur is Dying* (MTV, 2006), aims to bring development related issues to a mainstream audience. In this case, the HTSMG introduces players to a series of female characters who must negotiate difficult situations brought about by poverty and gender inequality. The goal is for players to "recruit more people into this global movement" as they take Radhika, the first character, on "a journey from oppression to opportunity," (Half the Sky Trailer, 2014). Radhika, a cartoon illustration of a woman from India, clothed in a pink and orange sari, is unable to afford medicine for her sick child. It's up to her, and you as the player controlling her, to find ways to earn money and change her life situation. The game weaves a development narrative based on self-help and empowerment into Radhika's journey as she sells mangoes in the market, applies for a microcredit loan, buys a goat and starts a business selling the goat's milk. The game isn't just about Radhika's participation in economic activities—various moments show her reading to her children and joining a women's empowerment group—but the emphasis in the narrative remains on the importance of Radhika securing a loan and starting a small business.

The story of Radhika helping herself via entrance into the global market reflects a broader trend in development that identifies poor women in the Global South as an "untapped resource" (Moser, 1993; Razavi & Miller, 1995). For many years, women were not included in development discourse or its projects: The early goal of international development was national economic growth and, because men were seen as the productive members of society, all of the resources and benefits of development were directed towards them (Kabeer, 1994; McEwan, 2009; Melkote & Steeves, 2001; Singh, 2007). It wasn't until the United Nations Decade for Women and the subsequent Women in Development (WID) movement of the 1970s that serious attention was given to women's role in international development. The main arguments of the WID movement, which fought for the inclusion of women's issues within the mainstream development framework, were based on ideas of efficiency: development resources should be directed towards women, and women included in development, because of the economic returns the inclusion of women could bring (Kabeer, 1994; Razavi & Miller, 1995). The thinking was, if women were included in the development process and given access to technology, credit, and income generating skills, their economic productivity would benefit development at both local and national levels (Razavi & Miller, 1995). While the focus of WID was on correcting the exclusion of women from the current development system, rather than an analysis of flaws within that system, two different, and sometimes competing, questions arose within the framework: How could development help women, and how could women help development (Connelly, Murray-Li, MacDonald & Parpart, 2002; Melkote & Steeves, 2001; Sen, 1999)?

By highlighting women's potential as economic producers, WID advocates fought against the depiction of women as needy welfare recipients and emphasized the benefits they would bring if both the development space and marketplace took them in (Razavi & Miller, 1995). Contemporary development representations of women as an "untapped resource" (see The Girl Effect, 2014 & HTSM, 2014) have continued to utilize the efficiency argument, heralding the inclusion of women in economic processes as the key to a variety of development issues, including population control, food crisis, environmental degradation, etc.; the WID approach remains the predominant development policy approach to women today (Moser, 1993; Razavi & Miller, 1995). Despite its popularity in mainstream development, the WID approach has seen sustained criticism. Critics argue that it isolates women as a categorical group from the rest of their lives, ignoring the relationships, structures and systems through which women's inequalities are reproduced (Kabeer, 1994). By merely bringing women *into* the existing system, without addressing the structures of power established within it, the WID approach, argue critics, fails to address the real problems women face and does little to support the redistribution of power necessary to achieve gender equity (Kabeer, 1994; Moser, 1993). Unlike WID, many Women and Gender (WAG) and Gender and Development (GAD) approaches critique the structural inequalities at play in the lives of poor women in the developing world, as well as the inherent biases towards men that have been established in the development industry itself (Elson, 1995; Kabeer, 1994; Razavi & Miller, 1995). The gender-oriented approaches to development highlight poverty and women's oppression as products of larger structural inequalities at the local level and as byproducts of global economic power structures (Kabeer, 1994). Approaches to gender and development that take a structural analysis into account question asymmetrical power dynamics at both macro and micro levels, and argue that the integration of women *into* the current development field, without challenging existing power structures, is itself problematic.

There is no one theory of development; the various approaches compete, overlap and borrow from one another often. Nevertheless, certain theories and ideologies, backed by more powerful voices, dominate at different moments in time. The sweeping changes in economic policies of the 1980s brought neoliberalism, with its focus on open markets and free trade, into many arenas, including that of international development. As a development ideology, neoliberalism has had tremendous staying power and its dominance has implications not only for the field but, more importantly, for the lives of women in the Global South. A series of gender-focused policies, dubbed the 'New Policy Agenda,' built on neoliberal economics and liberal democratic theory, helped construct a development discourse that emphasized the incorporation of poor women in the developing world into the global market (Alvarez, 1999). This approach saw self-help projects, microcredit loans and small businesses as the best path towards international development (Alvarez, 1999). Though the many negative impacts of globalization, free trade agreements, and microcredit loans on the lives of poor women have been well documented, a neoliberal approach to development has remained the dominant discourse (Aguilar & Lacsamana, 2004; Karim, 2008, 2011). Whereas the first two decades of development overlooked women altogether, the current neoliberal discourse brings women into sharp focus, framing them as the ultimate "untapped resource." Harnessing this resource, then, becomes the key to solving development issues.

When women are framed as neoliberal, individual entrepreneurs, they become responsible not only for their own development but for the development of society at large (Karim, 2011). The responsibility for this development rests fully with the individual and it is up to her to take the actions necessary to achieve it, regardless of the various constraints (e.g. lack of material resources, skills, education, childcare, etc.) she may face (Brown, 2003). As Brown argues, "The model neo-liberal citizen is one who strategizes for her/himself among various social, political and economic options, not one who strives with others to alter or organize these options" (Brown, 2003, p. 15). A neoliberal approach to development invites women in the developing world into the global marketplace, positing that the solution to development lies within the current system, rather than questioning what negative affects that very system has on peoples' lives or what an alternative system might look like. For instance, microloans, which are a key part of the HTSM's development project and a predominate goal in the HTSMG, are celebrated by many as the key to liberating poor women in the developing world (Sen, 1999). However, research shows that in actuality the micro-credit system oppresses women in the developing world in new ways, benefiting the middle class at the expense of the poorest (Karim, 2008, 2011). Further, a neoliberal discourse of women and efficiency, based on the assumed benefit of women's economic empowerment via entrance into the market, glosses over the role of capitalism and globalization in further burdening women in the developing world (Aguilar & Lacsamana, 2004). While women are discursively constructed as an untapped labor source, in reality they struggle as an already-over-tapped labor source—entrance into the market (where they are generally relegated to underpaid "women's work," often in the informal sector) creates new sources of oppression and inequality (Pearson, 2007). What a development discourse based on neoliberal ideology fails to do is question the asymmetrical North/South power structures and economic flows that contribute to the difficult reality of women in the developing world. Women's inequality, instead of becoming a challenge to a system that is inherently asymmetrical, is depoliticized and is used to promote new market subjects (Elson, 1995; Karim, 2011).

The conceptualization of development presented to the HTSMG's audience is one based on WID-like arguments of efficiency that emphasize the need to integrate poor women into the global market. Through the HTSMG, players meet Radhika, learn about her hardships, and encounter microloans and individual entrepreneurship as the best way to overcome them. Players are asked to join in on the development process, and they do so by unlocking sponsored donations through game play, making personal donations to the game's non-profit partners, and extending the network of developers by inviting friends to play along. In the case of the HTSMG, the audience asked to participate in this development project is overwhelmingly female: 80% of HTSMG players are female, and the top playing country is the U.S. (Half the Sky Movment, 2013). In creating a Facebook based game filled with female characters and illustrated in a distinctly cartoonish, childlike way, the HTSM and Games for Change, the organization that guided the game's production, consciously targeted the traditionally female social media gaming audience: studies show that 55% of all social media game players in the U.S. are female and their average age is 48 (PopCap, 2010; Ingram, 2010). As outlined previously, *DD* games present development issues situated in the Global South to a primarily Northern audience while constructing for them a particular understanding of what development should look like, how it should be done, and what their role is in it. In the case of the HTSMG, development is achieved by individual women in the Global South entering the global marketplace via microcredit loans and small businesses, and the role of the female game player, situated in the Global North, is to facilitate that productivity through material donations. The discourse of poor women and market participation that is woven into the game's narrative is not a new one; in fact it is quite common in the current development landscape. However, the strategic digital choices made by the HTSM have added an additional gendered layer to the development process: through the gaming platform, aesthetics, and narrative choices, individual female players are targeted as key actors in supporting neoliberal development work aimed at individual women in the Global South.

By playing *DD* games, players in the Global North learn what development is, what it should accomplish, and who is in charge of carrying it out. In other words, they learn about their position as developers in the Global North in relation to those in need of development – namely, women in the Global South. Like Kristoff and Wu-Dunn's upcoming book, "A Path Appears," the HTSMG acts as a kind of "road-map to becoming a conscientious global citizen" (Half the Sky, 2014). In this case, the citizen in question is a woman in the Global North, with her hand outstretched, inviting the poor women of the world to enter the global marketplace and join her.

Digital Interventions: Urgent EVOKE, 9-Minutes, Block by Block

The second category, *DI*, describes games intended for use as on-the-ground development interventions. These online and mobile phone games target individuals living in the Global South using digital formats as a new channel for carrying out health, education, and skill based projects. By making use of digital technologies and incorporating intervention messages into an entertaining, gaming context, practitioners hope to reach more people in need, connect people to one another through digital networks, and present information in engaging ways. This section analyzes three such games. The first, *Urgent EVOKE (EVOKE)*, is an online game created by the World Bank Institute, aimed at youth in sub-Saharan Africa (SSA). The second, *9-Minutes*, is a mobile phone game created by the HTSM targeted at women of reproductive age in India, Kenya and Tanzania. The final game, *Block by Block*, is a collaborative urban development project between Minecraft and the United Nations Human Settlements Programme (UN-Habitat).

EVOKE, a "ten-week crash course in saving the world" launched in March of 2010. It was funded by the World Bank Institute (WBI) and directed by award winning social game designer Jane McGonigal (Urgent, 2010). While the goal of the web-based game was "to help empower people all over the world to come up with creative solutions to our most urgent social problems," its target demographic was youth across SSA (Urgent, 2010). Home to 30% of the world's extreme poor, the SSA region of the continent has long been an important area for many international development organizations and projects (World Bank, 2014). But, despite decades of interventions, the area still faces issues of underdevelopment on a vast scale. In creating a free, web-based social network, *EVOKE* hoped to generate a new space for people living within the region to voice their own ideas about, and solutions to, development issues identified as important by the WBI.

That is, if the game could reach them.

Over the course of 10 weeks, 19,386 players from across the world registered to be Agents and were tasked with a new mission each week (Natoma, 2010). The missions dealt with topics such as social innovation, food security, the future of money, empowering women, and preserving indigenous knowledge. The Agents completed their missions over the course of three phases: Learn, Act, Imagine.

In the first phase, Learn, players were connected to information resources and asked to contribute blog posts or upload pictures and videos as evidence of what they had learned about the issue. The Act stage asked players to tackle those same issues by taking real-world action in their own communities and adding additional blog posts, photos, and videos as evidence of the solutions they found. In the final phase, Imagine, players posted a final set of blogs, photos, and videos outlining how they would address the mission's issue locally, and/or globally, in the future. The 142 players who completed all 10 missions were given a WBI certificate and recognized on the *EVOKE* website as a member of the *EVOKE* 2010 graduating class. Players were also given a chance to compete for a series of online mentorships and seed funding for their ideas, but only 72 players submitted applications (Natoma, 2010). While the launch of the game brought in close to 20,000 players, only 1,529 were from SSA. Further, of the SSA players, 1,010 (5.2% of total players) were from South Africa, while the other 519 (2.6% of total players) were from the rest of the SSA countries combined (Natoma, 2010). Compared to the 9,577 players in the United States, or the 1,672 players in Canada, the number of players from the target demographic seems scarce (Natoma, 2010).

In planning for the game's launch, the WBI conducted a focused marketing campaign in South Africa, building strategic partnerships with both university and high school teachers who were asked to use the game as part of their classroom curriculum (Natoma, 2010). The rest of the continent, however, was left to its own devices to discover and engage with the game – an approach that significantly skewed player participation. Not only were South African players overrepresented in terms of total SSA numbers, a post-game evaluation found that they were also more engaged with the game and spent more time playing than all other players in aggregate (Natoma, 2010). But in South Africa, *EVOKE* was not just a stand-alone digital development game; it was part of a larger strategic approach that secured beneficial relationships and reinforced campaign messages. The South African approach, which included the game as one of many intervention channels, was something more akin to a traditional, on-the-ground, social marketing-based development project than a strictly digital development solution. Based on the lack of success across the rest of SSA, the potential of *DI* games to succeed *without* additional resources and social marketing strategies must be questioned.

When compared to the data on South African players, other SAA players' engagement and participation in the game is at best minimal, and often non-existent. It's important to note that even within South Africa the majority of players came from a specific demographic: high-school and university students (Natoma, 2010). Presumably these players came from classrooms targeted by the WBI's outreach campaign, and were instructed to play and given the time and resources to do so. Even if a strategic social marketing campaign were used to spread awareness about the game's existence outside of South Africa, it's unlikely that the majority of would-be-players would have the technological access or skills necessary to do so.

Reliable and affordable Internet access is the most obvious barrier to player participation in *EVOKE*: fewer than 16% of the total population of Africa has access to the Internet (Internet World Stats, 2012). But beyond a player's ability to get online, issues of gender, language, and social class must also be taken into account when considering who gets to play. Limiting factors include language skills (*EVOKE* was programmed in English only, requiring at least functional fluency); access to additional technological resources and equipment skills (players were asked to post evidence as part of the game, including blogs, photos, and video); and Web 2.0 skills, which require a high level of Internet literacy. Players who already have access to the hardware, and have acquired the necessary language, literacy, and technological skills, are most likely players who come from more privileged backgrounds within SSA societies. As noted in the *EVOKE* evaluation, "These characteristics are more likely to be met by users at universities; these users, on this account and on others, are likely to be members of privileged, if not elite, groups within their countries" (Natoma, 2010, p. 32). If the purpose of *EVOKE* is to act as a *DI* that empowers the youth of SSA by creating access to knowledge, social networks, and encouraging problem-solving skills, then the WBI must acknowledge the ways in which an online game that requires access to specific material and immaterial resources is beyond the reach of the majority of SSA youth, ultimately precluding the majority of their target demographic from participating. *EVOKE* did support access via mobile telephone, a more accessible technology platform than computers for many in the region, but phone-based access of the game was rare and the experience was less than satisfactory for those players (Natoma, 2010). A stronger emphasis on mobile play in future iterations of *EVOKE* could be a way to reduce at least some material barriers to participation.

If the goal of *EVOKE* is to empower all SSA youth, the effects of gender as a barrier to play must also be considered alongside more general issues of access, skills and literacy. Although gender as a barrier to play isn't included in the game evaluation, it is mentioned in a post-game blog written by the *EVOKE* development team. In a group blog post titled "What Went Right, What Went Wrong: Lessons from Season 1 of *EVOKE*," Robert J. Hawkins, executive producer and education specialist, writes, "While outreach in South Africa was successful, we would like to reach more participants in Africa outside of SA. Also, we did not reach enough female participants; it was roughly a 75%/25% split. Our graphic novel aesthetic may have been inadvertently skewed to aesthetics that resonate with men" (Urgent, 2010).

While game aesthetics may have been one deterrent, gendered access to education and ICTs, even via informal routes such as cybercafés, is not mentioned by the EVOKE development team (Steeves, forthcoming). This gendered, asymmetrical access, which is a serious issue in South Africa and beyond, has important implications for who gets to join the project, but isn't outlined as a consideration for the EVOKE development team in pre or post evaluations of the game. Setting aside issues of access and education, a recent study on gendered videogame play by young South Africans suggests that men and women's approach to videogame play is influenced by the hypermasculine South African culture (Amory & Molomo, 2012). While both inexperienced men and women chose similar games to play and felt games were designed for both genders, 83% of men and 43% of women thought that men were better at playing video games, an attitude that may impact who chooses to play games like *EVOKE* (Amory & Molomo, 2012). Perhaps even more pertinent to overall player participation is the fact that, when given a selection of games to play, both male and female young South Africans gave the educational game the lowest rating and said they disliked the game's focus on solving complex problems and negotiating nonlinear activities; both men and women reported preferring sports and action-based games to the educational ones on offer (Amory & Molomo, 2012). The question, then, is whether young game players in South Africa or other SSA locations would choose to play the cognitively challenging, problem-solving based game of *EVOKE* if not motivated to do so by a teacher or other organizational leader. Despite these drawbacks, the World Bank is currently partnering with Arizona State University's Center for Science and the Imagination to add additional stories and scenarios to the *EVOKE* game for future deployments in Africa and other regions of the world (Eschrich, 2014). While both ASU and the World Bank are excited about the prospect of "developing solutions to a range of complex global challenges" and "empowering young people," by bringing the work of science fiction authors, futurists, visual artists and subject area experts together to collaborate on new narratives in the games, it is unclear if and how the various barriers to play that specifically affect young people across SSA will be addressed (Eschrich, 2014). It seems that the potential for web-based *DI* games to stand alone as digital development tools, without additional on-the-ground, strategic communication outreach or an emphasis on facilitating access to necessary resources, is seriously limited by the various barriers to play faced by target audiences. *DI* games, as one part of a larger intervention package, may prove to be an engaging new channel for development related messaging and network building, but additional tools and strategies are necessary to ensure that engagement.

While *EVOKE* was designed for computer based play, other organizations are looking to mobile phones as a way to bring *DI* games to their target audience. Based on the best-selling book "Half the Sky: Turning Oppression into Opportunity for Women Worldwide" by journalists Nicholas Kristof and Sheryl WuDunn, the HTSM has developed into a multi-donor, multi-media initiative that seeks to "ignite the change needed to put an end to the oppression of women and girls worldwide" (Half the sky, 2014). With guidance from social cause game producers Games for Change, and funding from USAID, the HTSM developed a series of educational, mobile phone based games aimed at the "hardest to reach": millions of mobile-phone users in the developing world who lack regular access to computer and land-line telephone technology (Half the Sky, 2014). More than 65% of the world's 3.5 billion mobile phone users live in developing countries, making mobile technology an attractive platform for bringing projects that address development issues (Half the Sky, 2014). With the mobile phone game *9-Minutes*, the HTSM hopes to tackle the high rates of child and maternal mortality in India and East Africa, an issue that has long been a focus of international development and aid agencies. The United Nations' Millennium Development Goals (MDGs), a 2000 agreement among 189 countries, put international pressure on development organizations and national leaders to address and reduce child and maternal deaths by two-thirds and three-quarters, respectively, by 2015 (Dasgupta, Tureski, Lenzi, Bindu, & Nanda, 2012). According to the United Nations, the concerted efforts put towards these issues have had positive effects: there has been a global decrease in under-five child mortality rates since 1990, and all nations across the globe have made progress in decreasing maternal mortality rates (UN, 2014). However, the impact of these issues remains most damaging in the less developed regions of the world—an *increasing* proportion of all child deaths are occurring in SSA and Southern Asia, and the maternal mortality rate in developing regions is still 14 times higher than that of developed regions (UN, 2014). Beyond increasing access to health care facilities and trained health care personnel, development practitioners have seen a need to encourage attitude change towards antenatal care, institutional delivery, and nutrition in order to address the issues in these regions (Dasgupta et al., 2012). But how can organizations get this important health information to millions of women living in developing regions? And how can they present this information in such a way as to encourage attitudinal and behavioral change? For organizations like the HTSM, mobile phone-based games present a way to try and do just that.

The HTSM is looking to mobile phone based games as a new way to address traditional development concerns in the developing world. Because of the high penetration of mobile phones and the popularity of digital games on mobile devices the HTSM saw mobile phone based games as a new way to bring maternal and child health development projects to communities in need in India, Kenya, and Tanzania. By incorporating pregnancy health information into a game, the organization hoped to take advantage of the potential of edutainment games to affect positive health-related changes, and influence women who had been overlooked or untouched by traditional health messaging approaches (Dasgupta et al., 2012).

The pregnancy health-education game *9-Minutes* exposes players to information on safe-pregnancy and delivery by condensing the nine-month gestational process into a nine-minute game that rewards players for keeping a mother-to-be and the baby inside her safe and healthy (Half the Sky, 2014). The game was initially designed for players in India, a country that, despite major strides, still has extremely high maternal and neonatal death rates (Dasgupta et al., 2012). Beyond increasing knowledge around pregnancy health, the game encourages players to change their attitudes and behavioral intentions towards the game's prescribed safe pregnancy and delivery methods as they work through the decisions an expectant mother must make (Dasgupta, 2012). The main emphasis in the game is on accessing appropriate pre and antenatal services provided by trained professionals in an institutional setting. Given that research on the effectiveness of educational video games in changing attitudes and behaviors has shown mixed results, USAID and the HTSM commissioned a pre-launch study to look at the effects of the game on players, compared to players who were exposed to the game alongside a broader intervention package (Dasgupta et al., 2012). The study included a group of 608 married Indian women, aged 18-44, who were pregnant or intended to become pregnant within a year, and 308 men married to women who were pregnant or intended to become pregnant within the next year (Dasgupta et al., 2012). Half of the participants only played the game, while the other half played the game, watched a video, and were part of a short discussion group. The study found that participants who were exposed to the *9-Minutes* intervention package, which included the video and a post-game discussion along with gameplay, as well as those who were exposed to the game only, had measurable changes in knowledge, attitudes and behavioral intentions towards the HTSM's prescribed pregnancy and delivery actions. Participants felt more positively about institutional delivery and its benefits and were more confident in their ability to access such care. They also showed significant increase in their knowledge of the number of optimal antenatal care visits and key *9-Minutes* pregnancy "do's" and "don'ts" (Dasgupta et al., 2012). Perhaps because mobile games were already a fairly popular form of entertainment for participants (41.6% reported playing a mobile game at least once per week, and 23.1% reported playing on a daily basis), the *9-Minutes* game proved to be a successful way to deliver relevant information to a target audience (Dasgupta et al., 2012). However, based on the previously mentioned study of players' game preferences (Amoroy & Molomo, 2012) it remains to be seen if players will choose to engage with educational-based *DI* games if not encouraged to do so through non-digital, on-the-ground interventions or as part of focus groups, as was the case in the study referenced here.

While the previous two games were created specifically to achieve development related goals, a recent collaboration between the United Nations Human Settlement Programme (UN-Habitat) and Mojang's popular game *Minecraft*, provides an example of how *DI* might make use of already existing gaming technology. February of 2013, the UN-Habitat held its first *Minecraft* workshop in Kibera, a large slum in Nairobi, Kenya (Westerberg, 2013). The organization had been working with the Nairobi City Council for almost a year to come up with solutions for upgrading a popular multi-use site, but community members had difficulty picturing what the upgrades would mean for their individual uses and needs (Westerberg, 2013). The site is home to a school, a vegetable garden, a community hall, sports facilities, and a market space, and the various people who use it had conflicting opinions on what kinds of upgrades would be truly beneficial (Westerberg, 2013). Almost a year after the project started, the UN-Habitat decided to integrate *Minecraft*, a game that lets players construct spaces in a 3D open world, into its projects. The game is not designed around achieving specific goals; rather it operates as an open world that allows players to freely design and interact with the space. For UN-Habitat, using *Minecraft* to help communities virtually move through the upgraded space proved helpful in moving the project forward: Pontus Westerberg, a UN-Habitat staff member at the 2013 workshop, said "The mood in the room changed when the 3D model was presented – for the first time the participants could really understand what was in front of them. And some disagreements that had been doing on for a while were also finally settled!" (Westerberg, 2013). After the success of this first collaboration, UN-Habitat and Mojang joined together in a four-year partnership to support the Sustainable Urban Development Network, which aims to upgrade 300 public spaces by 2016 (Block by Block, 2014). Current projects include upgrading a play park and creating a public urban walkway in Les Cayes, Haiti, improving water system management and revitalizing public spaces in Kirtipur, Nepal, and turning a neglected garden into a playground that will be maintained and preserved by the community in Mumbai, India (Block by Block, 2014). By incorporating existing gaming technology into its projects, UN-Habitat is using *Minecraft* as a tool for participatory project planning and facilitating inclusive processes in which community members help redesign spaces for communal use (Block by Block, 2014). The UN-Habitat has found an innovative way to use existing gaming technology as a tool for participatory project planning that includes community members in visualizing, designing, and carrying out improvements to their public spaces. In using *Minecraft* to facilitate inclusive processes in which community members help redesign spaces, UN-Habitat has presented an interesting possibility for new directions in the gamification of development: rather than creating a game with specific, predetermined development goals, the use of an established, open world game might allow for greater participation from those at whom the development project is aimed and a more active role for participants in determining the processes and goals of such a project.

Critical Play: Haki, 3rd World Farmer and The Invisible Hand

The final category, *CP*, refers to games that address structural inequalities as the root cause of many development issues. Rather than presenting players with specific development solutions, as seen in *DD* and *DI* games, *CP* games highlight the broad, complex systems of power that impact the lives of individuals in complex ways. Corporate environmental degradation, exploitative trade policies, corrupt government practices, and the inherent instability of an ever fluctuating agricultural market are all pointed to as factors at play in the lives of the world's poor. Through *CP* games, players learn about these forces and the obstacles they create for those living in the Global South. Unlike the previous examples, these games are often made independently of large international development institutions and/or are produced by local companies for a local audience. They're also the least represented of the three types of digital development games. This section looks at several *CP* games and game producers.

The mission of Afroes, a digital media production company, is to create "uniquely African mobile applications and tools for social development agencies" (Afroes, 2014). From its bases in South Africa and Kenya, Afroes consciously works to make content that is contextually relevant and easily accessible for youth audiences across the two countries. Games like the *Haki* series, which addresses environmental rights, and *Moraba*, a game about gender based violence modeled after a traditional African board game, work to instill messages of "hope and possibility in young people" through content that celebrates "Africa's rich heritage" (Afroes, 2014). In order to reach as many young people as possible, and to ensure they engage those with the least access to information resources, all of Afroes' content is created for mobile platforms. Currently, the company is working with the Nelson Mandela Children's Fund "Champion for Children" campaign on a series of mobile phone games about child safety, as well as an SMS platform for increased public participation in reporting child abuse and promoting child safety (Afroes, 2014). Afroes was born out of a Southern African startup incubator called mLab which provides mobile technology entrepreneurs with support and resources to help them create and distribute locally made content for audiences in Southern and Eastern Africa (mLab, 2014).

In Afroes' recently released *Haki 2: Chaguo Ni Lako*, players join the Underground, "a group of heroes who strive for peace and tranquility" as they attempt to stop Mboss, an evil mastermind trying to "destabilize the country by causing discontent, disunity, disharmony and civil unrest" (Afroes, 2014). Players are asked to be a "champion of peace" by solving puzzles and quizzes that hold clues to how they can stop Mboss from reaching his destructive goals (Afroes, 2014). The game is a follow-up to *Haki 1: Shield and Defend*, which gave players the opportunity to "mend the wrongs that tear at the social fabric and in the process defend [their] rights" (Afroes, 2014). The first in what will eventually be a series of similarly themed games, *Haki 1* focuses on the protection of environmental rights as an important factor of human rights. Players go on a mission to stop illegal logging in a protected forest. The game opens with a call to action, "...Oh the beautiful green forest is being destroyed. Defend our Haki (Rights). Join the Underground!" (Haki, 2014). Players get points for defeating the evil agents and are told, "Haki (Justice) gives you wings" (Haki, 2014). The *Haki* series was designed in partnership with the TUVUKE Peace Initiative, a "countrywide collective platform" launched in 2011 to promote peaceful, free and fair elections in Kenya (Haki Facebook, 2014). After the violence that erupted during the 2007-2008 Kenyan elections, TUVUKE saw a need for community involvement in order to ensure more peaceful and inclusive election processes in the future, and to proactively deter the gender based violence that followed the previous election (TUVUKE, 2014). The *Haki* games are meant to bolster this process by inspiring a commitment to peace and tolerance in Kenyan youth. In a promotional YouTube video for *Haki 2* a young man playing the game tells others to "Get inspired. Think about your actions. Find out where you stand. Play for peace" (Haki 2 Video, 2014). For TUVUKE, a focus on responsible and accountable media in Kenya is one way to "contribute to entrenching a sustainable peace movement for inclusive public participation and a culture of constitutionalism" in the country (TUVUKE, 2014). Games like *Haki 2* are meant to further the movement's goals and improve the relationships between land and natural resource dependent communities, engage youth in civil governance processes and support safer, peaceful, diversified communities (TUVUKE, 2014). The construction of the issues, goals, and actors at play in processes of development is radically in *CP* games than in *DD* and *DI* games. For instance, rather than offer up ways to enter the global capitalist system, as seen in the HTSMG, *Haki* looks at how such a system negatively affects those living in the developing world. By highlighting global corporate environmental degradation and illegal logging as systems that create and reinforce issues associated with underdevelopment, the game asks players to fight against the causes of underdevelopment, rather than consider solutions that deal only with the symptoms of such issues. Like traditional critical approaches to development as outlined by Melkote and Steeves (2001), *CP* games challenge the tenets of modernization and point to structural inequalities as the root of underdevelopment.

While some *CP* production companies, such as Afroes, create *CP* content for a local audience, other games in this category have been created for a global audience, independent of large gaming and development institutions. The game titled *3rd World Farmer*, developed as a student project at the IT-University in Copenhagen in 2005, is one such example. In *3rd World Farmer*, players manage an African farm while navigating "some of the real-world mechanisms that cause and sustain poverty in 3rd World countries" (3rd World, 2014). Varying crop prices, draughts, disease, poachers and raids by armed guerilla forces all impact the wellbeing of the farm and the family tending it. As the game developers note, in the real world, it's not always possible to get ahead, even if you do make the "right" choices:

Just like real people are dying from starvation in desperate situations they never asked to be put in, all it takes for things to go wrong in this game is one bad harvest, an unfortunate encounter with corrupt officials, a raid by guerillas, a civil war, a sudden fluctuation in market prices, or any of the many other game events, that might never happen to families in industrialized countries (3rd World, 2014).

In addition to buying crops and livestock, the game's farmers can also purchase crop insurance, support schools and infrastructure, or, for 800 game dollars, secure a representative who supports peace, health and prosperity. In-game purchases don't translate to real-world donations or aid, as in some *DD* games, but players can get involved with development projects directly by visiting the organizations and relief agencies on the game's "Take Action" page. In one of the game's many scenarios, a sickness in the family cancels out the positive outcome of the year's farming: "You have spend [sic] most of your savings of [sic] expensive foreign medicine, praise patent laws! (One family member loses health, and living costs increase this year)" (3rd World Farmer, 2014). Rather than pointing to what development should do and how it should be done, *3rd World Farmer* highlights the various economic, environmental and political constraints that impact the lives of poor people living in a rural, developing region. Although the game's narrative is represented using characters in a single family, players learn that obstacles to development go beyond individual choices and actions.

Italian production company Koala Games' approach takes this analysis a step further, highlighting the inequalities built into the global economic system and its impacts on people in the developing world. As dramatic music plays, the trailer for Koala Games' *The Invisible Hand: Challenge For A Fair World* opens with a provocative question, "Did you ever wonder what globalisation [sic] means?" (Invisible, 2014). The game uses an analysis of the international cocoa trade to critique the free market policies of the World Trade Organization (WTO), offering up Fair Trade as a much needed alternative to an inherently biased system. Players carry out 13 missions that take them from the "opulence of the Western nations to the injustices of the South of the world" while fighting a global consumerist lifestyle and exploitative labor and trade policies (Koala Games, 2014). The game teaches players to recognize problematic multinational products, reveals harsh working conditions in African cocoa plantations, and shows players how to help the Fair Trade market (Invisible, 2014). The final mission in the game involves sneaking into the WTO in order to change the system, an act that is radically different from those in *DD* and *DI* games that emphasize entrance *into* the global marketplace, rather than disruption to it, as the solution to development. For a donation, players can download the video game; the player then chooses how his or her donation will be spent. In a system that the Invisible Hand's website refers to as a "new economic sustainable model," players decide how much (if any) of their money will go to ongoing development of the game and how much will go to an NGO project of their choosing (Koala Games, 2014).

The emphasis in *CP* games is on highlighting and analyzing issues of structural inequality—whether economic, political, or social—that affect those living in the developing world. Rather than proposing development solutions within the current framework, *CP* games ask players to scrutinize and fight against the existing system, pointing to asymmetrical power dynamics within it as a cause of underdevelopment. Much like the traditional critical approaches to development, *CP* games offer up critiques, rather than specific solutions. Because of this, the same critique that is lodged against critical development theory can be applied to *CP* games—an analysis of power structures is important to our understanding of development, but if it doesn't work to provide alternatives, how does it help move the field forward? As Wilkins and Mody (2001) argue, a critical approach to development communication, one that questions the guiding theoretical and epistemological conventions of the field, is integral to development work, but it must not come at the expense of an awareness of "the very material resources people need to survive" (p. 386). Thus, *CP* games that propose alternatives alongside a critique of current development systems may have more viability in development practice.

SOLUTIONS AND RECOMMENDATIONS

According to both entertainment-education and gamification scholars, digital games have the potential to be effective tools in carrying out development projects. By integrating educational and social change messages into an entertaining format, games can affect positive attitudinal and behavior change at an individual level, as seen in HTSM's *9-Minutes*. Further, games can be used to bring development related issues to new audiences, as well as to bring more people into the development process and facilitate more participatory practices. However, for games to be effective digital development tools, it's important to consider issues of access, relevancy, and representation. By producing games for mobile phones, organizations have the opportunity to reach a broader audience, as most in the developing world have greater access to mobile devices than to computers or landline telephones. If computer-based games are used, they should be integrated into a strategic project that facilitates access to the necessary hardware and skills. Communication and outreach campaigns that establish partnerships with classrooms and encourage the use of games in their curriculum have greater chance for success than games launched without additional on-the-ground resources.

In constructing awareness and fundraising games for audiences in the Global North, organizations should be critically aware of the impacts of the development solutions they propose, as well as the effects of their particular development discourse on audiences' understanding of the relationship between the Global North and South. Including issues of structural inequalities and global power dynamics into game narratives has the potential to create a more nuanced understanding of the issues at play, as well as the role of players in both exacerbating those issues and in generating solutions to them. Finally, organizations should look to the potential of games to generate greater participation in development at the local level. By using the model of open world games, organizations should consider how they might create game environments that allow communities and individual players to have greater control in shaping the development projects meant to serve them. When it comes to the question of "Who should get to decide what 'better' looks like?" the answer should be "those who will live with it." Beyond participation in gameplay, organizations should work to support local game production industries to produce culturally relevant content. Not only does this help ensure that games are relevant to players' lives, both in terms of the narratives presented and the issues addressed, it also works to support growing industries and the development of technical skills at the local level.

FUTURE RESEARCH DIRECTIONS

As digital games continue to gain popularity in the field of international development several important areas of research should be addressed. First, the new relationships established between the private, commercial gaming industry and the development industry must be analyzed. These relationships have important implications for how development projects are conceptualized and carried out. Further, funding for game production by large international development organizations impacts the production and viability of local gaming industries, as well as the role of local communities in constructing an approach to development on their own terms.

A continued analysis of individual games is important to an understanding of how games reinforce or subvert dominant narratives of development, and thus how they close off or make room for innovative approaches to both talking about and doing development.

Because material resources are necessary for gameplay, an ongoing analysis of the production processes of digital hardware, such as mobile phones and computers, is important to understanding how such production impacts social and environmental conditions in the developing world. The mining of precious metals, the disposal of e-waste, the global supply chain and the labor practices at various stages of production aggravate and sustain many of the issues development games are meant to address.

CONCLUSION

This chapter outlined how digital games, as the most recent iteration in a long line of technological tools, are used to facilitate myriad approaches to development. Broadly, the field of games created over the last decade breaks down into three categories: Developing Developers, Digital Interventions, and Critical Play. Each has important implications for how our collective knowledge of international development is constructed, as well as who stands to benefit from such an understanding. As tools, digital games are used to further development discourse and carry out development practice, the parameters of which are set by the organizations responsible for producing them.

Game play can affect attitude and behavior change, and they certainly play an important role in constructing a discourse that frames the development issues, solutions, and actors at play, all of which has the potential to impact the lives of real people in the developing world in meaningful ways. But, it's also apparent that games take many approaches to development—at best, many of these approaches miss their target audience altogether; at worst they reinforce problematic social and environmental conditions. To assume that increasing gameplay exponentially will save the world and lead to a sort of development utopia is naïve at best. Rather, we must continue to critically analyze these games in order to understand how they operate as communication *for* development and *about* development, as well as how they can be used to successfully attend to the goal of development: the advancement of socially beneficial goals (Wilkins & Mody, 2001).

REFERENCES

Afroes website. (n.d.). Afroes Games. Retrieved 5 June 2014 from http://www.afroes.com/games/

Aguilar, D. D., & Lacsamana, A. E. (2004). *Women and globalization*. Amherst, NY: Humanity Books.

Alvarez, S. E. (1999). Advocating feminism: The Latin American feminist NGO 'boom.' *International Feminist Journal of Politics*, *1*(2), 181–209. doi:10.1080/146167499359880

Amory, A., & Molomo, B.Amory & Molomo. (2012). Gendered play and evaluation of computer video games by young South Africans. *Gender, Technology and Development*, *16*(2), 177–196. doi:10.1177/097185241201600203

Block by Block website. (n.d.). Block by Block. Retrieved from http://blockbyblock.org/about

Brown, W. (2003). Neo-liberalism and the end of liberal democracy. *Theory & Event, 7*(1).

Cameron, J., & Haanstra, A. (2008). Development made sexy: How it happens and what it means. *Third World Quarterly*, *29*(8), 1475–1489. doi:10.1080/01436590802528564

Connelly, M. P., Murray-Li, T., MacDonald, M., & Parpart, J. L. (2002). Feminisms and development: Theoretical perspectives. In J. Parpart, P. Connelly, & V. U. Barritreau (Eds.), *Theoretical perspectives on gender and development* (pp. 51–160). Ontario, Canada: International Development Research Centre.

Connolly, T. M., Boyle, E. A., MacArthur, E., Hainey, T., & Boyle, J. M. (2012). A systematic literature review of empirical evidence on computer games and serious games. *Computers & Education*, *59*(2), 661–686. doi:10.1016/j.compedu.2012.03.004

Curtis, D., & Lawson, M. (2002). Computer Adventure Games as Problem-solving Environments. *International Education Journal*, *3*(4), 43–56.

Dasgupta, P., Tureski, K., Lenzi, R., Bindu, K., & Nanda, G. (2012). Half the Sky Movement multimedia communication initiative: An evaluation of the 9-Minutes mobile game and video. Washington, DC: C-Change/FHI 360.

Deterding, S., Khaled, R., Nacke, L., & Dixon, D. (2011). *Gamification: Toward a definition*. Retrieved from http://hci.usask.ca/uploads/219-02-Deterding,-Khaled,-Nacke,-Dixon.pdf

Egenfeddt-Nielsen, S. (2007). Third genderation educational use of computer games. *Journal of Educational Multimedia and Hypermedia*, *16*(3), 263–281.

Egenfeldt-Nielsen, S. (2006). Overview of research on the educational use of video games. *Digital Kompetanse*, *3*(1), 184–213.

Elson, D. (1995). *Male bias in the development process*. Manchester, UK: Oxford University Press.

Eschrich, J. (2014, July 8). ASU center partners with World Bank on sci-fi, gaming and social innovation. Retrieved from https://asunews.asu.edu/20140708-world-bank-evoke

Escobar, A. (1984). Discourse and Power in Development: Michael Foucault and the Relevance of his Work to the Third World. *Alternatives, 10*(3), 377–400. doi:10.1177/030437548401000304

Federation of American Scientists. (2006). Summit on educational games: Harnessing the power of video games for learning. Retrieved from http://www.fas.org/programs/ltp/policy_and_publications/summit/Summit%20on%20Educational%20Games.pdf

Gaible, E., & Dabla, A. (2010, December 13). Project Evaluation EVOKE. The Natoma Group. Retrieved from http://siteresources.worldbank.org/EDUCATION/Resources/ProjectEVOKE-evaluation-final-16oct11.pdf

Gee, J. P. (2003). What video games have to teach us about learning and literacy. *ACM Computers in Entertainment, 1*(1), 1–4. doi:10.1145/950566.950595

Gee, J. P. (2005). Good video games and good learning. *Phi Kappa Forum, 85*(2), 33-37.

Gudykunst, W. B., & Mody, B. (2002). *Handbook of international and intercultural communication.* Thousand Oaks, CA: Sage Publications.

Haki 1: Shield and Defend [Mobile game]. (2012). *Afroes Games*. Retrieved from http://www.afroes.com/games/

Haki 2: Chaguo Ni Lako [Mobile game]. (2013). *Afroes Games*. Retrieved from http://www.afroes.com/games/

Haki 2 Video. (2013, February 10). *Afroes Games*. Retrieved from https://www.youtube.com/watch?v=1UvkProPh-U

Haki Facebook page. (n.d.). Afroes Games. Retrieved from https://www.facebook.com/pages/Afroes-Games/185317804821699

Half the Sky Movement. The Game (2012, January 1). Half the Sky Movement. Retrieved from https://www.facebook.com/HalftheGame

Mobile Games: Reaching the hardest to reach. (n.d.). Half the Sky Movement. Retrieved from http://www.halftheskymovement.org/pages/mobile-games

Hermund, F., Toubro, O. F., Nielsen, J. E., Spycher, R., & Salqvist, B. (2005). *3rd World Farmer: A simulation to make you think.* [Online game]. Retrieved from http://www.3rdworldfarmer.com/About.html

Hewmanne, S. (2006). Participation? My blood and flesh is being sucked dry: Market-based development and Sri Lanka's Free Trade Zone women workers. *Journal of Third World Studies, 23*, 51–74.

Ingram, M. (2010, February 17). *Average social gamer is a 43-year-old woman.* Retrieved 5 June 2014 from http://gigaom.com/2010/02/17/average-social-gamer-is-a-43-year-old-woman/

Internet World Stats. (2012). Miniwatts Marketing Group. Retrieved from http://www.internetworldstats.com/stats.htm

Johnson, L., Smith, R., Willis, H., Levine, A., & Haywood, K. (2011). The 2011 Horizon Report. Austin, Texas: The New Media Consortium. Retrieved from http://net.educause.edu/ir/library/pdf/HR2011.pdf

Kabeer, N. (1994). *Reversed realities: Gender hierarchies in development thought.* London, UK: Verso.

Karim, L. (2008). Demystifying micro-credit: The Grameen Bank, NGOs, and Neoliberalism in Bangladesh. *Cultural Dynamics, 20*(1), 5–29. doi:10.1177/0921374007088053

Karim, L. (2011). *Microfinance and its discontents: Women in debt in Bangladesh.* Minneapolis, MN: University of Minnesota Press.

Klimmt, C. (2009). Serious games and social change: Why they (should) work. In U. Ritterfeld, M. Cody, & P. Vorderer (Eds.), *Serious games: Mechanisms and effects.* New York, NY: Routledge.

Kwami, J., Wolf-Monteiro, B., & Steeves, H. L. (2011). Toward a 'macro-micro' analysis of gender, power and ICTs: A response to Mickey Lee's feminist political economic critique of the human development approach to new ICTs. *The International Communication Gazette, 73*(6), 539–549. doi:10.1177/1748048511412290

Lee, J. J., & Hammer, J. (2011). Gamification in education: What, how, Why Bother? Definitions and uses. *Exchange Organizational Behavior Teaching Journal, 15*(2), 1–5.

Lerner, D. (1958). *The passing of traditional society: Modernizing the Middle East.* Glencoe, IL: Free Press.

Leye, V. (2009). Information and communication technologies for development: A critical perspective. *Global Governance: A Review of Multilateralism and International Organizations, 15*(1), 29-35.

Malone, T. W. (1980). What makes things fun to learn? Heuristics for designing instructional computer games. *Proceedings of the 3rd ACM SIGSMALL symposium and the first SIGPC symposium on Small systems – SIGSMALL '80 (pp. 162-169). New York, New York: ACM Press.* doi:10.1145/800088.802839

McClarty, K. L., Orr, A., Frey, P. M., Dolan, R. P., Vassileva, V., & McVay, A. (2012). A literature review of gaming in education: Research report. Pearson. Retrieved from http://researchnetwork.pearson.com/wp-content/uploads/Lit_Review_of_Gaming_in_Education.pdf

McEwan, C. (2009). *Postcolonialism and development.* New York, NY: Routledge.

McGonigal, J. (Speaker). (2010, March). Jane McGonigal: Gaming can make a better world [TED Talk]. Retrieved from http://www.ted.com/talks/jane_mcgonigal_gaming_can_make_a_better_world.html

Melkote, S., & Steeves, H. (2001). *Communication for development in the Third World.* Thousand Oaks: Sage Publications.

mLab (n.d.). Retrieved 5 June 2014 from http://www.mlab.co.za/about/

Moser, C. (1989). Gender planning in the Third World: Meeting practical and strategic gender needs. *World Development, 17*(11), 1799–1825. doi:10.1016/0305-750X(89)90201-5

Raise the Village [Mobile app]. (2010). New Charity Era. Retrieved from http://purposefulgames.info/post/17528621162/raise-the-village

Nicholson, S. (2012). *A user-centered theoretical framework for meaningful gamficiation.* Paper presented at the June 2012 meeting of Games+Learning+Society 8.0, Madison, WI.

Ogan, C., Bashir, M., Camaj, L., Luo, Y., Gaddie, B., & Pennington, R. et al. (2009). Development communication: The state of research in an era of ICTs and globalization. *International Communication Gazette, 71*(8), 655–670. doi:10.1177/1748048509345060

Online game "Food Force" Puts Players on Front Lines of Hunger. (2011, November 30). *World Food Program USA*. Retrieved from http://wfpusa.org/blog/online-game-food-force-puts-players-front-lines-hunger

Parpart, J., Rai, S., & Staudt, K. (Eds.). (2002). *Rethinking empowerment: Gender and development in a global/local world*. New York, NY: Routledge.

Pearson, R. (2007). Reassessing paid work and women's empowerment: Lessons from the global economy. In A. Cornwall, E. Harrison, & A. Whitehead (Eds.), Feminisms in development: Contradictions, contestations and challenges, (201-213). London, UK: Zed Books.

Playerthree (2005). *Food Force* [Flash game]. Retrieved from http://www.food-force.com/

PopCap. (2010). Social gaming research. Information Solutions Group, p. 1-72. Retrieved from http://www.infosolutionsgroup.com/2010_popcap_social_gaming_research_results.pdf

Rao, L. (1963). Communication and development: A study of two Indian villages. Doctoral Dissertation. University of Minnesota, St. Paul.

Razavi, S., & Miller, C. (1995, February). From WID to GAD: Conceptual shifts in the Women and Development discourse. Presented to the United Nations Research Institute for Social Development Programme. Retrieved from http://iupuebla.com/Doctorado/Docto_Generoyderecho/MA_Doctorado_Genero/MA_from%20wid%20to%20gad.pdf

Rogers, E. M. (1973). *Communication strategies for family planning*. New York, NY: Free Press.

Rogers, E. M. (1976). Where are we in Understanding the Diffusion of Innovations? In W. Schramm & D. Lerner (Eds.), *Communication and Change* (pp. 204–222). Honolulu: University Press of Hawaii.

Rogers, E. M., & Hardt, W. B. (2002). The histories of international, intercultural and development communication. In W. B. Gudykunst & B. Mody (Eds.), *Handbook of international and intercultural communication*. Thousand Oaks, CA: Sage Publications.

Rosas, R., Nussbaum, M., Cumsille, P., Marianov, V., Correa, M., & Flores, P. et al. (2003). Beyond Nintendo: Design and assessment of educational video games for first and second grade students. *Computers & Education, 40*(1), 71–94. doi:10.1016/S0360-1315(02)00099-4

Rughinis, R. (2013). Gamification for productive interaction: Reading and working with the gamification debate in education. Presented at the June 2013 Information Systems and Technologies (CISTI) 8th Iberian Conference. Retrieved from http://www.academia.edu/5758624/Gamification_for_Productive_Interaction._Reading_and_Working_with_the_Gamification_Debate_in_Education

Ruiz, S., York, A., Stein, M., Keating, N., & Santiago, K. (2006). *Darfur is Dying* [Flash game]. Retrieved from htpp://www.darfurisdying.com

Schoech, D., Boyas, J. F., Black, B. M., & Elias-Lambert, N. (2013). Gamification for Behavior Change: Lessons from Developing a Social, Multiuser, Web-Tablet Based Prevention Game for Youths. *Journal of Technology in Human Services, 30*(3), 197–217. doi:10.1080/15228835.2013.812512

Schramm, W. (1964). *Mass Media and National Development*. Stanford, CA: Stanford University Press.

Sen, A. (1999). *Development as freedom*. Oxford, UK: Oxford University Press.

Shaffer, D. W. (2004, June). Epistemic frames and islands of expertise: Learning from infusion experiences. Paper presented at the International Conference of the Learning Sciences (ICLS), Santa Monica, CA. Retrieved from http://epistemicgames.org/cv/papers/epistemicframesicls04.pdf

Singhal, A., & Rogers, E. M. (1999). *Entertainment-education: A communication strategy for social change*. Mahwah, NJ: Lawrence Erlbaum Associates, I.

Squire, K. (2002). Cultural framing of computer/video games. *Game Studies, 2*(1). Retrieved from http://gamestudies.org/0102/squire/%3fref%3dHadiZayifla

Squire, K. (2003). Video games in education. *International Journal of Intelligent Games & Simulation, 2*(1), 49–62.

Steeves, H. L. & Kwami, J. (in press). ICT4D, gender divides and development: The case of Ghana.

Sydell, L. (2013, November 29). For advocacy groups, video games are the next frontier. NPR. Retrieved from http://www.npr.org/blogs/alltechconsidered/2013/11/29/247515389/for-advocacy-groups-video-games-are-the-next-frontier

The Invisible Hand: The Challenge for a Fair World [Flash game]. (2011). TiconBlu. Retrieved from http://www.koalagames.it/koalaweb/pages/TIH/Index.aspx

Tuvuke Initiative. (2014). Retrieved from http://tuvuke.org/pages/Tuvuke_Initiative.htm

Urgent EVOKE (2010). Retrieved from http://www.urgentevoke.com/

Transforming American education: Learning powered by technology. (2010, November). U.S. Department of Education. Retrieved from http://www.ed.gov/sites/default/files/netp2010-execsumm.pdf

Wastiau, P., Kearney, C., & Van den Berghe, W. (2009). How are digital games used in schools? *European Schoolnet*. Retrieved from http://games.eun.org/upload/gissynthesis_report_en.pdf

Wilkins, K. G. (1999). Development discourse on gender and communication in strategies for social change. Retrieved from http://nabilechchaibi.com/resources/Karin.pdf

Wilkins, K. G., & Mody, B. (2001). Reshaping Development Communication: Developing communication and communicating development. *Communication Theory, 11*(4), 385–396. doi:10.1111/j.1468-2885.2001.tb00249.x

KEY TERMS AND DEFINITIONS

Critical Play: Describes games that address structural inequalities as the root cause of underdevelopment, asking players to challenge local and global power structures through gameplay.

Developing Developers: Describes games that construct an understanding of development for an audience in the Global North by presenting them with development issues situated in the Global South. These games often ask players to participate directly in development projects through material donations.

Development Interventions: Describes games that are intended for use as on-the-ground health, education and skill based development interventions in the Global South.

Digital Development: An approach to international development that uses digital channels in place of, or in addition to, traditional on-the-ground development practices.

Global North: Refers to the area of the world often defined as the First World, or the developed world.

Global South: Refers to the area of the world often defined as the Third World, or developing world.

Serious Games: Digital games created as tools for achieving educational, problem-solving, or skill training goals.

Social Cause Games: Digital games created as tools for social change. These games address social issues, work for social justice, and/or present prescribed solutions to social problems.

Chapter 13
Gamified Self:
Factors Influencing Self-Tracking Technology Acceptance

Rachelle DiGregorio
Big Spaceship, USA

Harsha Gangadharbatla
University of Colorado, USA

ABSTRACT

Gamified self has many dimensions, one of which is self-tracking. It is an activity in which a person collects and reflects on their personal information over time. Digital tools such as pedometers, GPS-enabled mobile applications, and number-crunching websites increasingly facilitate this practice. The collection of personal information is now a commonplace activity as a result of connected devices and the Internet. Tracking is integrated into so many digital services and devices; it is more or less unavoidable. Self-tracking engages with new technology to put the power of self-improvement and self-knowledge into people's own hands by bringing game dynamics to non-game contexts. The purpose of this chapter's research is to move towards a better understanding of how self-tracking can (and will) grow in the consumer market. An online survey was conducted and results indicate that perceptions of ease of use and enjoyment of tracking tools are less influential to technology acceptance than perceptions of usefulness. Implications and future research directions are presented.

INTRODUCTION

One day, Robin Barooah decided that his addiction to coffee had gone too far. His relationship with the caffeinated substance had gone on for almost 28 years, and he was beginning to suspect that it was causing his mood swings and productivity crashes. He had lasted this long as a coffee drinker because he believed that it helped him be productive, but it didn't seem worth it anymore.

Robin's previous attempts to quit "cold turkey" had proven unsuccessful, so he crafted a new plan to stop drinking coffee for good. His plan consisted of brewing the same pot of coffee every morning, but

DOI: 10.4018/978-1-4666-8651-9.ch013

gradually decreasing the amount he consumed by 20 milliliters every week. Robin stuck to this precise scheme for almost four months until he was down to less than one ounce of coffee per day. That is when he decided he could stop drinking it altogether.

For an unrelated experiment, Robin was also keeping track of his daily hours of productivity. One day, a few months after he quit drinking coffee, he was feeling unproductive and thought a quick cup of caffeine would get him back on track. Before following through with this urge, Robin decided to examine how his productivity had previously been affected by coffee. He used his collected data to produce the chart below, which is very clear that caffeine has a negative influence on Robin's ability to concentrate and be productive (Barooah, 2009).

By comparing his change in coffee intake to his hours of productivity, Robin had turned his body and self into an experiment and knowingly or unknowingly employed game dynamics to achieve the desired outcome. He set goals and used numbers and self-tracking to better understand his behavior and see the consequences of his actions. His meticulous method for collecting his personal data eventually paid off in the form of self-knowledge (Wolf, 2010).

Robin Barooah's story is one of many examples of a practice called self-tracking, in which a person collects and reflects on their personal information over time and thereby brings game dynamics to non-game contexts. Robin's experience is one of the many examples described in an article titled, "The Data-Driven Life," in *The New York Times Magazine* in 2010 and was penned by Gary Wolf, the co-founder of a subculture movement devoted to self-tracking called the Quantified Self or Gamified Self. Robin's story is one of the quintessential examples of this interesting phenomenon.

There is no doubt that self-tracking has become a subject of major media interest. To accompany its appearance in *The New York Times*, many other prestigious and influential news outlets have covered the Quantified Self, including *The Economist, Wired, The Atlantic, The Guardian*, and *Forbes*. As another example, the volume of Google searches for the term "quantified self," for example, has spiked repeatedly since 2011, reflecting repeated surges of news references starting in mid-2010. Even renound scientist and inventor Stephen Wolfram is talking about self-tracking. In a recent blog post, Wolfram claimed: "It won't be long before…everyone will be doing it, and wondering how they could have ever gotten by before" (Wolfram, 2012).

What does all of this attention on self-tracking mean? Is everyone destined for a life of meticulously monitoring their caffeine intake and measuring it against their daily productivity? Will they all be consulting spreadsheets for diet advice before they know it? Is gamifying self the next big thing?

The answer is no, probably not. The real growth of self-tracking (and reason for its extensive media attention) is happening within the consumer product sector. Self-tracking dynamics are making a (relatively) quiet ascension within the technology industry through consumer products that help people easily track their fitness, finances, sleep, food, productivity, and many other types of information. These devices, mobile applications, and websites are called commercial self-tracking tools. They are usually simple, designed to be easy enough for anyone to use, oriented around a goal (such as weight loss), and their prime audience reaches beyond the scope of early technology adopters.

The production of self-tracking services by large corporations is one of the most obvious indications that the practice is growing in the consumer market. Nike first integrated strike sensors into its running shoes in May 2006 and now has a multi-faceted Nike+ product line including sensors for shoes, mobile applications, wearable wrist monitors, and more. Other large companies, such as Nokia and Garmin, had success marketing a range of new tracking products employing Global Positioning Systems (GPS), heart monitors, and other technologies during the subsequent five years. The fact that these global companies are investing heavily in self-tracking tools suggests that the trend of self-tracking has grown significantly in the consumer market and will continue to grow in the future.

A quick comparison between a tool that helps people track their fitness, like Nike+, and Robin Barooah's self-experiment reveals that the use of commercial self-tracking tools can be quite unlike highly personalized Quantified Self projects, even though both activities fall under the umbrella of self-tracking. People who use commercial self-tracking tools usually operate under a different self-tracking philosophy than members of the Quantified Self or Gamified Self movement. They use self-tracking tools to reach goals and improve themselves, instead of seeking self-knowledge. The development of self-tracking within the consumer market looks very different from the Quantified Self movement, which encourages self-trackers to seek self-knowledge.

This distinction is not very clear in the media coverage of self-tracking. News articles often refer to commercial self-tracking tools as part of the Quantified Self or Gamified Self without clarifying the difference. For example, the Nike+ FuelBand that was released in January of 2012 is a simple wristband that tracks users' progress towards a daily activity goal. Influential culture and technology blogs, including BetaBeat, Cool Hunting, and PSFK, referenced the Quantified Self in their coverage of the Nike+ FuelBand, misleading readers to think of the in the same way (Kamer, 2012). While "quantified self" is a convenient term to reference the rising influence of self-tracking activities and the gamified self movement, it is often used in an ambiguous way to describe commercial self-tracking tools, too. This is especially true when news articles link their discussion to the Quantified Self website, where experimenters like Robin Barooah share their experiences.

Commercial self-tracking tools are the focus of this research because of their potential to develop and influence the culture of the general population. While growth is also likely to happen within the Quantified Self community, it will be more specialized and among more of a pioneering, early-adopter, and cutting-edge audience. The purpose of making the distinction between the Quantified Self movement and commercial self-tracking tools is to show that an analysis of consumer self-tracking tools must occur outside of the Quantified Self context. If the most influential growth is happening in the consumer sector, it needs to be understood outside of the self-tracking philosophies of self-experimenters and early adopters. That is the purpose of the following research.

The research presented in this paper seeks to understand how self-tracking will grow in general acceptance by examining perceptions of self-tracking tools and the factors that influence these perceptions. This is accomplished through a case study of fitness tracking tools, which are the most pervasive type of commercial self-tracking tool. Using Technology Acceptance Model (TAM) as a framework, we investigate the factors that drive acceptance and use of self-tracking tools.

BACKGROUND

The trend of self-tracking and Gamified Self is not a new phenomenon, but it has seen a large growth in popularity and interest in the past decade. This movement is all about using technology that is capable of data acquisitions and introducing game dynamics on all aspects of an individual's life including but not limited to health and fitness, finances, physical and emotional states (e.g., arousal, mood, heart rate etc.). There are many tools available both online and in the form of mobile apps that facilitate this gamification of self. A few examples of self-tracking tools are Nike+ FuelBand, Mint.com, Foursquare, RunKeeper, GymPact, Fitbit, and Fitocracy. This growth, in terms of technology acceptance, is occurring in a variety of venues, from communities of early adopters to commercial product lines. Our society's current cultural and technological environments support the progress of self-tracking and make this a great time for the practice to thrive.

While self-tracking in its current form may seem like a recent development, the practice has existed for many centuries. From the time when hieroglyphics were the main medium for recording personal stories, to when diaries came into use in the 11th Century, to the current self-tracking practices people use today, humans have always been keeping track of themselves (Makdisi, 1986). Self-tracking is currently enjoying an invigoration with the development of digital tools that boost collection and reflection of personal data. Developments in technology and current cultural attitudes take self-tracking to new levels. New technologies have made the practice of self-tracking more useful, easier, and fun, and they are proving to be both popular and influential. The descriptions that follow provide a framework for the technological and cultural developments that have helped, and will continue to help, the gamification of self and self-tracking thrive.

Technological and Cultural Support for Gamified Self

In general, technological devices are becoming a bigger part of the average person's life. From laptops to smartphones, technology is more powerful and easier to use than ever before. Technological progress plays a large role in the development and acceptance of self-tracking tools. Advances in sensor technology make self-tracking capabilities more compact, cheaper and accordingly more accessible for the average person. Increasing accessibility is a key factor that can influence the acceptance of self-tracking technology. If the tools are easier to acquire, people are more likely to accept them. Paired with the pervasiveness of access to the Internet, advanced sensor technology can communicate with numerous devices so that collected personal data can be processed and visualized for reflection (Li, 2011).

The communication between technological devices on a large scale leads to the concept of ubiquitous computing. Ubiquitous computing is a computer-human interaction (CHI) model in which computing technology is integrated into everyday objects and activities. The model evolves society beyond the desktop computer paradigm, towards a world where computers are effortlessly integrated into the human environment, to a point where they are almost invisible to users (Borriello, 2008).

With the help of ubiquitous computing, personal information can be collected actively, passively, comprehensively, and most of all, easily. Sensor technology and pervasive Internet access have provided the practice of self-tracking with a huge boost, allowing for the advancement of tracking tools. Mobile phones, specifically smartphones, which connect to the Internet, are an important example of the combination of sensors and connected technology. With built-in accelerometers and constant access to the Web, smartphones are a great tool for self-tracking. Many popular commercial tracking tools exist as mobile phone applications, including Foursquare and MapMyRun. Additionally, smartphone usage is growing considerably, a fact that is evident in the number of smartphone shipments, which increased globally by 61.3% between 2010 and 2011 ("Global Mobile Statistics"). These technological advances and increased use of mobile technology support the growth of self-tracking enabled by digital tools by making the practice easier and more accessible.

Self-tracking tools are also affected and supported by many technology trends, most notably, the increase in social and gaming dynamics as characteristics of digital tools. According to Pew Internet Research, 66% of online adults use social media sites while over half of adults, and 80% of young adults, play video games (Smith, 2011; Lenhart, 2008). These cultural interests have been translated to technological development and now many devices and services, including self-tracking tools, incorporate social and gaming dynamics. They make self-tracking more fun and a more natural fit into existing popular culture.

Technological advances continue to make self-tracking practices more useful, easy and enjoyable. The evolution of sensor technology, increasing access to the Internet, the rise of ubiquitous and mobile technology, along with the increased incorporation of social and gaming dynamics into tools, support the development and adoption of self-tracking. The way people and culture interact with technology is always changing and these changes also influence the acceptance of self-tracking technology. Currently, society is enjoying an increase in people's comfort and familiarity with technology due to its pervasiveness in their everyday lives. This is especially true for young people, for whom technology is an expectation, not an innovation. Their existing digital lifestyles break down barriers towards technology acceptance, and more specifically, self-tracking adoption. The current cultural environment also supports the self-discovery and self-improvement philosophies that are so important to self-tracking practice.

Comfort with technology is a key component of self-tracking technology acceptance because if people are not comfortable with it, they will not use the tools. The growth in digital literacy, driven by increasing access to the Internet, has led to a culture of self-empowerment through discovery online. The Internet has taught people to find and share information on their own, without the help of institutions or the barriers of bureaucracy. This cultural shift in knowledge seeking means that many people feel that they don't need government or academic validation to trust information (Czerski, 2012). In the same way, people are now less likely to find a doctor's evaluation necessary in their journey towards a healthier lifestyle through fitness. These sentiments directly relate to self-tracking practices, in which people are empowered to discover information about themselves on their own.

As a result of high digital literacy and social media use, people are increasingly "embrac(ing) multiple modes of self-expression" (Kohut, 2010). This means that expressing their identity through quantified data is a behavior that can come easily to many people. Their quantified information can be just another piece of their curated identity. Cultural ideologies like self-empowerment through digital networks and identity curation align with the philosophies of self-tracking, thus supporting the practice's increased adoption.

The growth of self-tracking is simultaneously occurring in a variety of settings. Two notable and very different venues of expansion are The Quantified Self community and the commercial self-tracking tool market. The following section describes the characteristics of each environment of self-tracking.

The Quantified or Gamified Self

The first place that digital self-tracking theories and practices were purposefully brought together is a website called The Quantified Self. This website has become the premier resource for information about self-tracking. The growth of the website, along with the formation of a community around it, has positioned The Quantified Self at the cutting-edge of self-tracking experimentation and early adoption. The website was founded by technology thought leaders and journalists Kevin Kelly and Gary Wolf in 2007 as a "users group" for self-tracking. By creating The Quantified Self (QS) to be a users group, the founders established it as an "informal but deeply engaged learning (community) operating outside the normal channels of academic and commercial authority" (Wolf, 2010).

Besides the online community, the QS community also meets offline, in an annual Quantified Self conference and 59 meetups around the world. These offline gatherings are a testament to the growth of QS. Between 2007 and mid-2012, the meetup membership list grew from two individuals to over nine thousand (Quantified Self). The QS community acts as a resource for all kinds of tracking practices, but caters to highly specialized and experimental types of self-tracking. The community's most active members use the website to share and inspire cutting-edge technologies and personalized exploration through numbers. When self-trackers share their personal projects at QS meetups and on the website, they are asked to structure their presentations in three parts, by answering the questions: "What did you do?," "How did you do it?," and "What did you learn?" (Wolf, 2009, 2010). These three questions provide insight into the ideologies by which The Quantified Self operates.

The first question suggests that each self-tracker's experience is unique. This is common in the QS community because trackers usually begin their exploration with a question they want to answer about themselves. Past QS projects have begun with questions like "Does my coffee intake affect my productivity?" "How do the words I use to describe reality reflect my personality type?," or "Does moving my legs while at the computer change how many breaks I need to take?" (Wolf, 2010; Novak, 2012; Leavitt, 2012). The questions tend to be specific to the person's own life, so, like the community, the tracking experiences are very diverse. The second question speaks to the wide variety of methods QS trackers use to answer their questions. From one tool, to many tools, to self-made tools, to hacked tools, the methods people use to collect and reflect on their personal information are almost endless. The third question best illustrates the QS philosophy, and consequently, its motto: "Self-knowledge through numbers." For QS trackers, the purpose of self-tracking is to better understand themselves (Li, 2011).

The lack of a fourth question, which could ask something along the lines of "What did you change?" further clarifies the QS philosophy. For QS trackers, self-tracking is not about changing their behavior, but simply understanding it. As Gary Wolf (2010) wrote in his article for *The New York Times*, self-tracking in the Quantified Self context is "not ... a tool of optimization, but of discovery." While behavior change is often a result of increased self-knowledge, it is not an emphasis or requirement in the QS community.

The active participants of the Quantified Self community are on the cutting edge of self-tracking innovation. They are early adopters of technology and their self-experiments run the gamut from monitoring caffeine intake to measuring movement's effect on sitting endurance. Their signature approach to self-tracking usually begins with a personal question, uses a variety of tools to explore that question, and ends with reflection on the results of the exploration. Quantified Self trackers place little emphasis on changing their behavior after reflection, and that is what sets them apart from the people who use commercial self-tracking tools.

Commercial Self-Tracking Tools

The enthusiasm and interest for self-tracking seen within The Quantified Self community is also manifested in the variety of commercial tools that have been specifically developed for self-tracking. These tools are making their way into general markets and are the main channel by which the awareness of self-tracking behavior is growing beyond the scope of early adopters. Similar to the tracking methods of the QS community, commercial self-tracking tools are very diverse. Tracking can be facilitated by anything from a wearable device, to a website, to a mobile phone application. Access to these tools is increasing with the pervasiveness of mobile phone use as well as the trend for large retailers, like Best Buy and Sports Authority, to put these tools on their shelves. Simple tools like pedometers are part of this category, but many of the tools are identified by their brand names.

A few notable examples of these commercial self-tracking tools are the Nike+ FuelBand, FitBit, and Foursquare. The Nike+ FuelBand is a wearable device that looks similar to a bracelet and tracks daily activity through a metric called NikeFuel. It displays the wearer's Fuel points along with a progress bar to show them how close they are to their daily activity goal ("Nike+ FuelBand"). The Nike+ FuelBand is a less complex version of Fitbit, a wearable monitor that records steps taken, calories burned, distance traveled, and sleep efficiency. Fitbit is less expensive and collects more personal data, but doesn't have the big brand name like the FuelBand. Both tools have online and mobile platforms where data collected over time can be reflected on. Foursquare is a free mobile application that tracks a person's location. With the tap of a button, people can "check-in" wherever they are and receive points, badges, or even designation as that location's "mayor." The application is social so people can share their locations with friends and compete for the highest scores or number of mayorships within their social circle.

All of these commercial tracking tools and more fall under the self-tracking umbrella with The Quantified Self or Gamified Self community, but most of them are used in ways that depart from the QS philosophy. Because commercial tracking tools are usually built for a general audience, they cannot be easily customized to address trackers' specific and personal questions, which is a key component of the QS approach to self-tracking. They are best put to use by helping trackers change their behavior. Considerations for change and action are often built directly into the products. Especially with tools like the Nike+ FuelBand, data is collected for the sole purpose of helping the user reach and improve upon a set goal. The Quantified Self is only one side of the self-tracking spectrum and while the philosophy doesn't consider optimization to be a priority, behavior change is present in many other areas along the spectrum, like with commercial self-tracking tools.

THEORETICAL FRAMEWORK

The goal of the research presented in this chapter is to understand how technology acceptance of self-tracking tools works. This area of exploration is necessary in order to assess how self-tracking tools will develop in the consumer market. The research begins with literature reviews of Ian Li's "Stage-Based Model of Personal Informatics" and Fred D. Davis' "Technology Acceptance Model." These models provide insight into the process of tracking one's personal information and the process of accepting and using a new technology. Then, the choice to focus on fitness tracking tools as a case study for self-tracking tool acceptance is explained and elaborated.

The literature review and fitness discussion provide background information for the survey, which is the last section of the paper. The primary research conducted through the survey evaluates the factors that influence self-tracking technology acceptance.

The Self-Tracking Process

To assess the factors that influence self-tracking tool acceptance, it is helpful to establish how the process of self-tracking works and observe how tools can enable it. Self-tracking practices and the tools that facilitate them are diverse and depend on each self-tracker's personal process. Ian Li's (2010, 2011) research from the Human-Computer Interaction Institute at Carnegie Mellon University informs the discussion of these distinctions. His research also provides a theoretical model that outlines the process of self-tracking by identifying the stages that a tracker goes through on their way to self-knowledge and/or optimization.

While every self-tracker's experience is unique, Ian Li's (2010, 2011) "Stage-Based Model of Personal Informatics" identifies the stages that all trackers go through as they collect and reflect on their personal information (note: personal informatics is another name for self-tracking and gamified self). Li's (2010, 2011) identifies five stages of self-tracking.

The first stage of self-tracking is preparation. During this stage, a person finds motivation to collect their personal information, determines what kind(s) of information they want to record, and how they want to record it. Once they have decided on these things, they move on to the collection stage, in which they collect their personal information. Once the information is collected, a person must prepare, combine and transform the data for reflection. This stage is called integration. Next comes the reflection stage in which the person reflects on all of the personal information that was collected. The last stage, the action stage, is when the person decides what to do with the information and insight they found in the reflection stage. It could be that during the action stage, they make a decision to change their behavior based on their discoveries in the reflection stage (Li, Dey, Forlizzi, 2010).

This model makes the difference between the Quantified Self philosophy of self-tracking and the use of commercial tracking tools clearer. The distinction between these two types of self-tracking lies in the action stage. Commercial tracking tools usually revolve around self-improvement and behavior optimization, which reflect on collected data and suggest actions to take as a result. The Quantified Self community limits its focus to the reflection stage, which answers the last of their three main questions: "What did you learn?"

Most self-trackers utilize tools to help them collect and reflect on their personal information. These tools are often digital and vary in a number of different characteristics. They make collection much easier through automation and data organization. They also make reflection more valuable through their increased capacity to create meaningful visualizations and suggest paths of action (Li, 2011).

Both the collection and reflection stages can be manually driven by the user, automated by the tool, or a combination of both. Each stage can operate with any number of facets, from the collection or reflection of one type of information to many types of information. Collection and reflection processes can also vary in the amount of customization they allow, and their hedonic (pleasure-oriented) or utilitarian (productivity-oriented) design. Commercial self-tracking tools usually have a similar set of characteristics. They are, for the most part, automated in collection and reflection, requiring little work on the part of the user. They usually collect between one and four types of information and have limited options for customization. The most popular commercial self-tracking tools are a mix of hedonic and utilitarian design to provide value to users, but also make the process of tracking fun.

The self-tracking process, especially as it relates to the use of commercial self-tracking tools, is an important factor in the discussion of tracking technology acceptance. In order to assess tool acceptance, an understanding of tool use is necessary. The next section lays the groundwork for a discussion and exploration of commercial self-tracking tool acceptance.

Technology Acceptance Model

The main goal of this research is to understand how people accept self-tracking technology. A theoretical model called the "Technology Acceptance Model," which identifies the factors that influence technology acceptance, aids in an investigation of this subject. "The Technology Acceptance Model," developed by Fred D. Davis in 1985, is a theoretical framework for describing the "motivational processes that mediate between system characteristics and user behavior" (Davis, 1985). It was created in order to understand the process of technology acceptance and to provide a basis for acceptance testing. This research will utilize the Technology Acceptance Model (TAM) in a survey to better understand how people's perceptions of a specific technology influence their acceptance of that technology.

The Technology Acceptance Model was chosen for this research based on its history of use in technology analysis. Davis's first article on TAM has been cited by 1569 other articles and is considered to be the "most influential and commonly employed theory for describing an individual's acceptance of information systems" (Lee, Kozar, & Larsen, 2003). The extensive academic employment of TAM has proven its robustness; as the model has been tested on a variety of technologies including word processors, email clients, and websites, with a diversity of control factors such as gender and environment (Lee, Kozar, & Larsen, 2003). The TAM has "ceaselessly evolved" since its introduction, with at least 8 other scholars besides Davis making significant changes and amendments (Lee, Kozar, & Larsen, 2003). As a result, current versions of TAM are very complicated and include more information about technology acceptance than is required for this research. The following description of TAM covers the basic information necessary for a preliminary study on technology acceptance.

The TAM defines technology acceptance to be the actual use of a technology system. If a person has accepted a technology, it means that they have used it repeatedly. The first version of TAM explains a person's attitude towards using a certain technology as a function of their perceived usefulness and perceived ease of use of the tool, which are influenced by the tool's design features. The person's attitude towards using the technology then influences their acceptance and actual use of the tool. These relationships are demonstrated in the figure 1 below, modified from Davis's 1985 paper on TAM.

This research focuses on the perceptions of tools that eventually influence acceptance. Davis defines perceived usefulness as "the degree to which an individual believes that using a particular system would enhance his or her…performance." Perceived ease of use is defined as "the degree to which an individual believes that using a particular system would be free of physical and mental effort" (Davis, 1985, p. 26). In 1992, Davis and his colleagues Richard Bagozzi and Paul Warshaw experimented with another factor of influence on technology acceptance, a person's expected enjoyment. They defined expected enjoyment as "the extent to which the activity of using the (technology) is perceived to be enjoyable in its own right" (Davis, Bagozzi, Warshaw, 1992). This factor fits well with the analysis of modern technology, as many current technological devices and programs incorporate some amount of fun-oriented components.

Two variables can be relevant and potentially exogenous to perceived usage (PU) and perceived ease of use (PEU) in the specific context of self-tracking tools—personality and demographics. For example, locus of control is a personality variable that refers to the extent to which individuals believe they can

Figure 1.

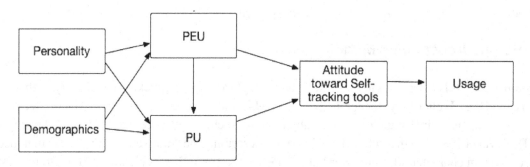

control the events that affect them (Phares, 1976; Rotter, 1966). Individuals who believe they can control the events of their life are said to have an internal locus of control whereas those who believe that life is controlled by environmental factors, which they cannot control, are said to have an external locus of control (Rotter, 1966, 1975). For self-tracking, it can be hypothesized that individuals high on internal locus of control would see these tools as more useful than someone high on external locus of control.

However, based on the simplified description of the Technology Acceptance Model, and for the purposes of this research, technology acceptance is considered to be function of a user's perceived usefulness, perceived ease of use and expected enjoyment. In other words, the current study applies the theory of the TAM to the technology used for self-tracking. An efficient way to do this is to examine a specific example of self-tracking that currently has high acceptance and to measure the perceptions of that type of technology. Fitness tracking technologies were chosen for this task because their high level of consumer acceptance can provide a strong example for evaluation.

Fitness Tracking Tools

Of the many different kinds of personal information that people track, physical activity data is one of the most popular. The sheer number of tools that people use for fitness tracking is a testament to this statement, along with the fact that many big brands are investing in the production of fitness tracking tools. Based on their impressive prevalence, fitness-tracking tools offer a valuable case study for the acceptance of self-tracking technology in general. There are many reasons why fitness-tracking provides an interesting case study, but the primary reason it was chosen for this research is its relatively long and sustained popularity in the technology market, which has given the category more of a chance to mature than newer ones. By looking at the relatively established category of fitness tracking, we can speculate how the acceptance of newer categories of self-tracking will mature.

A comprehensive guide to self-tracking tools on the Quantified Self website includes a list of 124 tools under its "fitness" category. The list is not exhaustive and new tools are being developed everyday, so the number is likely to be much higher. The success of fitness tracking is also evident in the fact that large companies like Nike have been on the fitness-tracking trail for a while now. Nike began its incorporation of self-tracking in 2006 with the launch of Nike + Ipod and has been developing the Nike+ line ever since.

High awareness of fitness tracking also suggests popularity of these tools. It shows that fitness-tracking technologies are not just collecting dust in the App Store or on store shelves, they are actually being used. Of all of the people who were surveyed for this paper's primary research, 93% said they have heard of people using fitness-tracking tools. Compared to other categories of self-tracking, fitness had the highest awareness followed by food-tracking (81% awareness) and financial tracking (69% awareness). Not only is tool development booming in the fitness arena, but so is the awareness of fitness tracking. This awareness may have an influence on the high technology acceptance rates that fitness-tracking tools enjoy. This theory is tested in the primary research section.

The relatively long-term success of fitness tracking technology could be due to the fact that quantification and physical activity compliment each other well. Sports historians and health professionals have linked the two together for years, and they have been the focus of many research studies. Self-tracking and fitness have been paired together since the time of the Roman Empire. Goal-oriented fitness, a category that includes both sports and personal fitness, almost always requires some sort of quantification so that progress can be tracked and compared for competition. Ian Li (2011) reaffirms this point by claiming that exercise is a popular category for self-tracking because it is an activity for which people want to monitor their progress. From this it is clear that quantitative tracking is a modern necessity for goal-oriented physical activity. Commercial fitness tracking embodies the simplicity of aligning physical activity with quantification.

Fitness tracking, like all forms of self-tracking, can be facilitated with a wide variety of tools. Examples of the popular commercial fitness tracking tools tend to be mobile applications or devices specifically built for simple self-tracking towards a specified goal. Some of the tools that receive the most recognition among fitness trackers are Nike+, Fitbit, MyFitnessPal, LoseIt, and MapMyRun. One commercial fitness-tracking tool that has received a lot of media attention recently is the Nike+ FuelBand. It is the newest, simplest, and most fun-oriented tool in the Nike's product line of fitness tracking devices, Nike+. The overall interest and publicity surrounding the tool provide an interesting example of a self-tracking tool developed for the masses, which has the power to convert many new people into self-trackers. Analysis of the marketing of this tool is a great way to understand how marketers are trying to influence self-tracking technology acceptance (and increase their use and sales).

The Nike+ FuelBand (NFB) was introduced through television commercials and online social marketing to a wide audience of people who may or may not have considered tracking their physical activity before. The company's choice of a general audience is evident in their marketing efforts, which position the FuelBand as a tool that "makes life a sport" for athletes of all types and fitness levels ("Nike+ FuelBand"). The product messaging emphasizes the simplicity of the tool and how fun it is to use. This approach to marketing seems to have had the right effect. Both pre-sales of the NFB sold out in less than 3 minutes (Kamer, 2012). It is important to note that Nike believes "if you have a body, you are an athlete" ("About Nike, Inc."). Clearly, the FuelBand was developed for use by everyone, a large majority of which has never tracked their personal information before. The Nike+ FuelBand most likely appeals to such a wide audience because of its emphasis on simplicity and fun.

The Nike+ product line had the highest tool awareness among the people surveyed for this research and the FuelBand itself had the third-highest awareness. This is likely due to the fact that the Nike+ tools are attached to a very well known brand name and are marketed towards every kind of "athlete." The example of the NFB illustrates how self-tracking activities are becoming more acceptable and popular. In fact, numerous technology experts have acknowledged that Nike's presence in the self-tracking market could increase adoption of self-tracking behaviors in general ("Apple Joins"). Fitness tracking is the most well-established and popularly accepted type of self-tracking. The plentiful amount of tools developed to facilitate it, along with the high awareness of fitness tracking in the general population make it a valuable category to study. Insights from the analysis of fitness tracking tool acceptance could lead to an understanding of how self-tracking in general will mature and increase in adoption. The following section of this paper seeks to understand the actual factors that influence technology acceptance through a survey about fitness tracking tools.

PRIMARY RESEARCH

Fitness Tracking Survey

The purpose of the survey is to collect primary data related to the general acceptance of consumer self-tracking technologies in order to understand the factors that influence self-tracking tool acceptance. Based on the category's pervasiveness and popularity, fitness tracking was selected as the focus of the survey. The sample of research subjects is intentionally diverse, including people who practice fitness tracking and people who don't. The survey participants span a wide range of ages, employment statuses, and education levels. The varied sample allows for a balanced representation of the perceptions and evaluations of a general audience.

The principal section of the survey is modeled after Fred D. Davis' (1985) "Technology Acceptance Model" (TAM), which defines technology acceptance as a function of perceived usefulness, perceived ease of use, and expected enjoyment. TAM is a widely used theoretical model that is useful because of its clear categorization of the factors that influence technology acceptance.

The survey seeks to answer the research question:

How do perceptions of fitness tracking tools influence their acceptance?

The research explores this question by measuring people's perceived usefulness, perceived ease of use, and expected enjoyment of fitness tracking tools. Other information is gathered to check for additional influences on technology acceptance, as well as to compare fitness tracking to other types of self-tracking. Results from the survey suggest that people's perceived usefulness of fitness tracking tools has a greater influence on their acceptance than their perceived ease of use or expected enjoyment.

Survey Method

The 55-question survey was produced and distributed online using Qualtrics Online Survey Software. The survey was distributed through email and social media outlets (Facebook and Twitter) using a snowball sampling method. In total, there were 121 fully completed responses. In addition to the participants who completed the survey, many people began it but did not finish. Including the partial completions, the survey had 198 total responses. Survey participants are 66% female, 33% male, and fall between the ages of 18 and 76. The majority of the sample is employed (85%) and 22% are in school. Almost all of the participants (98%) are high school graduates and 30% have a degree higher than undergraduate. Their daily technology use relies heavily on desktop and laptop computers (63%, 79% respectively) and 62% own smartphones.

The survey is designed in a funnel form so that the questions move from general to specific. The questions begin with the topic of self-tracking, get more specific by asking about self-tracking tools, and then finally narrow down to the subject of fitness tracking tools. Within the fitness tracking section, the survey evaluates participants' awareness of the tools, then perceptions, and then use. This funnel-shaped format gradually acquaints non-familiar participants with the concepts of self-tracking.

The main focus of the survey is to measure three types of information about fitness tracking tools: participants' awareness, perceptions, and use. First, awareness of fitness tool use is measured by asking the sample the extent to which they agree with the statement: "I have heard of people using digital tools to track their personal fitness data." Survey participants can select an answer on a scale from one to five, where one represents strong disagreement, three represents neutral agreement ("neither agree nor disagree"), and five represents strong agreement. Participants' awareness of self-tracking tools, along with the general concept of self-tracking, is also evaluated in order to put their previous answers into a broader context.

Survey participants' perceptions of fitness tracking tools are next assessed through a simplified version of Davis's *Technology Acceptance Model* (TAM), which defines technology acceptance as a function of perceived usefulness and ease of use of a tool. A third factor of influence, expected enjoyment, is added to this equation in order to account for the increasing incorporation of gaming dynamics into fitness tracking tools.

The simplified version of TAM allows for a solid and concise analysis of self-tracking technology acceptance, but requires the researcher to make some assumptions. First, the simplified TAM assumes that awareness of fitness tool use is a valid form of exposure to fitness tracking technology. The survey's version of TAM also simplifies the acceptance process by removing Davis's factor of "attitude towards use" from mediating between perceptions and acceptance. The simplified TAM assumes that perceptions of fitness tracking tools lead directly towards acceptance of the tools.

Perceptions of fitness tools are measured by asking the sample the extent to which they agree with the statements: "Digital tools that track personal fitness data seem useful/easy to use/enjoyable." Again, participants can select their level of agreement on a scale from one to five, where one signifies strong disagreement and five signifies strong agreement. Potential factors that motivate each of three perceptions (usefulness, ease of use, and enjoyment) are explored through open-ended questions designed to collect information on why participants choose their selected level of agreement. The last main section of the survey distinguishes the people who have experience fitness tracking from those who don't. Information about which participants use tracking tools is fundamental to measuring how perceptions affect acceptance of fitness tracking tools. Participants who say they haven't used digital tools to collect and reflect on their personal fitness data, or the "non-trackers," are asked a set of questions to gauge their interest in beginning to use fitness tracking tools

Participants who report having used digital tools to track their fitness data are asked a serious of questions to collect information on how they collect their personal information and why they do it. This small portion of the survey takes inspiration from Ian Li's Personal Informatics Survey, which provided much of the research for his Stage Based Model of Personal Informatics (Li, 2010). In the survey for this paper, the group of "trackers" is asked about their motivation to track their fitness, the tool(s) they use for their fitness tracking, why they use those tools, and what motivated them to first try those tools. These questions are designed to get to the heart of the factors that influence fitness tracking technology acceptance.

Survey Results

The results from the survey are organized into three sections. The first answers the main research question, "How do perceptions of fitness tracking tools influence their acceptance?" by testing the hypothesis that perceived usefulness, perceived ease of use, and expected enjoyment equally influence fitness tracking tool acceptance. The second section explores other influences on fitness tracking acceptance by examining information collected about trackers' experiences. The last section compares the perceptions of fitness tracking to those of other types of self-tracking in order to place the preceding information in a broader context.

1.   Perceptions of Fitness Tracking Tools

Perceptions of fitness tracking tools comes from the section of the survey that uses the simplified TAM to measure participants' perceptions of usefulness, ease of use, and expected enjoyment of fitness tracking tools. It tests the hypothesis that people's perceived usefulness, ease of use, and enjoyment of fitness tracking tools equally influence their acceptance of fitness tracking tools. The survey results provide sufficient information to reject this hypothesis, showing that each factor has a different level of influence on technology acceptance.

Participants were asked to select the extent to which they agreed with the statements: "Digital tools that track personal fitness data seem useful/easy to use/enjoyable." Survey participants selected their agreement on a scale from one to five. In order to directly assess how these perceptions affect tool acceptance, only the answers from participants who have actually accepted fitness tracking tools, defined as "trackers," are considered for this section. On average, trackers agreed that fitness tracking tools are useful, but were on the fence between being neutral and agreeing that they are easy to use and enjoyable.

These sentiments are expressed through the mean levels of agreement about usefulness, ease of use, and enjoyment, which came out to be 4.19, 3.67, and 3.39 respectively, on the scale from 1 to 5. The numbers show that for fitness tracking tools, perceptions of usefulness have more influence on technology acceptance than perceived ease of use and expected enjoyment do. Trackers' high level of agreement that fitness-tracking tools seem useful (4.19) is based on their feelings that the tools help them reach goals, provide motivation, and help them understand their fitness. These categories came from an evaluation of answers to open-ended questions that asked participants why they selected their level of agreement.

Many trackers expressed that fitness tracking tools' usefulness is a result of the tools' ability to help users achieve their goals and stay change their behavior. This sentiment was affirmed by Participant 25 (P25) who stated that "keeping track of your fitness helps to keep you motivated and reach your fitness goal," and by Participant 4 who said "If I track my progress and achievements, it helps keep me motivated." Trackers also expressed that fitness tracking tools are useful because they help users better understand their fitness and "allow you to see patterns" (Participant 9). The neutral level of agreement that fitness trackers displayed with the statement that fitness tracking tools seem useful (3.67) is a result of many factors. Their evaluations of ease of use are varied, but largely based on the simplicity of tools, their integration with mobile technology, the time it takes to track fitness in general, and the wide variety of tools.

Participant 9 expressed the ease of use associated with mobile integration by stating, "I'm already using my smart phone ... everyday, connected easily to tools therefore making it easy to track myself." Other participants were not as convinced of the ease of using fitness tracking tools, saying "It seems to take quite a bit of time, that makes it harder to use" (Participant 102) and "It depends on the tool" (Participant 31). Overall, sentiments leaned towards positivity and optimism, a trend embodied in P56's comment that "many (fitness tracking tools) are pretty easy to use, and technology keeps improving."

Perceptions of expected enjoyment were even more neutral than those of ease of use, with a mean level of agreement of 3.39. Trackers expressed that expected enjoyment is a matter of personal preference, but that getting feedback and seeing progress is often enjoyable along with the competitive dynamics incorporated into some fitness tracking tools. Participants acknowledged that expected enjoyment "depends on the person" (P53). Participant 31 said, "For me, the tool would be 'functional,' not 'enjoyable.' It's a tool, not an ice cream bar" while P41 said "I don't know about other people, but I'm a data geek, and it pleases me immensely to see my data in various quantitative representations." Both of these participants, among others, agreed that expected enjoyment depends are personal preferences.

Survey participants cited observing their personal progress and feeling like they were playing a game as enjoyable functions of fitness tracking tools. Participants expressed that "These tools help achieve goals, achieving goals feels awesome" (P76) and "(Fitness tracking tools) can make something difficult and critical feel more like a game" (P4). The reported negative factors of fitness tracking tools were related to the time and effort required to self-track. Participants claimed that this could detract from one's ability to enjoy the tool, saying, "(Fitness tracking tools) can be motivating, but also time consuming" (P56).

All of the data collected on trackers' perceptions of fitness tracking tools boils down to show that ease of use and enjoyment are not as important or influential to fitness tracking technology acceptance as usefulness is.

The above results concerning trackers' perceptions of fitness tracking tools must be presented in conjunction with the assumptions that they are based upon and the potential threats that could decrease their validity. The results are based on the assumptions that the TAM can be applied to fitness tracking tools, that awareness of fitness tracking tools doesn't affect a person's perceptions of them, and that the use of fitness tracking tools doesn't affect perceptions of them. Each assumption is explored in order to assess its potential for decreasing the results' validity.

First, there is the assumption that TAM can be applied to fitness tracking tools. To test whether or not the model can be applied, a linear regression was set up between use of fitness tracking tools and the three types of perceptions to see how the variables are related. Unfortunately, the regression is only able to show correlations between the variables, it cannot prove causation. Despite this limitation, the equation can provide some evidence as to the relationship between each variable. The linear regression equation is

$$T = \alpha_1 \cdot x_1 + \alpha_2 \cdot x_2 + \alpha_3 \cdot x_3 + k$$

where T represents fitness tracking tool use (yes or no), each x represents the perceptions of fitness tracking tools (x_1 = usefulness, x_2 = ease of use, x_3 = enjoyment), each α is the coefficient for the corresponding perception, and k is a constant. TAM can potentially be applied to fitness tracking tools if the relationship between tracking and each perception, represented by the coefficients α_{1-3}, is positive. This would mean that the factors are correlated.

Three hypotheses, one for each type of perception, were developed to test the validity of applying TAM to fitness tracking tools:

H1: $\alpha_1 > 0$, or perceived usefulness is positively correlated with tracking
H2: $\alpha_2 > 0$, or perceived ease of use is positively correlated with tracking
H3: $\alpha_3 > 0$, or expected enjoyment is positively correlated with tracking

Each hypothesis is accepted because the regression showed that $\alpha_1 = .25$, $\alpha_2 = .209$, and $\alpha_3 = .232$. These values were each accompanied by a p-value of .001 or less, meaning that they are statistically valid. The fact that each α has a positive value allows for an acceptance of all three hypotheses and shows that tracking is positively correlated with perceptions of fitness tracking tools.

As mentioned before, correlation doesn't imply causation, so these results are unclear as to whether or not the perceptions influence the technology acceptance or vice versa. However, the proof of correlation is a good start and, combined with the TAM's history of use on many different types of technology (Lee et al, 2003), suggests that it is acceptable to apply the TAM to fitness tracking tools.

The second assumption of the results concerning perceptions of fitness tracking tools is that a person's awareness of fitness tracking tool use doesn't affect their perceptions of fitness tracking tools. This assumption may be incorrect, but it is difficult to evaluate because there are only five people in the sample who said they had not heard of people using digital tools to track their fitness data. Even though the comparison is lopsided, evaluation showed that perceptions of ease of use and enjoyment were an average of .98 higher for those aware of fitness tool use compared to those who are not aware. This result means that the tracker's perceptions of fitness tracking tools evaluated earlier may be higher than the perceptions of people who aren't aware of fitness tracking tools use. This could mean that the data is not generalizable or applicable to people who don't know about fitness tracking.

The third assumption is that a person's use of fitness tracking tools doesn't affect their perceptions of them. This assumption could be false and if so, would mean that the correlations found between perceptions and use could have the reverse relationship than suggested by the TAM. Evaluation showed that tracker's perceptions of fitness tracking tools (usefulness, ease of use, and enjoyment) were an average of 0.4 higher than those of non-trackers. This could mean that tracker's perceptions of fitness tracking tools are higher as a result of their use of the tools, which could then mean that the survey results are not applicable to people who don't use fitness tracking tools. These evaluations of the assumptions made by the survey results show that the relationships between perceptions and acceptance of fitness tracking tools may not be as simple as previously suggested. Future studies must be designed to test for causation, as well as to test for the effects of awareness and use.

By evaluating the survey results concerning tracker's perceptions of fitness tracking tools, the relationship between the perceptions and the acceptance of these tools becomes clearer. Assuming that the TAM can be applied to fitness tracking tools, and that awareness and use of the tools doesn't affect perceptions, the data suggests that a person's perceived usefulness of a fitness-tracking tool is more influential to their acceptance of that tool than their perceived ease of use or expected enjoyment.

2.   Additional Factors of Technology Acceptance

This portion of the survey results comes from the series of questions that evaluate why fitness trackers use the tools they use. This section was meant to explore any other influences on fitness tracking tool acceptance. It was discovered that many trackers, 63% of those who took the survey, are motivated to accept fitness tracking tools by person-to-person connections and experiences.

When trackers were asked about what motivated them to try the fitness tracking tools they have used, 46% said that friends and family members had recommended the tools to them. This was the most common response. Additional selections concerning personal connections like observing someone's fitness tracking experience online or offline also had high response rates of 4% online and 13% offline, respectively. These results show that person-to-person experiences and connections play a large role in fitness tracking tool acceptance.

The only threat to validity in this section of the results is a survey design mistake. In the question that asked trackers what motivated them to use their fitness tracking tool(s), the "Other" option did not have a space for text entry. This mistake could have lost some valuable insight because 28% of the sample of trackers selected the "Other" option, but could not elaborate. The 28% could have suggested another strong influencer of acceptance, or further illustrated that person-to-person experiences affect fitness tracking tool acceptance. Despite this mistake, the 63% of trackers who cited their motivation to accept a fitness tracking tool as a result of a personal connection is still a strong insight into what influences acceptance.

3.   Fitness Tracking Compared to Self-Tracking in General

The last portion of the survey results show how perceptions of fitness tracking tools compare to perceptions of self-tracking tools in general. This information is taken from the questions that ask participants about self-tracking tools before the survey narrows down to fitness-tracking tools. Each question asks to what extent the participant agrees with the statements: "Digital tools that track personal data seem useful/easy to use/enjoyable." Survey participants selected an answer on a scale from one to five, where one represents strong disagreement and five represents strong agreement. Answers from trackers and non-trackers alike are evaluated for this section because it is simply comparing perceptions and not relating them to actual use.

The hypothesis, based on the knowledge that fitness-tracking tools are very popular, is that perceptions of fitness tracking tools are higher than perceptions of self-tracking tools in general. This hypothesis is rejected, based on the data from the survey, which showed that, compared with self-tracking tools in general, fitness tracking tools have a similar perception of usefulness, a lower perception of ease of use, and a higher perception of enjoyment.

These sentiments are expressed through the mean levels of agreement about usefulness, ease of use, and enjoyment for fitness tracking tools, which came out to be 3.99, 3.42, and 3.37 respectively. Compared with the means for self-tracking tools in general, which came out to be 3.95, 3.56, and 3.18, respectively, it is clear that perceptions of fitness tracking tools are not all higher than those of self-tracking tools in general. The lower perceptions of ease of use for fitness tracking tools could be related to the idea that "fitness is often too complicated to easily track" (P60) that some participants expressed. Higher expectations of enjoyment could be the result of people's appreciation for the gaming and competition dynamics built into many fitness tracking tools.

It should also be noted that fitness tracking tools had the highest awareness and perceptions when directly compared to other types of self-tracking tools. Participants were asked to pick the top 3 categories of tracking tools they thought to be most useful/easy to use/enjoyable out of fitness, productivity, time management, finance, physical health, food, goals, mood, sleep, location, and online activity. Fitness had the highest number of selections in awareness, perceived usefulness, perceived ease of use, and expected enjoyment. This could be a result of the affect high awareness may have on perceptions. The only threat to validity for this section of research insights is that fitness was one of the categories included in the self-tracking tools discussion. This means that the comparison between fitness tracking tools and self-tracking tools in general is weaker because the two variables are not independent or mutually exclusive.

Discussion of Results

The survey had three main insights:

1. Usefulness is more important/influential to fitness tracking technology acceptance than ease of use and enjoyment.
2. Person-to-person experiences and connections play a large role in fitness tracking tool acceptance.
3. Compared with self-tracking tools in general, fitness-tracking tools have a similar perception of usefulness, a lower perception of ease of use, and a higher perception of enjoyment.

The survey, although focused on fitness tracking tools, was conducted in order to better understand the process of acceptance of self-tracking tools. Each survey insight can be expanded to demonstrate a bigger insight about self-tracking as a whole.

The first survey result says that perceptions of usefulness are the most influential factor of technology acceptance for fitness tracking tools. This could suggest that perceived usefulness is also the most influential factor of acceptance for other types of self-tracking tools, or for all types of self-tracking tools. This could then mean that if the developers of other types of self-tracking tools want to play to their audience's perceptions of fitness tracking tools, they should emphasize the usefulness of their tools because ease of use and enjoyment are less important influencers of acceptance. The results could also be interpreted to mean that for the developers of other types of tracking tools, ease of use and enjoyment are opportunities to improve perceptions of self-tracking tools. This could be why Nike was so successful in its marketing of the Nike+ Fuel Band as simple and fun.

The second survey insight suggests that personal recommendations are an important part of self-tracking tool acceptance. This could have interesting implications for other types of self-tracking tools in the realm of marketing and advertising. If person-to-person experiences are one of the main motivators for tracking tool acceptance, tool developers could potentially grow their business by marketing their product through the peers of potential users. This strategy could be employed in a number of ways, for example, by giving current users incentives to share their experiences with their friends and family.

The third insight from the survey simply shows that fitness tracking tools, while more popular than other categories of self-tracking tools, don't necessarily have higher perceptions than the whole category. The durability of these perceptions is an important point to discuss, especially because the insights from the survey are meant to inform evaluations of the future of self-tracking. Perceptions of usefulness, ease of use, and enjoyment are likely to change as any type of technology matures and users' comfort with the technology increases. These shifts in perceptions are likely to happen gradually, and in the long run. Therefore, the survey results are valid in the short run, which is acceptable because self-tracking's rise to technology acceptance is very likely to happen in the short run, based on all of the press and attention it is getting.

LIMITATIONS AND FUTURE RESEARCH DIRECTIONS

The current study is based on a few assumptions that may compromise the validity of the results. Each assumption is evaluated and analyzed for its effect on the results found in the survey. First, the simplification of the TAM assumes that awareness of fitness tool use is a valid form of exposure and that perceptions of a technology lead directly to its acceptance. Many factors of influence are ignored this simplified model, but as Younghwa Lee and colleagues suggest in their paper "The Technology Acceptance Model: Past, Present, and Future," the TAM is a complicated and fluid model that has gone through significant changes over the course of its existence. Therefore, the simplified version of TAM may only be an acceptable model for preliminary research on technology acceptance, like this survey.

The second factor that may compromise the validity of the survey results is the fact that the survey sample is a convenience sample. This means that participants were selected at the convenience of the researcher. Research that utilizes convenience samples is difficult to generalize to a wider population because the sample is usually not random or representative of the entire population.

Thirdly, the open-ended definition of fitness tracking may have been too broad to insure that all survey participants had the same level of understanding of what a fitness tracking tool is. Fitness tracking tools are defined in the survey as the tools that help people collect and reflect on their personal fitness information. This definition is followed by three examples of fitness tracking tools: a pedometer, Nike+,

FitBit and MapMyRun. The definition and examples leave room for some variance in interpretation, especially if the survey participant was unfamiliar with examples. Some participants could have been thinking of simple and easy tools while others could have been thinking of more complicated ones.

The last threat to validity is the potential that high awareness of fitness tracking affected participant's perceptions of the categories. If awareness has a large influence on technology acceptance, it is possible that the results concerning fitness tracking tools couldn't be easily scaled and generalized to other categories of self-tracking tools.

Future research could do a number of things to account for and address these issues and threats to validity. First, it would need to be designed in order to test for more direct causation between perceptions and acceptance, not just correlation. This could be achieved by recruiting a large and random sample, and separating participants into groups based on their interest in fitness, interest in self-tracking, and interest in self-tracking tools. The study would also benefit from using one definite example of a fitness-tracking tool, in order to control the issue of different interpretations of the term "fitness tracking tools."

Other interesting areas that future studies could explore are the perceptions outside of those suggested by the TAM, the direct comparisons between fitness tracking and another category of self-tracking, and the use of more than one tool in the self-tracking process. Many people interested in self-tracking are researching how self-trackers can combine different tools to enhance their tracking experience. Ian Li focuses on this topic in his dissertation "Personal Informatics and Context: Using Context to Reveal Factors That Affect Behavior." Along with examining the acceptance of tracking tools by themselves, a second study could explore how multiple self-tracking tools could potentially be accepted in conjunction with each other.

CONCLUSION

Self-tracking is an activity in which a person collects and reflects on their personal information over time. One of the distinguishing features of games and game dynamics is a constant feedback loop of where one is in the game. Self-tracking serves as this feedback mechanism wherein game dynamics are brought into non-game contexts. Digital tools increasingly facilitate this practice and its presence in the consumer market is quickly growing.

The collection of personal information is now a commonplace activity as a result of connected devices and the Internet. Tracking is integrated into so many digital services and devices; it is more or less unavoidable. Self-tracking engages with new technology to put the power of self-improvement and self-knowledge into people's own hands. Currently, self-tracking activities are increasing their presence in a number of environments, most notably, with early-adopters and experimenters of the Quantified or Gamified Self community, and with commercial self-tracking tools within the consumer market.

Based on insights about the self-tracking process, it was established that the development of self-tracking within the consumer market looks very different from the increasing popularity of the Quantified Self movement. For this reason, an analysis of consumer self-tracking tools was performed outside of the context of Quantified Self.

Exploration of commercial self-tracking tools, and the conditions necessary for their growth, was implemented through both secondary and primary research. A thorough review of literature about technology acceptance and the self-tracking process supported investigations of self-tracking tool acceptance. Then, a survey about fitness tracking provided primary data on how perceptions of fitness tracking tools influence their acceptance. This research moves towards a better understanding of how self-tracking can (and will) grow in the consumer market. Based on findings from both secondary and primary research, it was found that perceptions of ease of use and enjoyment of tracking tools are less influential to technology acceptance than perceptions of usefulness. Fitness tracking tools provided a valuable case study for self-tracking tool acceptance because they are the most pervasive type of commercial self-tracking tool.

As self-tracking technologies become more useful, easier to use, and more fun, their acceptance is likely to increase. Increases in acceptance, if on a large enough scale, can then lead to increases in pervasiveness of these tools. Thought leaders in technological innovation, like Biz Stone of Twitter and Steven Wolfram of Mathematica, have been quoted predicting that everyone will be tracking their personal data soon. They suggest that the practice itself could become ubiquitous and invisible, much like the technology it employs.

The growth of self-tracking has many implications in the technology industry and beyond. As people create more data about themselves, data and privacy standards will need to evolve. This is especially true if the trend towards integrating data from multiple sources and tools continues. Additionally, people will want to keep their personal information safe to avoid minimal issues such as broadcasting their embarrassing behavior, but also serious issues like identity theft (Wolf, 2009, 2010).

The ascension of self-tracking, especially in the category of fitness, also has countless implications for healthcare. If low-cost personal health tracking becomes more accessible to those who need it most, and they accept the technology, there could be major changes in the healthcare system. There is a community of healthcare and technology professionals who are already planning for this transition. They are calling the next phase of healthcare Health 2.0. (Rowley). Implications for the growth of self-tracking activities are vast and could change the way people in the future interact with their own behaviors, their environment, and each other.

Leaders of self-tracking innovation frame self-tracking as a new context for knowledge generation. It is more than just a few people's hobby, it is a lens through which people see and create the world around them. An understanding of self-tracking is vital to our assessment of society's digital evolution, especially as the practice continues to grow in popularity and influence.

REFERENCES

Barooah, R. (2009, October 19). The False God of Coffee. *Quantified Self*. Retrieved from http://quantifiedself.com/2009/10/the-false-god-of-coffee/

Borriello, G. (2008). Invisible computing: automatically using the many bits of data we create. *Philosophical Transactions of the Royal Society of London A: Mathematical, Physical and Engineering Sciences, 366*(1881), 3669-3683.

Czerski, P. (2012, February 15). We, the Web Kids. Trans. Marta Szreder. Pastebin, Retrieved from http://pastebin.com/0xXV8k7k

Davis, F. D. (1985). A Technology Acceptance Model for Empirically Testing New End-User Information Systems: Theory and Results. [Doctoral Dissertation]. Sloan School of Management, Massachusetts Institute of Technology.

Davis, F. D., Bagozzi, R. P., & Warshaw, P. R. (1992). Extrinsic and Intrinsic Motivation to Use Computers in the Workplace. *Journal of Applied Social Psychology, 22*(14), 1109–1130. doi:10.1111/j.1559-1816.1992. tb00945.x

Fleming, N. (2011, December 2). Know Thyself: The Quantified Self Devotees Who Live by Numbers. *The Guardian*. Retrieved from http://www.theguardian.com/science/2011/dec/02/psychology-human-biology

Global Mobile Statistics. (2012). *MobiThinking*. Retrieved from http://mobithinking.com/mobile-marketing-tools/latest-mobile-stats

Hill, K. (2011, April 7). Adventures in Self-Surveillance, Aka The Quantified Self, Aka Extreme Navel-Gazing. *Forbes*. Retrieved from http://www.forbes.com/sites/kashmirhill/2011/04/07/adventures-in-self-surveillance-aka-the-quantified-self-aka-extreme-navel-gazing/

Hutchings, E. (2012, January 20). Track Your Daily Activity and Improve Your Health with The Nike Fuelband. *PSFK*. Retrieved from http://www.psfk.com/2012/01/track-your-activity-with-the-nike-fuelband.html

Kamer, F. (2012, February 23). Nike's Fuelband, the Shiny IOS-Powered New Fitness Gadget, Sold Out in Four Minutes. *Observer*. Retrieved from http://observer.com/2012/02/nike-fuelband-apple-sold-out-02232012/

Kohut, A., Taylor, P., & Keeter, S. (2010). The Millennials: Confident. Connected. Open to Change. *Pew Research Center*. Pew Research Center, Retrieved from http://www.pewsocialtrends.org/2010/02/24/millennials-confident-connected-open-to-change/

Leavitt, M. (2012). *HealthESeat*. Portland, OR: PDX Quantified Self Show and Tell. Wieden and Kennedy.

Lee, Y., Kozar, K. A., & Larsen, K. R. (2003). The technology acceptance model: Past, present, and future. *Communications of the Association for Information Systems, 12*(1), 50.

Lenhart, A., Jones, S., & Macgill, A. (2008). Adults and Video Games. *Pew Internet*. Pew Research Center, Retrieved from http://www.pewinternet.org/2008/12/07/adults-and-video-games/

Li, I. (2010). *Survey*. Personal Informatics Lab.

Li, I. (2011). Personal Informatics and Context: Using Context to Reveal Factors That Affect Behavior [Doctoral Dissertation]. Carnegie Mellon University.

Li, I., Dey, A., & Forlizzi, J. (2010). A Stage-Based Model of Personal Informatics Systems. *Proceedings of CHI '10 Conference*. New York City.

Phares, E. J. (1976). *Locus of control in personality*. Morristown, NJ: General Learning Press.

Rotter, J. B. (1966). Generalized expectancies for internal versus external control of reinforcement. *Psychological Monographs, 80*(1), 1–28. doi:10.1037/h0092976 PMID:5340840

Rotter, J. B. (1975). Some problems and misconceptions related to the construct of internal versus external control of reinforcement. *Journal of Consulting and Clinical Psychology, 43*(1), 56–67. doi:10.1037/h0076301

Rowley, R. (2012). *Health Care and Wellness Are Converging Concepts. EHR Bloggers*. Practice Fusion.

Selinger, E. (2012, March 9). Why It's OK to Let Apps Make You a Better Person. *The Atlantic*. Retrieved from http://www.theatlantic.com/technology/archive/2012/03/why-its-ok-to-let-apps-make-you-a-better-person/254246/

Smith, A. (2011). Why Americans Use Social Media. *Pew Internet*. Pew Research Center, Retrieved from http://www.pewinternet.org/files/old-media/Files/Reports/2011/Why%20Americans%20Use%20Social%20Media.pdf

The Economist (2012, March 3). The Quantified Self: Counting Every Moment. *The Economist*. Retrieved from http://www.economist.com/node/21548493

Wolf, G. (2009, June 22). Know Thyself: Tracking Every Facet of Life, from Sleep to Mood to Pain, 24/7/365. *Wired.com*. Retrieved from http://archive.wired.com/medtech/health/magazine/17-07/lbnp_knowthyself?currentPage=all

Wolf, G. (2010). The Data-Driven Life. *The New York Times*. Retrieved from http://www.nytimes.com/2010/05/02/magazine/02self-measurement-t.html?_r=0

Wolfram, S. (2012). The Personal Informatics of My Life. *StephanWolfram.com*. Retrieved from http:\\www.stephenwolfram.com

ADDITIONAL READING

Alkhatib, A., & Boellstorff, T. (2014). *Quantified Self: Ethnography of a Digital Culture* [Doctoral dissertation, Doctoral dissertation]. University of California. Retrieved from http://alialkhatib.com/presentations/QSThesisFinal.pdf

Barreto, P., Borgeld, R., de Graaf, K., & Tromp, S. (2013, October 25). Games4Health. *MediaLAB*. Retrieved from http://medialab.hva.nl/wp-content/uploads/2014/02/Research-report.pdf

Bildl, S. (2014). Gamification of the Quantified Self. In P. Lindemann, T. Stockinger, M. Koelle, & M. Kranz (Eds.), Advances in embedded interactive systems, 2(3) (pp. 4–9). Passau, Germany: University of Passau; Retrieved from http://www.eislab.fim.uni-passau.de/files/publications/2014/TR2014-FunSecureEmbedded.pdf

Fleming, N. (2012). The end of the average person. *New Scientist*, *215*(2876), 40–43. doi:10.1016/S0262-4079(12)62024-7

Jacquez, G. M., & Rommel, R. The quantified self and crowd sourcing of the genome+, exposome and behavome: Perspective and call for action.

Kelly, K. (2007). *What is the quantified self?* The Quantified Self.

Khaled, R. (2015). Gamification and culture 11. *The Gameful World: Approaches, Issues, Applications*, 301.

Kukulska-Hulme, A. (2014). Mobile, Wearable, Companionable: Emerging technological challenges and incentives for learning.

Lupton, D. (2014). *Self-tracking Cultures: Towards a Sociology of Personal Informatics. Mekky, S.* Wearable Computing and the Hype of Tracking Personal Activity. doi:10.1145/2686612.2686623

Millington, B. (2014). Smartphone apps and the mobile privatization of health and fitness. *Critical Studies in Media Communication, 31*(5), 479–493. doi:10.1080/15295036.2014.973429

Neumann, U., & Cho, Y. (1996, July). A self-tracking augmented reality system. In *Proceedings of the ACM Symposium on Virtual Reality Software and Technology* (pp. 109-115).

Rapp, A. (2014). A SWOT Analysis of the Gamification Practices: Challenges, Open Issues and Future Perspectives. *Advances in Affective and Pleasurable Design, 19*, 476.

Rapp, A., & Cena, F. (2014). Self-monitoring and Technology: Challenges and Open Issues in Personal Informatics. In Universal Access in Human-Computer Interaction. Design for All and Accessibility Practice (pp. 613-622). Springer International Publishing.

Rich, E., & Miah, A. (2014). Understanding digital health as public pedagogy: A critical framework. *Societies, 4*(2), 296–315. doi:10.3390/soc4020296

Sjöklint, M. (2014, September). The measurable me: the influence of self-quantification on the online user's decision-making process. In *Proceedings of the 2014 ACM International Symposium on Wearable Computers: Adjunct Program* (pp. 131-137). ACM. doi:10.1145/2641248.2642737

Spillers, F., & Asimakopoulos, S. (2014). Does Social User Experience Improve Motivation for Runners? (pp. 358-369). In A. Marcus (Ed.), Design, User Experience, and Usability. User Experience Design Practice. Springer International Publishing. doi:10.1007/978-3-319-07638-6_35

Swan, M. (2013). The quantified self: Fundamental disruption in big data science and biological discovery. *Big Data, 1*(2), 85–99. doi:10.1089/big.2012.0002

Till, C. (2014). Exercise as labour: Quantified self and the transformation of exercise into labour. *Societies, 4*(3), 446–462. doi:10.3390/soc4030446

Wagner, D., & Schmalstieg, D. (2006, March). Handheld augmented reality displays. In *Virtual Reality Conference* (pp. 321-321). IEEE.

Whitson, J. R. (2013). Gaming the quantified self. *Surveillance & Society, 11*(1/2), 163–176.

Wolf, G., Carmichael, A., & Kelly, K. (2010). The quantified self. *TED*. Retrieved from http://www. ted. com/talks/gary_wolf_the_quantified_self. html

KEY TERMS AND DEFINITIONS

Gamification: The use of game thinking and game dynamics in non-game contexts in order to engage users to solve problems, increase their participation, provide them feedback, and ultimately achieve the set objectives or goals.

Gamified Self: The idea of incorporating self-tracking and feedback mechanism into one's daily activities such as fitness, health, finances, and other goal-oriented behaviors in order to achieve set objectives and monitor ones progress.

Personal Infomatics: A class of tools that help people collect personally relevant information for the purpose of self-reflection and self-monitoring.

Quantified Self: The generation of self-knowledge through self-tracking.

Self-Tracking Tools: A class of tools that help individuals collect personal information for the purposes of self-monitoring and self-reflection.

Technology Acceptance Model (TAM): An information systems theory that models how users come to accept and use a particular technology.

Wearable Technology: Accessories and clothing that incorporate electronic and advance computing technologies for the purposes of self-tracking, monitoring, recording and/or providing information to its users.

Section 5
Gamification and Journalism

Chapter 14
Games and Quizzes in Online Journalism:
Reaching Users via Interactivity and Customization

Bartosz W. Wojdynski
University of Georgia, USA

ABSTRACT

The competition for online news page views increasingly involves strategies designed to promote the "viral" nature of content, and to capitalize on the content's spread by ensuring that the content does not quickly lose timeliness or relevance. As a result of the pressure for these stories, news experiences which can be revisited by consumers are at a premium. In this ecosystem, interactive games and quizzes which can be played to receive different feedback or reach a different ending offer promise for news organizations to receive ongoing and widespread reward for their efforts. This chapter provides an overview of the state of gamification in journalism, challenges and opportunities for the growth of games in online news, and discusses evidence for the impact of increasingly gamified news content on how users process and perceive news information.

INTRODUCTION

The most-viewed news story in 2013 was not really a news story at all.

Published on December 21st, "How Y'All, Youse, and You Guys Talk," the most-viewed story on the *New York Times'* site was an online quiz based on linguistic research from a Harvard student, as seen from the point of view of a former North Carolina State statistics student who was working at the *Times* as an intern. In the last 11 days of the year, the story managed to receive the most traffic of any *Times* story all year (New York Times Co., 2014).

The premise for the quiz was simple: users were served 25 multiple-choice questions, each of which asked about a specific example of word choice or pronunciation (for example, "What do you call the long sandwich that contains cold cuts, lettuce, and so on?"). Once users answered all 25 questions,

DOI: 10.4018/978-1-4666-8651-9.ch014

they received a result that matched their answers to the part of the country – often a small region – that matched their specific diction and pronunciation the best.

How did this story top coverage of news in a year filled with the Boston Marathon bombing and the rollout of new federal healthcare legislation? The answer lies in the increasingly socially mediated landscape of online news, in which content that offers users an emotional payoff, a novelty, and a chance to discover and share something about themselves is at a premium. The increased incentivization of these content aspects provides opportunities for news organizations to use news games and quizzes to not only deliver news value to audiences, but to drive traffic to their Websites. Increasingly, news organizations are providing audiences with interactive games and quizzes that provide users with an interactive experience that maybe highly related to a current news topic, or may just provide a diversion to users and traffic to the news organizations' Web servers. The integration of online news and online games has received attention as part of a broader rise of "gamification" across a variety of industries (see [*introductory chapter, this volume*]; Deterding, Dixon, Khaled, & Nacke, 2011). Although motivating individuals to learn or act by using game-like elements has been hailed for its potential when done well (e.g., Kapp, 2012; Deterding, Björk, Nacke, Dixon, & Lawley, 2013), the adoption of news games by news organization has, to date, focused on creating discrete news consumption experiences, only some of which seem to incentivize learning or news consumption.

This chapter provides an overview of the role of games and quizzes in the journalism industry. It begins by discussing the state of the online journalism industry today, including changes in how audiences reach news content, how such content is consumed, and how news organizations seek to monetize content. The following section discusses the role of games and quizzes within this landscape, and discusses their contribution to news organizations and audiences from a functional perspective. This is followed by a section on best practices in the design of online news games and quizzes. This section is followed by descriptions of four types of news games and quizzes: identity quizzes, knowledge quizzes, simulations, and topical play. The final section of the chapter outlines challenges to and opportunities for the growth of news games and quizzes, and suggests necessary research for understanding how these formats change the relationships between audiences and the news.

THE ONLINE NEWS LANDSCAPE

Although Internet adoption in the United States has leveled off in recent years, consumption of news via the Web continues to grow by all metrics. Digital advertising revenue continues to grow (Holcomb & Mitchell, 2014), and new digital-first news organizations have emerged on to the scene, fueled by venture capital (Pew, 2014). Online news video consumption continues to slowly increase (Pew, 2014). As news consumers receive a growing portion of their news online, the market for news content grows less localized; news producers have found themselves in competition with national and global outlets. The competition for news consumers – whether measured in digital subscriptions, unique page views, minutes spent on the site, Facebook "Likes" – has never been more fierce. As famed journalist Glen Greenwald told the *New York Times* in 2014:

No one, not The New York Times, no one, is entitled to an audience. The ability to thrive is directly dependent upon your ability to convince people that you're providing something valuable and unique (Carr, 2014)."

The growth of online news consumption has been partially fueled by the increase in traffic from social networking sites to news content. Individuals browsing their customized social media feeds encounter links to news content shared by friends, often with commentary by friend who posted it, and a thread of responses by others. The rise of user-distributed content (Villi, 2012; Villi, Matikainen, & Khaldarova, 2014) not only influences the exposure of others to news, but also the practice of news production. In recent years, as time spent on social networking services has skyrocketed (Short, 2013, p. 39), consumers get more of their news from posts by members of their social network, and less of it by choosing from a news organization homepage or aggregator (Thompson, 2014). Posted outbound links from Facebook to content publishers grew from 62 million in 2012 to 161 million in 2013 (Thompson, 2014). Half of U.S. Facebook users get news there (Mitchell, 2014) and nearly a third say that keeping up with news and current events is a major reason why they use Facebook (Smith, 2014). This growth in link sharing is important to news publishers, given that their audience is likely to spend a much larger portion of its time visiting social network sites than news Web sites. The average American aged 18-64 spends 3.2 hours per day using social media (Ipsos, 2013), while spending only 70 minutes consuming news across all platforms (Heimlich, 2010).

In this new ecosystem of socially-mediated news consumption, the stories that get the most traffic are the ones that are shared the most often. Although the propensity of a given news story to be shared depends on the interplay of a number of factors and concurrent situational events, researchers have begun to examine factors that increase sharing of content. A study by Berger and Milkman (2012) showed that emotionally-laden content is shared more often than other content, and that high-arousal emotions are the ones more likely to fuel sharing. The notion that effective news reaches its viewers on a emotional level is not a new one, but it may be enhanced in an era in which users increasingly access stories directly and not via an interface. This behavior has found to influence sharing and speed of sharing news stories on Twitter (Stieglitz & Dang-Xuan, 2013). Differences between individual users play a key role as well; to receive news through social media, individuals must have friends who pass on news articles. They also must be willing to potentially interrupt their social media browsing by opening a link to the news content. Enduring differences between individuals including personality type (Kim, Kim, & Seo, 2014), and situational differences in factors such as availability of attention, device, bandwidth, and others.

In addition to shareability, a second characteristic of news stories that lends them currency in the economy of the viral is staying power. Editors have long known that evergreen stories have their value not just for filling in the news hole on a slow news day, but also for taking a longer time to become stale. On the Web, this allows a piece a larger window of time in which to gather page views and draw unique visitors, two metrics of success important to publishers and their advertisers (Cherubini, 2014). Staying power also allows the online word-of-mouth process that takes place through social networks to reach users that may be more on the periphery of their networks, those who have fewer connections, or those who utilize the network less frequently. A review of top traffic published by BuzzFeed, a provider of news and entertainment content that both hosts its own stories and partners with other news organizations to display them, illustrates the evergreen nature of frequently shared stories (Thompson, 2014). Much of the list is populated by "listicles," or list articles, which break content down into simple chunks (e.g., "30 Signs You're Almost 30").

Not every news story is well-suited to trade in either emotional impact or staying power, and most online news organizations have to dedicate much of their resources to covering time-sensitive, newly developing events. Such stories necessarily have a short shelf life, and are often more focused on efficiently presenting the available information than making an emotional impression. This creates a juxtaposition between the kinds of stories that last and those who are only viewed within the first 12 hours of publication. Publishers strive for a mix of the two – longer, evergreen pieces that may continue to pull in new readers to the site over a period of months, or longer.

Scholars have noted that the increased competition for audience may have a negative effect on its quality. "Tabloidization" describes the process of producing stories and story-promoting elements (such as links and headlines) in a manner that is "designed to be stimulating and exciting (McLachlan & Golding, 2000). A perceived rise in tabloidization is not unique to online media (e.g., Tulloch, 2000; Bek, 2004), an era of increasing tabloidization has seen a shift toward more coverage of "soft news" rather than "hard news" (Kurtz, 1993), or scenarios in which "the cheap, easy, and popular story often wins out over the expensive, difficult, and less popular one (Bird, 2009)." Research has shown that presenting stories in a tabloidized or sensationalized style leads to lower perceptions of news organization credibility (Mackay & Bailey, 2012), although conflicting effects have been found on participants' enjoyment of news consumption (Johansson, 2008; Mackay & Bailey, 2012).

A key shift in the way online news is consumed has been driven by the increased portion of news traffic that occurs via SNSes. Because social media recommendations take the form of a link to a specific page, users recommending a news feature will post a link directly to that feature, bypassing the news organization's home page. However, a particular component of a multimedia packages can serve as the entry point to accessing the rest of package content – when a user lands at the first component, the interior navigation of the package can guide the user to the other content nodes. News games are often presented as part of a larger multimedia package (George-Palilonis and Spillman, 2011). Socially shared news games may also help facilitate incidental news exposure (see Tewksbury, Weaver, & Maddex, 2001) to headlines and "top stories" on the site.

Metrics for digital news success – directly tied to the ability to monetize the viewing of news content by selling advertising – have also seen a shift over recent years. Contemporary Web news rooms, aided by analytics software from companies like Chartbeat and Outbrain, pay granular attention to how content performs in terms of page views, video starts, and time on pages, and use this information to negotiate rates with advertisers, as well as to position and promote content (Tandoc, 2014). One aspect of the increased social mediation of news exposure is that engagement on the news site tends to be much lower for users arriving via social media than for users who access the site directly. A recent study showed that direct visitors to a specific site spend an average of nearly three times longer per visit, visit a specific site three times as often, and view five times as many pages over the course of a month than visitors who access the content through social media (Mitchell, Olmstead, & Jurkowitz, 2014).

An additional consideration for news organizations with regard to investment in games is the rapid growth in news consumption on mobile platforms. News consumers across the world are increasingly getting their online news via smartphone or tablet, although computers still remain slightly more popular (Reuters, 2013). Although mobile gaming is a booming industry overall, Web-based mobile news consumption poses several challenges to news organizations seeking to use news games to present and promote their content. While many legacy-based online news providers have been slow to adapt their delivery methods to an increasingly mobile-based audience (Nel & Westlund, 2012), the promise of news games in attracting mobile audience (through the promise of play, geographical awareness, and other factors) is counterbalanced by several challenges.

First, a number of technological constraints make it difficult for developers to ensure a consistent experience across platforms. A number of interactive games still utilize Adobe Flash technology to handle animation, interactivity and video streaming, but certain mobile devices (such as Apple's iPhone) have refused to support Flash's platform. Games which contain high-resolution images or video require a lot of bandwidth, which poses two potential barriers: users who do not have fast data coverage my get a sub-optimal experience with a lot of waiting, and users who do not pay for unlimited data access may choose to spend their data on more necessary or efficient content.

A second, but potentially related problem is news consumers' own preferences: they are much more likely to prefer mobile devices for consuming quick news, but not for in-depth experiences (Reuters, 2013); and they consume traditional journalistic content far more often than online-specific content (Wolf & Schnauber, 2014) Users access news via mobile in different settings and scenarios than they do from computers, often accessing content in gaps between their routines (Dimmick, Feaster, & Hoplamazian, 2011). As a result, they may be less likely to choose a game that requires attention and immersion over text content, which can be downloaded and consumed quickly.

On the other hand, mobile devices offer several benefits that game devices can harness to make news gamers' experience more customized to the situation in which users may play them. Perhaps chief among these is the potential of geolocation. Smartphone hardware has made it easy for application to access a user's precise geographical location, and a variety of general online games and applications have harnessed this ability to serve users unique features based on where they are, or to allow user to compete or interact with others in the same area. This feature also allows games to integrate other smartphone applications, such as maps or recommendation services, to add situationally relevant content. One could imagine an update to the *New York Times'* distracted driving simulation that replaces the background with satellite pictures from the users' surroundings. The ability for games to offer different user experiences based on user location may also add to the likelihood of repeat play.

GAMES AND QUIZZES AS NEWS CONTENT

The need for emotion-laden, sharable content with staying power highlights the role that non-traditional, interactive news features like games and quizzes can play in driving traffic to news sites and drawing attention to news stories. News games (often stylized as "newsgames") use unique properties of digital media to merge some of the functions of news with the ability of the user to interact with content and compete with herself or others. Relative to other digital games, games tied to news events need to be easy to play to have an appeal beyond frequent gamers (Bogost, Ferrari, & Schweitzer, 2010, p. 18). Sicart (2008) positions news games as a narrower subset of serious games (see Michael & Chen, 2005; Ritterfeld, Cody, & Vorderer, 2009) that use the notion of play and/or game mechanics for purposes that go beyond leisure. Proponents of serious games have argued that games can be used not only to provide recreation or diversion, but also to educate and help identify solutions to complex problems (McGonigal, 2011).

The inclusion of news-related games and quizzes as journalism is relatively new, and not without controversy. Some of the controversy stems from the function these games fulfill for their users and producers. Simon Ferrari has argued that "that most games called "newsgames" don't have the same intentions or goals as traditional reporting, or "the news," but rather those of the op-ed piece: to persuade; therefore, we should label these digital opinion pieces as "editorial" rather than "news. (Ferrari, 2009). The relationship between gameplay experience and news events also manifests itself in the creation of video games that are based on news. As noted by George-Palilonis & Spillman (2011), the 2005 video documentary "Playing the News" profiled the story of a company that developed a video game based on the United States' siege of Fallujah during the Iraq conflict in 2004. Other examples include PRISM the game and Eddy's Run: The Prism Prison, both based on the whistleblower Edward Snowden's revelations about government surveillance. These games, usually distributed freely online, are not developed by news organizations, and may often play a role that is more critical or persuasive than informative. For example, Eddy's Run, which puts the game player in the character of Snowden trying to evade government officials, was created by German development studio Binji as an "artistic game-homage" to Snowden (Pitcher, 2013).

Journalism is often described in terms of the functions it fulfills for its consumers, which vary across individuals and situations. These functions evolve over time with changes to the journalism industry and to audience expectations. Kovach and Rosenstiel, in their book "Blur: How to Know What's True in the Age of Information Overload," propose eight contemporary functions, that of authenticator, investigator, witness bearer, smart aggregator, forum organizer, and role model, empowerer, and sense-maker (Kovach & Rosenstiel, 2010, pp. 176-180). News games are well suited to play the latter two of these roles. News games can help empower the user by giving her a perspective she hasn't had before, by giving her the power to explore relationships between sets of data, or by allowing her to test or discover an aspect of her ability, or her personality. They can also help the user make sense of dimensions of a news story that other news forms do not present as well. Through the use of animation and simulation, games can certainly convey a sense of elapsed time and physical space that does not come across in still images and text, though may still be there in video. The added element of interactivity, which gives the user control over elements of the content or of the experience, can give users of news games an enhanced ability to discover, explore, and understand.

An important step in mapping out the landscape for a particular news form involves defining its boundaries and inclusion criteria. Beyond merely facilitating interaction between a user and content the interaction needs to be linked to a particular goal, score, or outcome (Bogost et al, 2010). The increased presence of games in the news landscape may be viewed in relation to a broaderrise in interest in and use of gamification across a wide variety of disciplines (Hamari, Koivisto, & Sarsa, 2014; Hanus & Fox, 2015; Lister, West, Canon, Sax, & Brodegard, 2014; Snyder & Hartig, 2013). Gamification, which has been defined as "the use of game design elements principles in non-game contexts (Deterding et al, 2013)," seeks to give the user intrinsic or extrinsic motivation for engaging with content, often by giving the user a task linked to a scoring system, timer or other gauge of performance. Gamification often seeks to motivate users to improve their knowledge or change their behavior, and reviews of gamification studies show some evidence that game-like elements can shape desired outcomes (Hamari et al., 2014). News games and quizzes may gamify current events and information by testing users' existing knowledge or ability or by providing users with an evaluation of their selves based on user interaction,

Gamification, however, is not a necessary component of news games; news organizations also deploy games that are very much traditional games, but which bring attention to a news topic through their subject matter or links to additional content. Additionally, organizations publish news graphics and documentary features allow the user to interact with content, but do not seek to "gamify" this interaction. Framing these types of user interactions as games connotes the idea that users voluntarily choose to engage with the content for the purpose of entertainment. However, such a simplistic causal explanation can also be inverted; as Deterding (2014) has argued, because gameplay involves voluntary decisions to start and stop playing, it fulfills a need for autonomy.

A second necessary element in any definition of news games is that the content of the game needs be related to an issue of contemporary interest. However, the nature of this relationship can vary widely. News games close to the subject matter can include knowledge quizzes pertaining to a breaking or ongoing news topic. However, games, quizzes, and simulations can also be relevant to news based on only the overall topic domain, on the inclusion of characters from current events, or on the release of data related to a news topic. To illustrate the breadth of news games, the Knight News Game Award presented by the John S. and James L. Knight Foundation includes the following in its scope: current events, infographic news games, puzzle news games, literacy games, community news games, and news game platforms. Much as the format can vary, the relationship of the gameplay to the news topic itself may be central or tangential.

The news games discussed in this chapter are games that are used for the purpose of conveying or promoting news information online, thus intentionally excluding commercial and recreational games that may also refer to current events. Other scholars have defined news games more broadly, such as "computer games used to participate in the public sphere with the intention of explaining or commenting on current news (Sicart, 2008)." The above definition duly notes that news games can fulfill the role of informational content or editorial content, explaining the news with an objective veneer or with a specific persuasive intent.

Key Variables in News Game Design

Although the ultimate success of a news game owes a lot to timing and competition, there are a number of design considerations that increase the odds of success, either by maximizing user engagement with the content or by increasing the ease with which the game's popularity can spread. These factors may underlie a news organization's decision to deploy an interactive game or quiz, even though its creation might require greater time and personnel resources than creating a text or video story. While these factors may not be unique to news games in comparison to other game formats, they constitute a set of relatively new criteria for news producers and publishers to consider when making content production decisions, and a set of characteristics that may be used to classify and manipulate characteristics of news for empirical research into their effects.

1.   Level and Type of Interactivity

At the heart of successful gameplay is the user's ability to submit information and receive information based on what was transmitted. This type of affordance of digital media forms is usually referred to as "interactivity," and it has been viewed as a hallmark of a variety of digital media types for decades. Specific definitions of user-system interactivity tend to focus either on the relatedness of the messages being transmitted between the user and the interface (e.g., Rafaeli & Ariel, 2007), or on the amount and type of content control afforded to the user (Kalyanaraman & Wojdynski, 2015). Message-contingency definitions of interactivity focus on how interrelated the information submitted by the user and the information returned by the system are, with the assumption that perceived message contingency drives beneficial effects of interactivity (Sundar, Bellur, Oh, Jia, & Kim, 2014).

News games are predicated on interactivity; in order to have the outcome of the game not be randomly generated, the game needs to collect input from the user, and the input needs to affect the result accordingly. Interactivity influences both the outcomes of news consumption and the nature of the news consumption itself. The nature of the news consumption is fundamentally shifted to an experience that is tailored, in real-time, to suit characteristics of the user and the situation in which she is consuming the feature. Maximizing user interaction is not the same as maximizing users' control over the content or increasing their satisfaction; certain calls to interact with content may be too demanding vis-à-vis the reward obtained (e.g., Sundar, Kalyanaraman, & Brown, 2003). Likewise, the interface features that maximize user interaction may not be the same as those that facilitate the best perception. One study of six interaction modalities found that allowing users to access content by sliding it across the screen led to greater memory, while access via mouse-over or cover-flow led to greater user interaction (Sundar, Xu, Bellur, Oh, & Jia, 2011).

In general, research that has compared non-interactive content to interactive content, as well as that which has compared less interactive content to more interactive content, has found that greater interactivity tends to lead to more positive attitudes toward the content. This has carried across to attitude toward brands (Lee, Park, & Wise, 2013). For news organization, the presence of interactive games and quizzes may contribute to users perceiving the news site itself as interactive, which for some users can improve quality of information processing and preference for the site (Broekhuizen & Hoffmann, 2012).

Individual differences between news consumers also affect the degree to which they are likely to seek out interactive content, how they engage with it, and the outcomes of the interaction. One overarching difference is that of user experience and self-efficacy with interactive content. These concepts have often been studied together, as "power usage" (Sundar & Marathe, 2010). Interactive graphics may increase users' motivation to process the content (Burmester, Mast, Tille, & Weber, 2010), but they may only do so for users who come to the content with low levels of involvement in the topic (Wojdynski, 2014).

Within the context of gaming, several aspects of the user interaction may influence perceptions. Successful design of interaction for news games manifests itself in a low bar to entry for less-experienced users. The interface must be intuitive to use, and the headline and other introductory text must explain the purpose or goal of the feature. While innovation certainly can give cachet, the level and type of interactivity should be somewhat in line with user expections for that particular content domain or gameplay type (Sohn, Ci, & Lee, 2007), or users may be disappointed or confused. Interactivity within videos games brings with it a set of dimensions that do not apply to other digital media, including character customization and perceptual persuasiveness and thus ought to be studied using distinct measures and classification criteria (Weber, Behr, & DeMartino, 2014). The level of technological advancement of a game has been shown to increase players' involvement, excitement, and physiological arousal in the context of the game (Ivory & Kalyanaraman, 2007).

2.   Design for Repeated Use

Another factor influencing the appeal and longevity of news games is the extent to which users are inclined to play the game more than once. While a singular experience may be rewarding enough for a player to decide to recommend the game to friends, repeated visits to an online feature provide chances for the player to play experience the game in different settings in his own life, some of which may more conducive than others to triggering the desire to share. Players may first access the game on a device on which they don't access their social networks, or through an Internet connection on which social network services are restricted.

The nature of play involved in the news game is one determinant of the likelihood for repeated play. Simulations and other games in which the objective is to reach a particular stage, play for as long as possible without error, or set a high score are designed to entice the user to improve her performance. However, incentivizing the reaching of certain scores, levels, times with the promise of additional features or content is a hallmark of digital gaming, and can be a powerful motivator (Richter, Raban, & Rafaeli,

2015), steering users to keep playing to reach higher levels of success. Interactive games in educational contexts have been shown to influence users' intrinsic motivation for achievement (Kang & Tan, 2014; Miller, Shell, Khandaker, & Soh, 2010).

With quizzes and question-based games, users may want to see if they can beat their initial score. However, if question-specific feedback is provided, in many games this becomes a matter of rote memorization. However, one way of adding variety to users' gameplay is by varying elements of the presentation of the quiz question and answers. This can include simply varying the order in which questions or answer choices are presented, or it can include varying the questions or answers themselves. Dynamic loading of content from a database (for example, using random number generation to load a different subset from a list of possible content each time) introduces a notion of repeated serendipity and discovery to the user experience: Each time the quiz is opened, the user doesn't know which questions she is going to receive. If the content is humorous or otherwise engaging, users may revisit the content several times to make sure that they have viewed all the possible questions or content nodes. The ability to compare one's score to others may also motivate users to continue playing (Yee, 2006).

Repeated use of a game also may enhance effects of the game on how users perceive the content. One mechanism through which repetition may shape effects is that of desensitization; exposure to serious news content in the context of a game may lead to desensitize users to the serious consequences of those issues. For example, repeated play of video games has been shown to lead to desensitization toward violence (Breuer, Scharkow, & Quandt, 2014; Brockmyer, 2015). However, studies have also shown that exposure to prosocial behavior and characters that act counter to stereotypes can lead to positive short-term and long-term effects on players' attitudes and behavior (see Greitemeyer & Mügge, 2014 for a meta-analysis). Both of these outcomes might be less likely in online news games than the broader video game world due to the differences in content; news games more typically do not have the depth of character development and game play afforded by console games.

3. The Ability to Acquire New Knowledge

News games take place in the domain of informational content. While the opportunity for play may serve as an initial driver to the news game, the opportunity to learn something new in the process may enhance user's motivations. Games that are tied to current issues in the news can offer users an engaging way to learn details about the topic while in pursuit of gaming goals. Quizzes are more directly designed to not only measure players' knowledge, but to identify gaps and provide the information therein. Quizzes published alongside informational content can also serve to reinforce the key points, dates, or individuals in a news story, likely increasing the likelihood of the user remembering this information at a future date

Some news games can offer specific context to a news story that is difficult for journalists to provide through another form. Simulation games (see the discussion of "Battle of the Bags" in the following section) can position the viewer in the role of a particular character in the news story, and give the user gaming tasks to recreate a particular moment or test a virtual skill. First-person video clips or animations can let the game player "see" what the character in the news story might see. In the role of the story character, the users can make decisions on the fly that shape the outcome. Through this process, the user obtains not factual knowledge, but a simulated experiential knowledge. This knowledge may not only create empathy for the specific participants in a story, but can help provide a context for the factual information contained in the game or in adjacent story content.

A TYPOLOGY OF GAMES AND QUIZZES IN ONLINE NEWS

News games vary widely in their interface design, purpose, subject matter, and mode of game play. Because novelty is a key element in the attention a game might receive, and thus its potential for viral spread, developers of news games and quizzes are often looking to re-invent the proverbial wheel in terms of presentation and opportunities for user interaction. This relative premium on uniqueness poses a challenge to creating an exhaustive and exclusive typology of news games. However, sorting games on the basis of the type and purpose of user interaction involved in game play allows for the creation of categories that have meaning to both producers and consumers.

Other typologies for interactive news content have placed an emphasis on a different scope. George-Palilonis and Spillman (2011) created a five-category typology of interactive graphics, drawing on earlier work by Nichani and Rajamanickam (2003), which included *serious games* as one broad category, but separate categories for *simulations* and *instructives* that could also include gamified elements. They suggest several criteria that serious games must include, including use of game strategies (such as having a story line that pulls users through the game), featuring some form of winning and losing or other payoff at the end, have an explanation of the rules of play, and involve tasks that can be achieved via a computer interface (George-Palilonis & Spillman, 2011, p. 173). Bogost et al (2010) developed a news-game-specific categorization scheme on the basis of their content and intent, although different categories refer to either content topic or presentation format, rendering the categories not exclusive. Their typology, which includes games about current events, infographic news games, documentary news games, puzzle, literacy news games, and community news games, provides useful labels for analyzing a broad set of games created by different parties that relate to news events.

Although the previous taxonomies have much value in providing some labels that can be used to differentiate some examples of interactive content from others, this chapter proposes a streamlined classification for games and quizzes used by news organizations based on the functions these games fulfill for both the news organization and the news audience. These classifications draw on the work of the authors above, based primarily on the nature of the user interaction involved in the game, the information necessary to develop the game, and the news values the game format can convey to its players.

There may be many reasons why a news organization would choose to devote resources to the development and promotion of game content. Games are a vehicle for technological innovation that may be rewarded by accolades from journalistic peers and increased public attention to a specific reporting project, new Web site, or new publication. Games may lure a player by providing a diversion, but spark that player's interest in consuming additional content on that topic. Games can even serve as a digital beta test of interface elements and formats that can be later applied to more serious content. However, it's also important to consider the ways in which games shape users' interaction with the news information itself – their interest in engaging with the content, their knowledge, their ability to understand complex processes or ideas, and their attitudes toward the issues raised in the content.

Games can also provide consumers of online news with an experience that other news content cannot match. One of the strongest ways that online games provide users with an experience that analog media cannot match is through their ability to provide customization of information. Kalyanaraman and Sundar (2006) define customization as matching aspects of the content to aspects of the self. The agency model of customization (Sundar, 2008) suggests that customization influences information processing chiefly by making the user a gatekeeper for his own information. Web-based technologies allow scalable and rapid customization of content, either through actively collecting data from the user, or through passive means of determining user interest and preferences. While news organizations often use these forms (see Thurman, 2011), the ability of users to choose their own paths and answers in online news games brings the notion of active control into the news environment. Research has shown that users have higher satisfaction with news content that is personalized based on their interest (Sela, Lavie, Inbar, Oppenheim, & Meyer, 2014).

Games created by online news organizations can take many forms, although the classifications below are designed to encompass the breadth in scope, gameplay, and news function represented by existing news games, and provide a framework for journalists and scholars that aids in the creation and study of future games as well.

Type 1: Identity Quiz

One type of news game that saw a spike in popularity with the growth of BuzzFeed in 2013 was the customizable quiz or identity quiz. Identity quizzes allow users to answer a series of questions, typically in a multiple choice format, to find out the answer to an overarching question, which is usually framed as providing information about the user. BuzzFeed's many quizzes show the breadth, and often lighthearted tone, of this genre, ranging from topics such as "Which children's book character are you?" and "Which pop star should be your best friend?" to "Which state do you actually belong in" and "What career should you actually have?" These questions arouse potential players' curiosity, and they complete the quiz as a means of interacting with an online oracle – seeking a dose of self-knowledge in addition to amusement. While BuzzFeed may be strongly associated with these quizzes, other publishers such as Bitecharge, Zimbio, and Playbuzz have found a large audience for similar content.

The gameplay experience for identity quizzes is straightforward. The user is presented with a series of questions, either in a single vertical scrolling page or spread across consecutive pages. The number of answer choices for each question typically varies from four to nine. Once the user has answered all questions, the user receives the answer to her question. Sometimes this is presented in the form of a numerical score, but more often, the user receives a categorical response, along with an explanation. For example, upon completing BuzzFeed's quiz about pop-star best friends, one might receive the following response:

You got: Beyoncé. Beyoncé has a lot going on in her life and might not always be available, but go out of her way to make you feel loved. She's endlessly inspirational, and would always be fun and interesting to talk to. (Perpetua, 2014).

The compelling draw of identity quizzes to players is the same characteristic that makes them spread with relative ease: At the end of the quiz, the user receives customized payoff in the form of information about himself. Sharing information about one's self has been shown to be intrinsically more rewarding than sharing other information (Tamir & Mitchell, 2012), and so consumers who are steered toward a customized result should be more likely to broadcast the information. Researchers have found that individuals place a high value on being able to communicate information about themselves, including forgoing payment to answer more questions about themselves than others (Tamir & Mitchell, 2012). Self-disclosure from others also leads individuals to disclose information about themselves (Dindia, 2002; Sprecher, Treger, Wondraw, Hilaire, & Wallpe, 2013). While the propensity to share information may be moderated by personality differences such as extraversion (Wang, 2013), social media users in general disclose information in a way that allows them to demonstrate their tastes and optimized self-image (Qiu, Lin, Leung, & Tov, 2012; Wang, 2013).

While many widely-disseminated identity quizzes are frivolous in nature, their popularity and share-ability provides opportunities for news organizations to capitalize on their appeal. One such opportunity is the launch of such quizzes to coincide with the release of large data sets. By actually allowing the real-time processing and accessing of data, online news sites have an advantage over traditional media forms in handling data stories. Top news organizations have already capitalized on these abilities by publishing interactive interfaces which allow users to view subsets of data based on demographic (e.g., the *New York Times'* "American Time Use Survey") or geographic variables (e.g., the *Seattle Times'* "What Your Seattle Address Says About You") by allowing users to click on or hover over a map, or delimit data using radio buttons and drop-down menus. Pairing a data front-end with an interactive quiz allows the user to see how she compares to the individuals whose data make up the data set. In some cases, the quizzes may also collect and store user-submitted data and integrate aggregate user data into future iterations of the content; such practices raise the privacy risks to the individual consumer considerably, particularly in combination with cookies, log-ins, or other forms users tracking (for a broader discussion, see the "User Data and Privacy Concerns" section of this chapter). Content generated by users within online games is likely to be in line with other user-generated content in online news, which typically does not involve users in the news production process, but rather promotes news consumption (Jönsson & Örnebring, 2011).

Identity quizzes lack some traditional elements of gamification. They have no storyline, and motivation for play comes in the form of self-discovery rather than attaining a level or score. However, these games appeal to users on the basis of the result they offer, and users complete the quiz in order to view this result. This may take the form of honestly answering questions for an accurate outcome, or of trying to frame one's answers to reach a specific desired outcome. Either way, they seem tailor-made for self-disclosure through social media sharing.

Example: "How Millennial Are You?"

Title: "How Millennial Are You?"
Publisher: Pew Research Center
Date Published: February 23, 2010
Created by: Leah Melani Christian, Russell Heimlich, Michael Keegan, Scott Keeter, Alicia Parlapiano, Michael Piccorossi and Paul Taylor, an Courtney Kennedy, Pew Resarch Center.
Available at: www.pewresearch.org/quiz/how-millennial-are-you/
Description: The Pew Research Center, a U.S.-based organization that releases social science survey data on a variety of topics, has published identity quizzes with some of their data sets. Their 2010 report, "The Millennials: Confident. Connected. Open to Change" consisted of the following components: An executive summary, written much like a news story announcing the release of a data set; the full report containing questions, results, and graphs; videos from a day-long conference timed with the release of the data set; and a 14-item quiz titled "How Millennial Are You?" The quiz consisted of multiple-choice and yes-or-no questions about users' recent media consumption and beliefs, with the final question asking participants to select their age-range for the purposes of collecting how people of different ages do on the quiz. The response page assigned participants a "Millennial score" between 0 and 100, and showed the score on an axis which anchored average

scores for various generational cohorts. Beneath this axis, users were shown how respondents of various age groups responded to each question, and were allowed to modify their original response to see its effect on their overall score. The interface also included buttons which allowed users to share the quiz and their results through social media channels; users who clicked one of these buttons while signed in to their social network received a pop-up window with a pre-written message, "How Millennial Are You? I scored (score)," along with a link to the quiz. To capitalize on this as a potential entry point to the rest of the package, the quiz homepage included a description of and link to the Millennial report itself. Thus not only can Pew use the quiz as a means of increasing the audience for its report, but it also gains a tool for collecting expanded data beyond the original phone survey on which the report was based.

Type 2: Knowledge Quiz

Unlike identity quizzes, knowledge quizzes require players to submit information that is much less personal. Although the nature of the interaction is similar, the success of knowledge quizzes is based in part on the degree of challenge they offer to users. Much like classroom assessements, these games gauge users' ability to correctly answer a series of questions that measure their knowledge, usually by selecting the correct choice from a series of options. Knowledge quizzes are likely to have a shorter shelf life than identity quizzes, as the both the newsworthiness of the topic and the accuracy of the answers may change with time. These quizzes can be news story specific, or very general (e.g., Huffington Post's "How Well Do You Know Your Geography?"). *The Daily Mirror* celebrated the return to television of the cult classic "Danger Mouse" with a 15-item quiz measuring participants' recall of the original television series. *The New York Times*, long renowned for challenging print readers with its crossword puzzle, added an online Weekly News Quiz as part of its education outreach blog, "The Learning Network."

Although knowledge quizzes can consist solely of text-based questions, the possibility to incorporate graphic elements allows the ability to test other forms of knowledge; interfaces can also move beyond the school-quiz approach by including rich media and gestural interactions. Users can be challenged with their ability to recognize the faces of key players in the news, or by testing their ability to identify geographic locations on a map. *The Guardian's* "The Toughest Maps Quiz… In the World" challenged users to decode the topic of six interactive data visualizations embedded from Google charts. *The Telegraph's* "Name that Tennis Player's Grunt" quiz combines Soundcloud audio clips with a drag-and-drop interface that allows users to match player names and faces to each audio clip. Like identity quizzes, knowledge quizzes provide user with an end results that may facilitate viral sharing: in this case, a performance score.

The effects of online quiz use on news learning have not been well established, although there is some support for interactive quizzes stimulating learning. The inclusion of game-like elements has been shown toincrease learner motivation and performance in educational courses (Barata, Gama, Jorge, & Goncalves, 2012; Moreno, 2012; Squire, 2006), although much of this research focuses on process-based learning. Interactive quizzes in museum kiosks have been shown to lead to improved knowledge compared to paper materials (Mikalef, Giannakos, Chorianopoulos, & Jaccheri, 2013). Knowledge quizzes in a news context might also demonstrate these effects, although whether and how users complete quizzes in relation to consuming other content on the topic is likely to play a role.

Example: "Staying in Bounds"

Title: "Staying in Bounds"
Publisher: Raleigh News & Observer
Date Published: December 16, 2010
Created by: Kristen Long, Pressley Baird, and Seth Wright, RFDN
Available at: http://reesenews.org/2010/12/16/staying-in-bounds/7929
Description: One example of thinking beyond the confines of text-based knowledge quizzes is "Staying in Bounds," an interactive knowledge quiz gamecreated by the student-led Reese Felts Digital Newsroom at UNC-Chapel Hill and later published by the Raleigh *News & Observer*. Published in the aftermath of a National Collegiate Athletics Association (NCAA) investigation into the eligibility of several UNC football players, the game puts the user in the role of a lauded collegiate athlete negotiating the tricky line between acceptable benefits and NCAA eligibility violations. Players are asked to input their first name, and then taken on a ten-question odyssey of potential pitfalls, which were developed with the aid of the director of compliance for UNC's athletic department. Each scenario consists of a slide containing an image of a potential benefit provider – an assistant coach, a sorority sister at your college, etc. – a benefit scenario, and two options from which the user can complete the narrative.

In one scenario, a car dealer in the player's college town asks to use the player's name to promote the dealership in a trivia contest. In another, a local lawyer offers to field inquiries from agents on behalf of the player, to avoid improper contact. After the user accepts or declines each offer, a short message pops up offering brief feedback without revealing whether the choice was correct. After ten questions, the user receives a message describing whether the actions taken violated NCAA regulations, and whether the player missed any opportunities to receive permissible benefits. The user can roll over each question number to see question-specific information, including excerpts from the relevant section of the NCAA compliance guide.

"Staying in Bounds" has several features that make it a successful example of a knowledge quiz. First, although the material is based on knowledge of the NCAA rules, the quiz is presented in the form of a narrative, pulling the user into a storyline. Each scenario within the game relates to a specific section of the NCAA policy, and the user gets to see the actual policy wording at the end. Secondly, the game draws its ten questions from a database containing more than 20, so the user gets a novel experience on subsequent visits, increasing the odds that a single user will play multiple times. Finally, this quiz straddles the line between timely and evergreen news events – while its initial deployment coincided with the NCAA's investigation of UNC, its content is valid for as long as the current NCAA rules stay on the books; thus, the quiz is well-positioned for future spikes of popularity when other athletes run afoul of the rules.

Type 3: Simulation

While identity and knowledge quizzes trade primarily in information, online simulations can provide players with a realistic vicarious experience that takes greater advantage of the technologies available via the Web. Simulation-based games allow the user to engage in virtual actions that mirror, with some degree of accuracy, actions that take place in the real world. Virtual simulations In the context of news, simulations can be used to increase the degree of empathy between the news consumer and the subjects of the news story. Often, this is done using animation, first-person perspective, and some sort of virtual experience. In most cases, the simulation ends after a set amount of time has elapsed, or a specific goal has been reached, and the player receives a grade based on their performance in the virtual task.

Simulations typically allow the user to act in the role of one of the subjects in a news story. Examples such as MSNBC.com's "Battle of the Bags" and "Can You Spot the Threat?" allow the user to view realistic approximations of baggage scanners and grocery store check-out counters, and engage in tasks that approximate real-world interactions with the equipment. Similarly, The *New York Times'* "Gauging Your Distraction" typifies the value of simulation in the context of a news story. Published to coincide with a news story about the hazards of distracted driving, the game simulates driving while trying to receive, type, and send text messages. Although the demands on the user to successfully complete the driving task consist only of pushing a single button every two or three seconds to enter the appropriate lane, the interface also includes a virtual smartphone which requires interaction to read messages and type responses. The split visual interface and concurrent demands on attention effectively convey the difficulties involved in task switching while driving safely.

Another category of simulations focuses less on approximating behavior than on giving users an interface which allows them to make decisions in the role of another party. Features such as *Washington Post's* "Oscars Ballot Builder," *New York Times'* "You Fix the Budget" allow users to view the world from the perspective of Academy voters and legislators, respectively. Although these game Over the course of the 2008 and 2012 U.S. Presidential Election, a number of organizations created graphical map-based calculators that allowed users to view election scenarios by assigning a winner to each state. Another professional simulation, PBS's "Decisions on Deadline," may hit closer to home for journalists. Launched by PBS's Independent Lens documentary series to coincide with a video documentary about plagiarism, the game puts the player in the role of a journalist in a fictional town trying to report and publish salient details about a series of news topics while working against deadline pressure and a budget

In both "Gauging Your Distraction" and "Can You Spot the Threats" (see box below), the game does not achieve its news value by providing the user with additional factual information. While the accompanying news stories provide the timeliness and the facts, the simulations allow the user an approximate understanding of the issue being discussed. This affords the users a different facet of understanding, one that is rooted in the simulated experience rather than information processing. The ultimate effects of playing such simulations on how users perceive and remember the news is unclear. Classroom studies of whether interactive simulations improve learning outcomes vis-à-vis traditional learning methods show higher cognitive gains for simulations, although user preferences may vary by gender, with females being more likely to prefer simulations (Vogel et al, 2006). However, while most classroom learning simulations are developed with specific cognitive, skill-based, or affective learning outcomes (Krieger, 1993; Wilson et al, 2009) in mind, news simulations are more likely to be geared toward engaging the user in the subject matter and perhaps drawing the user to other site content.

Simulation games are only as effective as the gameplay is engaging and relevant to the task being simulated. Because both engagement and verisimilitude are task-specific, every simulation game will generally require unique design and development. While such games can provide an inimitable contribution to news packages covering a current event, the time and planning required to create a successful simulation makes this a difficult format for time-sensitive events.

Simulation games pose another challenge when the simulation involves actual events. Such games, by their nature, offer users a multitude of scenarios rather than offering a specific path through evidence like an article or video might (see Bogost et al, 2010, p.70). Empowering the user with the ability to make events unfold in a different manner than they did historically has the potential to shape viewers' perceptions of the actual event, though there is little evidence to show such effects. How the gameplay occurs and the manner in which the factual events are presented may play a role. Immersive online games demand sizable cognitive resources and task working memory, which may leave the player with fewer resources to allocate to information presented separately (Kalyuga & Plass, 2009; Schrader & Bastiaens, 2012).

Example: "Can You Spot the Threats?"

Title: Baggage Screening: Can You Spot the Threats?
Publisher: NBCNews.com
Date Published: 2002
Created By: Alex Johnson, Ashley Wells, Fred Birchman, Asim Khan
Available At: http://www.nbcnews.com/id/34623505/ns/us_news-security/t/can-you-spot-threats/

Although this game is now over a decade old, it still serves as a benchmark for using simulations to add value to an online news story. Published in the aftermath of the attacks on the United States on September 11th, this game allows users a chance to step into the role of an airport baggage screener. The timed game features a scrolling series of cross-sectional x-ray photographs of luggage. The player can choose to flag each piece of luggage as containing an explosive, gun, or knife, or let the luggage pass through unflagged. The user is allowed to stop and start the scrolling as if it were a real conveyor belt, to adjust the level of zoom of the images, and to toggle between color and black-and-white views of the luggage. At the end of the two-minute timer, the player views a results screen listing the percentage of threats correctly identified, the number of threats missed, and the number of false alarms. In addition, a sentence provides summary feedback, such as "Letting even one threat by would get a fully trained screener fired." When the scrolling images are stopped, the user is serenaded by audio clips of impatient passengers ("Hey buddy, can you get this operation moving a little bit faster here?"), adding a sense of pressure and realism.

"Can You Spot the Threats?" has a somewhat dated feel due to the game's size and audio quality. Although it's Flash based, most of the graphics are bitmaps, and stretching the window beyond its 525-by-400-pixel size decreases the quality of the graphics. The game's narration, by MSNBC's Natalie Morales, is tough to understand at times. While these factors may limit the games telepresence, they don't detract from the game's ultimate "message," if there is one: that expediently and effectively locating threats by looking at x-rayed baggage is difficult.

Type 4: Topical Play

Classifying content into the fourth category of news games is easiest to define by the absence of inclusion in the first three. Topical play focuses on games that do not substantially engage the user in content-related issues, but nonetheless provide a gaming experience that is topically related to the news content. In other words, these games may attract users to a news organization's site on the basis of the gameplay experience, but only relate to a news topic by virtue of the characters, the setting, or the objective. Such games, therefore, are similar to multitudes of other digital games, but have ties to a news organization and a news topic.

Topical play games often involve a re-skinning or repurposing of existing, familiar digital or analog games. The Guardian's "Beat the Bard," offers a head-to-head matchup of character attributes, similar to card-based roleplaying games such as Magic the Gathering and Pokemon. Users compete against a computer-controlled "Bard" to pick the traits for which the card in their hand may be superior. Published to coincide with Shakespeare's 450th birthday, the game may provide a treat for Shakespeare devotees who know the characters, their traits, and their words well, but the simple nature of the gameplay makes such knowledge unnecessary for enjoyment. Other examples of topical play have included online memory challenges published to coincide with a feature about a competitive memory champion (*New York Times*), or a game that allows users to seat members of the Supreme Court by seniority (*Washington Post*). These games foster interaction with elements of a news story in ways that do not rely on specific knowledge, but rather usually some dimension of skill or luck.

Simply playing a game that relates to a news topic or persons in the news may influence the way game players feel toward those issues and individuals, particularly if the game serves as a first exposure. Much research has demonstrated that individuals view information that seems familiar more positively (Zajonc, 1968). Moreover, this mere exposure effect is greater for information that is not consciously perceived (Bornstein & D'Agostino, 1992). These effects have demonstrated in studies of online advertising games, with participants' accessibility of favorable attitudes (Glass, 2007). Advergaming research also suggests that the congruity between the game play and the subject matter itself may be an important moderator of effects; games in which game and product have been congruent lead to greater recall of the product (Gross, 2010), more positive attitudes toward the product (Huang & Yang, 2012), and a greater carryover effects from liking the game to liking the product (Wise, Bolls, Kim, Venkataraman, & Meyer, 2008). While the broad

In sum, topical play games involve little gamification of news consumption, and instead rely more the incorporation of games into the topic and setting of news content.

Example: "Rock-Paper-Scissors"

Title: "Rock-Paper-Scissors: You Vs. The Computer"
Publisher: *New York Times*
Date Published: October 7, 2010
Created by: Gabriel Dance and Tom Jackson
Available at: http://www.nytimes.com/interactive/science/rock-paper-scissors.html
Description: Topical play can take a wide variety of forms. In October 2010, as part of a months-long series of features on developments in artificial intelligence, the *New York Times* published this quiz as a feature that could be accessed from various story pages in the series. The nature of the gameplay is simple. After selecting a skill-level ("novice" or "veteran"), the user gets to play an infinite number of rounds of the classic choice game Rock-Paper-Scissors against a virtual opponent. The user indicates her choice of throws for each round by clicking one of three buttons, and then sees a brief animation of two hands, each throwing one the hand-gestures. When the throws are shown, the screen automatically updates with feedback about who won the hand. Additionally, on the computer-player's side of the screen, the user views a stream of feedback about what information the computer is using to learn how the game works, what logic rules the computer used to determine which hand to throw. A linked feature at the bottom of the screen allows the user to share her score after a minimum of 20 rounds played.

This game is a typical example of topical play. While the feature is promoted as sheds a little bit of light into basic operations related to computer intelligence, most of the screen interface is dedicated to simply keeping track of the competition between user and virtual agent. The other stories in the series are not linked here, although one later Times article about computer intelligence is linked at the bottom. Nonetheless, the cheap virtual game allows the user a level of competition that is tied to the other content in the series, and may serve as both an entry point to users seeking more information about the broader topic and a way to prolong the time readers of the articles in the series spend on the *Times'* site.

OPPORTUNITIES AND CHALLENGES IN THE STUDY OF NEWS GAMES

Although news games may play an increasingly important role in the creation of online multimedia packages, the design and creation of news games poses a number of challenges that will likely keep the deployment of such games to special features. First and foremost, the creation of news games is relatively time-consuming and expensive in comparison to other formats. The design of news games requires the development of a storyline and game mechanics (Wei, 2013), and usually necessitates the work of personnel with varied skillsets – a reporter for the information and content, a graphic designer for the visual appearance, and a programmer to create a functional, interactive product, not to mention an individual to design (and refine) the gameplay and user experience.

The time and budget costs associated with production can be diminished with an attention to platform. Just as BuzzFeed's integration of a quiz-builder into their publishing system enabled mass production of quizzes, organizations' investment in the building of reusable code and interfaces can pay off in the economy of scale, and lead to the widespread of dissemination of a particular game format or design. A second issue is whether the mere act of playing a game triggers users to apply a different schema than they might to traditionally presented news content, and whether this affects persuasive and cognitive outcomes of playing news games.

User Data and Privacy Concerns

Playing a news game or quiz requires user interaction of some sort, and often requires users to submit information about themselves. The same characteristics of identity quizzes that make the compelling to complete and to share may also keep certain users away. One aspect of identity quizzes that may curb their steep rise in popularity is their potential role in gathering data about the player and using that data for advertising purposes. While black market personal info about customers may be relatively inexpensive for cyber-thieves to procure (Hill & Greenburg, 2010), data sets that include answers about viewers' preferences and desires can be useful for online marketers. While popular-press outlets have begun to raise awareness that these data may be collected, the average user may still be unlikely to be dissuaded from the fun of completing and sharing quiz results. Blogger Dan Barker highlighted some of the data that BuzzFeed sends along with quiz responses, including participants' gender, age, country, whether they've connected via Facebook, and how often they've shared BuzzFeed stories. This data is transmitted alongside quiz answers, which can range from the benign to the highly personal, as Barker highlighted with selections from the quiz "How Privileged Are You," which asked about participants' race, comfort with their gender, and history of sexual abuse, among other questions. Barring a substantial privacy-fueled backlash, however, identity quizzes allow users a personal entry point to the news that allows them to learn and share information about themselves and their friends.

The Ethics of Playing With the News

News is rooted in real events that often have a profound physical, emotional, or economic impact on real human beings. Presenting those issues in a way that treats the subjects and the audience ethically is a challenge in any platform. Games such as simulations or topical play construct a representational world in which complex realities are often simplified or misrepresented. In video games, such worlds often include stereotypical representations of others based on race (Burgess, Dill, Stermer, Burgess, & Brown, 2011; Chan, 2005) and gender (Fox & Tang, 2014). While many news games are not very character-driven, the use of images or drawings to represent real individuals leaves a lot in the hands of the designer. While the representations within games may perpetuate stereotypes, simulation games that place the reader in the role of an out-group member may also be capable of reducing negative stereotypes (Alhabash & Wise, 2014).

A second ethical issue that is specific to journalistic games involves the presentation of fact or truth in the game. Because news games are deliberately released to capitalize on current events, users may encounter them while searching for factual information. While designers may assume a certain level of media literacy on the part of their intended audience, the potential impact of the information in news games on how users perceive the issues warrants discussion of ethical standards in issue presentation. Games that address military conflicts, serious medical issues, and other sensitive issues should be subject to the same close editing that traditional news stories on these issues receive. Professional guidelines and ethical standards should be updated to include ethics in content design.

Future Research Directions in News Games

News games, especially presented in the context of news by news organizations, are relatively recent addition to consumer choices in browsing online news. The content domain of news games changes monthly to include new manners of user interaction, and the development of platform-based changes can lead to the proliferation of a specific type of content (recall BuzzFeed's addition of a quiz-builder to their CMS, which allowed staff members without programming skills to build quizzes). As these formats and their uses evolve, the role these quizzes play in explaining, augmenting, or advertising the news may become clearer. Because of this rapid evolution, content analyses of news games that valuable insight into news game topics, types, interface elements, scoring and results systems, characters, and other attributes are needed to help practitioners and researchers understand the playing field.

Several streams of research into processes and effects of video games warrant extension and re-examination in the context of news games. One of these focuses on the role of individual differences in shaping selective exposure to and outcomes of news games. Much is known about individual characteristics that pre-dispose individuals to play games and play heavily (Seounmi, Lee, & Doyle, 2003; Westwood & Griffiths, 2010), although the average age of gamers has increased as kids who grew up playing video games turned into adults. Individual differences may intervene at several stages in the process of news game consumption: certain users may be more likely to select or search for news games, more capable of playing advanced games or processing complex information; more likely to be inspired by game play to seek additional content; or more likely to be persuaded based on gaming experience.

In order to fully understand the potential of news games, more robust empirical research is needed examining how presenting news content in the form of a game, rather than a linear format, affects users' attention, understanding, and recall of the content. While some studies have shown positive relationships between playing of certain video games and cognitive performance, the evidence is mixed, and often clouded by methodological problems (see Boot, Blakely, and Simons, 2011). The challenge for the study of format in news involves the difficulty of creating stimulus materials that include the same content presented in multiple formats; game design requires time and expertise, trying to hold and trying to holding the content constant between a simulation game and a text story requires much subjective decision making. While these challenges make such research time-consuming and cost-intensive, they also potentially heighten the value of the findings. In addition, because such games are often meant to complement more informative stories, more research is needed examining the effects of link structure and positioning within such news story packages on selection and engagement. Finally, the continued growth in mobile news consumption also signals a need for examining how devices may shape news game interaction through screen size, input modality, or a number of other characteristics.

CONCLUSION

This chapter began with the premise that the rise in digital and mobile news consumption and the increased role of social media in driving traffic posed an opportunity for news organizations to leverage interactive games and quizzes to attract attention and build their audience. The desire for news organizations to have their content stand out from the clutter in their consumers' social media streams means that content should be accessible and engaging, two strengths of news games. While research has shown that users respond to effective interactive content with favorable attitudes toward the content and its source, findings regarding the impact of interactivity on cognitive processing vary greatly by content domain, situation, and individual differences. Due to the resources involved in the production of news games, they are not likely to represent a large portion of the content published by news organizations any time soon, or perhaps ever. However, the ability to publish content in these novel forms gives producers additional tools that can be used – effectively or poorly – to convey a news story to an audience, or to seek to draw a larger and different audience than conventional story forms.

While games and quizzes may hold a lot of potential, the rush of news organizations into the world of game creation is not without its drawbacks. For one, games and quizzes may be viewed by audience members already skeptical of tabloidized news content that the publishing organization prioritizes diversion over covering serious issues. Conversely, audience members may view certain news stories or their consequences as less serious when those news stories become fodder for a game. In addition to changing the relationship between news and consumer, games that allow users to submit information about their preferences, behavior, or knowledge may invite exploitive use of collected data by the news organization. At the very least, they introduce potential privacy risks that do not exist in more traditional news formats.

While identity quizzes, knowledge quizzes, simulations and topical play are likely to continue to represent only a sliver of content published by news organizations, their potential effects in helping spread information and recruit new consumers to news make them a promising development in the competition for online audiences. As the utilization of these formats continues to grow, we will better be able to examine how consuming news by playing shapes the way we perceive the world around us.

REFERENCES

Alhabash, S., & Wise, K. (2014). Playing their game: Changing stereotypes of Palestinians and Israelis through videogame play. *New Media & Society, 1461444814525010*. doi:10.1177/1461444814525010

Bek, M. G. (2004). Research note: Tabloidization of news media an analysis of television news in Turkey. *European Journal of Communication, 19*(3), 371–386. doi:10.1177/0267323104045264

Berger, J., & Milkman, K. L. (2012). What Makes Online Content Viral? *JMR, Journal of Marketing Research, 49*(2), 192–205. doi:10.1509/jmr.10.0353

Bogost, I., Ferrari, S., & Schweizer, B. (2010). *Newsgames: Journalism at play.* Cambridge, MA: MIT Press.

Boot, W. R., Blakely, D. P., & Simons, D. J. (2011). Do action video games improve perception and cognition? *Frontiers in Psychology, 2.* PMID:21949513

Breuer, J., Scharkow, M., & Quandt, T. (2014). Tunnel vision or desensitization? The effect of interactivity and frequency of use on the perception and evaluation of violence in digital games. *Journal of Media Psychology: Theories, Methods, and Applications, 26*(4), 176–188. doi:10.1027/1864-1105/a000122

Brockmyer, J. F. (2015). Playing Violent Video Games and Desensitization to Violence. *Child and Adolescent Psychiatric Clinics of North America, 24*(1), 65–77. doi:10.1016/j.chc.2014.08.001 PMID:25455576

Broekhuizen, T., & Hoffmann, A. (2012). Interactivity Perceptions and Online Newspaper Preference. *Journal of Interactive Advertising, 12*(2), 29–43.

Burgess, M. C. R., Dill, K. E., Stermer, S. P., Burgess, S. R., & Brown, B. P. (2011). Playing With Prejudice: The Prevalence and Consequences of Racial Stereotypes in Video Games. *Media Psychology, 14*(3), 289–311. doi:10.1080/15213269.2011.596467

Burmester, M., Mast, M., Tille, R., & Weber, W. (2010). How Users Perceive and Use Interactive Information Graphics: An Exploratory Study. Proceedings of *Information Visualisation (IV), 2010 14th International Conference* (pp. 361–368). doi:10.1109/IV.2010.57

Carr, D. (2014, August 3). Inside Glenn Greenwald's Mountaintop Home Office. *The New York Times.* Retrieved from http://www.nytimes.com/2014/08/04/business/media/inside-glenn-greenwalds-mountaintop-home-office.html

Chan, D. (2005). Playing with race: The ethics of racialized representations in e-games. *International Review of Information Ethics, 4*(12), 24–30.

Cherubini, F. (2014, August 1). When Data Drives the News: A Look at Analytics Beyond the Page View. *Mediashift. PBS.* Retrieved from http://www.pbs.org/mediashift/2014/08/when-data-drives-the-news-a-look-at-analytics-beyond-the-page-view/

Deterding, S. (2014). Eudaimonic Design, or: Six Invitations to Rethink Gamification (SSRN Scholarly Paper No. ID 2466374). Rochester, NY: Social Science Research Network; Retrieved from http://papers.ssrn.com/abstract=2466374

Deterding, S., Björk, S. L., Nacke, L. E., Dixon, D., & Lawley, E. (2013). Designing Gamification: Creating Gameful and Playful Experiences. Proceedings of CHI '13 Extended Abstracts on Human Factors in Computing Systems (pp. 3263–3266). New York, NY, USA: ACM; doi:10.1145/2468356.2479662

Deterding, S., Dixon, D., Khaled, R., & Nacke, L. (2011, September). From game design elements to gamefulness: defining gamification. *Proceedings of the 15th International Academic MindTrek Conference: Envisioning Future Media Environments* (pp. 9-15). ACM. doi:10.1145/2181037.2181040

Dimmick, J., Feaster, J. C., & Hoplamazian, G. J. (2011). News in the interstices: The niches of mobile media in space and time. *New Media & Society*, *13*(1), 23–39. doi:10.1177/1461444810363452

Dindia, K. (2002). Self-disclosure research: Knowledge through meta-analysis. *Interpersonal communication research: Advances through meta-analysis*, 169-185.

Ferrari, S. (2009, June 2). Newsgame or Editorial Game? Retrieved from http://newsgames.gatech.edu/blog/2009/06/newsgame-or-editorial-game.html

Fox, J., & Tang, W. Y. (2014). Sexism in online video games: The role of conformity to masculine norms and social dominance orientation. *Computers in Human Behavior*, *33*, 314–320. doi:10.1016/j.chb.2013.07.014

George-Palilonis, J., & Spillman, M. (2011). Interactive Graphics Development: A framework for studying innovative visual story forms. *Visual Communication Quarterly*, *18*(3), 167–177. doi:10.1080/15551393.2011.599286

Glass, Z. (2007). The effectiveness of product placement in video games. *Journal of Interactive Advertising*, *8*(1), 23–32. doi:10.1080/15252019.2007.10722134

Gross, M. L. (2010). Advergames and the effects of game-product congruity. *Computers in Human Behavior*, *26*(6), 1259–1265. doi:10.1016/j.chb.2010.03.034

Hamari, J., Koivisto, J., & Sarsa, H. (2014, January). Does gamification work?--A literature review of empirical studies on gamification. Proceedings of *System Sciences (HICSS), 2014 47th Hawaii International Conference on* (pp. 3025-3034). IEEE.

Hanus, M. D., & Fox, J. (2015). Assessing the effects of gamification in the classroom: A longitudinal study on intrinsic motivation, social comparison, satisfaction, effort, and academic performance. *Computers & Education*, *80*, 152–161. doi:10.1016/j.compedu.2014.08.019

Heimlich, R. (2010, September 12). Americans Spending More Time Following the News. *Pew Research Center for the People and the Press*. Retrieved from http://www.people-press.org/2010/09/12/americans-spending-more-time-following-the-news/

Hill, K., & Greenburg, Z. O. (2010, November 29). *The Black Market Price Of Your Personal Info. Forbes.* Retrieved from http://www.forbes.com/2010/11/29/black-market-price-of-your-info-personal-finance.html

Holcomb, J., & Mitchell, A. (2014, March 26). The Revenue Picture for American Journalism and How It Is Changing. *Pew Research Center's Journalism Project.* Retrieved from http://www.journalism.org/2014/03/26/the-revenue-picture-for-american-journalism-and-how-it-is-changing/

Huang, J. H., & Yang, T. K. (2012). The Effectiveness of In-Game Advertising: The Impacts of Ad Type and Game/Ad Relevance. *International Journal of Electronic BusinessManagement*, *10*(1), 61.

Ivory, J. D., & Kalyanaraman, S. (2007). The effects of technological advancement and violent content in video games on players' feelings of presence, involvement, physiological arousal, and aggression. *Journal of Communication*, *57*(3), 532–555. doi:10.1111/j.1460-2466.2007.00356.x

Johansson, S. (2008). Gossip, sport and pretty girls. *Journalism Practice*, *2*(3), 402–413. doi:10.1080/17512780802281131

Jönsson, A. M., & Örnebring, H. (2011). User-generated Content and the News: Empowerment of citizens or interactive illusion? *Journalism Practice*, *5*(2), 127–144. doi:10.1080/17512786.2010.501155

Kalyanaraman, S., & Sundar, S. S. (2006). The psychological appeal of personalized content in web portals: Does customization affect attitudes and behavior? *Journal of Communication*, *56*(1), 110–132. doi:10.1111/j.1460-2466.2006.00006.x

Kalyanaraman, S., & Wojdynski, B. W. (2015). Affording control: How interactivity, customization and navigability affect psychological responses to communication technology. In S. S. Sundar (Ed.), *The Handbook of the Psychology of Communication Technology* (pp. 425–444). New York: Wiley-Blackwell. doi:10.1002/9781118426456.ch19

Kalyuga, S., & Plass, J. L. (2009). Evaluating and managing cognitive load in games. In R. E. Ferdig (Ed.), *Handbook of Research on Effective Electronic Gaming in Education* (pp. 719–737). Hershey, PA: Information Science Reference. doi:10.4018/978-1-59904-808-6.ch041

Kang, B., & Tan, S. (2014). Interactive Games: Intrinsic and Extrinsic Motivation, Achievement, and Satisfaction. *Journal of Management and Strategy*, *5*(4), 110. doi:10.5430/jms.v5n4p110

Kapp, K. M. (2012). *The gamification of learning and instruction: game-based methods and strategies for training and education*. San Francisco, CA: John Wiley & Sons.

Kim, J., Kim, J.-H., & Seo, M. (2014). Toward a person × situation model of selective exposure: Repressors, sensitizers, and choice of online news on financial crisis. *Journal of Media Psychology: Theories, Methods, and Applications*, *26*(2), 59–69. doi:10.1027/1864-1105/a000111

Kovach, B., & Rosenstiel, T. (2010). *Blur: How to Know What's True in the Age of Information Overload*. Bloomsbury Publishing USA.

Kurtz, H. (1993). *Media circus: The trouble with America's newspapers*. New York, NY: Times Books.

Lee, J., Park, H., & Wise, K. (2013). Brand interactivity and its effects on the outcomes of advergame play. *New Media & Society*. doi:10.1177/1461444813504267

Lister, C., West, J. H., Cannon, B., Sax, T., & Brodegard, D. (2014). Just a Fad? Gamification in Health and Fitness Apps. *JMIR Serious Games*, *2*(2), e9. doi:10.2196/games.3413 PMID:25654660

McGonigal, J. (2011). *Reality is broken: Why games make us better and how they can change the world*. London, UK: Penguin.

McLachlan, S., & Golding, P. (2000). Tabloidization in the British press: A quantitative investigation into changes in British Newspapers. In C. Sparks & J. Tulloch (Eds.), *Tabloid tales: Global debates over media standards* (pp. 76–90). Lanham, MD: Rowman and Littlefield.

Michael, D. R., & Chen, S. L. (2005). *Serious games: Games that educate, train, and inform.* Muska & Lipman/Premier-Trade.

Mikalef, K., Giannakos, M. N., Chorianopoulos, K., & Jaccheri, L. (2013). Does informal learning benefit from interactivity? The effect of trial and error on knowledge acquisition during a museum visit. *International Journal of Mobile Learning and Organisation*, 7(2), 158–175. doi:10.1504/IJMLO.2013.055620

Miller, L. D., Shell, D., Khandaker, N., & Soh, L. K. (2010). Teaching using computer games. *Journal of Educational Technology Systems*, 39(3), 321–343. doi:10.2190/ET.39.3.g

Mitchell, A., Jurkowitz, M., & Olmstead, K. (2013, March 14). Social, search and direct: Pathways to digital news. Pew Research Journalism Project. Retrieved from http://www.journalism.org/2014/03/13/social-search-direct/

Moreno, J. (2012). Digital Competition Game to Improve Programming Skills. *Journal of Educational Technology & Society*, 15(3), 288–297.

Nel, F., & Westlund, O. (2012). THE 4C'S OF MOBILE NEWS: Channels, conversation, content and commerce. *Journalism Practice*, 6(5-6), 744–753. doi:10.1080/17512786.2012.667278

The New York Times's Most Visited Content of 2013. (2014, January 17). The New York Times Company. Retrieved from http://www.nytco.com/the-new-york-timess-most-visited-content-of-2013/

Nichani, M., & Rajamanickam, V. (2003). Interactive Visual Explainers–A Simple Classification. *Elearning post*. Retrieved from http://www.elearningpost.com/articles/archives/interactive_visual_explainers_a_simple_classification

O'Donovan, C. (2014, February 19). Are quizzes the new lists? What BuzzFeed's latest viral success means for publishing. *Nieman Journalism Lab*. Retrieved from http://www.niemanlab.org/2014/02/are-quizzes-the-new-lists-what-buzzfeeds-latest-viral-success-means-for-publishing/

Perpetua, M. (2014, March 24). *Which Pop Star Should Be Your Best Friend? BuzzFeed*. Retrieved July 28, 2014, from http://www.buzzfeed.com/perpetua/which-pop-star-should-be-your-best-friend

Pew Research Center's Journalism Project Staff. (2014, March 26). Key Indicators in Media & News. Retrieved from http://www.journalism.org/2014/03/26/state-of-the-news-media-2014-key-indicators-in-media-and-news/

Pitcher, J. (2013, August 12). *German studio creates game based on Edward Snowden. Polygon*. Retrieved from http://www.polygon.com/2013/8/12/4613202/binji-create-game-based-on-edward-snowden

Qiu, L., Lin, H., Leung, A. K., & Tov, W. (2012). Putting Their Best Foot Forward: Emotional Disclosure on Facebook. *Cyberpsychology, Behavior, and Social Networking*, 15(10), 569–572. doi:10.1089/cyber.2012.0200 PMID:22924675

Rafaeli, S., & Ariel, Y. (2007). Assessing interactivity in computer-mediated research. In A. N. Joinson, K. Y. A. McKenna, T. Postmes, & U. D. Rieps (Eds.), *The Oxford handbook of internet psychology, 71--88.* Oxford University Press.

The Growth of Multi-Platform News. *Digital News Report 2013.* (2013). Reuters Institute for the Study of Journalism. Retrieved from http://www.digitalnewsreport.org/survey/2013/the-growth-of-multi-platform-news-2013/

Richter, G., Raban, D. R., & Rafaeli, S. (2015). Studying gamification: The effect of rewards and incentives on motivation. In T. Reiners & L. C. Woods (Eds.), *Gamification in Education and Business* (pp. 21–46). Springer International Publishing. doi:10.1007/978-3-319-10208-5_2

Ritterfeld, U., Cody, M., & Vorderer, P. (Eds.). (2009). *Serious Games: Mechanisms and Effects*. New York, London: Routledge.

Schrader, C., & Bastiaens, T. J. (2012). The influence of virtual presence: Effects on experienced cognitive load and learning outcomes in educational computer games. *Computers in Human Behavior, 28*(2), 648–658. doi:10.1016/j.chb.2011.11.011

Sela, M., Lavie, T., Inbar, O., Oppenheim, I., & Meyer, J. (2014). Personalizing news content: An experimental study. *Journal of the Association for Information Science and Technology,* n/a–n/a. doi:10.1002/asi.23167

Seounmi, Y., Lee, M., & Doyle, K. O. (2003). Lifestyles of online gamers: A psychographic approach. *Journal of Interactive Advertising, 3*(2), 49–56. doi:10.1080/15252019.2003.10722073

Short, J. E. (2013). *How much media? 2013: Report on American consumers.* Global Information Industry Center, UC San Diego. Available at http://hmi.ucsd.edu/howmuchinfo.php

Sicart, M. (2008, September). Newsgames: Theory and Design. *Proceedings of the 7th International Conference on Entertainment Computing* (pp. 27-33). Springer-Verlag.

Smith, A. (2014, February 3). 6 new facts about Facebook. Retrieved from http://www.pewresearch.org/fact-tank/2014/02/03/6-new-facts-about-facebook/

Snyder, E., & Hartig, J. R. (2013). Gamification of board review: A residency curricular innovation. *Medical Education, 47*(5), 524–525. doi:10.1111/medu.12190 PMID:23574079

Sohn, D., Ci, C., & Lee, B. K. (2007). The moderating effects of expectation on the patterns of the interactivity-attitude relationship. *Journal of Advertising, 36*(3), 109–119. doi:10.2753/JOA0091-3367360308

Sprecher, S., Treger, S., Wondra, J. D., Hilaire, N., & Wallpe, K. (2013). Taking turns: Reciprocal self-disclosure promotes liking in initial interactions. *Journal of Experimental Social Psychology, 49*(5), 860–866. doi:10.1016/j.jesp.2013.03.017

Squire, K. (2006). From content to context: Videogames as designed experience. *Educational Researcher, 35*(8), 19–29. doi:10.3102/0013189X035008019

Stieglitz, S., & Dang-Xuan, L. (2013). Emotions and Information Diffusion in Social Media—Sentiment of Microblogs and Sharing Behavior. *Journal of Management Information Systems*, *29*(4), 217–248. doi:10.2753/MIS0742-1222290408

Sundar, S. (2008). The MAIN model: A heuristic approach to understanding technology effects on credibility. In M. Metzger & A. Flanagin (Eds.), *Digital media, youth, and credibility* (pp. 73–100). Cambridge, MA: MIT Press.

Sundar, S. S., Bellur, S., Oh, J., Jia, H., & Kim, H.-S. (2014). Theoretical Importance of Contingency in Human-Computer Interaction Effects of Message Interactivity on User Engagement. *Communication Research*. doi:10.1177/0093650214534962

Sundar, S. S., Kalyanaraman, S., & Brown, J. (2003). Explicating Web Site interactivity impression formation effects in political campaign sites. *Communication Research*, *30*(1), 30–59. doi:10.1177/0093650202239025

Sundar, S. S., & Marathe, S. S. (2010). Personalization Versus Customization: The Importance of Agency, Privacy, and Power Usage. *Human Communication Research*, *36*(3), 298–322. doi:10.1111/j.1468-2958.2010.01377.x

Sundar, S. S., Xu, Q., Bellur, S., Oh, J., & Jia, H. (2011). Beyond Pointing and Clicking: How Do Newer Interaction Modalities Affect User Engagement? Proceedings of CHI'11 Extended Abstracts on Human Factors in Computing Systems (pp. 1477–1482). New York, NY, USA: ACM; doi:10.1145/1979742.1979794

Tamir, D. I., & Mitchell, J. P. (2012). Disclosing information about the self is intrinsically rewarding. *Proceedings of the National Academy of Sciences of the United States of America*, *109*(21), 8038–8043. doi:10.1073/pnas.1202129109 PMID:22566617

Tandoc, E. C. Jr. (2014). Journalism is twerking? How Web analytics is changing the process of gatekeeping. *New Media & Society*, *16*(4), 559–575. doi:10.1177/1461444814530541

Tewksbury, D., Weaver, A. J., & Maddex, B. D. (2001). Accidentally Informed: Incidental News Exposure on the World Wide Web. *Journalism & Mass Communication Quarterly*, *78*(3), 533–554. doi:10.1177/107769900107800309

Thompson, D. (2014, February 12). *The Facebook Effect on the News. The Atlantic*. Retrieved from http://www.theatlantic.com/business/archive/2014/02/the-facebook-effect-on-the-news/283746/

Thurman, N. (2011). Making "The Daily Me": Technology, economics and habit in the mainstream assimilation of personalized news. *Journalism*, *12*(4), 395–415. doi:10.1177/1464884910388228

Tulloch, J. (2000). The eternal recurrence of new journalism. In C. Sparks & J. Tulloch (Eds.), *Tabloid tales: Global debates about media standards* (pp. 13–46). Lanham, MD: Rowman & Littlefield.

Vogel, J. J., Vogel, D. S., Cannon-Bowers, J., Bowers, C. A., Muse, K., & Wright, M. (2006). Computer Gaming and Interactive Simulations for Learning: A Meta-Analysis. *Journal of Educational Computing Research*, *34*(3), 229–243. doi:10.2190/FLHV-K4WA-WPVQ-H0YM

Wang, S. S. (2013). "I Share, Therefore I Am": Personality Traits, Life Satisfaction, and Facebook Check-Ins. *Cyberpsychology, Behavior, and Social Networking*, *16*(12), 870–877. doi:10.1089/cyber.2012.0395 PMID:23992473

Weber, R., Behr, K.-M., & DeMartino, C. (2014). Measuring Interactivity in Video Games. *Communication Methods and Measures, 8*(2), 79–115. doi:10.1080/19312458.2013.873778

Wei, S. (2013, July 11). *Creating Games for Journalism. ProPublica*. Retrieved from http://www.propublica.org/nerds/item/creating-games-for-journalism

Westwood, D., & Griffiths, M. D. (2010). The role of structural characteristics in video-game play motivation: A Q-methodology study. *Cyberpsychology, Behavior, and Social Networking, 13*(5), 581–585. doi:10.1089/cyber.2009.0361 PMID:20950185

Wise, K., Bolls, P. D., Kim, H., Venkataraman, A., & Meyer, R. (2008). Enjoyment of advergames and brand attitudes: The impact of thematic relevance. *Journal of Interactive Advertising, 9*(1), 27–36. doi: 10.1080/15252019.2008.10722145

Wojdynski, B. W. (2014). Interactive data graphics and information processing: The moderating role of involvement. *Journal of Media Psychology*; Advance online publication. doi:10.1027/1864-1105/a000127

Wolf, C., & Schnauber, A. (2014). News Consumption in the Mobile Era: The role of mobile devices and traditional journalism's content within the user's information repertoire. *Digital Journalism*. Advance online publication. Doi:10.1080/21670811.2014.942497

Yee, N. (2006). Motivations for play in online games. *Cyberpsychology & Behavior, 9*(6), 772–775. doi:10.1089/cpb.2006.9.772 PMID:17201605

Chapter 15
The Gamification of Journalism

Raul Ferrer Conill
Karlstad University, Sweden

Michael Karlsson
Karlstad University, Sweden

ABSTRACT

Traditional news outlets are on the decline and journalism has embraced digital media in its struggle to survive. New models of delivering news to the public are being explored in order to increase the levels of readership and user engagement.The narrative of this chapter focuses on the future of journalism and media, and the potential benefits and dangers of gamifying journalism. Since gamification is a new trend, a thorough look at the intersection between the enhancements of public mobility, the digitalization of news services, and the engagement of gamified systems can bring better understanding of future channels of reading news to the users, to researchers, and to the industry. This chapter aims to bridge the gap between gamification as an emerging practice in news distribution and yet a vastly uncharted area or research.

INTRODUCTION

No group of young people has ever had more choices to make regarding — or more control over — its own information, amusement and politics. Rock spawned one culture; TV, another; movies, hip-hop, computers, video games, still more. (Katz, 1993)

The previous quote is as relevant now as it was more than two decades ago. What Katz probably did not foresee is the converging use of media that has led to an entanglement of information, amusement, and politics. In the current media landscape the processes of mediatization, commercialization, and individualization (Lundby, 2009), spurred by the ubiquity of mobile technologies and pervasive connectivity (Dimmick, Feaster, & Hoplamazian, 2010; Van Dijck, 2013), have derived in a myriad of news services competing for the audience's attention.

As newspapers' sales plunge and traditional news outlets decline, new models of delivering news to the public are being explored in order to increase levels of readership and user engagement. Gamifica-

DOI: 10.4018/978-1-4666-8651-9.ch015

tion is one of these new models news outlets have adopted to engage young audiences, sparking the need for a new strand of research on the intersection of journalism and gamification (Ferrer Conill, 2014).

The narrative of this chapter focuses on the future of journalism and media, and the potential benefits and dangers of gamifying journalism. Since gamification is a new trend, a thorough look at the intersection between the enhancements of public mobility, the digitalization of news services, and the engagement of gamified systems can bring better understanding of future channels of reading news to the users, to researchers, and to the industry. This text aims to bridge the gap between gamification as an emerging practice in news distribution and yet a vastly uncharted area or research.

This chapter departs by discussing two of the conflicting logics of the journalistic field: the professional logic, which regards audiences as citizens; and the commercial logic, which regards audiences as consumers. Based on these tensions, it continues addressing the aims of applying gamification to news services, offering an account of potential benefits and pitfalls of using game-mechanics in order to engage young audiences. We aim to provide a nuanced view of the gamification of news beyond the commercial determinism and the democratic functionalism of journalism (Schudson, 1997). Next, we discuss how these new configurations of game-like news fit within the current context of media convergence, new journalism formats, audience reconfigurations, setting the context on which digital game elements can be formally applied to news. For this reason we analyze how game elements are currently implemented in journalism, to then discuss other ways to create gamified interfaces that have the potential of enhancing the democratic and civic purposes of journalism while engaging younger users, or center the news experience about the games, and not the news. The chapter concludes providing a set of challenges and needs for research, intending to propose an agenda for future research on gamification's place within journalism.

THE CONFLICTING LOGICS OF THE JOURNALISTIC FIELD

Journalism and the production of news is not any odd work, in fact it is not even any odd information or media work. To properly understand and relate to how and why journalism is produced in a meaningful theoretical and practical way, one must consider its place within society and democracy. Journalism's *raison d'être* is, in short, to serve the public with qualified information so that people can make informed decisions in their capacity as citizens holding those in power accountable (Cushion, 2012; McNair, 2000). This is the ideal and the high ground journalists and their protagonists claim when news media and journalism are under attack. But it is also, more importantly, an established empirical fact that the media environment and the contents of news have effect on how informed and engaged people are in society (Aalberg & Curran, 2011; Scheufele, Shanahan, & Kim, 2002; Shaker, 2014). In short, media matters and contributes to the quality of democracy. Journalism's status in society is also recognized formally as countries such as United States and Sweden regulate it, as the only commercial operation, in their constitutions.

Another equally important and conflicting dimension in the discourse about journalism, news media, and their function in society, is that they regularly fall short of their own standards and deliver false, irrelevant or inaccurate information. This is due to a number of different factors and obstacles such as influence from consumer demands, advertisers, owners, sources, trade and industry, as well as technological developments and the overall ideology of any given society (McManus, 1994; Schudson, 2003; Shoemaker & Reese, 1996).

This part of the chapter sets up and describes two, often conflicting, logics or regimes – one being a professional logic and the other a commercial logic – that saturate journalism practice and, subsequently, journalism studies (Croteau & Hoynes, 2001; McManus, 2009; Schudson, 2003). Any introduction of new ideas, practices or technologies, such as gamification, will be appropriated within the framework of these logics. Although there are other ways to describe and deal with tensions and different forces in journalism, these logics are adequate for the purpose of this chapter as they pinpoint the relationship between journalism and users. The tensions between these two actors, journalists and users, and the two logics, professional and commercial, sets the context for gamified news articles and systems.

Professional Logic

Earlier incarnations of journalism were far from the objective enterprise we take for granted today. Instead, journalism was expected to be strongly partial and sensationalistic (Barnhurst & Nerone, 2009; Hartley, 2009; Schudson, 1978). However, since then, standards and protocols have been developed to promote journalism as a, broadly speaking, merchant of truth seeking. That is – journalists must seek and have much higher standards than other information workers (Kovach & Rosenstiehl, 2001; Zelizer, 2004). This must also be communicated to the audience, making journalism a, to paraphrase Tuchman (1972), strategic ritual, which the public can discern and evaluate. In practice, this is manifested by journalists when they are employing techniques such as verifying information before publishing, relying on more than one source, and being able to answer questions of when, who, what, where, why and how an event unfolded (Kovach & Rosenstiehl, 2001; Singer, 2008). In addition to be true, it is of immense importance that the information is *relevant* to the audience in the role of citizens. Thus, true but irrelevant information about celebrities, sports and entertainment is less useful to people in their capacity as citizens, than true but relevant information about politics, society and economics (Reinemann, Stanyer, Scherr, & Legnante, 2011).

Overall, journalism is to a large extent understood as process of verifying, refining, and upgrading mere 'information' to useful and unbiased facts and analysis. This process contains several steps where first raw information of various origins and shifting quality is gathered by journalists, then selected/disregarded by editors and transformed to 'facts and truth' through journalistic scrutiny, standardized routines and procedures. As a final step the finished product is distributed to the willing and able audience (Karlsson, 2011; Kovach & Rosenstiehl, 2001; Seib, 2001). Should journalists produce misleading, inaccurate or irrelevant news, it does not only have results for peoples' capacity to keep themselves informed, but also pose a serious threat to the existence of journalism as it undermines its very foundations.

In short, the professional logic addresses audiences and readers primarily as citizens. True and relevant news have constituted the backbone of journalism for close to a century, but journalism has also been embedded in a commercial logic for an even longer time period.

Commercial Logic

Not only is news and journalism important for democracy but they also represent a billion dollar industry (Croteau & Hoynes, 2001; McManus, 1994). Journalism, and especially its printed incarnations, has operated within a mass-market framework since at least the mid nineteenth century due to, for instance, increased printing capacity, urbanization, and literacy. Thus, as Hartley (2009) has pointed out, modern journalism has always had, in one way or another, to relate and adjust to popular taste. The professional logic above is in essence an ideal construct on how journalism should operate, while journalism in practice is urged to follow or influence market demand to be able to support its operations. This information market is driven within other parameters than the idealistic notion of journalism, and there is evidence that this, implicitly and explicitly, shapes news content (Hamilton, 2004; Shoemaker & Reese, 1996).

Since *news is a commodity, not a mirror of reality* (Hamilton, 2004, p.7) it is essential to point out how consumer preferences, among other things, drive news coverage. Hamilton (2004) has, inspired by the 'why, where, who, what, when' dimensions of the professional logic, put together a particularly useful set of corresponding questions viable in the market context: *Who cares about a particular piece of information? What are they willing to pay to find it, or what are others willing to pay to reach them? Where can media outlets or advertisers reach these people? When it is profitable to provide the information? Why is it profitable?* As evident, only the first two questions relate explicitly to the taste of the audience while the rest regard the audience as a commodity, logistics, pricing structure and production costs that needs to be taken into consideration. Accordingly, the relationship between these questions is intrinsically complex, demonstrated, for instance, by the fact that advertisers traditionally have provided the lion's share of media corporations income while not being too interested in reaching every citizen since their products are niched to target audiences (Schudson, 2003). Additionally, it becomes lucrative for media corporations to provide content that enables the tailoring of audiences to advertisers (Hamilton, 2004; Shoemaker & Reese, 1996). Further, in contrast to the professional logic, the five questions posed by Hamilton have, in themselves, absolutely nothing to do with what kind of information will be produced or the quality of that information. Yet, these parameters set up the boundaries of the competitive marketplace in which journalism and the media industry have to work. Of course, it is still plausible that people will request information that makes it easier for them to participate in society, but there are other information demands as well – information that makes it easier to work, or consume for pure entertainment reasons (Hamilton, 2004). Thus, if professional logic regards audiences and readers as citizens, the commercial logic addresses them primarily as consumers.

Conflicting Logics and the Future of Journalism

Ideally, these logics, professional and commercial, would work in tandem: readers would prefer qualified information over other types of information available, journalists would only produce true and relevant news, advertisers would not care about ratings or which audiences they reach, media corporations would not prioritize profit, and different actors would not try to spin the news. However, this is not and has never been the case. On the contrary, it is widely understood that the commercial logic is gaining ground at the expense of the professional logic, as journalism and news media are increasingly anchored in the digital environment. For instance, digital publishing allows live readings of ratings that shape what news are being published and how those news are being framed (Anderson, 2011; Karlsson & Clerwall, 2013; MacGregor, 2007). Previous research convincingly shows a slow, and sometimes faster, shift from harder to softer news, indicating that journalists are being forced to digress from the professional logic in favor of the commercial logic (Bird, 2009; Connell, 1998; Currah, 2009; Cushion, 2012; Sparks & Tulloch, 2000; Uribe & Gunter, 2004). Karlsson, (in press), took stock on how news have developed in the digital environment, finding that the process is even more accelerated there.

Furthermore, faced with this abundance of choices in the information environment more people are decreasing their news consumption or are checking out from journalism completely (De Waal & Schoenbach, 2010; Prior, 2007; Stromback, Djerf-Pierre, & Shehata, 2012). This is due to the fact that the digital era presents consumers with more opportunities to choose what they want, no longer being restrained to what a few media outlets chose to publish. In the digital world, journalism has to work within these premises instead of the near monopoly situation in the analogue media system, adjusting even more to audience demands, or find ways to increase motivation for news consumption. Something that can prove very difficult as a telling study by Boczkowski and Mitchelstein (2013) illustrates, where journalists and users have diverging priorities as the former promotes public affair stories but the latter, to a larger extent opt for useful, bizarre or controversial bits of information.

It is against this background and in this setting and framework that the gamification of journalism needs to be analyzed. On the one hand as a tool to increase interest in and engagement with news, on the other hand as a tool to further transform and adjust journalism to the demands of the audience.

THE AIMS OF GAMIFYING JOURNALISM

The future of journalism seems to be attached to popular demands. However, as Martin Conboy (2010) suggests, it needs to maintain certain distance from the mainstream discourses of general entertainment while reclaiming the attention of audiences and readers, and their drive to learn about what happens in the world. Literature about youth and news consumption usually points to the issue of engagement (Tufte & Enghel, 2009). The narratives that aim to explain the lack of engagement take various departing points: a reconfiguration of social structures and generational change on media habits (Bimber, 2012; Bennet et al., 2012; Van Dijck, 2013); a disconnect between current content and formats of news distribution (Reese & Lee, 2012); lack of entertainment or even entertainment media becoming a source of distraction (Delli Carpini, 2012). Particularly incisive is Robert Putman's (2000) suggestion that the amount of time used consuming popular and entertainment media is using up the limited time from citizens and users, time they could be using engaging in public and civic activities or *quality media*. Admittedly, Putman's argument has underlying speculative tones, as the logics of causality do not lead to believe that stopping consuming entertainment would necessarily lead to civic activities. However, in the age of multipurpose devices, it is worth considering that media services must strive for the users' attention, competing with several other affordances such devices have to offer, and depending on the amount of hours the device is being used.

While gamification is already being used in real life journalism context, the ideal implementation with the applied system does not always match. As it has been mentioned earlier, the notion of journalism is rather unspecific in digital settings. There are several *flavors* of journalism, and so, we feel compelled to constrain our narrative to the transition of legacy news media (specifically newspapers) to their digital counterparts, in the most idealist type of journalism, watchdog, investigative, and informative journalism. This section tackles the potential usefulness and dangers of introducing gamification techniques to journalism. If there are surely proponents of gamifying the news, there are for sure reasons to not gamify the news.

Engaging with Games

Historically, the use of games in traditional newspapers had been relegated to the use of simple game-like pastimes such as quizzes, crosswords, or even *sudokus*, in order to attract certain demographics (Shortz, 2006). Other approaches used by legacy media to engage and create habit are programs like

The Washington Post's Points, which is an analogue loyalty program tied to annual subscriptions with the possibility of redeeming accumulated points for physical presents.

However, adapting to the rise of new media, news organizations have tried to generate internal structures that aim to approach and engage with the public in their own terms, through the new channels established by social media and games (Kwak et al., 2010; Gil de Zúñiga, Jung, & Valenzuela, 2012). Newsrooms started introducing editors and employees with new skills and competencies. At the same time, interfaces have provided room for users to interact with.

While those traditional game-like pastime features such as quizzes have been successfully translated into the digital arena (Schultz, 1999), it is videogames to their full extent the type of new media that is reported to be majorly engaging younger audiences, and on its turn, as Putman would suggest, *distracting* teens from civic media use. A Pew (2008) study reports that 97% of American teens play videogames on a regular basis and do so in a variety of devices. Gaming has become a pervasive form of media consumption that transcends all layers of the socioeconomic fabric of Western societies. Furthermore, 72% of players use their mobile phones to play, which adds the option of mobility and communication through the same medium for play. Beyond the basic outcome of entertainment, gaming, especially multiplayer gaming, provides sources for participatory action, social interaction, and often simulates civic action.

New behaviors are embedded within the interactions of the social and the technical, but also depend on the media and news environment available. This taps into the reasoning of engagement or lack of it. According to the OMA Framework (Strömbäck, Djerf-Pierre, & Shehata, 2012), any behavior such as media choice or civic engagement is contingent upon a combination of opportunity, motivation, and ability. Motivation and ability are individual-level factors, but opportunity, in news consumption, refers to the availability and accessibility to different types of news and non-news media. Coincidentally, this behavioral framework is strikingly similar to Fogg's (2009) behavioral model for persuasive design, which is composed of motivation, ability, and triggers. Thus, these two frameworks are equal with the exception that one takes the reference from the media system (opportunity), and the other one takes the focus from what the technology itself interacts with the user (triggers). It is not that surprising that, games themselves use a similar triadic model to engage users by fostering autonomy, mastery, and relatedness.

There is an ambivalent set of results on the effects of playing video games and the level of engagement of youth with news media and civic activities (Williams, 2006). Studies show that hard core gamers have lower social capital, however, it is difficult to discern whether those who turn to games are disengaged, or the other way around. What it is clear is that gaming is in part a media-centric activity embedded in the daily habits of young citizens' everyday life, and that the media literacy achieved during early years is carried throughout later stages in life. As we mentioned before, the habits and traditions of media consumption are fundamentally linked to a generational context. If new generations do not read news, but are extremely engaged in playing games, the trend is only going to increase as one generation replaces the other.

Hence, if Coleman and Blumber (2012) are right, and one of the basic norms of democracy requires informed, balanced, and consequential citizens, then media needs to find methods that engage users to be informed. So why not games? To the question of '*why gamify the news?*' the basic response is to engage users to be informed, to be balanced, and to be consequential. In other words, to use the nature of games to empower users, and to cement one of the pillars of democracy. At least this is why we think news could expand the already ongoing experimentation with game elements, and why researchers need to investigate the feasibility of news and games. This is, we argue, the ideal scenario. Of course, as we will see later in this section, the reasons and consequences of gamifying the news might be different for those who have the power to implement these strategies.

The Potential Benefits of Gamifying the News

As it tends to happen with new approaches to old problems, there are proponents and opponents. Gamification is no exception and sustains a large group of enthusiasts and equally large group of skeptics. The champions of gamification (McGonigal, 2011; Zichermann & Linder, 2013; Herger, 2014) are convinced that gamification is the cure to many ailments, especially if they are customer engagement ailments. But McGonigal in particular makes a rather compelling argument that by using game elements into everyday environments, we can turn those environments into an equally fun and engaging environment as games themselves. Reality is too slow, too boring to keep individuals who grew up playing videogames engaged. And in a way, we have seen that this is true, at least in the realm of journalism. If McGonigal's assertion is right, youth have adopted games as their means of entertainment and have left news behind because it is not an engaging environment.

So how does the application of game elements in non-engaging environments work? In its most basic form, the introduction of gamified applications to a wide range of users and audiences provides a new way to develop new heuristics, design patterns, and dynamics of games, with the aim of improving user experience and user engagement (Deterding et al. 2011:a; Deterding et al., 2011:b). And while there has been a considerable degree of hype in the industry, gamification has shown to be an effective method to attract the attention and engagement of users in various domains such as marketing and business oriented applicability (Zichermann & Linder, 2010; Huotari & Hamari, 2012; Paharia, 2013), technology (Fujikawa & Manki, 2013), education (Prensky, 2010; Sheldon, 2011; Muntean, 2011; Kapp, 2012), and health (McCallum, 2012).

Certainly, gamification is a by-product of other meta-process such as mediatization (Lundby, 2009), individualization, and commercialization, but the gamification of everything (Rolland & Eastman, 2011) responds to a generational shift into *digital natives* (Bennet, Maton, & Kervin, 2008) that not only have grown with the omnipresence of the Internet and networked technologies, but that are the first generation to have been born into a world filled with digital games within the context of home and everyday life.

Alas, the implementation rush during the first years of gamification seemed to follow the old method of throwing badges to everything and see where they stuck. And while old (analogue) loyalty programs are still used in several industries, the digitalization of services, such as newspapers, unveils new pathways for experimentation with gamified systems. The reasoning behind the application of gamification in web-based system, or a mobile app, is to enhance engagement, grant choices, reaffirm progression, and provoke social habit (Werbach & Hunter, 2012). Applied to news consumption, there is a vast opportunity to introduce game elements in systems that aim to create experiences that foster a sense of autonomy, mastery, and relatedness, as users become more informed about the world. Coincidentally, these three concepts are what motivational theories, such as Self-Determination Theory (Deci & Ryan 1985; Pink, 2009), propose as the igniters of intrinsic motivation. In addition, gamification gives the tools for users to participate and engage with other users, broadening the network of consumers to a particular service. The aim is to create a user experience that is more attractive and enticing to the new mobile lifestyle of today's consumers, especially youth, who have slowly discarded news from the mix of their media consumption.

Thus, a gamified news service has the potential to engage users (and particularly youth) to read news, to inform themselves, and most importantly, to foster an intrinsic motivation to consume news while creating a habit out of it. Whether this leads to a more democratic and civic society willing to participate in public debate is a discussion that escapes the ambitions of this chapter, but that should be central to the gamification of news research. Additionally, introducing game mechanics to news websites could very well become a profitable business model. This assumption is done twofold: on the one hand, a more engaged community of users remains longer in the site, visits more often, and interacts more with the service, making it a service much more attractive to advertisers; on the other hand, games (and specifically mobile games) have achieved incredible profit figures with services that are free to play while offering virtual goods (Quah, 2003) that can be purchased by the player. Such a monetizing model allows for dynamic pricing that can be encompassed to carefully timed events. If games have achieved such successful business models by offering their main content for free, it should be also at the grasp of the news industry to do so. Another benefit of gamifying journalism is no other than avoiding the *tabloidization* effect (Bird, 2009; Reese & Lee, 2012). The shift towards *entertainment* content could very well be due to the fact that the format is not entertaining. If newspapers focus on crafting a packaging that is interesting and that offers a truly entertaining news experience in itself, then content could be delivered intact, thus reducing tabloidization. The final benefit to be discussed here is the one attempted by one of the examples briefly discussed in the following section, Bleacher Report, which introduced gamification in order to engage their news producers and contributors, instead of the audience. This last benefit is much harder to achieve but it could certainly make the production of news a more engaging experience.

The Potential Pitfalls of Gamifying the News

As we mentioned earlier, there are also critics and opponents that offer a less optimistic view of gamification. The critical voices usually come from the field of game studies, digital labor, and surveillance studies. The rationale for critique is different, with varying degrees of emotional involvement. Ian Bogost (2011), famed researcher in game design puts it this way:

"Gamification is bullshit. More specifically, gamification is marketing bullshit, invented by consultants as a means to capture the wild, coveted beast that is videogames and to domesticate it for use in the grey, hopeless wasteland of big business. It takes games – a mysterious, magical, powerful medium that has captured the attention of millions of people – and it makes them accessible in the context of contemporary business"

Bogost's livid statement represents a line of thought that considers gamification a bastardization of gaming, instrumentalizing Game Design Theory for commercial purposes only. As a newsgames proponent, Bogost does not find value in the whole range of purposes of gamification, and only focuses in the commercialization perspective. However, this line of critique can easily apply to news if the gamified layer does not suit the experience that news wants to convey, being a completely gratuitous set of game elements poorly implemented. A corresponding caveat can emerge from the other end, and it is to generate a game so powerful that users forget that the goal of the experience is being informed about current events. There is a line of journalists that would see the use of games in journalism as a threat to creative journalism, selling the core values of journalism to entertainment media.

A similar strand of thought but oriented directly to the idea of digital labor or exploitation has been gaining traction. Gamification benefits from new technological advances to automatically generate content based on the users' actions. On the one hand, this user-generated content is packaged and offered to the user (sometimes even at a price!) while being owned by the service provider. On the other hand, using the power of games, gamification can be used to manipulate and exploit people behind the veil of fun and leisure. This line of thought is best exemplified by PJ Rey's (2012) statement:

"Gamification is a mechanism for de-coupling alienation from capitalist production. By masking work as play, capitalist production moves exploitation out of the work places and infiltrates our leisure time. Play loses its innocence. It is no longer an escape from the system, it is just another branch of it. Waste is no longer wasted. Playbour is part of capitalism´s effort to colonize every last moment in the waking day"

The pervasive and ubiquitous tracking and measuring techniques embedded in gamification systems, result in the third line of criticism of gamification, which has to do with the ethical questions of continuously being surveilled. In the majority of cases, the user is not only complacent with monitoring, but it is often the initiator. This notion of self-surveillance challenges the traditional ideas behind surveillance, but as Whitson (2013) points out, when the gamified systems are promoted in working environments, the quantification of everyday life could lead to ethical questions in the relations of power of those measured and those who have access to the data. Thus, news outlets could indeed use a gamified experience to exploit their users, either by manipulating their reading choices through game mechanics, or by only monetizing the content and data they generate while they interact with the system. This could become a serious privacy risk involved with tracking the users' every move, while owning such data. It is at least ethically dubious (O'Donnell, 2014).

Furthermore, there is the implication that journalism, in the aim to compete with a wider range of digital services, gives in completely to the commercial logic by enticing users with game elements to engage users with news, but also catering news to the demand of popularized content, disregarding the professional logic. Even though gamification has the potential to abstract format from content, an excessive stress on the gratifications of the system offers an equally strong potential to forgetting or altering the reasons why such gamified format is there in the first place. If the goal of gamifying the news is to engage youth and creating the habit of consuming news by providing a service that taps into their format expectations, the effect can counter this goal and turning the game mechanics and the interface into the central aspect, relegating news to a secondary role. In a similar note, there could be serious conflicts of editorial choice when hard news of disturbing nature is channeled through a gamified format. The dissonance of news that aims to inform citizens about injustices and challenges of our times disseminated through a lighthearted gaming environment can diminish the gravitas of the issues being covered.

It is a matter of balance between the core of journalism and the engaging factors of games. With this in mind, Gamification can also be seen from a more neutral perspective. As Werbach (2014) redefines it, gamification could simply be *the process of making activities game-like.* This is in fact a much more useful standpoint for research, as gamification is not the tool that will either save or enslave journalism (or any other industry for that matter). Borrowing from behavioral economics scholar Dan Ariely (2011), gamification is a perfect example of reward substitution, which is *doing the right thing for the wrong reasons.* If by using game mechanics news outlets could trigger extrinsic and intrinsic motivators that engage youth to consume news, it is worth a try to implement, and subsequently researching on it.

The ever-present tensions between the professional and commercial logic is now played under new and different conditions. Before analyzing concrete examples of the application of gamification within journalism contexts we need to outline how journalism has been fundamentally changed by digitalization and how journalists, the media industry, and the audience relate to this change.

NEWS IN TRANSITION: DIGITALIZATION, SHIFTING AUDIENCES, NEWS PATHS, AND USER ENGAGEMENT

The introduction of the Internet and the process of digitalization of news did nothing but exacerbate the conflict of logics outlined above. It would be an oversimplification to assume that the complex phenomenon in which society adopted digital technologies to consume media is reduced to pure economic and technological reasons. The new wave of commercial and technological advances, based on computing, convergence, and digitalization, is merely an amplified account of similar historical instances based on printing culture, audiovisual culture, and broadcasting media, such as the telegraph, the radio, or the television (Schudson, 1978; Briggs & Burke, 2002; Bondebjerg, 2002; Ekström & Djerf-Pierre, 2013).

However, while the decline of journalism in terms of quality is a matter of debate, the decline of the news industry in commercial terms is undeniable. The transition to digital journalism was majorly done following a free-for-all strategy, hoping that newspapers' subscriptions and online advertising would provide a sustainable business model (Meyer, 2009). After several years, newspaper sales keep dropping and advertising revenues have shifted to other digital services that attract more users (Picard, 2008; Gallaugher, Auger, & BarNir, 2001).

This part of the chapter aims to map the adoption and evolution of digital news both by its producers and its consumers. The idea is to provide a clear image of where the news industry is now: *what are the formats provided by the producers? what are the media habits of consumers?,* and finally *how does the introduction of gamification fit within the industry?*

New Channels, New Formats, and News Consumption

Journalism, as many other forms of audiovisual communication, is in the midst of a process of convergence. Technologically, various types of media are mixed and integrated in unified digital distribution points that can be accessed and consumed via a single medium, such as smartphones, tablets, or computers (Mitchell, Rosenstiel, & Christian, 2012). Culturally, news conglomerates that used to operate in departmentalized structures face arduous challenges as the increasing importance of multimedia and technical aspects to the craft of journalism (Deuze, 2004, Deuze, 2005; Thurman & Lupton, 2008). The new media landscape amalgamates several content providers, expanding competition in all shapes of entertainment and communication sources, spurring a change of habits in media consumption. New efforts have been introduced in order to capture the emerging individual structures of the self, through engagement with technological systems that turn life towards short-term, fragmented information, *on the go* life styles (Elliott & Urry, 2010; Urry, 2002), transforming media interaction into a prominently social experience (Jenkins, 2006). It is not technology *per se* that matters, but the way technology is used.

The concept of traditional news is a blurred. What constitutes news is contested. The integration of digital network technologies enable and encourage social participation (Lewis, 2012), shaking the barriers between producers and consumers. The public has the ability to be everywhere, all the time, thus having the advantage on immediacy to organized journalism (Peters, 2012). This results in users decreasing their attention to mainstream media and increasing interaction within social networks, collecting atomized information from source to destination in different forms, forging a reconfigured model of news medium (Baresch, Hsu, & Reese, 2010)

The need to adapt to the new *milieu* and embrace technology (Singer, 2004; Deuze, 2009; Westlund, 2012) has opened doors to a myriad of new channels and formats. New forms of storytelling that depart from print formats including audio, video, slide shows, and interactive features have steadily been incorporated in the digital editions of news outlets (Kleis Nielsen, 2012; Karlsson & Clerwall, 2012; Thurman & Walters, 2013). Traditional game-like pastimes like knowledge quizzes as well as unconventional formats like newsgames (Bogost, Ferrari, & Schweizer, 2010; Gómez García & Navarro Sierra, 2013) and gamification (Jacobson, 2012) have found a place in digital journalism. The interface becomes a proxy for automated interaction, by introducing technology as a persuasive actor (Fogg, 2002). The triggers and experiences that digital games have embedded in our new digital culture, help explain why media choice is much more prone towards games than news in younger generations. Games provide specific gratifications, but most importantly feed back to the users experiences that fulfill psychological needs that intrinsically motivates them to seek more interactions with the medium (Przybylski, Ryan, and Rigby, 2010; Tamborini et al., 2010). However, it is widely accepted that the new forms of expression multimedia has to offer have been massively underused by mainstream news organizations (Lillie, 2011).

Thus, the extremely varied type of news media use poses a threat to major legacy news outlets. News consumption fluctuates according to the users' everyday life (Jansson & Lindell, 2014), and it becomes a less immersive form of news acquisition, embedded in brief exchanges of media content afforded by the multimodality of the medium (Schroder, 2014). News aggregators, social media, and services like *Summly* or *BuzzFeed* offer an innovative model of news consumption, allowing personalization, and adapting to new users' personal contexts. Audiences evolve, and traditional news must evolve with them or eventually they will be replaced by a newer breed of news services (Carey & Elton, 2010).

Transforming Audiences, User Agency, and Crisis of Engagement

The effects of convergence seem to have a tighter grip on audiences. Media consumers used to be regarded as *publics*, *audiences,* or even *readers*. The common connotative aspect of these terms is an apparent passivity (Humphreys & Grayson, 2008). But new media and the multiple services available to media consumers have ignited a debate on the role of consumers, from a passive approach to a much more active role as media users (Rosen, 2006). We adopt the word *user* as our unit of study, particularly because it keeps us from dwelling in the bipolar notion of producer and consumer (Van Dijck, 2009), and most importantly, it provides a much wider potentiality of media interaction. Personal, contextual, and experiential factors are combined to define the interaction between the user, the choice of media, and the news service (Hartmann, 2009). And while activities within the spectrum of consumption and production are always developed to a certain degree, one of the important additions to the users' roles is that of the data provider. Metadata and digital behaviors are automatically logged and become, regardless of the content, a main feature of the digital cultural practice (Murray, 2012). In an increasingly mechanized and automated news production process (Clerwall, 2014), user-generated content (Örnebring & Jönsson, 2011, Holt & Karlsson, 2011), and most importantly, user-generated data have introduced new drives for economic development. The conceptual debate around the commodification of audience labor, *playbor* (Kücklich, 2005), and the subdued exploitation has sparked ambivalent reactions within the scientific community.

The addition of digital news sites has derived into a change of habits that are connected to a generational bias. Older generations have adopted digital media as a complementary source of news. In younger generations, the trend has been of displacement, as digital news has replaced traditional newspapers

(Westlund & Färdigh, 2011). However, it is the younger users, the *DotNet* generation, the so called *millennials* who show a growing disregard for news both in paper and digital. This generation of users is the only one that significantly consumes less news both in paper and online (Wadbring & Bergström, 2014). While actual figures and definitions tend to shift from source to source, we name "young news users" to those under 30-35 years of age.

The current trend in online news distributors is to offer paywall models that combine subscription models with only certain amount of content for free (Myllylahti, 2014). This move is not particularly well received among a generation of internet users who are used to access a service for free, and in most cases, receive and consume their news through entertainment media instead of the traditional news media.

The shift from traditional news consumption to more "soft news" is often viewed as an indicator of a decline in democratic and civic engagement of media users (Macedo, 2005; Bennet, 2008). However, younger generations are engaged in media in different ways than what traditional media regard as valid (Westlund & Bjur, 2014). Thus, if being informed is a serious indicative of human and social capital that enhances democratic values (and we believe it is so), traditional news might need to expand their methods to engage younger audiences with even bolder and faster approaches that grasp the millennial ideals of what is worth their time.

GAMIFIED INTERFACES IN DIGITAL JOURNALISM

The first mention on the use of gamification and the news industry in a scholarly publication is 2012 Susan Jacobson's analysis of multimedia journalism published on nytimes.com. While discussing new storytelling techniques in news websites, Jacobson addresses the rising research interest on the impact of digital games on digital news. The stress is placed on serious games as a storytelling technique and their ability to provide the audience with a medium to explore news stories on their own terms. Currently there are various projects that are studying the intersection of journalism and gamification, such as *The Impact of Gamification on Journalism* at the University of Jyväskylä, Finnland, and the *Going Mobile* project at Karlstad University, Sweden (Ferrer Conill, 2014). Admittedly, research on serious games (Stapleton, 2004) and the so-called newsgames (Burton, 2005; Bogost et al., 2010; Siitonen & Varsaluoma, 2013) has gained more traction than the gamification of news, and that might be because game studies scholars feel more at home with the study of newsgames than with gamification, which has received a more controversial attention from the game design community. The difference, as Sicart (2008) explains, is that newsgames are *computer games used to participate in the public sphere with the intention of explaining or commenting on current news*, while, as we mentioned, gamification does not attempt to create a full-fledged game, but simply apply game elements to a digital service.

To simplify this, it could be argued that newsgames bring news to games, and the gamification of journalism brings games to news. However, newsgames and gamification of news share a similar mission, which is majorly considered to convey current events in an engaging manner to an audience that responds and is engaged by the language of video games (Ruffino, 2014). What differs both approaches is the procedural rhetoric (Treanor & Mateas, 2009), as newsgames carry along a self-contained narrative that is to be explored by the users. Gamification on the other hand intends to maintain the original news piece narrative and offer a game-like experience that can relate to that particular piece, or extend to the overall interaction with the news service as a whole. Interestingly, while newsgames sparked a great scholarly debate, it is gamification the one that has managed to contribute with more varied applications in real life journalism settings, which in no doubt is responsible for the current rise for interest in the gamification of news, both in the bloggosphere, but also in media studies. The reason for this could be explained by the higher resource demands of newsgames against a limited impact. On the one hand newsgames require a game design and implementation process for each story while making a serious impact only on that particular story. The results, attention span, and most important of all, information acquisition might be powerful, but as a change of habit and general news consumption impact is still limited. On the other hand, gamification still requires the game design and implementation process, but it is normally on a website or service level, which reduces resources per piece, and at the same time attempts to have an effect on the overall news consumption habits of readers in the long term, creating long-standing adherence to news services.

This section aims to reroute the previous section by detailing some of the game elements that are more recurrent in gamified news services. As a trend in the industry and for the sake of brevity, we take a look at the *triforce* of gamification, the omnipresent PBLs (points, badges, and leaderboards), and discuss the way they have been introduced in news websites and how they intend to engage with the users.

Points, Badges, and Leaderboards

As it has been pointed out, PBLs are the main game components that gamification initiatives include in their systems. Journalism and news services are not an exception.

Points aim to provide a sense of progress. Earning points for performing actions or achieving milestones becomes an automatic feedback mechanism that prompts the user to keep using the system. Journalism is no stranger to the points craze. As mentioned above, there are existing analogue approaches, like the *PostPoints* loyalty program from The Washington Post. This program offers a seemingly crude approximation of a game system where points are exchanged for gifts and discounts. The points are earned in a rather unclear way by reading the paper but also by shopping at third party establishments. The instant feedback loop is lost as a reward here. A completely different type of interaction occurs in a gamified digital system like the one over at Bleacher Report, a sports news website. B/R turns journalists into users by awarding them with points according to their writing career statistics regarding their contribution to the site. Number of reads, number of comments, number of lead stories, and other metrics keep adding points defining each author's reputation level. Almost immediately, journalists can evaluate the impact of their work in the organization and compels them to keep contributing to the site.

Badges function as a graphical representation of a one-time achievement or a cumulative achievement of other metrics (Antin & Churchill, 2011). One of the infamous use of badges in news gamified systems is that of Google News Badges. Google News, launched in September 2002, is a news aggregator gathering news from 25,000 publishers and offering a country-specific version for international users in 27 languages. As most news aggregators, they provide a personalized news experience, allowing the user to select the type of news they want to appear in their news feed, as well as which news publishers they want the content to be pulled from (Galbraith, 2008). In 2011 Google introduced Google News Badges with a set of 500 theme badges that could be leveled up. The new gamified layer intended to allow the user to track reading habits, create a more personalized news experience, and find articles on favorite topics. One year later, the system was phased out due to lack of impact. What Google missed here is that the system relied on providing vague feedback on what users already did. There was no real outcome for advancing in the game other than leveling up the badges. On top of that, there was very limited focus on persuading users to expand their content types, which would lead to broaden the variety of badges earned. Instead, Google News Badges resulted in users narrowing the number of chosen topics and providers, reinforcing users' selective exposure. A much more elegant use of badges was crafted by the football news-oriented NFL.com network in their system NFL Fan Rewards, rolled out in 2012. The badges in this gamified layer resembled patches on a football jersey and represented the user's rank in a team, from *Rookie* to *Hall of Fame*. Each patch was awarded by cumulative points and by completing *drives* of news and videos the user would have to read or view. The NFL Fan Rewards system excelled in its design because it managed to mimic American Football culture. The digital patches, just like the real ones in the game, served to show the status of each user within the community.

Leaderboards are a more ambivalent and complex game component. Leaderboards include the social aspect to the gamified system, as they represent the user's performance when compared to other users. On the one hand, they are great motivators as they show how much more progress is needed to increase a position in the ranking. On the other hand, assessing a very large gap between the higher-ranked users can demotivate a user and provoked leaving the system. To enhance the motivating effects and alleviate the demotivating ones, the Times Points program by media conglomerate Times Internet Limited, India's largest internet network, integrated two different leaderboards. This gamified system is integrated across 12 different media sites that offer a wide and eclectic range of content, including traditional news, real state, music streaming, feminine entertainment, masculine entertainment, and car deals. Thus, each website participant in the program offers both a site specific leaderboard and a global leaderboard that combines all users across websites. Finally, one of the most publicized gamified initiatives was a very simple system implemented by The Guardian, which implemented an investigative journalism crowdsourcing campaign to sieve through a large set of leaked documents that would trigger a major political scandal anchored in the UK's parliamentary expenses and the misuse of allowances by Members of Parliament. The Guardian created a specific page where all the documents could be openly accessed by their readers. Each user had the possibility to flag documents as "Not interesting", "Interesting but known", "Interesting", and "Investigate this!". Additionally, a progress bar showing the amount of data covered was implemented, as well as a leaderboard that displayed the top users and the number of items reviewed. The gamified crowdsourcing campaign had 20,000 readers review 170,000 in the first 80 hours harnessing the willpower of users to do a joint investigative journalism initiative. The engagement of users was driven by a combination of a shared goal by the community, a clear sensation of progress, and a sense of status as they mentioned in the leaderboards. In further iterations of the system, they allowed users to focus on the documents that tackled their own MPs in order to make the experience more relevant to their personal context (Daniel & Flew, 2010). Interestingly, The Guardian managed to create an article-level gamified news which does not extend to the whole website, which opens horizons for small scale approaches to gamifying the news.

Another great example of a gamified news article that incorporates PBLs is Al Jazeera's *Pirate Fishing: An Interactive Investigation*. This particular piece transforms viewers into players, aiming to "come up with an original, interactive, investigative story that would transform viewers into players and capture their attention" (Ruhfus, 2014). Juliana Ruhfus and her team created a storytelling interface including videos, maps, photos, and other documents to submerge the reader into the process of reporting, with the reference of illegal fishing in Sierra Leone. Here the user is prompted to view videos and read documents to collect *Investigation Points*, which in turn take the view from a *Junior Researcher* position up to *Senior Reporter*. As the user advances stages, by accessing to different notebooks, identifying evidence, and exploring maps, it is possible to acquire badges such as *Activist*, *City Explorer*, or *Corruption Investigation*. This is a particularly insightful approach as how to expand the boundaries of digital news storytelling, attempting to engage users with game mechanics and other elements.

CRAFTING THE EXPERIENCE: BEYOND THE PBLs

The examples discussed above have different ways to approach users, but it is important to note the game mechanics they use do not affect the actual news pieces' content. This is probably the main reason to experiment with the gamification of news as a way to engage users to consume news. The strategies and tools to use in a gamified layer need to enrich the news experience by adapting the interface and user interaction to the users' needs while keeping the content a matter of editorial choice. If journalism is to continue to uphold certain democratic and civic function, then on the one hand, the gap between news and entertainment must remain open when it comes to content, and on the other hand, it should slowly disappear when it comes to format. The aim is to keep content and format as independent as possible.

We have discussed the possible reasons for gamifying the news. This section aims to connect the dots in the attempt to motivate for news consumption. For that reason we try to conceptualize young news readers as game players to understand what they crave. Consequently, we analyze the strategies and game mechanics that could be persuasive and engaging while remaining as little intrusive to the news experience as possible.

Expanding Gamification to News Consumption

According to Diddi and LaRose (2006) habit strength is the most powerful predictor of news consumption. That is a great place to start analyzing the gamification of news. The narrative of a gamified system should lead to the creation of new habits for the users. Accordingly, there needs to be a clear description of what the target behaviors that would derive into new habits are. Tracking behaviors during the interaction with the interface and setting success metrics is key to the system. Metrics can range in terms of engagement (news accessed, unique visits, time on the site), loyalty (users return, engaging other users), virality (sharing, social media, and social connections), and monetization (conversion rates and virtual goods) (Meloni & Gruener, 2012).

At this point the users/gamers need to be defined. Who are the players that will interact with the interface? There is a tradition in the gamification literature to use Bartle's (1996) player type model, however, the model was developed for Massively Multiplayer Online Games (MMOGs) and Bartle himself has mentioned his concerns about using the model for other type of "games". Bartle's original taxonomy divided players into four categories: *killers*, *achievers*, *socializers*, and *explorers*. For the purposes of a journalism gamified system, players can be typified differently by looking at what is behind the user's motives for each choice (Krcmar & Strizhakova, 2009). Most of gamified programs tend to reward killers, as those are the ones who respond to leaderboards and ranks, but killers are probably not the target of those who seek civic engagement. Thus, the key here is to find what are the type of players that want to read news. Explorers and socializers seem good news player types. The first could be engaged by finding new content and unveiling stories. The latter could be engaged by interacting with other users. Additional player types for journalism could be contributors, those who are engaged by providing content, and watchdogs, those who could be engaged by pointing out misleading information that has been published.

In the next step, the *activity loops* as well as the *progression loops* have to be defined. What is to be considered an activity, whether it is reading an entire article, watching a video, writing a comment in the forum, exploring new news sections, providing with content for news or even reporting wrong information. Each activity loop is composed of an action conducted by the user, upon which the system offers feedback, creating engagement and motivation to keep performing the action. Progression loops aim to make visible the improvement of each user, from the onboarding stage to an eventual mastering of the system.

Finally, the actual elements that will be placed in the interface to produce the feedback need to be chosen. Points, badges, and leaderboards are only the tip of the iceberg, but certainly they could be viable in a news website for different purposes. Leaderboards for general readers seem to be problematic, but certainly for investigative crowdsourcing (as previously mentioned in The Guardian example) could be particularly enticing. Achievements for different reads, content unlocking, social graphs, collections, and virtual goods are other game components that could easily fit the needs of the users. As it has been discussed, there are a wide range of game elements that can be included in the interface to enhance user experience (Zichermann & Cunningham, 2011; Witt, Scheiner, & Robra-Bissantz, 2011;), and they need to be applied on a case to case basis, both for desktop and mobile devices (Crowley et al., 2012) with adaptable and personalized experiences.

In sum, there are four main areas that new to be closely planned from a multidiscipline perspective with game designers, journalists, and business strategists. The first one is the progress paths. The notion of progress is a very powerful motivator (see Amabile & Kramer, 2011). The journey from novice to mastery needs to be something acknowledged. Challenges and current affairs knowledge tests presented as in system games can be a way to go. Secondly, timely feedback and rewards are necessary to keep the users informed of their progress. Once again, the rewards need to be appealing to the users and have to be related to the activities. A comment is an activity a socializer is most plausible to do. Similarly, explorers would appreciate rewards for curiosity, but not reading more than others. Hence being rewarded with status for such a feat is a reward that does not motivate a socializer. Status might resonate more with a watchdog user type, for example. Getting such reward for uncovering wrong doing publicly might be a better match. Third, the social connection. The transition to digital news have turned the news experience a social one, especially with the new role of social media when disseminating the news (Hermida, 2010; Moe, 2013). Harnessing social networks, both internally and externally in order to control the path of news, but also to create competition, camaraderie, and support is hugely important. The social aspect is usually what provides the notion of relatedness. Finally, the interface and user experience. Gamification is a persuasive technology (Llagostera, 2012), thus the aesthetics, design, and sophistication of the system has to entice the user to keep using it. These four areas must be taken into consideration as a whole, blending them into one functioning news experience, while keeping the balance that would appeal to all user types. It is not an easy feat, but failing to get each part right or deal with them as isolated components of a system might lead to failure (Palmer, Lunceford & Patton, 2012).

Ultimately, the goal is to generate a feeling of competence, autonomy, and relatedness to generate the intrinsic motivation of consuming news in the user (Przybylski, Rigby & Ryan, 2010). Simultaneously, it is vital to keep news content out of the equation. Maintaining the news untouched is key to this process if the notion of democratic values is to be upheld. The gamification process is meant to provide new value to the user, personalizing the news experience with relevant, targeted news, embedded in a social environment, while keeping the quality of the news intact, and always aiming for a broadening of views, avoiding selective exposure, and emphasizing improvement of the users' knowledge.

CHALLENGES AND NEEDS FOR RESEARCH

In media studies, every ground breaking technological innovation and every new medium have been accepted with the widespread fear that scientific paradigms as we know them might be shattered. The idea that the effects of new technology might be detrimental to society, and might aid those in power to control and exploit users has been a recurrent one since the dawn of this discipline (Jensen & Rosengren, 1990; Scannell, 2007). Interestingly, when the dust settles, research and life moves on, waiting for the next ground-shaking innovation.

Journalism is a long and well-established research tradition and paradoxically, as the actual news industry is immersed in a world-wide crisis, the academic field of journalism is thriving. Gamification, on the other hand, is a rather new field of study, and while Hamari, Koivisto and Pakkanen (2014) demonstrate that research on gamification has been extremely prolific since 2011, much still needs to be done. Furthermore, gamification is a profoundly multidisciplinary field, which allows for comparative research, but also for research projects that combine different approaches and traditions that could lead to a better understanding of such a complex phenomenon. However, the focus so far has been on the practice and implementation of gamification, and particularly on the technologies used to apply game mechanics in user interfaces. This means that focus on media research on gamification has only started. There is a an apparent disregard for an inclusive approach that attempts to introduce a multiplicity of factors, such as the medium, the effects game elements have on users, but also on the perspective of how non-game media is affected by those game elements. Similarly, a look into the effects that pervasive, continuous, and ubiquitous games have on media consumption and creation is still merely on its infancy. The issues of time and space have been not been optimally researched.

It is exciting to think that at this stage, research on the gamification of journalism has a lot to conquer. We need more studies that cover how to effectively apply games to journalism without breaking the essence of what journalism should be. Newsgames cover parts of this, but there are a lot of new formats that do not require creating a full-fledged game to convey a message. We need to understand how new rituals and habits of youth and their new mobile lifestyles affect their perception of the role of news (Bolin & Westlund, 2009). We should certainly look into what are the main motivators that could lead to change those rituals in order to create a habit of news consumption. Additionally, we need to know how gamifying the interface of a news website could affect news producers and journalism practice. Equally important is to study if the premise of leaving the content of news untouched is true or if, as some suspect, gamifying the news would necessarily change the content of news, trivializing the news experience.

Some of the challenges linked to the research of gamified news carry methodological challenges that should be confronted. Longitudinal studies, multidisciplinary approaches, and mix-methods designs are hard to conduct, normally requiring more than one team of researchers. However, it is essential to conduct multifaceted research including as many factors as possible to fully understand the effects of game elements in news environments.

Finally, other challenges must be bridged. Disentangling studies from time and space is a particularly difficult thing to do, especially when it is connected use of media that happens everywhere, all the time. There is a need looking into the context of news consumption as a whole, and not only as an interface to exploit. We need to understand what are the contextual factors that require a unique set of *affordances of fun, motivation, and learning* that journalism could offer to its users (Deterding, 2014).

Thus, we call for experimental design including aspects of mobility and habits, looking for ecological validity, thinking on the setting and context first in order to grasp much more nuanced results from empirical research. Surveys, focus groups, and ethnographic and participatory observation are methods that can help complement studies that deepen in all aspects of each study conducted.

We encourage researchers to cross boundaries and engage colleagues from other disciplines to join them conduct their studies. Mixing perspectives and theoretical frameworks from journalism studies with different traditions, expanding both the current body of knowledge in journalism research and gamification. If adding game elements to news is crossing certain boundaries, studying this particular phenomenon should invite to cross boundaries of conventional research too.

CONCLUSIONS: GAMIFICATION'S FUTURE PLACE WITHIN JOURNALISM AND JOURNALISM RESEARCH

The current tensions of the journalistic field, from a professional logic to a commercial logic, combined with the expansion of the internet and mobile technologies have led to a decline of news industry. Similarly, the apparition of new channels of media, the reconfiguration of audiences, and decreasing engagement of youth with news consumption has derived in the experimentation with new formats and models designed to make the consumption of news a much more engaging experience.

At the same time, gamification, by applying game mechanics to non-gaming environments, has proven to be capable of engaging users and leading to the creation of habits and social change in several disciplines.

There is an undeniable theoretical benefit from applying gamification into digital news outlets. Motivating younger generations to adopt new media rituals while providing them with agency (van Dijck, 2009), could lead to enhancing the democratic aims of journalism (Schudson, 1997). It offers the potential to generate the stimuli to amplify small wins generating engagement, user habit, and finally feeding a progress loop that leads to social change. However, there is risk of centering the news experience on the game rather than the content or even worse, perverting the gamified system for sole purpose of commercialization. There is also skepticism and resistance from the news industry. Surely, there is a whole lot to learn.

Concerning gamification's place within journalism research one is tempted to ask, "What place?" since there is so little written about it. Much more theoretical and empirical research is needed in the intersection between journalism and gamification. From this chapter we can see that much is at stake and that gamification is already in practice in some news outlets, but that there is a serious lack of research in the area. Future research projects could include, but not be limited to, explorations on how journalists view and appropriate gamification elements in the production of news; how gamification is being implemented on various platforms – computer, tablet, smartphone – and in different publishing contexts – countries, traditions; how users view and relate to gamification features; how does mobility and gamification shape news consumption; if and how gamification affects what news is being published and how users are affected by it. Obviously, answering these research questions is a gigantic task that would need collaborations and many different methodological approaches. But it is a task that is needed since only systematic, comparative and empirical research can shed a light on what gamification, for better or for worse, will do with journalism.

REFERENCES

Aalberg, T., & Curran, J. (2011). *How Media Inform Democracy*. New York, NY: Routledge.

Amabile, T., & Kramer, S. (2011). *The progress principle. Using small wins to ignite joy, engagement, and creativity at work*. Boston, MA: Harvard Business Review Press.

Anderson, C. W. (2011). Deliberative, agonistic, and algorithmic audiences: Journalism's vision of its public in an age of audience transparency. *International Journal of Communication, 5*, 529–547.

Antin, J., & Churchill, E. F. (2011). Badges in social media: A social phsychological perspective. *Proceedings of the Computer Human Interaction (CHI) conference, May 2011, Vancouver, BC, Canada*. ACM.

Ariely, D. (2011). *The upside of irrationality: The unexpected benefits of defying logic at home and at work*. Harper. doi:10.1109/AERO.2011.5747214

Baresch, B., Hsu, S.-H., & Reese, S. D. (2010). The power of framing: New challenges for researching the structure of meaning in news. In S. Allan (Ed.), *The Routledge companion to news and journalism*. New York, NY: Routledge.

Barnhurst, K., & Nerone, J. (2009). Journalism history. In K. Wahl-Jorgensen & T. Hanitzsch (Eds.), *The Handbook of Journalism Studies* (pp. 17–28). New York, NY: Routledge.

Bartle, R. (1996). *Hearts, clubs, diamonds, spades: Players who suit MUDs*. Retrieved from http://www.mud.co.uk/richard/hcds.htm

Bennet, W. L. (2008). Changing citizenship in the digital age. In W. L. Bennet (Ed.), *Civic life online: Learning how digital media can engage youth* (pp. 1–24). Cambridge, MA: MIT Press.

Bennet, W. L., Freelon, D. G., Hussain, M. M., & Wells, C. (2012). Digital media and youth engagement. In H. Semetko & M. Scammell (Eds.) The Sage handbook of political communication. London: SAGE Publications. doi:10.4135/9781446201015.n11

Bennett, S., Maton, K., & Kervin, L. (2008). The 'digital natives' debate: A critical review of the evidence. *British Journal of Educational Technology, 39*(5), 775–786. doi:10.1111/j.1467-8535.2007.00793.x

Bimber, B. (2012). Digital media and citizenship. In H. Semetko & M. Scammell (Eds.), The Sage handbook of political communication. London: SAGE Publications. doi:10.4135/9781446201015.n10

Bird, E. (2009). Tabloidization: What is it, and does it really matter? In B. Zelizer (Ed.), *The changing faces of journalism. Tabloidization, technology and truthiness* (pp. 40–50). New York, NY: Routledge.

Boczkowski, P., & Mitchelstein, E. (2013). *The news gap. When the information preferences of the media and the public diverge*. Cambridge, MA: MIT Press. doi:10.7551/mitpress/9780262019835.001.0001

Bogost, I. (2011). Gamification is bullshit. Retrieved from http://www.bogost.com/blog/gamification_is_bullshit.shtml

Bogost, I., Ferrari, S., & Schweizer, B. (2010). *Newsgames. Journalism at play*. Cambridge, MA: MIT Press.

Bolin, G., & Westlund, O. (2009). Mobile generations: The role of mobile technology in the shaping of Swedish media generations. *International Journal of Communication, 3*, 108–124.

Bondebjerg, I. (2002). Scandinavian media histories. A comparative study. *Nordicom Review, 23*(1-2), 61–79.

Briggs, A., & Burke, P. (2002). *A social history of the media: From Gutenberg to the Internet.* Cambridge, MA: Polity Press.

Burton, J. (2005). News-game journalism: History, current use and possible futures. *Australian Journal of Emerging Technologies and Society, 3*(2), 87–99.

Carey, J., & Elton, M. C. J. (2010). *When media are new: Understanding the dynamics of new media adoption and use.* Digital Culture Books. doi:10.3998/nmw.8859947.0001.001

Clerwall, C. (2014). Enter the robot journalism: Users' perceptions of automated content. *Journalism Practice,* (ahead-of-print), 1-13.

Coleman, S., & Blumler, J. G. (2012). The Internet and citizenship: Democratic opportunity or more of the same? In H. Semetko & M. Scammell (Eds.) The Sage handbook of political communication. London: SAGE Publications.

Conboy, M. (2010). The paradoxes of journalism history. *Historical journal of film, radio and television, 30*(3), 411-420.

Connell, I. (1998). Mistaken identities: Tabloid and broadsheet news discourse. *Javnost (Ljubljana), 5*(3), 11–31. doi:10.1080/13183222.1998.11008680

Croteau, D., & Hoynes, W. (2001). *The Business of Media. Corporate Media and the Public Interest.* Thousand Oaks: Pine Forge Press.

Crowley, D. N., Brestlin, J. G., Corcoran, P., & Young, K. (2012). Gamification of citizen sensing through mobile social reporting. Proceedings of *Games Innovation Conference (IGIC), 2012 IEEE International,* (pp. 1-5). IEEE Xplore. doi:10.1109/IGIC.2012.6329849

Currah, A. (2009). *What's happening to our news. An investigation into the likely impact of the digital revolution on the economics of news publishing in the UK.* Oxford: Reuters Institute for the Study of Journalism.

Cushion, S. (2012). *The democratic value of news. Why public service media matter.* Houndmills: Palgrave Mcmillan.

Daniel, A., & Flew, T. (2010, November 15-16). The Guardian reportage of the UK MP expenses scandal: a Case study of computational journalism. Proceedings of *Communications Policy and Research Forum 2010,* Sydney.

De Waal, E., & Schoenbach, K. (2010). News sites' position in the mediascape: Uses, evaluations and media displacement effects over time. *New Media & Society, 12*(3), 477–496. doi:10.1177/1461444809341859

Deci, E. L., & Ryan, R. M. (1985). *Intrinsic motivation and self-determination in human behavior.* New York, NY: Plenum. doi:10.1007/978-1-4899-2271-7

Delli Carpini, M. X. (2012). Entertainment media and the political engagement of citizens. In H. Semetko & M. Scammell (Eds.) The Sage handbook of political communication. London: SAGE Publications. doi:10.4135/9781446201015.n2

Deterding, S. (2014). Eudaimonic design, or: Six invitations to rethink gamification. In M. Fuchs et al. (Eds.), *Rethinking gamification* (pp. 305–333).

Deterding, S., Dixon, D., Khaled, R., & Nacke, L. (2011b). From game design elements to gamefulness: Defining gamification. *Proceedings of the 15th International Academic MindTrek Conference: Envisioning Future Media Environments*, (pp. 9-15). ACM. doi:10.1145/2181037.2181040

Deterding, S., Sicart, M., Nacke, L., O'Hara, K., & Dixon, D. (2011a). Gamification, using game-design elements in non-gaming contexts. *Proceedings of the 2011 annual conference extended abstracts on Human factors in computing systems PART 2* (pp. 2425-2428). ACM.

Deuze, M. (2004). What is multimedia journalism? *Journalism Studies*, 5(2), 139–152. doi:10.1080/1461670042000211131

Deuze, M. (2005). What is journalism? Professional identity and ideology of journalists considered. *Journalism*, 6(4), 442–464. doi:10.1177/1464884905056815

Deuze, M. (2009). Journalism, citizenship, and digital culture. In Z. Papacharissi (Ed.), *Journalism and citizenship: New agendas in communication*. New York, NY: Routledge.

Diddi, A., & LaRose, R. (2006). Getting hooked on news: Uses and gratifications and the formation of news habits among college students in an Internet Environment. *Journal of Broadcasting & Electronic Media*, 50(2), 193–210. doi:10.1207/s15506878jobem5002_2

Dimmick, J., Feaster, J. C., & Hoplamazian, G. J. (2010). News in the interstices: The niches of mobile media in space and time. *New Media & Society*, 13(1), 23–39. doi:10.1177/1461444810363452

Ekström, M., & Djerf-Pierre, M. (2013). Approaching broadcast history: An introduction. In *A history of Swedish broadcasting*. Gothenburg: Nordicom.

Elliott, A., & Urry, J. (2010). *Mobile lives*. Routledge.

Ferrer Conill, R. (2014). Going mobile: Gamifying digital news in mobile devices. Proceedings of Persuasive Technology: Persuasive, motivating, empowering videogames. Padova, Italy, May 2014. Adjunct proceedings, (pp. 86-89). University of Padova.

Fogg, B. J. (2002). *Persuasive technology: using computers to change what we think and do. Ubiquity, 2002, art. 5*. New York, NY: ACM.

Fogg, B. J. (2009). A behavior model for persuasive design. In *Proceedings of the 4th international Conference on Persuasive Technology*, (p. 40). ACM.

Fujikawa, Y., & Manki, M. (2013). A new environment for algorithm research using gamification. In *2013 IEEE International Conference on Electro/Information Technology (EIT)*, (pp. 1-6). IEEE. doi:10.1109/EIT.2013.6632668

Galbraith, J. (2008). A Squatter on the Fourth Estate: Google News. *Journal of Library Administration, 46*(3-4), 191–206. doi:10.1300/J111v46n03_13

Gallaugher, J. M., Auger, P., & BarNir, A. (2001). Revenue streams and digital content providers an empirical investigation. *Information & Management, 38*(7), 473–485. doi:10.1016/S0378-7206(00)00083-5

Gil de Zúñiga, H., Jung, N., & Valenzuela, S. (2012). Social media use for news and individuals' social capital, civic engagement and political participation. *Journal of Computer-Mediated Communication, 17*(3), 319–336. doi:10.1111/j.1083-6101.2012.01574.x

Gómez García, S. & Navarro Sierra, N. (2013). Videogames and information. An approach about Spanish newsgames as new informative perspective. *Icono 14, 11*(2), 31-51.

Hamari, J., Koivisto, J., & Pakkanen, T. (2014). Do Persuasive Technologies Persuade? – A Review of Empirical Studies. In A. Spagnolli et al. (Eds.), *Persuasive Technology, LNCS 8462* (pp. 118–136). Switzerland: Springer International Publishing. doi:10.1007/978-3-319-07127-5_11

Hamilton, J. (2004). *All the news that's fit to sell. How the market transforms information into news.* Princeton, NJ: Princeton university press.

Hartley, J. (2009). Journalism and Popular Culture. In K. Wahl-Jorgensen & T. Hanitzsch (Eds.), *The Handbook of Journalism Studies* (pp. 310–324). New York, NY: Routledge.

Hartmann, T. (Ed.). (2009). *Media choice: A theoretical and empirical overview.* New York, NY: Routledge.

Herger, M. (2014). Enterprise gamification: Engaging people by letting them have fun. ISBN:1470000644.

Hermida, A. (2010). Tweet the news: Social media streams and the practice of journalism. In S. Allan (Ed.), *The Routledge companion to news and journalism.* New York, NY: Routledge.

Holt, K., & Karlsson, M. (2011). Edited participation: Comparing editorial influence on traditional and participatory online newspapers in Sweden. Javnost - the public, 18(2), 19-36.

Humphreys, A., & Grayson, K. (2008). The intersecting roles of consumer and producer: A critical perspective on co-production, co-creation and presumption. *Social Compass, 2,* 1–18.

Huotari, K., & Hamari, J. (2012). Defining gamification: a service marketing perspective. *Proceedings of the 16th International Academic MindTrek Conference,* (pp. 17-22). ACM. doi:10.1145/2393132.2393137

Jacobson, S. (2012). Transcoding the news: An investigation into multimedia journalism published on nytimes.com 2000-2008. *New Media & Society, 14*(5), 867–885. doi:10.1177/1461444811431864

Jansson, A., & Lindell, J. (2014). News media consumption in the transmedia age. *Journalism Studies.* doi:10.1080/1461670X.2014.890337

Jenkins, H. (2006). *Convergence culture: Where old and new media collide.* New York University Press.

Jensen, K. B., & Rosengren, K. E. (1990). Five traditions in search of the audience. *European Journal of Communication, 5*(2), 207–238. doi:10.1177/0267323190005002005

Kapp, K. M. (2012). *The gamification of learning and instruction: Game-based methods and strategies for training and education.* Pfeiffer & Co.

Karlsson, M. (2011). The immediacy of online news, the visibility of journalistic processes and a restructuring of journalistic authority. *Journalism, 12*(3), 279–295. doi:10.1177/1464884910388223

Karlsson, M., & Clerwall, C. (2012). Patterns and origins in the evolution of multimedia on broadsheet and tabloid news sites: Swedish online news 2005-2010. *Journalism Studies, 13*(4), 550–565. doi:10.1080/1461670X.2011.639571

Karlsson, M., & Clerwall, C. (2013). Negotiating professional news judgment and "Clicks". Comparing tabloid, broadsheet and public service traditions in Sweden. *Nordicom Review*.

Katz, J. (1993, November 25). The media's war on kids: from the Beatles to Beavis and Butt-head. *Rolling Stone*.

Kleis Nielsen, R. (2012). How newspapers began to blog. *Information Communication and Society, 15*(6), 959–978. doi:10.1080/1369118X.2012.694898

Kovach, B., & Rosenstiehl, T. (2001). *The elements of journalism. What newspeople should know and the public should expect.* New York, NY: Crown Publishers.

Krcmar, M., & Strizhakova, Y. (2009). Uses and gratifications as media choice. In T. Hartmann (Ed.), Media choice: A theoretical and empirical overview. Routledge.

Kücklich, J. (2005). Precarious playbor: modders and the digital game industry. *The Fibreculture Journal, 5*.

Kwak, H., Lee, C., Park, H., & Moon, S. (2010). What is Twitter, a social network or a news media? In *Proceedings of the 19th International Conference on World Wide Web*, (pp.591-600). Raleigh, NC. doi:10.1145/1772690.1772751

Lewis, S. C. (2012). The tension between professional control and open participation. *Information Communication and Society, 15*(6), 836–866. doi:10.1080/1369118X.2012.674150

Lillie, J. (2011). How and why journalists create audio slideshows. *Journalism Practice, 5*(3), 350–365. doi:10.1080/17512786.2010.530977

Llagostera, E. (2012). On gamification and persuasion. *Proceedings of XI SBGames 2012.* Brasilia, Brazil.

Lundby, K. (Ed.). (2009). *Mediatization: concept, changes, consequences.* Peter Lang.

Macedo, S. (2005). *Democracy at risk: How political choices undermine citizen participation, and what we can do about it.* Washington, DC: Brookings Institution.

MacGregor, P. (2007). Tracking the online audience. *Journalism Studies, 8*(2), 280–298. doi:10.1080/14616700601148879

McCallum, S. (2012). Gamification and serious games for personalized health. In *Proceedings of the 9th International Conference on Wearable Micro and Nano Technologies for Personalized Health. Studies in Health Technology and Informatics, 177*, 85–96. PMID:22942036

McGonigal, J. (2011). *Reality is Broken.* New York, NY: Penguin Press.

McManus, J. H. (1994). *Market-Driven Journalism: Let the Citizen Beware?* Thousand Oaks: Sage.

McManus, J. H. (2009). The Commercialization of News (pp. 218–233). In K. Wahl-Jorgensen & T. Hanitzsch (Eds.), *The Handbook of Journalism Studies*. New York, NY: Routledge.

McNair, B. (2000). *Journalism and democracy. An evaluation of the political public sphere*. London, UK: Routledge.

Meloni, W. & Gruener, W. (2012). *Gamification in 2012: Market update, consumer and enterprise market trends*. M2 Research.

Meyer, P. (2009). *The vanishing newspaper: Saving journalism in the information age*. University of Missouri Press.

Mitchell, A., Rosenstiel, T., & Christian, L. (2012). Mobile devices and news consumption: Some good signs for journalism. *The Pew Research Center's project for excellence in journalism: The state of the news media 2012*.

Moe, H. (2013). Public service broadcasting and social networking sites: The Norwegian broadcasting corporation on Facebook. *Media International Australia, 146*, 114–122.

Muntean, C. I. (2011). Raising engagement in e-learning through gamification. In *Proceedings of the 6th International Conference on Virtual Learning. ICVL*, (pp. 323-329).

Murray, J. H. (2012). *Inventing the medium: Principles of interaction design as a cultural practice*. The MIT Press.

Myllylahti, M. (2014). Newspaper paywalls – the hype and the reality. *Digital journalism, 2*(2), 179-194.

O'Donnell, C. (2014). Getting played: Gamification, bullshit, and the rise of algorithmic surveillance. *Surveillance & Society, 12*(3), 349–359.

Örnebring, H., & Jönsson, A. M. (2011). User-generated content and the news: Empowerment of citizens or an interactive illusion? *Journalism Practice, 5*(2), 127–144. doi:10.1080/17512786.2010.501155

Paharia, R. (2013). *Loyalty 3.0: How to revolutionize customer and employee engagement with big data and gamification*. McGraw-Hill.

Palmer, D., Lunceford, S., & Patton, A.J. (2012). The engagement economy: How gamification is re-shaping business. *Deloitte Review*, 11.

Peters, C. (2012). Journalism to go: The changing spaces of news consumption. *Journalism Studies, Special Issue: The Future of Journalism 2011. Developments and Debates, 13*(5-6), 695–705.

Picard, R. G. (2008). Shifts in newspaper advertising expenditures and their implications for the future of newspapers. *Journalism Studies, 9*(5), 704–716. doi:10.1080/14616700802207649

Pink, D. (2009). *Drive: The surprising truth about what motivates us*. Riverhead Books.

Prior, M. (2007). *Post-Broadcast democracy. How media choice increases inequality in political involvement and polarizes elections*. Cambridge: Cambridge University Press.

Przybylski, A. K., Rigby, C. S., & Ryan, R. M. (2010). A motivational model of video game engagement. *Review of General Psychology, 14*(2), 154–166. doi:10.1037/a0019440

Putman, R. (2000). *Bowling alone: The collapse and revival of American community*. New York: Simon and Schuster.

Quah, D. (2003). *Digital goods and the new economy. CEP discussion paper; CEPDP0563, 563*. London, UK: Centre for Economic Performance, London School of Economics and Political Science.

Reese, S. D., & Lee, J. K. (2012). Understanding the content of news media. In H. Semetko & M. Scammell (Eds.) The Sage handbook of political communication. London: SAGE Publications. doi:10.4135/9781446201015.n21

Reinemann, C., Stanyer, J., Scherr, S., & Legnante, G. (2011). Hard and soft news: A review of concepts, operationalizations and key findings. *Journalism*, *13*(2), 221–239. doi:10.1177/1464884911427803

Rey, P. J. (2012). Gamification, Playbor & Exploitation. Retrieved April 25, 2014, from http://pjrey.wordpress.com/2012/12/27/gamification-playbor-exploitation/

Rolland, A., & Eastman, J. (2011). *The gamification of everything. Analyst briefing*. PWC PricewaterhouseCoopers LLP.

Rosen, J. (2006, June 27). The people formerly known as the audience. *Press Think*. Retrieved from http://archive.pressthink.org/2006/06/27/ppl_frmr.html

Ruffino, P. (2014). From engagement to life, or: How to do things with gamification? In M. Fuchs et al. (Eds.), *Rethinking gamification* (pp. 47–60).

Ruhfus, J. (2014). Why we decided to gamify investigative journalism at Al Jazeera. Retrieved from https://medium.com/@julianaruhfus/pushing-the-boundaries-of-news-why-we-decided-to-gamify-investigations-and-current-affairs-db6b13d64a46

Scannell, P. (2007). *Media and Communication*. London: Sage.

Scheufele, D., Shanahan, J., & Kim, S.-H. (2002). Who cares about local politics? Media influences on local political involvement, issue awareness, and attitude strength. *Journalism & Mass Communication Quarterly*, *79*(2), 427–444. doi:10.1177/107769900207900211

Schroder, K. C. (2014). News media old and new. *Journalism Studies*. doi:10.1080/1461670X.2014.890332

Schudson, M. (1978). *Discovering the News*. New York, NY: Bacis Books.

Schudson, M. (1997). Toward a troubleshooting manual for journalism history. *Journalism & Mass Communication Quarterly*, *74*(3), 463–476. doi:10.1177/107769909707400302

Schudson, M. (2003). *The sociology of news*. New York: Norton.

Schultz, T. (1999). Interactive options in online journalism: A content analysis of 100 US newspapers. *Journal of Computer-Mediated Communication, 5*(1), 0.

Seib, P. (2001). *Going live. Getting the news right in a real-time online world*. Lanham: Rowman & Littlefield.

Shaker, L. (2014). Dead newspapers and citizens' civic engagement. *Political Communication*, *31*(1), 131–148. doi:10.1080/10584609.2012.762817

Shoemaker, P. J., & Reese, S. D. (1996). *Mediating the message: Theories of influences on mass media content*. White Plains: Longman.

Shortz, W. (Ed.). (2006). *The New York Times everyday Sunday crossword puzzles: America's most popular crosswords anytime, anywhere*. Macmillan.

Sicart, M. (2008, September 25-27). Newsgames: Theory and design. *Proceedings of the 7th International Conference of Entertainment Computing*, (pp. 27-33), Pittsburgh, PA, USA. Springer.

Siitonen, M., & Varsaluoma, J. (2013). "I'm so going to nuke Helsinki" - Newsgames in the Nordic media landscape. *Proceedings of DiGRA 2013: DeFragging Game Studies*.

Singer, J. B. (2004). Strange bedfellows: The diffusion of convergence in four news organizations. *Journalism Studies*, *5*(1), 3–18. doi:10.1080/1461670032000174701

Singer, J. B. (2008). Five Ws and an H: Digital challenges in newspaper newsrooms and boardrooms. *International Journal on Media Management*, *10*(3), 122–129. doi:10.1080/14241270802262468

Sparks, C., & Tulloch, J. (2000). *Tabloid tales. Global debates over media standards*. Lanham: Rowman & Littlefield.

Stapleton, A. J. (2004). Serious games: Serious opportunities. Proceedings of Australian Game Developers' Conference 2004, Academic Summit, Melbourne.

Strömbäck, J., Djerf-Pierre, M., & Shehata, A. (2012). The dynamics of political interest and news media consumption: A longitudinal perspective. *International Journal of Public Opinion Research*.

Tamborini, R., Bowman, N. D., Eden, A., Grizzard, M., & Organ, A. (2010). Defining media enjoyment as the satisfaction of intrinsic needs. *Journal of Communication*, *60*(4), 758–777. doi:10.1111/j.1460-2466.2010.01513.x

Teens, video games, and civics - Teens' gaming experiences are diverse and include significant social interaction and civic engagement. (2008). *Pew Internet & American Life Project*.

Thurman, N., & Lupton, B. (2008). Convergence calls: Multimedia storytelling at British news websites. *Convergence (London)*, *14*(4), 439–455. doi:10.1177/1354856508094662

Thurman, N., & Walters, A. (2013). Live blogging – Digital journalism's pivotal platform? *Digital Journalism*, *1*(1), 82–101. doi:10.1080/21670811.2012.714935

Treanor, M., & Mateas, M. (2009). Newsgames: Procedural rhetoric meets political cartoons. In *Breaking new ground: Innovation in games, play, practice and theory. Proceedings of DIGRA 2009*. DIGRA.

Tuchman, G. (1972). Tuchman 1972 Objectivity as a Strategic ritual. *American Journal of Sociology*, *77*(4), 660–679. doi:10.1086/225193

Tufte, T., & Enghel, F. (2009). Youth engaging with media and communication. Different, unequal and disconnected? In Tufte & Enghel (eds.) Youth engaging with the world. Media, communication and social change. Gothenburg, Nordicom.

Uribe, R., & Gunter, B. (2004). The Tabloidization of British Tabloids. *European Journal of Communication*, *19*(3), 387–402. doi:10.1177/0267323104045265

Urry, J. (2002). Mobility and proximity. *Sociology, 36*(2), 255–274. doi:10.1177/0038038502036002002

Van Dijck, J. (2009). Users like you? Theorizing agency in user-generated content. *Media Culture & Society, 31*(1), 41–58. doi:10.1177/0163443708098245

Van Dijck, J. (2013). *The culture of connectivity. A critical history of social media.* Oxford University Press. doi:10.1093/acprof:oso/9780199970773.001.0001

Wadbring, I., & Bergström, A. (2014, February 26-28). A print crisis or a local crisis? Local news use over 27 years. Presented at Local journalism around the world: Professional practices, economic foundations, and political implications conference, University of Oxford.

Werbach, K. (2014). (Re)Defining gamification: A process approach. In Spagnolli, et al. (Eds.), Proceedings of Persuasive 2014, LNCS 8462 (pp. 266–272). Springer.

Werbach, K., & Hunter, D. (2012). *For the win: How game thinking can revolutionize your business.* Wharton Digital Press.

Westlund, O. (2012). Producer-centric versus participation-centric: On the shaping of mobile media. *Northern Lights, 10*(1), 107–121. doi:10.1386/nl.10.1.107_1

Westlund, O. (2013). Mobile news. *Digital Journalism, 1*(1), 6–26. doi:10.1080/21670811.2012.740273

Westlund, O., & Bjur, J. (2014). Media life of the young. *Young, 22*(1), 21–41. doi:10.1177/1103308813512934

Westlund, O., & Färdigh, M. A. (2011). Displacing and complementing effects of news sites and newspapers 1998-2009. *International Journal on Media Management, 13*(3), 177–194. doi:10.1080/14241277.2011.595020

Whitson, J. R. (2013). Gaming the Quantified Self. *Surveillance & Society, 11*(1/2), 163–176.

Williams, D. (2006). Groups and goblins: The social and civic impact of online game. *Journal of Broadcasting & Electronic Media, 50*(4), 651–670. doi:10.1207/s15506878jobem5004_5

Witt, M., Scheiner, C., & Robra-Bissantz, S. (2011). Gamification of online idea competitions: Insights from an explorative case. Proceedings of Informatik 2011, Lecture Notes in Informatics, Band P192. TUBerlin.

Zelizer, B. (2004). When facts, truth and reality are God terms. On journalism's uneasy place in cultural studies. *Communication and Critical. Cultural Studies, 1*(1), 100–119.

Zichermann, G., & Cunningham, C. (2011). *Gamification by design: Implementing game mechanics in web and mobile apps.* Sebastopol, CA: O'Reilly Media.

Zichermann, G., & Linder, J. (2013). *The gamification revolution: How leaders leverage game mechanics to crush the competition.* McGraw-Hill.

KEY TERMS AND DEFINITIONS

Gamification: The use of game mechanics and game elements within environments that are normally not considered games themselves.

Journalism: The activity of surveying and interpreting matters of public interest and then delivering such information through a wide variety of channels and formats to a community or society at large.

Media Convergence: The process of integration and amalgamation of different types of media content and media technologies affecting the creating, dissemination, and consumption of media.

News: The principal output of journalism, based on information derived from recent or previously unknown events, often embedded with opinion and editorial content.

Newsgames: A broad genre of digital games that incorporate journalistic principles, content and narratives to full-fledged games.

User Agency: The activities, capacities, status, and motivations of users exerted while interacting with a system and that are embedded in the multifaceted nature of their role as facilitators, producers, consumers, and data providers.

User Engagement: A psychological state where users are either cognitively or emotionally involved with the system they are interacting with.

Compilation of References

Aalberg, T., & Curran, J. (2011). *How Media Inform Democracy*. New York, NY: Routledge.

Aarseth, E. J. (2003). Cybertext: Perspectives on ergodic literature. Baltimore, M.D.: Johns Hopkins University Press.

About Badgeville. (2012). Badgeville. Retrieved from http://www.badgeville.com/about

Abt, C. C. (1987). *Serious games*. Boston, MA: University Press of America.

Adamou, B. (2011). The Future of Research Through Gaming. Paper presented at the 2011 CASRO Online Research Conference. Retrieved from http://www.casro.org/?page=2011ORC&hhSearchTerms=%22adamou%22&#rescol_765745

Adamou, B. (2014). Research Games as a methodology: The impact of online ResearchGames and game components upon participant engagement and future ResearchGame participation. Proceedings of the 2013 Association of Survey Computing Conference.

Afroes website. (n.d.). Afroes Games. Retrieved 5 June 2014 from http://www.afroes.com/games/

Age of Empires [computer software]. (1997 Ensemble Studios. Microsoft.

Aguilar, D. D., & Lacsamana, A. E. (2004). *Women and globalization*. Amherst, NY: Humanity Books.

Aguinis, H. (2009). *Performance Management* (2nd ed.). Upper Saddle River, NJ: Pearson Prentice Hall.

Ajzen, I. (1991). The theory of planned behavior. *Organizational Behavior and Human Decision Processes*, *50*(2), 179–211. doi:10.1016/0749-5978(91)90020-T

Albrecht, S. C. (2012). *The game of happiness – Gamification of positive activity interventions* [Doctoral thesis]. Maastricht University, Netherlands. Retrieved from http://arno.unimaas.nl/show.cgi?fid=26239

Alhabash, S., & Wise, K. (2014). Playing their game: Changing stereotypes of Palestinians and Israelis through videogame play. *New Media & Society*, *1461444814525010*. doi:10.1177/1461444814525010

Allen, K. (2005). Online learning: Constructivism and conversation as an approach to learning. *Innovations in Education and Teaching International*, *42*(3), 247–256. doi:10.1080/01587910500167985

Almala, A. H. (2006). Applying the principles of constructivism to a quality e-learning environment. *Distance Learning*, *3*, 33–40.

Alvarez, S. E. (1999). Advocating feminism: The Latin American feminist NGO 'boom.' *International Feminist Journal of Politics*, *1*(2), 181–209. doi:10.1080/146167499359880

Amabile, T., & Kramer, S. (2011). *The progress principle. Using small wins to ignite joy, engagement, and creativity at work*. Boston, MA: Harvard Business Review Press.

Amabile, T., & Kramer, S. (2011). *The progress principle: Using small wins to ignite joy, engagement, and creativity at work*. Harvard Business Press.

America's Army. (2014). Retrieved from https://www.americasarmy.com/assets/americas_army_backgrounder.doc

American Educational Research Association. (1999). *Standards for educational and psychological testing*. Washington, D.C.: Author.

Amory, A. (2007). Game object model version II: A theoretical framework for educational game development. *Educational Technology Research and Development*, *55*(1), 51–77. doi:10.1007/s11423-006-9001-x

Amory, A., & Molomo, B.Amory & Molomo. (2012). Gendered play and evaluation of computer video games by young South Africans. *Gender, Technology and Development*, *16*(2), 177–196. doi:10.1177/097185241201600203

Amory, A., Naicker, K., Vincent, J., & Adams, C. (1999). The use of computer games as an educational tool: Identification of appropriate game types and game elements. *British Journal of Educational Technology*, *30*(4), 311–321. doi:10.1111/1467-8535.00121

Anderson, A., Huttenlocher, D., Kleinberg, J., & Leskovec, J. (2013, May). Steering user behavior with badges.*Proceedings of the 22nd International Conference on World Wide Web*, Rio de Janeiro, Brazil, 95-106.

Anderson, C. W. (2011). Deliberative, agonistic, and algorithmic audiences: Journalism's vision of its public in an age of audience transparency. *International Journal of Communication*, *5*, 529–547.

Ang, C. S., Avni, E., & Zaphiris, P. (2008). Linking pedagogical theory of computer games to their usability. *International Journal on E-Learning*, *7*, 533–558.

Ankeny, J. (2013). Playing for keeps. *Entrepreneur*, *41*(9), 62–64.

Antin, J., & Churchill, E. (2011, May). *Badges in Social Media: A Social Psychological Perspective*. Paper presented at the CHI 2011 Conference, Vancouver, BC, Canada.

Antin, J., & Churchill, E. F. (2011). Badges in social media: A social phsychological perspective. *Proceedings of the Computer Human Interaction (CHI) conference, May 2011, Vancouver, BC, Canada*. ACM.

Antin, J., & Churchill, E. F. (2011). Badges in social media: A social psychological perspective. Proceedings from CHI 2011 gamification workshop, Vancouver, BC, Canada. ACM.

Aparicio, A. F., Gutiérrez Vela, F. L., González Sánchez, J. L., & Isla Montes, J. L. (2012, October 1-2). Analysis and application of gamification. *Proceedings of Interaccion 2012*, Elche, Alicante, Spain.

Apperley, T. H. (2006). Genre and game studies: Toward a critical approach to video game genres. *Simulation & Gaming*, *37*(1), 6–23. doi:10.1177/1046878105282278

Aranda, J. (2006, October 22). Cheap shots at the Gartner Hype Cycle. *Catenary*. Retrieved from http://catenary.wordpress.com/2006/10/22/cheap-shots-at-the-gartner-hype-curve/

Ariely, D. (2011). *The upside of irrationality: The unexpected benefits of defying logic at home and at work*. Harper. doi:10.1109/AERO.2011.5747214

Aronson, E. (1978). *The jigsaw classroom*. Oxford, UK: Sage.

Arthur, W., Woehr, D. J., & Maldegen, R. (2000). Convergent and discriminant validity of assessment center dimensions: A conceptual and empirical reexamination of the assessment center construct-related validity paradox. *Journal of Management*, *26*, 813–835.

Ashraf, N., Bandiera, O., & Jack, B.K. (2014). No margin, no mission? A field experiment on incentives for public service delivery. *Journal of Public Economics*, *120*, 1–17. doi:10.1016/j.jpubeco.2014.06.014

Assessing the Representativeness of Public Opinion Surveys. (2012). *Pew Research Center*. Retrieved from http://www.people-press.org/2012/05/15/assessing-the-representativeness-of-public-opinion-surveys/

Austin, D. (2014). The Gamification of Energy Conservation Retrieved from http://www.dzone.com/articles/gamification-energy

Ayers, R. S. (2013). Building goal alignment in federal agencies' performance appraisal programs. *Public Personnel Management*, *42*(4), 495–520. doi:10.1177/0091026013496077

Badgeville. (2014). Deloitte augments their leadership development program. *Case Study*: Deloitte Leadership Academy. Retrieved from http://badgeville.com/customer/case-study/deloitte

Bailenson, J. N., & Beall, A. C. (2006). Transformed social interaction: Exploring the digital plasticity of avatars. In R. Schroeder & A.-S. Axelsson (Eds.), *Avatars at work and play: Collaboration and interaction in shared virtual environments* (pp. 1–16). New York: Springer-Verlag. doi:10.1007/1-4020-3898-4_1

Bailenson, J. N., Beall, A. C., Loomis, J., Blascovich, J., & Turk, M. (2004). Transformed social interaction: Decoupling representation from behavior and form in collaborative virtual environments. *Presence (Cambridge, Mass.)*, *13*(4), 428–441. doi:10.1162/1054746041944803

Bailey, R., Wise, K., & Bolls, P. (2009). How Avatar Customizability Affects Children's Arousal and Subjective Presence During Junk Food–Sponsored Online Video Games. *Cyberpsychology & Behavior*, *12*(3), 277–283. doi:10.1089/cpb.2008.0292 PMID:19445632

Bandura, A. (1977). *Social learning theory*. New Jersey: Prentice Hall.

Bandura, A. (1982). Self-efficacy mechanism in human agency. *The American Psychologist*, *37*(2), 122–147. doi:10.1037/0003-066X.37.2.122

Bandura, A. (1986). *Social foundations of thought and action: A social cognitive theory*. Englewood Cliffs, NJ: Prentice-Hall.

Bandura, A. (1997). *Self-efficacy: The exercise of control*. New York, NY: W H Freeman/Times Books/ Henry Holt & Co.

Baranowski, T., & Frankel, L. (2012). Let's get technical! Gaming and technology for weight control and health promotion in children. *Childhood Obesity*, *8*(1), 34–37. PMID:22799477

Barber, A. E. (1998). *Recruiting employees: Individual and organizational perspectives*. Thousand Oaks, CA, US: Sage Publications, Inc.

Barber, A. E., & Roehling, M. V. (1993). Job postings and the decision to interview: A verbal protocol analysis. *The Journal of Applied Psychology*, *78*(5), 845–856. doi:10.1037/0021-9010.78.5.845

Baresch, B., Hsu, S.-H., & Reese, S. D. (2010). The power of framing: New challenges for researching the structure of meaning in news. In S. Allan (Ed.), *The Routledge companion to news and journalism*. New York, NY: Routledge.

Barnhurst, K., & Nerone, J. (2009). Journalism history. In K. Wahl-Jorgensen & T. Hanitzsch (Eds.), *The Handbook of Journalism Studies* (pp. 17–28). New York, NY: Routledge.

Barooah, R. (2009, October 19). The False God of Coffee. *Quantified Self*. Retrieved from http://quantifiedself.com/2009/10/the-false-god-of-coffee/

Bartle, R. (1996). *Hearts, clubs, diamonds, spades: Players who suit MUDs*. Retrieved from http://www.mud.co.uk/richard/hcds.htm

Bartle, R. (1996). Hearts, Clubs, Diamonds, Spades: Players Who suit MUDs. Retrieved from http://www.mud.co.uk/richard/hcds.html

Bartle, R. A. (1996). Hearts, clubs, diamonds, spades: Players who suit MUDs. *Journal of MUD Research, 1*(1). Retrieved from http://mud.co.uk/richard/hcds.htm

Bartle, R. A. (2004). *Designing virtual worlds*. San Francisco, CA: New Riders Publishing.

Bataille, G. (1991). The Accursed Share: an Essay on General Economy: Vol. 1. *Consumption*. Cambridge: Zone Books.

Bateman, I. J., Day, B. H., Jones, A. P., & Jude, S. (2009). Reducing gain–loss asymmetry: A virtual reality choice experiment valuing land use change. *Journal of Environmental Economics and Management, 58*(1), 106–118. doi:10.1016/j.jeem.2008.05.003

Bateson, G. (1956). The message, "This is play. In B. Schaffner (Ed.), *Group processes*. New York: Josiah Macy.

Baudrillard, J. (1981a). Hypermarket and Hypercommodity (S. F. Glaser, Trans.) Simulacra and Simulation (pp. 75-78). Ann Arbor: University of Michigan Press.

Baudrillard, J. (1981b). The Precession of Simulacra (S. F. Glaser, Trans.) Simulacra and Simulation (pp. 1-42). Ann Arbor: University of Michigan Press.

Baudrillard, J. (1979). *Seduction*. Montreal: New World Perspective.

Baudrillard, J. (1998a). *The Drama of Leisure or the Impossibility of Wasting One's Time The Consumer Society: Myths and Structures* (pp. 151–158). Thousand Oaks: Sage.

Baudrillard, J. (1998b). *The Social Logic of Consumption The Consumer Society: Myths and Structures* (pp. 49–68). Thousand Oaks: Sage.

Baudrillard, J. (1998c). *Towards a Theory of Consumption The Consumer Society: Myths and Structures* (pp. 69–86). Thousand Oaks: Sage.

Baudrillard, J. (2005). *The System of Objects* (J. Benedict, Trans.). London: Verso.

Bauer, K. N., Callan, R. C., Cavanaugh, K. J., & Landers, R. N. (2014, May). *The application of goal-setting theory to gamification*. Poster presented at the 29th Annual Conference of the Society for Industrial and Organizational Psychology, Honolulu, HI.

Bauer, T. N., Truxillo, D. M., Sanchez, R., Craig, J., Ferrera, P., & Campion, M. A. (2001). Development of the Selection Procedural Justice Scale (SPJS). *Personnel Psychology, 54*(2), 387–419. doi:10.1111/j.1744-6570.2001.tb00097.x

Bauer, T. N., Truxillo, D. M., Tucker, J. S., Weathers, V., Bertolino, M., Erdogan, B., & Campion, M. A. (2006). Selection in the information age: The impact of privacy concerns and computer experience on applicant reactions. *Journal of Management, 32*(5), 601–621. doi:10.1177/0149206306289829

Baumgartner, H., & Steenkamp, J. E. M. (2001). Response Styles in Marketing Research: A Cross-National Investigation. *JMR, Journal of Marketing Research, 38*(2), 143–156. doi:10.1509/jmkr.38.2.143.18840

Bedwell, W. L., Pavlas, D., Heyne, K., Lazzara, E. H., & Salas, E. (2012). Toward a taxonomy linking game attributes to learning: An empirical study. *Simulation & Gaming: An Interdisciplinary Journal, 43*(6), 729–760. doi:10.1177/1046878112439444

Beed, P. L., Hawkins, E. M., & Roller, C. M. (1991). Moving learners toward independence: The power of scaffolded instruction. *The Reading Teacher*, *44*, 648–655. Retrieved from http://www.reading.org/general/Publications/Journals/RT.aspx

Bek, M. G. (2004). Research note: Tabloidization of news media an analysis of television news in Turkey. *European Journal of Communication*, *19*(3), 371–386. doi:10.1177/0267323104045264

Bellotti, F., Berta, R., De Gloria, A., Lavagnino, E., Dagnino, M. F., Antonaci, A., & Ott, M. (2013). A gamified short course for promoting entrepreneurship among ICT engineering students. Proceedings of *13ᵗʰ International Conference on Advanced Learning Technologies*. doi:10.1109/ICALT.2013.14

Bem, D. J. (1972). In L. Berkowitz (Ed.), *Self-perception theory* (Vol. 6, pp. 1–62). Advances in experimental social psychologySan Diego, CA: Academic Press.

Benbunan-Fich, R., & Arbaugh, J. B. (2006). Separating the effects of knowledge construction and group collaboration in learning outcomes of web-based courses. *Information & Management*, *43*(6), 778–793. doi:10.1016/j.im.2005.09.001

Bennet, W. L., Freelon, D. G., Hussain, M. M., & Wells, C. (2012). Digital media and youth engagement. In H. Semetko & M. Scammell (Eds.) The Sage handbook of political communication. London: SAGE Publications. doi:10.4135/9781446201015.n11

Bennett, S., Maton, K., & Kervin, L. (2008). The 'digital natives' debate: A critical review of the evidence. *British Journal of Educational Technology*, *39*(5), 775–786. doi:10.1111/j.1467-8535.2007.00793.x

Bennet, W. L. (2008). Changing citizenship in the digital age. In W. L. Bennet (Ed.), *Civic life online: Learning how digital media can engage youth* (pp. 1–24). Cambridge, MA: MIT Press.

Berger, J., & Milkman, K. L. (2012). What Makes Online Content Viral? *JMR, Journal of Marketing Research*, *49*(2), 192–205. doi:10.1509/jmr.10.0353

Bernandin, T., Kemp-Robertson, P., Stewart, D. W., Cheng, Y., Wan, H., Rossiter, J. R., & Fukawa, N. (2008). Envisioning the future of advertising creativity research: Alternative perspectives. *Journal of Advertising*, *37*(4), 131–150. doi:10.2753/JOA0091-3367370411

Bimber, B. (2012). Digital media and citizenship. In H. Semetko & M. Scammell (Eds.), The Sage handbook of political communication. London: SAGE Publications. doi:10.4135/9781446201015.n10

Binning, J. F., & Barrett, G. V. (1989). Validity of personnel decisions: A conceptual analysis of the inferential and evidential bases. *The Journal of Applied Psychology*, *74*(3), 478–494. doi:10.1037/0021-9010.74.3.478

Bird, E. (2009). Tabloidization: What is it, and does it really matter? In B. Zelizer (Ed.), *The changing faces of journalism. Tabloidization, technology and truthiness* (pp. 40–50). New York, NY: Routledge.

Blair, E. (2009, March). A further education college as a heterotopia. *Research in Post-Compulsory Education*, *14*(1), 93–101. doi:10.1080/13596740902717465

Block by Block website. (n.d.). Block by Block. Retrieved from http://blockbyblock.org/about

Boczkowski, P., & Mitchelstein, E. (2013). *The news gap. When the information preferences of the media and the public diverge*. Cambridge, MA: MIT Press. doi:10.7551/mitpress/9780262019835.001.0001

Boellstorff, T. (2006). A Ludicrous Discipline? Ethnography and Game Studies. *Games and Culture*, *1*(1), 29–35. doi:10.1177/1555412005281620

Boellstorff, T., Nardi, B., Pearce, C., & Taylor, T. L. (2012). *Ethnography and virtual worlds: A handbook of method.* Princeton, N.J.: Princeton University Press.

Bogost, I. (2007, July). *Persuasive games: The expressive power of videogames.* Cambridge, M.A.: The MIT Press.

Bogost, I. (2010). Cow clicker: The making of an obsession. Retrieved from http://bogost.com/writing/blog/cow_clicker_1/

Bogost, I. (2011). Gamification is Bullshit. Retrieved from http://kotaku.com/5829210/gamification-is-bullshit

Bogost, I. (2011). Gamification is bullshit. Retrieved from http://www.bogost.com/blog/gamification_is_bullshit.shtml

Bogost, I. (2011). Persuasive Games: Exploitationware. Retrieved from http://www.gamasutra.com/view/feature/134735/persuasive_games_exploitationware.php

Bogost, I. (2011a, August 9). Gamification is bullshit. *The Atlantic.* Retrieved from http://www.theatlantic.com/technology/archive/2011/08/gamification-is-bullshit/243338/

Bogost, I. (2011b, May 3). Persuasive games: Exploitationware. *Gamasutra.* Retrieved from http://www.gamasutra.com/view/feature/6366/persuasive_games_exploitationware.php

Bogost, I., Ferrari, S., & Schweizer, B. (2010). *Newsgames. Journalism at play.* Cambridge, MA: MIT Press.

Bogost, I., Ferrari, S., & Schweizer, B. (2010). *Newsgames: Journalism at play.* Cambridge, MA: MIT Press.

Bolin, G., & Westlund, O. (2009). Mobile generations: The role of mobile technology in the shaping of Swedish media generations. *International Journal of Communication, 3*, 108–124.

Bondebjerg, I. (2002). Scandinavian media histories. A comparative study. *Nordicom Review, 23*(1-2), 61–79.

Boot, W. R., Blakely, D. P., & Simons, D. J. (2011). Do action video games improve perception and cognition? *Frontiers in Psychology, 2.* PMID:21949513

Borriello, G. (2008). Invisible computing: automatically using the many bits of data we create. *Philosophical Transactions of the Royal Society of London A: Mathematical, Physical and Engineering Sciences, 366*(1881), 3669-3683.

Bourdieu, P. (1993). *The field of cultural production: Essays on art and literature.* Boston: Polity Press.

Bower, B. (2013). Life: Chimps play fair when it counts: Critics question extent to which apes cooperate. *Science News, 183*(3), 16–16. doi:10.1002/scin.5591830316

Bowman, S. L. (2010). *The functions of role-playing games: How participants create community, solve problems and explore identity.* McFarland.

Boylorn, R. M. (2008, October). As seen on TV: An autoethnographic reflection on race and reality television. *Critical Studies in Media Communication, 25*(4), 413–433. doi:10.1080/15295030802327758

Brands, L. (2014, May 7). May sales report podcast. *LB.com.* Retrieved from http://www.lb.com/investors/financial_information/sales_earnings.aspx

Breaugh, J. A. (1992). *Recruitment: Science and practice.* Boston, MA: PWS-Kent.

Breuer, J., Scharkow, M., & Quandt, T. (2014). Tunnel vision or desensitization? The effect of interactivity and frequency of use on the perception and evaluation of violence in digital games. *Journal of Media Psychology: Theories, Methods, and Applications, 26*(4), 176–188. doi:10.1027/1864-1105/a000122

Briggs, A., & Burke, P. (2002). *A social history of the media: From Gutenberg to the Internet.* Cambridge, MA: Polity Press.

Brightman, J. (2013, November 13). PlayStation Plus has seen "significant growth" says Sony [Blog]. *Gamesindustry.biz*. Retrieved from http://www.gamesindustry.biz/articles/2013-11-13-playstation-plus-has-seen-significant-growth-says-sony

Brockmyer, J. F. (2015). Playing Violent Video Games and Desensitization to Violence. *Child and Adolescent Psychiatric Clinics of North America, 24*(1), 65–77. doi:10.1016/j.chc.2014.08.001 PMID:25455576

Broekhuizen, T., & Hoffmann, A. (2012). Interactivity Perceptions and Online Newspaper Preference. *Journal of Interactive Advertising, 12*(2), 29–43.

Brown, W. (2003). Neo-liberalism and the end of liberal democracy. *Theory & Event, 7*(1).

Brown, J. S. (2006). New learning environments for the 21st century: Exploring the edge. *Change, 38*(5), 18–24. doi:10.3200/CHNG.38.5.18-24

Brown, S., & Vaughan, C. (2009). *Play: how it shapes the brain, opens the imagination and invigorates the soul*. New York: Avery.

Brown, V. R., & Vaughn, E. (2011). The writing on the (Facebook) wall: The use of social networking sites in hiring decisions. *Journal of Business and Psychology, 26*(2), 219–225. doi:10.1007/s10869-011-9221-x

Bryce, J., & Rutter, J. (2005). Gendered gaming in gendered space. In J. Raessens & J. Goldstein (Eds.), Handbook of computer game studies (pp. 301-310). Cambridge, M.A.: The MIT Press.

Bryce, J., & Rutter, J. (2002). Spectacle of the Deathmatch: Character and narrative in first person shooters. In G. King & T. Krzywinska (Eds.), *ScreenPlay: Cinema/videogames/interfaces* (pp. 66–80). Wallflower Press.

Bryceson, K. (2007). The online learning environment—A new model using social constructivism and the concept of 'Ba' as a theoretical framework. *Learning Environments Research, 10*(3), 189–206. doi:10.1007/s10984-007-9028-x

Bryson, J. (1988). Strategic planning: Big wins and small wins. *Public Money & Management, 8*(3), 11–15. doi:10.1080/09540968809387483

Bucholz, C. (2013, May 23). Four important rule changes that make every game more fun. www.cracked.com/blog/4-important-rule-changes-that-make-every-game-more-fun/

Bunchball. (2013). It's no game: Gamification is transforming the call center. Bunchball White Paper. Retrieved from http://www.bunchball.com/resources/its-no-game-gamification-transforming-call-center

Burgess, M. C. R., Dill, K. E., Stermer, S. P., Burgess, S. R., & Brown, B. P. (2011). Playing With Prejudice: The Prevalence and Consequences of Racial Stereotypes in Video Games. *Media Psychology, 14*(3), 289–311. doi:10.1080/15213269.2011.596467

Burgess, M. L., Slate, J. R., Rojos-LeBouef, A., & LaPrairie, K. (2010). Teaching and learning in Second Life: Using the community of inquiry (CoI) model to support online instruction with graduate students in instructional technology. *The Internet and Higher Education, 13*(1/2), 84–88. doi:10.1016/j.iheduc.2009.12.003

Burgun, K. (2014). What makes a game? *Gamasutra: The art and business of making games*.www.gamasutra.com/view/features/167418/what_makes_a_game?

Burke, B. (2013, January 21). The gamification of business. *Forbes.com*. Retrieved from http://www.forbes.com/sites/gartnergroup/2013/01/21/the-gamification-of-business/

Burke, K. (1965). Permanence and change: An anatomy of purpose (2nd ed.). Indianapolis, I.N.: The Bobbs-Merrill Company, Inc.

Burke, K. (1966). Language as symbolic action: Essays on life, literature, and method. Berkeley, C.A.: The University of California Press.

Burke, K. (1969). A rhetoric of motives. Berkeley, C.A.: The University of California Press.

Burke, L. A., & Hutchins, H. M. (2007). Training transfer: An integrative literature review. *Human Resource Development Review*, *6*(3), 263–296. doi:10.1177/1534484307303035

Burmeister, B. (2014). Befriend the trend: Gaming goes to work. *Finweek, 1/2/2014,* 7.

Burmester, M., Mast, M., Tille, R., & Weber, W. (2010). How Users Perceive and Use Interactive Information Graphics: An Exploratory Study. Proceedings of *Information Visualisation (IV), 2010 14th International Conference* (pp. 361–368). doi:10.1109/IV.2010.57

Burnett, M., Clayton, P., Crispin, G., Dingee, K., Gotkin, B., & Hudson, C. … Tice, D. (2014). *Candidate Experience 2013.* Retrieved from http://nam.thecandidateexperienceawards.org/2013-cande-results/

Burrill, D. A. (2005). Out of the box: Performance, drama, and interactive software. *Modern Drama*, *48*(3), 492–512. doi:10.3138/md.48.3.492

Burton, J. (2005). News-game journalism: History, current use and possible futures. *Australian Journal of Emerging Technologies and Society*, *3*(2), 87–99.

Burton, J. K., Moore, D. M., & Magliaro, S. G. (2004). Behaviorism and instructional technology. In D. H. Jonasses (Ed.), *Handbook of Research on Educational Communications and Technology* (2nd ed.). Mahwah, NJ: Lawrence Erlbaum Associates.

Byrne, T. (2012). The evolving digital workplace. *KM World*, *21*(9), 12–14.

Cable, D. M., & Judge, T. A. (1996). Person-organization fit, job choice decisions, and organizational entry. *Organizational Behavior and Human Decision Processes*, *67*(3), 294–311. doi:10.1006/obhd.1996.0081

Cable, D. M., & Yu, K. Y. T. (2006). Managing job seekers' organizational image beliefs: The role of media richness and media credibility. *The Journal of Applied Psychology*, *91*(4), 828–840. doi:10.1037/0021-9010.91.4.828 PMID:16834508

Cabrera, M. A. M., & Nguyen, N. T. (2001). Situational judgment tests: A review of practice and constructs assessed. *International Journal of Selection and Assessment*, *9*(1-2), 103–113. doi:10.1111/1468-2389.00167

Caillois, R. (1961). *Man, Play and Games* (M. Barash, Trans.). New York: Free Press.

Calhoun, C. (2000). Pierre Bourdieu. In G. Ritzer (Ed.), *The Blackwell Companion to Major Sociological Theorists* (pp. 696–730). Malden: Blackwell.

Callan, R. C., Bauer, K. N., Armstrong, M. B., & Landers, R. N. (2014, May). *Gamification in psychology: A review of theory and potential pitfalls.* Poster presented at the 29th Annual Conference of the Society for Industrial and Organizational Psychology, Honolulu, HI.

Callan, R. C., Bauer, K. N., & Landers, R. N. (2014). How to avoid the dark side of gamification: Ten business scenarios and their unintended consequences. In T. Reiners & L. Wood (Eds.), *Gamification in Education and Business.* New York, NY: Springer.

Calleja, G. (2010). Digital Games and Escapism. *Games and Culture*, *5*(4), 335–353. doi:10.1177/1555412009360412

Calvert, S. L. (2005). Cognitive effects of video games. In J. Raessens & J. Goldstein (Eds.), Handbook of computer game studies (pp. 125-131). Cambridge, M.A.: The MIT Press.

Calvillo-Gámez, E. H., Cairns, P., & Cox, A. L. (2009, September). Assessing the core elements of the gaming experience. Retrieved from http://www.eduardocalvillogamez.info/2009/09/assessing-core-elements-of-gaming.html

Calvillo-Gámez, E. H., Cairns, P., & Cox, A. L. (2011). Assessing the core elements of the gaming experience. In R. Bernhaupt (Ed.), *Evaluating user experience in games: Concepts and methods* (pp. 41–71). London: Springer.

Cameron, J. (2001). Negative effects of reward on intrinsic motivation—a limited phenomenon: Comment on Deci, Koestner, and Ryan (2001). *Review of Educational Research, 71*(1), 29–42. doi:10.3102/00346543071001029

Cameron, J., Banko, K. M., & Pierce, W. D. (2001). Pervasive negative effects of rewards on intrinsic motivation: The myth continues. *The Behavior Analyst, 24*, 1–44. Retrieved from https://www.abainternational.org/journals/the-behavior-analyst.aspx PMID:22478353

Cameron, J., & Haanstra, A. (2008). Development made sexy: How it happens and what it means. *Third World Quarterly, 29*(8), 1475–1489. doi:10.1080/01436590802528564

Cameron, J., & Pierce, W. D. (1994). Reinforcement, reward, and intrinsic motivation: A meta-analysis. *Review of Educational Research, 64*(3), 363–423. doi:10.3102/00346543064003363

Camilleri, V., Busuttil, L., & Montebello, M. (2011). Social interactive learning in multiplayer games. In M. Ma, A. Oikonomou, & L. C. Jain (Eds.), *Serious games and edutainment applications* (pp. 481–501). London, England: Springer-Verlag. doi:10.1007/978-1-4471-2161-9_23

Campbell, J., McCloy, R., Oppler, S., & Sager, C. (1993). A theory of performance. Personnel Selection in Organizations, (1983).

Campbell, M. (2011). The audacious plan to make the world into a game. *New Scientist, 209*(2794), 2.

Carey, J. (1989). *Communication as Culture*. New York: Routledge.

Carey, J., & Elton, M. C. J. (2010). *When media are new: Understanding the dynamics of new media adoption and use.* Digital Culture Books. doi:10.3998/nmw.8859947.0001.001

Carpenter, J. E., & Doverspike, D. (2014, May). *Altering images during selection: Assessment content matters.* Poster session presented at the meeting of the Society for Industrial and Organizational Psychologists, Honolulu, HI.

Carr, D. (2014, August 3). Inside Glenn Greenwald's Mountaintop Home Office. *The New York Times*. Retrieved from http://www.nytimes.com/2014/08/04/business/media/inside-glenn-greenwalds-mountaintop-home-office.html

Carse, J. P. (1987). *Finite and Infinite Games: A Vision of Life as Play and Possibility.* New York: Ballantine.

Cary, J. W. (1989). *Mass Communication and Cultural Studies Communication as Culture: Essays on Media and Society* (pp. 37–68). Boston: Unwin Hyman.

Castronova, E. (2005). *Synthetic Worlds: The Business and Culture of Online Games.* Chicago: Chicago University Press.

Cato, S., & Gordon, J. (2012, March). Relationship of the strategic vision alignment to employee productivity and student enrollment. *Research in Higher Education Journal, 15*, 1.

Cavaliere, V. (2013, February 12). Former grad student sues Lehigh University for $1.3 million over average grade. *New York Daily News.* Retrieved from http://www.nydailynews.com/news/national/ex-student-sues-school-1-3m-grade-article-1.1261784

Cerasoli, C. P., Nicklin, J. M., & Ford, M. T. (2014). Intrinsic motivation and extrinsic incentives jointly predict performance: A 40-year meta-analysis. *Psychological Bulletin, 140*(4), 980–1008. doi:10.1037/a0035661 PMID:24491020

Chambers, J. H., & Ascione, F. R. (1987, December). The effects of prosocial and aggressive videogames on children's donating and helping. *The Journal of Genetic Psychology, 148*(4), 499–505. doi:10.1080/00221325.1987.10532488 PMID:3437274

Chan, D. (2005). Playing with race: The ethics of racialized representations in e-games. *International Review of Information Ethics, 4*(12), 24–30.

Chang, B.-H., Lee, S.-E., & Kim, B.-S. (2006, April). Exploring factors affecting the adoption and continuance of online games among college students in South Korea: Integrating uses and gratification and diffusion of innovation approaches. *New Media & Society, 8*(2), 295–319. doi:10.1177/1461444806059888

Chapin, A. (2011). The Future is a Videogame. *Canadian Business, 84*(4), 46–48.

Chapman, L. (2014, June 4). Ambition Solutions raises $2M for new ways to gamify sales. *The Wall Street Journal.* Retrieved from http://blogs.wsj.com/venturecapital/2014/06/04/ambition-systems-raises-2m-for-new-ways-to-gamify-sales/

Charles, D., Charles, T., McNeill, M., Bustard, D., & Black, M. (2011). Game-based feedback for educational multi-user virtual environments. *British Journal of Educational Technology, 42*(4), 638–654. doi:10.1111/j.1467-8535.2010.01068.x

Chatfield, T. (2009, September). Videogames now outperform Hollywood movies: Titles such as Halo: ODST are drawing people away from cinemas, television, and DVDS. *The Guardian.* Retrieved from http://www.theguardian.com/technology/gamesblog/2009/sep/27/videogames-hollywood

Cheng, J. (2008). The Success Secrets of Michael Jordan. Retrieved from http://www.jordancheng.net

Cherubini, F. (2014, August 1). When Data Drives the News: A Look at Analytics Beyond the Page View. *Mediashift. PBS.* Retrieved from http://www.pbs.org/mediashift/2014/08/when-data-drives-the-news-a-look-at-analytics-beyond-the-page-view/

Chesebro, J. L., & McCroskey, J. C. (2001, January). The relationship of teacher clarity and immediacy with student state receiver apprehension, affect, and cognitive learning. *Communication Education, 50*(1), 59–68. doi:10.1080/03634520109379232

Chiang, O. (2010). When playing video games at work makes dollars and sense. *Forbes.* Retrieved from http://www.forbes.com/2010/08/09/microsoft-workplace-training-technology-videogames.html

Chiang, O. (2010, October 15). FarmVille Players Down 25% since Peak, Now Below 60 Million. *Forbes.* Retrieved from http://www.forbes.com/sites/oliverchiang/2010/10/15/farmville-players-down-25-since-peak-now-below-60-million/

Chickering, A. W., & Gamson, Z. F. (1987). Seven principles for good practice in undergraduate education. *AAHE Bulletin, 39*, 3–7.

Chipotle Mexican Grill. (2014). Food with integrity. *Chipotle.* Retrieved from https://www.chipotle.com/en-us/fwi/fwi.aspx

Choi, Y. K., & Lee, J.-G. (2012). The Persuasive Effects of Character Presence and Product Type on Responses to Advergames. *Cyberpsychology, Behavior, and Social Networking, 15*(9), 503–506. doi:10.1089/cyber.2012.0012 PMID:22897431

Chorney, A. (2012). Taking the game out of gamification. *Dalhousie Journal of Interdisciplinary Management, 8*(1), 1–14. doi:10.5931/djim.v8i1.242

Chow, S., & Chapman, D. (2013, October). Gamifying the employee recruitment process. In Proceedings of Gamification '13, Stratford, ON, Canada. doi:10.1145/2583008.2583022

Chow, S., & Chapman, D. (2014, May). *A novel approach to employee recruitment: Gamification.* Poster presented at the 29th Annual Conference of the Society for Industrial and Organizational Psychology, Honolulu, HI.

Chuang, Y.-C. (2006). Massively multiplayer online role-playing game-induced seizures: A neglected health problem in internet addiction. *Cyberpsychology & Behavior*, *9*(4), 451–456. doi:10.1089/cpb.2006.9.451 PMID:16901249

Chung, J. (2014, June 20). Gukeng runs out of eggs in cigarette butts battle. *Taipei Times.* Retrieved from http://www.taipeitimes.com/News/taiwan/archives/2014/06/20/2003593232

Clark, M. C., & Rossiter, M. (2008). Narrative learning in adulthood. *New Directions for Adult and Continuing Education*, *119*(119), 61–70. doi:10.1002/ace.306

Clavio, G., Kraft, P. M., & Pedersen, P. M. (2009). Communicating with consumers through video games: An analysis of brand development within the video gaming segment of the sports industry. *International Journal of Sports Marketing & Sponsorship*, *10*(2), 143–156.

Clerwall, C. (2014). Enter the robot journalism: Users' perceptions of automated content. *Journalism Practice,* (ahead-of-print), 1-13.

Cohen, A. (2011, September-October). The gamification of education. *The Futurist*, 16–17.

Colarelli, S. M. (1984). Methods of communication and mediating processes in realistic job previews. *The Journal of Applied Psychology*, *69*(4), 633–642. doi:10.1037/0021-9010.69.4.633

Coleman, S., & Blumler, J. G. (2012). The Internet and citizenship: Democratic opportunity or more of the same? In H. Semetko & M. Scammell (Eds.) The Sage handbook of political communication. London: SAGE Publications.

Collins, E., Freeman, J., & Chamarro-Premuzic, T. (2012). Personality traits associated with problematic and non-problematic massively multiplayer online role playing game use. *Personality and Individual Differences*, *52*(2), 133–138. doi:10.1016/j.paid.2011.09.015

Colman, F. J. (2012). Play as an Affective Field for Activating Subjectivity: Notes on The Machinic Unconscious. *Deleuze Studies*, *6*(2), 250–264. doi:10.3366/dls.2012.0061

Comer, B. (2012). Gamification GROWS UP. *Pharmaceutical Executive*, *32*(6), 30–35.

Conboy, M. (2010). The paradoxes of journalism history. *Historical journal of film, radio and television, 30*(3), 411-420.

Connell, I. (1998). Mistaken identities: Tabloid and broadsheet news discourse. *Javnost (Ljubljana)*, *5*(3), 11–31. doi:10.1080/13183222.1998.11008680

Connelly, B. L., Certo, S. T., Ireland, R. D., & Reutzel, C. R. (2011). Signaling theory: A review and assessment. *Journal of Management*, *37*(1), 39–67. doi:10.1177/0149206310388419

Connelly, M. P., Murray-Li, T., MacDonald, M., & Parpart, J. L. (2002). Feminisms and development: Theoretical perspectives. In J. Parpart, P. Connelly, & V. U. Barritreau (Eds.), *Theoretical perspectives on gender and development* (pp. 51–160). Ontario, Canada: International Development Research Centre.

Connolly, T. M., Boyle, E. A., MacArthur, E., Hainey, T., & Boyle, J. M. (2012). A systematic literature review of empirical evidence on computer games and serious games. *Computers & Education*, *59*(2), 661–686. doi:10.1016/j.compedu.2012.03.004

Consalvo, M. (2005). Rule sets, cheating, and magic circles: Studying games and ethics. *International Review of Information Ethics*, *4*(2), 7–12.

Consalvo, M. (2009). There is No Magic Circle. *Games and Culture*, *4*(4), 408–417. doi:10.1177/1555412009343575

Cook, W. (2013). Five reasons you can't ignore gamification. *Incentive, 187*, 22-23. Retrieved from http://www.incentivemag.com/Incentive-Programs/Non-Sales/Articles/5-Reasons-You-Can-t-Ignore-Gamification/

Coonradt, C. A. (2007). The Game of Work: How to Enjoy Work as Much as Play [Kindle ed.]. Salt Lake City: Gibbs Smith.

Corbett, S. (2010, September 15). Learning by playing: Video games in the classroom. *The New York Times*. Retrieved from http://www.nytimes.com/2010/09/19/magazine/19video-t.html?_r=1

Corbett, S. (2010, September 15). Learning by playing: Video games in the classroom. *The New York Times*. Retrieved from http://www.nytimes.com/2010/09/19/magazine/19video-t.html?_r=2&

Costea, B., Crump, N., & Holm, J. (2005). Dionysus at Work? The Ethos of Play and the Ethos of Management. *Culture and Organization, 11*(2), 139–151. doi:10.1080/14759550500091069

Couldry, N. (2000). *Inside Culture: Re-imagining the Method of Cultural Studies*. Tousand Oaks, CA: Sage.

Coulter, G. (2007). Jean Baudrillard and the Definitive Ambivalence of Gaming. *Games and Culture, 2*(4), 358–365. doi:10.1177/1555412007309530

Cowles, L. (2011). The spectacle of bloodshed in Roman society. *Constructing the Past, 12*(1).

Crogan, P. (2003). Gametime: History, narrative, and temporality in combat flight simulator 2. In M. J. P. Wolf & B. Perron (Eds.), *The video game theory reader* (pp. 275–301). New York, N.Y.: Routledge.

Crogan, P. (2007). Remembering (Forgetting) Baudrillard. *Games and Culture, 2*(4), 405–413. doi:10.1177/1555412007309531

Cronbach, L. J. (1951). Coefficient alpha and the internal structure of tests. *Psychometrika, 16*(3), 297–334. doi:10.1007/BF02310555

Cronk, M. (2012, June). Using gamification to increase student engagement and participation in class discussion. Proceedings of *World conference on education multimedia, hypermedia, and telecommunications* (Vol. 2012, No.1, pp. 311-315).

Croson, R., & Gneezy, U. (2009). Gender differences in preferences. *Journal of Economic Literature, 47*(2), 448–474. doi:10.1257/jel.47.2.448

Croteau, D., & Hoynes, W. (2001). *The Business of Media. Corporate Media and the Public Interest*. Thousand Oaks: Pine Forge Press.

Crowe, E., & Higgins, E. T. (1997). Regulatory focus and strategic inclinations: Promotion and prevention in decision-making. *Organizational Behavior and Human Decision Processes, 69*(2), 117–132. doi:10.1006/obhd.1996.2675

Crowley, D. N., Brestlin, J. G., Corcoran, P., & Young, K. (2012). Gamification of citizen sensing through mobile social reporting. Proceedings of *Games Innovation Conference (IGIC), 2012 IEEE International,* (pp. 1-5). IEEE Xplore. doi:10.1109/IGIC.2012.6329849

Csikszentmihályi, M. (1990). The domain of creativity. In M. A. Runco & R. S. Albert (Eds.), *Theories of creativity* (pp. 190–212). Thousand Oaks, CA, US: Sage Publications, Inc.

Csikszentmihalyi, M. (1997). *Finding flow*. New York, NY: Basic Books.

Csikszentmihályi, M. (1997). *Finding flow: The psychology of engagement with everyday life*. New York, NY, US: Basic Books.

Csikszentmihalyi, M., & Csikzentmihaly, M. (1991). *Flow: The psychology of optimal experience*. New York: Harper Perennial.

Csikszentmihályi, M., & LeFevre, J. (1989). Optimal experience in work and leisure. *Journal of Personality and Social Psychology*, *56*(5), 815–822. doi:10.1037/0022-3514.56.5.815 PMID:2724069

Csikszentmihaly, M. (1990). *Flow: The Psychology of Optimal Experience*. New York: Harper & Row.

Currah, A. (2009). *What's happening to our news. An investigation into the likely impact of the digital revolution on the economics of news publishing in the UK*. Oxford: Reuters Institute for the Study of Journalism.

Curtis, D., & Lawson, M. (2002). Computer Adventure Games as Problem-solving Environments. *International Education Journal*, *3*(4), 43–56.

Cushion, S. (2012). *The democratic value of news. Why public service media matter*. Houndmills: Palgrave Mcmillan.

Czerski, P. (2012, February 15). We, the Web Kids. Trans. Marta Szreder. Pastebin, Retrieved from http://pastebin.com/0xXV8k7k

Danforth, L. (2011). Gamification and Libraries. *Library Journal*, *136*(3), 84–84.

Daniel, A., & Flew, T. (2010, November 15-16). The Guardian reportage of the UK MP expenses scandal: a Case study of computational journalism. Proceedings of *Communications Policy and Research Forum 2010*, Sydney.

Darnold, T. C., & Rynes, S. L. (2013). *Recruitment and job choice research: Same as it ever was?* (pp. 104–142). In I. B. Weiner (Ed.), Handbook of Psychology (2nd ed). New York: Wiley.

Dasgupta, P., Tureski, K., Lenzi, R., Bindu, K., & Nanda, G. (2012). Half the Sky Movement multimedia communication initiative: An evaluation of the 9-Minutes mobile game and video. Washington, DC: C-Change/FHI 360.

Davidson, D. (2003, August). *Games and rhetoric: A rhetorical look at gameplay, the IGDA ivory tower column*. Paper presented at the International Game Developers Association (IGDA), San Jose, CA.

Davis, F. D. (1985). A Technology Acceptance Model for Empirically Testing New End-User Information Systems: Theory and Results. [Doctoral Dissertation]. Sloan School of Management, Massachusetts Institute of Technology.

Davis, J. (2014, April 15). Tabletop strategy games still popular, create a sense of community. *The Beacon News*. Retrieved from http://stingydungeon1921.wordpress.com/2014/04/11/tabletop-strategy-games-still-popular-create-sense-of-community/

Davis, F. D., Bagozzi, R. P., & Warshaw, P. R. (1992). Extrinsic and Intrinsic Motivation to Use Computers in the Workplace. *Journal of Applied Social Psychology*, *22*(14), 1109–1130. doi:10.1111/j.1559-1816.1992.tb00945.x

Davison, H., Maraist, C., & Bing, M. N. (2011). Friend or foe? The promise and pitfalls of using social networking sites for HR decisions. *Journal of Business and Psychology*, *26*(2), 153–159. doi:10.1007/s10869-011-9215-8

De Certeau, M. (1984). *The practice of everyday life*. Retrieved from http://danm.ucsc.edu/~dustin/library/de%20certeau,%20the%20practice%20of%20everyday%20life.pdf

De Freitas, S., & Griffiths, M. (2008). The onvergence of gaming practices with other media forms: What potential for learning? A review of the literature. *Learning, Media and Technology*, *33*(1), 11–20. doi:10.1080/17439880701868796

De Geode, M. E. E., Van Vianen, A. E. M., & Klehe, U.-C. (2011). Attracting applicants on the web: PO fit, industry culture stereotypes, and website design. *International Journal of Selection and Assessment*, *19*(1), 51–61. doi:10.1111/j.1468-2389.2010.00534.x

de Souza e Silva, A.de Souza e Silva. (2006). From Cyber to Hybrid: Mobile Technologies as Interfaces of Hybrid Spaces. *Space and Culture*, *9*(3), 261–278. doi:10.1177/1206331206289022

De Waal, E., & Schoenbach, K. (2010). News sites' position in the mediascape: Uses, evaluations and media displacement effects over time. *New Media & Society, 12*(3), 477–496. doi:10.1177/1461444809341859

DeAndrea, D. C. (2014). Advancing warranting theory. *Communication Theory, 24*(2), 186–204. doi:10.1111/comt.12033

Deci, E. L., Koestner, R., & Ryan, R. M. (1999). A meta-analytic review of experiments examining the effects of extrinsic rewards on intrinsic motivation. *Psychological Bulletin, 125*(6), 627–668. doi:10.1037/0033-2909.125.6.627 PMID:10589297

Deci, E. L., Koestner, R., & Ryan, R. M. (2001). Extrinsic rewards and intrinsic motivation in education: Reconsidered once again. *Review of Educational Research, 71*(1), 1–27. doi:10.3102/00346543071001001

Deci, E. L., & Ryan, R. M. (1985). *Intrinsic motivation and self-determination in human behavior*. Springer. doi:10.1007/978-1-4899-2271-7

Deci, E. L., & Ryan, R. M. (1985). The general causality orientations scale: Self-determination in personality. *Journal of Research in Personality, 19*(2), 109–134. doi:10.1016/0092-6566(85)90023-6

Deci, E. L., & Ryan, R. M. (1987). The support of autonomy and the control of behavior. *Journal of Personality and Social Psychology, 53*(6), 1024–1037. doi:10.1037/0022-3514.53.6.1024 PMID:3320334

Deci, E. L., & Ryan, R. M. (2000). The 'what' and 'why' of goal pursuits: Human needs and the self-determination of behavior. *Psychological Inquiry, 11*(4), 227–268. doi:10.1207/S15327965PLI1104_01

Deci, E. L., Ryan, R. M., & Koestner, R. (2001). The pervasive negative effects of rewards on intrinsic motivation: Response to Cameron (2001). *Review of Educational Research, 71*(1), 43–51. doi:10.3102/00346543071001043

Delgado, M. R., Labouliere, C. D., & Phelps, E. A. (2006). Fear of losing money? Aversive conditioning with secondary reinforcers. *Social Cognitive and Affective Neuroscience, 1*(3), 250–259. doi:10.1093/scan/nsl025 PMID:17332848

Delli Carpini, M. X. (2012). Entertainment media and the political engagement of citizens. In H. Semetko & M. Scammell (Eds.) The Sage handbook of political communication. London: SAGE Publications. doi:10.4135/9781446201015.n2

Delo, C. (2012). What is gamification, and how can I make it useful for my brand? *Advertising Age, 83*(9), 58–58.

Deloitte (2014). *Virtual Tour - Life at Deloitte*. Retrieved from http://mycareer.deloitte.com/cn/en/life-at-deloitte/virtual-tour

Deloitte China Virtual Tour [Internet website application]. (2014). Deloitte. Retrieved from http://workatdeloitte.cn/virtualtour/

DeNisi, A., & Smith, C. E. (2014). Performance appraisal, performance management, and firm-level performance: A review, a proposed model, and new directions for future research. *The Academy of Management Annals, 8*(1), 127–179. doi:10.1080/19416520.2014.873178

Denny, P. (2013, May). The effect of virtual achievements on student engagement. *Proceedings of CHI 2013: Changing Perspectives* (pp. 763-772), Paris, France. doi:10.1145/2470654.2470763

Deterding, S. (2012). Gamification: designing for motivation. *interactions, 19*(4), 14-17. doi: 10.1145/2212877.2212883

Deterding, S. (2014). Eudaimonic design, or six invitations to rethink gamification. In S. Fizek, M. Fuchs, P. Ruffino & N. Schrape (Eds.), *Rethinking Gamification*. Lüneburg, Germany: Meson Press. Retrieved from http://projects.digital-cultures.net/meson-press/files/2014/06/9783957960016-rethinking-gamification.pdf

Deterding, S. (2014). Eudaimonic Design, or: Six Invitations to Rethink Gamification (SSRN Scholarly Paper No. ID 2466374). Rochester, NY: Social Science Research Network; Retrieved from http://papers.ssrn.com/abstract=2466374

Deterding, S., Björk, S. L., Nacke, L. E., Dixon, D., & Lawley, E. (2013). Designing Gamification: Creating Gameful and Playful Experiences. Proceedings of CHI '13 Extended Abstracts on Human Factors in Computing Systems (pp. 3263–3266). New York, NY, USA: ACM; doi:10.1145/2468356.2479662

Deterding, S., Dixon, D., Khaled, R., & Nacke, L. (2011). From game design elements to gamefulness: Defining "gamification". In A. Lugmayr, H. Franssila, C. Safran, & I. Hammouda (Eds.) *Proceedings of the 15th International Academic MindTrek Conference: Envisioning future media environments* (pp. 9-15). New York, NY: ACM.

Deterding, S., Dixon, D., Khaled, R., & Nacke, L. (2011). From game design elements to gamefulness: Defining "gamification". Proceedings from MindTrek '11. *Proceedings of the 15th International Academic MindTrek Conference: Envisioning future media environments.* Tampere, Finland. ACM. doi:10.1145/2181037.2181040

Deterding, S., Dixon, D., Khaled, R., & Nacke, L. (2011, September 28-30). From game design elements to gamefulness: Defining "gamification". *Proceedings of the 15th International Academic MindTrek Conference*, Tampere, Finland. Retrieved from https://www.cs.auckland.ac.nz/courses/compsci747s2c/lectures/paul/definition-deterding.pdf

Deterding, S., Dixon, D., Khaled, R., & Nacke, L. (2011b, September 28-30). *From game design elements to gamefulness: Defining "gamification."* Paper presented at the MindTrek '11, Tampere, Finland. Retrieved from https://www.cs.auckland.ac.nz/courses/compsci747s2c/lectures/paul/definition-deterding.pdf

Deterding, S., Khaled, R., Nacke, L., & Dixon, D. (2011). *Gamification: Toward a definition.* Retrieved from http://hci.usask.ca/uploads/219-02-Deterding,-Khaled,-Nacke,-Dixon.pdf

Deterding, S., Sicart, M., Nacke, L., O'Hara, K., & Dixon, D. (2011, May). Gamification: Using game-design elements in non-gaming contexts. In CHI'11 Extended Abstracts on Human Factors in Computing Systems (pp. 2425-2428). ACM. doi:10.1145/1979742.1979575

Deterding, S., Sicart, M., Nacke, L., O'Hara, K., & Dixon, D. (2011a). Gamification, using game-design elements in non-gaming contexts. *Proceedings of the 2011 annual conference extended abstracts on Human factors in computing systems PART 2* (pp. 2425-2428). ACM.

Deterding, S., Sicart, M., Nacke, L., O'Hara, K., & Dixon, D. (2011a, May 7-12). *Gamification: Using game design elements in non-gaming contexts.* Paper presented at the CHI 2011, Vancouver, BC, Canada. Retrieved from http://gamification-research.org/wp-content/uploads/2011/04/01-Deterding-Sicart-Nacke-OHara-Dixon.pdf

Deterding, S. (2014). Eudaimonic design, or: Six invitations to rethink gamification. In M. Fuchs et al. (Eds.), *Rethinking gamification* (pp. 305–333).

Deterding, S., Sicart, M., Nacke, L., O'Hara, K., & Dixon, D. (2011). Gamification: Toward a definition.*Proceedings of the CHI 2011 Gamification Workshop*, Vancouver, BC, Canada.

Deterding, S., Sicart, M., Nacke, L., O'Hara, K., & Dixon, D. (2011). *Gamification: Using game design elements in non-gaming contexts. CHI'11 Extended Abstracts on Human Factors in Computing Systems, 2425-2428.* New York, New York: ACM.

Deuze, M. (2004). What is multimedia journalism? *Journalism Studies, 5*(2), 139–152. doi:10.1080/1461670042000211131

Deuze, M. (2005). What is journalism? Professional identity and ideology of journalists considered. *Journalism, 6*(4), 442–464. doi:10.1177/1464884905056815

Deuze, M. (2009). Journalism, citizenship, and digital culture. In Z. Papacharissi (Ed.), *Journalism and citizenship: New agendas in communication.* New York, NY: Routledge.

Diamond, J., & Bond, A. B. (2003). A Comparative Analysis of Social Play in Birds. *Behaviour, 140*(8), 1091–1115. doi:10.1163/156853903322589650

Dibbell, J. (2006). *Play money: Or, how I quit my day job and made millions trading virtual loot.* New York, NY: Basic Books.

Dickey, M. (2006). Game design narrative for learning: Appropriating adventure game design narrative devices and techniques for the design of interactive learning environments. *Educational Technology Research and Development, 54*(3), 245–263. doi:10.1007/s11423-006-8806-y

Dickey, M. (2007). Game design and learning: A conjectural analysis of how massively multiple online role-playing games (MMORPGs) foster intrinsic motivation. *Educational Technology Research and Development, 55*(3), 253–273. doi:10.1007/s11423-006-9004-7

Diddi, A., & LaRose, R. (2006). Getting hooked on news: Uses and gratifications and the formation of news habits among college students in an Internet Environment. *Journal of Broadcasting & Electronic Media, 50*(2), 193–210. doi:10.1207/s15506878jobem5002_2

Dietrich, H. (2007). Wizards veterans conjure new trading card company. *Puget Sound Business Journal.* Retrieved from http://www.bizjournals.com/seattle/stories/2007/03/19/story9.html?page=all

Dijkstra, P., Kuyper, H., van der Werf, G., Buunk, A. P., & van der Zee, Y. G. (2008). Social comparison in the classroom: A review. *Review of Educational Research, 78*(4), 828–879. doi:10.3102/0034654308321210

Dimmick, J., Feaster, J. C., & Hoplamazian, G. J. (2011). News in the interstices: The niches of mobile media in space and time. *New Media & Society, 13*(1), 23–39. doi:10.1177/1461444810363452

Dindia, K. (2002). Self-disclosure research: Knowledge through meta-analysis. *Interpersonal communication research: Advances through meta-analysis,* 169-185.

Dineen, B. R., & Soltis, S. M. (2011). Recruitment: A review of research and emerging directions. In S. Zedeck (Ed.), APA handbook of industrial and organizational psychology: Vol. 2. *Selecting and developing members for the organization* (pp. 43–66). Washington, DC, US: American Psychological Association; doi:10.1037/12170-002

Disaster: Day of Crisis [Software]. (2007Monolith Soft. Nintendo.

Domínguez, A., Saenz-de-Navarrete, J., de-Marcos, L., Fernández-Sanz, L., Pagés, C., & Martínez-Herráiz, J.-J. (2013). Gamifying learning experiences: Practical implications and outcomes. *Computers & Education, 63*, 380–392. doi:10.1016/j.compedu.2012.12.020

Donath, J. (2007). Signals in social supernets. *Journal of Computer-Mediated Communication, 13*(1), 231–251. doi:10.1111/j.1083-6101.2007.00394.x

Doran, G. T. (1981). There's a S.M.A.R.T. way to write management's goals and objectives. *Management Review, 70*, 35–36.

Dormehl, L. (2014, May 26). Your web presence just picked your next job. *Wired.* Retrieved from http://www.wired.co.uk/magazine/archive/2014/05/features/web-presence-employment

Dovey, J., & Kennedy, H. W. (2006). *Game Cultures: Computer Games as New Media.* New York: Open University Press.

Downes Le-Guin, T., Baker, R., Mechling, J., & Ruyle, E. (2012). Myths and realities of respondent engagement in online surveys. *International Journal of Market Research, 54*(5), 613–633. doi:10.2501/IJMR-54-5-613-633

Downs, S., Farr, R. M., & Colbeck, L. (1978). Self-appraisal: A convergence of selection and guidance. *Journal of Occupational Psychology*, *51*(3), 271–278. doi:10.1111/j.2044-8325.1978.tb00423.x

Driscoll, M. P. (2000). *Psychology of learning for instruction*. Boston: Allyn & Bacon.

Duggan, R. (2013, September 19). Sporting events bring people together and create a sense of community for fans of all teams. *Washington County Enterprise and Pilot Tribune online*. Retrieved from http://m.enterprisepub.com/dakotacountystar/opinion/columns/sporting-events-bring-people-together-and-create-a-sense-of/article_25ccc47c-2158-11e3-a2f9-0019bb30f31a.html?mode=jqm

DuVernet, A. M., & Popp, E. (2014). Gamification of workplace practices. *The Industrial-Organizational Psychologist*, *52*, 39–44.

DuVernet, A. M., & Popp, E. (2014). Practitioners' forum: Gamification of workplace practices. *The Industrial-Organizational psychologist*, *52*(1), 39–44.

Dweck, C. S. (1986). Motivational processes affecting learning. *The American Psychologist*, *41*(10), 1040–1048. doi:10.1037/0003-066X.41.10.1040

Dyer-Witheford, N., & de Peuter, G. (2009). *Games of Empire: Capitalism and Video Games*. Minneapolis: University of Minnesota Press.

Dyer-Witheford, N., & De Peuter, G. (2009). *Games of empire: Global capitalism and video games*. Minneapolis, MN: University of Minnesota Press.

Edwards, J. L. (2004). Echoes of Camelot: How images construct cultural memory through rhetorical framing. In C. A. Hill & M. Helmers (Eds.), *Defining visual rhetorics* (pp. 179–194). Mahwah, N.J.: Lawrence Erlbaum Associates, Publishers.

Egenfeddt-Nielsen, S. (2007). Third gendaration educational use of computer games. *Journal of Educational Multimedia and Hypermedia*, *16*(3), 263–281.

Egenfeldt-Nielsen, S. (2006). Overview of research on the educational use of video games. *Digital Kompatense*, *1*, 184–213.

Egenfeldt-Nielsen, S. (2006). Overview of research on the educational use of video games. *Digital Kompetanse*, *3*(1), 184–213.

Eiben, C., Siegel, J., Bale, J., Cooper, S., Khatib, F., & Shen, B. et al. (2012). Increased Diels-Alderase activity through backbone remodeling guided by Foldit players. *Nature Biotechnology*, *30*(2), 190–192. Retrieved from http://www.nature.com/nbt/journal/v30/n2/full/nbt.2109.html doi:10.1038/nbt.2109 PMID:22267011

Eigen, M., & Winkler, R. (1981). *Laws of the Game: How the principles of nature govern chance*. New York, New York: Random House.

Ekström, M., & Djerf-Pierre, M. (2013). Approaching broadcast history: An introduction. In *A history of Swedish broadcasting*. Gothenburg: Nordicom.

Elden, S. (2008). Eugene Fink and the question of the world. *Parrhesia*, *5*, 48–59.

Electronic Arts Reports Q1 FY14 Financial Results [Press release]. (2013, July 23). Electronic Arts. Retrieved from http://investor.ea.com/releasedetail.cfm?ReleaseID=779751

Elliott, A., & Urry, J. (2010). *Mobile lives*. Routledge.

Elson, D. (1995). *Male bias in the development process*. Manchester, UK: Oxford University Press.

Entertainment Software Association (2014). *Industry facts: Sales and genre data*.

Entertainment Software Association. (2011). *Video game and the economy*. Washington, D.C.: Entertainment Software Association, 2011. Retrieved from http://www.theesa.com/gamesindailylife/economy.pdf

Entertainment Software Association. (2014). Essential facts about the computer and video game industry: Sales, demographic and usage data [Annual report]. Retrieved from http://www.theesa.com/facts/pdfs/esa_ef_2014.pdf

Environment, B. t. (2012). Gamification Revolutionizes Consumer Recycling Incentives. *Business & the Environment, 23*, 10-11.

Equal Employment Opportunity Commission. (1978). Uniform guidelines on employee selection procedures. *Federal Register, 43*(166), 38295–38309.

Ertmer, P. A., & Newby, T. J. (1993). Behaviorism, cognitivism, constructivism: Comparing critical features from an instructional design perspective. *Performance Improvement Quarterly, 6*(4), 50–72. doi:10.1111/j.1937-8327.1993.tb00605.x

Eschrich, J. (2014, July 8). ASU center partners with World Bank on sci-fi, gaming and social innovation. Retrieved from https://asunews.asu.edu/20140708-world-bank-evoke

Escobar, A. (1984). Discourse and Power in Development: Michael Foucault and the Relevance of his Work to the Third World. *Alternatives, 10*(3), 377–400. doi:10.1177/030437548401000304

Eskelinen, M. (2001). Towards computer game studies.*Proceedings of SIGGRAPH*.

ESOMAR. (2013). *Global Market Research 2013*. Amsterdam: ESOMAR (the European Society for Opinion and Market Research). Retrieved from http://www.esomar.org

Esposito, R. (2011). *Immunitas: The Protection and Negation of Life*. Cambridge: Polity.

Essential facts about the computer and video game industry. (2014). Entertainment Software Association. Retrieved from http://www.theesa.com/facts/pdfs/esa_ef_2014.pdf

Extra Credits. (2012, May 13). *Extra Credits: Gamifying Education* [Video file]. Retrieved from https://www.youtube.com/watch?v=MuDLw1zIc94

Fagen, R. (1981). *Animal play behavior*. New York: Aldine.

Falk, E. (2012). *Becoming a new instructor: A guide for college adjuncts and graduate students*. New York, NY: Taylor& Francis.

Farmville. [Online Application]. (2009). Zynga. Facebook

Fassett, D., & Warren, J. T. (2007). *Critical communication pedagogy*. Thousand Oaks, CA: Sage.

Federation of American Scientists. (2006). Harnessing the power of video games for learning. Retrieved from http://www.fas.org/gamesummit/Resources/Summit%20on%20Educational%20Games.pdf

Federation of American Scientists. (2006). Summit on educational games: Harnessing the power of video games for learning. Retrieved from http://www.fas.org/programs/ltp/policy_and_publications/summit/Summit%20on%20Educational%20Games.pdf

Ferrara, J. (2013). Games for persuasion: Argumentation, procedurality, and the lie of gamification. *Games and Culture, 8*(4), 289–304. doi:10.1177/1555412013496891

Ferrari, S. (2009, June 2). Newsgame or Editorial Game? Retrieved from http://newsgames.gatech.edu/blog/2009/06/newsgame-or-editorial-game.html

Ferrer Conill, R. (2014). Going mobile: Gamifying digital news in mobile devices. Proceedings of Persuasive Technology: Persuasive, motivating, empowering videogames. Padova, Italy, May 2014. Adjunct proceedings, (pp. 86-89). University of Padova.

Ferro, L., & Walz, S. (2013, April). *Like this: How game elements in social media and collaboration are changing the flow of information.* Paper presented at the CHI 2013 Conference, Paris, France.

Festinger, L. (1954). A theory of social comparison processes. *Human Relations, 7*(2), 117–140. doi:10.1177/001872675400700202

Filiciak, M. (2003). Hyperidentities: Postmodern identity patterns in massively multiplayer online role-playing games. In M. J. P. Wolf & B. Perron (Eds.), *The video game theory reader* (pp. 87–102). New York, N.Y.: Routledge.

Fink, E., Saine, U., & Saine, T. (1968). The Oasis of Happiness: Toward an Ontology of Play. *Yale French Studies,* (41): 19–30. doi:10.2307/2929663

Fishbein, M., & Ajzen, I. (1975). *Belief, attitude, intention, and behavior: An introduction to theory and research.* Reading, MA: Addison-Wesley.

Fitz-Walter, Z. (2013). *A brief history of gamification.* Retrieved from http://zefcan.com/2013/01/a-brief-history-of-Gamification/

Fitz-Walter, Z., Tjondronegoro, D., & Wyeth, P. (2011, November) Orientation passport: Using gamification to engage university students.*Proceedings of the 23rd Australian Computer-Human Interaction Conference,* Canberra, Australia, 122-125. doi:10.1145/2071536.2071554

Fleming, N. (2011, December 2). Know Thyself: The Quantified Self Devotees Who Live by Numbers. *The Guardian.* Retrieved from http://www.theguardian.com/science/2011/dec/02/psychology-human-biology

Fogg, B. J. (2002). *Persuasive technology: using computers to change what we think and do. Ubiquity, 2002, art. 5.* New York, NY: ACM.

Fogg, B. J. (2009). A behavior model for persuasive design. In *Proceedings of the 4th international Conference on Persuasive Technology,* (p. 40). ACM.

Foo, C. Y., & Koivisto, E. M. I. (2004). Defining grief play in MMORPGs: Players and developer perceptions. In R. Nakatsu, M. Billinghurst, & G. Yu (Eds.), *Proceedings of the 2004 ACM SIGCHI International Conference on Advances in Computer Entertainment Technology* (pp. 245-250). New York, NY: ACM.

Foo, C. Y. (2008). *Grief play management: A qualitative study of grief play management in MMORPGs.* Saarbrücken, Germany: VDM Verlag.

Food Deserts. (n.d.). *USDA.gov.* Retrieved from http://apps.ams.usda.gov/fooddeserts/fooddeserts.aspx

Foucault, M., & Blasius, M. (1993). About the Beginnings of the Hermenuetics of the Self: Two Lectures at Dartmouth. *Political Theory, 21*(2), 198–227. doi:10.1177/0090591793021002004

Foucault, M., & Miskowiec, J. (1986, Spring). Des Espaces Autres.[Of Other Spaces]. *Diacritics, 16*(1), 22–27. doi:10.2307/464648

Fox, Z. (2012, May 31). Best-selling book turns into mobile game for women in developing countries. *Mashable.* Retrieved from http://mashable.com/2012/05/31/half-the-sky-movement-game/

Fox, J., & Tang, W. Y. (2014). Sexism in online video games: The role of conformity to masculine norms and social dominance orientation. *Computers in Human Behavior, 33,* 314–320. doi:10.1016/j.chb.2013.07.014

Frasca, G. (1998). Ludology meets narratology: Similitude and differences between (video)games and narrative.

Frederick, C. M., & Ryan, R. M. (1995). Self-determination in sport: A review using cognitive evaluation theory. *International Journal of Sport Psychology, 26*, 5–23.

Freire, P. (2000). Pedagogy of the oppressed (30th Anniversary ed.). New York, NY: Continuum International Publishing Group.

Freitas, A. L., & Higgins, E. T. (2002). Enjoying goal-directed action: The role of regulatory fit. *Psychological Science, 13*(1), 1–6. doi:10.1111/1467-9280.00401 PMID:11892772

Freitas, A. L., Liberman, N., & Higgins, E. T. (2002). Regulatory fit and resisting temptation during goal pursuit. *Journal of Experimental Social Psychology, 38*(3), 291–298. doi:10.1006/jesp.2001.1504

Freud, S. (2003). *Beyond the pleasure principle and other writings* (J. Reddick, Trans.) (Original work published 1920). London: Penguin Books.

Frymier, A. B., & Shulman, G. M. (1994, November). *Development and testing of the learner empowerment instrument in a communication based model*. Paper presented at the Speech Communication Association annual convention, New Orleans, LA.

Fuchs, M. (2012). Ludic interfaces. Driver and product of gamification. *GAME Journal of Game Studies, 1*(1).

Fujikawa, Y., & Manki, M. (2013). A new environment for algorithm research using gamification. In *2013 IEEE International Conference on Electro/Information Technology (EIT)*, (pp. 1-6). IEEE. doi:10.1109/EIT.2013.6632668

Fülöp, M. (2009). Happy and unhappy competitors: What makes the difference? *Psihologijske Teme, 18*, 345–367. Retrieved from http://hrcak.srce.hr/index.php?show=clanak&id_clanak_jezik=74342

Gabris, G. T., & Ihrke, D. M. (2000). Improving employee acceptance towards performance appraisal and merit pay systems: The role of leadership credibility. *Review of Public Personnel Administration, 20*(1), 41–68. doi:10.1177/0734371X0002000104

Gagné, M., & Deci, E. (2005). Self-Determination Theory and work motivation. *Journal of Organizational Behavior, 362*, 331–362.

Gaible, E., & Dabla, A. (2010, December 13). Project Evaluation EVOKE. The Natoma Group. Retrieved from http://siteresources.worldbank.org/EDUCATION/Resources/ProjectEVOKE-evaluation-final-16oct11.pdf

Galbraith, J. (2008). A Squatter on the Fourth Estate: Google News. *Journal of Library Administration, 46*(3-4), 191–206. doi:10.1300/J111v46n03_13

Galesic, M., & Bosnjak, M. (2009). Effects of questionnaire length on participation and indicators of response quality in a web survey. *Public Opinion Quarterly, 73*(2), 349–360. doi:10.1093/poq/nfp031

Gallaugher, J. M., Auger, P., & BarNir, A. (2001). Revenue streams and digital content providers an empirical investigation. *Information & Management, 38*(7), 473–485. doi:10.1016/S0378-7206(00)00083-5

Galloway, A. R. (2007). Radical Illusion (A Game Against). *Games and Culture, 2*(4), 376–391. doi:10.1177/1555412007309532

Gamers use satellites to spot deforestation: New 'Forest Guardians' game relies on crowd to monitor illegal forest destruction [Blog]. (2014, March 28). MobLab Team. Retrieved from http://www.mobilisationlab.org/gamers-use-satellites-to-spot-deforestation/

Games for Cats. (2012). *Nestle Purina Petcare Company*. Retrieved from http://gamesforcats.com/

Ganster, D. C., Hennessey, H. W., & Luthans, F. (1983). Social desirability response effects: Three alternative models. *Academy of Management Journal, 26*(2), 321–331. doi:10.2307/255979

Garcia, S. M., Tor, A., & Gonzalez, R. (2006). Ranks and rivals: A theory of competition. *Personality and Social Psychology Bulletin, 32*(7), 970–982. doi:10.1177/0146167206287640 PMID:16738029

Gardiner, B. (2014, March). Gamification the new game changer? How enterprise gamification is enhancing innovation, change management, and collaboration. *CIO*. Retrieved from http://www.cio.com.au/article/539654/gamification_new_game_changer_/

Garg, M. (2014). Structural gamification for onboarding employees. In *K. M. Kapp, L. Blair & R. Mesch's The Gamification of Learning and Instruction Fieldbook: Ideas into Practice*. John Wiley & Sons.

Garris, R., Ahlers, R., & Driskell, J. E. (2002). Games, motivation, and learning: A research and practice model. *Simulation & Gaming, 33*(4), 441–467. doi:10.1177/1046878102238607

Gartner (2011, August 10). Gartner's 2011 hype cycle special report evaluates the maturity of 1,900 technologies. *Gartner.com*. Retrieved from http://www.gartner.com/newsroom/id/1763814

Gartner (2012a, August 16). Gartner's 2012 hype cycle for emerging technologies identifies "tipping point" technologies that will unlock long-awaited technology scenarios. *Gartner.com*. Retrieved from http://www.gartner.com/newsroom/id/2124315

Gartner (2012b, November 27). Gartner says by 2014, 80 percent of current gamified applications will fail to meet business objectives primarily due to poor design. *Gartner.com*. Retrieved from http://www.gartner.com/newsroom/id/2251015

Gartner (2013, August 19). Gartner's 2013 hype cycle for emerging technologies maps out evolving relationship between humans and machines. *Gartner.com*. Retrieved from http://www.gartner.com/newsroom/id/2575515

Gartner Predicts Over 70 Percent of Global 2000 Organisations Will Have at Least One Gamified Application by 2014. (2011). Gartner, Inc. Retrieved from http://www.gartner.com/newsroom/id/1844115

Gartner Says by 2014, 80 Percent of Current Gamified Applications Will Fail to Meet Business Objectives Primarily Due to Poor Design . (2012). Gartner, Inc. Retrieved from http://www.gartner.com/newsroom/id/2251015

Gartner says by 2015 more than 50 percent of organizations that manage innovation processes will gamify those processes. (2011, April). Retrieved from http://www.gartner.com

Gartner Says Worldwide Video Game Market to Total $93 Billion in 2013 [Press release]. (2013, October 29). Gartner. Retrieved from http://www.gartner.com/newsroom/id/2614915

Gartner, Inc. (2011, November 9). *Gartner predicts over 70 percent of Global 2000 organisations will have at least one gamified application by 2014*. Retrieved from http://www.gartner.com/newsroom/id/1844115

Gartner, Inc. (2012, November 27). *Gartner says by 2014, 80 percent of current gamified applications will fail to meet business objectives primarily due to poor design*. Retrieved from http://www.gartner.com/newsroom/id/2251015

Gears, D., & Braun, K. (2013, April). Gamification in business: Designing motivating solutions to problem situations. *Proceedings of the CHI 2013 Designing Gamification Workshop*, Paris, France.

Gee, J. P. (2005). Good video games and good learning. *Phi Kappa Forum, 85*(2), 33-37.

Gee, J. P. (2007). What video games have to teach us about learning and literacy (Revised and updated edition ed.). New York, N.Y.: Pelgrave Macmillan.

Gee, J. P. (2007a). What video games have to teach us about learning and literacy (Rev. and updated ed.). New York: Palgrave Macmillan.

Gee, J. P. (2003). What video games have to teach us about learning and literacy. *ACM Computers in Entertainment*, *1*(1), 1–4. doi:10.1145/950566.950595

Gee, J. P. (2004). *What video games have to teach us about learning and literacy.* New York, N.Y.: Palgrave Macmillan.

Gee, J. P. (2007b). *Good video games + good learning: Collected essays on video games, learning and literacy.* New York: Peter Lang.

Geimer, J. L., & O'Shea, P. G. (2014). Design considerations to maximize the utility of gamification for selection. In *E. C. Popp* (Chair), *Challenges and innovations of using game-like assessments in selection.* Proceedings of the 29th Annual Conference of the Society for Industrial and Organizational Psychology, Honolulu, HI.

George-Palilonis, J., & Spillman, M. (2011). Interactive Graphics Development: A framework for studying innovative visual story forms. *Visual Communication Quarterly*, *18*(3), 167–177. doi:10.1080/15551393.2011.599286

George, S., Clark, M., & Crotty, M. (2007). Development of the Adelaide driving self-efficacy scale. *Clinical Rehabilitation*, *21*(1), 56–61. doi:10.1177/0269215506071284 PMID:17213242

Geuter, S. (2012). Did you think gamification was a new concept? Think again! Retrieved from http://wonnova.es/2012/07/did-you-think-gamification-was-a-new-concept-think-again/

Gil de Zúñiga, H., Jung, N., & Valenzuela, S. (2012). Social media use for news and individuals' social capital, civic engagement and political participation. *Journal of Computer-Mediated Communication*, *17*(3), 319–336. doi:10.1111/j.1083-6101.2012.01574.x

Giles, D. C. (2002). Parasocial interaction: A review of the literature and a model for future research. *Media Psychology*, *4*(3), 279–205. doi:10.1207/S1532785XMEP0403_04

Glas, R. (2013). Breaking reality: Exploring pervasive cheating in Foursquare. *Transactions of the Digital Games Research Association, 1*(1). Retrieved from http://todigra.org/index.php/todigra/article/view/4

Glass, Z. (2007). The effectiveness of product placement in video games. *Journal of Interactive Advertising*, *8*(1), 23–32. doi:10.1080/15252019.2007.10722134

Global Mobile Statistics. (2012). *MobiThinking.* Retrieved from http://mobithinking.com/mobile-marketing-tools/latest-mobile-stats

Goggin, J. (2011). Playbour, farming and labour. *Ephemera: Theory and Politics in Organization*, *11*(4), 357–368.

Goldstein, J. (2005). Violent video games. In J. Raessens & J. Goldstein (Eds.), Handbook of computer game studies (pp. 341-357). Cambridge, M.A.: The MIT Press.

Goldstein, I. L., & Ford, J. K. (2002). *Training in organizations: Needs assessment, development, and evaluation* (4th ed.). Belmont, CA, US: Wadsworth/Thomson Learning.

Gómez García, S. & Navarro Sierra, N. (2013). Videogames and information. An approach about Spanish newsgames as new informative perspective. *Icono 14, 11*(2), 31-51.

Gonsalves, A. (2011, September 29). Shaker Consulting culls weak job seekers with online games. *Bloomberg*. Retrieved from http://www.bloomberg.com/news/2011-09-26/shaker-consulting-culls-weak-job-seekers-with-online-games.html

Gonzalez, A. (2012). Gamifying my classes. Retrieved from http://www.educatoral.com/wordpress/2012/07/16/gamifying-my-classes/

Gopaladesikan, S. (2012). Gamification: Envisioning a New Tomorrow. *Forward Thinking*, from http://weplay.co/gamification-envisioning-a-new-tomorrow/

Gray, C. B. (2007). *Philosophy of Man at Recreation and Leisure*. New York: Peter Lang.

Greenberg, B. S., Sherry, J., Lachlan, K., Lucas, K., & Holmstrom, A. (2010). Orientations to video games among gender and age groups. *Simulation & Gaming*, *41*(2), 238–259. doi:10.1177/1046878108319930

Greene, A. (2012, August 15). Song Premiere: Devo, 'Don't Roof Rack Me, Bro! (Seamus Unleashed). *Rolling Stone*. Retrieved from http://www.rollingstone.com/music/news/song-premiere-devo-dont-roof-rack-me-bro-seamus-unleashed-20120815

Greenfield, P. M. (1984). *Mind and media: The effects of television, video games and computers*. Cambridge, MA: Harvard University Press.

Green, M. C., & Brock, T. C. (2000). The role of transportation in the persuasiveness of public narratives. *Journal of Personality and Social Psychology*, *79*(5), 701–721. doi:10.1037/0022-3514.79.5.701 PMID:11079236

Green, M. C., Brock, T. C., & Kaufman, G. F. (2004). Understanding media enjoyment: The role of transportation into narrative worlds. *Communication Theory*, *14*(4), 311–327. doi:10.1111/j.1468-2885.2004.tb00317.x

Gregory, C. A. (1997). *Savage money: the anthropology and politics of commodity exchange*. Amsterdam: Harwood Academic.

Griffiths, M., & Davies, M. N. O. (2005). Does video game addiction exist? In J. Raessens & J. Goldstein (Eds.), Handbook of computer game studies (pp. 359-369). Cambridge, M.A.: The MIT Press.

Grodal, T. (2003). Stories for eye, ear, and muscles: Video games, media, and embodied experiences. In M. J. P. Wolf & B. Perron (Eds.), *The video game theory reader* (pp. 129–155). New York, N.Y.: Routledge.

Groh, F. (2012). Gamification: State of the art definition and utilization. In N. Asaj, B. Könings, M. Poguntke, F. Schaub, B. Wiedersheim, & M. Weber (Eds.), RTMI '12 - Proceedings of the 4th Seminar on Research Trends in Media Informatics (pp. 39–46). Retrieved from http://vts.uni-ulm.de/query/longview.meta.asp?document_id=7866

Groh, F. (2012, February 14). Gamification: State of the art definition and utilization. In N. Asaj, B. Konings, M. Poguntke, F. Schaub, B. Wiedersheim & M. Weber (Eds.), *Proceedings of the 4th Seminar on Research Trends in Media Informatics*. Ulm University, Germany. Retrieved from http://vts.uni-ulm.de/docs/2012/7866/vts_7866_11380.pdf

Gross, M. L. (2010). Advergames and the effects of game-product congruity. *Computers in Human Behavior*, *26*(6), 1259–1265. doi:10.1016/j.chb.2010.03.034

Gudykunst, W. B., & Mody, B. (2002). *Handbook of international and intercultural communication*. Thousand Oaks, CA: Sage Publications.

Guillen-Nieto, V., & Aleson-Carbonell, M. (2012). Serious games and learning effectiveness: The case of *It's a Deal! Computers & Education*, *58*(1), 435–448. doi:10.1016/j.compedu.2011.07.015

Guion, R. M. (2011). *Assessment, measurement, and prediction for personnel decisions* (2nd ed.). New York, NY, US: Routledge/Taylor & Francis Group.

Gunter, B. (2005). Psychological effects of video games. In J. Raessens & J. Goldstein (Eds.), Handbook of computer game studies (pp. 145-160). Cambridge, M.A.: The MIT Press.

Haki 1: Shield and Defend [Mobile game]. (2012). *Afroes Games*. Retrieved from http://www.afroes.com/games/

Haki 2 Video. (2013, February 10). *Afroes Games*. Retrieved from https://www.youtube.com/watch?v=1UvkProPh-U

Haki 2: Chaguo Ni Lako [Mobile game]. (2013). *Afroes Games*. Retrieved from http://www.afroes.com/games/

Haki Facebook page. (n.d.). Afroes Games. Retrieved from https://www.facebook.com/pages/Afroes-Games/185317804821699

Half the Sky Movement. The Game (2012, January 1). Half the Sky Movement. Retrieved from https://www.facebook.com/HalftheGame

Hamari, J., & Eranti, V. (2011, September 14-17). *Framework for designing and evaluating game achievements*. Paper presented at the Proceedings of DiGRA 2011 Conference: Think Design Play, Hilversum, Netherlands. Retrieved from http://www.quilageo.com/wp-content/uploads/2013/07/Framework-for-Designing-Eval-11307.59151.pdf

Hamari, J., Koivisto, J., & Sarsa, H. (2014). Does gamification work? -- A literature review of empirical studies on gamification. Proceedings of the *2014 47th Hawaii International Conference on System Sciences*.

Hamari, J., Koivisto, J., & Sarsa, H. (2014, January). Does gamification work?--A literature review of empirical studies on gamification. Proceedings of *System Sciences (HICSS), 2014 47th Hawaii International Conference on* (pp. 3025-3034). IEEE.

Hamari, J. (2013). Transforming homo economicus into homo ludens: A field experiment on gamification in a utilitarian peer-to-peer trading service. *Electronic Commerce Research and Applications*, *12*(4), 236–245. doi:10.1016/j.elerap.2013.01.004

Hamari, J., Koivisto, J., & Pakkanen, T. (2014). Do Persuasive Technologies Persuade? – A Review of Empirical Studies. In A. Spagnolli et al. (Eds.), *Persuasive Technology, LNCS 8462* (pp. 118–136). Switzerland: Springer International Publishing. doi:10.1007/978-3-319-07127-5_11

Hamari, J., Koivisto, J., & Sarsa, H. (2014, January 6-9). Does Gamification Work? – A Literature Review of Empirical Studies on Gamification.*Proceedings of the 47th Hawaii International Conference on System Sciences*. Hawaii, USA. doi:10.1109/HICSS.2014.377

Hamilton, J. (2004). *All the news that's fit to sell. How the market transforms information into news*. Princeton, NJ: Princeton university press.

Hamori, M. (2010). Who gets headhunted—and who gets ahead? The impact of search firms on executive careers. *The Academy of Management Perspectives*, *24*, 46–59.

Handler, C., Popp, E., Brodbeck, C. C., Geimer, J., Kubisiak, C., Moye, N., et al. (2014, May). *Challenges and innovations of using game-like assessments in selection*. Proceedings of the Society for Industrial and Organizational Psychologists, Honolulu, HI.

Hannafin, M. J., & Hooper, S. R. (1993). Learning principles. In M. J. Fleming & W. H. Levie (Eds.), *Instructional Message Design: Principles from the Behavioral and Cognitive Sciences* (2nd ed.). Englewood Cliffs, NJ: Educational Technologies Publications.

Hanus, M. D., & Fox, J. (2015). Assessing the effects of gamification in the classroom: A longitudinal study on intrinsic motivation, social comparison, satisfaction, effort and academic performance. *Computers & Education, 80*, 152–161. doi:10.1016/j.compedu.2014.08.019

Harjani, P. (2011, August 29). 'Angry Anna' gains a virtual victory. *CNN Travel*. Retrieved from http://travel.cnn.com/mumbai/life/team-anna-eliminates-indias-corrupt-politicians-well-virtually-386861

Hartley, J. (2009). Journalism and Popular Culture. In K. Wahl-Jorgensen & T. Hanitzsch (Eds.), *The Handbook of Journalism Studies* (pp. 310–324). New York, NY: Routledge.

Hartmann, T. (Ed.). (2009). *Media choice: A theoretical and empirical overview*. New York, NY: Routledge.

Harviainen, J. T. (2012). Ritualistic Games, Boundary Control, and Information Uncertainty. *Simulation & Gaming, 43*(4), 506–527. doi:10.1177/1046878111435395

Hattie, J., & Timperley, H. (2007, March). The Power of Feedback. *Review of Educational Research, 77*(1), 81–112. doi:10.3102/003465430298487

Hausknecht, J., Day, D. V., & Thomas, S. C. (2004). Applicant reactions to selection procedures: An updated model and meta-analysis. *Personnel Psychology, 57*(3), 639–683. doi:10.1111/j.1744-6570.2004.00003.x

Haythornthwaite, C. (2002). Strong, Weak and Latent Ties and the Impact of New Media. *The Information Society: An International Journal., 18*(5), 385–401. doi:10.1080/01972240290108195

Heath, T. (2010, January 19). U.S. cellphone users donate $22 million to Haiti earthquake relief via text. *Washington Post*. Retrieved from http://www.washingtonpost.com/wp-dyn/content/article/2010/01/18/AR2010011803792.html

Heimlich, R. (2010, September 12). Americans Spending More Time Following the News. *Pew Research Center for the People and the Press*. Retrieved from http://www.people-press.org/2010/09/12/americans-spending-more-time-following-the-news/

Hellwege, B., & Robertson, C. (2012, October). Entertain, engage, educate.*Proceedings of ACEC 2012*. Perth, Australia: ACEC.

Hense, J., & Mandl, H. (2014). Learning in or with games?: Quality criteria for digital learning games from the perspectives of learning, emotion, and motivation theory. In *Digital Systems for Open Access to Formal and Informal Learning* (pp. 181–193). Springer. doi:10.1007/978-3-319-02264-2_12

Herd Wisdom. (2013, May 22). Gamifying recruitment: Increase interest and results. Retrieved from http://www.herd-wisdom.com/blog/gamifying-recruitment-increase-interest-and-results/

Herger, M. (2014). Enterprise gamification: Engaging people by letting them have fun. ISBN: 1470000644.

Herman, D., Jahn, M., & Ryan, M. (2005). Narrative, games and play. In D. Herman, M. Jahn, & M. Ryan (Eds.), *Routledge Encyclopedia of Narrative Theory*. London: Routledge.

Hermida, A. (2010). Tweet the news: Social media streams and the practice of journalism. In S. Allan (Ed.), *The Routledge companion to news and journalism*. New York, NY: Routledge.

Hermund, F., Toubro, O. F., Nielsen, J. E., Spycher, R., & Salqvist, B. (2005). *3ʳᵈ World Farmer: A simulation to make you think*. [Online game]. Retrieved from http://www.3rdworldfarmer.com/About.html

Hewmanne, S. (2006). Participation? My blood and flesh is being sucked dry: Market-based development and Sri Lanka's Free Trade Zone women workers. *Journal of Third World Studies, 23*, 51–74.

Higgins, E. T. (1998). Promotion and prevention: Regulatory focus as a motivational principle. *Advances in Experimental Social Psychology, 30*, 1–46. doi:10.1016/S0065-2601(08)60381-0

Higgins, E. T. (2002). How self-regulation creates distinct values: The case of promotion and prevention decision making. *Journal of Consumer Psychology, 12*(3), 177–191. doi:10.1207/S15327663JCP1203_01

Hill, K. (2011, April 7). Adventures in Self-Surveillance, Aka The Quantified Self, Aka Extreme Navel-Gazing. *Forbes*. Retrieved from http://www.forbes.com/sites/kashmirhill/2011/04/07/adventures-in-self-surveillance-aka-the-quantified-self-aka-extreme-navel-gazing/

Hill, K., & Greenburg, Z. O. (2010, November 29). *The Black Market Price Of Your Personal Info. Forbes*. Retrieved from http://www.forbes.com/2010/11/29/black-market-price-of-your-info-personal-finance.html

Holcomb, J., & Mitchell, A. (2014, March 26). The Revenue Picture for American Journalism and How It Is Changing. *Pew Research Center's Journalism Project*. Retrieved from http://www.journalism.org/2014/03/26/the-revenue-picture-for-american-journalism-and-how-it-is-changing/

Holt, K., & Karlsson, M. (2011). Edited participation: Comparing editorial influence on traditional and participatory online newspapers in Sweden. Javnost - the public, 18(2), 19-36.

Hoorens, V., & Van Damme, C. (2012). What do people infer from social comparisons? Bridges between social comparison and person perception. *Social and Personality Psychology Compass, 6*(8), 607–618. doi:10.1111/j.1751-9004.2012.00451.x

Hope Lab. (2014). Innovative solutions. *Hope Lab*. Retrieved from http://www.hopelab.org/innovative-solutions/

Horton, D., & Wohl, R. R. (1956). Mass communication and para-social interaction: Observations on intimacy at a distance. *Psychiatry, 19*(3), 215–229. PMID:13359569

Ho, S., Putthiwanit, C., & Chia-Ying, L. (2011). May I continue or should I stop? The effects of regulatory focus and message framings on video game players' self-control. *International Journal of Business and Social Science, 2*(12), 194–200.

Hough, L. M., & Johnson, J. W. (2013). Use and importance of personality variables in work settings. In N. W. Schmitt, S. Highhouse, & I. B. Weiner (Eds.), Handbook of psychology: Vol. 12. *Industrial and organizational psychology* (2nd ed., pp. 211–243). Hoboken, NJ, US: John Wiley & Sons Inc.

House, G. (2012) *Engage or die: Gamify your sales process*. Pleasanton, CA: Retrieved from http://www.calliduscloud.com/wp-content/uploads/2012/09/callidus_gamification_whitepaper_v12.pdf?utm_source=mysalesgame&utm_medium=CTA2&utm_campaign=whitepaper

Howitt, G. (2014, February 21). Writing video games: can narrative be as important as gameplay? *The Guardian*. Retrieved from http://www.theguardian.com/culture/australia-culture-blog/2014/feb/21/writing-video-games-can-narrative-be-as-important-as-gameplay

Hsu, S., Chang, J., & Lee, C. (2013). Designing attractive gamification features for collaborative storytelling websites. *Cyberpsychology, Behavior, and Social Networking, 16*(6), 428–435. doi:10.1089/cyber.2012.0492 PMID:23438264

Huang, H.-M. (2002). Toward constructivism for adult learners in online learning environments. *British Journal of Educational Technology, 33*(1), 27–37. doi:10.1111/1467-8535.00236

Huang, J. H., & Yang, T. K. (2012). The Effectiveness of In-Game Advertising: The Impacts of Ad Type and Game/Ad Relevance. *International Journal of Electronic BusinessManagement, 10*(1), 61.

Huizinga, J. (1950). Homo Ludens: A Study of the Play-Element. In *Culture*. Boston: Beacon Press.

Hulsey, N., & Reeves, J. (2014). The Gift that Keeps on Giving: Google, Ingress, and the Gift of Surveillance. *Surveillance & Society, 12*(3), 389–400.

Humphreys, A., & Grayson, K. (2008). The intersecting roles of consumer and producer: A critical perspective on co-production, co-creation and presumption. *Social Compass, 2*, 1–18.

Humphreys, S. (2003). Online multi-user games. *Australian Journal of Communication, 30*(1), 79–91.

Hunicke, R., LeBlanc, M., & Zubek, R. (2004) MDA: A formal approach to game design and game research.*Proceedings of the Association for the Advancement of Artificial Intelligence 2004 Work Shop on Challenges in Game Artificial Intelligence*, 1-5.

Huotari, K., & Hamari, J. (2012, October 3-5). Defining gamification - A service marketing perspective. *MindTrek, 17-22. Proceedings of the 16th International Academic MindTrek Conference*, Tampere, Finland. Retrieved from http://www.hubscher.org/roland/courses/hf765/readings/p17-huotari.pdf

Huotari, K., & Hamari, J. (2012). Defining gamification: a service marketing perspective.*Proceedings of the 16th International Academic MindTrek Conference*, (pp. 17-22). ACM. doi:10.1145/2393132.2393137

Hutchings, E. (2012, January 20). Track Your Daily Activity and Improve Your Health with The Nike Fuelband. *PSFK*. Retrieved from http://www.psfk.com/2012/01/track-your-activity-with-the-nike-fuelband.html

Iles, P. A., & Robertson, I. T. (1989). The impact of personnel selection procedures on candidates. In P. Herriot (Ed.), *Assessment and selection in organizations* (pp. 257–271). Chichester, UK: John Wiley & Sons.

Ingram, M. (2010, February 17). *Average social gamer is a 43-year-old woman.* Retrieved 5 June 2014 from http://gigaom.com/2010/02/17/average-social-gamer-is-a-43-year-old-woman/

Insanely driven: Reckitt Benckiser. (n. d.). *Reckitt Benckiser.* Retrieved from http://insanelydriven.archive.lessrain.co.uk/

Internet World Stats. (2012). Miniwatts Marketing Group. Retrieved from http://www.internetworldstats.com/stats.htm

Isaacson, W. (2011). *Steve Jobs.* New York: Simon and Schuster.

Ivory, J. D., & Kalyanaraman, S. (2007). The effects of technological advancement and violent content in video games on players' feelings of presence, involvement, physiological arousal, and aggression. *Journal of Communication, 57*(3), 532–555. doi:10.1111/j.1460-2466.2007.00356.x

Jacobson, S. (2012). Transcoding the news: An investigation into multimedia journalism published on nytimes.com 2000-2008. *New Media & Society, 14*(5), 867–885. doi:10.1177/1461444811431864

Jakobsson, M. (2011). The achievement machine: Understanding Xbox 360 achievements in gaming practices. *Game Studies, 11*(1). Retrieved from http://gamestudies.org/1101

Jakobsson, M., & Taylor, T. L. (2003). The Sopranos meets EverQuest: Social networking in massively multiplayer online games. In *Proceedings of the 2003 Digital Arts and Culture (DAC) Conference.* (pp.81-90). Melbourne: RMIT School of Applied Communication.

Jamieson, D. (2014). *A look at luck in game design. Tuts+ Game Development article.* Retrieved from http://gamedevelopment.tutsplus.com/articles/a-look-at-luck-in-game-design--gamedev-14195

Jansson, A., & Lindell, J. (2014). News media consumption in the transmedia age. *Journalism Studies.* doi:10.1080/1461670X.2014.890337

Jansz, J., & Tanis, M. (2007). Appeal of playing online first person shooter games. *Cyberpsychology & Behavior*, *10*(1), 133–136. doi:10.1089/cpb.2006.9981 PMID:17305460

Jegers, K. (2007). Pervasive game flow: Understanding player enjoyment in pervasive gaming. *ACM Computers in Entertainment*, *5*(1), 1–11. doi:10.1145/1236224.1236238

Jenkins, H. (2006). *Convergence culture: Where old and new media collide*. New York, NY: New York University Press.

Jensen, K. B., & Rosengren, K. E. (1990). Five traditions in search of the audience. *European Journal of Communication*, *5*(2), 207–238. doi:10.1177/0267323190005002005

Jesper, J. (2003). The game, the player, the world: Looking for a heart of gameness. In M. Copier & J. Raseens (Eds.), *Level Up: Digital Games Research Conference Proceedings, Utrecht, Netherlands*, 30-45. Retrieved from http://www.jesperjuul.net/text/gameplayerworld/

Jewell, R. T., Moti, A., & Coates, D. (2012). A brief history of violence and aggression in spectator sports. In R.T. Jewell (Ed.), Violence and Aggression in Sporting Contests (pp. 11–26). Springer New York. doi:10.1007/978-1-4419-6630-8

Johansson, P., & Gardenfors, P. (2005). Introduction to cognition, education, and communication technology. In P. Gardenfors & P. Johansson (Eds.), *Cognition, education and communication technology*. London: Lawrence Erlbaum Associates.

Johansson, S. (2008). Gossip, sport and pretty girls. *Journalism Practice*, *2*(3), 402–413. doi:10.1080/17512780802281131

Johnson, B. (2009, June 1). How Tetris conquered the world, block by block. *The Guardian*. Retrieved from http://www.theguardian.com/technology/gamesblog/2009/jun/02/tetris-25anniversary-alexey-pajitnov

Johnson, L., Smith, R., Willis, H., Levine, A., & Haywood, K. (2011). The 2011 Horizon Report. Austin, Texas: The New Media Consortium. Retrieved from http://net.educause.edu/ir/library/pdf/HR2011.pdf

Johnson, D. I. (2007, April). Using out-of-class quizzes to promote cognitive engagement. *Communication Teacher*, *21*(2), 35–38. doi:10.1080/17404620701529431

Johnson, D. W., Johnson, R. T., & Stanne, M. B. (2000). *Cooperative learning methods: A meta-analysis*. Minneapolis: University of Minnesota.

Jones, S. (Ed.). (2003). *Encyclopedia of new media*. Thousand Oaks: Sage. doi:10.4135/9781412950657

Jönsson, A. M., & Örnebring, H. (2011). User-generated Content and the News: Empowerment of citizens or interactive illusion? *Journalism Practice*, *5*(2), 127–144. doi:10.1080/17512786.2010.501155

Juul, J. (2003, November). *The game, the player, the world: Looking for a heart of gameness*. Paper presented at the Level Up: Digital Games Research Conference. Retrieved from http://www.jesperjuul.net/text/gameplayerworld/

Juul, J. (2004, July 9). Introduction to game time. *ElectronicBookReview.com*. Retrieved from http://www.electronicbookreview.com/thread/firstperson/teleport

Juul, J. (2005). Games telling stories? In J. Raessens & J. Goldstein (Eds.), Handbook of computer game studies (pp. 219-226). Cambridge, M.A.: The MIT Press.

Kabeer, N. (1994). *Reversed realities: Gender hierarchies in development thought*. London, UK: Verso.

Kahne, J., Middaugh, E., & Evans, C. (2008). *The civic potential of video games*: CERG and MacArthur Foundation. Retrieved from http://www.civicsurvey.org/sites/default/files/publications/Civic_Pot_Video_Games.pdf

Kahneman, D., & Tversky, A. (1984). Choices, values, and frames. *The American Psychologist*, *39*(4), 341–350. doi:10.1037/0003-066X.39.4.341

Kalyanaraman, S., & Sundar, S. S. (2006). The psychological appeal of personalized content in web portals: Does customization affect attitudes and behavior? *Journal of Communication*, *56*(1), 110–132. doi:10.1111/j.1460-2466.2006.00006.x

Kalyanaraman, S., & Wojdynski, B. W. (2015). Affording control: How interactivity, customization and navigability affect psychological responses to communication technology. In S. S. Sundar (Ed.), *The Handbook of the Psychology of Communication Technology* (pp. 425–444). New York: Wiley-Blackwell. doi:10.1002/9781118426456.ch19

Kalyuga, S., & Plass, J. L. (2009). Evaluating and managing cognitive load in games. In R. E. Ferdig (Ed.), *Handbook of Research on Effective Electronic Gaming in Education* (pp. 719–737). Hershey, PA: Information Science Reference. doi:10.4018/978-1-59904-808-6.ch041

Kamer, F. (2012, February 23). Nike's Fuelband, the Shiny IOS-Powered New Fitness Gadget, Sold Out in Four Minutes. *Observer*. Retrieved from http://observer.com/2012/02/nike-fuelband-apple-sold-out-02232012/

Kang, Y. W. (2011). *Hybrid interactive rhetoric engagements in Massively Multiplayer Online Role-Playing Games (MMORPGs): Examining the role of rhetors and audiences in generative rhetorical discourses.* [Dissertation]. The University of Texas at El Paso, 2011.

Kang, B., & Tan, S. (2014). Interactive Games: Intrinsic and Extrinsic Motivation, Achievement, and Satisfaction. *Journal of Management and Strategy*, *5*(4), 110. doi:10.5430/jms.v5n4p110

Kapp, K. M. (2014, Spring). What L&D professionals need to know about gamification. *Training Industry Magazine*, 16-19. Retrieved from [REMOVED HYPERLINK FIELD]http://www.nxtbook.com/nxtbooks/trainingindustry/tiq_2014spring/

Kappen, D. L., & Nacke, L. E. (2013, October). The kaleidoscope of effective gamification: Deconstructing gamification in business applications. Proceedings of Gamification '13, Stratford, ON, Canada. doi:10.1145/2583008.2583029

Kapp, K. (2012). *The gamification of learning and instruction: Game-based methods and strategies for training and education.* San Francisco, CA: Pfeifer.

Kapp, K. M. (2012). *The gamification of learning and instruction: game-based methods and strategies for training and education.* John Wiley & Sons.

Kapp, K. M., Blair, L., & Mesch, R. (2013). *The Gamification of Learning and Instruction Fieldbook: Ideas Into Practice.* John Wiley & Sons.

Karim, L. (2008). Demystifying micro-credit: The Grameen Bank, NGOs, and Neoliberalism in Bangladesh. *Cultural Dynamics*, *20*(1), 5–29. doi:10.1177/0921374007088053

Karim, L. (2011). *Microfinance and its discontents: Women in debt in Bangladesh.* Minneapolis, MN: University of Minnesota Press.

Karlsson, M. (2011). The immediacy of online news, the visibility of journalistic processes and a restructuring of journalistic authority. *Journalism*, *12*(3), 279–295. doi:10.1177/1464884910388223

Karlsson, M., & Clerwall, C. (2012). Patterns and origins in the evolution of multimedia on broadsheet and tabloid news sites: Swedish online news 2005-2010. *Journalism Studies*, *13*(4), 550–565. doi:10.1080/1461670X.2011.639571

Karlsson, M., & Clerwall, C. (2013). Negotiating professional news judgment and "Clicks". Comparing tabloid, broadsheet and public service traditions in Sweden. *Nordicom Review*.

Kato, P. M., Cole, S. W., Bradlyn, A. S., & Pollock, B. H. (2008). A video game improves behavioral outcomes in adolescents and young adults with cancer: A randomized trial. *Pediatrics*, *122*(2), e305–e317. doi:10.1542/peds.2007-3134 PMID:18676516

Katz, J. (1993, November 25). The media's war on kids: from the Beatles to Beavis and Butt-head. *Rolling Stone*.

Kaul, A. Narang, R. & Shant,M. (2014). Gamijoint: Improving Conjoint Through Gamification. Paper presented at the 2014 CASRO Digital Research Conference, San Antonio, TX. Retrieved from http://c.ymcdn.com/sites/www.casro.org/resource/collection/E0F10496-BE87-48E8-8746-521D403EE4A2/Paper_-_Anil_Kaul_and_Rajat_Narang_-_AbsolutData_Analytics.pdf

Keats, A. (2011). Loyalty is the greatest value of location-based marketing. *PRWeek (U.S.)*, *14*(12), 26–26.

Keith, N., & Frese, M. (2005). Self-Regulation in Error Management Training: Emotion Control and Metacognition as Mediators of Performance Effects. *The Journal of Applied Psychology*, *90*(4), 677–691. doi:10.1037/0021-9010.90.4.677 PMID:16060786

Keller, J.M. (1987). The systematic process of motivational design. *Performance + Instruction, 26*(9-10), 1-8.

Keller, J. M. (1984). The use of the ARCS model of motivation in teacher training. *Aspects of Educational Technology*, *17*, 140–145.

Kennedy, D. (2014). What can 'gamification' do for lawyers? *ABA Journal*. Retrieved online: http://www.abajournal.com/magazine/article/what_can_gamification_do_for_lawyers/

Kerr, S. (1995). An academy classic. On the folly of rewarding A, while hoping for B. *The Academy of Management Perspectives*, *9*(1), 7–14. doi:10.5465/AME.1995.9503133466

Keys, B., & Wolfe, J. (1990). The role of management games and simulations in education and research. *Journal of Management*, *16*(2), 306–336. doi:10.1177/014920639001600205

Khatib, F., & DiMaio, F., & the Foldit Contenders Group. Foldit Void Crushers Group, Cooper, S., Kazmierczyk, M., ... Baker, D. (2011). Crystal structure of a monomeric retroviral protease solved by protein folding game players. *Nature Structural & Molecular Biology*, *18*(10), 1175–1177. Retrieved from http://www.nature.com/nsmb/journal/v18/n10/full/ nsmb.2119.html

Khatib, F., Cooper, S., Tyka, M. D., Xu, K., Makedon, I., & Popovic, Z. et al. (2011). Algorithm discovery by protein folding game players. *Proceedings of the National Academy of Sciences of the United States of America*, *108*(47), 18949–18953. doi:10.1073/pnas.1115898108 PMID:22065763

Kheops Studio. (2004). *Return to Mysterious Island* [computer software]. The Adventure Company.

Kim, B. (2012). Harnessing the power of game dynamics. *College & Research Libraries News*, *73*(8), 465–469.

Kim, J., Kim, J.-H., & Seo, M. (2014). Toward a person × situation model of selective exposure: Repressors, sensitizers, and choice of online news on financial crisis. *Journal of Media Psychology: Theories, Methods, and Applications*, *26*(2), 59–69. doi:10.1027/1864-1105/a000111

King, D., Delfabbo, P., & Griffiths, M. (2010). Video game structural characteristics: A new psychological taxonomy. *International Journal of Mental Health and Addiction*, *8*(1), 90–106. doi:10.1007/s11469-009-9206-4

Kiousis,S.(2002).Interactivity:Aconceptexplication.*NewMedia&Society*,*4*(3),355–383.doi:10.1177/146144480200400303

Kirkpatrick, D. L. (1959). Techniques for evaluating training programs. *Journal of ASTD*, *11*, 1–13.

Kirkpatrick, D. L. (1976). Evaluation. In R. L. Craig (Ed.), *Training and development handbook: A guide to human resource development* (pp. 301–319). New York: McGraw-Hill.

Kirriemuir, J., & McFarlane, A. (2004). Literature review on games and learning. (Report No. 8). *NESTA*. Retrieved from http://archive.futurelab.org.uk/resources/documents/lit_reviews/Games_Review.pdf

Kirsch, I., Lynn, S. J., Vigorito, M., & Miller, R. R. (2004). The role of cognition in classical and operant conditioning. *Journal of Clinical Psychology*, *60*(4), 369–392. doi:10.1002/jclp.10251 PMID:15022268

Klabbers, J. H. G. (2003, November 4-6). *The gaming landscape: A taxonomy for classifying games and simulations.* Paper presented at the LEVEL UP: Digital Games Research Conference, University of Utrecht, The Netherlands.

Kleis Nielsen, R. (2012). How newspapers began to blog. *Information Communication and Society*, *15*(6), 959–978. doi:10.1080/1369118X.2012.694898

Klimmt, C. (2009). Serious games and social change: Why they (should) work. In U. Ritterfeld, M. Cody, & P. Vorderer (Eds.), *Serious games: Mechanisms and effects*. New York, NY: Routledge.

Kluemper, D. H., & Rosen, P. A. (2009). Future employment selection methods: Evaluating social networking web sites. *Journal of Managerial Psychology*, *24*(6), 567–580. doi:10.1108/02683940910974134

Koenig-Lewis, N., Marquet, M., & Palmer, A. (2013). The effects of gamification on market research engagement and response. Paper presented at the Academy of Marketing conference. Retrieved from http://marketing.conference-services.net/resources/327/3554/pdf/AM2013_0291_paper.pdf

Kohut, A., Taylor, P., & Keeter, S. (2010). The Millennials: Confident. Connected. Open to Change. *Pew Research Center*. Pew Research Center, Retrieved from http://www.pewsocialtrends.org/2010/02/24/millennials-confident-connected-open-to-change/

Koivisto, J., & Hamari, J. (2014). Demographical differences in perceived benefits from gamification. *Computers in Human Behavior*, *35*, 179–188. doi:10.1016/j.chb.2014.03.007

Kolowich, S. (2014, January 22). Completion rates aren't the best way to judge MOOCs, researchers say [Blog post]. Retrieved from http://chronicle.com/blogs/wiredcampus/completion-rates-arent-the-best-way-to-judge-moocs-researchers-say/49721

Kotler, P., & Lee, N. R. (2008). *Social marketing: Influencing behaviors for good* (3rd ed.). Thousand Oaks: Sage.

Kovach, B., & Rosenstiehl, T. (2001). *The elements of journalism. What newspeople should know and the public should expect*. New York, NY: Crown Publishers.

Kovach, B., & Rosenstiel, T. (2010). *Blur: How to Know What's True in the Age of Information Overload*. Bloomsbury Publishing USA.

Kraiger, K., & Culbertson, S. S. (2013). In I. B. Weiner (Ed.), *Understanding and facilitating learning: Advancements in training and development* (2nd ed., pp. 244–261). Handbook of PsychologyNew York: Wiley.

Kranstuber, H., Carr, K., & Hosek, A. M. (2012, January). "If you can dream it, you can achieve it." Parent memorable messages as indicators of college student success. *Communication Education*, *61*(1), 44–66. doi:10.1080/03634523.2011.620617

Krcmar, M., & Strizhakova, Y. (2009). Uses and gratifications as media choice. In T. Hartmann (Ed.), Media choice: A theoretical and empirical overview. Routledge.

Kristof, A. L. (1996). Person-organization fit: An integrative review of its conceptualizations, measurement, and implications. *Personnel Psychology*, *49*(1), 1–49. doi:10.1111/j.1744-6570.1996.tb01790.x

Kristof-Brown, A. L., & Stevens, C. K. (2001). Goal congruence in project teams: Does the fit between members' personal mastery and performance goals matter? *The Journal of Applied Psychology*, *86*(6), 1083–1095. doi:10.1037/0021-9010.86.6.1083 PMID:11768052

Krogue, K. (2012). 5 gamification rules from the grandfather of gamification. Retrieved from http://www.forbes.com/sites/kenkrogue/2012/09/18/5-gamification-rules-from-the-grandfather-of-gamification/

Krosnick, J. A. (1991). Response strategies for coping with the cognitive demands of attitude measures in surveys. *Applied Cognitive Psychology*, *5*(3), 213–236. doi:10.1002/acp.2350050305

Kubisiak, C., Stewart, R., Thornbury, E., & Moye, N. (2014, May). Development of PDRI's learning agility simulation. In *E. C. Popp* (Chair), *Challenges and innovations of using game-like assessments in selection*. Symposium presented at the 29th Annual Conference of the Society for Industrial and Organizational Psychology, Honolulu, HI.

Kücklich, J. (2005). Precarious playbor: modders and the digital game industry. *The Fibreculture Journal, 5*.

Kücklich, J. (2005). Precarious playbour: Modders and the digital games industry. *The Fibreculture Journal, 1*(5). Retrieved from http://five.fibreculturejournal.org/fcj-025-precarious-playbour-modders-and-the-digital-games-industry/

Kücklich, J. (2009). A Techno-Semiotic Approach to Cheating in Computer Games: Or How I Learned to Stop Worrying and Love the Machine. *Games and Culture*, *4*(2), 158–169. doi:10.1177/1555412008325486

Kücklich, J. (2009). Virtual worlds and their discontents: Precarious sovereignty, govermentality, and the ideaology of play. *Games and Culture*, *4*(4), 340–352. doi:10.1177/1555412009343571

Kuczaj, S. A., & Highfill, L. E. (2005). Dolphin play: Evidence for cooperation and culture? *Behavioral and Brain Sciences*, *28*(05), 705–706. doi:10.1017/S0140525X05370129

Kuo, I. (2013, December 18). Gartner: 80% of poorly designed gamification initiatives still on track to fail by 2014. *Gamification.co*. Retrieved from http://www.gamification.co/2013/12/18/gartner-bad-gamification-initiatives-still-fail-2014/

Kuo, I. (2014, February 3). Gartner's latest gamification research for 2014 with Brian Burke. *Gamification.co*. Retrieved from http://www.gamification.co/2014/02/03/gartners-gamification-research-2014-brian-burke/

Kurtz, H. (1993). *Media circus: The trouble with America's newspapers*. New York, NY: Times Books.

Kwak, H., Lee, C., Park, H., & Moon, S. (2010). What is Twitter, a social network or a news media? In *Proceedings of the 19th International Conference on World Wide Web*, (pp.591-600). Raleigh, NC. doi:10.1145/1772690.1772751

Kwami, J., Wolf-Monteiro, B., & Steeves, H. L. (2011). Toward a 'macro-micro' analysis of gender, power and ICTs: A response to Mickey Lee's feminist political economic critique of the human development approach to new ICTs. *The International Communication Gazette*, *73*(6), 539–549. doi:10.1177/1748048511412290

Kyle, D. (2007). *Sport and Spectacle in the Ancient World*. Malden, MA: Blackwell.

Ladley, P. (2011). Gamification, education and behavioural economics [Entire issue]. *Games: innovation in learning*. Retrieved from http://www.games-ed.co.uk/resources/Gamification-Education-and-Behavioural-Economics-v1.pdf

Lagel, E. (2010, August 27). Randomness in games . . . why? *Gamasutra*. Retrieved fromwww.gamasutra.com/blogs/EricLagel/20100827/Randomness-in-games-why.php

Landers, R. N. (2013, April). Gamification: A new approach to serious games in training. In M.A. Lodato (Chair), R.C. Brusso (Co-Chair), & R. Wisher (Discussant), *I-O's role in emerging training technologies*. Symposium presented at the 28th Annual Conference of the Society for Industrial and Organizational Psychology, Houston, TX.

Landers, R. N., & Armstrong, M. B. (in Press). Enhancing instructional outcomes with gamification: An empirical test of the Technology-Enhanced Training Effectiveness Model [Unpublished manuscript, submitted for publication].

Landers, R. N., & Callan, R. C. (2011) Casual social games as serious games: The psychology of gamification in undergraduate education and employment training. In M. Ma, A. Oikonomou & L.C. Jain (Eds.), Serious Games and Edutainment Applications (pp. 399-423). Springer.

Landers, R. N. (2014). Developing a theory of gamified learning: Linking serious games and gamification of learning. *Simulation & Gaming*.

Landers, R. N., Bauer, K. N., Callan, R. C., & Armstrong, M. B. (2014). Psychological theory and the gamification of learning. In T. Reiners & L. Wood (Eds.), *Gamification in Education and Business*. New York, NY: Springer.

Landers, R. N., & Callan, R. C. (2011). Casual social games as serious games: The psychology of gamification in undergraduate education and employee training. In M. Ma, A. Oikonomou, & L. C. Jain (Eds.), *Serious Games and Edutainment Applications* (pp. 399–424). Surrey, UK: Springer. doi:10.1007/978-1-4471-2161-9_20

Landers, R. N., & Callan, R. C. (2012). Training evaluation in virtual worlds: Development of a model. *Journal of Virtual Worlds Research*, 5(3), 1–20.

Landers, R. N., & Landers, A. K. (2014). An empirical test of the Theory of Gamified Learning: The effect of leaderboards on time-on-task and academic performance. *Simulation & Gaming*.

Landers, R. N., Sackett, P. R., & Tuzinski, K. A. (2011). Retesting after initial failure, coaching rumors, and warnings against faking in online personality measures for selection. *The Journal of Applied Psychology*, 96(1), 202–210. doi:10.1037/a0020375 PMID:20718510

Landy, F. J. (2007). The validation of personnel decisions in the twenty first century: Back to the future. In S. M. McPhail (Ed.), *Alternate validation strategies: Developing and leveraging existing validity evidence* (pp. 409–426). San Francisco: Jossey-Bass.

Lane, R. J. (2008). *Jean Baudrillard* (2nd ed.). New York: Routledge.

Laster, J. (2010, March 23). At Indiana U., a class on game design has students playing to win [Blog post]. Retrieved from http://chronicle.com/blogs/wiredcampus/at-indiana-u-a-class-on-game-design-has-students-playing-to-win/21981

Latham, G. P., & Seijts, G. H. (1999). The effects of proximal and distal goals on performance on a moderately complex task. *Journal of Organizational Behavior*, 20(4), 421–429. doi:10.1002/(SICI)1099-1379(199907)20:4<421::AID-JOB896>3.0.CO;2-#

Lave, J., & Wenger, E. (1991). *Situated learning: Legitimate peripheral participation*. Cambridge, UK: Cambridge University Press. doi:10.1017/CBO9780511815355

Lazzaro, N. (2004, March 8). Why we play games: Four keys to more emotion without story. *XeoDesign.com*. Retrieved from http://xeodesign.com/xeodesign_whyweplaygames.pdf

Lazzaro, N. (2009). Understading emotions. In C. Bateman & R. Bartle (Eds.), *Beyond Game Design: Nine Steps Towards Creating Better Videogames* (pp. 3–47). Hampshire: Cengage Learning.

Le Fevre, M., Matheny, J., & Kolt, G. S.(2003). Eustress, distress, and interpretation in occupational stress. *Journal of Managerial Psychology*, 18(7), 726–744. doi:10.1108/02683940310502412

Leach, G. J., & Sugarman, T. S. (2005). Play to win! Using games in library instruction to enhance student learning. *Research Strategies*, 20(3), 191–203. doi:10.1016/j.resstr.2006.05.002

Leavitt, M. (2012). *HealthESeat*. Portland, OR: PDX Quantified Self Show and Tell. Wieden and Kennedy.

Lee, D. W., & LaRose, R. (2007). A socio-cognitive model of video game usage. *Journal of Broadcasting & Electronic Media, 51*(4), 632–650. doi:10.1080/08838150701626511

Lee, J. J., & Hammer, J. (2011). Gamification in education: What, how, Why Bother? Definitions and uses. *Exchange Organizational Behavior Teaching Journal, 15*(2), 1–5.

Lee, J. J., & Hammer, J. (2011). Gamification in education: What, how, why bother? *Academic Exchange Quarterly, 15*, 1–5.

Lee, J., Park, H., & Wise, K. (2013). Brand interactivity and its effects on the outcomes of advergame play. *New Media & Society*. doi:10.1177/1461444813504267

Lee, K. M. (2004). Presence, explicated. *Communication Theory, 14*(1), 27–50. doi:10.1111/j.1468-2885.2004.tb00302.x

Leeson, C. (2013). Driving KM behaviors and adoption through gamification. *KM World, 22*, 10-11; 20.

Lee, Y., Kozar, K. A., & Larsen, K. R. (2003). The technology acceptance model: Past, present, and future. *Communications of the Association for Information Systems, 12*(1), 50.

Lefebvre, H. (1991). *The Production of Space* (D. Nicholson-Smith, Trans.). Malden, MA: Blackwell-Wiley.

Lenhart, A., Jones, S., & Macgill, A. (2008). Adults and Video Games. *Pew Internet*. Pew Research Center, Retrieved from http://www.pewinternet.org/2008/12/07/adults-and-video-games/

Lenhart, A., Jones, S., & Macgill, A. R. (2008). *Pew Internet Project data memo*. Pew Research Center. Retrieved from http://www.pewinternet.org/files/old-media//Files/Reports/2008/PIP_Adult_gaming_memo.pdf.pdf

Lepper, M. R., Greene, D., & Nisbett, R. E. (1973). Undermining children's intrinsic interest with extrinsic reward: A test of the ''overjustification'' hypothesis. *Journal of Personality and Social Psychology, 28*(1), 129–137. doi:10.1037/h0035519

Lerner, D. (1958). *The passing of traditional society: Modernizing the Middle East*. Glencoe, IL: Free Press.

less rain. (2014). *Insanely driven*. Retrieved from http://insanelydriven.archive.lessrain.co.uk/

Levy, P. E. (2012). *Industrial organizational psychology: Understanding the workplace* (4th ed.). New York, NY: Worth Publishers.

Lewin, T. (2013, December 10). After setbacks, online courses are rethought. *New York Times*. Retrieved from http://www.nytimes.com/2013/12/11/us/after-setbacks-online-courses-are-rethought.html?_r=1&

Lewis, C., Wardrip-Fruin, N., & Whitehead, J. (2012). Motivational game design patterns of 'ville games. *Proceedings of the International Conference on the Foundations of Digital Games* (pp. 172-179). ACM. doi:10.1145/2282338.2282373

Lewis, S. C. (2012). The tension between professional control and open participation. *Information Communication and Society, 15*(6), 836–866. doi:10.1080/1369118X.2012.674150

Leye, V. (2009). Information and communication technologies for development: A critical perspective. *Global Governance: A Review of Multilateralism and International Organizations, 15*(1), 29-35.

Li, I. (2011). Personal Informatics and Context: Using Context to Reveal Factors That Affect Behavior [Doctoral Dissertation]. Carnegie Mellon University.

Li, I., Dey, A., & Forlizzi, J. (2010). A Stage-Based Model of Personal Informatics Systems. *Proceedings of CHI '10 Conference.* New York City.

Lieberman, D. A. (2001). Management of chronic pediatric diseases with interactive health games: Theory and research findings. *The Journal of Ambulatory Care Management, 24*(1), 26–38. doi:10.1097/00004479-200101000-00004 PMID:11189794

Lieberman, D. A. (2006). What can we learn from playing interactive games? In P. Vorderer & J. Bryant (Eds.), *Playing video games: Motives, responses, and consequences.* Mahvah, New Jersey: Lawrence Erlbaum Associates.

Lievens, F., Peeters, H., & Schollaert, E. (2007). Situational judgment tests: A review of recent research. *International Journal of Selection and Assessment, 37,* 426–441.

Li, I. (2010). *Survey.* Personal Informatics Lab.

Likert, R. (1932). A technique for the measurement of attitudes. *Archives de Psychologie, 1*(55), 140.

Lillie, J. (2011). How and why journalists create audio slideshows. *Journalism Practice, 5*(3), 350–365. doi:10.1080/1 7512786.2010.530977

Limber, J. (1977). Language in child and chimp? *The American Psychologist, 32*(4), 280–295. doi:10.1037/0003-066X.32.4.280

Lim, S., & Reeves, B. (2010). Computer agents versus avatars: Responses to interactive game characters controlled by a computer or other player. *International Journal of Human-Computer Studies, 68*(1-2), 57–68. doi:10.1016/j. ijhcs.2009.09.008

Lister, C., West, J. H., Cannon, B., Sax, T., & Brodegard, D. (2014). Just a Fad? Gamification in Health and Fitness Apps. *JMIR Serious Games, 2*(2), e9. doi:10.2196/games.3413 PMID:25654660

Liu, M., & Peng, W. (2009). Cognitive and psychological predictors of the negative outcomes associated with playing MMOGs (massively multiplayer online games). *Computers in Human Behavior, 25*(6), 1306–1311. doi:10.1016/j. chb.2009.06.002

Livingstone, S. (2002). *Young people and new media.* London: Sage.

Liyakasa, K. (2012a). *GAME ON!. CRM Magazine,* 28–32.

Liyakasa, K. (2012b). *Serious About Gamification. CRM Magazine,* 33–33.

Liyakasa, K. (2012c). Turning Business into Pleasure. *CRM Magazine, 16*(3), 14–14.

Llagostera, E. (2012). On gamification and persuasion.*Proceedings of XI SBGames 2012.* Brasilia, Brazil.

Llamas, S., & Barberie, S. (2014, April). *eSports Digital Games Market Trends Brief.* SuperData. Retrieved from http://www.superdataresearch.com/blog/esports-brief/

Locke, E. A. (1968). Effects of knowledge of results, feedback in relation to standards, and goals on reaction-time performance. *The American Journal of Psychology, 81*(4), 566–574. doi:10.2307/1421061 PMID:5760037

Locke, E. A. (1968). Toward a theory of task motivation and incentives. *Organizational Behavior and Human Performance, 3*(2), 157–189. doi:10.1016/0030-5073(68)90004-4

Locke, E. A., & Latham, G. P. (1990). *A theory of goal setting and task performance.* Englewood Cliffs, NJ: Prentice-Hall.

Locke, E. A., & Latham, G. P. (2002). Building a practically useful theory of goal setting and task motivation: A 35-year odyssey. *The American Psychologist, 57*(9), 705–717. doi:10.1037/0003-066X.57.9.705 PMID:12237980

Locke, E. A., Shaw, K. N., Saari, L. M., & Latham, G. P. (1981). Goal setting and task performance: 1969–1980. *Psychological Bulletin, 90*(1), 125–152. doi:10.1037/0033-2909.90.1.125

Loftus, G., & Loftus, F. (1983). *Mind at play: The psychology of video games.* New York: Basic Books.

Lovata, L. M. (1987). Behavioral theories relating to the design of information systems. *Management Information Systems Quarterly, 11*(2), 147–149. doi:10.2307/249354

Lucas, K., & Sherry, J. L. (2004). Sex differences in video game play: A communication-based explanation. *Communication Research, 31*(5), 499–523. doi:10.1177/0093650204267930

Lucero, A., Karapanos, E., Arrasvuori, J., & Korhonen, H. (2014). Playful or gameful? Creating delightful UX. *Interactions (New York, N.Y.), 21*(3), 34–39. doi:10.1145/2590973

Lugtigheid, A. & Rathod, S. (2005). *Questionnaire Length and Response Quality: Myth or Reality?* Stamford CT: Survey Sampling International.

Lu, H., & Wang, S. (2008). The role of internet addiction in online game royalty: An exploratory study. *Internet Research, 18*(5), 499–519. doi:10.1108/10662240810912756

Lui, Y., Alexandrova, T., & Nakajima, T. (2011, December). *Gamifying intelligent environment.* Paper presented at the International ACM Workshop on Ubiquitous Meta User Interfaces, Scottsdale, AZ.

Lundby, K. (Ed.). (2009). *Mediatization: concept, changes, consequences.* Peter Lang.

Luscombe, B. (2009). Zynga harvests the cyberfarmer. *Time, 174*(21), 59–60. PMID:19891392

Lynch, K. (2013, October 8). Confirmed; Grand Theft Auto 5 Breaks 6 Sales World Records. *Guinness Book of World Records.* Retrieved from http://www.guinnessworldrecords.com/news/2013/10/confirmed-grand-theft-auto-breaks-six-sales-world-records-51900/

M+R. (2014). Benchmarks 2014. Retrieved from http://mrbenchmarks.com/

Macedo, S. (2005). *Democracy at risk: How political choices undermine citizen participation, and what we can do about it.* Washington, DC: Brookings Institution.

MacGregor, P. (2007). Tracking the online audience. *Journalism Studies, 8*(2), 280–298. doi:10.1080/14616700601148879

Maddow, R. (2012, January 12). Insensitivity, gaffes dog Romney [Video file]. *NBC News.* Retrieved from http://www.nbcnews.com/video/rachel-maddow/45980205#45980205

Major, B., Testa, M., & Bylsma, W. H. (1991). Responses to upward and downward social comparisons: The impact of esteem-relevance and perceived control in social comparison. In J. Suls & T. A. Wills (Eds.), *Contemporary Theory and Research* (pp. 237–260). Hillsdale, N.J.: Erlbaum.

Makuch, E. (2014, August 5). World of Warcraft Loses 800,000 Subscribers in Three Months [Blog]. Gamespot. Retrieved from http://www.gamespot.com/articles/world-of-warcraft-loses-800-000-subscribers-in-thr/1100-6421529/

Malaby, T. M. (2007). Beyond Play: A New Approach to Games. *Games and Culture, 2*(2), 95–113. doi:10.1177/1555412007299434

Malone, T. W. (1980). What makes things fun to learn? Heuristics for designing instructional computer games. *Proceedings of the 3rd ACM SIGSMALL symposium and the first SIGPC symposium on Small systems – SIGSMALL '80 (pp. 162-169). New York, New York: ACM Press.* doi:10.1145/800088.802839

Malone, T. W. (1981). Toward a theory of intrinsically motivating instruction. *Cognitive Science, 5*(4), 333–369. doi:10.1207/s15516709cog0504_2

Marczewski, A. (2014, November 20). Is it gamification if....? Retrieved from http://www.gamified.co.uk/2014/11/20/gamification/

Marx, K. (1997). The German Ideology [extract]. In D. McLennan (Ed.), *Karl Marx--Selected Writings*. Oxford: Oxford University Press.

Maslow, A. H. (1970). *Motivation and Personality*. New York: Harper & Row.

Massey, D. (1992). Politics and space/time. *New Left Review, 196*, 65–84.

Mathieu, J. E., Heffner, T. S., Goodwin, G. F., Salas, E., & Cannon-Bowers, J. (2000). The influence of shared mental models on team process and performance. *The Journal of Applied Psychology, 85*(2), 273–283. doi:10.1037/0021-9010.85.2.273 PMID:10783543

Mauss, M. (2000). *The Gift: The Form and Reason for Exchange in Archaic Societies*. New York: W.W. Norton & Co.

McCallum, S. (2012). Gamification and serious games for personalized health. In *Proceedings of the 9th International Conference on Wearable Micro and Nano Technologies for Personalized Health. Studies in Health Technology and Informatics, 177*, 85–96. PMID:22942036

McClarty, K. L., Orr, A., Frey, P. M., Dolan, R. P., Vassileva, V., & McVay, A. (2012). A literature review of gaming in education: Research report. Pearson. Retrieved from http://researchnetwork.pearson.com/wp-content/uploads/Lit_Review_of_Gaming_in_Education.pdf

McClelland, D. C. (1961). *The achieving society*. Princeton, NJ: Van Nostrand. doi:10.1037/14359-000

McCormick, T. (2013, June 24). Gamification: A short history. *Foreignpolicy.com.* Retrieved from http://foreignpolicy.com/2013/06/24/gamification-a-short-history/

McEwan, C. (2009). *Postcolonialism and development*. New York, NY: Routledge.

McGonigal, J. (2003). A real little game: The performance of belief in pervasive play. *Level Up.* Retrieved from http://www.avantgame.com/MCGONIGAL%20A%20Real%20Little%20Game%20DiGRA%202003.pdf

McGonigal, J. (2010, February). Gaming can make a better world. *TED.* Retrieved from http://www.ted.com/talks/jane_mcgonigal_gaming_can_make_a_better_world

McGonigal, J. (2012, October 15). How might video games be good for us? *Big Questions Online.* www.bigquestionsonlin.com/content/how-might-video-games-be-good-us

McGonigal, J. (Speaker). (2010, March). Jane McGonigal: Gaming can make a better world [TED Talk]. Retrieved from http://www.ted.com/talks/jane_mcgonigal_gaming_can_make_a_better_world.html

McGonigal, J. (2007). Why I love bees: A case study in collective intelligence gaming. In K. Salem (Ed.), *The ecology of games: Connecting youth, games, and learning* (pp. 199–227). Cambridge, MA: The MIT Press.

McGonigal, J. (2011). *Reality is broken*. London: Jonathan Cape.

McGonigal, J. (2011). *Reality is Broken*. New York, NY: Penguin Press.

McGonigal, J. (2011). *Reality Is Broken: Why Games Make Us Better and How They Can Change the World*. New York, NY: Penguin Press.

McGonigal, J. (2011). *Reality is Broken: Why games make us better and how they can change the world*. New York: Penguin.

McGonigal, J. (2011). *Reality is broken: Why games make us better and how they can change the world*. Penguin.

McLachlan, S., & Golding, P. (2000). Tabloidization in the British press: A quantitative investigation into changes in British Newspapers. In C. Sparks & J. Tulloch (Eds.), *Tabloid tales: Global debates over media standards* (pp. 76–90). Lanham, MD: Rowman and Littlefield.

McManus, J. H. (1994). *Market-Driven Journalism: Let the Citizen Beware?* Thousand Oaks: Sage.

McManus, J. H. (2009). The Commercialization of News (pp. 218–233). In K. Wahl-Jorgensen & T. Hanitzsch (Eds.), *The Handbook of Journalism Studies*. New York, NY: Routledge.

McNair, B. (2000). *Journalism and democracy. An evaluation of the political public sphere*. London, UK: Routledge.

Mekler, E. D., Brühlmann, F., Opwis, K., & Tuch, A. N. (2013, October). Do points, levels and leaderboards harm intrinsic motivation? An empirical analysis of common gamification elements. Proceedings of Gamification '13, Stratford, ON, Canada. doi:10.1145/2583008.2583017

Melkote, S., & Steeves, H. (2001). *Communication for development in the Third World*. Thousand Oaks: Sage Publications.

Meloni, W. & Gruener, W. (2012). *Gamification in 2012: Market update, consumer and enterprise market trends*. M2 Research.

Metcalfe, S. (2014). Capitalism and evolution. *Journal of Evolutionary Economics*, *24*(1), 11–34. doi:10.1007/s00191-013-0307-7

Meyer, P. (2009). *The vanishing newspaper: Saving journalism in the information age*. University of Missouri Press.

Michael, D. R., & Chen, S. L. (2005). *Serious games: Games that educate, train and inform*. Cincinnati, OH: Muska & Lipman Publishing.

Michael, D., & Chen, S. (2005). *Serious games: Games that educate, train, and inform*. Boston, MA: Thomson Course Technology.

Microsoft by the numbers [Infographic]. (2014). *Microsoft, Inc.* Retrieved from http://news.microsoft.com/bythenumbers/index.html

Microsoft Flight [computer software]. (2012 Microsoft Studios. Microsoft.

Mikalef, K., Giannakos, M. N., Chorianopoulos, K., & Jaccheri, L. (2013). Does informal learning benefit from interactivity? The effect of trial and error on knowledge acquisition during a museum visit. *International Journal of Mobile Learning and Organisation*, *7*(2), 158–175. doi:10.1504/IJMLO.2013.055620

Mikulincer, M. (1988). Reactance and helplessness following exposure to unsolvable problems: The effects of attributional style. *Journal of Personality and Social Psychology*, *54*(4), 679–686. doi:10.1037/0022-3514.54.4.679 PMID:3367284

Mikulincer, M. (1989). Cognitive interference and learned helplessness: The effects of off-task cognitions on performance following unsolvable problems. *Journal of Personality and Social Psychology*, *57*(1), 129–135. doi:10.1037/0022-3514.57.1.129

Miller, C. (2009) Respondent technology preferences in surveys: plain text versus rich media. Paper presented at the CASRO Technology Conference, New York.

Miller, J., & Baker-Prewitt, J. (2009). Beyond 'Trapping' the Undesirable Panelist: The Use of Red Herrings to Reduce Satisficing. Paper presented at the 2009 CASRO Panel Quality Conference. Retrieved from http://www.burke.com/library/conference/beyond%20trapping%20the%20undesirable%20panelist_final.pdf

Miller, K. (2005). *Communication theories, perspectives, processes and context* (2nd ed.). New York: McGraw-Hill.

Miller, L. D., Shell, D., Khandaker, N., & Soh, L. K. (2010). Teaching using computer games. *Journal of Educational Technology Systems*, *39*(3), 321–343. doi:10.2190/ET.39.3.g

Mitchell, A., Jurkowitz, M., & Olmstead, K. (2013, March 14). Social, search and direct: Pathways to digital news. Pew Research Journalism Project. Retrieved from http://www.journalism.org/2014/03/13/social-search-direct/

Mitchell, A., Rosenstiel, T., & Christian, L. (2012). Mobile devices and news consumption: Some good signs for journalism. *The Pew Research Center's project for excellence in journalism: The state of the news media 2012*.

mLab (n.d.). Retrieved 5 June 2014 from http://www.mlab.co.za/about/

Mobile Games: Reaching the hardest to reach. (n.d.). Half the Sky Movement. Retrieved from http://www.halftheskymovement.org/pages/mobile-games

Mobile Technology Fact Sheet. (2014). *Pew Research Internet Project*. Retrieved from http://www.pewinternet.org/fact-sheets/mobile-technology-fact-sheet/

Moe, H. (2013). Public service broadcasting and social networking sites: The Norwegian broadcasting corporation on Facebook. *Media International Australia*, *146*, 114–122.

Molesworth, M., & Denegri-Knott, J. (2007). Digital Play and the Actualization of the Consumer Imagination. *Games and Culture*, *2*(2), 114–133. doi:10.1177/1555412006298209

Mone, E. M., & London, M. (2014). *Employee engagement through effective performance management: A practical guide for managers*. New York, NY: Routledge.

Monkey Tales [computer software]. (2010 Larian Studios & die Keure. Larian Studios.

Montola, M. (2012). Social Constructionism and Ludology: Implications for the Study of Games. *Simulation & Gaming*, *43*(3), 300–320. doi:10.1177/1046878111422111

Montola, M., Nummenmaa, T., Lucero, A., Boberg, M., & Korhonen, H. (2009, September). Applying game achievement systems to enhance user experience in a photo sharing service.*Proceedings of the 13th International MindTrek Conference: Everyday Life in the Ubiquitous Era (pp.94-97), Tampere, Finland*. doi:10.1145/1621841.1621859

Montola, M., Stenros, J., & Waern, A. (2009). *Pervasive games: experiences on the boundary between life and play*. Burlington: Morgan Kaufman Publishers.

Moore, E. S. (2006). It's child's play: Advergaming and the online marketing of food to children. *Kaiser Family Foundation Report*. Retrieved from http://kaiserfamilyfoundation.files.wordpress.com/2013/01/7536.pdf

Moreno, J. (2012). Digital Competition Game to Improve Programming Skills. *Journal of Educational Technology & Society*, *15*(3), 288–297.

Morschheuser, B. S., Rivera-Pelayo, V., Mazarakis, A., & Zacharias, V. (2014). Interaction and reflection with quantified self and gamification: An experimental study. *Journal of Literacy and Technology*, *15*(2), 136–156.

Mosca, I. (2012). +10! Gamification and deGamification. *GAME Journal of Game Studies, 1*(1).

Moser, C. (1989). Gender planning in the Third World: Meeting practical and strategic gender needs. *World Development, 17*(11), 1799–1825. doi:10.1016/0305-750X(89)90201-5

Moyer-Gusé, E. (2008). Toward a theory of entertainment persuasion: Explaining the persuasive effects of entertainment-education messages. *Communication Theory, 18*(3), 407–425. doi:10.1111/j.1468-2885.2008.00328.x

Moyer-Gusé, E., & Nabi, R. L. (2010). Explaining the persuasive effects of narrative in an entertainment television program: Overcoming resistance to persuasion. *Human Communication Research, 36*(1), 25–51. doi:10.1111/j.1468-2958.2009.01367.x

Mt. Auburn Associates. (2011). *Measuring Collaboration: The Benefits and Impacts of Nonprofit Centers.* Prepared for The NonprofitCenters Network. Retrieved from http://www.tides.org/fileadmin/user/ncn/Measuring_Collaboration_Executive_Summary.pdf

Multon, K. D., Brown, S. D., & Lent, R. W. (1991). Relation of self-efficacy beliefs to academic outcomes: A meta-analytic investigation. *Journal of Counseling Psychology, 38*(1), 30–38. doi:10.1037/0022-0167.38.1.30

Mumford, L. (1934). *Technics and Civilization.* New York: Harcourt Brace & Company.

Munson, L. (2013, December 31). New year, new workplace! SIOP announces the top 10 workplace trends for 2014. Retrieved from https://www.siop.org/article_view.aspx?article=1203

Muntean, C. I. (2011). Raising engagement in e-learning through gamification. *Proceedings of the 6th International Conference on Virtual Learning* (pp. 323-329). Retrieved from http://icvl.eu/2011/disc/icvl/documente/pdf/met/ICVL_ModelsAndMethodologies_paper42.pdf

Muntean, C. I. (2011). Raising engagement in e-learning through gamification. In *Proceedings of the 6th International Conference on Virtual Learning. ICVL,* (pp. 323-329).

Murray, J. H. (2006). Toward a cultural theory of gaming: Digital games and the co-evolution of media, mind, and culture. *Popular Communication, 4*(3), 185–202. doi:10.1207/s15405710pc0403_3

Murray, J. H. (2012). *Inventing the medium: Principles of interaction design as a cultural practice.* The MIT Press.

My Marriott Hotel™ opens its doors on Facebook: Marriott uses social media gaming to help attract tens of thousands of employees. (2011). *Marriott International, Inc.* Retrieved from http://news.marriott.com/2011/06/my-marriott-hotel-opens-its-doors-on-facebook.html

Myllylahti, M. (2014). Newspaper paywalls – the hype and the reality. *Digital journalism, 2*(2), 179-194.

Myron, D. (2012). *Going Against the Grain with Gamification and NLU.* CRM Magazine, 2.

Nardi, B. (2010). My life as a night elf priest: An anthropological account of world of warcraft. Ann Arbor, M.I.: University of Michigan Press.

Nauert, R. (2009). Leisure Play is important for human collaboration. PsychCentral. Retrieved from http://psychcentral.com/news/2009/04/17/leisure-play-is-important-for-human-collaboration/5398.html

Naughton, K. (2003). PIXELS to PAVEMENT. *Newsweek, 141*(10), 46.

Nel, F., & Westlund, O. (2012). THE 4C'S OF MOBILE NEWS: Channels, conversation, content and commerce. *Journalism Practice, 6*(5-6), 744–753. doi:10.1080/17512786.2012.667278

Nelson, E. (2013, October 16). *Gamification*. Opening remarks for the Education Technology Innovation Summit. Retrieved from www.youtube.com/watch?v=F6iBcvRuiQI

Netcentric Campaigns. (2013). *The Moving Maryland Forward Network | Year 2 Final Report*. Washington, DC: Casey.

Netcentric Campaigns. (2014). *PreventObesity.net Analytics February 2014*. Washington, DC: Brooks.

Networking for Policy Change: An Advocacy Training Manual. (1999). The Policy Project. Retrieved from http://www.policyproject.com/pubs/AdvocacyManual.pdf

Newman, J., & Oh, S. (2014). 8 things you should know about MOOCs. Retrieved from http://chronicle.com/article/8-Things-You-Should-Know-About/146901/

Nichani, M., & Rajamanickam, V. (2003). Interactive Visual Explainers–A Simple Classification. *Elearning post*. Retrieved from http://www.elearningpost.com/articles/archives/interactive_visual_explainers_a_simple_classification

Nicholson, S. (2012). *A user-centered theoretical framework for meaningful gamficiation*. Paper presented at the June 2012 meeting of Games+Learning+Society 8.0, Madison, WI.

Nicholson, S. (2012). *A User-Centered Theoretical Framework for Meaningful Gamification*. Proceedings of Games+Learning+Society 8.0. Madison, WI.

Nicholson, S. (2013). *Exploring gamification techniques for classroom management*. Paper presented at Games+Learning+Society 9.0, Madison, WI.

Nike +. (2014). Nike. Retrieved from https://secure-nikeplus.nike.com/plus/

Nippert-Eng, C. (2005). Boundary Play. *Space and Culture*, *8*(3), 302–324. doi:10.1177/1206331205277351

Nunes Castellar, E., Van Looy, J., Szmalec, A., & de Marez, L. (2014). Improving arithmetic skills through gameplay: Assessment of the effectiveness of an educational game in terms of cognitive and affective learning outcomes. *Information Sciences*, *264*, 19–31. doi:10.1016/j.ins.2013.09.030

Nunnally, J. C. (1978). *Psychometric theory* (2nd ed.). New York: McGraw-Hill.

O'Donnell, C. (2014). Getting played: Gamification, bullshit, and the rise of algorithmic surveillance. *Surveillance & Society*, *12*(3), 349–359.

O'Donovan, C. (2014, February 19). Are quizzes the new lists? What BuzzFeed's latest viral success means for publishing. *Nieman Journalism Lab*. Retrieved from http://www.niemanlab.org/2014/02/are-quizzes-the-new-lists-what-buzzfeeds-latest-viral-success-means-for-publishing/

O'Reilly, C. A. III, Chatman, J., & Caldwell, D. F. (1991). People and organizational culture: A profile comparison approach to assessing person-organization fit. *Academy of Management Journal*, *34*(3), 487–516. doi:10.2307/256404

O'Toole, J. (2014, February 28). Mobile apps overtake PC Internet usage in U.S. *CNN Money online*. Retrieved from http://money.cnn.com/2014/02/28/technology/mobile/mobile-apps-internet/

O'Brien, H. L., & Toms, E. G. (2007). What is user engagement? A conceptual framework for defining user engagement with technology. *Journal of the American Society for Information Science and Technology*, *59*(6), 938–955. doi:10.1002/asi.20801

Office of Naval Research. (2014). Game-based training and education. *U.S. Navy*. Fact sheet. Retrieved from http://www.onr.navy.mil/en/Media-Center/Fact-Sheets/Game-Based-Training.aspx

Ogan, C., Bashir, M., Camaj, L., Luo, Y., Gaddie, B., & Pennington, R. et al. (2009). Development communication: The state of research in an era of ICTs and globalization. *International Communication Gazette, 71*(8), 655–670. doi:10.1177/1748048509345060

Ones, D. S., & Viswesvaran, C. (1998). The effects of social desirability and faking on personality and integrity assessment for personnel selection. *Human Performance, 11*(2-3), 245–269. doi:10.1080/08959285.1998.9668033

Online game 'Cerberus' launching today to help relief effort in the Philippines uses VHR satellite imagery [Press Release]. (2013, November 14). European Space Imaging. Retrieved from http://www.directionsmag.com/pressreleases/online-game-cerberus-launching-today-to-help-relief-effort-in-the-philippin/367285

Online game "Food Force" Puts Players on Front Lines of Hunger. (2011, November 30). *World Food Program USA.* Retrieved from http://wfpusa.org/blog/online-game-food-force-puts-players-front-lines-hunger

Ordioni, J. (2013, April 26). Game on for employee gamification. *ERE Daily.* Retrieved from http://www.ere.net/2013/04/26/game-on-for-employee-gamification/

Organ, D. W. (1988). *Organizational citizenship behavior: The good soldier syndrome.* Lexington, MA, England: Lexington Books/D. C. Heath and Com.

Orosz, G., Farkas, D., & Roland-Lévy, C. (2013). Are competition and extrinsic motivation reliable predictors of academic cheating? *Frontiers in Psychology, 4*(87), 1–16. doi:10.3389/fpsyg.2013.00087 PMID:23450676

Owen's blog. (2011, October 20). Why gamification misses the point. [Blog post]. Retrieved from http://www.gurudigitalarts.com/tips/IXD/gamification

Paharia, R. (2013). *Loyalty 3.0: How to Revolutionize Customer and Employee Engagement with Big Data and Gamification.* McGraw Hill Professional.

Paharia, R. (2013). *Loyalty 3.0: How to revolutionize customer and employee engagement with big data and gamification.* McGraw-Hill.

Pajares, F. (2002). Overview of social cognitive theory and of self-efficacy. Retrieved from http://www.emory.edu/EDUCATION/mfp/eff.html

Palmer, D., Lunceford, S., & Patton, A.J. (2012). The engagement economy: How gamification is reshaping business. *Deloitte Review, 11.*

Palmer, D., Lunceford, S., & Patton, A. J. (2012). The engagement economy: How gamification is reshaping businesses. *Deloitte Review, 11,* 51–69.

Pappano, L. (2012, November 2). The Year of the MOOC. *New York Times.* Retrieved from http://www.nytimes.com/2012/11/04/education/edlife/massive-open-online-courses-are-multiplying-at-a-rapid-pace.html?pagewanted=all&_r=0

Paradise, A., & Patel, L. (2013). *State of the Industry: ASTD's Annual Review of Trends in Workplace Learning and Performance.* Alexandria, VA: ASTD.

Parker, J. (2007, June 8). Romney Strapped Dog to Car Roof. *ABC News.* Retrieved from http://abcnews.go.com/blogs/politics/2007/06/romney-strapped/

Parpart, J., Rai, S., & Staudt, K. (Eds.). (2002). *Rethinking empowerment: Gender and development in a global/local world.* New York, NY: Routledge.

Pashupati, K., Courtright, M. & Pettit, A. (2013, March 7-8). Battle Of The Scales: Examining Respondent Scale Usage across 10 Countries. Paper presented at the 2013 CASRO Online Research Conference, San Francisco.

Pearson, R. (2007). Reassessing paid work and women's empowerment: Lessons from the global economy. In A. Cornwall, E. Harrison, & A. Whitehead (Eds.), Feminisms in development: Contradictions, contestations and challenges, (201-213). London, UK: Zed Books.

Peng, W. (2006). *Using a computer game to promote a healthy life style to college students.* [Doctoral dissertation]. University of Southern California, Los Angeles, CA.

Peng, W. (2009). Design and evaluation of a computer game to promote a healthy diet for young adults. *Health Communication, 24*(2), 115–127. doi:10.1080/10410230802676490 PMID:19280455

Pereira, C. (2014, January 15). Steam tops 75 million users [Blog]. *IGN.* Retrieved from http://www.ign.com/articles/2014/01/15/steam-tops-75-million-users

Performance Management: Overview & History. (2014). *Office of Personnel Management.* Retrieved from http://www.opm.gov/policy-data-oversight/performance-management/overview-history/

Perlroth, N. (2013, March 24). Luring young Web warriors is priority. It's also a game. *The New York Times.* Retrieved from http://www.nytimes.com/2013/03/25/technology/united-states-wants-to-attract-hackers-to-public-sector.html

Perpetua, M. (2014, March 24). *Which Pop Star Should Be Your Best Friend? BuzzFeed.* Retrieved July 28, 2014, from http://www.buzzfeed.com/perpetua/which-pop-star-should-be-your-best-friend

Peters, C. (2012). Journalism to go: The changing spaces of news consumption. *Journalism Studies, Special Issue: The Future of Journalism 2011. Developments and Debates, 13*(5-6), 695–705.

Pew Research Center's Journalism Project Staff. (2014, March 26). Key Indicators in Media & News. Retrieved from http://www.journalism.org/2014/03/26/state-of-the-news-media-2014-key-indicators-in-media-and-news/

Phares, E. J. (1976). *Locus of control in personality.* Morristown, NJ: General Learning Press.

Picard, R. G. (2008). Shifts in newspaper advertising expenditures and their implications for the future of newspapers. *Journalism Studies, 9*(5), 704–716. doi:10.1080/14616700802207649

Pickering, A. (1995). The mangle of practice: Time, agency, & science. Chicago, I.L.: The University of Chicago Press.

Pierce, D. (2013, November 25). Any given Sunday: Inside the chaos and spectacle of the NFL on Fox. *The Verge.* Retrieved from http://www.theverge.com/2013/11/25/5141600/any-given-sunday-the-chaos-and-spectacle-of-nfl-on-fox

Pink, D. (2009). *Drive: The surprising truth about what motivates us.* Riverhead Books.

Pink, D. (2011). *Drive: the surprising truth about what motivates us.* New York, NY: Penguin Group, Inc.

Pintrich, P. R., & Schrauben, B. (1992). Students' motivational beliefs and their cognitive engagement in classroom academic tasks. In D. H. Schunk & J. L. Meece (Eds.), *Student Perceptions in the Classroom* (pp. 149–183). London: Routledge.

Pitcher, J. (2013, August 12). *German studio creates game based on Edward Snowden. Polygon.* Retrieved from http://www.polygon.com/2013/8/12/4613202/binji-create-game-based-on-edward-snowden

Play Mission US: A Cheyenne Odyssey. (2014). Games for Change. Retrieved from http://www.gamesforchange.org/play/mission-us-a-cheyenne-odyssey/

Playerthree (2005). *Food Force* [Flash game]. Retrieved from http://www.food-force.com/

Ployhart, R. E., & Moliterno, T. P. (2011). Emergence of the human capital resource: A multilevel model. *Academy of Management Review*, *36*(1), 127–150. doi:10.5465/AMR.2011.55662569

PopCap. (2010). Social gaming research. Information Solutions Group, p. 1-72. Retrieved from http://www.infosolutionsgroup.com/2010_popcap_social_gaming_research_results.pdf

Popp, E. (2014, May). Addressing practical challenges in developing game-like assessments. In *E. C. Popp* (Chair) & *C. Handler* (Discussant), *Challenges and innovations of using game-like assessments in selection*. Symposium presented at the 29th Annual Conference of the Society for Industrial and Organizational Psychology, Honolulu, HI.

Prensky, M. (2001). The games generations: How learners have changed. In *Digital game-based learning* (pp. 02-1-02-26). Retrieved from http://www.marcprensky.com/writing/prensky%20-%20ch2-digital%20game-based%20learning.pdf

Prensky, M. (2005). Computer games and learning: Digital game-based learning. In J. Raessens & J. Goldstein (Eds.), Handbook of computer game studies (pp. 97-122). Cambridge, M.A.: The MIT Press.

Prensky, M. (2005). Engage me or enrage me: What today's learners demand. *EDUCAUSE Review*, 60–64.

Prensky, M. (2006). *Don't bother me mom- I'm learning*. St. Paul, MN: Paragon House.

Priebatsch, S. (2010). The game layer on top of the world. *TED*. Retrieved from http://www.ted.com/talks/seth_priebatsch_the_game_layer_on_top_of_the_world.html

Priebatsch, S. (2010, July). The game layer on top of the world. *TED*. http://www.ted.com/talks/seth_priebatsch_the_game_layer_on_top_of_the_world

Priebatsch, S. (2012, August). When the game means freedom. *CNN*. Retrieved from http://edition.cnn.com/interactive/2012/08/tech/gaming.series/prison.html

Principles for the validation and use of personnel selection procedures (4th ed.). (2003). *Society for Industrial and Organizational Psychology, Inc.* Bowling Green, OH: Society for Industrial Organizational Psychology. Retrieved from http://www.siop.org/_principles/principles.pdf

Prior, M. (2007). *Post-Broadcast democracy. How media choice increases inequality in political involvement and polarizes elections*. Cambridge: Cambridge University Press.

Przybylski, A. K., Rigby, C., & Ryan, R. M. (2010). A motivational model of video game engagement. *Review of General Psychology*, *14*(2), 154–166. doi:10.1037/a0019440

Przybylski, A. K., Weinstein, N., Ryan, R. M., & Rigby, C. S. (2009). Having to versus wanting to play: Background and consequences of harmonious versus obsessive engagement in video games. *Cyberpsychology & Behavior*, *12*(5), 485–492. doi:10.1089/cpb.2009.0083 PMID:19772442

Puleston, J. (2012). What It Is and What It Is Not: 8 Things Everyone is Asking about Gamification. Retrieved from http://www.lightspeedresearchblog.com/data-quality/what-it-is-and-what-it-is-not-8-things-everyone-is-asking-about-gamification/

Puleston, J., & Eggers, M. (2012). Dimensions of Online Survey Data Quality: What Really Matters? [White paper]. *GMI-Lightspeed Research*. Retrieved from http://www.gmi-mr.com/uploads/file/PDFs/gmi_formatted_whitepaper_DimensionsWhatReallyMatters.pdf

Puleston, J. (2011). *Market Research Game Theory*. Bellevue, WA: Global Market Insight, Inc.

Putman, R. (2000). *Bowling alone: The collapse and revival of American community*. New York: Simon and Schuster.

Qin, G., Rau, P.-L. P., & Salvendy, G. (2009). Perception of interactivity: affects of four key variables in mobile advertising. *International Journal of Human-Computer Interaction, 25*(6), 479–505. doi:10.1080/10447310902963936

Qiu, L., Lin, H., Leung, A. K., & Tov, W. (2012). Putting Their Best Foot Forward: Emotional Disclosure on Facebook. *Cyberpsychology, Behavior, and Social Networking, 15*(10), 569–572. doi:10.1089/cyber.2012.0200 PMID:22924675

Quah, D. (2003). *Digital goods and the new economy. CEP discussion paper; CEPDP0563, 563.* London, UK: Centre for Economic Performance, London School of Economics and Political Science.

Raessens, J., & Goldstein, J. (2005). Introduction. In J. Raessens & J. Goldstein (Eds.), Handbook of computer game studies (pp. xi-xvii). Cambridge, M.A.: The MIT Press.

Rafaeli, S., & Ariel, Y. (2007). Assessing interactivity in computer-mediated research. In A. N. Joinson, K. Y. A. McKenna, T. Postmes, & U. D. Rieps (Eds.), *The Oxford handbook of internet psychology, 71--88.* Oxford University Press.

Rafiq, S. (2014, June 26). Gamification of thrones. *World Bank Blog.* Retrieved from http://blogs.worldbank.org/developmenttalk/gamification-thrones

Raftopoulos, M., & Walz, S. (2013, April). *Designing events as gameful and playful experiences.* Paper presented at the CHI 2013 Conference, Paris, France.

Raise the Village [Mobile app]. (2010). New Charity Era. Retrieved from http://purposefulgames.info/post/17528621162/raise-the-village

Rampell, C. (2014, January 26). Your next job application could involve a video game. *The New York Times.* Retrieved from http://www.nytimes.com/2014/01/26/magazine/your-next-job-application-could-involve-a-video-game.html?_r=2

Randel, J. M., Morris, B. A., Wetzel, C. D., & Whitehill, B. V. (1992). The effectiveness of games for educational purposes: A review of recent research. *Simulation & Gaming, 23*(3), 261–276. doi:10.1177/1046878192233001

Rao, L. (1963). Communication and development: A study of two Indian villages. Doctoral Dissertation. University of Minnesota, St. Paul.

Rao, V. (2013, April). *Challenges of Implementing Gamification for Behavior Change: Lessons Learned from the Design of Blues Buddies.* Paper presented at the CHI 2013 Conference, Paris, France.

Raynauld, L. (2005). Click reading: Screenwriting and screen-reading practices in film and multimedia fictions. In J. Raessens & J. Goldstein (Eds.), Handbook of computer game studies (pp. 81-95). Cambridge, M.A.: The MIT Press.

Razavi, S., & Miller, C. (1995, February). From WID to GAD: Conceptual shifts in the Women and Development discourse. Presented to the United Nations Research Institute for Social Development Programme. Retrieved from http://iupuebla.com/Doctorado/Docto_Generoyderecho/MA_Doctorado_Genero/MA_from%20wid%20to%20gad.pdf

Red Bull Musketeers: Red Bull. (n. d.). *Red Bull.* Retrieved from http://www.redbullusa.com/cs/Satellite/en_US/Red-Bull-Musketeers/001243067960808

Reese, S. D., & Lee, J. K. (2012). Understanding the content of news media. In H. Semetko & M. Scammell (Eds.) The Sage handbook of political communication. London: SAGE Publications. doi:10.4135/9781446201015.n21

Reeve, J., & Deci, E. L. (1996). Elements of the competitive situation that affect intrinsic motivation. *Personality and Social Psychology Bulletin, 22*(1), 24–33. doi:10.1177/0146167296221003

Reeves, B., & Read, J. L. (2010, April 27). Ten ingredients of great games. *ASTD.org.* Retrieved from http://www.astd.org/Publications/Newsletters/ASTD-Links/ASTD-Links-Articles/2010/04/Ten-Ingredients-of-Great-Games

Reeves, B., & Read, J. L. (2009). *Total engagement: How games and virtual worlds are changing the way people work and businesses compete*. Boston, MA: Harvard Business Publishing.

Reeves, B., & Read, J. L. (2009). *Total engagement: Using games and virtual worlds to change the way people work and businesses compete*. New York, NY: Harvard Business School Press Books.

Reinemann, C., Stanyer, J., Scherr, S., & Legnante, G. (2011). Hard and soft news: A review of concepts, operationalizations and key findings. *Journalism, 13*(2), 221–239. doi:10.1177/1464884911427803

Rey, P. J. (2012). Gamification, Playbor & Exploitation. Retrieved April 25, 2014, from http://pjrey.wordpress.com/2012/12/27/gamification-playbor-exploitation/

Richter, G., Raban, D. R., & Rafaeli, S. (2015). Studying gamification: The effect of rewards and incentives on motivation. In T. Reiners & L. C. Woods (Eds.), *Gamification in Education and Business* (pp. 21–46). Springer International Publishing. doi:10.1007/978-3-319-10208-5_2

Ritterfeld, U., Cody, M., & Vorderer, P. (Eds.). (2009). *Serious Games: Mechanisms and Effects*. New York, London: Routledge.

Rizzo, S. (2008). The promise of cell phones: from people power to technological nanny. *Convergence (London), 14*(2), 135–143. doi:10.1177/1354856507087940

Roberts, J. M., Arth, M. J., & Bush, R. R. (1959). Games in Culture. American Anthropologist, *61*(4), 597–605.

Robinson, D., & Bellotti, V. (2013). A preliminary taxonomy of gamification elements for varying anticipated commitment. *Proceedings of ACM CHI 2013 Workshop on Designing Gamification: Creating Gameful and Playful Experiences*. Retrieved from http://gamification-research.org/wp-content/uploads/2013/03/Robinson_Bellotti.pdf

Robinson, J. (2013, November 13). Creators of Myst hope for come-back with new fan-funded game. *NW News Network*. Retrieved from http://nwnewsnetwork.org/post/creators-myst-hope-comeback-new-fan-funded-game

Robinson, D., & Bellotti, V. (2013). A preliminary taxonomy of gamification elements for varying anticipated commitment.*Proceedings of the CHI 2013 Designing Gamification Workshop*, Paris, France.

Rodgers, R., Hunter, J. E., & Rogers, D. L. (1993). Influence of top management commitment on management program success. *The Journal of Applied Psychology, 78*(1), 151–155. doi:10.1037/0021-9010.78.1.151

Roeger, K., Blackwood, A., & Pettijohn, S. (2010). *Nonprofit Almanac 2012*. Urban Institute Press.

Rogers, E. M. (1973). *Communication strategies for family planning*. New York, NY: Free Press.

Rogers, E. M. (1976). Where are we in Understanding the Diffusion of Innovations? In W. Schramm & D. Lerner (Eds.), *Communication and Change* (pp. 204–222). Honolulu: University Press of Hawaii.

Rogers, E. M., & Hardt, W. B. (2002). The histories of international, intercultural and development communication. In W. B. Gudykunst & B. Mody (Eds.), *Handbook of international and intercultural communication*. Thousand Oaks, CA: Sage Publications.

Rolland, A., & Eastman, J. (2011). *The gamification of everything. Analyst briefing*. PWC PricewaterhouseCoopers LLP.

Ronald, F., & Jens, F. (2001). The effects of promotion and prevention cues on creativity. *Journal of Personality and Social Psychology, 81*(6), 1001–1013. doi:10.1037/0022-3514.81.6.1001 PMID:11761303

Rooij, A. J., & van, . (2009). Compulsive internet use: The role of online gaming and other internet applications. *The Journal of Adolescent Health, 47*(1), 51–57. doi:10.1016/j.jadohealth.2009.12.021 PMID:20547292

Rosas, R., Nussbaum, M., Cumsille, P., Marianov, V., Correa, M., & Flores, P. et al. (2003). Beyond Nintendo: Design and assessment of educational video games for first and second grade students. *Computers & Education, 40*(1), 71–94. doi:10.1016/S0360-1315(02)00099-4

Rosen, J. (2006, June 27). The people formerly known as the audience. *Press Think*. Retrieved from http://archive.pressthink.org/2006/06/27/ppl_frmr.html

Rosewater, M. (2002a, March 11). Our three favorite players: Timmy, Johnny, and Spike. *Wizards of the Coast*. Retrieved from http://archive.wizards.com/Magic/Magazine/Article.aspx?x=mtgcom/daily/mr11

Rosewater, M. (2002b, March 11). Our three favorite players: Timmy, Johnny, and Spike. *Wizards of the Coast*. Retrieved from http://archive.wizards.com/Magic/Magazine/Article.aspx?x=mtgcom/daily/mr11b

Rotter, J. B. (1966). Generalized expectancies for internal versus external control of reinforcement. *Psychological Monographs, 80*(1), 1–28. doi:10.1037/h0092976 PMID:5340840

Rotter, J. B. (1975). Some problems and misconceptions related to the construct of internal versus external control of reinforcement. *Journal of Consulting and Clinical Psychology, 43*(1), 56–67. doi:10.1037/h0076301

Rowley, R. (2012). *Health Care and Wellness Are Converging Concepts. EHR Bloggers*. Practice Fusion.

Ruey, S. (2010). A case study of constructivist instructional strategies for adult online learning. *British Journal of Educational Technology, 41*(5), 706–720. doi:10.1111/j.1467-8535.2009.00965.x

Ruffino, P. (2014). From engagement to life, or: How to do things with gamification? In M. Fuchs et al. (Eds.), *Rethinking gamification* (pp. 47–60).

Ruggiero, T. (2000). Uses and gratifications theory in the 21st century. *Mass Communication & Society, 3*(1), 3–37. doi:10.1207/S15327825MCS0301_02

Rughinis, R. (2013). Gamification for productive interaction: Reading and working with the gamification debate in education. Presented at the June 2013 Information Systems and Technologies (CISTI) 8th Iberian Conference. Retrieved from http://www.academia.edu/5758624/Gamification_for_Productive_Interaction._Reading_and_Working_with_the_Gamification_Debate_in_Education

Ruhfus, J. (2014). Why we decided to gamify investigative journalism at Al Jazeera. Retrieved from https://medium.com/@julianaruhfus/pushing-the-boundaries-of-news-why-we-decided-to-gamify-investigations-and-current-affairs-db6b13d64a46

Ruiz, S., York, A., Stein, M., Keating, N., & Santiago, K. (2006). *Darfur is Dying* [Flash game]. Retrieved from htpp://www.darfurisdying.com

Rushkoff, D. (2005). Renaissance now! The gamers' perspective. In J. Raessens & J. Goldstein (Eds.), Handbook of computer game studies (pp. 415-421). Cambridge, M.A.: The MIT Press.

Ryan, R. M., & Deci, E. L. (2000). Self-determination theory and the facilitation of intrinsic motivation, social development, and well-being. *The American Psychologist, 55*, 68–78. doi: 10.1037110003-066X.55.1.68

Ryan, A., & Ployhart, R. E. (2014). A century of selection. *Annual Review of Psychology, 65*(1), 693–717. doi:10.1146/annurev-psych-010213-115134 PMID:24050188

Ryan, M.-L. (1999). Immersion vs. interactivity: Virtual reality and literary theory. *SubStance, 28*(2), 110–137. doi:10.1353/sub.1999.0015

Ryan, R. M., & Deci, E. L. (2000). Self-determination theory and the facilitation of intrinsic motivation, social development, and well-being. *The American Psychologist, 55*(1), 68–78. doi:10.1037/0003-066X.55.1.68 PMID:11392867

Ryan, R. M., & Deci, E. L. (2001). On happiness and human potentials: A review of research on hedonic and eudaimonic well-being. In S. Fiske (Ed.), *Annual Review of Psychology 52* (pp. 141–166). Palo Alto, CA: Annual Reviews, Inc. doi:10.1146/annurev.psych.52.1.141

Ryan, R. M., Rigby, C. S., & Przybylski, A. K. (2006). Motivational pull of video games: A self-determination theory approach. *Motivation and Emotion, 30*(4), 347–365. doi:10.1007/s11031-006-9051-8

Rynes, S. L. (1991). Recruitment, job choice, and post-hire consequences: A call for new research directions. In M. D. Dunnette & L. M. Hough (Eds.), *Handbook of industrial and organizational psychology* (2nd ed., Vol. 2, pp. 399–444). Palo Alto, CA, US: Consulting Psychologists Press.

Sailer, M., Hense, J., Mandl, H., & Klevers, M. (2013). Psychological Perspectives on Motivation through Gamification. *Interaction Design and Architecture(s). Journal, 19,* 28–37. Retrieved from http://www.fml.mw.tum.de/

Salas, E., & Cannon-Bowers, J. (2001). The science of training: A decade of progress. *Annual Review of Psychology, 52*(1), 471–499. doi:10.1146/annurev.psych.52.1.471 PMID:11148314

Salas, E., Cannon-Bowers, J., Rhodenizer, L., & Bowers, C. A. (1999). In G. R. Ferris (Ed.), *Training in organizations: Myths, misconceptions, and mistaken assumptions* (pp. 123–161). US: Elsevier Science/JAI Press.

Salen, K., & Zimmerman, E. (2003). *Rules of Play.* Cambridge: MIT Press.

Salen, K., & Zimmerman, E. (2004). *Rules of play.* Cambridge: MIT Press.

Salen, K., & Zimmerman, E. (2004). *Rules of play: Game design fundamentals.* Cambridge, MA: The MIT Press.

Salgado, J. F., & Moscoso, S. (2002). Comprehensive meta-analysis of the construct validity of the employment interview. *European Journal of Work and Organizational Psychology, 11*(3), 299–324. doi:10.1080/13594320244000184

Sarner, A. (2013, September 13). Why game based marketing is relevant for anyone – who markets anything. Retrieved from http://blogs.gartner.com/adam-sarner/2013/09/13/why-game-based-marketing-is-relevant-for-anyone-who-markets-anything/

Scannell, P. (2007). *Media and Communication.* London: Sage.

Schell, J. (2010). *Visions of the Gameocolypse.* Proceedings of Gameification Summit. San Francisco, CA.

Schell, J. [msc81]. (2010, July 17). *Jesse Schell @ DICE2010 (Part 1)* [Video file]. Retrieved from http://www.youtube.com/watch?v=DLwskDkDPUE

Schell, J. (2008). *The art of game design.* Burlington, MA: Morgan Kaufman.

Schell, J. (2008). *The Art of Game Design: A Book of Lenses.* Burlington, MA: Elsevier.

Scheufele, D., Shanahan, J., & Kim, S.-H. (2002). Who cares about local politics? Media influences on local political involvement, issue awareness, and attitude strength. *Journalism & Mass Communication Quarterly, 79*(2), 427–444. doi:10.1177/107769900207900211

Schleiner, A.-M. (2001, June). Does Lara Croft wear fake polygons? Gender and gender-role subversion in computer adventure games. *Leonardo, 34*(3), 221–226. doi:10.1162/002409401750286976

Schmidt, F. L., & Hunter, J. E. (1998). The validity and utility of selection methods in personnel psychology: Practical and theoretical implications of 85 years of research findings. *Psychological Bulletin, 124*(2), 262–274. doi:10.1037/0033-2909.124.2.262

Schmitt, N., Ford, J. K., & Stults, D. M. (1986). Changes in self-perceived ability as a function of performance in an assessment center. *Journal of Occupational Psychology, 59*(4), 327–335. doi:10.1111/j.2044-8325.1986.tb00233.x

Schneider, B. (1987). The people make the place. *Personnel Psychology, 40*(3), 437–453. doi:10.1111/j.1744-6570.1987.tb00609.x

Schoech, D., Boyas, J. F., Black, B. M., & Nada, E. (2013). Gamification for behavior change: Lessons from developing a social, multiuser, web-tablet based prevention same for youths. *Journal of Technology in Human Services, 31*(3), 197–217. doi:10.1080/15228835.2013.812512

Schooling, P., & Toth, M. (2013). *The Critical Importance of a Common Language of Instruction*. Learning Science International.

Schrader, C., & Bastiaens, T. J. (2012). The influence of virtual presence: Effects on experienced cognitive load and learning outcomes in educational computer games. *Computers in Human Behavior, 28*(2), 648–658. doi:10.1016/j.chb.2011.11.011

Schramm, W. (1964). *Mass Media and National Development*. Stanford, CA: Stanford University Press.

Schroder, K. C. (2014). News media old and new. *Journalism Studies*. doi:10.1080/1461670X.2014.890332

Schrodt, P., Witt, P. L., Myers, S. A., Turman, P. D., Barton, M. H., & Jernberg, K. A. (2008, April). Learner empowerment and teacher evaluations as functions of teacher power use in the college classroom. *Communication Education, 57*(2), 180–200. doi:10.1080/03634520701840303

Schudson, M. (1978). *Discovering the News*. New York, NY: Bacis Books.

Schudson, M. (1997). Toward a troubleshooting manual for journalism history. *Journalism & Mass Communication Quarterly, 74*(3), 463–476. doi:10.1177/107769909707400302

Schudson, M. (2003). *The sociology of news*. New York: Norton.

Schultz, T. (1999). Interactive options in online journalism: A content analysis of 100 US newspapers. *Journal of Computer-Mediated Communication, 5*(1), 0.

Scofidio, B. (2012). Get Serious About Gamification. *Corporate Meetings & Incentives, 31*(7), 2.

Seay, A. F., Jerome, W. J., Lee, K. S., & Kraut, R. E. (2004). Project massive: A study of online gaming communities. In E. Dykstra-Erickson, & M. Tscheligi (Eds.) *Proceedings of CHI EA '04 Extended Abstracts on Human Factors in Computing Systems* (pp. 1421-1424). New York, NY: ACM. doi:10.1145/985921.986080

Seib, P. (2001). *Going live. Getting the news right in a real-time online world*. Lanham: Rowman & Littlefield.

Sela, M., Lavie, T., Inbar, O., Oppenheim, I., & Meyer, J. (2014). Personalizing news content: An experimental study. *Journal of the Association for Information Science and Technology*, n/a–n/a. doi:10.1002/asi.23167

Selinger, E. (2012, March 9). Why It's OK to Let Apps Make You a Better Person. *The Atlantic*. Retrieved from http://www.theatlantic.com/technology/archive/2012/03/why-its-ok-to-let-apps-make-you-a-better-person/254246/

Selye, H. (1964). *From dream to discovery*. New York, NY: McGraw-Hill.

Sen, A. (1999). *Development as freedom*. Oxford, UK: Oxford University Press.

Sennott, S. (2005). Gaming the Ad. *Newsweek, 145*(5), E2-E2.

Seounmi, Y., Lee, M., & Doyle, K. O. (2003). Lifestyles of online gamers: A psychographic approach. *Journal of Interactive Advertising, 3*(2), 49–56. doi:10.1080/15252019.2003.10722073

Shaer, M. (2012). Game of Life. *Polar Science, 280*(2), 54–77.

Shaffer, D. W. (2004, June). Epistemic frames and islands of expertise: Learning from infusion experiences. Paper presented at the International Conference of the Learning Sciences (ICLS), Santa Monica, CA. Retrieved from http://epistemicgames.org/cv/papers/epistemicframesicls04.pdf

Shaffer, D. W., Squire, K. R., & Gee, J. P. (2004). Video games and the future of learning. Retrieved from http://www.academiccolab.org/resources/gappspaper1.pdf

Shaffer, D. W. (2005). Epistemic frames for epistemic games. *Computers & Education, 43*, 223–234.

Shaker, L. (2014). Dead newspapers and citizens' civic engagement. *Political Communication, 31*(1), 131–148. doi:10.1080/10584609.2012.762817

Sheldon, L. (2010). Syllabus [Blog post]. Retrieved from http://gamingtheclassroom.wordpress.com/syllabus/

Sheldon, K. M., & Filak, V. (2008). Manipulating autonomy, competence and relatedness support in a game-learning context: New evidence that all three needs matter. *The British Journal of Social Psychology, 47*(2), 267–283. doi:10.1348/014466607X238797 PMID:17761025

Shelley, R. (1989). *The Lottery Encyclopedia*. Austin, TX: Byron Publishing Services.

Shepard, S. (2012, August 6). Sorry, Wrong Number. *National Journal*. Retrieved from http://www.nationaljournal.com/magazine/who-responds-to-telephone-polls-anymore-20120719

Sherry, J. L., Lucas, K., Greenberg, B., & Lachlan, K. (2006). Video game uses and gratifications as predictors of use and game preference. In P. Vorderer & J. Bryant (Eds.), *Playing computer games: Motives, responses, and consequences* (pp. 213–224). Mahwah, NJ: Lawrence Erlbaum.

Shoemaker, P. J., & Reese, S. D. (1996). *Mediating the message: Theories of influences on mass media content*. White Plains: Longman.

Short, J. E. (2013). *How much media? 2013: Report on American consumers*. Global Information Industry Center, UC San Diego. Available at http://hmi.ucsd.edu/howmuchinfo.php

Shortz, W. (Ed.). (2006). *The New York Times everyday Sunday crossword puzzles: America's most popular crosswords anytime, anywhere*. Macmillan.

Sicart, M. (2008). Defining Game Mechanics. *Game Studies, 8*(2). Retrieved from http://gamestudies.org/0802/articles/sicart

Sicart, M. (2008, September 25-27). Newsgames: Theory and design. *Proceedings of the 7th International Conference of Entertainment Computing*, (pp. 27-33), Pittsburgh, PA, USA. Springer.

Sicart, M. (2008, September). Newsgames: Theory and Design.*Proceedings of the 7th International Conference on Entertainment Computing* (pp. 27-33). Springer-Verlag.

Sidelinger, R. J., Bolen, D. M., Frisby, B. N., & McMullen, A. L. (2011, July). When instructors misbehave: An examination of student-to-student connectedness as a mediator in the college classroom. *Communication Education, 60*(3), 340–361. doi:10.1080/03634523.2011.554991

Siitonen, M., & Varsaluoma, J. (2013). "I'm so going to nuke Helsinki" - Newsgames in the Nordic media landscape. *Proceedings of DiGRA 2013: DeFragging Game Studies.*

Simoes, J., Redondo, R. D., & Vilas, A. F. (2013). A social gamification framework for a K-6 learning platform. *Computers in Human Behavior, 29*(2), 345–353. doi:10.1016/j.chb.2012.06.007

Simon, S. (2014, February 8). What a week in Sochi, Russia! *Weekend Edition - National Public Radio.*

Simon, B. (2007). What if Baudrillard was a Gamer?: Introduction to a Special Section on Baudrillard and Game Studies. *Games and Culture, 2*(4), 355–357. doi:10.1177/1555412007309535

Singer, J. B. (2004). Strange bedfellows: The diffusion of convergence in four news organizations. *Journalism Studies, 5*(1), 3–18. doi:10.1080/1461670032000174701

Singer, J. B. (2008). Five Ws and an H: Digital challenges in newspaper newsrooms and boardrooms. *International Journal on Media Management, 10*(3), 122–129. doi:10.1080/14241270802262468

Singh, A., Taneja, A., & Mangalaraj, G. (2009). Creating online surveys: Some wisdom from the trenches tutorial. *IEEE Transactions on Professional Communication, 52*(2), 197–212. doi:10.1109/TPC.2009.2017986

Singhal, A., & Rogers, E. M. (1999). *Entertainment-education: A communication strategy for social change.* Mahwah, NJ: Lawrence Erlbaum Associates, I.

Siwek, S. E. (2014). *Video games in the 21st century: The 2014 report.* Washington, D.C.: The Entertainment Software Association.

Skalski, P., Tamborini, R., Shelton, A., Buncher, M., & Lindmark, P. (2011). Mapping the road to fun: Natural video game controllers, presence, and game enjoyment. *New Media & Society, 13*(2), 224–242. doi:10.1177/1461444810370949

Skinner, B. F. (1948). 'Superstition' in the pigeon. *Journal of Experimental Psychology, 38*(2), 168–172. doi:10.1037/h0055873 PMID:18913665

Skinner, B. F. (1953). *Science and human behavior.* Oxford, England: Macmillan.

Skinner, B. F. (1958). Teaching machines. *Science, 128*(3330), 969–977. doi:10.1126/science.128.3330.969 PMID:13592277

Skinner, B. F. (1968). *The technology of teaching.* Englewood Cliffs, NJ: Prentice-Hall.

Sleep, D., & Puleston, J. (2011). *Measuring the Value of Respondent Engagement: Summary of Research Findings.* Bellevue, WA: Global Market Insight, Inc.

Smith, (2014, April 1). This is what Candy Crush Saga does to your brain [Blog]. *The Guardian.* Retrieved from http://www.theguardian.com/science/blog/2014/apr/01/candy-crush-saga-app-brain

Smith, A. (2011). Why Americans Use Social Media. *Pew Internet.* Pew Research Center, Retrieved from http://www.pewinternet.org/files/old-media/Files/Reports/2011/Why%20Americans%20Use%20Social%20Media.pdf

Smith, A. (2014, February 3). 6 new facts about Facebook. Retrieved from http://www.pewresearch.org/fact-tank/2014/02/03/6-new-facts-about-facebook/

Smith, R. (n.d.). *The future of work is play: Global shifts suggest rise in productivity games.* Retrieved from http://www.42projects.org/docs/The_Future_of_Work_is_Play.pdf

Smither, J. W., Reilly, R. R., Millsap, R. E., Pearlman, K., & Stoffey, R. W. (1993). Applicant reactions to selection procedures. *Personnel Psychology, 46*(1), 49–76. doi:10.1111/j.1744-6570.1993.tb00867.x

Smith, P. L., & Ragan, T. J. (2005). *Instructional design* (3rd ed.). Hoboken, NJ: Wiley.

Smith, R. (2010). The long history of gaming in military training. *Simulation & Gaming*, *41*(1), 6–19. doi:10.1177/1046878109334330

Snyder, E., & Hartig, J. R. (2013). Gamification of board review: A residency curricular innovation. *Medical Education*, *47*(5), 524–525. doi:10.1111/medu.12190 PMID:23574079

Society for Human Resource Management. (2014, January 22). Future insights: The top trends for 2014 according to SHRM's HR subject matter expert panels. Retrieved from http://www.shrm.org/Research/FutureWorkplaceTrends/Documents/13-0724%202014%20Panel%20Trends%20Report%20v4.pdf

Society for Industrial and Organizational Psychology. (2003). *Principles for the validation and use of personnel selection procedures*. Retrieved from http://www.siop.org/_principles/principles.pdf

Sohn, D., Ci, C., & Lee, B. K. (2007). The moderating effects of expectation on the patterns of the interactivity-attitude relationship. *Journal of Advertising*, *36*(3), 109–119. doi:10.2753/JOA0091-3367360308

Sonmez, J. (2011, April 13). Why Rules Rule. Elegant Code blog. *Elegantcode.com*. Retrieved from Elegantcode.com/2011/04/13/why-rules-rule/

Spariosu, M. (1989). *Dionysus Reborn*. Ithaca, N.Y.: Cornell University Press.

Sparks, C., & Tulloch, J. (2000). *Tabloid tales. Global debates over media standards*. Lanham: Rowman & Littlefield.

Spence, M. (1973). Job market signaling. *The Quarterly Journal of Economics*, *87*(3), 355–374. doi:10.2307/1882010

Spicer, A., Alvesson, M., & Kärreman, D. (2009). Critical performativity: The unfinished business of critical management studies. *Human Relations*, *62*(4), 537–560. doi:10.1177/0018726708101984

Spiegel, S., Grant-Pillow, H., & Higgins, E. T. (2004). How regulatory fit enhances motivational strength during goal pursuit. *European Journal of Social Psychology*, *34*(1), 39–54. doi:10.1002/ejsp.180

Spitzberg, B. H. (1983, July). Communication competence as knowledge, skill and impression. *Communication Education*, *32*(3), 323–329. doi:10.1080/03634528309378550

Sprague, J. (1992, April). Critical perspectives on teacher empowerment. *Communication Education*, *41*(2), 181–203. doi:10.1080/03634529209378879

Sprecher, S., Treger, S., Wondra, J. D., Hilaire, N., & Wallpe, K. (2013). Taking turns: Reciprocal self-disclosure promotes liking in initial interactions. *Journal of Experimental Social Psychology*, *49*(5), 860–866. doi:10.1016/j.jesp.2013.03.017

Squire, K. (2002). Cultural framing of computer/video games. *Game Studies, 2*(1). Retrieved from http://gamestudies.org/0102/squire/%3fref%3dHadiZayifla

Squire, K. R. (2002). Cultural framing of computer / video games. *The International Journal of Computer Game Research, 2*. Retrieved from http://gamestudies.org/0102/squire/

Squire, K. (2003). Video games in education. *International Journal of Intelligent Games & Simulation*, *2*(1), 49–62.

Squire, K. (2006). From content to context: Videogames as designed experience. *Educational Researcher*, *35*(8), 19–29. doi:10.3102/0013189X035008019

Stajkovic, A. D., & Luthans, F. (1998). Social cognitive theory and self-efficacy: Going beyond traditional motivational and behavioral approaches. *Organizational Dynamics*, *26*(4), 62–74. doi:10.1016/S0090-2616(98)90006-7

Stanley, R. (2014, March 24). Top 25 best examples of gamification in business, *ClickPedia: A ClickSoftware Blog*. Retrieved from http://blogs.clicksoftware.com/clickipedia/top-25-best-examples-of-gamification-in-business/

Stapleton, A. J. (2004). Serious games: Serious opportunities. Proceedings of Australian Game Developers' Conference 2004, Academic Summit, Melbourne.

Statista, daily time spent playing video games per capita in the United States in 2008, 2013 and 2018 (in minutes). (2014a). *Statista*. Retrieved from http://www.statista.com/statistics/186960/time-spent-with-videogames-in-the-us-since-2002/

Statista, global video games revenue from 2012 to 2015 (in billion U.S. dollars). (2014b). *Statista*. Retrieved from http://www.statista.com/statistics/237187/global-video-games-revenue/

Steeves, H. L. & Kwami, J. (in press). ICT4D, gender divides and development: The case of Ghana.

Steinkuehler, C. A. (2006). The Mangle of Play. *Games and Culture*, *1*(3), 199–213. doi:10.1177/1555412006290440

Steinkuehler, C. A., & Williams, D. (2006). Where everybody knows your (screen) name: Online games as "third place". *Journal of Computer-Mediated Communication*, *11*(4), 885–909. doi:10.1111/j.1083-6101.2006.00300.x

Stevens, S. H. (2013). How gamification and behavior science can drive social change one employee at a time. In A. Marcus (Ed.) *Design, User Experience, and Usability. Health, Learning, Playing, Cultural, and Cross-Cultural User Experience.Proceedings of Second International Conference, DUXU 2013* (pp. 597-601). New York, NY: Springer. doi:10.1007/978-3-642-39241-2_65

Stieglitz, S., & Dang-Xuan, L. (2013). Emotions and Information Diffusion in Social Media—Sentiment of Microblogs and Sharing Behavior. *Journal of Management Information Systems*, *29*(4), 217–248. doi:10.2753/MIS0742-1222290408

Stott, A., & Neustaedter, C. Analysis of gamification in education. Retrieved from http://carmster.com/clab/uploads/Main/Stott-Gamification.pdf

Strömbäck, J., Djerf-Pierre, M., & Shehata, A. (2012). The dynamics of political interest and news media consumption: A longitudinal perspective. *International Journal of Public Opinion Research*.

Subrahmanyam, K., & Greenfield, P. (1994). Effect of video game practice on spatial skills in girls and boys. *Journal of Applied Developmental Psychology*, *15*(1), 13–32. doi:10.1016/0193-3973(94)90004-3

Subrahmanyam, K., Greenfield, P., Kraut, R., & Gross, E. (2001). The impact of computer use on children's and adolescent's development. *Applied Developmental Psychology*, *22*(1), 7–30. doi:10.1016/S0193-3973(00)00063-0

Sukoco, B. M., & Wu, W.-Y. (2011). The effects of advergames on consumer telepresence and attitudes: A comparison of products with search and experience attributes. *Expert Systems with Applications*, *38*(6), 7396–7406. doi:10.1016/j.eswa.2010.12.085

Sundar, S. S., Xu, Q., Bellur, S., Oh, J., & Jia, H. (2011). Beyond Pointing and Clicking: How Do Newer Interaction Modalities Affect User Engagement? Proceedings of CHI '11 Extended Abstracts on Human Factors in Computing Systems (pp. 1477–1482). New York, NY, USA: ACM; doi:10.1145/1979742.1979794

Sundar, S. (2008). The MAIN model: A heuristic approach to understanding technology effects on credibility. In M. Metzger & A. Flanagin (Eds.), *Digital media, youth, and credibility* (pp. 73–100). Cambridge, MA: MIT Press.

Sundar, S. S., Bellur, S., Oh, J., Jia, H., & Kim, H.-S. (2014). Theoretical Importance of Contingency in Human-Computer Interaction Effects of Message Interactivity on User Engagement. *Communication Research*. doi:10.1177/0093650214534962

Sundar, S. S., Kalyanaraman, S., & Brown, J. (2003). Explicating Web Site interactivity impression formation effects in political campaign sites. *Communication Research*, *30*(1), 30–59. doi:10.1177/0093650202239025

Sundar, S. S., & Limperos, A. M. (2013). Uses and grats 2.0: New gratifications for new media. *Journal of Broadcasting & Electronic Media, 57*(4), 504–525. doi:10.1080/08838151.2013.845827

Sundar, S. S., & Marathe, S. S. (2010). Personalization Versus Customization: The Importance of Agency, Privacy, and Power Usage. *Human Communication Research, 36*(3), 298–322. doi:10.1111/j.1468-2958.2010.01377.x

Sundar, S. S., & Nass, C. (2001). Conceptualizing sources in online news. *Journal of Communication, 51*(1), 52–72. doi:10.1111/j.1460-2466.2001.tb02872.x

Super Mario Wiki. (2014, July 30). Retrieved from http://www.mariowiki.com/Main_Page

Surveys: Tracking Opinion. Special Report. (2011). National Science Foundation. Retrieved from http://www.nsf.gov/news/special_reports/survey/index.jsp?id=question

Susi, T., Johannesson, M., & Backlund, P. (2007). *Serious games: An overview* [Technical Report HS- IKI -TR-07-001]. School of Humanities and Informatics University of Skövde, Sweden. Retrieved July 8, 2014, from http://www.diva-portal.org/smash/get/diva2:2416/FULLTEXT01.pdf

Sutton-Smith, B. (1997). *The Ambiguity of Play*. Cambridge: Harvard University Press.

Swallow, E. (2012, September 18). Can gamification make customer support fun? *Forbes.* Retrieved from http://www.forbes.com/fdc/welcome_mjx.shtml

Swan, C. (2012). Gamification: A new way to shape behavior. *Communication World, 29*(3), 13–14.

Sydell, E., & Brodbeck, C. (2014, May). The predictive power of game-like assessments compared to traditional tests. In *E. C. Popp* (Chair) & C. Handler (Discussant), *Challenges and innovations of using game-like assessments in selection.* Symposium presented at the 29th Annual Conference of the Society for Industrial and Organizational Psychology, Honolulu, HI.

Sydell, L. (2013, November 29). For advocacy groups, video games are the next frontier. NPR. Retrieved from http://www.npr.org/blogs/alltechconsidered/2013/11/29/247515389/for-advocacy-groups-video-games-are-the-next-frontier

Take-Two Interactive Software, Inc. Reports Record Results for Fiscal Year 2014. (2014). Take-Two Interactive Software, Inc. Retrieved from http://ir.take2games.com/phoenix.zhtml?c=86428&p=irol-newsArticle&ID=1930485&highlight=

Tamborini, R., Bowman, N. D., Eden, A., Grizzard, M., & Organ, A. (2010). Defining media enjoyment as the satisfaction of intrinsic needs. *Journal of Communication, 60*(4), 758–777. doi:10.1111/j.1460-2466.2010.01513.x

Tamborini, R., Grizzard, M., Bowman, N. D., Reinecke, L., Lewis, R. J., & Eden, A. (2011). Media enjoyment as need satisfaction: The contribution of hedonic and nonhedonic needs. *Journal of Communication, 61*(6), 1025–1042. doi:10.1111/j.1460-2466.2011.01593.x

Tamir, D. I., & Mitchell, J. P. (2012). Disclosing information about the self is intrinsically rewarding. *Proceedings of the National Academy of Sciences of the United States of America, 109*(21), 8038–8043. doi:10.1073/pnas.1202129109 PMID:22566617

Tandoc, E. C. Jr. (2014). Journalism is twerking? How Web analytics is changing the process of gatekeeping. *New Media & Society, 16*(4), 559–575. doi:10.1177/1461444814530541

Tanes, Z., & Cemalcılar, Z. (2010). Learning from SimCity: An empirical study of Turkish adolescents. *Journal of Adolescence, 33*(5), 731–739. doi:10.1016/j.adolescence.2009.10.007 PMID:19931157

Tang, S., & Hall, V. C. (1995). The overjustification effect: A meta-analysis. *Applied Cognitive Psychology, 9*(5), 365–404. doi:10.1002/acp.2350090502

Tavinor, G. (2005). Videogames and interactive fiction. *Philosophy and Literature*, *29*(1), 24–40. doi:10.1353/phl.2005.0015

Tay, L. (2010, May 18). Employers: Look to gaming to motivate staff. Gamer rewards could boost employee engagement. *itnews*. Retrieved from http://www.itnews.com.au/News/169862,employers-look-to-gaming-to-motivate-staff.aspx

Taylor, F. W. (1914). Scientific management. *The Sociological Review*, *7*(3), 266–269. doi:10.1111/j.1467-954X.1914.tb02387.x

Taylor, J., & Taylor, J. (2009). A content analysis of interviews with players of massively multiplayer online role-play games (MMORPGs): Motivating factors and the impact on relationships. *Online Communities and Social Computing*, *5621*, 613–621. doi:10.1007/978-3-642-02774-1_66

Taylor, T. L. (2003). Multiple pleasures: Women and online gaming. *Convergence*, *9*(1), 21–46.

Taylor, T. L. (2006). *Play Between Worlds: Exploring online game culture*. Cambridge: MIT Press.

Taylor, T. L. (2009). The Assemblage of Play. *Games and Culture*, *4*(4), 331–339. doi:10.1177/1555412009343576

Taylor, T. L., & Kolko, B. E. (2003). Boundary Spaces: Majestic and the uncertain status of knowledge, community and self in a digital age. *Information Communication and Society*, *6*(4), 497–522. doi:10.1080/1369118032000163231

Teens, video games, and civics - Teens' gaming experiences are diverse and include significant social interaction and civic engagement. (2008). *Pew Internet & American Life Project*.

Tegtmeyer, K. (2007). Data, data, data – but how to keep track of it all. *American Journal of Lifestyle Medicine*, *1*(2), 144–145. doi:10.1177/1559827606297324

Tewksbury, D., Weaver, A. J., & Maddex, B. D. (2001). Accidentally Informed: Incidental News Exposure on the World Wide Web. *Journalism & Mass Communication Quarterly*, *78*(3), 533–554. doi:10.1177/107769900107800309

Thaler, R. H., & Johnson, E. J. (1990). Gambling with the house money and trying to break even: The effects of prior outcomes on risky choice. *Management Science*, *36*(6), 643–660. doi:10.1287/mnsc.36.6.643

The Economist (2012, March 3). The Quantified Self: Counting Every Moment. *The Economist*. Retrieved from http://www.economist.com/node/21548493

The Elder Scrolls IV: Oblivion. [computer software]. (2006). Bethesda Game Studios, 2K Games.

The Entertainment Software Association. (n. d.). Retrieved from http://www.theesa.com/facts/salesandgenre.asp

The Growth of Multi-Platform News. *Digital News Report 2013*. (2013). Reuters Institute for the Study of Journalism. Retrieved from http://www.digitalnewsreport.org/survey/2013/the-growth-of-multi-platform-news-2013/

The Invisible Hand: The Challenge for a Fair World [Flash game]. (2011). TiconBlu. Retrieved from http://www.koalagames.it/koalaweb/pages/TIH/Index.aspx

The New York Times's Most Visited Content of 2013. (2014, January 17). The New York Times Company. Retrieved from http://www.nytco.com/the-new-york-timess-most-visited-content-of-2013/

The play's the thing. (2011). *Economist*, *401*(8763), 10-11.

The Scarecrow. [Software]. (2013). Moonbot Studios. Chipotle Mexican Grill Inc. Retrieved from http://www.scarecrowgame.com/index.html

The standards for educational and psychological testing. (1999American Educational Research Association, American Psychological Association, & National Council on Measurement in Education. Washington, DC: AERA Publications.

Thier, D. (2014, May 13). *Grand Theft Auto V* Has Sold Nearly $2 billion. *Forbes*. Retrieved from http://www.forbes.com/sites/davidthier/2014/05/13/grand-theft-auto-5-has-sold-nearly-2-billion-at-retail/

Thomas, R. K. (2014). Fast and Furious… or Much Ado About Nothing? Sub-Optimal Respondent Behavior and Data Quality. *Journal of Advertising Research, 54*(1), 17–31. doi:10.2501/JAR-54-1-017-031

Thompson, D. (2014, February 12). *The Facebook Effect on the News. The Atlantic*. Retrieved from http://www.theatlantic.com/business/archive/2014/02/the-facebook-effect-on-the-news/283746/

Thorhauge, A. M. (2013). The Rules of the Game—The Rules of the Player. *Games and Culture, 8*(6), 371–391. doi:10.1177/1555412013493497

Thurman, N. (2011). Making "The Daily Me": Technology, economics and habit in the mainstream assimilation of personalized news. *Journalism, 12*(4), 395–415. doi:10.1177/1464884910388228

Thurman, N., & Lupton, B. (2008). Convergence calls: Multimedia storytelling at British news websites. *Convergence (London), 14*(4), 439–455. doi:10.1177/1354856508094662

Thurman, N., & Walters, A. (2013). Live blogging – Digital journalism's pivotal platform? *Digital Journalism, 1*(1), 82–101. doi:10.1080/21670811.2012.714935

Tibbles, D., Richmond, V. P., McCroskey, J. C., & Weber, K. (2008, July). Organizational orientations in an instructional setting. *Communication Education, 57*(3), 389–407. doi:10.1080/03634520801930095

Tippins, N. (2009). Internet alternatives to traditional proctored testing: Where are we now? *Industrial and Organizational Psychology, 2*(1), 2. doi: 1754-9426/09

Titsworth, S., Quinlan, M. M., & Mazer, J. P. (2010, October). Emotion in teaching and learning: Development and validation of the classroom emotions scale. *Communication Education, 59*(4), 431–452. doi:10.1080/03634521003746156

Tong, S. T., Van Der Heide, B., Langwell, L., & Walther, J. B. (2008). Too much of a good thing? The relationship between number of friends and interpersonal impressions on Facebook. *Journal of Computer-Mediated Communication, 13*(3), 531–549. doi:10.1111/j.1083-6101.2008.00409.x

Transforming American education: Learning powered by technology. (2010, November). U.S. Department of Education. Retrieved from http://www.ed.gov/sites/default/files/netp2010-execsumm.pdf

Treanor, M., & Mateas, M. (2009). Newsgames: Procedural rhetoric meets political cartoons. In *Breaking new ground: Innovation in games, play, practice and theory. Proceedings of DIGRA 2009*. DIGRA.

Tripathi, K. N. (1992). Competition and intrinsic motivation. *The Journal of Social Psychology, 132*(6), 709–715. doi: 10.1080/00224545.1992.9712101

Trippenbach, P. (2013, April 17). Kill it with fire: Why gamification sucks and game dynamics rule. *Trippenbach.com*. Retrieved from http://trippenbach.com/2013/04/17/kill-it-with-fire-gamification-sucks-game-dynamics/

Trygstad, K. (2012, December 23). The Most Expensive House and Senate Races of 2012. *Forbes*. Retrieved from http://www.rollcall.com/news/the_most_expensive_house_and_senate_races_of_2012-220314-1.html?pg=2&dczone=politics

Tuchman, G. (1972). Tuchman 1972 Objectivity as a Strategic ritual. *American Journal of Sociology, 77*(4), 660–679. doi:10.1086/225193

Tufte, T., & Enghel, F. (2009). Youth engaging with media and communication. Different, unequal and disconnected? In Tufte & Enghel (eds.) Youth engaging with the world. Media, communication and social change. Gothenburg, Nordicom.

Tulloch, J. (2000). The eternal recurrence of new journalism. In C. Sparks & J. Tulloch (Eds.), *Tabloid tales: Global debates about media standards* (pp. 13–46). Lanham, MD: Rowman & Littlefield.

Tulloch, R. (2014). The Construction of Play: Rules, Restrictions, and the Repressive Hypothesis. *Games and Culture*, *9*(5), 335–350. doi:10.1177/1555412014542807

Turkle, S. (1984). *The second self: Computers and the human spirit*. New York, N.Y.: Simon and Schuster.

Turkle, S. (2011). *Alone together: Why we expect more from technology and less from each other*. New York, N.Y.: Basic Books.

Turner, J. S. (2006). Book reviews. *The Quarterly Journal of Speech*, *92*, 109–112.

Tuvuke Initiative. (2014). Retrieved from http://tuvuke.org/pages/Tuvuke_Initiative.htm

Urgent EVOKE (2010). Retrieved from http://www.urgentevoke.com/

Uribe, R., & Gunter, B. (2004). The Tabloidization of British Tabloids. *European Journal of Communication*, *19*(3), 387–402. doi:10.1177/0267323104045265

Urry, J. (2002). Mobility and proximity. *Sociology*, *36*(2), 255–274. doi:10.1177/0038038502036002002

Utz, S. (2010). Show me your friends and I will tell you what type of person you are: How one's profile, number of friends, and type of friends influence impression formation on social network sites. *Journal of Computer-Mediated Communication*, *15*(2), 314–335. doi:10.1111/j.1083-6101.2010.01522.x

Vallerand, R. J., Gauvin, L. I., & Halliwell, W. R. (1986). Negative effects of competition on children's intrinsic motivation. *The Journal of Social Psychology*, *126*(5), 649–656. doi:10.1080/00224545.1986.9713638

van Benthem, J. (2003). Logic Games are Complete for Game Logics. *Studia Logica*, *75*(2), 183–203. doi:10.1023/A:1027306910434

Van Dijck, J. (2009). Users like you? Theorizing agency in user-generated content. *Media Culture & Society*, *31*(1), 41–58. doi:10.1177/0163443708098245

Van Dijck, J. (2013). *The culture of connectivity. A critical history of social media*. Oxford University Press. doi:10.1093/acprof:oso/9780199970773.001.0001

Van Iddekinge, C. H., & Ployhart, R. E. (2008). Developments in the criterion-related validation of selection procedures: A critical review and recommendations for practice. *Personnel Psychology*, *61*(4), 871–925. doi:10.1111/j.1744-6570.2008.00133.x

van Reijmersdal, E. A., Rozendaal, E., & Buijzen, M. (2012). Effects of Prominence, Involvement, and Persuasion Knowledge on Children's Cognitive and Affective Responses to Advergames. *Journal of Interactive Marketing*, *26*(1), 33–42. doi:10.1016/j.intmar.2011.04.005

VandeWalle, D. (1997). Development and validation of a work domain goal orientation instrument. *Educational and Psychological Measurement*, *57*(6), 995–1015. doi:10.1177/0013164497057006009

VandeWalle, D. (2003). A goal orientation model of feedback seeking behavior. *Human Resource Management Review*, *13*(4), 581–604. doi:10.1016/j.hrmr.2003.11.004

Vigneron, F., & Johnson, L. W. (1999). A review and a conceptual framework of prestige-seeking consumer behavior. *Academy of Marketing Science Review, 1999(1)*. Retrieved from http://www.academia.edu/4793340/Vigneron_and_Johnson_A_Review_and_a_Conceptual_Framework_of_Prestige_A_Review_and_a_Conceptual_Framework_of_Prestige-Seeking_Consumer_Behavior

Vogel, J. J., Vogel, D. S., Cannon-Bowers, J., Bowers, C. A., Muse, K., & Wright, M. (2006). Computer Gaming and Interactive Simulations for Learning: A Meta-Analysis. *Journal of Educational Computing Research, 34*(3), 229–243. doi:10.2190/FLHV-K4WA-WPVQ-H0YM

Voter Turnout. (n.d.). Fair Vote, The Center for Voting and Democracy. Retrieved from http://www.fairvote.org/research-and-analysis/voter-turnout/

Vroom, V. H. (1964). *Work and motivation*. New York: Wiley.

Wadbring, I., & Bergström, A. (2014, February 26-28). A print crisis or a local crisis? Local news use over 27 years. Presented at Local journalism around the world: Professional practices, economic foundations, and political implications conference, University of Oxford.

Wälder, R. (1933). The psychoanalytic theory of play. *The Psychoanalytic Quarterly, 2*, 208–224.

Walther, J. B., & Parks, M. (2002). Cues filtered out, cues filtered in: Computer mediated communication and relationships. In M. L. Knapp, J. A. Daly, & G. R. Miller (Eds.), *The handbook of interpersonal communication* (3rd ed., pp. 529–563). Thousand Oaks, CA: Sage.

Walther, J. B., Van Der Heide, B., Hamel, L., & Shulman, H. C. (2009). Self-generated versus other-generated statements and impressions in computer-mediated communication: A test of warranting theory using facebook. *Communication Research, 36*(2), 229–253. doi:10.1177/0093650208330251

Walz, S. P. (2004). Delightful identification & persuasion: Toward an analytical and applied rhetoric of digital games. *Works and Days, 22*(1&2), 185–200.

Wan, C., & Chiou, W. (2006a). Why are adolescents addicted to online gaming? An interview study in Taiwan. *Cyberpsychology & Behavior, 9*(6), 762–766. doi:10.1089/cpb.2006.9.762 PMID:17201603

Wan, C., & Chiou, W. (2006b). Psychological motives and online games addiction: A test of flow theory and humanistic needs theory for Taiwanese adolescents. *Cyberpsychology & Behavior, 9*(3), 317–324. doi:10.1089/cpb.2006.9.317 PMID:16780399

Wanenchak, S. (2014, January 27). Player vs. Game: Design, narrative, and power. *The Society Pages – Cyborgology*. Retrieved from http://thesocietypages.org/cyborgology/2014/01/27/player-vs-game-design-narrative-and-power/

Wang, S. S. (2013). "I Share, Therefore I Am": Personality Traits, Life Satisfaction, and Facebook Check-Ins. *Cyberpsychology, Behavior, and Social Networking, 16*(12), 870–877. doi:10.1089/cyber.2012.0395 PMID:23992473

Wanous, J. P. (1973). Effects of a realistic job preview on job acceptance, job attitudes, and job survival. *The Journal of Applied Psychology, 58*(3), 327–332. doi:10.1037/h0036305

Warburton, S. (2009). Second Life in higher education: Assessing the potential for and the barriers to deploying virtual worlds in learning and teaching. *British Journal of Educational Technology, 40*(3), 414–426. doi:10.1111/j.1467-8535.2009.00952.x

Wastiau, P., Kearney, C., & Van den Berghe, W. (2009). How are digital games used in schools? *European Schoolnet*. Retrieved from http://games.eun.org/upload/gissynthesis_report_en.pdf

Watson, J. (2013, September 21). Gamification: Don't say it, don't do it, just stop. *Media Commons*. Retrieved from http://mediacommons.futureofthebook.org/question/how-does-gamification-affect-learning/response/gamification-dont-say-it-dont-do-it-just-sto

Watts, A. (1995). Work as Play. In M. A. Watts (Ed.), *The Essential Alan Watts*. London: Celectial Arts.

Weber, K. (2004, Fall). The relationship between student interest and teacher's use of behavior alteration techniques. *Communication Research Reports*, *21*(4), 428–436. doi:10.1080/08824090409360007

Weber, K., Martin, M. M., & Cayanus, J. L. (2005, January). Student interest: A two-study re-examination of the concept. *Communication Quarterly*, *53*(1), 71–86. doi:10.1080/01463370500055996

Weber, K., & Patterson, B. R. (2000, Winter). Student interest, empowerment and motivation. *Communication Research Reports*, *17*(1), 22–29. doi:10.1080/08824090009388747

Weber, R., Behr, K.-M., & DeMartino, C. (2014). Measuring Interactivity in Video Games. *Communication Methods and Measures*, *8*(2), 79–115. doi:10.1080/19312458.2013.873778

Wei, S. (2013, July 11). *Creating Games for Journalism. ProPublica*. Retrieved from http://www.propublica.org/nerds/item/creating-games-for-journalism

Weisheimer, A., & Giordano, G. (2013). Perceptions of truthfulness and communication anxiety in online employment interviews. *Drake Management Review*, *3*, 48–56.

Wells, B. M., & Skowronski, J. J. (2012). Evidence of choking under pressure on the PGA tour. *Basic and Applied Social Psychology*, *34*(2), 175–182. doi:10.1080/01973533.2012.655629

Werbach, K. (2014). (Re)Defining gamification: A process approach. In Spagnolli, et al. (Eds.), Proceedings of Persuasive 2014, LNCS 8462 (pp. 266–272). Springer.

Werbach, K., & Hunter, D. (2012). *For the win: How game thinking can revolutionize your business*. Wharton, PA: Digital Press.

Westerman, D., Spence, P. R., & Van Der Heide, B. (2012). A social network as information: The effect of system generated reports of connectedness on credibility on Twitter. *Computers in Human Behavior*, *28*(1), 199–206. doi:10.1016/j.chb.2011.09.001

Westervelt, E. (2013). The online education revolution drifts off course. Retrieved from http://www.npr.org/2013/12/31/258420151/the-online-education-revolution-drifts-off-course

Westlund, O. (2012). Producer-centric versus participation-centric: On the shaping of mobile media. *Northern Lights*, *10*(1), 107–121. doi:10.1386/nl.10.1.107_1

Westlund, O. (2013). Mobile news. *Digital Journalism*, *1*(1), 6–26. doi:10.1080/21670811.2012.740273

Westlund, O., & Bjur, J. (2014). Media life of the young. *Young*, *22*(1), 21–41. doi:10.1177/1103308813512934

Westlund, O., & Färdigh, M. A. (2011). Displacing and complementing effects of news sites and newspapers 1998-2009. *International Journal on Media Management*, *13*(3), 177–194. doi:10.1080/14241277.2011.595020

Westwood, D., & Griffiths, M. D. (2010). The role of structural characteristics in video-game play motivation: A Q-methodology study. *Cyberpsychology, Behavior, and Social Networking*, *13*(5), 581–585. doi:10.1089/cyber.2009.0361 PMID:20950185

What makes a successful advocacy network? These Seven Elements [Blog]. (n.d.). Retrieved from http://www.netcentriccampaigns.org

What we do. (2014). The Institute for the Future. Retrieved from http://www.iftf.org/what-we-do/

Whitson, J. (2010). FCJ-106 rule making and rule breaking: Game development and the governance of emergent behavior. *The Fiberculture Journal, 16.* Retrieved from http://sixteen.fibreculturejournal.org/rule-making-and-rule-breaking-game-development-and-the-governance-of-emergent-behaviour/

Whitson, J. R. (2013). Gaming the Quantified Self. *Surveillance & Society, 11*(1/2), 163–176.

Why we play games: Four keys to more emotion without story. (2004, March 8). *Xeodesign.com.* Retrieved from http://www.xeodesign.com/xeodesign_whyweplaygames.pdf

Wikipedia. Service Awards. (2014, October 22) In *Wikipedia.* Retrieved from http://en.wikipedia.org/wiki/Wikipedia:Service_awards

Wilkins, K. G. (1999). Development discourse on gender and communication in strategies for social change. Retrieved from http://nabilechchaibi.com/resources/Karin.pdf

Wilkins, K. G., & Mody, B. (2001). Reshaping Development Communication: Developing communication and communicating development. *Communication Theory, 11*(4), 385–396. doi:10.1111/j.1468-2885.2001.tb00249.x

Williams, D. (2005, December). Bridging the methodological divide in game research. *Simulation & Gaming, 36*(4), 1–17. doi:10.1177/1046878105282275

Williams, D. (2006). Groups and Goblins: The social and civil impact of an online game. *Journal of Broadcasting & Electronic Media, 50*(4), 651–670. doi:10.1207/s15506878jobem5004_5

Williams, D., Caplan, S., & Xiong, L. (2005). Can you hear me now? The impact of voice in an online gaming community. *Human Communication Research, 33*(4), 427–449. doi:10.1111/j.1468-2958.2007.00306.x

Williams, R. (1989). Culture is Ordinary. In B. Highmore (Ed.), *The Everyday Life Reader* (pp. 91–100). New York: Routledge.

Wilson, K. A., Bedwell, W. L., Lazzara, E. H., Burke, C. S., & Estock, J. L. et al. (2009). Relationships between game attributes and learning outcomes. *Simulation & Gaming, 40*(2), 217–266. doi:10.1177/1046878108321866

Winn, W. (2004). Cognitive perspective in psychology. In D. H. Jonasses (Ed.), *Handbook of Research on Educational Communications and Technology* (2nd ed.). Mahwah, NJ: Lawrence Erlbaum Associates.

Winston, M. (2001, November). The Importance of Leadership Diversity: The Relationship between Diversity and Organizational Success in the Academic Environment. *College & Research Libraries, 62*(6), 517–526. doi:10.5860/crl.62.6.517

Wise, K., Bolls, P. D., Kim, H., Venkataraman, A., & Meyer, R. (2008). Enjoyment of advergames and brand attitudes: The impact of thematic relevance. *Journal of Interactive Advertising, 9*(1), 27–36. doi:10.1080/15252019.2008.10722145

Witt, M., Scheiner, C., & Robra-Bissantz, S. (2011). Gamification of online idea competitions: Insights from an explorative case. Proceedings of Informatik 2011, Lecture Notes in Informatics, Band P192. TUBerlin.

Wojdynski, B. W. (2014). Interactive data graphics and information processing: The moderating role of involvement. *Journal of Media Psychology*; Advance online publication. doi:10.1027/1864-1105/a000127

Wolf, C., & Schnauber, A. (2014). News Consumption in the Mobile Era: The role of mobile devices and traditional journalism's content within the user's information repertoire. *Digital Journalism*. Advance online publication. Doi:10.1080/21670811.2014.942497

Wolf, G. (2009, June 22). Know Thyself: Tracking Every Facet of Life, from Sleep to Mood to Pain, 24/7/365. *Wired.com*. Retrieved from http://archive.wired.com/medtech/health/magazine/17-07/lbnp_knowthyself?currentPage=all

Wolf, G. (2010). The Data-Driven Life. *The New York Times*. Retrieved from http://www.nytimes.com/2010/05/02/magazine/02self-measurement-t.html?_r=0

Wolfram, S. (2012). The Personal Informatics of My Life. *StephanWolfram.com*. Retrieved from http:\\www.stephen-wolfram.com

World of Warcraft [computer software]. (2004). Blizzard Entertainment.

World of Warcraft. (2012, October 9). *Wikipedia*. Retrieved from http://en.wikipedia.org/wiki/World_of_Warcraft

Wouters, P., van der Spek, E. D., & van Oostendorp, H. (2009). Current practices in serious game research: A review from a learning outcomes perspective. In T. Connolly, M. Stansfield, & L. Boyle (Eds.), *Games-Based Learning Advancements for Multi-Sensory Human Computer Interfaces: Techniques and Effective Practices*. Hershey, PA: IGI Global. doi:10.4018/978-1-60566-360-9.ch014

Wright, P. M., George, J. M., Farnsworth, S. R., & McMahan, G. C. (1993). Productivity and extra-role behavior: The effects of goals and incentives on spontaneous helping. *The Journal of Applied Psychology*, 78(3), 374–381. doi:10.1037/0021-9010.78.3.374

Wright, W. (1993). *SimCity 2000* [computer software]. Maxis.

Wu, H.-K., Lee, S. W.-Y., Chang, H.-Y., & Liang, J.-C. (2013). Current status, opportunities and challenges of augmented reality in education. *Computers & Education*, 62, 41–49. doi:10.1016/j.compedu.2012.10.024

Xu, Y. (2011, April). Literature review on web application gamification and analytics. *CSDL Technical Report 11-05*. Retrieved from http://csdl.ics.hawaii.edu/techreports/11-05/11-05.pdf

Yan, J., & Randell, B. (2005). A systematic classification of cheating in online games. *Proceedings of 4th ACM SIGCOMM Workshop on Network and System Support for Games*. (pp. 1-9). New York, NY: ACM. doi:10.1145/1103599.1103606

Yee, N. (2006). Motivations for play in online games. *Cyberpsychology & Behavior*, 9(6), 772–775. doi:10.1089/cpb.2006.9.772 PMID:17201605

Yee, N. (2006). The psychology of MMORPGs: Emotional investment, motivations, relationship formation, and problematic usage. In R. Schroeder & A. Axelsson (Eds.), *Avatars at Work and Play: Collaboration and Interaction in Shared Virtual Environments* (pp. 187–207). London: Springer-Verlan. doi:10.1007/1-4020-3898-4_9

Yee, N. (2006, January). The labor of fun: How video games blur the boundaries of work and play. *Games and Culture*, 1(1), 68–71. doi:10.1177/1555412005281819

Zagal, J., Chan, S. S., & Zhang, J. (2011). *Measuring flow experience of computer game players*. Paper presented at the AMCIS 2010 Proceedings (pp. 137). Retrieved from http://aisel.aisnet.org/amcis2010/137

Zagal, J., Rick, J., & His, I. (2006). Collaborative games: Lessons learned from board games. *Simulation & Games*, 37(1), 24–40. doi:10.1177/1046878105282279

Zahavi, A. (1975). Mate selection – a selection for a handicap. *Journal of Theoretical Biology*, 53(1), 205–214. doi:10.1016/0022-5193(75)90111-3 PMID:1195756

Zaphiris, P., & Wilson, S.Chee Siang Ang. (2010). Computer Games and Sociocultural Play: An Activity Theoretical Perspective. *Games and Culture*, *5*(4), 354–380. doi:10.1177/1555412009360411

Zelizer, B. (2004). When facts, truth and reality are God terms. On journalism's uneasy place in cultural studies. *Communication and Critical. Cultural Studies*, *1*(1), 100–119.

Zicherman, G., & Cunningham, C. (2011). *Gamification by design: implementing game mechanics in web and mobile apps*. New York: O'Reilly Media.

Zicherman, G., & Linder, J. (2010). *Game-based marketing: inspire customer loyalty through rewards, challenges and contests*. New Jersey: Wiley.

Zichermann, G. (2011, August 23). Gamification is here to stay (and it's not bullshit). *Kotaku*. Retrieved from http://kotaku.com/5833631/gamification-is-here-to-stay-and-its-not-bullshit

Zichermann, G., & Cunningham, C. (2011). *Gamification by Design*. Sebastopol, CA: O'Reilly Media.

Zichermann, G., & Cunningham, C. (2011). *Gamification by design: Implementing game mechanics in web and mobile apps*. Sebastopol, CA: O'Reilly Media.

Zichermann, G., & Linder, J. (2010). *Game-based marketing: Inspire customer loyalty through rewards, challenges, and contests*. New York, NY: John Wiley & Sons.

Zichermann, G., & Linder, J. (2013). *The gamification revolution: How leaders leverage game mechanics to crush the competition*. McGraw-Hill.

Zichermann, G., & Linder, J. (2013). *The Gamification revolution: How leaders leverage game mechanics to crush the competition*. New York: McGraw Hill.

Zuk, R. (2012). Get in the game: How communicators can leverage gamification. *Public Relations Tactics*, *19*(2), 7.

About the Contributors

Harsha Gangadharbatla (Ph.D., University of Texas) is an associate professor and the founding chair of the department of advertising, public relations and media design in the college of media, communication and information at the University of Colorado Boulder. His research focuses on new and emerging media, social and economic effects of advertising, and environmental communication. He has authored (or co-authored) over 40 publications including conference proceedings.

Donna Z. Davis earned a Ph.D. in Mass Communication from the University of Florida studying the strength of relationships formed in virtual worlds. Her current research extends to the development of community and interpersonal relationships in virtual environments and other emerging social media with a focus on health and disability communities. Her interests also focus on new media technologies that shape the human condition and change behavior via gamification. Prior to life in academia, she had a successful career of more than 25 years in public relations and development, while teaching at the College of Journalism and Communication at UF.

***

Michael B. Armstrong is a Ph.D. student and research assistant at Old Dominion University studying Industrial and Organizational Psychology. He graduated from Western Kentucky University in 2013 with a Bachelor of Arts in Psychology. Michael's research interests focus upon the Internet and related technologies as they affect human capital. He is particularly interested in the effectiveness of gamification in human resource management. Michael is a student affiliate of the Society for Industrial and Organizational Psychology.

Jacqueline Carpenter is a consultant with Shaker and earned her Ph.D. in Industrial-Organizational Psychology from the University of Akron. She has worked with clients across industries to develop and implement web-based pre-employment assessments, many of which have included gamified job simulations. Her research interests include corporate image perceptions, organizational attraction, and applicant reactions, particularly in the contexts of technology enhanced assessment for selection and web-based recruitment.

Andrew B. Collmus graduated Cum Laude from Colorado State University in 2014 with a BS in Psychology. He is working toward his doctorate in industrial-organizational psychology at Old Dominion

University, with an expected completion date in 2019. He researches the use of technology in training and selection, including virtual worlds, e-learning, gamification, and augmented reality.

Raul Ferrer Conill is a PhD candidate in Media and Communication at Karlstad University, Sweden. His current research focuses on the applications of Gamification as a tool to investigate the transition from traditional journalism to mobile and digital news consumption. Other research interests cover social media, motivation, and technology. Raul has 14 years of experience as a web designer and developer.

Carlos Cruz is a PhD candidate currently attending The Ohio State University. His research interests include gamification and credibility in online environments.

Rachelle DiGregorio is a digital strategist making it happen in NYC with Big Spaceship. Her expertise includes strategic planning, qualitative and quantitative research skills – unearthing the insights that drive surprising and effective brand experiences. In her spare time, she loves reading classic novels and eating a good medium-rare steak, not necessarily at the same time.

Nikki M. Dudley is a Senior Consultant and Partner at Shaker. She received her Ph.D. at George Mason University. She has worked with numerous Fortune 100 clients creating cutting edge mobile and web-based assessment solutions. Current research interests include innovative measurement methodologies for knowledge, skills, and personality; high-fidelity simulations; 'day in the life' assessments; and applicant reactions. She has also received the Edwin A. Fleishman award for her research on knowledge and skill measurement and the G. Klopfer Award for distinguished contribution to the literature in personality.

Jared Z. Ferrell is a consultant with Shaker and is currently a PhD candidate in the Industrial-Organizational Psychology program at the University of Akron. He earned his MA in Industrial-Organizational Psychology from the University of Akron in 2011. Jared has been involved in the development and implementation of numerous gamified recruitment and selection initiatives across a wide variety of industries and roles during his time at Shaker. He has also presented at numerous professional conferences and published in peer-reviewed journals, as well as books on personnel selection. His research interests include organizational attraction, applicant reactions to assessments, training in virtual settings, social networking websites, and gamification's impact on HR processes.

Jolene Fisher is a Doctoral Candidate at the University of Oregon and will graduate with her PhD in Media Studies in 2016. She received her MS in Communication and Society at the University of Oregon in 2012, where she researched issues of gender, development and new media. She writes and presents widely on the use of video games in international development and is the author of *Toward a Political Economic Framework for Analyzing Digital Development Games: A Case Study of Three Games for Africa* (2016, *Communication, Culture & Critique*).

Scott A. Goodman. As a founding member of Shaker, Scott's primary focus has been on developing and implementing pre-employment assessments to solve complex quality of hire challenges for Fortune 500 firms and niche market leaders. His thought leadership and insightful consulting have contributed to staffing process improvement initiatives around the globe and he has been involved in the development and deployment of numerous gamified assessment solutions. He has spent more than 20 years working with groups and companies around the world to assist them in aligning their people's performance with business strategies. He received his Ph.D. from the University of Akron.

Michael D. Hanus is a Ph.D. candidate at The Ohio State University. His work focuses on new, interactive technology and its applications to gamification, persuasion, and motivation.

Nathan Hulsey is currently a doctoral candidate at the Communication, Rhetoric and Digital Media program at North Carolina State University. His current research involves a critical approach to the history of gamification with a focus on surveillance tactics, spatiality and biopolitics. He also contributes research to the fields of Game Studies and Mobilities.

Yowei Kang holds a Ph.D. in Rhetoric and Writing Studies. His research specialties focus on digital game rhetoric, experiential rhetoric, new media technologies, and rhetorical analysis.

Michael Karlsson is a Professor in Media and Communication at Karlstad University, Sweden. His research interest is primarily digital journalism and he has been widely published in journals such as Journalism Studies, Journalism Theory, Practice and Criticism and New Media and Society.

Marty Kearns pioneered the integration of network-centric principles into civic organizing and social change work. As the Founder and President of Netcentric Campaigns, he drives their strategy, vision and development, working with advocacy leaders from nonprofits and foundations to further their understanding of the powerful role networks of people can play in all elements of their work.

Richard N. Landers earned his PhD in Industrial/Organizational Psychology in 2009, at which point he began as Assistant Professor of Industrial/Organizational Psychology at Old Dominion University. There, he has won the Teaching with Technology Award and was twice nominated for the State Council for Higher Education for Virginia Outstanding Faculty Awards. His research explores the intersection between technology research and industrial/organizational psychology with an emphasis on quantitative social scientific analytic approaches. In particular, he focuses on the use and influence of the Internet on assessment and human learning, primarily within the workplace. Specific Internet-related topics of focus include video games, gamification, social network sites, mobile devices, 3D multi-user virtual environments, crowdsourcing, and web-based learning.

Darcy Osheim graduated from San Jose State with a BA in Communication Studies in '09 and a MA in '13. A California native, she moved to Maine to follow her partner Richard and is currently working at Maine Maritime Academy as an adjunct instructor of Composition in their Arts and Sciences department. She recently gave birth to a beautiful baby girl, Lorelei.

Selcen Öztürkcan continues her academic career as a Faculty of the Social Sciences Institute at Istanbul Bilgi University. After graduating from Tarsus American High School (1995), she has earned a B.Sc. degree in Engineering from Middle East Technical University with honors (1999), and an M.B.A. degree from Bilkent University on merit-scholarship (2001). She continued her Ph.D. studies, again on merit-scholarship, first at the College of Business Administration of the University of South Florida (2002-2003), then at the Faculty of Management of the Istanbul Technical University (2003-2007) where she was awarded with the Outstanding Ph.D. Award of the Turkish Educational Foundation (2007). After 3 years of mid-managerial experience in the ICT sector, she joined the academia. She has taught Advertising Management, Applied Quantitative Research Methods, Consumer Behavior, Consumer Behavior Seminar, e-Business, e-Marketing, Information and Communication Technologies Management, Information Technologies Management, Integrated Marketing Communications, International Marketing, Introduction to Sectors, Marketing, Marketing Strategy, Marketing Theory, Organizational Theory, Principles of Marketing, Production and Operations Management, Qualitative Marketing Research, Sales Management, Strategic Management, and Web Site Management courses at University of South Florida (USA), Istanbul Bilgi University, Marka Okulu, Sabanci University, Ozyegin University, Bahcesehir University, Yeditepe University, Lancaster University (UK), IPAG (France), and ISCTE (Portugal). She renders occasional executive education and consultancy services to various institutions including Jones Lang LaSalle, Goldman Sachs' 10 000 Women, Mazda, Mapfre, Vatan Computer, Vestel, IngBank, Yatırımbank, and ACEV (the Mother Child Education Foundation). Sabancı University (2006-2008) and Ozyegin University (2008-2010) have hosted her Post-Doc Research activities. Her research has been awarded funding from Istanbul Metropolitan Municipality, Istanbul Chamber of Commerce and TUBITAK (The Scientific and Technological Research Council of Turkey) and received Encouragement Award from TUBA (The Turkish Academy of Sciences), Sabanci University, and Istanbul Bilgi University. Her work has been listed among the All Time Hits of the SSRN (Social Sciences Research Network). Dr. Öztürkcan's work has appeared as book chapters and case studies in books published by Cengage, Edward Elgar, Istanbul Chamber of Commerce and McGraw-Hill. She has published at ITU journal and Journal of Retailing and Consumer Services. She serves on the scientific board for the AVM Gazette, where she also authors practitioner-oriented articles. She gives seminars at the Marketingİst. Business oriented magazines such as Newsweek Turkey intermittently quote her evaluations and opinions for issues related with her research. She has served as Effie 2013 juror.

Kartik Pashupati is Research Director at Research Now. His passion for research extends across a career that includes market research, advertising and academia. After earning a Ph.D. from Michigan State University, Kartik spent 18 years as a full time academic, teaching courses in research methods, communication theory, and advertising strategy. He has served on the editorial review board of three journals, and is the author of more than 40 conference papers, peer-reviewed journal articles, and book chapters. He remains active in publishing and thought leadership projects. Along with colleagues at Research Now, he has co-authored papers that have been presented at industry conferences, and published in the Journal of Advertising Research. A paper co-authored by Kartik and three other colleagues from Research Now won the Best Methodological Paper award at the 2013 ESOMAR Congress, and also recognized as the best overall research paper for 2013/2014.

Pushkala Raman is an Associate Professor of Marketing in the Texas Woman's University School of Management. Her primary research interests include customer relationship management, data privacy, and online health care. Her research has been published in leading journals.

Sercan Şengün is a PhD student at the Department of Communications. More information and his academic work are available at www.sercansengun.com.

Zeynep Tanes is an assistant professor in the department of Journalism and Multimedia Arts, Duquesne University. She specializes on the effects of new media technologies on the individual and society. She examines the effects of messages transmitted via interactive and computer mediated platforms on cognition, attitudes, and behaviors. Her primary research is focused on the effects of player-game interaction on gaming experience and outcomes. She has been involved in designing and testing various serious games about risk communication. She teaches research methods, and various classes on multi-media advertising strategies and applications at Duquesne University focusing on their effects on the individual and society. She holds a Ph.D. from Purdue University, an M.S. from Istanbul Technical University – Maastricht University in Science, Technology and Society, and a B.A. from Koc University in Sociology.

William R. Upchurch is a doctoral candidate in the Department of Communication at the University of Pittsburgh. His dissertation is an oral history and autoethnography of an online message board community. His work touches on the rhetorics of online identity and community as well as the construction of masculinities in subcultures. He recently published an essay entitled Public Address as the Basic Communication Course, which argues for a basic course that respects our past while addressing the contemporary communication and pedagogical environments.

E. Daly Vaughn is a Senior Consultant with Shaker. He holds a Ph.D. from Auburn University and has developed and implemented innovative, custom, web- and mobile-based measures including measures of cognitive ability, situational judgment, biodata, qualitative responses, personality, and work simulations for a variety of Fortune 500 clients across a broad range of industries. His research interests include studying where innovative technology intersects with traditional human resource functions, encompassing implicit attitude measurement, legal challenges introduced by new technology, and the use of social media within a recruitment and selection context.

Susan M. Wildermuth is an Associate Professor of Communication at the University of Wisconsin-Whitewater. Her teaching and research interests include mediated communication, intercultural communication, and instructional communication.

Meredith Wise is the Digital Communications Strategist for Netcentric Campaigns. She oversees much of the writing and editing of content for both Netcentric Campaigns and their clients.

Bartosz W. Wojdynski is an Assistant Professor in the Department of Journalism at the Grady College of Journalism and Mass Communication at the University of Georgia. His research focuses on how interactivity, navigability, and design of digital information affects psychological responses including selection, attention, and cognition.

Index

Become an IRMA Member

Members of the **Information Resources Management Association (IRMA)** understand the importance of community within their field of study. The Information Resources Management Association is an ideal venue through which professionals, students, and academicians can convene and share the latest industry innovations and scholarly research that is changing the field of information science and technology. Become a member today and enjoy the benefits of membership as well as the opportunity to collaborate and network with fellow experts in the field.

IRMA Membership Benefits:

- **One FREE Journal Subscription**

- **30% Off Additional Journal Subscriptions**

- **20% Off Book Purchases**

- Updates on the latest events and research on Information Resources Management through the IRMA-L listserv.

- Updates on new open access and downloadable content added to Research IRM.

- A copy of the Information Technology Management Newsletter twice a year.

- A certificate of membership.

IRMA Membership $195

Scan code to visit irma-international.org and begin by selecting your free journal subscription.

Membership is good for one full year.

Printed in the United States
By Bookmasters